S0-BDL-194

Consumer-Driven Demand and Operations Management Models

A Systematic Study of Information-Technology-Enabled Sales Mechanisms

INT. SERIES IN OPERATIONS RESEARCH & MANAGEMENT SCIENCE

Series Editor: Frederick S. Hillier, Stanford University
Special Editorial Consultant: Camille C. Price, Stephen F. Austin State University
Titles with an asterisk (*) were recommended by Dr. Price

~A list of the early publications in the series is found at the end of the book~

Consumer-Driven Demand and Operations Management Models

A Systematic Study of Information-Technology-Enabled Sales Mechanisms

Edited by

Serguei Netessine
Christopher S. Tang

 Springer

Editors
Serguei Netessine
The Wharton School
University of Pennsylvania
3730 Walnut St.
Philadelphia, PA 19104-6340
USA
netessine@wharton.upenn.edu

Christopher S. Tang
UCLA Anderson School of Management
Box 951481
Los Angeles, CA 90095–1481
ctang@anderson.ucla.edu

Series Editor
Frederick S. Hillier
Stanford University
Stanford, CA, USA

ISSN 0884-8289
ISBN 978-0-387-98018-8   e-ISBN 978-0-387-98026-3
DOI 10.1007/978-0-387-98026-3
Springer Dordrecht Heidelberg London New York

Library of Congress Control Number: 2008944171

© Springer Science+Business Media, LLC 2009
All rights reserved. This work may not be translated or copied in whole or in part without the written permission of the publisher (Springer Science+Business Media, LLC, 233 Spring Street, New York, NY 10013, USA), except for brief excerpts in connection with reviews or scholarly analysis. Use in connection with any form of information storage and retrieval, electronic adaptation, computer software, or by similar or dissimilar methodology now known or hereafter developed is forbidden.
The use in this publication of trade names, trademarks, service marks, and similar terms, even if they are not identified as such, is not to be taken as an expression of opinion as to whether or not they are subject to proprietary rights.

Printed on acid-free paper

Springer is part of Springer Science+Business Media (www.springer.com)

Preface

To compete in today's volatile market with rapidly changing consumer tastes and fierce competition, companies in the manufacturing and service industries are deploying new mechanisms to increase sales, market shares, and profits. As an effective mechanism to segment a market comprising of consumers with different needs, preferences, and willingness-to-pay, many firms have used product (or service) variety with different price points to serve different segments of the market, see Ho (1998). Ideally, the price of each of these products (or services) targets a particular segment of customers. For example, airlines often use different terms of sales (refundable/non-refundable, upgradable/non-upgradable, direct/connecting flight, etc.) to sell economy class tickets at different prices. Likewise, retailers often sell the same product at different prices in different channels (company's own web site, dealers' web sites, or company's physical stores) or at different times (before, during, and after the selling season), see Talluri and van Ryzin (2005). Ample academic literature in Operations Management and other areas considered these strategies. However, as consumers become more knowledgeable about the product, pricing, organizational and operational policies that the companies deploy for products and services, their purchasing begins to change dramatically.

In the academic Operations Management literature, consumer demand is often assumed to be *exogenous* so that demand functions are usually modeled as well defined and exogenously specified functions of price and/or other product attributes such as quality. This type of modeling approach captures the "macro" view of consumer demand and many OM models shed light on strategic and managerial issues ranging from revenue management to supply chain management. Today, however, many companies are beginning to take the "micro" view by selling each product and service to a target segment by utilizing more sophisticated selling mechanisms enabled by information technologies (say, one-on-one marketing). Some of these sales mechanisms are the following:

1. Mixed sales channels – To offer customers more options and price points, Amazon.com sells both new books (owned by Amazon) and used books (owned by independent used book sellers) which compete for demand from consumers.

2. Automatic markdown pricing – To clear overstocked items, Landsend.com pre-announces their price markdown schedule in advance so that consumers can time their purchases according to the markdown schedule.

3. Portals – To provide the one-stop shopping experience for their customers, Orbitz.com sells airline tickets for multiple airlines thus putting them in direct competition with each other.

4. Group buying – To provide each individual consumer with the buying power of the collective group, thebuyinggroup.com offers their members group discount prices on items ranging from cell phones to office supplies.

5. Auctions – To create an online market for consumers who want to buy or sell their items, ebay.com constructs different online auction mechanisms.

Anecdotal and empirical evidences suggest that, in these sales mechanisms, consumer purchasing behavior is fundamentally different from that arising in more traditional retailing environments. For instance, there is plenty of anecdotal evidence suggesting that many consumers are becoming more *strategic* in the sense that they postpone their purchases due to an anticipation of future price decreases. Besides strategic purchasing behavior, there is empirical evidence indicating that consumer's purchasing decision is often affected by the purchasing decisions of other consumers. For instance, Bikhchandani et al. (1992) develop a theory to explain how information cascades can induce the *herd behavior* among customers. If a consumer's purchasing decision is affected by informational factors pertaining to pricing, product availability, product characteristics, and other consumers' purchasing decisions, the consumer demand becomes *endogenous* in the sense that it now depends on the underlying sales mechanism as well as on the realized (total) price that the consumer actually pays. As the demand pattern changes in response to firms' actions, firms must manage their supply operations effectively and efficiently in order to meet these new challenges. Thus, the study of different sales mechanisms and their implications for consumer demands and supply operations is very timely and is of immediate practical relevance.

This book contains a collection of state-of-the-art OM models that examine the implications of rational or strategic purchasing behavior under different retail formats. These models provide new insights into how firms should operate in these new channels using different sales mechanisms. The chapters in this book are written by leading scholars who have initiated the quest for a deeper understanding of consumer's rational purchasing behavior under various sales mechanisms. Moreover, these scholars have continued their efforts in developing innovative ways for companies to respond to this rational purchasing behavior.

We enjoyed the experience of working on this book and we sincerely hope that this book will stimulate researchers in Operations Management and other areas to explore further this exciting emerging area of research.

References

Bikhchandani S, Hirshleifer D, Welch I (1992) A theory of fads, fashion, custom, and cultural change as informational cascades. Journal of Political Economy 100(5):992–1026

Ho TH, Tang CS (1998) Product variety management: Research advances. Kluwer Publishers, Massachusetts

Talluri K, van Ryzin G (2005) The theory and practice of revenue management. Springer, New York

Fontainebleau, France, November 2008   *Serguei Netessine*
Los Angeles, November 2008   *Christopher S. Tang*

Introduction

One primary focus of research in Operations Management field is to find ways to make supply meet consumer demand. For decades, many OM researchers have developed various production planning and inventory control models and mathematical solution techniques with the intent of helping companies meet consumer demand effectively and at a low cost. These models have certainly helped many companies improve their internal operations. Our field continues to develop more sophisticated solution techniques for solving various classical Operations Management problems. However, another item on the agenda of our field is to broaden the scope of Operations Management, which is the key goal of this book.

In most Operations Management models consumer demand is assumed to be *exogenous* so that demand is usually taken to be a well-defined and pre-specified function of price and/or other product attributes such as quality. This modeling assumption is quite reasonable for capturing the consumer demand on an aggregate level. For example, there are many existing models explaining how firms can use product (or service) variety with different price points to serve different segments of the market (Ho and Tang 1998). However, to compete for market share, companies in the manufacturing and service industries are now deploying other novel mechanisms to segment a market comprising of consumers with different needs, preferences, and willingness-to-pay.

When buying different variants of a basic product (or service) at different prices with different terms of sales, consumers often need to process information about product characteristics and make their choices in a *rational* manner. Hence, each consumer's purchasing decision is affected by the way information is being conveyed to them, by the way information is being analyzed by the consumer, and by other consumers' decisions (such as the herding effect in Bikhchandani et al. 1992). In addition, organizational factors such as the choice of sales channels, marketing factors pertaining to product assortments (such as horizontal competition, see Hotelling 1929) and vertical competition (see Lilien et al. 1992), different sales mechanisms such as auctions (cf., Krishna 2002), and pricing (see Coase 1972 and Besanko and Winston 1990) as well as operational factors related to product availability can have direct impact on consumers' purchasing behavior. If these factors are considered by consumers, the consumer demand becomes *endogenous* in the sense that it depends on the underlying sales mechanism as well as on the realized price that the consumer actually pays.

To address these recent developments, this book presents a collection of state-of-the-art *Operations Management models with consumer-driven demand*. This is an emerging research area that focuses on the evaluation of different innovative product, services, and sales initiatives, and in all of these chapters it is critical to obtain a deeper understanding of consumer purchasing behavior first and then to develop efficient response to this behavior. Not only is each chapter motivated by various innovative service/product delivery mechanisms found in practice, but also the models presented in each chapter are based on various well-established theories in economics, marketing, operations management, and psychology that deal with consumer purchasing behavior.

Overall Structure

This book is comprised of 18 chapters that are divided into 5 parts. The first part (Chapters 1, 2, 3, and 4) examines *consumers' rational or strategic purchasing behavior* under different business environments. Anticipating consumers' behavior, firms in these chapters use different response mechanisms to mitigate the negative effect caused by the consumers' rational/strategic purchasing behavior. As a response to strategic customers, the second part (Chapters 5, 6, and 7) examines how different *organizational strategies* (such as sales channels and customer selection processes) can be deployed to increase profits. Chapters in the third part (Chapters 8, 9, 10, and 11) examine how companies can use *product strategies* to increase profits when consumers are strategic. To counteract the strategic customers' purchasing behavior, the fourth part (Chapters 12, 13, 14, and 15) examines how companies can use certain *operational strategies* (such as capacity/inventory/product availability and inventory display formats) to increase profits. Finally, in the fifth part (Chapters 16, 17, and 18) the book describes how different *pricing strategies* can enable firms to improve profits in the presence of strategic consumers.

Chapter Highlights

Part I: Rational Consumer Behavior: Endogenous Decision Making Mechanisms

In Chapter 1, Gad Allon and Achal Bassamboo set the stage for the book by examining situations in which consumers treat information provided by the sellers regarding product/service availability as unreliable. Thus, customers are strategic in the way they treat information and use it in decisions that they make regarding buying/waiting. While it is often assumed that consumers' purchasing behavior is purely driven by utility optimization, in Chapter 2, Matulya Bansal and Costis Maglaras examine a situation in which customers are "satisficers" instead of "optimizers". Specifically, the authors consider the case in which the customers seek to buy the cheapest product with quality above a certain customer-specific threshold which may reflect, for example, bounded rationality of consumers. In the same vein, in Chapter 3, Felipe Caro and Victor Marinez-de-Albeniz consider the case when customers are insatiable so that companies can increase sales by frequent new product introduction, and they determine how often the company should rotate its assortment. Laurens Debo and Senthil Veeraraghavan in Chapter 4 study consumer behavior in queues. In particular, they consider the issue of how customers might be able to infer product quality from the length of the queue and they endogenize customers' decision to select the queue to join.

Part 1 sets the stage by proposing that consumers are either *rational* (e.g., optimizers, satisficers, insatiable) or *strategic*. Specifically, consumers are *strategic* when they rationally anticipate and respond to future conditions. For example, anticipating future price drops, a strategic consumer may delay his/her purchasing decision. Therefore, dealing with rational/strategic consumers can be costly. As such, companies need to develop effective mechanisms to mitigate the negative effects of rational/strategic customers. This is the focus of the remainder of this book.

Part II: Organizational Strategies for Managing Rational/Strategic Consumer Behavior

Motivated by proliferation of multiple channels that target multiple customer segments, Barchi Gillai and Hau Lee examine in Chapter 5 the use of a secondary (e.g., Internet) market that can enable retailers to clear inventories unsold in the primary market. They demonstrate benefits of such strategies for retailers, manufacturers, and consumers. In Chapter 6, Basak Kalkanci and Jin Whang highlight the fact that it can be very costly to satisfy rational consumers (clients in a supply chain) in a heterogeneous market since their aggregate orders may induce the bullwhip effect. Instead, they suggest that a supplier can improve profitability by focusing on an optimal portfolio of clients that maximizes supplier's long-run expected profit. Considering situations when consumers are strategic and rationally respond to future market conditions, Xuanming Su and Fuqiang Zhang review several existing papers that demonstrate how decentralization can be beneficial to supply chain performance in Chapter 7. Interestingly, they find that, when customers are strategic, decentralized systems can outperform a centralized organization.

Part III: Product Strategies for Managing Rational/Strategic Consumer Behavior

As a way to entice rational/strategic consumers to make purchases, many companies now offer customized products to meet individual consumer's specification. In Chapter 8, Aydin Alptekinoglu, Alex Grasas, and Elif Akcali examine the impact of consumers' propensity to return products on product assortment decisions and show that, when return policies are relatively strict, firms may prefer to carry many eccentric products which are unlikely to be purchased by most consumers. In Chapter 9, Sergio Chayet, Panos Kouvelis, and Dennis Yu illustrate how a firm can optimally select production capacity and a set of products with different design quality levels to maximize profits when facing consumers who select the products in a self-interested manner by maximizing their consumption utilities. Kinshuk Jerarth, Serguei Netessine, and Senthil Veeraraghavan examine the conditions under which a firm can increase profits by selling opaque products to strategic consumers in Chapter 10. Opaque products allow an intermediary to hide identity of the products supplied by competing firms so as to reduce direct competition. Finally, in Chapter 11, Ali Parlaktürk considers firms' incentives to adopt mass customization in the presence of self-interested consumers. He shows that it may not be desirable to adopt mass customization even at zero cost due to its negative effect on price competition and that charging different prices for customized products would lead to a broader adoption of mass customization.

Part IV: Operational Strategies for Managing Rational/Strategic Consumer Behavior

This part examines how firms can use various operational instruments to reduce the negative effects associated with rational/strategic customers. Chapters 12, 13, 14, and 15 present different mechanisms to reduce the extent of "strategic waiting" behavior in which customers postpone their purchasing decisions in anticipation of future price drops. First, in Chapter 12, Yossi Aviv, Yuri Levin, and Mikhail Nediak introduce a general framework by exploring five different operational mechanisms: (a) credible price commitments (i.e., pre-announced pricing); (b) rationing capacity; (c) credible capacity commitments; (d) internal price matching policies; and (e) partial inventory information. Then Yossi Aviv, Christopher Tang, and Rui Yin show how inventory display formats and reservations and Gerard Cachon and Robert Swinney demonstrate how volume flexibility and design flexibility can provide effective mechanisms for reducing strategic waiting in Chapters 13 and 14, respectively. Finally, Qian Liu and Garrett van Ryzin explain how a firm can reduce strategic waiting behavior by using capacity rationing as a way to urge customers to purchase early rather than facing higher stock-out risks in Chapter 15.

Part V: Pricing Strategies for Managing Rational/Strategic Consumer Behavior

In this concluding section several authors examine different pricing mechanisms to mitigate the strategic consumer behavior. First, in Chapter 16, Eyal Biyalogorsky demonstrates how contingent pricing can be an effective tool to shape consumer demand so that inter-temporal price discrimination can be achieved when consumers endogenously decide when to show up in the market. In Chapter 17, Minho Cho, Ming Fan, and Yong-Pin Zhou show how threshold purchasing policy utilized by the strategic consumer can benefit both the firm selling the product and its consumers. Finally, in Chapter 18, Karan Girotra and Wenjie Tang illustrate how advanced purchase discounts can be an efficient pricing mechanism for achieving optimal outcomes for the firm and its strategic customers. Such discounts lead to better information sharing, superior risk bearing, reduced supply–demand mismatches and can lead to Pareto-improving outcomes for all actors in the supply chain.

References

Besanko D, Winston WL (1990) Optimal price skimming by a monopolist facing rational consumers. Management Science 36:555–567

Bikhchandani S, Hirshleifer D, Welch I (1992) A theory of fads, fashion, custom, and cultural change as informational cascades. Journal of Political Economy 100(5):992–1026

Coase RH, (1972) Durability and monopoly. Journal of Law and Economics 15(1):143–149

Ho TH, Tang CS (1998) Product variety management: Research advances. Kluwer Publishers, Massachusetts

Hotelling H (1929) Stability in competition. Economic Journal 39:41–57

Krishna V (2002) Auction theory. Academic Press, New York

Lilien G, Kotler P, Moorthy KS (1992) Marketing models. Prentice Hall, New Jersey

Acknowledgments

We would like to thank Professor Fred Hillier (Stanford University), the editor of Springer's *International Series in Operations Research and Management Science*, who has strongly encouraged us to work on this book from the very beginning. Clearly, this book would not exist without the strong support and commitment from our academic colleagues. Knowing the amount of time we withdraw from their busy schedule, we would like to express our sincere appreciation to the contributing authors for sharing their cutting-edge research with us (see table below). Last, but not least, we are grateful to Mirko Janc for typesetting each chapter beautifully and expeditiously. Of course, we are responsible for any errors that may occur in this book.

Affiliation (in alphabetical order)	Contributing authors (in alphabetical order)
Arizona State University, Mesa	Rui Yin
Carnegie Mellon University, Pittsburgh	Kinshuk Jerath
Clarkson University, Potsdam	Dennis Z. Yu
Columbia University, New York	Matulya Bansal, Costis Maglaras, Garrett van Ryzin
Hong Kong University of Science and Technology, New Territories	Qian Liu
University of Navarra, Pamplona	Victor Martínez-de-Albéniz
INSEAD, Fontainebleau	Karan Girotra, Wenjie Tang
Northwestern University, Chicago	Gad Allon, Achal Bassamboo
Queen's University, Ontario	Yuri Levin, Mikhail Nediak
Southern Methodist University, University Park	Aydin Alptekinolu
Stanford University, Stanford	Barchi Gillai, Basak Kalkanci, Hau L. Lee, Robert Swinney, SeungjinWhang
University of California, Berkeley	Xuanming Su
University of California, Davis	Eyal Biyalogorsky
University of California, Los Angeles	Felipe Caro, Christopher S. Tang
University of Chicago, Chicago	Laurens G. Debo
University of Florida, Gainesville	Elif Akçali, Alex Grasas
University of North Carolina, Chapel Hill	Ali K. Parlaktürk
University of Pennsylvania, Philadelphia	Gérard P. Cachon, Serguei Netessine, Senthil K. Veeraraghavan
University of Washington, Seattle	Minho Cho, Ming Fan, Yong-Pin Zhou
Washington University, St. Louis	Yossi Aviv, Sergio Chayet, Panos Kouvelis, Fuqiang Zhang

Contents

**3   The Effect of Assortment Rotation on Consumer Choice
and Its Impact on Competition** 63

Felipe Caro and Victor Martínez-de-Albéniz

4   Models of Herding Behavior in Operations Management 81

Laurens G. Debo and Senthil K. Veeraraghavan

Part II Organizational Strategies for Managing Rational/Strategic Consumer Behavior

Part III Product Strategies for Managing Rational/Strategic Consumer Behavior

8 Is Assortment Selection a Popularity Contest? 205

Aydın Alptekinoğlu, Alex Grasas, and Elif Akçalı

9 Product Design, Pricing, and Capacity Investment in a Congested Production System 229

Sergio Chayet, Panos Kouvelis, and Dennis Z. Yu

Part IV Operational Strategies for Managing Rational/Strategic Consumer Behavior

18 Strategic Behavior in Supply Chains: Information Acquisition 459
Karan Girotra and Wenjie Tang

Part I
Rational Consumer Behavior: Endogenous Decision Making Mechanisms

Chapter 1
Cheap Talk in Operations: Role of Intentional Vagueness

Gad Allon and Achal Bassamboo

Abstract Provision of real-time information by firms to their customers has become prevalent in recent years in both the service and retail sectors. Service providers use delay announcements to inform customers about anticipated service delays, whereas retailers provide the customers with information about the inventory level and the likelihood of a stockout. Often, this information cannot be credibly verified by the customers. The question of which information should the firm share with its customers is a complex one, and its answer depends among other things on the dynamics of the underlying operations and the customer behavior.

This chapter addresses these issues by proposing a model in which customers treat information provided by the service provider as unverified and non-binding. The model thus treats customers as strategic in the way they process information, as well as in making the decisions (that is, in service settings whether to join or balk, and whether to buy or wait in retail), and the firm as strategic in the way it provides the information. The customers and the firm are assumed to be self-interested in making their decisions: the firm in choosing which announcements to make and the customers in interpreting these and making the decisions. This allows us to characterize the equilibrium language that emerges between the firm and its customers. By doing that, not only do we relax the assumption that customers are naive in their treatment of the announcements, but we also demonstrate that many of the commonly used announcements arise in equilibrium in such a model.

Gad Allon
Kellogg School of Management, 2001 Sheridan Road Evanston, Chicago IL 60208, USA,
e-mail: g-allon@kellogg.northwestern.edu

Achal Bassamboo
Kellogg School of Management, 2001 Sheridan Road Evanston, Chicago IL 60208, USA,
e-mail: a-bassamboo@kellogg.northwestern.edu

S. Netessine, C.S. Tang (eds.), *Consumer-Driven Demand and Operations Management Models*, International Series in Operations Research & Management Science 131, DOI 10.1007/978-0-387-98026-3_1, © Springer Science+Business Media, LLC 2009

1.1 Introduction

Provision of real-time information by firms to their customers has become prevalent in recent years in both the service and retail sectors. Service providers use announcements to inform customers about anticipated delays, whereas retailers provide the customers with information about the inventory level and the likelihood of a stockout. Often, this information cannot be credibly verified by the customers. The question of which information should the firm share with its customers is a complex one, and its answer depends among other things on the dynamics of the underlying operations and the customer behavior.

Most of the Operations Management literature addressing this issue analyzed two categories of information provided to the customer: (i) full information – the state of the system, as known to the system manager when the customer arrives, and (ii) no information – where no information is provided, and customers must base their decisions on their expectation regarding the system performance. The main assumption made in the former category of literature is that customers treat the information provided regarding the state of the system as a priori verified (i.e., credible) and act accordingly in making their decisions. The two main issues with this assumption are the following: (i) Customers are seldom naive in their attitude toward any information provided by interested parties and thus take such announcements with a "grain of salt." Moreover, under the assumption of "naivety," it makes sense for the firm to deviate from the truth-telling policy. The option that the firm might *lie,* given that the customer always believes the firm, is never explored in the literature. (ii) Further, prior work implicitly assumes that the announcements have a literal meaning in terms of the availability (in retail) or delay (in services) or average waiting time. However, as stated above, many service providers use verbal messages that need to be further processed in order for customers to make the decision. For example, without processing, it is not clear what "high volume of calls" or "almost gone" mean in terms of delay in the system (in services) and availability of the product (in retail) in these commonly used statements. This problem is clearly a consequence of the first issue since, without processing, only announcements with literal meaning are possible. The combination of these two issues contributed to the fact that only simple (i.e., no-information or full-information) announcements were discussed, while in practice we observe a much richer variety of announcements.

This chapter surveys models that address these issues. In particular, the customers in these models treat information provided by the service provider as unverified and non-binding. These models, thus, treat customers as strategic in the way they process information, as well as in making the decisions (that is, in service settings whether to join or balk and whether to buy or wait in retail), and the firm as strategic in the way it provides the information. The customers and the firm are assumed to be self-interested in making their decisions: the firm in choosing which announcements to make and the customers in interpreting these and making the decisions. Note that, while previous models assumed customers to be strategic in the way they make decisions (being forward-looking) or in the way they form expectations, these models are the first to study settings in which customers are strategic in the way they *interpret* information provided by other parties. That is, customers do not take the messages or the information provided by the firm at their "face value."

This allows us to characterize the equilibrium language that emerges between the firm and its customers. By doing so, these models not only do relax the assumption that customers are naive in their treatment of the announcements but also demonstrate that many of the commonly used announcements arise in equilibrium. For example, in services, the spectrum of possible equilibria will range from announcements that are analogous to the verbal type, describing the volume of arriving customers as high or low to the detailed waiting time announcements, both common in service systems. In retail settings, it is shown that an informative language is not possible between a single retail and its customers. These models are among the first to show that the spectrum of announcements that exists in real-world applications can emerge as an equilibrium of a game between the provider and her customers.

This chapter surveys the emerging literature that deals with the strategic nature of the information transmission in a practical operational setting, where unverifiable, non-committal, real-time information is provided by a self-interested firm to selfish customers.

In this literature, the announcements made by the system manager is modeled as "cheap talk," i.e., pre-play communication that carries no cost. Cheap talk consists of costless,[1] non-binding, non-verifiable messages that may affect the customer's beliefs. It is important to note that while providing the information does not *directly* affect the payoffs, it has an indirect implication through the customer's reaction and the equilibrium outcomes. The information has no impact on the payoffs of the different players per se, i.e., the payoffs of both sides depend only on the actions taken by the customer and queueing dynamics. This, in turn, means that if the customer does not follow the recommendation made by the firm, he is not penalized, nor is he rewarded when he follows them. However, as it will be shown, the announcements do have an impact on the service provider's profits and the customers' utility, in equilibrium. This is in agreement with both the cheap talk literature (see Crawford and Sobel (1982)) and the operations management literature with strategic customers. (See Naor (1969) for a queueing application and Aviv and Pazgal (2008) for a retail application, where the information provided to the customer in the form of full visibility of the state of the system does not alter the customer's utility directly; however, it allows him to make a knowledgeable decision and thus affects his utility in an indirect manner.)

The focus of these models is dealing with the *strategic* interaction between the customer and the firm in a setting in which their incentives are *misaligned*, when *unverifiable, costless, and non-binding* information is provided to the customer. In all of the instances described in this chapter, the information is always unverifiable

---

[1] We assume that the cost associated with conveying the message is negligible. In most practical service organizations, while the provider needs to incur fixed costs, for example, by investing in a more sophisticated IT infrastructure to learn the state of the system, the marginal cost of providing the information to the customer is insignificant. There is a voluminous literature starting with Spence (1973) dealing with models where signaling is not costless, and the mere fact that players are willing to incur a cost provides a signal.

and has no contractual bearing. This is in contrast to service-level *guarantees*, such as those made by Dominos Pizza, Ameritrade, and E*trade to name a few, where the commitment is both contractually binding and verifiable.

A Reading Guide and Equilibrium Concept

The next section reviews the classical cheap talk model introduced by Crawford 1982. We discuss the challenges one faces in developing a framework that echoes the classical cheap talk model for dynamic operational settings. Section 1.3 describes the cheap talk game in a service setting, and Section 1.4 describes the cheap talk game in retail.[2] These sections are almost independent and can be read in any order. Section 1.5 summarizes the finding in the previous section and contrasts the equilibrium language in the queueing with the retail one. We conclude the chapter by surveying related literature and future direction. In this chapter, we refer to the equilibrium concept as Bayesian Nash Equilibrium. A careful reader would note the restrictions imposed are in fact for Markov Perfect Bayesian Nash Equilbrium. However, for brevity, we will omit the phrase Markov Perfect and simply use Bayesian Nash Equilibrium.

1.2 Classical Cheap Talk Game

In this section, we provide an overview of the cheap talk game introduced in Crawford and Sobel (1982). This is a game played between a *Sender* who has some private information and a *Receiver* who takes the action which impacts the payoff of both players. We next define the game and highlight the key findings.

1.2.1 Model

The game proceeds as follows: The Sender observes the state of the world, which we shall denote by Q, which is private information and is uniformly distributed on the unit interval. The Sender then sends a signal (or a message) denoted by $m \in \mathcal{M}$. (Here $\mathcal{M}$ denotes the set of all signals that can be used by the Sender.) The Receiver processes this information and chooses an action y which determines the players payoff. The Sender obtains an utility which depends on (a) the action taken by the Receiver y; (b) the state of the world Q; and (c) his bias which we denote by b and is given by $V(y, Q, b) = -(y - (Q + b))^2$. The Receiver, on the other hand, obtains an utility which depends only on (a) his own action y and (b) the state of the world, Q, and is given by $U(y, Q) = -(y - Q)^2$.[3]

---

[2] All the proofs of the results in Sections 1.3 and 1.4 are in Allon et al. (2007) and Allon and Bassamboo (2008), respectively.

[3] We adopt a notation that is different from the one used in Crawford and Sobel (1982). This is done in order to be consistent with the notation developed in the model used in the latter part of

The Bayesian Nash equilibrium of the above game requires that (a) the Sender's signaling rule yields an expected-utility maximizing action for each of the state of the world Q, fixing the action rule for the Receiver; and (b) the Receiver responds optimally to each possible signal using Bayes' rule to update his prior, taking into account the Sender's signaling rule and the message/signal received from the Sender.

1.2.2 Key Results

For this classical cheap talk game, there always exists an equilibrium where *no information* is transmitted from the Sender to the Receiver, irrespective of the parameters of the problem. In fact this is the only equilibrium of the game when the bias b exceeds $1/4$. However, when b is less than $1/4$, informative equilibria exist. All these equilibria share the same structure that they partition the state space (i.e., the unit interval) into finite number of intervals. On each of these intervals the Sender uses the same message. Further, they show that the number of intervals is bounded from above by an integer which is a function of the bias and is denoted by $N(b)$. The equilibrium where the sender partitions the state space into exactly $N(b)$ partitions is referred to as the *most informative equilibrium*. Further, it is shown that among all the equilibria, both the Sender and Receiver are better off in expectation under the most informative equilibrium.

1.2.3 Other Applications of the Classical Cheap Talk Model

A variety of papers study mixed-motive economic interaction involving private information and the impact of cheap talk on the outcomes. Farrell and Gibbons (1989) study cheap talk in bargaining; in political context cheap talk has been studied in multiple papers including Austen-Smith (1990) and Matthews (1989). A recent paper by Ren et al. (2007) studies a cheap talk game where a retailer shares forecast information with a supplier. These models almost exclusively focus on static environments. In operational systems information, transmission which is typically done in real time cannot be categorized in the classical model and the dynamic environment is, in general, multidimensional and complex.

1.2.4 Discussion

The framework used in this chapter echoes the cheap talk model proposed in Crawford and Sobel (1982). Driven by the applications in operations, the models have two novel features: first, the game is played with multiple receivers (customers)

---

the chapter. For instance, Q, which denotes the state of the world, would correspond to the queue length in services and the quantity on hand for retail.

whose actions have externalities on other receivers; and second, the stochasticity of the state of the world (i.e., the state of the system) is not exogenously given but is determined endogenously. In particular, the private information in these models (for example, the queue length or the inventory position at any given time in service and retail setting, respectively) is driven by the system dynamics, which in turn depend on the equilibrium strategies regarding the information and actions of both the firm and the customers. As we shall see, this multiplicity of receivers with externalities and the endogenization impact both the nature of the communication as well as the outcome for the various players. This endogeneity, which is crucial for modeling operational setting with customer interaction, is absent in the previous cheap talk literature.

To highlight the impact of the system dynamics, note that there are two types of uncertainties faced in these models: (i) Uncertainty regarding the state of the system when a customer arrives, which is a private information held by the service provider. This type of uncertainty exists in Crawford and Sobel's model as well. (ii) Uncertainty regarding the evolution of the system: Even after announcements are made and the customer decides on his action, both the service provider and the customers are exposed to uncertainty regarding the future dynamics. Note that the latter type of uncertainty is not modeled in Crawford and Sobel (1982). Hence, the definition of the equilibrium concept would require solving a dynamic optimization problem.

1.3 Service Application

In this section, we will survey an *endogenized* cheap talk model which studies the equilibrium language emerging in a service setting. This model is motivated by the prevalence of the practice of informing customers regarding anticipated delays. Call centers often use recorded announcements to inform callers of the congestion in the system and encourage them to wait for an available agent. While some of these announcements do not provide much information – such as the common message, "Due to high volume of calls, we are unable to answer your call immediately," some call centers go as far as providing the customer with an estimate of his waiting time or his place in the queue. In many service systems where the real state of the system is invisible to customers, delay announcements will affect customers' behavior and may, in turn, have significant impacts on the system performance.

1.3.1 Model

We consider a service provider, modeled as an *M/M/*1 system. Customers arrive to the system according to a Poisson process with rate λ. Service times are exponentially distributed with mean $1/\mu$. We assume that $\lambda < \mu$. We assume that all customers are ex ante symmetric: customers obtain a value R if they are served and incur a waiting cost that is proportional to the time spent in the system, with a unit waiting cost of c. Thus, a customer arriving to the system obtains the following utility:

$$U(y) = \begin{cases} R - cw & \text{if } y = \text{"join,"} \\ 0 & \text{if } y = \text{"balk,"} \end{cases} \tag{1.1}$$

where y is the decision made by this customer and w denotes its sojourn time in the system. Throughout the chapter, we shall assume that $R > c/\mu$; this assumption ensures that in the absence of delays, the service is beneficial to the customer, on average. Clearly, if $R < c/\mu$, no customer will join regardless of the system announcements. When a customer arrives, the system manager has private information regarding the number of customers currently waiting in queue, denoted by the random variable Q. Its distribution will depend on the equilibrium strategies of both the provider and the customers, unlike in the classical cheap talk games where the distribution of the state of the world is exogenous.

We assume that if the customer is satisfied (i.e., he obtains non-negative utility from the transaction), the service provider obtains a positive revenue of $\bar{v}$, while if the customer is dissatisfied (i.e., he obtains a negative utility), the service provider incurs a cost of $-\underline{v}$. Thus, the profit function captures the fact that the firm makes higher profit when the customer is satisfied versus when he is not.

Formally, depending on the action taken by the customer, and his actual sojourn time in the system, the firm obtains the following revenues:

$$\pi(y) = \begin{cases} \bar{v} > 0 & \text{if } y = \text{"join" and } R \geq cw, \\ \underline{v} \leq 0 & \text{if } y = \text{"join" and } R < cw, \\ 0 & \text{if } y = \text{"balk."} \end{cases} \tag{1.2}$$

Such profit functions arise naturally in several settings. One such environment is service processes outsourcing. Typically, the outsourcing firm requires the provider, (for example, a call center) to provide an adequate and timely service to the referred customers. The referring firm then pays the call center only for the satisfied customers and penalizes the provider for the dissatisfied ones. Such a structure will also arise in cases where the firm earns certain revenues from satisfied customers but loses goodwill with every dissatisfied ones. Further, we would like to point out that this analysis can be generalized for the setting where the firm's profit from a customer is a monotone decreasing function of the customer's waiting time. An alternative model is studied in Allon et al. (2007)

We assume that the customer decides whether to join or not based on the information he can infer from the system manager regarding the current state of the system, denoted by I, in order to maximize its expected utility. Therefore, the customer will join, if and only if $R \geq c\mathbb{E}(w|I)$, where I is the information provided to this customer.

Note that the customer's and the service provider's incentives are not completely misaligned: both prefer short waiting times, which result in higher utility for the customer and higher profits for the service provider. At the same time, we observe that the incentives are not perfectly aligned and this would lead to equilibria described in the next section. We refer the reader to Farrell and Rabin (1996) for a discussion of settings in which incentives are perfectly misaligned.

1.3.2 Problem Formulation

In this section we formally define the game between the service provider and the customers. The equilibrium concept we employ is one of Bayesian Nash equilibrium, which is simply a Nash equilibrium in the decision rules that relate agents' actions to their information and to the situation in which they find themselves. Recall that customers are indistinguishable and their strategies are ex ante symmetric, both in their interpretations of the signals and in their actions. Let $\mathcal{M} = \{m_1, m_2, \ldots\}$ represent the set of feasible signals that the firm can provide to the customer. We can represent the signaling rule by a function $g : \mathbb{Z} \mapsto \mathcal{M}$, where $g(q) = m$ if the firm uses the signal m when the queue length is q. Let $y : \mathcal{M} \mapsto \{0, 1\}$ denote the strategy of the customer, where $y(m)$ is the probability that a customer joins when the firm signals m. Consequently, we interpret $y(m) = 1$ as a "join" decision and $y(m) = 0$ as a "balk" decision and we will use this alternative terminology interchangeably. Note that the above signaling and action rules restrict attention to pure strategies. The requirements of a Bayesian Nash equilibrium in our context are rather intuitive. Given a signaling rule for the system, customers with an action rule that dictates joining the system when the signal is m will not deviate from this rule if their expected conditional utility, given by $\mathbb{E}[R - c((q+1)/\mu)|g(q) = m]$, will be negative by doing so. Given the customer's action rule $y(m)$, the firm will deviate from its signaling rule $g(q)$ if it maximizes its steady-state profit, i.e., if $g(q)$ solves an appropriate Markov decision process (see below) with respect to the action rule $y(m)$. The above is formalized in the following definition.

Definition 1. (Bayesian Nash Equilibrium) We say that the signaling rule $g(q)$ and the action rule $y(m)$ constitute a Bayesian Nash equilibrium (BNE), if they satisfy the following conditions:

1. Let $N = \inf\{q : y(g(q)) = 0\}$. Let p_q^N be the steady-state probability that the number of customers in an $M/M/1/N$ is q.[4] For each $m \in \mathcal{M}$, we have

$$
y(m) = \begin{cases} 1 & \dfrac{\sum_{\{q:g(q)=m\}} \left[R - c\frac{q+1}{\mu}\right] p_q^N}{\sum_{\{q:g(q)=m\}} p_q^N} \geq 0, \\ 0 & \text{otherwise.} \end{cases}
$$

---

[4] Note that p_q^N can be thought of as the beliefs of the agents on the state of the systems. These beliefs are consistent with the strategy of the other players.

2. With $f(j) = (\bar{v} - \underline{v})\mathbb{P}\{W(j+1) \leq R/c\} + \underline{v}$, there exist constants $J_0, J_1, \ldots$ and γ that solve the following set of equations:

$$
\begin{aligned}
J_0 &= \max_{m \in \mathcal{M}} \left\{ \frac{f(0)y(m) - \gamma}{\lambda} + J_0(1 - y(m)) + J_1 y(m) \right\} \\
&= \frac{f(0)y(g(0)) - \gamma}{\lambda} + J_0(1 - y(g(0))) + J_1 y(g(0)) \\
J_q &= \max_{m \in \mathcal{M}} \left\{ \frac{f(q)y(m) - \gamma}{\lambda + \mu} + \frac{\mu}{\lambda + \mu} J_{q-1} + \frac{\lambda}{\lambda + \mu}(J_q(1 - y(m)) + J_{q+1}y(m)) \right\} \\
&= \left\{ \frac{f(q)y(g(q)) - \gamma}{\lambda + \mu} + \frac{\mu}{\lambda + \mu} J_{q-1} \right. \\
&\quad \left. + \frac{\lambda}{\lambda + \mu}(J_q(1 - y(g(q))) + J_{q+1}y(g(q))) \right\}.
\end{aligned}
\tag{1.3}
$$

In the above definition of BNE, the first condition uses the Bayesian rule for the customer based on the signaling function g to determine whether to join or balk. The second condition states that the composite function $y \circ g$ solves the *admission control-type* MDP for the firm. In the optimality equations (1.3), the constant γ represents the long-run average profit made by the firm under optimal policy, and constants $J_0, J_1, \ldots$ represent the *relative cost* for states $0, 1, \ldots$.

1.3.3 Informative Equilibria

While the definition of the pure strategy BNE in the previous section is complete, it is not directly amenable for further analysis. Thus, the first step toward characterizing the equilibria is to show that any pure strategy BNE can be described using a threshold level. The next proposition shows that such a mapping always exists.

Proposition 1. *Let the pair $y(m)$ and $g(q)$ be a pure strategy BNE such that N defined in condition (1) of Definition 1 is finite. Then there exists a constant $\bar{q}$ such that the pair $(\tilde{g}(\cdot), \tilde{y}(\cdot))$ given by*

$$
\tilde{g}(q) = \begin{cases} m_1 & q \leq \bar{q}, \\ m_0 & \text{otherwise.} \end{cases}, \qquad \tilde{y}(m) = \begin{cases} 1 & m = m_1, \\ 0 & \text{otherwise.} \end{cases}
\tag{1.4}
$$

forms a BNE with the same firm profit and customer utility.

The above result implies that instead of studying the actions taken by customers and the announcement made by the firm in each state of the system (i.e., queue length), we can focus on the threshold queue length, below which the customer's action will be "join," while above which it will be "balk." Note that the equilibria characterized using the above proposition requires that the constant N in Definition 1 be finite. There may exist equilibria where the constant N is infinite. We shall discuss these in Section 1.3.4.

While every pure strategy BNE with finite N is equivalent to a pure strategy BNE induced by some threshold, the converse is not true, i.e., not all thresholds induce a pure strategy BNE. Indeed thresholds below q^* defined by (1.5) below and above a certain level cannot form a pure strategy BNE. Thus, given a threshold level, one needs to verify that it indeed induces a pure strategy BNE via the functions $\widetilde{g}$ and $\widetilde{y}$. Since we frequently use this notion, we formally define it below.

Definition 2. We say that the threshold $\bar{q}$ induces a pure strategy BNE if the pair $(\widetilde{g}(\cdot), \widetilde{y}(\cdot))$ given by (1.4) forms a BNE, and this pair is said to be the induced BNE by this threshold.

Before delving into the analysis of the model and the characterization of the equilibrium, we would like to take a step back and develop intuition into the possible regimes and outcomes. In order to do that, and knowing that we can focus on threshold levels, we characterize two important threshold levels: the first, q^*, denotes the threshold value above which a customer *will not* join, given that he has **full information** of the state of the system, and below which he *will join*. The second threshold level, $\widehat{q}$, is motivated by the service provider's point of view and denotes the threshold level below which the service provider would like the customers to join and above which she would like them to balk, if she had **full control** of their actions.

Full Information

We will define q^* to be the threshold value above which the customer will not obtain positive utility, in expectation, given full queue length information. It is easy to see that

$$q^* = \left[\frac{R\mu}{c} \right], \tag{1.5}$$

where $[\cdot]$ is the bracket function; i.e., q^* is the largest integer not exceeding $R\mu/c$. Note that this threshold pertains to the marginal customer who decides to balk. We will refer to this as the first-best from the customer's perspective, as this maximizes the utility for the individual (selfish) customer. Note that, as shown in Naor (1969), this threshold, which is based on self-optimization (to use Naor's (1969) terminology), falls short of maximizing the overall expected utility of the customer population.

Full Control

From the service provider's point of view, deciding on a threshold level amounts to deciding what should be the finite waiting space in an $M/M/1/k$ queueing system. For each value of k, the expected number of customers joining the queue per unit of time equals $\lambda[(1-\rho^k)/(1-\rho^{k+1})]$ where $\rho = \lambda/\mu$. Let $\widehat{q}$ denote the optimal waiting space. Thus, $\widehat{q}$ solves the following full control optimization problem:

$$\widehat{q} = \arg\max_k \ \lambda \frac{1-\rho^k}{1-\rho^{k+1}} \left[\bar{v}\beta(k) + \underline{v}(1-\beta(k)) \right], \tag{1.6}$$

where $\beta(k) = \mathbb{P}(W_k \leq R/c)$, and W_k is the steady-state sojourn time of the customers who join the $M/M/1/k$ queue. The following proposition is given to show that such a threshold exists and to discuss the properties of the objective function of the full control optimization problem faced by the service provider.

Proposition 2. *The function defined by*

$$\Pi(k) := \lambda \frac{1-\rho^k}{1-\rho^{k+1}} \left[\bar{v}\beta(k) + \underline{v}(1-\beta(k))\right]$$

is unimodal in k, i.e., there exists $k^* \in \{1, 2, \ldots, \infty\}$ such that the function $\Pi(k)$ is strictly increasing for $k < k^*$ and strictly decreasing for $k \geq k^*$.

Using these two quantities, q^* and $\widehat{q}$, which are based on unilateral optimization under full information to the customers and the full control of the service provider respectively, we can identify three regions. These regions are based on the misalignment between the customers and the service provider and correspond to different levels of the so-called *bias* in the cheap talk literature. Each of these regions results in a different type of conflict of interest and thus different equilibria and outcomes for both sides. Figure 1.1 depicts the different regions and the equilibrium announcements in each one, which we will discuss next. We will initially outline the key equilibrium in each of the three regions and the intuition behind them. The intuition will be followed by a formal statement in Proposition 3. The three cases are given below:

I. Complete alignment: $q^* = \widehat{q}$.   In this region, the interests of the two parties are completely aligned, and thus the pure strategy BNE is as follows. The firm gives two signals: (i) the first for low congestion, which can be denoted as "Low." This signal is announced if the queue length is below q^*. (ii) A second signal denoted

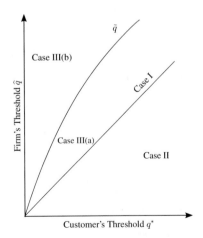

Fig. 1.1 The three regions as defined in Proposition 3.4, based on full control and full information. An informative equilibrium exists only in region IIIa and I.

by "High," which indicates high congestion, and is given when the queue length exceeds q^*. Thus we have $g(q) =$ "Low" if $q < q^*$ and $g(q) =$ "High" otherwise; the customer joins the queue when he/she receives the signal "Low" and balks otherwise, i.e., $y(\text{"Low"}) =$ "join", $y(\text{"High"}) =$ "balk."

As stated before, this is the key equilibrium in this region; however, this need not be the unique pure strategy BNE. As discussed in Allon et al. (2007) there are multiple equilibria in this model. However, it can be shown that even the more informative equilibria are equivalent to the one described above.

II. Overly patient customers: $q^* > \widehat{q}$. In this region, if customers are endowed with full information, they would like to join the system even when the service provider would like them to balk (if she had full control). Thus, we use the term "overly patient" to emphasize the fact that, in this case, customers are willing to join a more congested system than what the firm would like. Specifically, when the queue length is between $\widehat{q}$ and q^*, the customers would like to join whereas the firm would like them to balk.

We will show that there is no threshold which is immune to defection by both the customers and the firm and consequently that there is no BNE in pure strategies. Indeed, for pure strategy BNE to exist the firm should be able to signal "High" and customers who receive "High" should balk. The only threshold immune to profitable deviation by the firm is $\widehat{q}$. Given that under any pure strategy BNE, the customers respond to "High" by balking, a profitable deviation for the firm from any other candidate threshold is to announce "High" at $\widehat{q}$. The customers, however, know that $\widehat{q} < q^*$ so that $\widehat{q}$ cannot induce an equilibrium: an arriving customer that receives the signal that instructs him to "balk" can deviate from the prescribed equilibrium strategy by joining; the customer will then earn positive utility (since the *only* state in which he can receive such a signal is on the threshold itself, which is, by assumption, below q^*), and thus *detect* (on average) that such a deviation is profitable – hence ruling out the possibility of a pure strategy BNE.

III. Impatient customers: $q^* < \widehat{q}$. In this region, the service provider would like the customers to join a more congested system than the one they wish to join. Specifically, when the queue length is between q^* and $\widehat{q}$, the firm would like the customers to join, whereas the customers would like to balk. In order to study this region, we define $F(q)$ to be the customer's expected utility if he finds q customers in the system upon arrival and decides to join the queue; i.e., $F(q) := R - c(q+1)/\mu$. We define for $\ell < k$,

$$G(\ell,k) = \sum_{q=\ell}^{k-1} p_q^k F(q), \tag{1.7}$$

where $p_q^k := [\rho^q(1-\rho)]/(1-\rho^{k+1})$ is the steady-state measure of the $M/M/1/k$ queue. Here, $G(0,k)$ is interpreted as the average utility of a customer joining the $M/M/1/k$ queue.

Then, we have two subcases to consider:

(a) $G(0,\widehat{q}) \geq 0$: If the firm announces "Low" when the queue length is below $\widehat{q}$ and "High" otherwise, the customer would like to join when they get the "Low" signal, as their expected utility is positive (since $G(0,\widehat{q}) > 0$). Further, since in equilibrium "High" would be announced only when the queue exactly equals $\widehat{q}$, the customer would balk as they know that $q^* < \widehat{q}$. This is optimal for the firm and also describes our pure strategy BNE for this setting. Thus, the firm is capable of achieving its first-best profits and operates as if it has full control over the customer decisions.

(b) $G(0,\widehat{q}) < 0$: In this case there is no threshold-induced pure strategy BNE. For pure strategies to exist the firm should be able to signal "Low" and customers who receive "Low" should join. As in case II, the only threshold immune to profitable deviation of the firm is $\widehat{q}$. However, the customers know that $\widehat{q} > q^*$, thus the threshold $\widehat{q}$ cannot constitute an equilibrium: an arriving customer that receives a signal that instructs him to "join" would obtain negative expected utility and thus can deviate from the prescribed equilibrium strategy by balking and obtaining zero utility. This rules out the possibility of a threshold-induced pure strategy BNE.

The intuition of the above is as follows: if the expected utility of the customers under an $M/M/1/\widehat{q}$ system, as given by $G(0,\widehat{q})$, is positive, they will have no incentive to deviate. Any deviation here will lead to zero utility for the customers. If, on the other hand, their utility is negative, they would be better off by not joining at all. Consequently, the threshold $\widehat{q}$ cannot induce a pure strategy BNE. Further, no other threshold is immune to profitable deviation on the firm's part. Thus, in case III(b) there does not exist a pure strategy BNE. We emphasize, however, that in case III(a) the customer can be lured, by using intentional vagueness, to join the system even in states in which they obtain negative expected utility as long as their utility averaged over all state in which they join is positive.

We turn now to the formal statement and proof of the equilibria we have discussed thus far. To this end, we let Π_{FI} and Π_{FC} be the firm's profit under full information and full control, respectively. Let U_{FI} and U_{FC} denote the expected utility of the customers under full information and full control, respectively. As discussed before, Π_{FC} is the first-best profit for the firm and U_{FI} is the first-best utility for the customer. The next proposition summarizes the above result and also compares the firm's profit and expected customer utility under the different equilibria.

Proposition 3. *I. If $q^* = \widehat{q}$, then q^* induces a pure strategy BNE. Under this equilibrium the firm's profit equals Π_{FC} and the expected utility of the customers is U_{FI}.*
  II. If $q^* > \widehat{q}$, there is no finite q that induces a pure strategy BNE.
  III. If $q^* < \widehat{q}$, then:
    (a) If $G(0,\widehat{q}) > 0$, $\widehat{q}$ induces a pure strategy BNE. Under this equilibrium the firm's profit equals Π_{FC} and the expected utility of the customers is U_{FC}.
    (b) If $G(0,\widehat{q}) \leq 0$, there is no finite q that induces a pure strategy BNE.

To summarize the findings so far: we have identified three regions, each with a different equilibrium behavior. We observed that a pure strategy BNE exists only if the firm's and the customers' incentives are perfectly aligned or if the customers are mildly impatient. We find that in these equilibria, only a two-signal language is required, thus providing analytical support to the common "high congestion/low congestion" announcement observed in practice. Proposition 3 establishes conditions for the existence of pure strategy *informative* BNE's as a function of the system parameters and characterizes these whenever they exist. It also raises two important questions: are the equilibria outlined above (where they exist) the only equilibria. Further, does the lack of equilibria (for the appropriate regions) suggest that no equilibrium language whatsoever is possible. To discuss these questions, we shall consider these two types of equilibria. First, we show the existence of a *babbling* equilibria, where the firm provides no information. Next, we extend the definition of BNE to allow customers to randomize their actions. We characterize the *non-informative* as well as the *informative mixed* strategy BNE. Here, the informative mixed strategy BNE is again a two-signal language. While other equilibria can be constructed as well, they are equivalent to the two-signal equilibrium.

1.3.4 Non-informative and Other Equilibria

The equilibria constructed above are based on a signaling rule with two signals. In practice, however, there are many service providers that share no information whatsoever with the customer, whether it is direct information or one that is implicit in the type of recorded music heard while waiting. Are these systems, where no information is transmitted, in equilibrium? It turns out that such an equilibrium may indeed exist in our setting. When it does exist, it is referred to as a "babbling" equilibrium, to denote that no information is transmitted, and any information provided is treated by the customers as meaningless. In the setting of Crawford and Sobel (1982), such an equilibrium mostly exists and is sometimes the only possible one. In our model, however, such an equilibrium-in-pure-strategies exists only under certain conditions derived below. In our model, a "babbling equilibrium" exists in pure strategies if, in the absence of information, all customers join (otherwise, given that customers know that all customers balk, they have an incentive to join and earn positive utility). If all customers join, the resulting queueing system is an $M/M/1$ queue (i.e., with infinite waiting space), in which case the average waiting time is $E[W] = 1/(\mu - \lambda)$ and customers join if $R \geq cE[W]$, i.e., if $R \geq c/(\mu - \lambda)$. In this equilibrium, if indeed all customers join, the system manager can obtain the following profits

$$\pi^{NI} = \lambda e^{-(\mu-\lambda)(R/c)}(\bar{v} - \underline{v}) + \lambda \underline{v}.$$

Observe that if $R < c/(\mu - \lambda)$, we cannot have a babbling equilibrium. This underscores one of the differences between the setting of Crawford and Sobel (1982) and our setting. While the uncertainty in Crawford and Sobel (1982) is independent of the equilibrium dynamics, in our setting there is a clear dependence between the uncertainty (as embedded in the steady-state distribution of the queue) and the resulting equilibrium. This manifests itself in the fact that the babbling equilibrium may not exist. To provide rigorous characterization we have the following result.

Proposition 4. *There exists a pure strategy babbling equilibrium if and only if $R \geq c/(\mu - \lambda)$. Further, if $q^* < \widehat{q}$ and $G(0,\widehat{q}) < 0$, i.e., Case III(b) of Proposition 3, there does not exist a pure strategy babbling equilibrium.*

The following proposition shows that even though a babbling equilibrium may exist, the firm's profit obtained under it is dominated by the firm's profits under the two-signal equilibria described above. Further, the overall customer's expected utility is lower under the babbling equilibrium as compared to that achieved under the two-signal one.

Proposition 5. *Assume that $R \geq c/(\mu - \lambda)$ so that the babbling equilibrium is a pure strategy BNE. The firm's profits under babbling equilibrium are always dominated by the two-signal equilibrium described in Proposition 3, if it exists. Further, the customers' expected utility is higher under the equilibrium described in Proposition 3 than under the babbling equilibrium, if it exists.*

Proposition 5 emphasizes the value of communication. Even though a non-informative (babbling) equilibria does exist, both the service provider and the customers are always better off when they move to more informative equilibria if such equilibria exist, i.e., to a two-signal equilibria. This communication does not necessarily maximize the customer's overall expected utility but it does improve it. The logic behind Proposition 5 is as follows: Naor (1969) shows that when customers are self-interested and can observe the length of the queue prior to joining, their optimal threshold q^* will be higher than what the social optimum prescribes but it will be finite. In our setting, we observe that for the two-signal equilibrium, the threshold queue length is at least as high as q^*. Further, for the babbling equilibrium, when it exists, the threshold is infinite. Thus, using information improves the customer's overall expected utility when compared to settings where the service provider is giving no information. Note that this improvement is present in the absence of any verification or credibility of the information provided by the service provider.

At this point, we remind the reader that in the region where the customers are very impatient (region III(b)), there is no pure strategy BNE that is either informative or non-informative. Without expanding the strategy set for the customer or the firm, it is unclear how the system would behave in this parameter regime. In particular, the customer behavior is unpredictable for the service provider. This issue is alleviated by considering randomization on the part of the customer. We next discuss these results in passing. For more details and formal analysis of these equilibria the reader is referred to Allon et al. (2007).

Mixed Strategy Non-informative Equilibria

With the restriction to pure strategies BNE we have shown above that babbling equilibria need not exist. When customers are allowed to use mixed strategies, such equilibria always exist.

The customers randomize among joining and balking, to form a mixed strategy BNE as follows: they choose a probability of joining θ that satisfies $R = c/(\mu - \theta\lambda)$, if $R < c/(\mu - \lambda)$ and $\theta = 1$ otherwise. Under this equilibria, the arrival process is thinned by the customer randomization such that an arriving customer is indifferent between joining and balking. In particular, the customers do not have any profitable deviation.

Informative cheap talk can be viewed as a mechanism to coordinate incentives of the service provider and the customers when credible information cannot be transmitted. If only babbling equilibrium exists, it might suggest that the non-creditability is hampering any possibility of coordination whatsoever between the players. This is exactly the issue we explore below when we examine whether there is a possibility of improvement in the coordination between the service provider and its customers.

Mixed Strategy Informative Equilibrium

Allon et al. (2007) shows that in addition to the babbling equilibria, there may exist more *informative* BNEs in mixed strategies. The results in Allon et al. (2007) imply that there are only two possible types of two-signal mixed strategy BNE in which randomization is used. The two types can be described as follows: The firm announces "High" and "Low" based on the threshold q_{mix}: (a) in the first type of BNE, which we shall refer to as *Join or Randomize* equilibria, the customers who receive "Low" join the system and the customers who receive "High" would join the system with probability $\theta \in (0, 1)$ and balk otherwise; (b) in the second type of BNE, which we shall refer to as *Randomize or Balk* equilibria, the customers who receive "Low" join the system with probability θ and balk otherwise, and the customers who receive "High" would balk. Note that both of these types of equilibria are completely defined by two parameters: the threshold q_{mix} used by the firm for signaling and the randomization parameter θ.

Intentional Vagueness

Allon et al. (2007) shows that unless the firm and the customer are perfectly aligned (that is, $q^* = \widehat{q}$), the equilibrium language always involves *intentional vagueness*. For example, under region (IIIa), the firm uses intentional vagueness to lure customer to join a system they would not join if they had full information. Under mixed strategy equilibria, the firm uses intentional vagueness to ensure that the customer randomizes between joining and balking.

Thus, the firm even though always tells the truth it is almost always an *incomplete* truth.

1.4 Retail Application

In this section we shall apply the above framework to a retail setting. Here, a retailer is trying to sell a product over a time horizon and provides availability information to the arriving customers who make a decision whether to buy or wait. For example, the web-retailer *sierratradingpost.com* uses the tag "almost gone!" for some of the products, and in its Frequently Asked Questions section explains this tag as follows:

> *If an "almost gone!" label appears next to the item, the sell out risk is very high. We rec-ommend that you place your order immediately.*

Several other web-based retailers, such as BarnesandNoble.com and Circuitc-ity.com, allow customers to search for the availability of specific products for in-store pick-up. Along the same lines, web-based travel agencies such as Expe-dia.com allow customers to view the availability of airline tickets on specific flights, prior to making the purchasing decision. Similarly, brick-and-mortar stores use dif-ferent display modes to inform customers about availability. The different displays range from showing ample stock per item to showing only a single item per available product. In all of these examples, the information shared cannot be fully verified by the customers. In the brick-and-mortar examples, a customer does not know if there are more than a single item available even if only one is displayed and cannot verify whether the stock is indeed low, even if a tag "almost gone!" is attached to an item in web-retailing. In this section, we shall study a formal model and study the emerging equilibrium language between the retailer and its customers. We shall also study the setting when there are multiple decentralized information channels available to the customers.

1.4.1 Model

Consider a firm that sells a product during a finite length regular season denoted by $[0, \tau]$ followed by a sales season. Here, τ is a stopping time whose distribution is known to both the firm and the customers. Thus, the sales period begins at a random time and both the firm and its customers observe it only once the sales season starts. Further, we assume that the cumulative distribution function of τ is F_τ. We shall make the following assumption with regard to the distribution of the length of the regular season, τ.

Assumption 1. $\mathbb{E}[\tau - t | \tau > t]$ *is a non-increasing function.*

Simply put, the above assumption requires that in expectation the "sales period" is getting closer as time goes on. The impossibility result described in the chapter would hold even under general conditions but to characterize the specific structure of the equilibrium we shall make this assumption. Let $Q = \{Q(t) : t \in [0, \tau]\}$ be the quantity on hand process, i.e., $Q(t)$ denotes the number of products on hand at time $t \in [0, \tau]$. Thus, $Q(0)$ denotes the initial inventory at the beginning of the regular sea-son. Similarly, $Q(\tau)$ denotes the inventory at the end of the regular season and hence the inventory which is being offered at a discounted price during the sales season. Note that the actual evolution of the quantity on hand process $Q(t)$ is determined by both the arrival process of the customers and their buying decisions, which depend on the information they have, which includes the information provided by the firm.

Customers arrive according to a Poisson process with rate λ. We denote this arrival process by $N = \{N(t) : t \in [0, \tau]\}$, where $N(t)$ is the number of customers that arrived in the interval $[0, t]$. We assume that the firm sells the product for the price p during the regular season. All units that are left at time τ are discounted and sold at a random price S. We assume that S is a random variable which is independent of all other stochasticity in the system and satisfies $\mathbb{P}(S \leq p) = 1$. Further, we assume that the products during the sales season are sold instantaneously at time τ. Thus, the firm's revenue is $p(Q(0) - Q(\tau)) + SQ(\tau)$. Customers are assumed to be ex ante symmetric and obtain value v for the purchased product. Here, we assume $v > p$. A customer that arrives at time $t \in [0, \tau]$ makes the decision whether to buy immediately or wait for the sales season. (If $Q(t) = 0$ then there is no decision to be made.) If he buys immediately, he obtains an utility of $v - p$ which we assume to be positive. If he decides to wait until the end of the period for the sale then he obtains the product with probability $A(Q(\tau))$, where $A(x)$ is the probability that any single customer can obtain the product during the sales period if the sale starts with x units on hand.[5] Depending on whether he is able to buy the product during the sales season or not, he obtains $(v - S) - c^W(\tau - t)$ or $-c^W(\tau - t)$, respectively. Here c^W is the waiting cost incurred by the customer, associated with the inconvenience of not obtaining the product immediately. Hence his expected utility is given by $\mathbb{E}[(v - S)A(Q(\tau)) - c^W(\tau - t)|\tau > t]$, where the expectation is over the quantity available at the beginning of the sales period, $Q(\tau)$. An alternative model where the firm chooses the discounted price and the time of markdown is explored in Allon and Bassamboo (2008).

We shall refer to $A(Q(\tau))$ as the *availability* of the product during the sales season. The customer has the option to leave the market and obtain zero utility, but it can be easily seen since $v > p$ that the option of leaving the market is dominated by the "buying now" option. One can envision a more elaborate model for the availability of the product during the sales season. All the structural results from the chapter will continue to hold, even if the availability function depends on other factors. However, since the focus of this chapter is on the communication, we restrict attention to the above described availability model.

1.4.2 No-Information and Full-Information Strategies

The main focus of this chapter is to characterize the ability (or lack thereof) to communicate unverifiable information to a strategic customer by a retailer. In order to be able to discuss the specific model of communication we will initially discuss the customers behavior under two benchmarks. These correspond to two possible strategies on the firm's part: (i) the strategy of providing no information, and (ii) the

---

[5] We assume the probability that a customer can obtain the product during the sales period depends on the demand during the period only through the number of sales that occurred. This corresponds, for example, to cases where there are other customers that arrive during the sales period, and do not arrive during the regular season. Cachon and Swinney (2007) describe these customers as "bargain hunters," who frequent the store only during the sales season. The resulting availability for a specific customer in their model is similar to ours.

strategy of providing the customer full information regarding the availability of the item upon his arrival. The question whether these strategies would emerge in equilibrium is a separate one and would be addressed later in the chapter when we study the game between the retailer and its customers. There (see Section 1.4.3), we will allow the firm to use different information sharing rules. We will next describe the customers behavior in response to both of these strategies, forming an equilibrium among themselves.

No-Information Solution

In this setting, we assume that the firm is not providing any information with regard to the inventory position. Note that this is equivalent to the case where the customers have decided to disregard any information provided by the firm. Since the customers cannot observe the state of the system, they have to rely on the time to make their decisions. Thus, the strategy of the customer shall simply be a function of time. The customer's strategy is represented by $y = \{y(t) : t \in [0,\infty)\}$, where $y(t) \in [0,1]$ is the probability that a customer arriving at time t buys the product if faced with a decision. (Note that if $t > \tau$ or $Q(t) = 0$ then the customer cannot buy the product and there is no decision to be made.) We next define the notion of Bayesian Nash equilibrium (NE) under no information:

Definition 3. We say that y forms a *BNE under no information*, if the following is satisfied for all $t \in [0,\tau]$:

$$y(t) \in \arg\max_{\theta \in [0,1]} \theta[(v-p)-(v-S)\mathbb{E}[A(Q_y(\tau))]+c^W(\tau-t)|\tau>t],$$

where $Q_y(\tau)$ is the quantity on hand at time τ if the customers follow strategy y.

The definition requires that the customer buys with probability one if his utility from buying is strictly greater than his utility from waiting, assuming other customers follow their time-dependent strategies y. Similarly, his probability of buying is zero if the utility from buying is strictly dominated by that obtained from waiting. If the utilities from buying and waiting are equal, he randomizes between buying and waiting.

The next result shows that there exists a BNE under no information in *pure* strategies, i.e., a BNE for which $y(m) \in \{0,1\}$.

Proposition 6. *There exists a NE under no information in pure strategies. Specifically, there exists $\hat{t}$ such that*

$$y(t) = \begin{cases} 1 & t \le \hat{t} \\ 0 & t > \hat{t} \end{cases}$$

forms a pure strategy NE.

The above theorem shows that there exists an equilibrium among the customers when the firm does not provide any information. One can view this equilibrium as self-organization of the customers among themselves in the absence of any information. Further, this equilibrium exists in pure strategy, i.e., the arriving customer would buy or wait with probability one, depending on the arrival epoch. Note that under the monotonicity assumption 1, we have that there exists a threshold $\hat{\tau}$ until which the customer buys and does not buy after that. However, if this assumption is relaxed, then there still exists pure strategy equilibrium in which multiple switch-over points exist, that is, a customer arriving up to time t_1 will purchase the product, a customer arriving between t_1 and t_2 will wait, and a customer arriving after t_2 will buy immediately, again.

Full Information Solution

In this setting we assume that the customers have perfect information regarding the quantity on hand, based on which they make their buying/waiting decisions. The customers' strategy in this setting is defined via a mapping $y : \mathbb{Z}_+ \times [0, \infty) \mapsto [0, 1]$, where $y(q,t)$ is the probability that a customer arriving at time t buys the product immediately when the quantity on hand is q and $t \leq \tau$. We next define the NE under full information.

Definition 4. We say that y forms a *NE under full information*, if the following is satisfied for all $t \in [0, \infty)$:

$$y(q,t) \in \underset{\theta \in [0,1]}{\arg \max} \, \theta \left[(v - p) - (v - \mathbb{E}[S]) \mathbb{E}[A(Q_y(\tau)) | Q(t) = q, \tau > t] \right.$$

$$\left. + c^W \mathbb{E}[(\tau - t) | \tau > t] \right],$$

where $Q_y(\tau)$ is the quantity on hand at time τ if the customers follow strategy y.

To characterize the NE under full information, without loss of generality we can restrict ourselves to threshold-induced NE. The reason for this is the fact that for any $q, t \in \mathbb{Z}_+ \times [0, \infty)$, if $y(q,t) = 0$ then $y(q',t) = 0$ for all $q' > q$. In addition, if two equilibria y and y' differ on a set of Lebesgue measure zero, then the outcomes of the games, in terms of the customers' utility and the firm's profit, are identical. We next define the customer strategy induced by a threshold function $\eta = \{\eta(t) : t \in [0, \infty)\}$.

Definition 5. We say that a function η induces the customer strategy y if

$$y(q,t) = \begin{cases} 1 & q < \eta(t) \\ 0 & \text{otherwise.} \end{cases}$$

Further, we say that η induces a NE under full information if η-induced customer strategy y forms a NE under full information.

The next result shows that there is a unique threshold η that induces a NE under full information. To this end, note that since $A(\cdot)$ is a non-increasing function, we have that A^{-1}, which denotes the inverse of A, is well defined and is also a non-increasing function.

Proposition 7. *There is a unique NE under full information and it is induced by* $\eta_{FI}(\cdot)$ *which is defined as the pointwise solution to the following equation:*

$$\eta_{FI}(t) = \left[A^{-1} \left(\frac{(v-p) + c^W \mathbb{E}[(\tau - t)|\tau > t]}{(v - \mathbb{E}[S])} \right) \right]. \tag{1.8}$$

One might suspect that the utility obtained by an average customer endowed with full information is higher than the utility obtained by an average customer under the no-information equilibrium. However, this is not always the case, as shown in the numerical study in Allon and Bassamboo (2008). Note that when we move from no information to full information, *all* the customers have more information. The utility obtained by a given customer in our model is driven not only by his own information but also by the actions of the other customers, which drive the availability of the product during the sales period. Further, these actions are driven by their own information set. When we move to full information, other customers are also making more informed decisions, thus the average customer may obtain lower utility.

1.4.3 Cheap Talk Equilibrium

In the last section, we fixed the strategy of the firm with regard to information sharing and studied the equilibrium emerging among the customers. In this section, we explore the game played between the firm and its customers, where the firm is allowed to use any information sharing strategy. In particular, the firm can choose full information as well as no information but is not restricted to do so. To define the single-retailer game formally, we shall start by defining the strategy of the customer followed by the strategy of the firm.

Let $\mathcal{M}$ be the Borel set which comprises of feasible signals that the firm can use. Let $y : \mathcal{M} \times [0, \infty) \mapsto [0, 1]$ represent the strategy of the customers. Here, $y(m,t)$ is the probability that a customer arriving at time t, receiving a signal $m \in \mathcal{M}$, buys the product immediately. Thus, this customer waits for the sales period which starts at time τ with probability $1 - y(m,t)$. Let the space of feasible strategies for the customer be denoted by $\mathcal{Y}$. Let $g : \mathbb{Z} \times [0, \infty) \times \mathcal{M} \mapsto \mathbb{R}$ represent the strategy of the firm. Here $g(q,t,\cdot)$ induces a probability measure on $\mathcal{M}$ from which the firm announces a realization, if the quantity on hand at time t is q. Thus, we will impose the condition that $\int_{\mathcal{M}} g(q,t,m)dm = 1$ for all $q \in \mathbb{Z}$ and $t \in [0, \infty)$. Let the space of feasible strategies for the firm be denoted by $\mathcal{G}$. Note that the quantity on hand process Q is determined by the customer's strategy as well as the firm's strategy g. Let $\mu_{g,y}(t)$ represent the distribution of the signal transmitted at time t if the firm follows strategy g and the customers follow strategy y. A r.v. with measure μ shall be represented by X_{μ}. Further, let the firm's profit under the strategy pair g,y be written as $\Pi(g,y)$, and $Q_{g,y}(t)$ be the inventory on hand process under the strategy pair g, y.

Definition 6. We say that the pair $(g,y) \in \mathscr{G} \times \mathscr{Y}$ forms a Bayesian Nash equilibrium (BNE) in the single-retailer game if and only if it satisfies the following two conditions:

1. For all $m \in \mathscr{M}$ and $t \in [0,\infty)$,

$$y(m,t) \in \arg\max_{y \in [0,1]} y\big[(v-p)$$

$$- \mathbb{E}[(v-s)A(Q_{g,y}(\tau)) - c^W(\tau-t)|\tau > t, X_{\mu_{g,y}(t)} = m]\big].$$

2. Fixing the strategy of the customers y, the strategy of the firm g solves:

$$g \in \arg\max_{\widetilde{g} \in \mathscr{G}} \Pi(y,\widetilde{g}).$$

The above definition requires that both the firm and the customers do not have any unilateral profitable deviation. Specifically, the first condition in the definition requires that fixing the strategy of the rest of the customers and the firm, a customer arriving at time t should not have any profitable deviation. Similarly, the second condition requires that given the customer's action rule y as fixed, the firm maximizes its profit by using strategy g.

Next, we characterize the emerging equilibria in the single retailer game. We prove that it is impossible for the firm to credibly communicate any information to its customers. This result is equivalent to saying that the only type of equilibria that may arise in such a game are non-informative. Thus, it is either the case that the firm provides no information or the firm provides information, but the customers disregard it in making their decisions due to the lack of credibility on the part of the firm. The equilibrium language that emerges in this game does not carry any information and is equivalent to babbling. We shall first define the class of equilibria which are non-informative, and hence referred to as *babbling* equilibria.

Definition 7. We say that the pair $(y,g) \in \mathscr{Y} \times \mathscr{G}$ forms a babbling equilibrium if and only if the pair (y,g) forms a BNE and $y(m_1,t) = y(m_2,t)$ for all $m_1, m_2 \in \mathscr{M}$ and for all $t \in [0,\tau]$.

This definition states that a BNE is a babbling equilibrium if the customer's actions in equilibrium do not depend on the information provided by the firm.

Note that Proposition 6 already established that such an equilibrium always exists in pure strategies in the single retailer game. We next show that babbling is the *only* type of equilibria that can arise in the single retailer game.

Proposition 8 (The impossibility result). *Under any BNE of the single-retailer cheap talk game, the customer's realized buying behavior satisfies the following:*

$$y(X_{\mu_{g,y}(t)},t) = y^*(t) \quad a.s.,$$

for almost all $t \in [0,\tau]$, where there exists a babbling equilibrium where the customer purchases with probability $y^*(t)$ at time $t \in [0,\tau]$.

Proof. Consider any pair $(y,g) \in \mathscr{Y} \times \mathscr{G}$ BNE of the above cheap talk game. We shall first show that at any point in time the firm would provide a signal that would maximize the probability of an arriving customer buying the product immediately. That is,

$$y(X_{\mu_{g,y}(t)}, t) = \max_{m' \in \mathscr{M}} y(m', t).$$

For this, consider condition 2 in the definition of the BNE in the single retailer game. It can be expressed using Markov decision process approach as follows: let $V(q,t)$ be the total expected profit starting from period t until the sales period and having q units on hand. Since the firm would maximize its revenue, $V(\cdot, \cdot)$ should solve:

$$\frac{\partial V(q,t)}{\partial t} = \max_{m \in \mathscr{M}} [\lambda y(m,t)(p + V(q-1,t)) + \lambda(1 - y(m,t))V(q,t)$$
$$+ h(t)\mathbb{E}[S]q - (\lambda + h(t))V(q,t)], \qquad (1.9)$$

where $h(t)$ is the hazard rate of τ which defines the beginning of the sales period. The above can be reexpressed as

$$\frac{\partial V(q,t)}{\partial t} = \max_{m \in \mathscr{M}} y(m,t)\lambda[p + V(q-1,t) - V(q,t)] + h(t)\mathbb{E}[S]q - h(t)V(q,t).$$
$$(1.10)$$

Further, we have $V(q,t) \le p + V(q-1,t)$. Thus, we get the desired result that the support of $g(q,t,s)$ is a subset of $\arg\max_{m \in \mathscr{M}} y(m,t)$. So, we have

$$y(X_{\mu_{g,y}(t)}, t) = \max_{m' \in \mathscr{M}} y(m', t), \quad \text{a.s.}$$

Define $\bar{y}(m,t) = \arg\max_{m' \in \mathscr{M}} y(m',t)$ for all $m \in \mathscr{M}$ and $t \in [0,\infty)$. We can easily verify that the pair $(\bar{y}, g)$ is again a BNE. Further, by construction it is a babbling equilibrium. This completes the proof. $\square$

The above proposition shows that no matter what signaling rule the firm uses, the customers would simply ignore all the signals and make their buying decisions irrespective of any information provided. Thus, in this cheap talk game no credibility whatsoever can be created.

While a babbling equilibrium exists in all variants of the Crawford and Sobel cheap talk game, Allon et al. (2007) demonstrate that it may fail to exist in games with endogenized cheap talk. The result that there exists a pure strategy babbling equilibrium in a retail setting is driven by the fact that customers want to mimic other customers. This is in contrast to Allon et al. (2007) where, if no customer joins/purchases the service, an individual customer would like to join the service. See Section 1.5 for a detailed discussion.

Generalization of the Impossibility Result

In this section, we consider the setting where the pricing and the timing are done endogenously by the firm. We assume that the valuation of the product at time t is given by $v(t)$. The firm chooses the regular season price p, the sales period price s, and the beginning of the sales period τ. An equilibrium for this generalized cheap talk game can be defined in an analogous manner to Definition 7 where the strategy of the firm now includes the pricing and timing as well. Next we state the generalization of the impossibility result.

Consider any equilibrium of the generalized cheap talk game. Fix the pricing and the timing strategy of the firm. The signaling strategy of the firm and the buying/waiting behavior of the customer must also form a BNE equilibrium of a modified game where the pricing and the length of the regular season are exogenously fixed. Further note that Proposition 8 also holds for the setting where the valuation is decreasing. Thus this equilibrium must be non-informative. Further, note that if there is no equilibrium for the generalized cheap talk game, the result holds trivially. Thus we have the following general result.

Proposition 9. *There does not exist any informative equilibrium for the generalized cheap talk game.*

The fact that only babbling equilibria exist in the single retailer game suggests that the inability to credibly disclose information is hampering any possibility of information sharing. We explore this issue next, examining whether it is possible to improve coordination between the retailer and its customers by offering several remedies and studying the resulting games.

1.4.4 Remedies and Discussion

Multiple Channels of Information

While the previous section showed that the only equilibrium that emerges in the single retailer game is a babbling one, we next study a decentralized setting where the existence of a second information provider enables the retailers to gain "some" credibility.

There are numerous cases in practice where multiple channels sell inventory from the same pool of inventory and independently provide availability information (this inventory may either be physically co-located, or virtually pooled). For example, *Dicks.com* and *Modells.com* – whose operations are both run by GSI commerce – compete on the same pool of potential customers yet provide information on the same pool of inventory for the same items. Many brick-and-mortar retailers such as *Barnes & Noble* and *Circuit City* allow the customer to check the availability at the different stores on their web sites. Furthermore, Wal-mart.com, BN.com, and Circuitcity.com have autonomy in managing their marketing and availability decisions. Demery (2004) explains, "Channels run under different responsibility centers and profit centers, so a dot-com, a catalog and brick-and-mortar store were run as separate businesses." We shall show that this multiplicity of information sources can actually help the firms to achieve some credibility. In cases in which such a system is not yet implemented, allowing customers to obtain information through multiple channels can be viewed as a remedy to the inability to communicate unverifiable information with only a single retailer.

To study this multiple-retailer setting and to explore how much credibility "decentralization" can create in this setting, we shall next define the model and proceed to analyze it. We consider multiple autonomous sales channels of the same retailer or multiple sellers sharing a common inventory whose status the customer cannot see or verify. In this setting the sellers' signals are based on the common inventory and the customers make their buying decisions based on both signals. We assume that the utility function and profit of the firms are similar to the previous section with the following modification: the firms receive the profits from the products that are sold through them. Note that similar analysis can be carried out for more general systems, where the retailers carry some inventory "on-site" and share the rest.

To illustrate that an informative equilibria exists in this setting, we shall restrict ourselves to pure strategies. To describe the game formally, we denote the strategies of the firms by functions $g_1 : \mathbb{Z} \times [0, \infty) \mapsto \mathcal{M}$ and $g_2 : \mathbb{Z} \times [0, \infty) \mapsto \mathcal{M}$ to represent the signaling rule for the two sellers and $y : \mathcal{M} \times \mathcal{M} \times [0, \infty) \mapsto$ {"buy," "buy-1," "buy-2," "wait," "wait-1," "wait-2"} to represent the purchasing behavior of the customer. Here $g_i(q,t)$ represents the signal given by the firm $i = 1, 2$ to a customer arriving at time t when the common inventory on hand is q at time t. Here $y(m_1, m_2, t)$ is "buy" if the customer arriving at time t decides to buy with equal probability from firm 1 and firm 2 when he receives the signals $m_1 \in \mathcal{M}$ and $m_2 \in \mathcal{M}$ from firm 1 and firm 2, respectively. The function y is "wait" if the customer decides to wait for the sales period and then buy from either one with equal probability. The action "wait-1" corresponds to the customer deciding to wait for the sales period and buy from retailer 1. The action "wait-2" is defined similarly where the customer buys from retailer 2 in the sales period. Similarly, the actions "buy-1" and "buy-2" correspond to the case when the customer decides to purchase from retailer 1 and 2 with probability one, respectively. Let $\mathcal{G}_1$ and $\mathcal{G}_2$ be the set of feasible strategies for the retailer 1 and 2. For $i = 1, 2$, let $\Pi^i(g_1, g_2, y)$ be the profit of the ith retailer if retailer 1 follows strategy g_1, retailer 2 follows strategy g_2, and the customers follow strategy y.

For the purpose of this study, we shall restrict our attention to threshold-induced strategies for the firms. We next define these strategies as follows:

Definition 8. Let $\eta_i(t)$ $i = 1, 2$ be a decreasing function over the time interval $[0, \infty)$. The triplet of strategies (g_1, g_2, y) induced by η is defined as follows:

$$g_i^{\eta_i}(q,t) = \begin{cases} M_1 & q \leq \eta_i(t) \\ M_2 & \text{otherwise} \end{cases} , \qquad (1.11)$$

$$y^{(\eta_1, \eta_2)}(m_1, m_2) = \begin{cases} \text{"buy"} & m_1 = m_2 = M_1 \\ \text{"wait"} & m_1 = m_2 = M_2 \\ \text{"wait} - 1\text{"} & m_1 = M_2 \text{ and } m_2 \neq M_2 \\ \text{"wait} - 2\text{"} & m_2 = M_2 \text{ and } m_1 \neq M_2 \end{cases} . \qquad (1.12)$$

Further, let Π_η be the total combined profit of the two firms under strategies $\eta_1 = \eta_2 = \eta$.

This definition is based on the following logic for the customer's action. Here M_1 corresponds to a "buy" state and M_2 corresponds to a "wait" state. Note that the announcement M_2 that induces "wait," can actually be a lack of a signal (i.e., the firm is "silent" about the inventory status, and signals only if M_1 is used). Thus, if the firms agree about the information, the customer makes the decision as if there is just one signal. However, if they disagree, then the customer decides not to buy and wait for the sales period. Further, during the sales period the customer (who came during the regular season) visits the firm that provided him the information that it has ample inventory (did not signal M_1) when the other firm did not provide a similar signal.

Next we define the BNE for strategies induced by threshold functions (η_1, η_2). For this let $Q_{\eta_1,\eta_2} = \{Q_{\eta_1,\eta_2}(t) : t \in [0,\infty)\}$ be the quantity on hand process, where $Q_{\eta_1,\eta_2}(t)$ is quantity on hand at time t under the strategies induced by (η_1, η_2).

Definition 9. We say that the triplet $(g_1, g_2, y) \in \mathcal{G} \times \mathcal{G} \times \mathcal{Y}$ induced by (η_1, η_2) forms a BNE in the multi-retailer game if and only if it satisfies the following three conditions:

1. For all $m_1, m_2 \in \{M_1, M_2\}$ and $t \in [0,\infty)$, y satisfies the following:

   a. $y(m_1, m_2, t)$ is "buy" if

   $$(v-p) \geq \mathbb{E}[(v-s)A(Q_{\eta_1,\eta_2}(\tau)) - c^w(\tau - t)|g_i^{\eta_i}(Q_{\eta_1,\eta_2}(t),t) = m_i$$
   $$\text{for } i = 1,2 \text{ and } \tau > t].$$

   b. $y(m_1, m_2, t)$ is "wait," "wait-1," or "wait-2" if

   $$(v-p) < \mathbb{E}[(v-s)A(Q_{\eta_1,\eta_2}(\tau)) - c^w(\tau - t)|g_i^{\eta_i}(Q_{\eta_1,\eta_2}(t),t) = m_i$$
   $$\text{for } i = 1,2 \text{ and } \tau > t].$$

2. Fixing η_2 (hence $g_2^{\eta_2}$) and y, η_1 solves

   $$g_1^{\eta_1} \in \arg\max_{g \in \mathcal{G}} \Pi^1(g, g_2^{\eta_2}, y).$$

3. Fixing η_1 (hence $g_1^{\eta_1}$) and y, η_2 solves

   $$g_2^{\eta_2} \in \arg\max_{g \in \mathcal{G}} \Pi^2(g_1^{\eta_1}, g, y).$$

In Section 1.4.3 we showed that a babbling equilibrium always exists. This equilibrium trivially exists also in the multi-retail game. The next proposition shows that there also exists a BNE where the firms reveal complete information regarding their inventory to their customers. This BNE is induced by the threshold functions

$\eta_i = \eta_{FI}$ for $i = 1, 2$, where η_{FI} is the function that induces the NE under full information defined in Section 1.4.2.

Proposition 10. *Let $p > 2s$. Then the strategy induced by $\eta_i(\cdot) = \eta_{FI}(\cdot)$ for $i = 1, 2$ forms a BNE.*

The importance of this result stems from the somewhat negative result obtained in Proposition 8, where it was shown that only a non-informative equilibria can exist in the single retailer game. Here, we show that the presence of another retailer sharing a common inventory can induce full revelation of the quantity in the common pool at any given time. Thus, we show that competition moved the information sharing from being completely non-informative to being fully informative.

This result also stands in stark contrast to the existing literature on cheap talk games with multiple senders providing information regarding variability in a single dimension. The key driver for the existence of a fully revealing equilibrium even though the inventory status is one-dimensional is the fact that the customer can "punish" the two senders differently given the signals. Even though both senders are identical, when faced with a signal which is off-the-equilibrium path, the customer punishes the senders in a differential manner. For example, if the quantity on hand is greater than $\eta(t)$, one firm announces "buy" and the other firm announces "wait": the customer punishes the firm announcing "buy" and rewards the one saying "wait" by purchasing in the sales period from the firm that announced "wait." In this manner, the customer punishes the firm deviating and rewards the other. Note that in some cases, such as when the equilibrium prescribes "buy," the customer punishes both firms if one firm deviates and tries to induce "wait." The intuition is that the customer may "need" to punish both firms to ensure that no firm tries to induce "buy" while the equilibrium prescribes "wait."

While the above proposition shows that the presence of competition or decentralization allows firms to credibly disclose information to their customers, one should note that decentralization may "destroy" the equilibrium as well if the gains of selling during the regular season are not high enough when compared to those gained during the sales season. Since both firms are competing on the same customer pool, it may create an incentive for a firm to deviate and defer their customers to the sales season in the hope of exclusivity.

Next we pose the question whether there are any other informative equilibria (which are induced by some function η) that are not equivalent to the above described fully revealing BNE, yet provide the customer with some information regarding the availability level.

Proposition 11. *There exist two functions $\underline{\eta}$ and $\overline{\eta}$ such that for any $\eta_1 = \eta_2 = \eta$, which induces strategies that form a BNE in the multi-retailer game, we have $\underline{\eta} \leq \eta \leq \overline{\eta}$.*

The above proposition shows that there exist two functions $\underline{\eta}$ and $\overline{\eta}$ such that any threshold which induces a BNE must lie between $\underline{\eta}$ and $\overline{\eta}$. Figure 1.2 illustrates this result. Under any η that induces an equilibrium, at any point in time t,

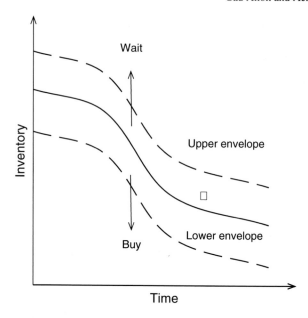

Fig. 1.2 Various thresholds that induce BNE. For each threshold function, the area below the threshold represents a "buy" region and the area above the threshold represents a "wait" region.

the signals provided by the retailers depend on whether the inventory on hand lies in the "buy" region or the "wait," corresponding to the region below and above the threshold, respectively. Note that the threshold function η must lie between $\underline{\eta}$ and $\overline{\eta}$ at each point in time. Furthermore, these envelopes themselves induce BNE. The exact characterization of these envelope thresholds is given in Allon and Bassamboo (2008). Here, we shall outline the intuition behind the characterization of these thresholds.

The informative equilibria corresponding to $\underline{\eta}$ and $\overline{\eta}$ exhibit two extreme consumer behaviors: one in which maximum volume of purchases is induced during the regular season and one in which minimum volume is induced. Note that in both of these equilibria the firms do not reveal the actual inventory level and use *intentional vagueness*. For example, in the BNE induced by $\overline{\eta}$, the number of purchases is maximized by luring the customers to purchase in states of the inventory they would not buy had they known the exact information. This is accomplished by giving one signal on the set over which the average utility obtained from waiting equals the utility obtained by buying the product immediately. To illustrate the idea behind intentional vagueness, consider the following scenario: Suppose at a certain point in time $t \in [0, \infty)$, $\overline{\eta}(t) = 5$, and say that $\tau > t$ and at this t had the customer known the exact status of the inventory they would have bought if the inventory was below 3. The firm uses the same signal as long as the inventory level is below 5, i.e., up to 3 (where the customer would have bought anyway) and also when the inventory is 4 (where the customer would *not* have bought). The firm, however, refrains from telling the truth for lower states, as it will not be able to induce customers to buy when the inventory level is 4. This is due to the fact that the customer would then be able to distinguish between the inventory being below 3 and the state being 4.

Noting the fact that there exist multiple equilibria, an important question to study is which equilibrium does the firm prefer among these. To answer this question we first note that any possible equilibrium must lie between the above-mentioned envelopes. Thus, while there is clearly multiplicity of equilibria in this model, one can bound both the threshold functions that induce equilibria and the possible outcomes for the firms.

Next, we identify the equilibrium which maximizes the profit for the firms. To that end, we shall denote this threshold by η^*. Thus we have

$$\eta^* \in \arg\max_{\eta \in \mathscr{B}} \Pi_\eta,$$

where $\mathscr{B}$ is the set of all decreasing functions that can induce a BNE and Π_η is the combined profit made by the firms under the BNE induced by η. Noting the fact that if η_1 and η_2 both induce BNE, and $\eta_1 \leq \eta_2$, then the firms' combined profit is higher under the BNE induced by η_2, i.e., $\Pi_{\eta_2} \geq \Pi_{\eta_1}$. Then, we have the following corollary.

Corollary 1. *If $p > 2s$ then the profit maximizing BNE in the multi-retailer game is induced by $\overline{\eta}$, i.e., $\eta^* = \overline{\eta}$.*

The above result shows that the presence of decenteralized information by multiple parties *may* improve the firms' profits, if managing to induce, non-cooperatively, equilibrium using the threshold function $\overline{\eta}$.

Third Party Endorsement

In many settings, organizations can create credibility by being endorsed by others, often called "third-party endorsement." These third parties typically do not have a vested interest in the specific firm: they can either be firms that provide certification or generate rating, or non-profit consumer organization. The same role can be played by weblogs covering the specific industry, or bulletin boards where consumers can share information regarding their purchasing experience. One can show that these institutions may allow the retailers to credibly disclose availability information. These third-party endorsements reduce the strategy space for the firm and improves both firm's credibility and the firm's profit.

1.5 Summary

In this chapter, we survey the emerging literature of information sharing between the firms and its customers. A novel framework of *endogenized* cheap talk is developed. In these models, the customers are not only strategic in their actions but also in the way they interpret information, while the firm is strategic in the way it provides information. The developed framework helps answer questions concerning the ability (or the lack thereof) to communicate credibly unverifiable *real-time* information. This framework uses a game-theoretic construct to study this type of communication and discusses the equilibrium language emerging between the firm and its customers. We survey applications of this framework as applied to two models, which are central to the Operations Management literature: the first is a service provider model, and the second is a retail or finite inventory model. We show that one obtains diametrically opposite results with regard to information sharing in service systems and retail systems.

In the setting of a single retailer, the only equilibrium language that may emerge is the one in which no information is revealed to the customer. This result is in contrast to the service setting where a single service provider can "create" some credibility with respect to sharing real-time system information. Further, in the service setting, non-informative, pure strategies equilibrium may not exist. These differences in the nature of equilibrium emerge due to the following distinguishing features of the service and retail operations: (a) In retail operations, the incentives of the customers and the firm are aligned for low inventory levels (i.e., both "agree" that the customer should purchase in these states) and misaligned for high inventory level (i.e., the firm would like the customers to purchase; however, given that the inventory is high the customers can improve their utility by postponing the purchase to the sales season). However, in service operations, the service provider's and its customers' incentives are aligned both when the number of customers waiting in the system is "high" or "low." The only misalignment is when the number of customers is moderate. Since misalignment is limited in the service setting it helps the provider create some credibility. Thus, the one-sided-only agreement in retail operations games prevents the firm from creating any credibility when it is providing the information on its own. (b) The non-existence of an equilibrium when no information is provided in the service setting is due to the "contrarian" behavior characteristic of queueing systems, i.e., customers prefer joining an empty system and resent joining a congested one. On the other hand, customer behavior in retail is one of mimicking, i.e., customers are more interested in buying if many customers buy during the regular season, due to the fear of low availability during the sales season.

One of the strongest phenomena common to both settings is the use of intentional vagueness. In the service setting, the firm might be vague either to lure customers to join the systems in states they would otherwise balk or to create credibility. In the retail setting, when an informative equilibrium exists (e.g., when the information is provided by multiple autonomous retailers), the firm would always favor using a language that is intentionally vague.

1.6 The Past and the Future

Recent literature in Operations Management analyzes and models the impact of strategic customers on managing operational systems. We begin by surveying this literature, both for queueing systems and inventory models.

Queueing Models with Strategic Customers

The literature on queueing models with strategic customers began with Naor (1969), who studied a system in which strategic customers observe the length of the queue prior to making the decision whether to join or balk. There is a (partial) conflict of interest between the self-interested customer and the interests of the social-welfare-maximizing service provider. Naor (1969) shows that pricing can be used to achieve the first-best solution. The follow-up literature that extends Naor (1969) can be broadly divided into two: one that studies models where the firm offers different grades of services (see Mendelson and Whang (1990) and the recent paper by Afeche (2004)), and the other that focuses on competition in the presence of congestion-sensitive customers (see Cachon and Harker (2002) and the recent paper by Allon and Federgruen (2007)). All of these papers assume that the announcements made by the firm are long-term averages (unlike real-time information), are credible, and are treated as such by customers.

Inventory Models with Strategic Customers

The literature on inventory models with strategic customers can be broadly divided into two categories: (a) models where no availability information is provided to the customer and (b) models where customer are provided complete information regarding availability.

Aviv and Pazgal (2008), which falls in the first category, study pricing strategies for a retailer facing a stochastic arrival stream of customers. When customers arrive, they have no information about the current state of the inventory, and thus their model with fixed-discount strategy corresponds to our no-information model. Cachon and Swinney (2007) consider a model of a retailer that sells a product with uncertain demand over a finite selling season. The authors characterize the rational expectation equilibrium between the firm, which sets its initial quantity level, and the strategic customers, who choose whether to buy during the selling season or during the clearance season. Cachon and Swinney (2007) study the impact of quick response and the interplay between the existence of strategic customers and this option. Su and Zhang (2007b) show that the presence of strategic customers can impact the performance of a centralized supply chain when the customers form rational expectation regarding quantities and prices. They show that, while firms cannot commit to specific levels of inventory, decentralized supply chains can use contractual arrangements as indirect commitment devices to attain the desired outcomes with commitment.

Yin et al. (2007) and Su and Zhang (2007a) belong to the second category. Yin et al. (2007) consider a retailer that announces the regular price and the sales season clearance price at the beginning of the selling season, as in our model. In the presence of either myopic customers or strategic customers, the authors compare two display modes: one where the retailers display all the available units (and corresponds to providing full information to the customers) and one where it shows only one unit. Customers treat this one unit as a verifiable proof that the firm has at least one unit in stock. The authors show that the retailers will earn higher expected profits under the "display one unit" format, when the customers are strategic. Su and Zhang (2007a) study the role of availability and its impact on consumer demand by analyzing a newsvendor model with strategic customers that incur some search cost in order to visit the retailer. They contrast the rational expectations equilibrium in a game where the availability information is not provided to the customer with the scenario where such information is provided. It is shown that the retailer can improve its profits in the latter. In order to deal with the lack of credibility of the above information, the authors study availability guarantees, in which the seller compensates the consumers in the event of stockouts.

Delay Announcements in Other Settings

There are several papers that study models in which either a service provider shares waiting time information or a make-to-stock manufacturer shares lead time information.

Hassin (1986) studies the problem of a price-setting, revenue-maximizing service provider that has the option to reveal the queue length to arriving customers, but may choose not to disclose this information, thus leaving the customers to decide whether to join the queue on the basis of the known distribution of the waiting times. The author shows that it may be – but not always – socially optimal to prevent suppression of information and that it is never optimal to encourage suppression when the revenue maximizer prefers to reveal the queue length. Armony and Maglaras (2004b) analyze a service system where arriving customers can decide whether to join, balk, or wait for the provider to call within a guaranteed time. The customers' decisions are based on the equilibrium waiting time (which is equivalent to not providing any information). Armony and Maglaras (2004a) extend the above model to allow the service manager to provide the customers an estimate of the delay, based on the state of the system upon their arrival. The authors show that providing information on the estimated delay improves the system performance. Armony et al. (2007) study the performance impact of making delay announcements to arriving customers who must wait before starting service in a many-server queue setting with customer abandonment. Customers who must wait are told upon arrival either the delay of the last customer to enter service or an appropriate average delay. Two approximations are proposed: (i) the equilibrium delay in a deterministic fluid model and (ii) the equilibrium steady-state delay in a stochastic model with fixed delay announcements. The authors show that within the fluid-model framework, under certain conditions, the actual delay coincides with the announced delay.

Duenyas and Hopp (1995) study the problem of quoting customer lead times in a manufacturing environment, both under infinite and finite capacity. For the latter, the authors prove the optimality of different forms of control limit policies for the situations where the lead time is dictated by the market and the firms are able to compete on the basis of the lead time. Ata and Olsen (2007) study a related problem for large systems under convex–concave cost structure.

Dobson and Pinker (2006) develop a stochastic model of a custom production environment with pricing, where customers have different tolerances for waiting. The authors model intermediate levels of information sharing (with a specific structure) ranging from none to complete state-dependent lead-time information and compare the performance from the firm's and the customer's perspectives. They show that for this specific structure it is not always the case that sharing information improves the profits of the firm. Guo and Zipkin (2007) study a model in which customers are provided with information and make decisions based on their expected waiting times, conditional on the provided information. Three types of information are studied: (i) no information, (ii) queue length, and (iii) the exact waiting time (in systems in which such information is available). The authors provide examples in which accurate delay information improves or hurts the system performance.

1.6.1 Future Research

The framework surveyed in this chapter can also be applied to other operations management settings where the customers cannot credibly verify the information provided to them. One scenario worth exploring is the setting where the firm and the customer engage in "long cheap talk," i.e., the customer is periodically receiving information regarding the inventory. This is common in many retail settings where customers can request to be notified about the future availability of products, and service systems where the customer is informed repeatedly while waiting to be served. It is also worth exploring how this framework applies to fashion retail operations where the customer's utility depends either on the "exclusivity" of the item or its "trendiness," usually conveyed by the retailer.

References

Afeche P (2004) Incentive-compatible revenue management in queueing systems: Optimal strategic idleness and other delaying tactics Working paper, Kellogg School of Management, Northwestern University

Allon G, Bassamboo A (2008) Buying from the babbling newsvendor: Availability information and cheap talk. Working paper, Kellogg School of Management, Northwestern University

Allon G, Bassamboo A, Gurvich I (2007) We will be right with you: Managing customers with vague promises and cheap talk. Working paper, Kellogg School of Management, Northwestern University

Allon G, Federgruen A (2007) Competition in service industries. Operations Research 55(1):37–55

Armony M, Maglaras C (2004a) Contact center with a call-back option and real-time delay information. Operations Research 52:527–545

Armony M, Maglaras C (2004b) On customer contact centers with a call-back options: Customer decisions, routing rules and system design. Operations Research 52:271–292

Armony M, Shimkin N, Whitt W (2007) The impact of delay announcements in many-server queues with abandonment. Working Paper, Stern School of Business, New York University, NY

Ata B, Olsen T (2007) Dynamic leadtime quotation under general customer utilities. Working paper, Kellogg School of Management, Northwestern University

Austen-Smith D (1990) Information transmission in debate. American Journal of Political Science 34(1):124–152

Aviv Y, Pazgal A (2008) Optimal pricing of seasonal products in the presence of forward-looking consumers. Manufacturing & service operations management 10(3): 339–359

Cachon G, Swinney R (2007) Purchasing, pricing and quick response in the presence of strategic consumers. Working paper, Wharton School of Business, University of Pennsylvania

Cachon G, Harker PT (2002) Competition and outsourcing with scale economies. Management Science 48(10):1314–1333

Crawford VP, Sobel J (1982) Strategic information transmission. Econometrica 50:1431–1451

Demery P (2004) The cross-channel ideal dismantling the application silos to support multi-channel selling. Internetretailer.com

Dobson G, Pinker J (2006) The value of sharing lead time information. IIE Transactions 38: 171–183

Duenyas I, Hopp W.J (1995) Quoting customer lead times. Management Science 41(1):43–57

Farrell J, Gibbons R (1989) Cheap talk can matter in bargaining. Journal of Economic Theory 48(1):221–237

Farrell J, Rabin M (1996) Cheap talk. The Journal of Economic Perspectives 10(3):103–118

Guo P, Zipkin P (2007) Analysis and comparison of queues with different levels of delay information. Management Science 53(6):962–970

Hassin R (1986) Consumer information in markets with random product quality: The case of queues and balking. Econometrica 54:1185–1195

Matthews S (1989) Veto threats: Rhetoric in a bargaining game. Quarterly Journal of Economics 104(2):347–370

Mendelson H, Whang S (1990) Optimal incentive-compatible priority pricing for the M/M/1 queue. Oper Res 38(5):870–883

Naor P (1969) The regulation of queue size by levying tolls. Econometrica 37:15–24

Ren ZJ, Cohen MA, Ho TH, Terwiesch C (2007) Information sharing in a long-term supply chain relationship: The role of customer review strategy. Working paper, The Wharton School of University of Pennsylvania.

Spence AM (1973) Job market signaling. Quarterly Journal of Economics 87: 355–374

Su X, Zhang F (2007a) On the value of inventory information and availability guarantees when selling to strategic consumers. Working paper, Haas School of Business, University of California, Berkeley

Su X, Zhang F (2007b) Strategic customer behavior, commitment, and supply chain performance. Working paper, Haas School of Business, University of California, Berkeley

Yin R, Aviv Y, Pazgal A, Tang CS (2007) Optimal markdown pricing: Implications of inventory display formats in the presence of strategic customers. Working paper, Olin School of Business, Washington University

Chapter 2
Product Design in a Market with Satisficing Customers

Matulya Bansal and Costis Maglaras

Abstract We study the product design problem of a revenue-maximizing firm that serves a market where customers are heterogeneous with respect to their valuations and desire for a quality attribute and are characterized by a perhaps novel model of customer choice behavior. Specifically, instead of optimizing the net utility that results from an appropriate combination of prices and quality levels, customers are "satisficers" in that they seek to buy the cheapest product with quality above a certain customer-specific threshold. This model dates back to Simon's work in the 1950s and can be thought of as a model of bounded rationality for customer choice. We characterize the structural properties of the optimal product menu for this model and explore several examples where such preferences may arise.

2.1 Introduction

How do consumers trade off price to quality of service in choosing a product among various substitutable alternatives offered by the same or by competing firms? As a concrete example, how do users tradeoff speed of an Internet service connection with the price they have to pay? How should a firm design its product menu to optimize its profitability taking into account the strategic consumer choice behavior? The answers to these questions depend crucially on our understanding of how consumers perceive delay (or, more generally, product quality), their degree of heterogeneity in terms of delay sensitivity, and value for the offered product and on how delay costs and the prices of the various product options are combined and

Matulya Bansal
Graduate School of Business, Columbia University, 3022 Broadway, New York, NY 10027, USA, e-mail: mbansal11@gsb.columbia.edu

Costis Maglaras
Graduate School of Business, Columbia University, 3022 Broadway, New York, NY 10027, USA, e-mail: c.maglaras@gsb.columbia.edu

S. Netessine, C.S. Tang (eds.), *Consumer-Driven Demand and Operations Management Models*, International Series in Operations Research & Management Science 131, DOI 10.1007/978-0-387-98026-3_2, © Springer Science+Business Media, LLC 2009

used in making a product choice decision. This chapter addresses the above questions under a novel model of choice behavior, where consumers rather than being utility maximizers of some sort are "satisficers" in that they seek to buy the cheapest product with quality above a certain consumer-specific threshold. This model dates back to Simon's work in the 1950s (Simon 1955, 1956).

As a running example we will consider a service provider (SP) offering a product, such as an ISP connection or software-on-demand that is susceptible to congestion effects and, therefore, delays; we use the terms consumer, customer, and, at times, user, interchangeably. Potential customers are heterogeneous in their valuations and delay sensitivities. Expected delay here captures the notion of quality, with lower delay implying higher quality. The SP's problem is to select a menu of product variants that are defined through their price and associated delay that maximizes its expected profits. A classical model of customer choice behavior for this problem is due to Mendelson and Whang (1990) which postulates that a customer with valuation v for the offered service enjoys a net utility of $u_i = v - (p_i + c(d_i))$ from the ith variant that is priced at p_i and has an associated delay of d_i time units and where $c(\cdot)$ is a customer-specific delay cost function expressed in $ per unit of delay. Mendelson and Whang (1990) used a linear delay cost function of the form $c(d_i) = c \cdot d_i$, Dewan and Mendelson (1990) use a delay cost of the form $c(d) = c \cdot (d - \theta)^+$, van Mieghem (1995) allowed for general, convex increasing delay functions, while Ata and Olsen (2008) introduced delay functions that are convex increasing and then become concave increasing after a point. Figure 2.1 shows the linear, quadratic, piecewise-linear (convex increasing), and the proposed cost function vs. delay. Given a set of product variants characterized by (p_i, d_i) a customer will select product

$$i^* = \arg\max_i \ \{v - (p_i + c(d_i)) \ : \ v \geq p_i + c(d_i)\}. \tag{2.1}$$

Another alternative model that is close to the vertical differentiation literature could postulate that the net utility associated with product variant i is $u_i = (v - p_i)g(d_i)$,

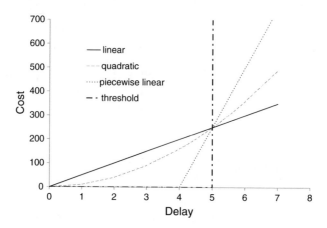

Fig. 2.1 The linear, quadratic, piecewise-linear, and proposed cost functions vs. delay.

where $g(\cdot)$ is a multiplicative factor whose magnitude depends on the quality of the offered product. Again, each customer would choose the product variant i that would maximize the resulting net utility.

Most of the above papers have focused on social welfare optimization as opposed to revenue maximization that is of interest in this chapter; in the cases where the revenue maximization objective has been considered, the emphasis has been on markets with two types of customers and product menus with two variants, Afeche (2005) and Maglaras and Zeevi (2006). The multi-type problem is hard, even in a deterministic setting, and, perhaps more importantly, assumes that the utility maximizing customers are solving an intricate problem in order to make their choice decision that in turn affects crucially the seller's product design decision.

In some practical settings it might be more realistic to assume that customers only care whether or not the product quality lies above a customer-specific threshold, and not by how much; e.g., video conferencing is associated with a bandwidth requirement, but additional bandwidth above that level is not necessarily beneficial. In those settings it might be appealing to assume that customer preferences with respect to the quality attribute are "dichotomous" such that all products with quality at least as good as a customer-specific quality threshold are acceptable to the customer, while all products with quality below the customer-specific threshold are unacceptable. From then on, among the acceptable products, if any, the customer buys the cheapest one, provided the price of this product does not exceed customer valuation.

An alternative motivation could be that the dichotomous decision rule is a simplification of the fully rational decision described earlier that is based on net utility calculations and serves as a "bounded rationality" surrogate for the potentially complex decision rule embodied in (2.1) or similar variants to it.

The baseline model that we will consider herein is that of a firm selling a good or service in a market of heterogeneous customers. The good or service is characterized by a one-dimensional quality attribute, such as delay, and to maximize revenues, the firm seeks to discriminate customers by creating multiple qualities and offering them at different prices. We assume that differentiation does not entail any cost. The firm offers M products, with p_j and q_j denoting, respectively, the price and quality of product j, $j = 1, \ldots, M$. The capacity available to the firm is denoted by C. We assume that there are N customer types that are segmented according to their quality preferences. Each type i customer has a valuation v_i for the product, which is an independent draw from a general distribution $F(\cdot)$ with support $[0, \bar{v}_i]$, and a strictly positive density $f_i(\cdot)$ on $[0, \bar{v}_i]$, and, a quality threshold θ_i, such that he or she is only willing to purchase product variants j whose quality q_j is at least as large as θ_i, i.e., $q_j \geq \theta_i$. The quality threshold is common across all type i customers. The size of the type i market segment is denoted by Λ_i. We assume that types are labeled in such a way that $\infty > \bar{\theta} > \theta_1 > \theta_2 > \cdots > \theta_N > \underline{\theta} > 0$, with a higher value implying the desire for a better quality, and $\infty \geq \bar{v}_1 \geq \bar{v}_2 \geq \cdots \geq \bar{v}_N > 0$, i.e., customers having higher quality thresholds have a maximum valuation at least as high as the maximum valuation of customers having lower quality thresholds. Let $\bar{F}_i(\cdot) = 1 - F(\cdot)$ be the complementary cumulative distribution function for type i

valuations. We will assume that $\lim_{p\to\infty} p\overline{F}_i(p) = 0$, $i = 1,\ldots,N$, i.e., the revenue from any customer type goes to 0 as the price goes to infinity (this holds trivially for class i if $\overline{v}_i < \infty$).

Customers are satisficers in that they strictly prefer the cheapest product whose quality exceeds their respective quality threshold and purchase that product if their valuation exceeds its price. In more detail all type i customers prefer product $\chi_i(p,q)$ given by

$$\chi_i(p,q) = \begin{cases} \arg\min p_j, & \exists\, q_j \geq \theta_i, \\ 0, & \text{otherwise,} \end{cases} \tag{2.2}$$

where p_j and q_j denote, respectively, the price and the quality of the jth product offered. If $\chi_i(p,q) = l$, $l \geq 1$, the demand from type i customers for this product is given by $\Lambda_i \overline{F}_i(p_l)$, and the revenue by $p_l \Lambda_i \overline{F}_i(p_l)$. If $\chi_i(p,q) = 0$, then type i customers do not find any product from the firm to be acceptable in terms of their quality.

The firm's revenue maximization problem is to choose the number of product variants to offer, M, as well as the corresponding prices and quality levels p_j, q_j for $j = 1,\ldots,M$ to solve the following problem:

$$\max_{p,q,M} \sum_{j=1}^{M} p_j \left[\sum_{i=1}^{N} \Lambda_i\, \overline{F}_i\, (p_j)\, 1_{\{\chi_i(p,q)=j\}} \right] \tag{2.3}$$

$$\text{s.t.} \sum_{j=1}^{M} \sum_{i=1}^{N} \Lambda_i\, \overline{F}_i\, (p_j)\, 1_{\{\chi_i(p,q)=j\}} \leq C, \tag{2.4}$$

$$0 \leq p < \infty,\ \ 0 \leq q < \infty, \tag{2.5}$$

$$1 \leq M < \infty,\quad M \text{ integer.} \tag{2.6}$$

The objective in (2.3) is the sum of revenues across the M products, where revenue for product j equals the price of the product multiplied by the number of customers that buy it. Equation (2.4) restricts the volume sold across customer types to be less than or equal to the available capacity C. For convenience, we have assumed that there exists a product 0 (corresponding to the case that customers do not find any product from the firm to be acceptable) and set $p_0 = 0$ and $q_0 = 0$.

This chapter lists several possible applications of this choice behavior for problems of practical interest, study the above mathematical problem, and sketch out several extensions. Our treatment is not exhaustive, but rather tries to highlight some structural result that hinges on this novel choice model, and hopefully motivates further work.

Satisficing is well known in the marketing and psychology literature, see, e.g., Iyengar (2006), and Schwartz et al. (2002), but seems to be novel in the context of the revenue management and operations management literatures. First, satisficing choice behavior can be the result of utility maximizing behavior in settings where the offered service and its anticipated usage are such that the disutility due to quality degradation is essentially flat until a certain threshold is reached and grows at a very rapid ("infinite") rate above that threshold. Perhaps more importantly, this threshold model of customer choice behavior can be motivated as an example of the "simple payoff" function as discussed in Simon (1955). Alternatively, this functional form can be motivated as the limiting case of the S-shaped utility functions, discussed, for example, in Kahneman and Tversky (1979) and Maggi (2004). For example, a utility function that would approximate $w(q)$ is the exponential S-shaped utility function

$$\tilde{w}(q) = \begin{cases} \dfrac{1}{\beta} + \dfrac{\beta-1}{\beta}(1 - e^{-\alpha(q-\bar{q})}), & \text{if } q \geq \bar{q}, \\[2ex] \dfrac{1}{\beta} e^{-\alpha(\bar{q}-q)}, & \text{if } q < \bar{q}, \end{cases} \tag{2.7}$$

where $\alpha > 0$, $\beta \geq 1$, with the approximation becoming exact when $\beta = 1$ and $\alpha = \infty$. This is illustrated in Figure 2.2.

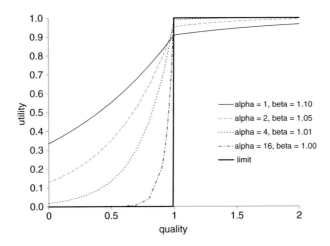

Fig. 2.2 This figure shows how threshold preferences arise as the limiting case of S-shaped utility functions discussed in prospect theory.

The satisficing model can be viewed as a limiting case of the vertical and horizontal differentiation models. In the context of vertical differentiation, satisficing choice behavior corresponds to using the function $g(q_i; \theta) = 1$ if $q_i \geq \theta$, and $g(q_i) = 0$, otherwise; our model would require the $g(\cdot)$ function to be type dependent, which is itself a slight extension of the vertical differentiation literature. In the context of horizontal differentiation, suppose customers differ in their preferences over a single-dimensional quality attribute θ in $[\underline{\theta}, \bar{\theta}]$. Under the traditional model of horizontal differentiation (Hotelling 1929), the quality cost $c(q)$ associated with a product of quality q to a customer with preference θ is $c(q) = t_1(\theta - q)$ if $q < \theta$, and $c(q) = t_2(q - \theta)$, otherwise, where the transportation costs t_1 and t_2 are typically assumed to be the same. Customers again find products that result in a non-negative utility acceptable and maximize their utility over acceptable products. In the limiting, asymmetric case where $t_1 = \infty$ and $t_2 = 0$, the horizontal model of customer choice behavior reduces to the threshold model of customer preferences.

The remainder of this chapter is organized as follows: Section 2.2 concludes with a brief literature review. Section 2.3 presents several examples where modeling customer behavior via threshold preferences is appealing. Section 2.4 characterizes the structure of the optimal solution to the product design problem. Section 2.5 discusses three extensions to the original model and Section 2.6 offers some concluding remarks.

2.2 Literature Survey

Our work builds upon several different areas of revenue management. The primary motivation for our work stems from the interface between marketing, psychology, and prospect theory focusing on customer behavior models. In his classic papers (1955; 1956), Simon questioned the pervasive assumption of agent rationality made in economic models. Citing constraints on information availability and computational capacities of individuals, (1955) Simon proposed "simple payoff functions" such as the one considered in this chapter as an approximation to model complex agent utility. Simon (1956) introduced the idea of "satisficing" to model the behavior of an organism facing multiple goals. In more recent research in psychology, researchers distinguish between "maximizers" and "satisficers," as discussed in Iyengar (2006) and Schwartz et al. (2002). Wieczorkowska and Burnstein (2004) refer to individuals exhibiting satisficing behavior as adopting an "interval" strategy as opposed to a "point" strategy (maximizing). Schwartz et al. (2002) mention that indeed individuals might not be maximizers or satisficers along all dimensions. In our case, customers satisfice with respect to quality while they maximize with respect to price.

In their famous paper Kahneman and Tversky (1979) propose that individual utility is concave for gains, while being convex for losses. Such utility functions are discussed in Maggi (2004). As discussed earlier, our utility function for quality attribute can be thought of as the limiting case for the S-shaped exponential utility function discussed here. The deadline delay cost structure discussed in Dewan and Mendelson (1990) prescribes zero cost for delay below a certain delay threshold and linear delay costs thereafter. Our delay cost function, like Dewan and Mendelson (1990), posits a zero cost for delay below a customer delay threshold and infinite (or large enough to deter customer from buying this product) costs thereafter.

The second stream of literature that is related to our work studies the second-degree price discrimination problem by a monopolist facing customers that differ in their preference for a quality attribute. Two classic papers are due to Mussa and Rosen (1978) and Moorthy (1984). In Mussa and Rosen (1978), customer utility is linear in quality, and quality is continuous. In Moorthy (1984), customer utility is allowed to be non-linear, but quality is discrete. In both cases, customers are maximizers. Both Moorthy (1984) and Mussa and Rosen (1978) discuss strategic degradation of quality by the monopolist to maximize revenues. This idea of intentionally degrading product quality when offering a product to less quality-sensitive customers so as to achieve differentiation is well known and also discussed in Afeche (2005) and Shapiro and Varian (1998) among other places. In addition to the above papers that discuss the product design problem under vertical differentiation, the product design problem has also been discussed under horizontal differentiation, e.g., Hotelling (1929) and Salop (1979). Duopoly models of product differentiation are considered in Moorthy (1988), Shaked and Sutton (1982), Wauthy (1996), etc. We also study the product design problem under threshold preferences to simultaneous and sequential duopoly models of market entry.

Each of the various application areas that we briefly touch upon later on has a potentially extensive literature that we will not review in this chapter in much detail, but rather simply offer a few passing references. In the area of revenue maximization for queues, in addition to the above-mentioned papers, we also highlight Katta and Sethuraman. There is a fast-growing literature in revenue management that considers the strategic consumer choice behavior, e.g., in deciding when to purchase a product in anticipation of the dynamic price path and associated rationing risk adopted by the seller. In this area we refer the reader to the review article by Shen and Su (2007), Liu and van Ryzin (2005), Su (2007), Cachon and Swinney (2007), and Bansal and Maglaras (2008). All of these assume a fully rational model of customer behavior. This chapter proposes a satisficing model of consumer choice behavior for this problem. Versioning of information goods has been studied in Bhargava and Choudhary (2004) and Ghose and Sundararajan (2005), while Shapiro and Varian (1998) presents several examples of versioning of information goods. Several researchers have addressed the problem of identifying the optimal inventory policy in the presence of multiple demand streams that differ in their tolerance for the minimum fillrate or the maximum leadtime they are willing to accept. Such a specification of acceptable quality levels closely mirrors our model of threshold-based preferences and is considered, for example, in Klejin and Dekker (1998). Finally, Kim and Chajjed (2002) study the product design problem of a monopolist firm offering a product with multiple quality attributes to a market of customers under the classic model of customer choice. The market consists of two customer segments, so at most two products need to be offered. We briefly discuss the extension of our model to the case of multiple quality attributes under some lexicographic ordering.

2.3 Applications and Variations to Basic Model

This section presents a non-exhaustive list of instances of product design problems where the study of customer satisficing behavior may be natural from a practical viewpoint.

2.3.1 Delay Differentiation

In the introduction we briefly reviewed an application of the proposed approach toward the problem of revenue maximization for a service that is susceptible to congestion effects and delay. Our model in this setting is based on a deterministic relaxation that disregards the equations that govern the steady state behavior of the queueing facility that is offering that service; this relaxation can be justified in an asymptotic setting where the market size of processing capacity of the system grows large along the lines of Maglaras and Zeevi (2006).

Delay sensitivity can also arise in other contexts, such as in retailing for fashion goods, where customers may be sensitive as to the time until which they wish to purchase the product; e.g., upon its introduction, in the middle of the regular selling season, after the season has ended. The resulting formulation is identical to the one discussed in the introduction.

2.3.2 Capacity Differentiation

There are several applications where the quality attribute corresponds to the capacity allocated to a customer, such as in the case of an Internet service provider (ISP) that offers bandwidth to domestic and business "end-users." Customers are heterogeneous in their valuations and have threshold preferences with respect to capacity, i.e., the minimum bandwidth they require. There are N customer classes, with class i customer valuations distributed as $F_i(\cdot)$ and class i having a capacity threshold θ_i, the minimum capacity that they desire. We assume that $\theta_1 > \theta_2 > \cdots > \theta_N$. Then denoting as c_j the capacity associated with product j offered by the firm, class i customers seek to buy the cheapest product j such that $c_j \geq \theta_i$. The firm's optimization problem can be stated as follows:

$$\max_{p,c,M} \sum_{i=1}^{N} \sum_{l=1}^{M} p_i \Lambda_i \overline{F}_i(p_i) 1_{\{\chi_i(p,c)=l\}} \tag{2.8}$$

$$\text{s.t. } \sum_{i=1}^{N} \sum_{l=1}^{M} \Lambda_i \overline{F}_i(p_i) c_i 1_{\{\chi_i(p,c)=l\}} \leq C, \tag{2.9}$$

$$0 \leq p < \infty, \quad 0 \leq c < \infty, \tag{2.10}$$

$$1 \leq M < \infty, \quad M \text{ integer.} \tag{2.11}$$

Equations (2.8), (2.10), and (2.11) are analogous to (2.3), (2.5), and (2.6) in the general problem, where c_i now denotes the quality of product i. Note that the capacity allocations c_i enter the seller's capacity constraint (2.9) in a way that is different than in the problem formulated in the introduction and potentially problematic due to the product terms $\overline{F}_i(p_i) c_i$; we show later on that due to the structure of the above problem, the capacity constraint simplifies and retains its tractability.

2.3.3 Rationing Risk Differentiation

Consider a monopolist firm that seeks to sell a homogeneous product to a market of heterogeneous, strategic customers that vary in their valuations and degree of risk aversion and where the firm seeks to discriminate its customers by creating rationing risk over time, i.e., by offering the product at different prices and fillrates at different times over the selling horizon; see, e.g., Liu and van Ryzin (2005) for the case where risk preferences are homogeneous and Bansal and Maglaras (2008) for a model where risk preferences may vary across customer types; both of these papers considered utility maximizing choice behavior. With satisficing behavior, customers will a threshold that corresponds to the minimum acceptable fillrate that they are willing to accept. Customers are strategic, observe (or know) the entire pricing and rationing risk trajectories used by the seller, and accordingly make the optimal timing decision to enter the market and purchase the product. The firm's product design problem is to identify the optimal number of products to offer to this market, along with their prices and fillrates. Fillrates r satisfy $0 \leq r \leq 1$, and a fillrate of r implies that only a proportion r of customer requests are fulfilled by the firm. Fillrates here correspond to our notion of quality, with a higher fillrate implying a better quality. There are N types and type i customers have a fillrate threshold θ_i, implying that type i customers prefer the cheapest product j with fillrate $r_j > \theta_i$ (notice we assume that the inequality is strict). We assume $1 > \theta_1 > \theta_2 > \cdots > \theta_N > 0$.

One possible way to motivate such choice behavior is by assuming that customers have a limit on the relative payoff variability they are willing to tolerate. The expected payoff to a customer with valuation v upon deciding to purchase a product with price p and fillrate r is given by $(v-p)r$ and the variance of this payoff is given by $(v-p)^2 r(1-r)$. Let A denote the customer threshold for the variability the customer is willing to tolerate. Hence this customer would seek to purchase the cheapest product such that

$$\frac{\text{stdev}}{\text{mean}} = \frac{\sqrt{(v-p)^2 r(1-r)}}{(v-p)r} \leq A, \tag{2.12}$$

where A is a fixed fraction. This reduces to $r \geq 1/(1+A^2)$, implying that customer has threshold preferences with respect to the rationing risk where the rationing threshold is given by $1/(1+A^2)$. Also, a low desire for variability leads to a higher rationing threshold, which is intuitive.

The optimization problem that the firm faces can be expressed as follows:

$$\max_{p,r,M} \sum_{i=1}^{N} \sum_{l=1}^{M} p_i \Lambda_i \overline{F}_i (p_i) r_i 1_{\{\chi_i(p,r)=l\}} \tag{2.13}$$

$$\text{s.t.} \sum_{i=1}^{N} \sum_{l=1}^{M} \Lambda_i \overline{F}_i (p_i) r_i 1_{\{\chi_i(p,r)=l\}} \leq C, \tag{2.14}$$

$$0 \leq p < \infty, \quad 0 \leq r \leq 1, \tag{2.15}$$

$$1 \leq M < \infty, \quad M \text{ integer.} \tag{2.16}$$

The objective (2.13) is the sum of revenue over the N classes, where class i revenue is the product of price p_i, the number of class i customers that are willing to buy at this price, $\Lambda_i \overline{F}_i (p_i)$, and the fillrate associated with this product, r_i. Equation (2.14) enforces the constraint that available capacity does not exceed sales, where the volume sold to class i customers is the product of class i demand and the fillrate corresponding to the product they purchase. The presence of the quality attribute r in the objective (2.13) and the capacity constraints (2.14) distinguishes this problem from the general problem (2.3), (2.4), (2.5), and (2.6).

2.3.4 No Capacity Constraint: Versioning of Information Goods

Consider a monopolistic software firm that serves a market of heterogeneous customers. To differentiate customers, the firm creates several versions of the software, and sells better versions at higher prices. Higher priced versions may have more features, a better user interface, and faster speed. Customers do not necessarily desire the fastest version, or the version with the most features, rather they seek to buy the cheapest product that satisfies their product and computational requirements. In such a setting it might be realistic to model customer choice behavior using threshold preferences. We will assume that the software product being sold by the firm is characterized by a one-dimensional quality attribute. The resulting revenue maximization problem is (2.3), (2.5), and (2.6).

2.3.5 Costly Quality Differentiation

So far quality differentiation has been costless, but this need not be the case. One popular example is in the sale of mp3 music players, such as the iPods. In particular, customers may have threshold preferences with respect to the mp3 player's storage capacity and seek to purchase the cheapest mp3 player with capacity above their specific threshold. The storage capacity of a mp3 player is a measure of the number of songs it can store, and customers that desire to carry along a larger number of songs have higher thresholds. The seller seeks to differentiate customers by selling mp3 players with different storage capacities at different prices, but in this case note that the higher quality products are more costly to produce. We will denote the marginal cost of a product with quality q_j as $s(q_j)$, where $s(\cdot)$ is a strictly increasing function of its argument. Then, the seller's product design problem can be formulated as follows:

$$\max_{p,q,M} \sum_{j=1}^{M} \sum_{i=1}^{N} \left(p_j - s(q_j) \right) \Lambda_i \, \overline{F}_i (p_j) \, 1_{\{\chi_i(p,q)=j\}} \tag{2.17}$$

$$\text{s.t. } \sum_{j=1}^{M} \sum_{i=1}^{N} \Lambda_i \, \overline{F}_i \, (p_j) \, 1_{\{\chi_i(p,q)=j\}} \leq C, \tag{2.18}$$

$$0 \leq p < \infty, \quad 0 \leq q < \infty, \tag{2.19}$$

$$1 \leq M < \infty, \quad M \text{ integer.} \tag{2.20}$$

Formulation (2.17), (2.18), (2.19), and (2.20) is the same as (2.3), (2.4), (2.5), and (2.6), except for the objective, which is modified to reflect that the profit upon selling a unit of product j changes from p_j to $p_j - s(q_j)$.

2.4 Analysis of General Model

2.4.1 Model Assumptions

Assumption A: 1. The hazard rates of the valuation distributions, $h_i(v) := f_i(v)/\overline{F}_i(v)$, are decreasing in desired quality levels, i.e., $h_i(v) < h_{i+1}(v)$, $\forall v \in [0, \overline{v}_{i+1}]$, $1 \leq i < N$. 2. $r_i(\lambda) = \lambda \overline{F}_i^{-1}(\lambda/\Lambda_i)$ is strictly concave in λ for $i = 1,\dots,N$.

Assumption B: $h_i(v)$ are decreasing and bounded below for $i = 1,\dots,N$.

Discussion of modeling assumptions: To facilitate exposition and analysis we have assumed that the set of threshold quality levels is discrete and as such there are a finite and discrete set of customer types; this can be viewed as a discretization of a potentially continuous distribution of quality threshold preferences. Assumption A (1) on the hazard rates is equivalent to assuming that $\eta_i(v) < \eta_{i+1}(v)$, $\forall v \in [0, \overline{v}_{i+1}]$, $1 \leq i < N$, where $\eta_i = v f_i(v)/\overline{F}_i(v)$ is the demand elasticity of customer class i. That is, customers that desire higher quality levels are more inelastic than those desiring lower quality levels and, therefore, are less likely to walk away as the price is increased. The assumptions that hazard rates are monotonic and that the per class type in terms of arrival rates is concave are not restrictive. For example, the uniform, exponential, pareto, half-logistic Rayleigh distributions satisfy these assumptions. Finally Assumption B can be replaced with either (a) $h_i(v)$ are non-decreasing for $i = 1,\dots,N$ or (b) $h_i(v)$ are decreasing and $\partial(1/h_i(v))/\partial v < 1$ for $i = 1,\dots,N$.

2.4.2 Structural Results

First, we show that without loss of generality the firm only needs to offer products with quality levels in the set $\{\theta_1, \theta_2, \dots, \theta_N\}$ and, second, that products with distinct prices must have distinct quality levels that are increasing in prices, and vice versa.

Lemma 1. *The following hold:*
(a) It suffices to offer quality levels that lie in the set $\{\theta_1, \theta_2, \ldots, \theta_N\}$.
(b) For any two distinct products (p_i, q_i) and (p_j, q_j), $q_i > q_j \Leftrightarrow p_i > p_j$.

Lemma 1 leads to the following corollary.

Corollary 1. *Suppose the firm offers $1 \leq k \leq N$ distinct products at qualities $\theta_{i_1}, \ldots, \theta_{i_k}$, $1 \leq i_1 < i_2 < \ldots < i_k \leq N$, at prices $p_{i_1}, p_{i_2}, \ldots, p_{i_k}$, respectively. Then $p_{i_1} > p_{i_2} > \ldots > p_{i_k}$ and (a) $p_{i_1} < \bar{v}_{i_1}$ and (b) $p_{i_k} > 0$.*

Lemma 2. *Any $k \leq N$ products partition the N customer classes into contiguous sets, i.e., if class $i-1$ and $i+1$ customers buy product j, then so do class i customers.*

Our next result shows that it is always optimal to offer the highest quality product.

Lemma 3. *The highest quality θ_1 is always offered.*

Lemma 3 leads to the following corollaries about the firm's one-product solution and the optimal product menu when the maximum valuations of all customer classes are the same.

Corollary 2. *The firm's one-product problem can be formulated as follows:*

$$\max_{p_1} \left\{ \sum_{i=1}^{N} p_1 \, \Lambda_i \, \overline{F}_i(p_1) \,\middle|\, \sum_{i=1}^{N} \Lambda_i \, \overline{F}_i(p_1) \leq C \right\}. \tag{2.21}$$

Corollary 3. *If $\bar{v}_i = \bar{v}$, $i = 1, \ldots, N$, then all classes buy a product from the firm.*

Lemmas 1–3 lead to the following formulation of the firm's revenue maximization problem.

Proposition 1. *The firm's problem (2.3), (2.4), (2.5), and (2.6) can be formulated as follows:*

$$\max_{p} \sum_{i=1}^{N} p_i \, \Lambda_i \, \overline{F}_i \, (p_i) \tag{2.22}$$

$$\text{s.t.} \sum_{i=1}^{N} \Lambda_i \, \overline{F}_i \, (p_i) \leq C, \tag{2.23}$$

$$p_N \leq p_{N-1} \leq \cdots \leq p_1, \quad i = 1, 2, \cdots, N, \tag{2.24}$$

$$p_i \leq \bar{v}_i \quad i = 1, 2, \ldots, N, \tag{2.25}$$

where p_i denotes the price of the product being offered at quality θ_i.

Proposition 1 simplifies considerably the firm's product design problem. The firm no longer needs to optimize over M and q, the number of qualities to offer and the vector of qualities, respectively, making the formulation (2.22), (2.23), and (2.24) more amenable to direct analysis.

Lemma 4. *Suppose qualities θ_m and θ_n are offered in the optimal solution, with $m+1 < n$. Then qualities θ_l, $m+1 \leq l \leq n-1$, are also offered.*

For homogeneous valuations, Lemma 4 leads to the following corollary.

Corollary 4. *If $\bar{v}_1 = \bar{v}_2 = \cdots = \bar{v}_N$, then it is optimal to offer exactly N products.*

2.4.3 Computation

The optimal solution to the revenue maximization problem can be easily computed. Under our assumption that $F_i(.)$ is continuous, this problem involves maximizing a continuous function over a compact set, and hence by Weierstrass theorem, an optimal solution exists. Compactness, note that the feasible set is bounded and that since the $F_i(.)$ are continuous, it is closed as well.

Instead of proceeding with a direct analysis of (2.22), (2.23), and (2.24), we will first restate the problem in terms of the demand rate vector as the optimization variable; this is typical in the revenue management literature. Specifically, for each class i, define $\lambda_i = \Lambda_i \bar{F}_i(p_i)$, so that $p_i = \bar{F}_i^{-1}(\lambda_i / \Lambda_i)$ because we assumed that $F_i(.)$ is continuous and increasing. We will also drop the monotonicity constraint (2.24) but later on verify that it is automatically satisfied by the optimal solution. The product design problem (2.22), (2.23), (2.24), and (2.25) reduces to

$$\max_{\lambda} \sum_{i=1}^{N} \lambda_i \, \bar{F}_i^{-1}\left(\frac{\lambda_i}{\Lambda_i}\right) \tag{2.26}$$

$$\text{s.t.} \sum_{i=1}^{N} \lambda_i \leq C, \tag{2.27}$$

$$0 \leq \lambda_i \leq \Lambda_i, \quad i = 1, \ldots, N, \tag{2.28}$$

which is a concave maximization problem over a polyhedron and the same problem that arises in the context of multi-product pricing problem studied in Maglaras and Meissner (1998). The first-order conditions are both necessary and sufficient to characterize the optimal solution for (2.22), (2.23), and (2.24) or equivalently (2.26) and (2.27).

Proposition 2. *The optimal solution to the product design problem (2.22), (2.23), (2.24), and (2.25) is given by*

$$p_i = \frac{\bar{F}_i(p_i)}{f_i(p_i)} + \mu - \frac{\eta_i}{f_i(p_i)}, \tag{2.29}$$

$$\mu\left(C - \sum_{i=1}^{N} \Lambda_i \bar{F}_i(p_i)\right) = 0, \tag{2.30}$$

$$\mu \geq 0, \quad C - \sum_{i=1}^{N} \Lambda_i \bar{F}_i(p_i) \geq 0, \tag{2.31}$$

$$\eta_i(\bar{v}_i - p_i) = 0, \quad \eta_i \geq 0, \quad \bar{v}_i - p_i \geq 0. \tag{2.32}$$

Here μ is the Lagrange multiplier associated with the capacity constraint (2.23) and η_i is the Lagrange multiplier associated with the constraint $p_i \leq \bar{v}_i$. Following the assumptions made earlier in this section, the optimal prices satisfy the monotonicity constraint (2.24).

It is worth noting that the product design problem with fully rational customers making decisions according to a decision rule of the form of (2.1) is intractable with more than two customer types $(N > 2)$. This arises for two reasons. First, the product design problem cannot be reformulated as a function of the demand rates λ_i, and as a result the objective need not be concave in prices. Second, the quality decisions complicate the seller's problem substantially. One popular approach is to formulate the problem as a direct mechanism that captures the behavior embodied in (2.1) through the incorporation of appropriate incentive compatibility and individual rationality constraints, but these may not be convex in general; when $N = 2$ the problem simplifies using algebraic manipulations that cannot be exploited when $N > 2$.

2.4.4 $k < N$ Products

For practical purposes the seller may only wish to restrict the number of products offered to the market. Such a strategy might be attractive when some customer types are similar or when administrative costs (not considered in our model) are high. It may also be driven by branding considerations (e.g., in the rationing example, the firm may not want to offer more than two products, so that customers that are rationed out do not discover that the product is available in a later period). We will assume that the firm seeks to offer $k < N$ products at qualities $\theta_{m_1}, \theta_{m_2}, \cdots, \theta_{m_k}$, with $1 \leq m_1 < m_2 < \cdots < m_k \leq N$, $m_{k+1} := N + 1$. Then, in a manner similar to Lemmas 1–3, it can be shown that it is optimal to set $m_1 = 1$, and $p_1 > p_2 > \cdots > p_k$. The firm's product design problem can be formulated as follows:

$$\max_{p} \sum_{l=1}^{k} p_l \sum_{j=m_l}^{m_{l+1}-1} \Lambda_j \overline{F}_j(p_l) \tag{2.33}$$

$$\text{s.t.} \sum_{l=1}^{k} \sum_{j=m_l}^{m_{l+1}-1} \Lambda_i \overline{F}_i(p_l) c \leq C, \tag{2.34}$$

$$0 \leq p_k \leq p_{k-1} \leq \ldots \leq p_1, \tag{2.35}$$

$$p_j \leq \bar{v}_{m_{j+1}-1}, \quad j = 1, \ldots, k. \tag{2.36}$$

In the following, we will assume that $\tilde{h}_l(\cdot)$ satisfies Assumptions A and B, where

$$\tilde{h}_l(v) = \frac{\sum_{j=m_l}^{m_{l+1}-1} f_j(v) \Lambda_j}{\sum_{j=m_l}^{m_{l+1}-1} \overline{F}_j(v) \Lambda_j}.$$

An example of a distribution that satisfies the above constraints is the exponential distribution with parameters $\alpha_1 < \alpha_2 < \cdots < \alpha_N$. Next, formulating the problem in terms of arrival rates, we obtain a concave maximization problem on a convex set, leading to the following characterization of optimal prices.

Proposition 3. *The optimal prices are characterized by*

$$p_l = \frac{\sum_{j=m_l}^{m_{l+1}-1} \overline{F}_j(p_l)\,\Lambda_j}{\sum_{j=m_l}^{m_{l+1}-1} f_j(p_l)\,\Lambda_j} + \mu - \frac{\eta_l}{\sum_{j=m_l}^{m_{l+1}-1} f_j(p_l)\,\Lambda_j}, \tag{2.37}$$

$$\mu \left(C - \sum_{l=1}^{k} \sum_{j=m_l}^{m_{l+1}-1} \overline{F}_j(p_l)\,\Lambda_j \right) = 0, \tag{2.38}$$

$$\mu \geq 0, \quad C - \sum_{l=1}^{k} \sum_{j=m_l}^{m_{l+1}-1} \overline{F}_j(p_l)\,\Lambda_j \geq 0, \tag{2.39}$$

$$\eta_l \, (v_{i_l-1} - p_l) = 0, \quad \eta_l \geq 0, \quad v_{i_l-1} - p_l \geq 0. \tag{2.40}$$

Here μ is the Lagrange multiplier associated with capacity constraint (2.34) and η_l is the Lagrange multiplier associated with constraint (2.36). The monotonicity of prices in (2.35) is ensured by our assumptions on $\widetilde{h}(\cdot)$.

The pricing problem given a preselected set of quality levels is simple, but the problem of identifying the optimal set of quality levels is combinatorial in nature. Since $m_1 = 1$ following Lemma 3, identifying the optimal k product solution requires solving $\binom{N-1}{k-1}$ problems. This can be computationally expensive for large k; however, solving the $k = 2$ problem requires solving $N - 1$ problems to identify m_2 and is hence easily done.

2.5 Extensions

We next discuss a few extensions to the model studied in the previous section. First, we look at the example of capacity differentiation to illustrate how the baseline model can be extended to address the applications mentioned in Section 2.2. Second, we briefly review how one could treat a model with two or more quality attributes for which customers have dichotomous preferences. Finally, we offer some results on optimal product menu design in a duopoly setting.

2.5.1 Capacity Differentiation

The extension of the results of the previous section to the case where the quality attribute is the capacity that is allocated to each type of customer is fairly straight-forward. For simplicity, in addition to the assumptions set forth in the previous section we will also restrict attention to valuation distributions for each customer type that have infinite support. In this setting, it is easy to verify that Lemmas 1 and 2 as

well as their associated corollaries continue to hold. For Lemma 3 and 4, we need
to slightly modify the proofs.

Lemma 5. *It is always optimal to offer the highest capacity product.*

The above result is slightly different from Lemma 3. In particular, we can no
longer say that the optimal single product offering involves selling the highest capacity product. However, adding the highest capacity product to the existing product
offering certainly increases revenues. Hence in the optimal product menu uncon-
strained by the number of products that are offered, the highest capacity product
will always be offered.

Lemma 6. *Suppose the firm offers products at capacities θ_m and θ_n, where $m+1 <
n$. Then it is optimal for the firm to offer products at capacity θ_l, $m+1 \leq l \leq n$.*

Together Lemmas 5 and 6 imply that if θ_k is the lowest capacity that is offered
by the firm, then it is optimal to offer products with capacities $\theta_1, \ldots, \theta_{k-1}$. The following corollary shows that in fact it is optimal to offer all N products at capacities
$\theta_1, \ldots, \theta_N$.

Corollary 5. *It is optimal to offer N products.*

Following Corollary 5, the service provider's revenue maximization problem can
be reformulated as follows:

$$\max_p \ \sum_{i=1}^{N} p_i \Lambda_i \overline{F}_i (p_i) \tag{2.41}$$

$$\text{s.t.} \ \sum_{i=1}^{N} \Lambda_i \overline{F}_i (p_i) \theta_i \leq C, \tag{2.42}$$

$$0 \leq p_N < p_{N-1} < \cdots < p_1 < \infty. \tag{2.43}$$

We can solve the firm's revenue maximization problem (2.41), (2.42), and (2.43) by
reformulating it in terms of arrival rates, wherein we obtain a concave maximization problem over a polyhedron. The first-order conditions lead to the following
characterization of the optimal prices.

Lemma 7. *The optimal prices are given by $p_i = \overline{F}_i(p_i)/f_i(p_i) + \mu \theta_i$, $i = 1, \ldots, N$,
where μ is the Lagrange multiplier associated with the capacity constraint.*

The $k < N$ products problem can also be solved in a similar fashion, though
solving it now requires $\binom{N}{k}$ effort.

2.5.2 Multiple Quality Attributes

Our results extend naturally to the case where customers have threshold preferences with respect to more than one quality attribute. For simplicity, we discuss
the two-attribute case here, which we will denote by θ_i and α_j, $i = 1, 2, \cdots, N_1$,

$j = 1, 2, \cdots, N_2$. Without loss of generality, we assume that $\infty > \theta_1 > \theta_2 > \cdots > \theta_{N_1} > 0$, $\infty > \alpha_1 > \alpha_2 > \cdots > \alpha_{N_2} > 0$, with higher values again denoting a desire for higher qualities. A type (i, j) customer is associated with the quality thresholds θ_i and α_j. Suppose the firm offers M products, where product l has price p_l and quality attributes q_l^1 and q_l^2. Then, a satisficing type (i, j) customer selects the following product:

$$\chi_{i,j}(p, q^1, q^2) = \begin{cases} \min_l p_l, & q_l^1 \geq \theta_i, \ q_l^2 \geq \alpha_j, \\ 0, & \text{otherwise.} \end{cases} \tag{2.44}$$

Analogous to the assumptions of Section 2.3, we assume that the supports of the valuation distributions satisfy the following ordering conditions $v_{1,j} > v_{2,j} > \cdots > v_{N,j}, \forall j$ and $v_{i,1} > v_{i,2} > \cdots > v_{i,M}, \forall i$. Also assume that

$$\frac{f_{i,1}(v)}{\overline{F}_{i,1}(v)} < \frac{f_{i,2}(v)}{\overline{F}_{i,2}(v)} < \cdots < \frac{f_{i,M}(v)}{\overline{F}_{i,M}(v)}, \quad \forall i,$$

$$\frac{f_{1,j}(v)}{\overline{F}_{1,j}(v)} < \frac{f_{2,j}(v)}{\overline{F}_{2,j}(v)} < \cdots < \frac{f_{N,j}(v)}{\overline{F}_{N,j}(v)}, \quad \forall j.$$

Hazard rates $f_{i,j}(p)/\overline{F}_{i,j}(p)$ are monotonic and $\lambda_{i,j}\overline{F}_{i,j}(\lambda_{i,j}/\Lambda_{i,j})$ is concave. Then, the results in Lemmas 1–4, Proposition 2, and their associated corollaries can be extended in a straightforward manner. As in Proposition 3, the k product problem can also be addressed, though the problem complexity increases significantly now (there are $\binom{N_1 N_2}{k}$ ways to choose k product quality combinations).

2.5.3 Duopoly

We finally consider some partial analysis of the case of two firms competing in a market with satisficing customers that satisfy the assumptions in Section 2.3. We examine the cases of simultaneous and sequential entry in order. As in Moorthy (1988), Shaked and Sutton (1982), and Wauthy (1996), we restrict attention to the case where each firm can offer only a single product and study a two-stage non-cooperative game. In the first stage, firms choose the quality level at which they seek to offer a product. In the second stage, given their and the competitor's quality, firms choose the prices at which to sell their product at. As in the above-mentioned papers, we focus on perfect Nash equilibria.

We begin by analyzing the second stage of the game, the price equilibrium. The two firms will not offer the same quality, else it will lead to a Bertrand game wherein profits would be zero. Hence we assume that firm 1 offers quality θ_i and firm 2 offers quality θ_j, $i < j$. Following Lemma 1 (which continues to hold), $p_i > p_j$ for two products to be offered. Then, the optimization problem for the firm offering quality θ_i can be written as follows:

$$\max_{p_i} \left\{ p_i \sum_{l=i}^{j-1} \overline{F}_l(p_i) \Lambda_l \ \middle| \ \sum_{l=i}^{j-1} \overline{F}_l(p_i) \Lambda_l \leq C, \ p_i \geq 0 \right\}. \tag{2.45}$$

Define p_1^* to be the optimal price in (2.45). The optimization problem for firm offering quality θ_j can be written as follows:

$$\max_{p_j}\left\{ p_j \sum_{l=j}^{N} \overline{F}_l(p_j)\, \Lambda_l \;\middle|\; \sum_{l=j}^{N} \overline{F}_l(p_j)\, \Lambda_l \leq C,\; p_1^* > p_j \geq 0 \right\}. \tag{2.46}$$

Define p_2^* to be the optimal price in (2.46). The following lemma characterizes the Nash equilibrium in prices.

Lemma 8. *Equations (2.45) and (2.46) define a Nash equilibrium in prices (given fixed qualities).*

For simultaneous entry case we obtain the following result.

Proposition 4. *The unique product equilibrium occurs with firm 1 selecting quality θ_1 and firm 2 selecting quality θ_2, if the following condition is satisfied:*

$$\max_{p_1}\{ p_1 \overline{F}_1(p_1)\, \Lambda_1 \mid \overline{F}_1(p_1)\, \Lambda_1 \leq C \}$$

$$\geq \max_{p_3}\left\{ p_3 \sum_{l=3}^{N} \overline{F}_l(p_3)\, \Lambda_l \;\middle|\; \sum_{l=3}^{N} \overline{F}_l(p_3)\, \Lambda_l \leq C, p_2^* > p_3 \geq 0 \right\}, \tag{2.47}$$

where $p_2^* = \arg\max_{p_2}\{ p_2 \overline{F}_2(p_2)\, \Lambda_2 \mid \overline{F}_2(p_2)\, \Lambda_2 \leq C \}$.

The analysis of the sequential entry is facilitated through the following notation:

$$R^1(l,p) = \{ p \overline{F}_l(p)\, \Lambda_l \mid \overline{F}_l(p)\, \Lambda_l \leq C \}, \tag{2.48}$$

$$R^1(l) = \max_{p} R^1(l,p), \quad p_1^l = \arg\max_{p} R^1(l,p), \tag{2.49}$$

$$\overline{R}^1(l,p) = \left\{ \sum_{u=l+1}^{N} p \overline{F}_u(p)\, \Lambda_u \;\middle|\; \sum_{u=l+1}^{N} \overline{F}_u(p)\, \Lambda_u \leq C,\quad p < p_1^l \right\}, \tag{2.50}$$

$$\overline{R}^1(l) = \max_{p < p_1^l} \overline{R}^1(l,p), \quad \overline{p}_1^l = \arg\max_{p < p_1^l} \overline{R}^1(l,p), \tag{2.51}$$

$$R^2(l,p) = \left\{ \sum_{u=l}^{N} p \overline{F}_u(p)\, \Lambda_u \;\middle|\; \sum_{u=l}^{N} \overline{F}_u(p)\, \Lambda_u \leq C,\quad p < \overline{p}_2^l \right\}, \tag{2.52}$$

$$R^2(l) = \max_{p < \overline{p}_2^l} R^2(l,p), \quad p_2^l = \arg\max_{p < \overline{p}_2^l} R^2(l,p), \tag{2.53}$$

$$\overline{R}^2(l,p) = \left\{ \sum_{u=1}^{l-1} p \overline{F}_u(p)\, \Lambda_u \;\middle|\; \sum_{u=1}^{l-1} \overline{F}_u(p)\, \Lambda_u \leq C \right\}, \tag{2.54}$$

$$\overline{R}^2(l) = \max_{p} \overline{R}^2(l,p), \quad \overline{p}_2^l = \arg\max_{p} \overline{R}^2(l,p). \tag{2.55}$$

$R^1(l,p)$ denotes the revenue achieved by firm 1, if it offers quality θ_l at price p and firm 2 decides to offer quality θ_{l+1}. $R^1(l)$ is the optimal revenue achieved in this case, and p_1^l denotes the revenue-maximizing price. $\overline{R}^1(l,p)$ denotes the revenue achieved by firm 2, if firm 1 offers quality θ_l at price p_1^l, and firm 2 offers quality θ_{l+1} at price p. $\overline{R}^1(l)$ denotes the optimal revenue achieved in this case, and $\overline{p}_1^l$ denotes the corresponding revenue-maximizing price. $R^2(l,p)$ denotes the revenue achieved by firm 1, if it offers quality l at price $p < \overline{p}_2^l$ and firm 2 decides to offer quality θ_1 at price $\overline{p}_2^l$. $R^2(l)$ is the optimal revenue achieved in this case, and p_2^l denotes the revenue-maximizing price. $\overline{R}^2(l,p)$ denotes the revenue achieved by firm 2, if firm 1 offers quality θ_l, and firm 2 offers quality θ_1 at price p. $\overline{R}^2(l)$ denotes the optimal revenue achieved in this case, and $\overline{p}_2^l$ denotes the corresponding revenue-maximizing price. The following proposition characterizes the optimal qualities to offer.

Proposition 5. *The first entrant chooses to offer quality*

$$i = \arg\max_{l=1,2,\ldots,N} R(l), \tag{2.56}$$

$$R(l) = \begin{cases} R^1(l), & \text{if } \overline{R}^1 \geq \overline{R}^2, \\ R^2(l) & \text{otherwise.} \end{cases} \tag{2.57}$$

The quality chosen by the second entrant then is θ_1 if $\overline{R}_i^1 < \overline{R}_i^2$, and θ_{i+1} otherwise.

We note that while in the simultaneous case the two best quality products are offered if an equilibrium exists, in the sequential entry case, neither of the two best qualities may be offered. This is in contrast with the optimal two-product solution of a monopolist firm, where the first product is always offered at the best quality, while the quality of the second product depends upon the problem parameters.

2.6 Concluding Remarks: Satisficers vs. Utility Maximizers

In this chapter, we have analyzed the product design problem for a seller facing a market of satisficing customers. The product design problem is tractable and enjoys several nice structural properties about the optimal number of products, the quality levels of the offered products, the structure of the product manu if the seller wants to restrict the number of offered products, and the structure of the optimal policy in a simplified duopoly setting. We also note that the ability to solve for the optimal menu in a multi-type market is a significant improvement over what can be done with classical models of vertical and horizontal product differentiations or mechanism design approaches for utility maximizing customers.

Satisficing provides a plausible approach to model bounded rationality in some revenue management and operations management contexts that we believe has both analytical and practical importance. An obvious issue that we have not addressed concerns the empirical validation of the satisficing customer choice behavior, which is an interesting problem that has been only partially addressed in the marketing and psychology literature.

2.7 Proofs

Proof of Lemma 1: Part (a). Since any customer class i is indifferent between the quality levels that lie in the interval $(\theta_{l-1}, \theta_l]$, $l = 1, \ldots, N$, where $\theta_0 := \overline{\theta}$, at most one price can be charged for any quality level in $(\theta_{l-1}, \theta_l]$, $l = 1, \ldots, N$. Hence, offering one quality level in $(\theta_{l-1}, \theta_l]$, $l = 1, \ldots, N$, suffices, which without loss of generality, we can fix to θ_l. Part (b). Following (a), the quality levels q_i and q_j lie in the set $\{\theta_1, \theta_2, \ldots, \theta_N\}$. Suppose $q_i > q_j$ while $p_i < p_j$. Then, every customer strictly prefers product i over product j. Hence the firm can drop product j from its product line without affecting its revenues. This would contradict our assumption that the firm only offers products that generate non-zero demand, and so $p_i > p_j$. Suppose now that $p_i > p_j$ but $q_i < q_j$. In this case, all customers strictly prefer product j to product i, which therefore generates zero demand. Again, this contradicts our assumption that the firm only offers products that generate non-zero demand and hence $q_i > q_j$. □

Proof of Corollary 1: The monotonicity of prices, $p_{i_1} > p_{i_2} > \cdots > p_{i_k}$, follows from Lemma 1. Part (a). If $p_{i_1} \geq \overline{v}_{i_1}$, then $\overline{F}_{i_1}(p_{i_1}) = 0$, implying that nobody will purchase this product, and it can be dropped. This violates our assumption that only products that offer a non-zero demand are offered. Hence, $p_{i_1} < \overline{v}_{i_1}$. Part (b). Suppose $p_{i_k} = 0$. Consider setting p_{i_k} to $0.5 \min\{p_{i_{k-1}}, \overline{v}_{i_k}\} > 0$ wherein the aggregate demand decreases while revenues increase. Note that $p_{i_{k-1}} > 0$, since products k and $k-1$ are distinct. Hence $p_{i_k} > 0$ in the optimal solution. □

Proof of Lemma 2: Since type $i-1$ buys product j, $q_j \geq \theta_{i-1} > \theta_i$, i.e., the quality of product j is higher than the quality threshold for type i. Since type $i+1$ buys product j, $p_j = \min_{q_l \geq \theta_{i+1}} p_l \leq \min_{q_l \geq \theta_i} p_l$, i.e., product j is the cheapest product offered by the firm with quality greater than or equal to θ_i. Hence it is optimal for type i to buy product j. □

Proof of Lemma 3: Let θ_k, $k > 1$, be the highest quality offered at price p to the market in the optimal solution. Also suppose that customers from classes l, $k \leq l \leq i$ are currently buying this product. Consider increasing the quality of the offered highest quality product from θ_k to θ_1 and increasing its price from p to $p + \varepsilon$, $\varepsilon > 0$, such that $\sum_{l=1}^{i} \overline{F}_l(p + \varepsilon)\Lambda_l = \sum_{l=k}^{i} \overline{F}_l(p)\Lambda_l$. The left hand side is continuous and decreasing in ε, exceeds the right hand side for $\varepsilon = 0$, and is less than the right hand side for $\varepsilon = \infty$. Hence, such an $\varepsilon > 0$ exists. Since the demand does not change while revenues increase (we increased the price), the original solution cannot be optimal and we have a contradiction. □

Proof of Corollary 2: Following Lemma 3, if a single product is offered by the firm, then it is offered at the highest quality θ_1. The one-product problem formulation then follows. □

Proof of Corollary 3: Since at least one product is offered, following Lemma 3, the highest quality product is offered. Let p_1 denote its price. Then $p_1 < \overline{v}$, else this product will generate zero demand. Since any other products would be offered at a lower quality level, and hence price (following Lemma 1), at least some customers from each class would buy from the firm. $\square$

Proof of Proposition 1: Following Lemma 3, quality θ_1 is always offered. Hence, all customer classes $1, \cdots, N$ would buy a product from the firm, subject to their valuations exceeding the price p_1. If $k < N$ products are offered in the optimal solution at qualities $\theta_{m_1}, \theta_{m_2}, \cdots, \theta_{m_k}$, with $m_1 < m_2 < \cdots < m_k \leq N$, $m_1 = 1, m_{k+1} := N+1$, and prices $p_{m_1} > p_{m_2} > \cdots > p_{m_k}$, then setting prices to be $p_j = p_{m_i}, m_i \leq j < m_{i+1}$, $i = 1, \cdots, k$, in the above formulation would lead to the same solution. Finally, any solution of (2.22), (2.23), and (2.24) is consistent with customer behavior, in that type i customers would buy the product priced at p_i. Hence the formulation is correct. $\square$

Proof of Lemma 4: Suppose it is optimal for the firm to offer $k < N$ products (lemma holds trivially if $k = N$). Then there exist indices $1 \leq i_1 < i_2 < \cdots < i_k \leq N$ such that product l, $1 \leq l \leq k$, is being offered at quality θ_{i_l}. Following Lemma 3, $i_1 = 1$. Suppose there exist indices m, n such that $m + 1 < n$, $i_l = m$, $i_{l+1} = n$ for some $1 \leq l \leq k - 1$. These correspond to products with qualities θ_m and θ_n, respectively. In case such indices do not exist (since $k < N$ and $i_1 = 1$, this case occurs only when the k products are offered at qualities $\theta_1, \ldots \theta_k$), the lemma holds. Even then for the first case of the following two, we set $m = k$, $n = N + 1$, $p_{N+1} = 0$, $\theta_{N+1} = 0$. For the second case, we consider only the possibility where such indices do exist. Let us denote the prices of these two products by p_m and p_n, respectively, with $p_m > p_n$ (since $\theta_m > \theta_n$ and following Lemma 1). There are two cases to consider.

Case (a): $p_m < \bar{v}_{m+1}$: Consider adding a product at quality level θ_{m+1} and price $p_m - \delta$, $\delta > 0$ such that $p_m - \delta > p_n$ and increasing the price of the product being offered at quality θ_m from p_m to $p_m + \varepsilon$, $\varepsilon > 0$, such that $p_m + \varepsilon < \bar{v}_m$ and $p_m + \varepsilon < p_{i_{l-1}}$, where $p_{i_{l-1}}$ is the price of the θ_{l-1} best quality product offered by the firm, if any, and ∞ otherwise. The change in demand $\Delta D = \Lambda_m \bar{F}_m(p_m + \varepsilon) + \sum_{u=m+1}^{n-1} \Lambda_u \bar{F}_u(p_m - \delta) - \Lambda_m \bar{F}_m(p_m) - \sum_{u=m+1}^{n-1} \Lambda_u \bar{F}_u(p_m)$. Using the first-order Taylor expansion, we can write $\Delta D = -\varepsilon \Lambda_m f_m(p_m) + \delta \sum_{u=m+1}^{n-1} \Lambda_u f_u(p_m) + o(\varepsilon) + o(\delta)$. Similarly, the change in revenue $\Delta R = \Lambda_m (p_m + \varepsilon) \bar{F}_m(p_m + \varepsilon) + (p_m - \delta) \times \sum_{u=m+1}^{n-1} \Lambda_u \bar{F}_u(p_m - \delta) - \Lambda_m p_m \bar{F}_m(p_m) - p_m \sum_{u=m+1}^{n-1} \Lambda_u \bar{F}_u(p_m)$. Again, $\Delta R = \varepsilon \Lambda_m (\bar{F}_m(p_m) - p_m f_m(p_m)) + \delta \sum_{u=m+1}^{n-1} \Lambda_u (p_m f_u(p_m) - \bar{F}_u(p_m)) + o(\varepsilon) + o(\delta)$.

We want to show that there exist δ, ε, small such that $\Delta D < 0$, $\Delta R > 0$. To this end, choose δ such that $\delta \sum_{u=m+1}^{n-1} \Lambda_u f_u(p_m) = \gamma \varepsilon \Lambda_m f_m(p_m)$, where $0 < \gamma < 1$. This implies that $\Delta D = -\varepsilon \Lambda_m f_m(p_m)(1 - \gamma) + o(\varepsilon) = -\delta[(1 - \gamma)/\gamma] \sum_{u=m+1}^{n-1} \Lambda_u f_u(p_m) + o(\delta)$, which is < 0 when ε (or equivalently δ) is small enough. Substituting this value of δ and simplifying, we get

$$\Delta R = \frac{\varepsilon \Lambda_m f_m(p_m) p_m}{\sum_{u=m+1}^{n-1} \Lambda_u f_u(p_m)} \left[\sum_{u=m+1}^{n-1} \Lambda_u f_u(p_m) \left(\frac{1}{\eta_m(p_m)} - 1 + \gamma - \frac{\gamma}{\eta_u(p_m)} \right) \right] + o(\varepsilon).$$

Now

$$\eta_m(p_m) < \eta_{m+1}(p_m) \leq \eta_u(p_m) \quad \Leftrightarrow \quad \frac{1}{\eta_m(p_m)} > \frac{1}{\eta_{m+1}(p_m)} \geq \frac{1}{\eta_u(p_m)}.$$

Hence, for ε sufficiently small, it suffices to show that

$$\frac{1}{\eta_m(p_m)} - 1 > \gamma\left(\frac{1}{\eta_{m+1}(p_m)} - 1\right),$$

which holds from above and the fact that we can choose any γ that satisfies $0 < \gamma < 1$.

Case (b): $p_m > \bar{v}_{m+1}$: In this case, classes $m+1 \leq u < n$ do not buy any product. Consider adding a product at quality level θ_{m+1} and price $\bar{v}_{m+1} - \varepsilon$, $\varepsilon > 0$, and increasing the price of the product offered at θ_n from p_n to $p_n + \delta$, $\delta > 0$ such that $p_n + \delta < \bar{v}_n$ and $\bar{v}_{m+1} - \varepsilon > p_n + \delta$. Let θ_r be the next best quality after θ_n that is offered by the firm (set it to $r = N+1$, $\theta_{N+1} = 0$, $p_{N+1} = 0$, as mentioned earlier, if there is none). The change in demand $\Delta D = \sum_{u=m+1}^{n-1} \bar{F}_u(\bar{v}_{m+1} - \varepsilon)\Lambda_u + \sum_{u=n}^{r-1} \bar{F}_u(p_n + \delta)\Lambda_{utj} - \sum_{u=n}^{r-1} \bar{F}_u(p_n)\Lambda_u$. Using the first-order Taylor expansion, $\Delta D = \varepsilon \sum_{u=m+1}^{n-1} f_u(\bar{v}_{m+1})\Lambda_u - \delta \sum_{u=n}^{r-1} f_u(p_n)\Lambda_u + o(\varepsilon) + o(\delta)$. Similarly, the change in revenue, $\Delta R = \sum_{u=m+1}^{n-1} \bar{F}_u(\bar{v}_{m+1} - \varepsilon)\Lambda_u(\bar{v}_{m+1} - \varepsilon) + \sum_{u=n}^{r-1} \bar{F}_u(p_n + \delta)\Lambda_u(p_n + \delta) - \sum_{u=n}^{r-1} \bar{F}_u(p_n)\Lambda_u p_n$, which can be written as $\Delta R = \bar{v}_{m+1}\varepsilon \sum_{u=m+1}^{n-1} f_u(\bar{v}_{m+1})\Lambda_u - \delta \sum_{u=n}^{r-1} \Lambda_u(p_n f_u(p_n) - \bar{F}_u(p_n)) + o(\varepsilon) + o(\delta)$. Choose $\varepsilon \sum_{u=m+1}^{n-1} f_u(\bar{v}_{m+1})\Lambda_u = \gamma\delta \sum_{u=n}^{r-1} f_u(p_n)\Lambda_u$, with $0 < \gamma < 1$, so that

$$\Delta R = \delta \sum_{u=n}^{r-1} f_u(p_n)\Lambda_u p_n \left(\frac{\bar{v}_{m+1}\gamma}{p_n} - 1 + \frac{\bar{F}_u(p_n)}{p_n f_u(p_n)}\right) + o(\delta).$$

For δ sufficiently small, a sufficient condition for $\Delta R > 0$ is that $\bar{v}_{m+1}\gamma/p_n > 1$, which is true if we choose $\gamma > p_n/\bar{v}_{m+1}$. This is possible, since the only restriction on our choice of γ was $0 < \gamma < 1$, and $p_n < \bar{v}_n \leq \bar{v}_{m+1}$.

Hence in both cases, we obtain a contradiction. □

Proof of Corollary 4: In the proof of Lemma 4, under the assumption that $\bar{v}_i = $ constant for all $i = 1, \ldots, N$, the second case in the proof never arises. The proof of the first part is applicable for all k, $1 \leq k < N$, irrespective of whether there are holes in the product offering or not. Hence we know that $\forall k < N$, offering $k+1$ products over k products increases revenues. Also from Lemma 1, we know that it suffices to offer at most N products. Hence, it is optimal to offer exactly N products. □

Proof of Lemma 5: Suppose that the highest quality product is being offered at capacity θ_k and price p_k in the optimal solution, where $k > 1$ (else the lemma holds). Note that $p_k < \infty$. Also suppose that the next highest quality product was being offered at θ_m, $m > k$. (Set $m = N+1$ if no other product is offered.) Consider introducing an additional product at capacity θ_1 and price $p_1 = p_k + \varepsilon$, $\varepsilon > 0$, such that $p_1 > p_k(\theta_1/\theta_k)$. Also, increase the price of product with capacity θ_k to $p_k + \delta$, $\delta > 0$, such that $\Delta D = \theta_1 \sum_{l=1}^{k-1} \Lambda_l \bar{F}_l(p_k + \varepsilon) + \theta_k \sum_{l=k}^{m-1} \Lambda_l [\bar{F}_l(p_k + \delta) - \bar{F}_l(p_k)] = 0$.

The first term is positive and decreases as ε increases, while the second term is negative and decreases as δ increases. Hence, there exist $\varepsilon > 0$, $\delta > 0$, such that $p_k + \delta < \bar{v}_k$, $p_k + \varepsilon < \bar{v}_1$, and $\Delta D = 0$. As a result, demand is unchanged, while the cost per unit capacity for products sold to classes $1 \ldots k$ increases to $\min\{p_1/\theta_1, (p_k + \delta)/\theta_k\} > p_k/\theta_k$. Hence the total revenue increases via the introduction of this product at θ_1. $\square$

Proof of Lemma 6: As in Lemma 4, consider two indices m, n where $m + 1 < n$, such that products are offered at θ_m and θ_n, but none in between. Following Corollary 1, $p_m < \infty$. Consider adding a product at θ_{m+1} and price $p_m - \delta$ while increasing the price of the product with capacity θ_m to $p_m + \varepsilon$. Then,

$$\Delta D = \sum_{l=m+1}^{n-1} \Lambda_l \bar{F}_l(p_m - \delta)\theta_{m+1} + \Lambda_m \bar{F}_m(p_m + \varepsilon)\theta_m$$

$$- \sum_{l=m}^{n-1} \Lambda_l \bar{F}_l(p_m)\theta_m = -\varepsilon\theta_m \Lambda_m f_m(p_m)$$

$$+ \delta\theta_{m+1} \sum_{l=m+1}^{n-1} \Lambda_l f_l(p_m) + (\theta_{m+1} - \theta_m) \sum_{l=m+1}^{n-1} \Lambda_l \bar{F}_l(p_m) + o(\varepsilon) + o(\delta).$$

Since $\theta_{m+1} < \theta_m$, choose δ sufficiently small so that $\Delta D < 0$. Similarly,

$$\Delta R = \sum_{l=m+1}^{n-1} \Lambda_l \bar{F}_l(p_m - \delta)(p_m - \delta) + \Lambda_m \bar{F}_m(p_m + \varepsilon)(p_m + \varepsilon)$$

$$- \sum_{l=m}^{n-1} \Lambda_l \bar{F}_l(p_m)p_m$$

$$= \varepsilon\Lambda_m \bar{F}_m(p_m) - \varepsilon\Lambda_m p_m f_m(p_m)$$

$$+ \sum_{l=m+1}^{n-1} \Lambda_l \delta[-\bar{F}_l(p_m) + p_m f_l(p_m)] + o(\varepsilon) + o(\delta).$$

Hence $\Delta R > 0$ if $\varepsilon\Lambda_m \bar{F}_m(p_m)(1 - \eta_m(p_m)) > \delta\sum_{l=m+1}^{n-1} \Lambda_l \bar{F}_l(p_m)(1 - \eta_l(p_m))$.

Define $A = \Lambda_m \bar{F}_m(p_m)(1 - \eta_m(p_m))$ and $B = \sum_{l=m+1}^{n-1} \Lambda_l \bar{F}_l(p_m)(1 - \eta_l(p_m))$. From our assumption on elasticities $\eta_m < \eta_l, m \leq l \leq n$. There are three possibilities:

(i) $A > 0, B > 0$: choose δ sufficiently small (compared to ε) $\implies \Delta R > 0$.

(ii) $A > 0, B < 0$: $\implies \Delta R > 0$.

(iii) $A < 0, B < 0$: choose ε sufficiently small (compared to δ) $\implies \Delta R > 0$.

Hence introducing a product at θ_{m+1} increases revenues. $\square$

Proof of Corollary 5: In the proof of Lemma 6, substituting $n = N + 1$, and introducing a dummy product with $\theta_{N+1} = 0$, $p_{N+1} = 0$, does not affect line of argument. Hence we conclude that if only first k capacities are being offered, introducing a product at capacity θ_{k+1} also increases revenues. Applying this argument iteratively and following Lemma 1, we conclude that it is optimal to offer exactly N products. $\square$

Proof of Lemma 8: Firm 1 has no incentive to change its price, since given the quality θ_i of its product, this is the optimal price for it to charge subject to its capacity. Firm 2 needs to offer a lower price than firm 1 to be able to generate non-zero revenues, since $\theta_i > \theta_j$. Hence, given its quality θ_j and capacity C, p_2^* is the optimal price for firm 2 to charge. Finally the resulting customer choice behavior is consistent with the formulation in (2.45) and (2.46). □

Proof of Proposition 4: Suppose the product equilibrium occurs at $1 < i < j \leq N$. Given choice of quality θ_j by firm 2, firm 1 will find it advantageous to offer quality θ_1, for it increases revenues when the price equilibrium with product qualities fixed is considered. Hence, in the Nash equilibrium, $i = 1$. Next consider the case where $j > 1$. In this case, given that firm 1 chooses to offer quality θ_1, firm 2 revenue would increase if it offers quality θ_2 instead of θ_j, given the price equilibrium that would occur with these qualities. Hence $j = 2$ in the Nash equilibrium. Next we consider whether $i = 1, j = 2$ constitutes a Nash equilibrium. Clearly, firm offering θ_2 does not have an incentive to deviate. As for the firm offering θ_1, the best alternative is to offer quality θ_3 instead. This happens only if

$$\max_{p_1}\{p_1 \, \overline{F}_1(p_1) \, \Lambda_1 \mid \overline{F}_1(p_1) \, \Lambda_1 \leq C\}$$

$$< \max_{p_3}\left\{p_3 \sum_{l=3}^{N} \overline{F}_l(p_3) \, \Lambda_l \,\middle|\, \sum_{l=3}^{N} \overline{F}_l(p_3) \, \Lambda_l \leq C, p_2^* > p_3 \geq 0\right\},$$

where $p_2^* = \arg\max_{p_2}\{p_2 \, \overline{F}_2(p_2) \, \Lambda_2 \mid \overline{F}_2(p_2) \, \Lambda_2 \leq C\}$. □

Proof of Proposition 5: Since firm 1 chooses its quality first, and with the knowledge that firm 2 will subsequently choose the optimal quality to offer following firm 1's choice, there are two situations to consider. Given firm 1's choice of quality θ_l, firm 2 would offer either a better quality, in which case it is optimal for firm 2 to offer θ_1, or a worse quality, in which case it is optimal for firm 2 to offer θ_{l+1}. The revenues resulting for firm 2 in these two situations are denoted by $\overline{R}^1(l)$ and $\overline{R}^2(l)$ for firm 2, respectively. Firm 2 chooses quality θ_1 if $\overline{R}^1(l) \geq \overline{R}^2(l)$, in which case the revenue achieved by firm 1 is given by $R^1(l)$ in equilibrium. If $\overline{R}^1(l) < \overline{R}^2(l)$, then firm 2 chooses quality θ_{l+1}, and consequently, firm 1 obtains $R^2(l)$ in revenue in equilibrium. This leads to (2.57). Given the optimal revenue achievable by firm 1 if it offers quality θ_l to the market, firm 1 then optimizes over qualities θ_l, $l = 1, \ldots, N$, to identify the optimal quality to offer, as summarized by (2.56). □

References

Afeche P (2005) Incentive compatible revenue management in queueing systems: Optimal strategic delay and other delay tactics. Working paper

Ata B, Olsen TL (2008) Congestion-based leadtime quotation and pricing for revenue maximization with heterogeneous customers. Working paper

Bansal M, Maglaras C (2009) Dynamic pricing in a market with strategic customers. Journal of Revenue and Pricing management, 8: 42–66

Bhargava HK, Choudhary V (2004) Research note: One size fits all? optimality conditions for versioning information goods. University of california, Davis

Cachon GP, Swinney R (2007) Purchasing, pricing, and quick response in the presence of strategic customers. Wharton School, University of Pennsylvania

Dewan S, Mendelson H (1990) User delay costs and internal pricing for a service facility. Management Science 36(12):1502–1517

Ghose A, Sundararajan A (2005) Software versioning or quality degradation. Columbia University

Hotelling H (1929) Stability in competition. Economic Journal 39:41–57

Iyengar SS (2006) Doing better but feeling worse, looking for the best job undermines satisfaction. Psychological Science 17(2):143–150

Kahneman D, Tversky A (1979) Prospect theory: An analysis of decision under risk. Econometrica XLVII:263–291

Katta AK, Sethuraman J (2005) Pricing strategies and service differentiation in queues – a profit maximization perspective. Columbia University

Kim K, Chhajed D (2002) Product design with multiple quality attributes. Management Science 48(11):1502–1511

Klejin MJ, Dekker R (1998) An overview of inventory systems with several demand classes, Econometric inst. rep. 9838/a, September

Liu Q, van Ryzin G (2005) Strategic capacity rationing to induce early purchases. Working paper. October

Maggi MA (2004) A characterization of s-shaped utility functions displaying loss aversion. April 2004

Maglaras C, Meissner J (1998) Dynamic pricing strategies for multi-product revenue management problems. Queueing Systems: Theory and Applications 30(1-2):89–148

Maglaras C, Zeevi A (2006) Models for differentiated services: Implications to customer behavior and system design. Working paper. Columbia University

Mendelson H, Whang S (1990) Optimal incentive-compatible priority pricing for the $m/m/1$ queue. Operations Research 38(5):870–883

Moorthy KS (1984) Market segmentation, self-selection and product-line design. Marketing Science 3(4):288–307

Moorthy KS (1988) Product and price competition in a duopoly. Marketing Science 7(2):141–168

Mussa M, Rosen S (1978) Monopoly and product quality. Journal of Economic Theory 18: 301–317

Salop SC (1979) Monopolistic competition with outside goods. Bell Journal Economics 10(1):146–156

Schwartz B, Ward A, Montersso J, Lyubomirsky S, White K, Lehman DR (2002) Maximizing versus satisficing: Happiness is a matter of choice. Journal of Personality and Social Psychology 83:1178–1197

Shaked A, Sutton J (1982) Relaxing price competition through product differentiation. The Review of Economic Studies 49(1):3–13

Shapiro C, Varian H (1998) Information Rules. Harvard Business School Press, Boston

Shen ZM, Su X (2007) Customer behavior modeling in revenue management and auctions: A review and new research opportunities. POMS 16(6): 713–728

Simon HA (1955) A behavioral model of rational choice. The Quarterly Journal of Economics 69(1):99–118

Simon HA (1956) Rational choice and the structure of the environment. Psychological Review 63(2)

Su X (2007) Inter-temporal pricing with strategic customer behavior. Management Science 53(5):726–741

van Mieghem JA (1995) Dynamic scheduling with convex delay costs: The generalized $c\mu$ rule. The Annals of Applied Probability 5(3):809–833

Wauthy X (1996) Quality choice in models of vertical differentiation. The Journal of Industrial Economics 44(3):345–353

Wieczorkowska G, Burnstein E (2004) Individual differences in adaptation to social change. International Journal of Sociology 34(3):83–99

Chapter 3
The Effect of Assortment Rotation on Consumer Choice and Its Impact on Competition

Felipe Caro and Victor Martínez-de-Albéniz

Abstract The recent success of fast fashion retailers has changed the (affordable) fashion industry dramatically. These companies, such as Zara, are characterized by a flexible supply chain that has allowed them to reduce design and production lead times to just a few weeks, rather than months. More importantly, they are using these capabilities to change the assortment (i.e., introduce new products) more frequently, which many practitioners claim increases sales, since there is evidence showing that customers visit more often the stores with fresher products. We propose in this chapter a customer consumption model with satiation and multiple competing retailers. The model implies that the consumers will spend a higher share of their budget in retailers that renovate the assortment at a faster pace. Using the insights from the model, we determine how often retailers should change the assortment in the competitive equilibrium.

3.1 Introduction

The fashion industry has seen enormous changes in the past years. We have witnessed the emergence of new firms that, over a decade, have continuously grown to become market leaders. The Inditex group from Spain, owner of the Zara chain, surpassed Gap in the first quarter of 2008 as the world's biggest clothing retailer, see The Guardian (2008). H&M from Sweden has also become a major player in the industry. These newcomers have recently offered higher profitability than traditional retailers, e.g., in 2007 H&M had a ROA of 32.6% and Inditex of 17.7% vs. 10.6% for Gap Inc.

Felipe Caro
UCLA Anderson School of Management, Los Angeles, CA 90095, USA,
e-mail: fcaro@anderson.ucla.edu

Victor Martínez-de-Albéniz
IESE Business School, University of Navarra, Barcelona, Spain, e-mail: valbeniz@iese.edu

S. Netessine, C.S. Tang (eds.), *Consumer-Driven Demand and Operations Management Models*, International Series in Operations Research & Management Science 131, DOI 10.1007/978-0-387-98026-3_3, © Springer Science+Business Media, LLC 2009

The main difference between these new players and traditional retailers is that H&M and Inditex are best of breed among *fast fashion* retailers. Fast fashion is a relatively new business strategy that can be succinctly defined as "cutting-edge fashion at an affordable price" for Zara, see Ferdows et al. (2002), or equivalently as "fashion and quality at the best price" for H&M, see H&M (2007). The fast fashion business strategy relies upon a distinctive operations strategy, which combines different elements. In what follows, we first present a detailed review of the fast fashion operations strategy. We then focus on a key factor of success that has received little attention in the past, namely, the role of assortment rotation to increase sales.

Structurally, fast fashion retailers exhibit a high level of vertical control, sometimes involving ownership of a large portion of the value chain, such as stores or even manufacturing facilities. In particular, the control over manufacturing implies that production is monitored closely, even when it is outsourced to external suppliers. Given the latter, information systems play an important role from production to point-of-sales data. The systems need not be very sophisticated, see McAfee et al. (2004) or McAfee (2004), but enable the feedback of real-time sales information into distribution, production, and even design decisions. The information provided by these systems is leveraged through the use of modern distribution platforms forwarding the merchandise to the stores under JIT principles.

Moreover, fast fashion retailers offer an assortment which is a mix of two types of products: *basic items*, e.g., a gray pull-over, a white T-shirt, a pair of plain blue jeans, and *fashion items*, e.g., the dress that a celebrity was wearing at the Oscar's. As a result, a fast fashion supply chain typically has a dual structure. It is combination of (i) *an* efficient supply chain, used for basic items that minimize cost, and (ii) *a responsive supply chain*, used for fashion items, following the definitions of Fisher (1997). As put by H&M (2007), "The time from an order being placed until the items are in the store may be anything from a few weeks up to six months. The best lead time will vary. For high-volume fashion basics and children's wear it is advantageous to place orders further in advance. In contrast, trendier garments in smaller volumes have to be in the stores much quicker." Indeed, basic items do not include a strong fashion component, are available every season, and have a stable and predictable demand. Hence, an efficient supply chain is the most appropriate for this class of products. It should minimize the total cost from factory to store, including raw materials (purchase in high volumes), production (outsourcing to low-labor-cost countries), and distribution (use of inexpensive shipping, e.g., maritime). In contrast, fashion items require a responsive supply chain that can bring the product quickly to the store if needed, since such a trendy product exhibits highly uncertain demand and is perishable. This implies a flexible production system that minimizes lead time, even at a higher cost. This can be achieved by minimizing the time from design to store, including raw materials (pre-positioning of raw materials and postponement of design), production (locally, reactive capacity through reservation contracts), and distribution (local sources, expedited shipping).

Following Hayes et al. (2005), the structural choices above are complemented with infrastructural decisions. These include a strong operations-driven culture, with a tendency for centralized decision-making. Decisions are taken in a coordinated fashion by cross-functional teams. This is perfectly aligned with the vertical control mentioned above. In particular, inventory at the stores is usually managed centrally from the headquarters and replenished more than once a week. This allows them to carry low levels of inventory at the stores, hence maximizing the effectiveness of shelf space. Also, production policies vary depending on the type of item. Fashion products are typically produced in small batches, whereas basics are made in large volumes. Finally, a main characteristic is that fast fashion retailers constantly adjust their assortment in the store. They introduce new products on a regular basis, e.g., weekly. In particular, fashion items have a very short life cycle, as they have to be replaced by trendier ones. As a result, the number of products offered by a fast fashion firm every year is much larger than that of a traditional retailer, even though the number of products in the store at any given time is similar. For example, in 2001, Zara offered 11,000 distinct products, compared to 2,000–4,000 offered by its key competitors, see Ghemawat and Nueno (2003).

Figure 3.1 illustrates these differences between two fast fashion retailers (Zara and H&M) and a traditional one (The Gap). Figure 3.2 shows the financials of these firms.

Some research has been done to link these operational characteristics to competitive advantage. The main focus has usually been the advantage derived from a responsive supply chain. This builds on the study of quick response (QR), which since 1980s has been described as the only viable strategy under the current conditions in

	Zara (Spain)	H&M (Sweden)	The Gap (U.S.A.)
Vertical integration [2007]	Fully integrated. Subcontracts cutting, sewing, and shipping	Controls every link in the chain but does not own factories	From design to store but outsources production
No. of stores worldwide [2007]	1,361	1,522	>1,572
No. of countries [2007]	68	28	21
Distribution of stores – Main locations [2007]	60% Southern Europe 13% Northern Europe 8% Latin America	64% Northern Europe 19% Southern Europe 12% North America	79% North America 9% United Kingdom 7% Japan
Assortment composition [2006]	40% Basic 60% Fashion	>70% Basic <30% Fashion	99% Basic
Sourcing – Main suppliers [2006]	50% Spain and prox. 34% Asia 14% Rest of Europe	>60% Asia <40% Europe	97% outside U.S.A.
Lead times - Dual SC [2006]	Efficient SC: 6 Months Responsive SC: 2–5 Weeks	Efficient SC: 6 Months Responsive SC: 3–6 Weeks	Efficient SC: 9 Months
Refreshment fashion [2006]	Twice a week	Daily	Occasionally
Pricing [2002]	Overall, higher than H&M (especially out of Spain)	Lowest among Fast Fashion	Comparable to Zara, if not higher
Marketing [2002]	0.3% of Revenues	3–4% of Revenues	Comparable to H&M

Fig. 3.1 Operating characteristics of Zara, H&M, and The Gap. Sources: annual reports and public press.

	Inditex (EUR)	H&M (SEK)	Gap Inc. (USD)
Revenue (Net Sales)	9,435	78,346	15,763
	8,196	68,400	15,923
Gross Margin	56.7%	61.1%	36.1%
	56.2%	59.5%	35.5%
Operating (EBIT) Margin	17.5%	23.5%	8.3%
	16.6%	22.4%	7.7%
Net Margin (ROS)	13.3%	17.3%	5.3%
	12.3%	15.8%	4.9%
Working Capital /Sales	-6.1%	9.7%	10.5%
	-6.1%	10.2%	17.3%
Inventory Turns	4.39	4.08	5.14
	4.54	3.90	4.93
Asset Turnover	1.33	1.88	2.01
	1.43	1.92	1.86
ROA	17.7%	32.6%	10.6%
	17.6%	30.4%	9.1%
Leverage	1.69	1.3	1.83
	1.67	1.28	1.65
ROE	30.0%	42.3%	19.5%
	29.3%	38.9%	15.0%
GMROI	5.74%	6.40%	2.90%
	5.83%	5.72%	2.71%

Fig. 3.2 Financials of the Inditex group (owner of Zara), H&M, and Gap Inc. In each entry, the first line is data for 2007, the second line for 2006 (1 USD = 0.65 EUR = 6.08 SEK). Source: annual reports.

the apparel market, similar to what just-in-time manufacturing has meant to the auto industry (Hammond and Kelly 1990). Single-firm models without competition that analyze QR include Fisher and Raman (1996) and Iyer and Bergen (1997). More recently, Caro and Martínez-de-Albéniz (2005) have examined the benefits of QR in inventory competition. Also, the impact of QR on strategic consumers has been explored by Cachon and Swinney (2007). On a different direction, given the more responsive supply chain, Caro and Gallien (2007) study how this can be leveraged to learn about demand and implement an optimal dynamic assortment.

Surprisingly, the role of assortment rotation on the competition for consumers has been relatively unexplored. Higher assortment rotation clearly sets apart fast fashion retailers from the rest, see Just-style.com (2005): "Fast fashion is a complete move away from the two seasons a year method. It accepts that if we're going to keep consumers interested and coming into our retail stores once a month, we've got to have a steady flow of new stuff for them to see." According to El País (2008), the strategy of launching two collections per year is "jurassic." "We acquire clothes 12 times a year, and every time that we enter a store we want to see something new. Otherwise, we get bored." [1] Thus, introducing products to the store more often is a

---

[1] Translation by the authors.

valuable way for retailers to increase their sales. In fact, anecdotal evidence suggests that this is a key lever to attract customers to the store. For instance, the H&M annual report (2007) states, "New items every day make the stores interesting and lively. Having a number of collections each season also means that the store changes its appearance often. The aim is that customers should always be able to find something new and exciting." Due to higher assortment rotation, Zara receives more visits to its stores than the competition: 17 visits per year per consumer on average vs. 3.5 in the industry, see Ghemawat and Nueno (2003).

The objective of this chapter is to shed light on how companies should use assortment rotation to increase customers' expenditure in the store. For this purpose, we propose a multi-period consumption model where *consumers become satiated*. Satiation occurs when they visit a store and realize that the assortment has not changed much from the previous visit. As a result, they consume less at that store. We model this effect by using a discounted utility model that takes into account the satiation level, a measure of aggregate previous consumption. We consider multiple retailers competing for the consumers' budget. The model implies that the consumers will spend a higher share of their budget in retailers that renovate the assortment at a faster pace. Using this insight, we determine how often a retailer should change the assortment, both when its competitors are passive and in the competitive equilibrium. The rest of this chapter is organized as follows. Section 3.2 reviews the literature. Section 3.3 presents the model and characterizes how the customers split their budget among the competing retailers. Section 3.4 determines the retailers' strategies regarding assortment rotation. We conclude in Section 3.5. Note that this chapter is based on research presented in Caro and Martínez-de-Albéniz (2009).

3.2 Literature Review

Assortment decisions have gained significant relevance as product variety has become a major component in the value proposition of an increasingly large number of companies. In terms of research, product variety and assortment planning have received plenty of attention in the marketing and operations literature. Here we briefly describe the findings that are related to the model which we present in the next section.

In the marketing literature, the work on variety-seeking is relevant to ours. Most of the research available is empirical and based on experiments or panel data. The focus has been on understanding and leveraging the purchase behavior among variety-seeking customers, which can be defined as the tendency to switch brands (or not repeat a recent purchase) induced by the utility derived from the change itself (Givon 1984, Kahn et al. 1986). At least three different possible explanations have been given for this phenomenon: (i) customers get bored or satiated with their most recent purchase; (ii) customers prefer to change due to external constraints; and (iii) customers switch brands in an attempt to diversify and hedge against uncertainty in their preferences (see Kahn (1995) for a detailed description). Note, however, that variety-seeking is not always prevalent. In some situations, by switching brands, a customer might derive disutility. This generates purchase inertia or a reinforcement behavior (variety-avoidance). Whether a customer seeks or avoids variety is idiosyncratic to the individual, but also depends on the type of product and the time elapsed between successive purchases (Chintagunta 1998).

In the operations literature, there are two strands of work that are relevant to our paper: assortment planning and product variety management. The work on assortment planning has centered on a single firm that wants to find the optimal set of products to offer, and the problem has been mostly studied as a single-shot decision (van Ryzin and Mahajan 1999, Smith and Agrawal 2000). The work by Caro and Gallien (2007) is one of the few exceptions that looks at assortment planning as a dynamic problem in which new products can be introduced with a two-fold purpose: to replace those that are not selling and also to test new variants. We refer the reader to Kök et al. (2008) for further references on assortment planning. In terms of the product variety management, the operations literature has focused on how companies can cope with product proliferation. Though a larger variety can increase revenue and market share (especially under the presence of variety-seeking customers), it comes at a cost. Therefore, a vast amount of research has been devoted to exploit product and process design to deliver a higher level of variety quickly and cheaply (see Ho and Tang 1998).

All the papers mentioned above look at a single firm. There has been some work that studies variety-based competition in which products are characterized by a reduced set of attributes (typically one or two), and offering more variety means more options available in terms of those attributes. Most of these models are either based on Hotelling (1929) single attribute locational model (e.g., Alptekinoğlu and Corbett 2008) or on the choice probabilities derived from the multinomial logit model (e.g., Cachon et al. 2008). We refer the reader to Lancaster (1990) and Anderson et al. (1992) for further references and discussion along these lines.

In our model, firms also compete for customers but the main competitive lever is the assortment rotation, i.e., the frequency of assortment changes. As mentioned in Section 3.1, there is evidence showing that stores that change the assortment more often are visited more frequently. Based on this observation, we view fast fashion shoppers as variety-seeking customers that are satiated with their previous purchase and look for stimulation in new garments. In order to capture this behavior, we propose a multi-period utility model with satiation that builds on the consumption model developed by Baucells and Sarin (2007). We expand their model by considering multiple choices competing for the same budget. A firm can decrease its customers' satiation rate (and increase their expenditure) by rotating the assortment more often. Moreover, since customers have a limited budget (to spend on apparel), the expenditure at a given firm will also depend on how often its competitors change their respective assortments. Therefore, a game arises. From the marketing literature, we allow for customer heterogeneity in terms of their preference for variety (or satiation sensitivity), and from the operations literature, we consider diverse cost structures to represent different process capabilities to offer variety.

As mentioned above, our model links a common operational lever, i.e., the assortment rotation strategy, with a typical market-oriented indicator, i.e., sales. For a single firm, this link has been studied mostly for durable goods such as personal computers, cellular phones, or toys (see Lim and Tang (2006) and the references therein). In contrast with the latter, this paper is motivated by the apparel industry, and to the best of our knowledge, our work would be the first to study the link between assortment rotation and sales in a competitive setting.

3.3 The Multi-period Utility Model with Satiation

In this section we present the utility model with satiation that we use later as a building block in the competitive game. Our approach builds on the consumption model by Baucells and Sarin (2007). We believe that a consumption model provides the right foundations since the goal of the chapter is to shed light on the optimal assortment renewal rate, rather than the optimal assortment at each point in time. Therefore, we only care about the expenditure at each retailer, and we do not model explicitly what the actual products are that are bought, as is usually the case in assortment models based on Hotelling's framework or on the multinomial logit (c.f. Section 3.2). Similarly, our model does not account explicitly for substitution or cannibalization effects, though they still might occur.

Consider an individual customer that maximizes its utility over T periods (say months). We think of an aggregate budget per period for the category (apparel) that can be shared in multiple retailers. Although one could integrate a saving decision into our model, it would unnecessarily complicate it. We assume that future consumption is less valuable to the consumer and is discounted at a rate δ per period. Let i and n denote one particular firm and the total number of firms, respectively. We denote by x_{it} the dollar amount spent at retailer i in period t.

As in Baucells and Sarin (2007), we assume that the contribution of the current consumption is an increment over the satiation level achieved due to previous consumption. Formally, when there has been previous consumption at retailer i, we model the incremental utility generated as a function of how many of the products are "old," i.e., they were already on display in the previous period. The customer already bought some of them and therefore exhibits some level of satiation with the previous purchases that remain in the current assortment. Thus, let y_{it} be the satiation level with the assortment at retailer i at the beginning of period t, which can be seen as a consumption stock level that remains from the previous period. The incremental utility derived from consuming x_{it} in period t is defined as $u_i(y_{it} + x_{it}) - u_i(y_{it})$, where $u_i(z)$ is an increasing and concave function that represents the utility derived from a consumption stock level z.

Of course, the relationship between y_{it} and $x_{i1}, \ldots, x_{it-1}$ depends on the retailer's assortment rotation policy. When the retailer keeps a share γ_i of the assortment untouched in between periods, then the average amount previously consumed that is still in the store is such that

$$y_{i,t+1} = \gamma_i(y_{it} + x_{it}), \tag{3.1}$$

where γ_i is called the satiation retention factor at retailer i. If the assortment changes completely, γ_i is 0, whereas it is equal to 1 if no changes occur between periods. Similarly, if 30% of the assortment changes between periods, then of the previously consumed products, only 70% is still on display. An implicit assumption is that the products that change in the assortment are picked at random, which may not be exact, but we believe it is a good first approximation.[2] Thus, depending on each retailer's policy for assortment rotation, the customer will experience a higher or lower satiation factor. We examine the retailer's problem in Section 3.4.

The customer problem can thus be defined as

$$
\max \sum_{t=0}^{T-1} \delta^t \left(\sum_{i=1}^{n} u_i(y_{it} + x_{it}) - u_i(y_{it}) \right)
$$

$$
\text{s.t.} \sum_{i=1}^{n} x_{it} = W_t \qquad\qquad \forall t = 0,\ldots,T-1 \qquad (3.2)
$$

$$
y_{i,t+1} = \gamma_i(y_{it} + x_{it}) \qquad \forall i = 1,\ldots,n, t = 0,\ldots,T-1
$$

$$
x_{it} \geq 0 \qquad\qquad \forall i = 1,\ldots,n, t = 0,\ldots,T-1.
$$

Here, W_t is the budget of the consumer for period t. Alternatively, using a dynamic programming formulation, with $V_t(y_t)$ the "utility-to-go" from period t to the last one, we can write

$$
V_t(y_t) = \max_{\substack{\sum_{i=1}^{n} x_{it} \leq W_t \\ x_{it} \geq 0}} \left\{ \sum_{i=1}^{n} u_i(y_{it} + x_{it}) - u_i(y_{it}) + \delta V_{t+1}(\gamma \bullet (y_t + x_t)) \right\} \qquad (3.3)
$$

and $V_T(\cdot) = 0$, where $\left(\gamma \bullet (y_t + x_t) \right)_i = \gamma_i(y_{it} + x_{it})$.

In order to avoid end-of-horizon effects, we consider the infinite horizon case $T = \infty$ with a stationary per period budget $W_t \equiv W$. As a result, V_t is stationary, i.e., $V_t \equiv V$ and satisfies the following Bellman equation (see Bertsekas 2000):

$$
V(y) = \max \left\{ \sum_{i=1}^{n} u_i(y_i + x_i) - u_i(y_i) + \delta V(\gamma \bullet (y + x)) \right\}. \qquad (3.4)
$$

In addition, let $v_i(z) \equiv u_i(z) - \delta u_i(\gamma_i z)$ be the (stationary) incremental utility function. If v_i is concave and v_i' is convex, it can be shown that, starting from a non-satiated state (i.e., for all i, $y_{i0} = 0$), the optimal policy x_{it}, y_{it} converges as $t \to \infty$ to levels $x_{i\infty}, y_{i\infty}$ such that $x_{i\infty} = (1 - \gamma_i) z_{i\infty}$ and $y_{i\infty} = \gamma_i z_{i\infty}$ where

$$
\frac{v_i'(z_{i\infty})}{1 - \delta \gamma_i} = \mu, \qquad (3.5)
$$

and μ ensures that $\sum_{i=1}^{n} (1 - \gamma_i) z_{i\infty} = W$.

---

[2] An alternative view is the following. If we know that a product at retailer i lasts on average ℓ_i periods in the store, then by Little's law, a fraction $1/\ell_i$ is replaced per period. Thus, $\gamma_i = 1 - 1/\ell_i$.

This result is non-trivial and the formal proof is given in Caro and Martínez-de-Albéniz (2009). Note that it complements the results in Baucells and Sarin (2007), in particular it supports the observation that consumptions tend to stabilize around an "equilibrium level" in the periods that are not in the beginning (impact of initial satiation state) or the end (impact of budget terminal value being zero).[3] In addition, our result is similar to the one found in Popescu and Wu (2007), in a different context. Popescu and Wu consider a dynamic pricing model where the current price proposed has an influence on the future demand. Interestingly, they show that all the optimal price paths converge to a steady-state price, which is similar to our convergence to steady-state consumption.

For the remainder of this chapter, we consider the steady-state consumption $x_{i\infty}$, given by μ, which depends on the particular per period budget W of the customer, and $y_{i\infty}$:

$$x_{i\infty} = \frac{1 - \gamma_i}{\gamma_i} y_{i\infty}. \tag{3.6}$$

3.4 Competing on Assortment Rotation

3.4.1 The Competitive Setting

In the previous section, we elucidated the relationship between assortment rotation at each retailer and the steady-state consumption $x_{i\infty}$ of an individual consumer. We build on the results above and study the behavior of the retailers under competition. We allow for heterogeneity among customers in terms of their preferences (utility function), and we use j and m to denote one (type of) customer and the total number of customers (or types), respectively.

The competition is based on assortment rotation, which we define as $r_i \equiv 1 - \gamma_i$. To be precise, each retailer i must choose r_i which represents the faction of the assortment that will change in between periods. The remaining fraction will still be available in the next period, and therefore the choice of r_i determines the satiation factor γ_i that customers experience at retailer i. We assume that the firms have stores that can hold a comparable number of SKUs, and hence we can work with the fraction rather than the absolute number of unchanged products. We are implicitly assuming that the satiation factor is the same for all consumers, which would be another departure from the model by Baucells and Sarin (2007). Note that the satiation model in Section 3.3 can be extended to the general case when the satiation factor is a consumer-specific function of the assortment rotation. However, this would add an extra layer of complexity and might deviate the attention from the main focus of

---

[3] It is worth noting that Baucells and Sarin (2007) consider a finite horizon and a total budget that is shared among the T periods.

the chapter. For a similar reason we have ignored price decisions and postponed it for future work.

We view the choice of r_i as a strategic decision for a retailer and cannot be changed easily. Indeed, the rotation has a very strong influence in many parts of the firm (see Ho and Tang 1998), in particular (1) the product development function, since rotating the assortment more implies developing higher number of products per period and (2) the supply chain, since introducing more products implies smaller production quantities, higher transportation costs, and smaller inventory levels. For a firm that rotates a fraction r_i of the assortment every period, we model its total costs as

$$\frac{C_i}{1-r_i}. \tag{3.7}$$

The parameter r_i is an idiosyncratic component and represents the firm's ability to offer variety over time. We model the total cost as an increasing and convex function of r_i to represent the fact that each marginal increase of the assortment rotation becomes increasingly harder to achieve.

Thus the average profit per customer for a given retailer in steady state is

$$\pi_i(r_i, r_{-i}) = \sum_{j=1}^{m} \theta_j x_{ij}(r_i, r_{-i}) - \frac{C_i}{1-r_i}, \tag{3.8}$$

where θ_j represents weight of customer (type) j and $x_{ij}(r_i, r_{-i})$ is the steady-state expenditure which is obtained from solving (3.5). If necessary, the cost parameter C_i can be normalized for the units in (3.8) to match. The weights θ_j can be given by a population distribution (for instance, $\theta_j = 1/m$ in the uniform case) or by the relative budget levels, i.e., $\theta_j = W_j / \sum_{j'} W_{j'}$, where $W_{j'}$ is the per period budget of customer (type) j'. The strategic assortment rotation game has a (pure) Nash equilibrium if there is an n-vector r^* such that no single firm can improve its profits by changing its assortment rotation unilaterally.

The steady-state expenditure is defined implicitly by (3.5). In order to obtain a closed-form expression we must specify the utility function u_{ij}. We use the power from utility function $u_{ij}(z_{ij}) = \alpha_{ij}^{\beta_j} z_{ij}^{1-\beta_j} / (1 - \beta_j)$ if $0 \leq \beta_j < 1$, and $u_{ij}(z_{ij}) = \alpha_{ij} \ln(z_{ij})$ if $\beta_j = 1$, which has been widely used because of its mathematical tractability (see Baucells and Sarin 2007). The parameters α_{ij} and β_j give us some degree of flexibility to model heterogenous customers. The α_{ij} parameters capture any preference not due to consumption, and the parameter β_j characterizes the customer's marginal utility: the larger the β_j, the more sensitive is the customer's marginal utility to changes in the consumption stock level.[4] In particular, if β_j equals zero, then the utility is linear and the consumer will spend all its budget at the retailer with the highest α_{ij}, regardless of whether the assortment changes or not. That would be the case of a customer who derives the same utility from repeating

---

[4] Formally, $\dfrac{d^2 u_{ij}}{dz_{ij}^2} \dfrac{z_{ij}}{u_{ij}} = -\beta_j$. Note that β_j also captures the customer's risk aversion, but in our deterministic setting that interpretation is less relevant.

a previous purchase (e.g., from buying again the same pair of pants or the same T-shirt) and does not care about new products and assortment rotation whatsoever. We use this to model consumers that are *rotation indifferent* and do not derive any additional utility from renewing their wardrobe.

Given the power form utility function, from (3.5) and (3.6), the steady-state expenditure can be expressed as follows:

$$
x_{ij}(r_i, r_{-i}) = \frac{\alpha_{ij} r_i \left(\dfrac{1 - \delta(1 - r_i)^{1 - \beta_j}}{1 - \delta(1 - r_i)} \right)^{1/\beta_j}}{\displaystyle\sum_{k=1}^{n} \alpha_{kj} r_k \left(\dfrac{1 - \delta(1 - r_k)^{1 - \beta_j}}{1 - \delta(1 - r_k)} \right)^{1/\beta_j}} W_j.
\tag{3.9}
$$

Unfortunately, the expression on the right hand side of (3.9) might not be unimodal in r_i since it could have a local maximum at one. This would pose some technical difficulties (the best-response function could eventually be discontinuous). However, $r_i = 1$ represents a 100% assortment rotation (i.e., the store is totally renewed each period), an extreme that is unrealistic if we consider periods to be months since it would be prohibitively expensive. In fact, even Zara, which is regarded as the fast fashion retailer with highest assortment rotation, still has some products that last a few months in the store (mostly basic items, see Figure 3.1). This provides further support for the choice of the cost function given by (3.7). Then, under mild conditions over C_i, it is possible to show that the best-response function for retailer i, which is derived from maximizing (3.8), is continuous in the competitors' actions r_{-i}. Since the action space is compact ($[0, 1]^n$), a Nash equilibrium is guaranteed to exist (see Caro and Martínez-de-Albéniz (2009) for details). Moreover, given that the profit function (3.8) is expressed in closed form, it is straightforward to verify (numerically) whether the equilibrium is unique, which was the case in all the experiments described below.

3.4.2 The Competitive Equilibrium

In this section, we study the outcome of the strategic assortment rotation game, under the assumption that consumers have power form utility functions. We begin by looking at the form of the best-response function of a given retailer. For that purpose, we consider the case with two firms ($n = 2$) and only one type of customers ($m = 1$, $\theta_1 = 1$), which is variety-seeking with $\beta = 0.5$. For simplicity, throughout this section we assume $\alpha_{ij} = 1 \ \forall i, j$ and we normalize the per period budget $W_j = 1 \ \forall j$.

In Figure 3.3 we plot the best-response function for the two retailers. For both, we consider two different cost structures: (L) $C_i = 0.05$ and (H) $C_i = 0.25$. We regard the first case (L) to represent a retailer that has a relatively low assortment rotation cost and therefore is prone to introduce new products very frequently. The second

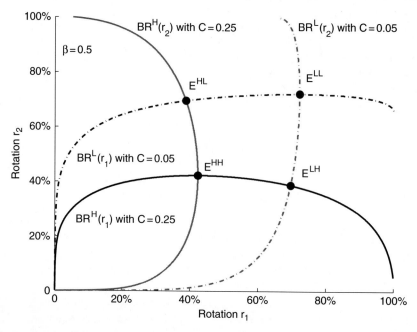

Fig. 3.3 Best responses and equilibriums LL, LH, and HH.

case (H) is the opposite and represents a retailer with a slow design process and rigid supply chain, and therefore new product introductions are more costly.

A first observation from Figure 3.3 is that the extremes $r_i = 1$ and $r_i = 0$ are never the best competitive response when $\beta_j > 0$. The fact that a 100% assortment rotation ($r_i = 0$) is never optimal is not a surprise, given our choice of the cost function in (3.7). Again, this is supported by what has been observed in practice (see the discussion after (3.9)). The fact that zero assortment rotation ($r_i = 0$) is not optimal either is also intuitive since we are considering variety-seeking customers ($\beta_j > 0$), and therefore satiation plays a role in how they allocate their budget. Note that Figure 3.3 seems to indicate that $r_i = 0$ is the best response to $r_{-i} = 0$ (and that would make it an equilibrium). However, the best-response curves do not actually intersect. In fact, if the competitor ($-i$) does not rotate its assortment at all, then it is optimal for retailer i to slightly change its assortment over time (i.e, select $r_i = \varepsilon$, with ε very small but strictly positive) to attract more expenditure to itself at a minimum cost (this is certain to occur since $\beta_j > 0$).

A second interesting observation in Figure 3.3 comes from comparing the equilibria under different cost structures. Consider retailer 1 who plays r_1, and suppose first that both retailers have low (L) assortment rotation costs. Then, the outcome is the (symmetric) equilibrium E^{LL} in which both retailers will rotate the most (around 72% in Figure 3.3). This would represent the exclusive competition between two (identical) fast fashion retailers (think of Zara vs. H&M). If retailer 2 is actually not as efficient managing variety and has high (H) assortment rotation costs, then the outcome becomes the (asymmetric) equilibrium E^{LH} in which the retailer 2 rotates significantly less (around 38%), but also retailer 1 will renovate its assortment slightly less often (only 68%). This would represent the competitive game between a fast and a traditional retailer (think of Zara or H&M vs. The Gap). The fact that competition becomes less intense slows down the assortment rotation at both retailers. If now retailer 1 also has a high (H) cost structure, then it will rotate even less and the outcome is equilibrium E^{HH}, in which both rotate 42%. What is surprising is that in this situation retailer 2 will decide to rotate more (compared to E^{LH}). In other words, when the cost of retailer 1 increases, the best response of retailer 2 is to rotate at a higher pace in order to regain some of the market share that retailer 1 must let go. Finally, if retailer 2 becomes the firm with low (L) assortment rotation costs, then its best response is to rotate even faster. Retailer 1 is not be able to keep up and will prefer to rotate further less. In that case, the outcome of the game becomes equilibrium E^{HL}, which is the mirror of E^{LH}.

The equilibrium transitions described above are further explored in Figure 3.4. The top and bottom graphs show the equilibrium action and the profits, respectively, for both retailers as a function of C_2, while the cost structure of retailer 1 is low (L) and high (H) in the left and right graphs, respectively. Note that the profits are normalized by π^{HH}, i.e., the profits obtained in the symmetric equilibrium E^{HH} when both firms have high (H) cost structures. Obviously, retailer 2 rotates less as it becomes harder (more costly). On the contrary, for retailer 1, the equilibrium assortment rotation first increases (when $C_2 < C_1$) and then decreases (when $C_2 > C_1$). In other words, if retailer 2 has a lower cost structure that gradually becomes more expensive, then retailer 1 can improve its profits by rotating the assortment faster. This is what occurs (reversed) in the transition from equilibrium E^{HH} to E^{HL} for retailer 1 and from equilibrium E^{LH} to E^{HH} for retailer 2. If the cost structure of retailer 2 continues to increase beyond C_1, then competition becomes less intense and retailer 1 can rotate less and still improve its profits. This is what occurs in the transition from equilibrium E^{LL} to E^{LH} for retailer 1 and (in reverse) from equilibrium E^{HL} to E^{LL} for retailer 2.

Finally, we consider the case when there are two types of customers. A fraction θ of the population is variety-seeking with $\beta_1 = 0.5$ as in the previous figures, and the remaining fraction $1 - \theta$ is rotation indifferent, i.e., has $\beta_2 = 0$. The equilibrium assortment rotation and profits as a function of $\theta \in [0, 1]$ are depicted in Figure 3.5 (for the profits, we use the same normalization constant as in Figure 3.4). When $\theta = 0$, none of the customers is affected by satiation, and therefore in equilibrium the assortments do not rotate (for both retailers). However, as the proportion of variety-seeking customers increases, the assortment rotation observed in equilibrium increases, just as expected. The profits decrease as θ increases since in order to remain competitive the retailer must rotate its assortment more often, which comes at an expense.

Based on Figure 3.5, in terms of assortment rotation, the competitive scenarios can be ordered as follows (for any proportion of variety-seeking customers θ):

$$r_1^{LL} \geq r_1^{LH} \geq r_1^{HH} \geq r_1^{HL}. \tag{3.10}$$

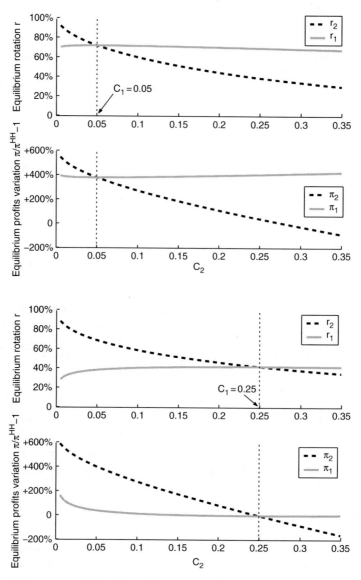

Fig. 3.4 Sensitivity of the equilibrium assortment rotation r_i with respect to C_2. Retailer 1 has $C_1 = 0.05$ (*left*) and $C_1 = 0.25$ (*right*).

The ordering indicates that for either a low (L) or high (H) cost structure, the assortment rotation is higher under symmetric competition vs. the asymmetric case (i.e., E^{LL} and E^{HH} compared to E^{LH} and E^{HL}, respectively). This has a direct implication on profits. In fact, the order of the competitive scenarios in terms of profits is the following:

$$\pi_1^{LH} \geq \pi_1^{LL} \geq \pi_1^{HL} \geq \pi_1^{HH}. \tag{3.11}$$

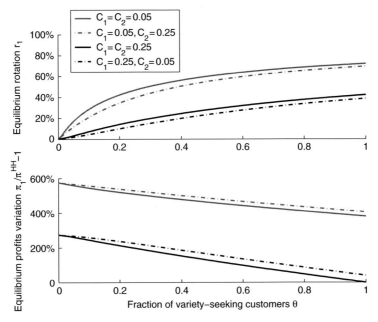

Fig. 3.5 Sensitivity with respect to the fraction of variety-seeking customers θ.

In other words, given a cost structure, a retailer prefers an asymmetric competitor. That a fast fashion retailer would prefer a traditional competitor is no surprise. However, what is less obvious is that a traditional retailer would also prefer the asymmetric case, i.e., it would rather compete against a fast fashion retailer than against another retailer that has high assortment rotation costs as well. The asymmetric competition is less intense and therefore is beneficial to both players. This is one of the key insights derived from the strategic game. Interestingly, we obtained a similar conclusion in a tactical model that we used to study the benefits of quick response under competition (see Caro and Martínez-de-Albéniz 2005).

3.5 Conclusions

We have developed a model that recognizes the importance of assortment rotation in a competitive setting and under the presence of variety-seeking customers. Our work is motivated by the abundant examples of apparel retailers that no longer plan their assortments based on static collections, but rather refresh and change the product offer on a regular basis. This strategy increases customers' expenditure at the store (possibly due to more frequent shopping visits), but also involves a higher operational cost.

Our study shows that for any retailer, some degree of assortment rotation is desirable (unless the entire population is indifferent to variety over time). The optimal rotation pace depends on the firm's cost structure, but it significantly pays off to develop capabilities that allow to manage variety efficiently. However, one of the key findings of this chapter is that firms would still prefer to remain non-identical (in terms of their assortment rotation costs) since then competition is less intense.

Despite the motivation, it is important to mention that our model is not exclusively for trendy items. Though changing the assortment seems natural for fashion products, what our model really emphasizes is the importance of the change itself, rather than the specific type of product that is being replaced. This could add a second dimension to the problem that would be worth exploring. In fact, selecting the right (type of) products to rotate might make a difference. Take, for instance, the cases of Zara and H&M. Zara is well known for mostly rotating the trendy items which are also the most expensive to produce (with a short lead time). H&M renovates its high fashion products as well (which represent a smaller fraction than at Zara, see Figure 3.1) and also rotates a large subset of products that have a fashion component but are not the latest trend. These items are actually produced in advance at a low cost. We believe this fact explains in part the difference in financial performance shown in Figure 3.2.

Other extensions that might be worth exploring are the following. We believe that our model captures one of the essential features that explains the success of fast fashion retailers. However, as it was mentioned in Section 3.1, there are other elements in fast fashion which could enrich our model. Similarly, besides the assortment rotation decision, it would be interesting to add price positioning as in Alptekinoğlu and Corbett (2008) and Cachon et al. (2008). Finally, an empirical validation of our model is a promising thread for future work.

References

Alptekinoğlu A, Corbett CJ (2008) Mass customization vs. mass production: Variety and price competition. Manufacturing and Service Operations Management 10(2):204–217

Anderson SP, de Palma A, Thisse J-F (1992) Discrete Choice Theory of Product Differentiation. MIT Press, Cambridge, MA

Baucells M, Sarin RK (2007) satiation in discounted utility. Operations Research 55(1): 170–181

Bertsekas DP (2000) Dynamic Programming and Optimal Control. Athena Scientific, Belmont, MA

Cachon G, Swinney R (2007) Purchasing, Pricing, and Quick response in the presence of strategic customers. Working paper, The Wharton School, University of Pennsylvania

Cachon G, Terwiesch C, Xu Y (2008) On the effects of consumer search and firm entry in a multiproduct competitive market. Marketing Science 27(3):461–473

Caro F, Gallien J (2007) Dynamic assortment with demand learning for seasonal consumer goods. Management Science 53(2):276–292

Caro F, Martínez-de-Albéniz V (2005) The Impact of Quick Response in Inventory-Based Competition. Working paper, IESE Business School, University of Navarra

Caro F, Martínez-de-Albéniz V (2009) Strategic Assortment Rotation. Working paper, IESE Business School, University of Navarra

Chintagunta PK (1998) Inertia and variety seeking in a model of brand-purchase timing. Marketing Science 17(3):253–270

Ferdows K, Machuca JAD, Lewis M (2002) Zara. The European case clearing house. Case 603-002-1

Fisher ML (1997) What is the Right Supply Chain for Your Product? Harvard Business Review, March–April, Reprint 97205

Fisher ML, Raman A (1996) Reducing the cost of demand uncertainty through accurate response to early sales. Operations Research 44(1):87–99

Ghemawat P, Nueno JL (2003) ZARA: Fast Fashion. Harvard Business School Multimedia Case 9-703-416

Givon M (1984) Variety seeking through brand switching. Marketing Science 3(1):1–22

The Guardian (2008) Zara Overtakes Gap to Become World's Largest Clothing Retailer. August 11

Hammond JH, Kelly MG (1990) Quick Response in the Apparel Industry. Harvard Business School Note 9-690-038

Hayes R, Pisano G, Upton D, Wheelwright S (2005) Operations, Strategy, and Technology. Pursuing the Competitive Edge. Wiley and Sons, Hoboken, NJ

H&M 2007 annual report

Ho T-H, Tang CS (1998) Product Variety Management: Research Advances. Kluwer Academic Publishers, Boston, MA

Hotelling H (1929) Stability in competition. Economic Journal 39(153):41–57

Iyer AV, Bergen ME (1997) Quick response in manufacturer-retailer channels. Management Science 43(4):559–570

Just-style.com (2005) Fast Fashion and Supply Chain Management. July 29

Kahn BE (1995) Consumer variety-seeking among goods and services: An integrative review. Journal of Retailing and Consumer Services 2(3):139–148

Kahn BE, Kalwani MU, Morrison DG (1986) Measuring variety-seeking and reinforcement behaviors using panel data. Journal of Marketing Research 23(2):89–100

Kök G, Fisher ML, Vaidyanathan R (2008) Assortment planning: Review of literature and industry practice. Retail Supply Chain Management, Eds. N. Agrawal and S. A. Smith, Kluwer Publishers. New York, NY

Lancaster K (1990) The economics of product variety: A survey. Marketing Science 9(3):189–206

Lim WS, Tang CS (2006) Optimal product rollover strategies. European Journal of Operational Research 174:905–922

McAfee A (2004) Do you have too much IT? MIT Sloan Management Review 45(3 Spring):18–22

McAfee A, Dessain V, Sjöman A (2004) ZARA: IT for Fast Fashion. Harvard Business School Case 9-604-081

El País (2008) Estrenar ropa dura segundos, January 2

Popescu I, Wu Y (2007) Dynamic pricing strategies with reference effects. Operations Research 55(3):413–429

Smith SA, Agrawal N (2000) Management of multi-item retail inventory systems with demand substitution. Operations Research 48(1):50–64

van Ryzin G, Mahajan S (1999) On the relationship between inventory costs and variety benefits in retail assortments. Management Science 45(11):1496–1509

Chapter 4
Models of Herding Behavior in Operations Management

Laurens G. Debo and Senthil K. Veeraraghavan

Abstract When new innovative products and services are introduced into the market, the consumers often do not have complete information about the quality of such products or services. Even though they collect information from several sources, their private information about the product is generally noisy and inaccurate. Under such cases, the consumers complement their private information with some available public information based on what /other/ consumers chose. For example, customers might look at the queue length information in choosing a restaurant/sports bar, or examine available sales information while choosing a recently released book, or observe stock-out information in buying a new electronic product. In these cases, the consumers might ignore their own private information and could decide to wait in the longer queue, or to purchase a more popular book, or to wait for a stocked-out electronic product. Modeling consumer behavior with such positive externalities causes the overall demand to be significantly different from traditionally modeled consumer demand. Not surprisingly, such consumer decision processes also significantly impact firms' capacity decisions: Long queues or stock-outs might signal better quality and thus generate more demand. Operations management literature in this area is nascent and emerging. In this chapter, we present current results in the operations management literature from papers that model consumer herding behavior and explore important future research directions.

Laurens G. Debo
Graduate School of Business, University of Chicago, 5807 S. Woodlawn Avenue, Chicago, IL 60637, USA
e-mail: laurens.debo@chicagobooth.edu

Senthil K. Veeraraghavan
The Wharton School, University of Pennsylvania, 3730 Walnut Street, Philadelphia, PA 19104, USA
e-mail: senthilv@wharton.upenn.edu

S. Netessine, C.S. Tang (eds.), *Consumer-Driven Demand and Operations Management Models*, International Series in Operations Research & Management Science 131, DOI 10.1007/978-0-387-98026-3_4, © Springer Science+Business Media, LLC 2009

4.1 Introduction

> *They also serve who only stand and waite.*
> John Milton (1608-1674), On His Blindness[1]

Queues are not only a nuisance in one's life. Queues can also attract potential customers to a service or product whose utility is not well known prior to the purchasing decision. In addition, for some goods, it is difficult for the seller to communicate precisely the information that allows determining the utility of the good to its potential customer base.[2] Think of a dinner at a restaurant, going to a play or a movie, or choosing a ride in an amusement park. These goods involve a 'physical' experience, a 'service' that is difficult to evaluate ex ante. The good can also be a product. Think of a new, innovative product such as a gadget with new features. Before buying the product, customers are not certain about the utility they will enjoy if they buy the product. The product could deliver some positive net surplus, or may not be worth the spent money. In many cases, customers do not know the net value of the product. A natural reaction to this lack of information is to seek complementary information about the product quality before making a purchasing decision. Such information could come from expert opinions, reviews, specialized literature, etc. In this chapter, we focus on another one such potential source of information that comes from the operational arena: the congestion level or queue length for a service or the waiting time for a product. Long waits indicate that many customers in the line have decided to buy the good, and hence, an arriving potential customer may infer that the waiting customers must have had a strong indication that it is worthwhile waiting for the product or service. Hence, *those who only stand and wait*, as Milton says in his poem, i.e., the customers that are in the queue, they also have a purpose (*they serve*): In our case, they have a signaling purpose. However, the customer's inference problem from a queue length is complicated by many factors. First of all, long lines or waiting times also are a nuisance that reduce the utility of the product. Consider, for example, a new gadget or toy that seems to be very popular and difficult to obtain during the holiday season when these ought to be given as gifts. If customers cannot obtain it during the holiday season, the joy or utility significantly decreases; or consider a restaurant with a long waiting line. Even though this may indicate that the food is of good quality, a hungry stomach may prefer joining a shorter queue at another restaurant.

Moreover, some customers in long lines may have better information than other customers. This knowledge could come from subscribing to specialized journals which provide more information on services/products. Serious theater-goers in New York (Broadway) and London (West End) presumably know more about shows and musicals, and their quality, than visiting tourists who might prefer to follow what others do. Typically, it is difficult to identify the individual customers who possess better information. Finally, on several occasions all the tables at the more popular restaurant may be occupied, or all seats for a particular play might have been sold

---

[1] We thank Christine Parlour for bringing this poem to our attention.

[2] These goods are thus experience goods.

out. Therefore, some customer may have been forced to choose their 'second-best' alternative due to capacity constraints. In that case, queue length information does not really matter. The above factors make inferring information from queue lengths non-trivial. We shall consider some specific examples that make the context we study interesting.

When hybrid cars were introduced, first by Honda (Insight) and then by Toyota (Prius), they were very novel products significantly different in design and performance from gasoline-based automobiles. Consequently, there was significant and widely prevalent uncertainty about which car was a better product. It has been widely acknowledged in several new articles that customers often had to wait as long as 6–8 months for the Prius (Boldt 2006) whereas the Honda hybrid car was immediately available (hybridcars.com 2008, Wards Auto Database 2006). Waiting time (and wait list numbers) was immediately available from dealerships. Individual experiences of several car owners are available at automotive sites such as hybridcars.com. It can be inferred that wait lines for Toyota Prius were generally significant and the queues for Honda Insight were empty (since they were immediately available). When it came to light hybrid sedans, many more customers purchased Toyota Prius cars than its competitor despite long queues. In 2006, Toyota Prius had much higher sales (more than 50,000) and by far was the market leader with more than 50% of the market that included luxury SUVs and hybrid SUVs and almost monopolized the light hybrid sedan market. In contrast, Honda Insight had really poor sales selling less than 500 cars (edmunds 2006) so much so that plans are currently afoot to shut down the production of Insight models. For this significant difference in success of seemingly similar products, we offer an explanation based on queuing.[3] Many new customers *might have taken* congestion information into account before deciding to wait for the more popular product.

It has been commonly observed that people queue up for innovative mobile phone (Lewis 2008), electronic goods such as Playstations (Pullen 2007), and even good coffee (Saporito et al. 2001). However, such herding behavior is not only restricted to consumer products such as cars, shows, books, and movies but could also occur in decisions by patients made in health-care sector. For instance, every year since 1998, more than 1,000 donated kidneys have gone unused in the United States. In 2005 alone, for example, 14.1% of recovered kidneys went unused, a disconcerting amount for a scarce commodity on which life depends. Zhang (2008) in a study of 275 donated kidneys at a major transplant center shows that herding behavior could explain such a loss. The quality of a donated kidney is uncertain, and a patient in the queue may reject a kidney (despite being way behind in the queue), because he infers that several patients ahead of him in the queue turned down that kidney. Such observation (given the knowledge of their queue position) decreases their confidence in the quality of the kidney available, and patients choose to wait for a better kidney.

---

[3] Other explanations also exist. Brand value and brand loyalty could explain some of the difference in sales. There were design issues that tempered the sales of some hybrid cars. For instance, Honda Insight was a two seater. Toward the end of this chapter, we discuss briefly some empirical issues associated with estimating the causes of such demand patterns.

In a famous example, Becker (1991) notes a puzzling context of two seafood restaurants in Palo Alto, one always crowded and the other nearly empty, even though they have similar prices and amenities, and writes,

> *Suppose that the pleasure from a good is greater when many people want to consume it, perhaps because a person does not wish to be out of step with what is popular or because confidence in the quality of food, writing or performance is greater when the restaurant, book or theater is more popular.*

Such an assumption would indicate that all customers have a higher ex post utility when they consume the more popular product. Becker's model is static and postulates that demand for a good is directly, positively influenced by other customers' demand or its popularity by assuming a functional form. However, customers could also be using other customers' decisions to bolster their own decisions. In fact, there is evidence that customers join longer queues when waiting to consume coffee (Adamy 2008), or lunch (Hill 2007).

Indeed, in several real scenarios customer decisions are influenced by others. Popular literature (Surowiecki 2003, Libert et al. 2007) discusses several noteworthy examples of such decision making in large populations. In general, customers do not decide in a 'vacuum' whether to buy a product whose quality is uncertain: Consumers are influenced by what they observe around them. Such customer-to-customer interactions are important determinants that shape a firm's demand or market share, especially for services with a high experiential content that cannot be communicated easily, or, for new, innovative products of which some features are unknown. Furthermore, operational levers like the service rate influence the queue length and hence play a role. In most operations management models, however, the demand for a product is exogenously given and is not directly affected by the characteristics of the operational system. For products or services with the characteristics described above, such independence between demand and operational characteristics like congestion level or queue lengths is not realistic: On one hand, queue lengths influence the demand for a product; on the other hand, the demand for a product also influences the queue lengths. As a result, the demand for a product and operational characteristics need to be determined simultaneously. We explore this simultaneity with great care in the models we develop and analyze.

For this chapter, we provide an overview of the theoretical underpinnings of the customer choice behavior in congestion-prone environments characterized by a high degree of quality uncertainty. We focus on how typical operational variables such as the *queue length* enter in the decision-making process of *rational Bayesian agents*. The formal study of rational Bayesian agents is a natural benchmark against which 'real customer behavior' needs to be compared. Such behavior can be tested, e.g., under laboratory-controlled circumstance. Finally, behavioral experiments as well as analytical models would form a theoretical basis for further empirical work helping us to unravel complex customer-to-customer interactions. The models presented in this chapter are thus a small first step to improve our understanding. Ultimately, a better understanding of such strategic customer behavior may allow firms better anticipate the product demand or change their capacity strategy, communication, or location strategy.

4.2 Related Literature

Our research objectives are closely linked to two broad literature but yet separate literature streams. The first stream deals with congestion: Naor (1969) is the seminal paper that analyzed congestion in systems with decentralized joining decisions. Naor's work, as well as the subsequent literature (notably, Mendelson 1985, Mendelson and Whang, 1990) that it triggered, mainly focusses on the complexities of negative externalities caused by congestion. Hassin and Haviv (2002) provide an excellent survey of this literature. Typically, agents arrive at a service system and need to decide whether to join the queue in front of a single facility or whether to balk, or, in case there are multiple facilities in front of which a queue is formed, they need to decide which queue to join, if any. Agents may or may not observe the system congestion upon arrival. Researchers study how the social welfare generated when agents make individual, utility maximizing decisions differs. when a central planner decides which customers to join. Naor found that too many customers joined a single queue in the decentralized case because they do not take into account the externalities (i.e., waiting costs) their joining decision imposes on other customers. Hence, in order to maximize the total welfare created, the expected welfare over the whole customer population, a tax needs to be imposed. Whinston (1977) considers a queue-selection problem, and shows that joining shorter queues minimizes the customers' expected waiting time, while also maximizing the total welfare, when the service times are exponentially distributed (assuming all customers join one of the two queues). Whitt (1986) provides a counterexample with non-exponential service times in which the total surplus is not maximized when customers join the shortest queue. In this literature, the value of the service for which the queue is created is generally known with certainty. In a related context, see Su and Zenios (2004, 2005), who study patient choice in kidney allocation in queues considering negative externalities.

In a separate literature stream, the impact of uncertainty about the (common) value of an asset when agents make a sequential decision about whether to purchase the asset or not is studied. Each agent has private but inaccurate information about the asset value and observes the outcome of the decisions (to buy the asset or not) of his predecessors. In their seminal papers, Banerjee (1992) and Bikhchandani et al. (1992) find that an equilibrium purchasing decision can be characterized by 'herding,' i.e., agents may ignore their private information and take the same decisions as the previously arrived agents. The authors demonstrate that the influence of the observed decisions of the predecessors could be so strong that individuals ignore completely their own information and follow their predecessor's decision. Herding can be socially inefficient as agents can make the wrong decision; i.e., buying an asset with negative value or not buying a high-value asset. The externalities present in herding models are positive: Due to their lack of information, customers follow each other's decisions. The herding literature typically assumes that arriving customers observe the full history of actions of their predecessors and do not consider waiting externalities.

Chamley (2004) notes that an analysis of the above interesting problem that employs 'optimization behavior for the consumers, and a dynamic analysis with imperfect information ...' remains to be done. This objective is the main focus of our chapter on ongoing research on herding behavior in operations management research. To our knowledge, there are only a few papers in herding literature that consider herding behavior under the limited amount of information. None of the papers consider customer waiting costs (negative externalities) that form the crux of issues related to queuing in services. Smith and Sorensen (1998) consider a model where all arriving agents sample exactly two observations. The actions that each agent observes are exogenously generated using a seed population. Smith and Sorensen are interested in the probability of convergence to the truth. In Banerjee and Fudenberg (2004), in each period a continuum of customers simultaneously choose their actions after observing exogenously chosen N previous actions. Callander and Horner (2006) focus on market heterogeneity, i.e., how the agents in the market are differentially informed, and argue how a minority of informed agents can cause other uninformed agents to follow shorter queues. The state space is restricted, and waiting costs are absent. We relax these assumptions and consider queue lengths upon arrival as a more natural but restricted, *endogenously censored* information set for an arriving customer.

There has been some literature on learning behavior and externalities in operations management. Gans (2002) studies customers who choose among various service providers with uncertain quality. Customers learn the true quality of every service provider through (expensive) repeated service sampling. There is no congestion externalities in the model (i.e., each customer learns about the service only by experiencing the service and not by observing the choices of other customers). Kumar and Parlakturk (2004) consider the behavior of self-interested customers in a general queueing network and show that a variety of scheduling rules lead to performance degradation of the network. Johari and Kumar (2008) consider positive and negative externalities in a network in a non-queueing context. For this chapter, we solely focus on positive and negative externalities caused by herding behavior combined with waiting costs.

In the remainder of this chapter, we analyze equilibrium outcomes with both *positive* (information) externalities and *negative* congestion externalities. We first present the simplest case in which there is one queue. Next, we extend the analysis to the two-queue case.

4.3 Herding in a Single Queue

In this section, we consider a single-queue system as in Debo et al. (2008b). We first develop a model and then explain the insights obtained from the analysis.

4.3.1 The Model

Debo et al. consider an experience good (a product or a service) of which the exact service value of the good or service, V, is the same for all customers, but unknown. It is the net utility of obtaining the service.[4] The quality of the good cannot be cred-

---

[4] We keep the price exogenous and only consider variations in the net utility.

ibly communicated to customers. V can take two values, $v_\omega \in \mathbb{R}$ for $\omega = \ell$ or h, with $v_\ell < v_h$. v_ℓ and v_h are common knowledge. The customers' prior belief that the product is high quality is p_h. It takes time to service (i.e., provide the good to) each customer. The service time is exponentially distributed with mean $\frac{1}{\mu}$ and is independent across customers. Consumers suffer disutility from waiting, with a waiting cost of $c \geq 0$ per unit time. Consumers are risk neutral and arrive sequentially at the market according to a Poisson process with parameter λ.[5] If agents arrive faster than they are serviced, they form a queue. The queue is served on a first-come first-served basis. Upon arrival at the market, all customers observe the queue length in front of each service facility; $n \in \mathbb{N} \triangleq \{0, 1, \cdots\}$. Besides observing the queue length, each customer receives a private signal $s \in \mathscr{S} \triangleq \{g, b\}$. This signal is an imperfect informer of which service facility provides the highest value in the market; $s \in \mathscr{S}$ is such that $\Pr(s = g \mid V = v_h) = \Pr(s = g \mid V = v_\ell) = q$, i.e., if the true state is that the product's value is high, each customer receives a signal $s = g$ ($s = b$) with probability q $(1 - q)$. Without loss of generality we assume $q \in \left(\frac{1}{2}, 1\right)$. Note that as q approaches 1, the signal becomes more informative (i.e., it has a high probability of being correct). On the other hand, as q approaches $\frac{1}{2}$, the signal becomes uninformative. Consider any customer that arrives at the market. Let $\mathscr{A} \triangleq \{0, 1\}$ be the set of possible actions that the customer can take upon arrival; $a = 1$ represents joining the queue and $a = 0$ represents the customer not entering the system. A mixed strategy for a customer is then a mapping $\sigma : \mathscr{A} \times \mathscr{S} \times \mathscr{N} \rightarrow [0, 1]$. $\sigma^j(a, s, n)$ denotes the probability that customer j joins the queue after observing state n. Thus, we have that $\sum_{a \in \mathscr{A}} \sigma^j(a, s, n) = 1$. Define *load factor* or *traffic intensity* as $\rho = \lambda \cdot (1/\mu)$. The arrival rate can be arbitrarily different compared to the service rate, $0 < \rho < \infty$. We make the following assumptions about the parameters.

Assumption 1. *(i) Either $c > 0$ or $\rho < 1$.*
(ii) $p_g v_h + (1 - p_g) v_\ell > c/\mu > p_b v_h + (1 - p_b) v_\ell$.

Part (i) ensures that the system is stationary, i.e., the expected queue length remains finite. If there are congestion costs (so that $c > 0$), even if all agents believe the good to be of high quality there is a maximum queue length. If there are no congestion costs, then the arrival rate of agents to the market is less than the service rate μ. Part (ii) states that an agent who acts only on the basis of her own signal and ignores any information in the observed queue length joins an empty queue if and only if her signal is good, i.e., when the updated valuation upon receiving a good (bad) signal is higher (lower) than the cost of waiting until the service is done. This is similar to the usual assumption in the cascades literature that an agent who ignores the information provided in other agents' actions will acquire the product if she has a good signal, but not if she has a bad one.

---

[5] Arrivals according to Poisson process is likely even when customers are *strategic*. In a recent paper, Lariviere and van Mieghem (2004) model a system in which customers find congestion costly and therefore plan to arrive when the system is under-utilized. They show that when customers choose arrival times strategically, the equilibrium arrival pattern approaches a Poisson process as the number of customers gets large.

Let $\sigma^j(a,s,n)$ be the strategy of customer j. As all customers are homogeneous ex ante, we consider symmetric strategies; $\sigma^j = \sigma$ for all customers j. Fix the strategy of all uninformed customers $j' \neq j$ at σ. Customer j's belief of that service value is high upon observing that n is $p_s'(n,\sigma)$. Due to the memoryless property of the exponential distribution, the expected time to serve each agent in the queue (including the one currently being served) is $1/\mu$. Thus, for the randomly arrived agent, the expected total waiting time before he leaves the system is $(n+1)(1/\mu)$. Given his signal and observed queue length (s,n), the agent's expected net utility from joining the queue is

$$u(s,n,\sigma) = \mathbb{E}(V \mid n,s;\sigma) - \frac{n+1}{\mu}c$$

$$= p_s'(n;\sigma)v_h + \left(1 - p_s'(n;\sigma)\right)v_\ell - \frac{n+1}{\mu}c. \qquad (4.1)$$

In a symmetric equilibrium, the agent's expected payoff in state (s,n) from playing the strategy σ is $\sigma(s,n)u(s,n,\sigma)$. Hence, σ defines a perfect Bayesian equilibrium if it maximizes this expected payoff in each state (s,n).

Definition 1. A strategy σ is a stationary Markov perfect Bayesian equilibrium if, for each $s \in \{g,b\}$ and each $n \in \mathbb{N}$,

$$\sigma(s,n) \in \underset{x\in[0,1]}{\arg\max}\ xu(s,n,\sigma), \qquad (4.2)$$

where $u(s,n,\sigma)$ is defined by (4.1) and $p'(s,n;\sigma)$ is defined by Bayes' rule for any n that is reached on the equilibrium path with a positive probability. As usual, perfect Bayesian equilibrium places no restrictions on belief $p'(s,n;\sigma)$ if n is not reached with a positive probability.

Let $p(s) = \Pr(V = v_h \mid s)$. Then, from Bayes' rule,

$$p(g) = \frac{p_h q}{p_h q + (1-p_h)(1-q)} \quad \text{and} \quad p(b) = \frac{p_h(1-q)}{p_h(1-q) + (1-p_h)q}.$$

For a given strategy vector σ, let $\pi_\omega(n,\sigma)$ be the long-run probability that the system state is n conditional on $V = v_\omega$, with σ representing the customer's strategy. With the PASTA property (Wolff, 1982), $\pi_\omega(n,\sigma)$ is also the probability that the queue is in state n for any randomly arriving customer, conditional on $V = v_h$. Using Bayes' Theorem, the updated density of the service value is

$$p'(s,n;\sigma) = \frac{\pi_h(n,\sigma)p(s)}{D(s,n,\sigma)}$$

where $D(s,n,\sigma)$ is a normalization constant:

$$D(s,n,\sigma) = \pi_h(n,\sigma)p(s) + \pi_\ell(n,\sigma)(1 - p(s)).$$

Let $BR(\sigma)$ be the best response to σ. Then, $\sigma \in BR(\sigma)$ if and only if

$$\begin{cases} u(s,n,\sigma) > 0 \Rightarrow \sigma(1,s,n) = 1, \\ u(s,n,\sigma) < 0 \Rightarrow \sigma(0,s,n) = 1. \end{cases} \tag{4.3}$$

Then σ^* is a pure strategy equilibrium if $\sigma^* \in BR(\sigma^*)$. A mixed strategy is determined analogously. We are now ready to characterize the equilibrium strategies of all customers, i.e., we characterize σ^*. The following lemma follows immediately.

Lemma 1. *The equilibrium strategy satisfies*

$$\sigma^*(s,n) = 1 \Leftrightarrow l(n,\sigma) > \frac{1-p(s)}{p(s)} \frac{((n+1)/\mu)c - v_\ell}{((n+1)/\mu)c + v_h}$$

where

$$l(n,\sigma) \doteq \frac{\pi_h(n,\sigma)}{\pi_\ell(n,\sigma)}$$

when $\pi_\ell(n,\sigma) > 0$ and $l(n,\sigma) = +\infty$ when $\pi_\ell(n,\sigma) = 0$.

The intuition is the following: The likelihood ratio, which is the ratio of the long run probability that the queue length is n when the true quality is $V = v_h$ over the long run probability that the queue length is n when the true quality is $V = v_\ell$, determines whether a customer with signal s joins the queue or not: when the likelihood ratio is higher than a certain function that depends on the signal, s, and is linearly increasing in the queue length. Obviously, $(1-p(b))p(b) > (1-p(g))/p(g)$, from which follows that if a customer with a bad signal joins the queue at a certain length, a customer with a good signal will do the same, but not the other way around. Next, we describe other insights that can be obtained from this model.

4.3.2 Insights from the Single-Queue Model

Debo et al. discuss the insights first that can be obtained from the case with $c = 0$. Then, the queue exerts a pure information externality: When the product quality is high ($V = v_h$), then more customers will obtain a good signal and, keeping all else equal, will be more likely to join the queue. As a result, it may be expected that queues are longer when the product quality is high. This is reflected in the following proposition that is proven in Debo et al. (2008b).

Proposition 1. *When $c = 0$,*
(i) $\sigma^*(1,g,0) > 0$ and $\sigma^*(1,g,n) = 1$ for all $n \geq 1$,
(ii) there exists an $\underline{n}_b \in \{1,2,3\}$ such that $\sigma^*(1,b,n) = 0$ for $0 \leq n < \underline{n}_b$ and $\sigma^*(1,b,n) > 0$ otherwise.

Proposition 1 introduces a lower threshold on the queue length: Below a certain queue length no customer that receives a bad signal ever joins the queue. Customers

with a good signal though join a queue of any length with a strictly positive probability. Hence, short queues are 'pushed forward' only by customers with a good
signal. Then, it is logical that as the queue length grows above a certain threshold
customers with a bad signal will ignore their private information and join the queue.
Debo et al. refer to this a 'local herding': Irrespective of their signals, all customers
join queues that are long enough. Note, however, that due to the service completion
process any arbitrarily long queue will dwindle to zero with probability 1. In that
case, the joining rate will again be determined by the customers with good signals
only, until the queue reaches again a certain length. Pure information externalities
introduce thus cyclic behavior. Similar behavior will be observed in the two-queue
system that will be discussed in the next section.

As an implication of this equilibrium queue joining behavior is that when, e.g.,
the prior that the product is of high quality, p, is 'strong,' say more than $\frac{1}{2}$, short
queues are undesirable: They filter out the customers with the bad signals, i.e., when
the true state of the world is high, not enough customers will have joined the queue
and hence consumed the product. It is easy to determine a measure of total customer
surplus (which is the ex ante utility of all customers that join the queue). Debo et al.
demonstrate the following proposition.

Proposition 2. *When $c = 0$, $v_\ell = -v_h$, and $\rho < (2p-1)/(p+q-1)$, there exists a
$\hat{\mu}$ such that the customer surplus decreases in the service rate for $\mu > \hat{\mu}$.*

The intuition is the following: As the prior is strong, it will be more likely that the
state of the world is high and thus that it is desirable from the customer's perspective
to join. When decreasing the service rate, the queue will dwindle less often to zero
and operate at lengths where all customers join.

It is natural to ask what will happen when queues also exert negative externalities, $c > 0$. For sure, as the value is finite and the waiting costs are a linearly increasing function of the queue length, there must exist a queue length above which
no customer joins. This is an intuitive threshold strategy discussed by Naor (1969)
and the subsequent queuing literature. It would be intuitive to conjecture that the
equilibrium strategy is determined by means of two thresholds: an upper threshold
above which no customer joins and a lower threshold below which no customer
joins. Such strategy structure would be a straightforward combination of queuing
and herding theory. The following proposition, derived by Debo et al., however,
demonstrates that the equilibrium joining strategies are in general not of the threshold type: 'holes' may exist. 'Holes' are queue lengths at which only customers with
a good signal join, while for queues that are just shorter or longer by one customer,
all customers join. This is a surprising finding. It indicates that the new insights can
be obtained from this model that are not present in either the herding or queuing
literature.

Proposition 3. *When $c > 0$, customers with a good signal play a threshold strategy:
(i) There exists an $\bar{n}$ such that $\sigma^*(1,g,n) > 0$ for $0 \leq n < \bar{n}$ and $\sigma^*(1,g,n) = 0$ for
all $n \geq \bar{n}$.
(ii) There exist parameter values for which the customers with a bad signal do not
play a threshold strategy.*

The intuition of this finding is the following: Waiting costs always increase linearly in the queue length. The updated valuation, however, always is between two bounds. When at some queue length the valuation for the customers with the bad signal is lower than the waiting costs, only customers with a good signal join the queue. This introduces a 'filter.' All customers with a bad signal observing a queue that is just only longer than the queue length at which no bad customer joins infer that only a customer with a good signal can have joined previously. This 'boosts' his belief that the quality is high. It may well be the case that the increase in value is higher than the extra waiting costs. Hence, a hole can be created. A hole is in essence a manifestation of combining both positive and negative externalities contained in queue lengths. Finally, Debo et al. address the question whether decreasing the service rate may still be beneficial for the customer surplus. From their numerical experiments, they find that when the waiting costs are not dominant, it may still be beneficial to decrease the service rate.

4.4 Herding and Queue Selection

In this section, we extend the previous model in different directions, based on Veeraghavan and Debo (2008a, b). We introduce (1) a two-queue system, without waiting costs and (Veeraraghavan and Debo, 2008a) with waiting costs (Veeraraghavan and Debo, 2008a, b), (2) finite buffer sizes (Veeraraghavan and Debo, 2008b), and (3) heterogeneity with respect to the signal quality: The signal strength may not be the same for all customers (Veeraraghavan and Debo, 2008b).

We discuss qualitatively how these features change the model set-up and insights that can be obtained from our analysis. We first discuss the most straightforward two-queue model of the single-queue model of the previous section: with a homogeneous customer base and finite buffers. Then, we extend the analysis to a heterogeneous base and large buffers. Finally, we present two applications of our models: In the first application, we compute the market share and blocking probability of two service facilities with a small buffer and a heterogeneous customer base; in the second application, we explore motivations of service facilities with small buffers to co-locate.

4.4.1 The Model

Now, we consider two service facilities whose values (V_1, V_2) are the same for all customers, but unknown. It is the net utility of obtaining the service.[6] Its joint distribution $F(v_1, v_2)$ over $[\underline{v}, \overline{v}] \times [\underline{v}, \overline{v}]$ with $\underline{v} < \overline{v} \in \mathbb{R}$ is common knowledge. Let

---

[6] We keep the price exogenous and only consider variations in the net utility. It may thus be that one facility is higher priced and brings more utility than the other; as long as the net utility is symmetrically distributed (which may be reasonable), our model is valid.

$f(v_1, v_2)$ be the density function of distribution of the valuations. We make no further distributional assumption on the $f(\cdot)$ except that it is symmetric and continuous.

Upon arrival at the market, all customers observe the queue length in front of each service facility; $\mathbf{n} = (n_1, n_2) \in \mathcal{N} \triangleq \{0, \cdots, N\} \times \{0, \cdots, N\}$. The market consists of K classes of customers.[7] α_k represents the fraction of customers belonging to class $k \in \mathsf{K} \triangleq \{1, ..., K\}$; therefore $\sum_{k \in \mathsf{K}} \alpha_k = 1$. Each customer of class k receives a private signal $s_k \in \mathcal{S} \triangleq \{1, 2\}$. For each customer class, this signal is a (possibly imperfect) informer of which service facility provides the highest value in the market; $s_k \in \mathcal{S}$ is such that $\Pr(s_k = 1 \mid V_1 > V_2) = \Pr(s_k = 2 \mid V_1 < V_2) = q_k$, i.e., if the true state is that server i provides better value than server j, each customer of type k receives a signal $s_k = i$ ($s_k = j$) with probability q_k $(1 - q_k)$. Without loss of generality we assume $q_k \in \left[\frac{1}{2}, 1\right]$ $\forall\, k$. Further, some customers have better (but not necessarily precise) information than others. We order the customer classes in descending order of private informedness or signal strength, i.e., class 1 customers have the sharpest information in the customer base and $q_n < q_m$ for $m < n$. Note that as q_k approaches 1, the signal becomes more informative (i.e., it has a high probability of being correct). On the other hand, as q_k approaches $\frac{1}{2}$, the signal becomes uninformative. Consider any customer that arrives at the market. Let $\mathcal{A} \triangleq \{0, 1, 2\}$ be the extended set of possible actions that the customer can take upon arrival; 1 represents joining server 1, 2 represents joining server 2, and 0 represents the customer not entering the system. A mixed strategy for a customer is then a mapping $\sigma_k : \mathcal{A} \times \mathcal{S} \times \mathcal{N} \to [0, 1]$. $\sigma_k^j(a, s, \mathbf{n})$ denotes the probability that customer j of class k joins queue a after observing state $\mathbf{n}$. Balking can be considered as the action of joining queue 0, i.e., a customer always balks if $\sigma_k^j(0, \mathbf{n}) = 1$. Further, we have $\sum_{a \in \mathcal{A}} \sigma_k^j(a, s, \mathbf{n}) = 1$.

Assumption 2. $E[V_i | V_i < V_{-i}] - Nc(1/\mu) > 0$.

We assume expected valuations are such that $E[V_i | V_i < V_{-i}] - Nc(1/\mu) > 0$ (and therefore $E[V_i | V_i > V_{-i}] - Nc(1/\mu) > 0$). Such service valuation ensures that a self-interested customer does not balk from a queue that is just $N - 1$ persons long. This assumption allows us to focus on the key phenomenon of interest: the equilibrium queue *selection* behavior as it eliminates cases of balking from the system merely because of waiting costs.

Let $\sigma_k^j(0, s, \mathbf{n})$ be the strategy of customer j of class k. As each server can contain N customers, all arriving customers are blocked when there is no waiting space, i.e., $\sigma_k^j(0, s, (N, N)) = 0$.[8] In other words, if the servers are full, the customers are blocked regardless of their type. When one queue is full and there is waiting space available in the other queue, customers join the other queue, even if it provides lower valuation than the blocked queue since the net utility from the queue is positive. Therefore, the actions are $\sigma_k^j(1, s, (n, N)) = 1$ and $\sigma_k^j(2, s, (N, n)) = 1$ (for

---

[7] For modeling purposes it suffices to consider heterogeneity in $K = 2$. However, all of our insights hold for several classes.

[8] No waiting customer is 'bumped' to accommodate another. The customers differ only in their private information (which is unidentifiable), not in service priority.

$n \in \{0,...,N-1\}$ and $\forall\, k,j$). The actions represent customers joining the queue of a competing service facility when their preferred server is full.

As all customers of a certain class are homogeneous ex ante, we consider symmetric strategies within each class (and allow for varying strategies across different classes); $\sigma_k^j = \sigma_k$ for all customers j in each class k. Fix the strategy of all uninformed customers $j' \neq j$ at $\sigma = \{\sigma_k, k \in K\}$ where σ_k represents the strategy of customers in class k. Customer j's belief of the service value upon observing $\mathbf{n}$ is $f_k'(v_1,v_2 \mid \mathbf{n},s;\sigma)$. Given his signal and observed queue length $(s,\mathbf{n})$, the agent's expected net utility from joining queue i is

$$u_k(i,s,\mathbf{n},\sigma) = \mathbb{E}_k\left(V_i \mid \mathbf{n},s;\sigma\right) - cn_i/\mu,$$

with

$$\mathbb{E}_k\left(V_i \mid \mathbf{n},s,\sigma\right) = \int_{\underline{v}}^{\overline{v}} \int_{\underline{v}}^{\overline{v}} v_i f_k'(v_1,v_2 \mid \mathbf{n},s;\sigma)\,dv_2 dv_1,\ i \in \{1,2\}.$$

Definition 2. A strategy σ is a stationary Markov perfect Bayesian equilibrium if, for each $s \in \{1,2\}$ and each $n \in \mathbb{N}$,

$$\sigma_k(i,s,\mathbf{n}) \in \arg\max_{x \in [0,1]} x u_k(i,s,\mathbf{n},\sigma), \tag{4.4}$$

where $f_k'(v_1,v_2 \mid \mathbf{n},s;\sigma)$ is defined by Bayes' rule for any $\mathbf{n}$ that is reached on the equilibrium path with a positive probability. Perfect Bayesian equilibrium places no restrictions on belief $f_k'(v_1,v_2 \mid \mathbf{n},s;\sigma)$ if $\mathbf{n}$ is not reached with a positive probability.

For a given strategy vector σ, let $\pi_i(\mathbf{n},\sigma)$ be the long run probability that the system state is $\mathbf{n}$ conditional on $V_i > V_{-i}$, with $-i$ denoting $2(1)$ if $i = 1(2)$, with σ representing the customer's strategy. With the PASTA property (Wolff, 1982), $\pi_i(\mathbf{n},\sigma)$ is also the probability that the queue is in state $\mathbf{n}$ for any randomly arriving customer, conditional on $V_i > V_{-i}$. Recall that the prior of the service values is symmetric. Define then $p_k(s)$ as the updated prior of a customer belonging to class k after obtaining signal s. Then, with Bayes' Theorem, it is easy to see that $p_k(1) = q_k$ and $p_k(2) = 1 - q_k$. Using Bayes' Theorem further, for all customer classes k, the updated density of the service value is

$$f_k'(v_1,v_2 \mid \mathbf{n},s;\sigma) = \begin{cases} \dfrac{p_k(s)\,\pi_i(\mathbf{n},\sigma)}{D_k(\mathbf{n},s,\sigma)} f(v_1,v_2) & v_1 > v_2 \\[2ex] \dfrac{(1 - p_k(s))\,\pi_{-i}(\mathbf{n},\sigma)}{D_k(\mathbf{n},1,\sigma)} f(v_1,v_2) & o/w \end{cases}$$

where $D_k(\mathbf{n},s,\sigma)$ is a normalization constant for customers in class k:

$$D_k(\mathbf{n},s,\sigma) = p_k(s)\,\pi_i(\mathbf{n},\sigma) \int_{\underline{v}}^{\overline{v}} \int_{\underline{v}}^{v_1} f(v_1,v_2)\,dv_2 dv_1$$

$$+ (1 - p_k(s))\,\pi_{-i}(\mathbf{n},\sigma) \int_{\underline{v}}^{\overline{v}} \int_{v_1}^{\overline{v}} f(v_1,v_2)\,dv_2 dv_1.$$

Let $BR_k(\sigma)$ be the best response of a customer of class k to σ. Then, $\sigma_k \in BR_k(\sigma)$ if and only if

$$
\begin{cases}
u_k(i,s,\mathbf{n},\sigma) > u_k(-i,s,\mathbf{n},\sigma) & \Rightarrow \sigma_k^j(i,s,\mathbf{n}) = 1 \\
u_k(-i,s,\mathbf{n},\sigma) > u_k(i,s,\mathbf{n},\sigma) & \Rightarrow \sigma_k^j(-i,s,\mathbf{n}) = 1 \\
\max\left(u_k(i,s,\mathbf{n},\sigma), u_k(-i,s,\mathbf{n},\sigma)\right) < 0 \Rightarrow \sigma_k^j(0,s,\mathbf{n}) = 1.
\end{cases}
\tag{4.5}
$$

Then σ^* is a pure strategy equilibrium if $\sigma_k^* \in BR_k(\sigma^*)\ \forall k \in K$. A mixed strategy is determined analogously. We are now ready to characterize the equilibrium strategies of all customers, i.e., we characterize σ^*. The following lemma follows immediately.

Lemma 2. *Assuming $n_1 > n_2$, the equilibrium strategy satisfies*

$$
\begin{cases}
\sigma_k^*(1,s,\mathbf{n}) = 1 \Leftrightarrow \dfrac{p_k(1)}{1-p_k(1)}\dfrac{\Delta + \frac{n_1-n_2}{\mu}c}{\Delta - \frac{n_1-n_2}{\mu}c} < l(\mathbf{n},\sigma) \\[2ex]
\sigma_k^*(s,s,\mathbf{n}) = 1 \Leftrightarrow \dfrac{p_k(2)}{1-p_k(2)}\dfrac{\Delta + \frac{n_1-n_2}{\mu}c}{\Delta - \frac{n_1-n_2}{\mu}c} < l(\mathbf{n},\sigma) < \dfrac{p_k(1)}{1-p_k(1)}\dfrac{\Delta + \frac{n_1-n_2}{\mu}c}{\Delta - \frac{n_1-n_2}{\mu}c} \\[2ex]
\sigma_k^*(2,s,\mathbf{n}) = 1 \Leftrightarrow \hspace{3cm} l(\mathbf{n},\sigma) < \dfrac{p_k(2)}{1-p_k(2)}\dfrac{\Delta + \frac{n_1-n_2}{\mu}c}{\Delta - \frac{n_1-n_2}{\mu}c}
\end{cases}
$$

where

$$
l(\mathbf{n},\sigma) \doteq \frac{\pi_1(\mathbf{n},\sigma)}{\pi_2(\mathbf{n},\sigma)}
$$

when $\pi_2(\mathbf{n},\sigma) > 0$ and $l(\mathbf{n},\sigma) = +\infty$ when $\pi_2(\mathbf{n},\sigma) = 0$ and $\Delta = E[V_1|V_1 > V_2] - E[V_2|V_1 < V_2]$.

Notice that similarity with Lemma 1: When the likelihood ratio of the long run probability of finding the system in state $\mathbf{n}$ with $n_1 > n_2$, conditional on $V_1 > V_2$, is higher than some function that depends on the signal s and is increasing in the difference in queue lengths, it is rational to join the longer (shorter) queue. Otherwise, in equilibrium, customers join the queue that is indicated by their private information. Due to the symmetry in values and service rates, when $n_1 = n_2$, the equilibrium action is $\sigma_k^*(s,s,\mathbf{n}) = 1$, i.e., 'follow the signal.' This is intuitive: When the two queues are equally long, no information about the relative value can be obtained; hence, in equilibrium, customers follow their private information.

Recall that for the single-queue case, Debo et al. defined 'local herding,' when a customer with a bad signal joined a queue only because it is long enough. In the two-queue case, we seek for situations where at some state 'join the longest queue' is part of an equilibrium. This is an interesting observation since action as without the quality uncertainty, which is fundamental to our framework, no rational customer would ever join the longest queue, provided both the servers are symmetric ex ante. We will interchangeably refer to 'joining the longest queue' behavior and 'herd' behavior in the remainder of this chapter.

4.4.2 Insights from the Two-Queue Model: Homogeneous Customer Bases and Small Buffers

Determination of equilibrium strategies with two queues is significantly more complex than with a single queue. The reason is that for a given strategy, σ the long run probabilities of a two-dimensional queuing system needs to be determined. As a single queue is a birth–death process, a closed form expression can be obtained easily. For two queues, no closed form expression is known to exist (Kingman, 1961). However, determining the long run probabilities is only a sub-problem when determining equilibrium strategies. For a given strategy σ needs to satisfy the conditions of Lemma 2. For $N = 25$, there are 676 possible states out of which 600 (excepting the diagonal and boundaries) need to be determined in equilibrium, giving rise to $3^{600} \approx 10^{286}$ candidate equilibrium profiles.

Hence, we start in this section with the lowest possible buffer space ($N = 2$) and homogeneous customers ($K = 1$), as in the single-queue case. Somewhat surprisingly, if *all* the customers are endowed with the *same* quality of private information, no customer will join the longest queue. In other words, the herding behavior that we identified for a single queue disappears! This at first puzzling result will reveal two important determinants of herd behavior in a queue selection setting: Buffer size and heterogeneity of the consumer base are necessary drivers of herd behavior in congestion-prone environments. Essentially, when there is not enough variation in the outcome (i.e., queue length) possible, no herd behavior will occur.

To illustrate this effect, we consider the strategies of the partially informed customers for whom $q_1 = q$. As we have only one customer class, we drop the subscript $_k$. When $N = 2$, all actions except for the states $(1, 0)$ and $(0, 1)$ are determined: On the boundary states, customers join the other queue; at $(2, 2)$, the system is full and customers balk. On the diagonal states, (n, n), customers follow their signal. Hence, in state $(1, 0)$ (and symmetrically in state $(0, 1)$), customers can follow their signal, the shortest queue, or the longest queue. Keeping the remaining aspects of the model the same as before, we explore the decisions of customers at state $(1, 0)$. We use notation $l(\mathbf{n}; \sigma)$ to represent the likelihood ratio function when customers play strategy σ at $\mathbf{n}$. Let l^L, l^F, and l^S indicate the likelihood ratios $l\big((1, 0); \sigma^L\big)$, $l\big((1, 0); \sigma^F\big)$, and $l\big((1, 0); \sigma^S\big)$.

To understand the equilibrium strategies better, we characterize the behavior of likelihood ratio functions with respect to the market parameters.

Lemma 3. *When $N = 2$, $c > 0$ and $K = 1$ with $q_1 = q$:*

1. *The likelihood ratios l^L, l^F, and l^S are all decreasing in ρ.*
2. $\lim_{\rho \to 0} l^L = \lim_{\rho \to 0} l^F = \lim_{\rho \to 0} l^S = q/(1-q) \geq 1.$
3. $\lim_{\rho \to \infty} l^L = \lim_{\rho \to \infty} l^F = \lim_{\rho \to \infty} l^S = 1.$
4. $l^F > l^L > l^S.$

We provide only a short description below. Lemma 3(1) shows that for a given q, the likelihood ratios are decreasing with the traffic intensity. Hence, as the traffic intensity increases, it becomes less likely to see a longer queue at the better server.

This is true for any queue joining strategy adopted by the customers. However, it is always true that the longer queue is more likely to occur at the better server since all likelihood ratios are more than one (from Lemma 3(3)). Thus, queue lengths do provide some information but do not provide perfect information. But they do not provide *perfect* information since all likelihood ratios are bounded by $q/(1-q)$ (Lemma 3(2)). Finally, note that $l^F > l^L > l^S$: If customers follow their signal, the longer queue is more indicative of quality more often than situations in which customers ignore their signals and follow the longer queue (or shorter queue). If arrival rates are low, boundary effects are minimal. When everyone follows their signal, the longer queue fully correlates to the better service provider. Hence, the likelihood ratios when all customers follow their signal are much higher than other likelihood ratios when the arrival rate is low (compared to the service rate). Now, we derive the following conditions on the equilibrium.

Proposition 4. *When $N = 2$, $c > 0$ and $K = 1$ with $q_1 = q$:*

1. *σ^L is never an equilibrium strategy.*
2. *When $0 \le c\tau < \Delta(2q-1)$, $\sigma^* = \sigma^F$.*
3. *When $\Delta(2q-1) \le c\tau < \Delta(2q-1)/[(1-q)^2+q^2]$, $\sigma^* = \sigma^F$ for $\rho \in (0,\overline{\rho})$ and $\sigma^* = \sigma^S$ for $\rho \in (\underline{\rho},\infty)$, where $\exists$ some $(\underline{\rho},\overline{\rho})$ such that $\underline{\rho} < \overline{\rho}$.*
4. *When $\Delta(2q-1)/[(1-q)^2+q^2] \le c\tau$, $\sigma^* = \sigma^S$.*

Notice that Proposition 4(1) presents an interesting result: Customers do *not* join the longer queue in a homogeneous customer base, even when waiting costs are zero. In other words, in a customer base with limited waiting space, when the information quality of all customers is the same, customers do not follow other customers, even when there are no waiting costs. Proposition 4 is also a markedly different result from Veeraraghavan and Debo (2008), where $c = 0$, but there is an infinite buffer space in front of each service facility ($N = \infty$). Thus, the size of the buffer space is a key determinant of the equilibrium joining behavior.

In the presence of waiting costs, the equilibrium behavior of customers is a complex function of waiting costs, traffic intensity, and signal strengths. In Proposition 4, results (2)–(4) specify the equilibria for every waiting cost and at all arrival rates.

Consider the case (2) when $c\tau < \Delta(2q-1)$. Recall Δ is the marginal updated valuation of the better service/product over the worse product. Since we assume $V_1 > V_2$ wlog, a customer arriving at $(1,0)$ expects an additional valuation Δ from facility 1 (longer queue), conditional on it being the better server. An arriving customer receives a private signal of strength q. Suppose she follows her signal. With probability q, the signal is 'correct' and she receives an additional utility Δ. With probability $1-q$ the signal is 'false' and she receives lower valuation and suffers a disutility $-\Delta$. Therefore, the expected additional utility for this customer from following her signal is $q\Delta + (1-q)(-\Delta) = \Delta(2q-1)$. If the customer held perfect private information (i.e., $q = 1$), then the updated valuation due to his perfect information equals Δ. Similarly, if the customer held fully imperfect private information (i.e., $q = 1/2$), then the noisy signal obfuscates all information about product quality (and $\Delta(2q-1) = 0$). Since the expected additional utility from following one's own signal $\Delta(2q-1)$ is greater than the waiting cost $c\tau$, all customers follow their signal, i.e., $\sigma^* = \sigma^F$; this result is captured in Proposition 4(2).

Let us examine result (4) to understand (3) better. To reason Proposition 4(4), let us examine the term

$$\Delta\frac{2q-1}{q^2+(1-q)^2}$$

in detail. First note that

$$\Delta\frac{2q-1}{q^2+(1-q)^2} \geq \Delta(2q-1)$$

since $q^2+(1-q)^2 \leq 1$.

What is the strongest information that a customer arriving at $(1,0)$ can infer about the valuation of the service through the choice of the previous customer? Suppose that the arriving customer is able to perfectly (by some means) know the private signal of the previous customer in the queue. Her confidence in the valuation of the service is highest when the previous customer's signal is identical to her own signal. Recall, the signals are independently and identically distributed, and each signal is 'true' with probability q. Therefore, conditional on observing two identical signals, the signals are correct with probability $q^2/[q^2+(1-q)^2]$ and they are both false with probability $(1-q)^2/[q^2+(1-q)^2]$.

When the signals are true, the customer receives an additional valuation Δ from following the signal. When they are false, she suffers some loss of utility $-\Delta$. Therefore the expected valuation in following her private (and an identical previous) signal is

$$\frac{q^2}{q^2+(1-q)^2}\Delta + \frac{(1-q)^2}{q^2+(1-q)^2}(-\Delta) = \frac{q^2-(1-q)^2}{q^2+(1-q)^2}\Delta = \frac{2q-1}{q^2+(1-q)^2}\Delta.$$

Note $\Delta(2q-1)/[q^2+(1-q)^2]$ is the strongest update on the valuation a customer can form based on her private signal, and by fully knowing the signal of the previous customer. If even this maximal information is less than additional waiting cost $c\tau$, the customer would have to forgo following her signal and instead join the shorter queue since waiting costs dominate. Therefore, if the waiting costs are such that $c\tau > \Delta(2q-1)/[q^2+(1-q)^2]$, the customers will *always* follow the shorter queue.

Now we focus our attention on the intermediate cost region defined in Proposition 4(3). This result combines information externality with queuing effects in an elegant way. This is the first known result in our knowledge that combines longer queue joining choice behavior with arrival traffic intensity. In general the customer (she) arriving at $(1,0)$ cannot perfectly infer the private signal of the customer who is currently in the queue. All she can infer from the public information (state of the system) is that there is currently one additional customer in the longer queue. Thus, updated valuation of the arriving customer is bounded above by $\Delta(2q-1)/[q^2+(1-q)^2]$ and bounded below by her own private information $\Delta(2q-1)$.

To elaborate, a customer arriving at state $(1,0)$ does not know with certainty whether she observes the state through a prior service departure (transitions from $(2,0)$ and $(1,1)$) or through a prior arrival (transition from $(0,0)$ to $(1,0)$). Therefore, she is not sure if the customer in the queue followed his signal or joined the shorter/longer queue when he joined the queue. In other words, service departure process complicates any information that can be gleaned about the private signal of the customer currently in the queue. If the previous event was an arrival, the customer currently in the queue (he) moved the state of the system from $(0,0)$ to $(1,0)$ by following his signal (since all customers follow their signals if the queue lengths are equal). However, the arriving customer is not sure if the previous event was an arrival. The more sure she is that the last event was an arrival, the higher the valuation she obtains from following her signal.

If the traffic intensity is very low, states with higher occupancy are less likely than $(0,0)$, and therefore the last event is more likely to be an arrival at $(0,0)$ (rather than a departure from less probable higher states). Thus, under low traffic intensity, arriving customers have higher updated valuation and hence can overcome the additional waiting cost and follow their signal.

When the traffic intensity is high, departures from $(2,0)$ and $(1,1)$ are more likely, and hence the customer's updated valuation is lower. When $\Delta(2q-1) \leq c\tau < \Delta(2q-1)/[(1-q)^2+q^2]$, the updated valuation is likely to be higher than the waiting cost $c\tau$ when the traffic is light than when the traffic intensity is high. Hence, customers follow their signal at low traffic (when $\rho < \overline{\rho}$) and join shorter queues under high traffic intensities (when $\rho > \underline{\rho}$). With the derived results we compare the equilibria in two similar markets in Section 4.4.4.

4.4.3 Insights from the Two-Queue Model: Heterogeneous Customer Bases and Large Buffers

In the previous section, we found that the herding behavior identified in a single-queue setting does not emerge in a two-queue setting with limited buffer space $(N = 2)$ and homogeneous customers $(K = 1)$. We show in this section that the buffer size and heterogeneity are key determinants of herding behavior. As for the single-queue case, it is convenient to split the discussion into the case with only positive information externalities; $c = 0$ as in Veeraraghavan and Debo, 2008a, and in the case with both positive informational externalities and negative waiting externalities. Veeraraghavan and Debo (2008a, b) analyze special cases: when $c = 0$ and $N = \infty$ and when $c > 0$ and $N = 2$. They extend their insights by means of a computational study for large values of N and $c > 0$. We first discuss the special case $c = 0$ (no waiting costs), $N = \infty$ (infinite buffer space), and $K = 1$ (homogeneous customer base). Moreover, we only look at one customer class; hence, we drop the index $_k$.

Proposition 5. *When $N = \infty$, $c = 0$, and $K = 1$, $\sigma^*(1, s, (n_1, 0)) = 1$ for $n_1 > 0$, $\sigma^*(2, s, (0, n_2)) = 1$ for $n_2 > 0$, and $\sigma^*(s, s, (0, 0)) = 1$.*

According to the proposition, without waiting costs or buffer limitations, joining the longer queue is an equilibrium. Only when both queues are empty will an arriving customer follow his/her signal. Veeraraghavan and Debo (2008a) show that customers arriving at $(n_1, 0)$ or $(0, n_2)$ are actually indifferent between joining the longer queue and following their signal. However, there cannot exist an equilibrium in which customers randomize between both strategies. Proposition 5 reveals some interesting implications: At any point in time, at least one server will be idling. The service provider with the truly higher quality will be busy $q\rho$ fraction of time, while the other service provider will be busy $(1 - q)\rho$ fraction of time (see Corollary 7 in Veeraraghavan and Debo, 2008a). As in the single-queue case, cycling occurs again. This time, the cycle is composed of one queue attracting all customers while the other queue remains empty. Depending on the signal strength, q, the higher quality queue will attract more cycles than the lower quality queue. Veeraraghavan and Debo consider a number of extensions to the base model and find that the qualitative properties of the equilibrium are robust to multiple servers for each queue and servers that 'go out of business' after idling for some time. The authors also discuss the case when the service rates are not known but are correlated with the service value: When better service is slower, they find that following the longer queue is again an equilibrium. In this case, as the service rate of the better service provider is the lowest, queues have a double signaling function: Long queues are not only 'traces' of customers' private signals but also an indication that the service process is slow and hence the quality is high. Both are reasons for joining the longer queue. The situation is different when better service is faster. Then, customers cannot solidly infer from long queues that the quality is high. Queues then provide mixed signals; hence, joining the longer queue is not an equilibrium when the difference in service rate between the high- and low-quality service provider is large.

Now, we turn to the case with waiting costs, $c > 0$. We consider two classes of customers: A fraction α of the population is perfectly informed about which service provider is the better one (i.e., they obtain a signal that is perfectly correlated with the state of the world, $q_1 = 1$), while the remainder of the population is uninformed (i.e., they obtain a signal that is not correlated with the state of the world, $q_2 = 1/2$). When $N = 2$, all actions except for the states $(1, 0)$ and $(0, 1)$ are determined: At $(1, 0)$ and $(0, 1)$ customers can follow their signal, the shortest queue, or the longest queue. We indicate these strategies by means of σ^F, σ^S, and σ^L, respectively, and the corresponding likelihood ratios at $(1, 0)$ as l^F, l^S, and l^L, respectively. The queue joining strategy of the perfectly informed customers is trivial: They join the queue that yields the highest net benefit: If their private information reveals $s = 1$, then they join queue 1 if $\Delta > [(n_1 - n_2)/\mu]c$. Otherwise, they join queue 2. For the uninformed customers, as their signal is uninformative, σ^F will never be part of the equilibrium. We can simply conjecture an equilibrium strategy and verify with Lemma 2 when all conditions are satisfied.

Proposition 6. *When $N = 2$, $c > 0$, and $K = 2$ with $q_1 = \frac{1}{2}$, $q_2 = 1$, $\alpha_1 = 1 - \alpha$, and $\alpha_2 = \alpha$, there exists a value of $\hat{\Delta}$ such that in a heterogeneous market with a fraction α of fully informed customers, the equilibria structure over all parameter values is as follows:*

1. *When $\hat{\Delta} < c\tau < \Delta$, $\sigma_2^* = \sigma^S$ is an equilibrium for all uninformed customers $\forall$ $\rho > 0$.*
2. *When $\alpha\Delta < c\tau < \hat{\Delta}$, there exist two values of ρ such that $\forall \rho \in (\underline{\rho}, \overline{\rho})$, such that $l^L > (\Delta + c/\mu)/(\Delta - c/\mu)$ and*

$$\begin{cases} \sigma_2^* = \sigma^L \ \forall \rho \in (\underline{\rho}, \overline{\rho}) \\ \sigma_2^* = \sigma^S \ \ \ \forall \rho > 0. \end{cases}$$

3. *When $c\tau < \alpha\Delta$, there exists a value of $\overline{\rho}$ such that $\forall \rho \in (0, \overline{\rho})$ such that $l^L > (\Delta + c/\mu)/(\Delta - c/\mu)$ and there exists a value of $\hat{\rho}$ such that $\forall \rho \in (\hat{\rho}, \infty)$ such that $l^S < (\Delta + c/\mu)/(\Delta - c/\mu)$ and*

$$\begin{cases} \sigma_2^* = \sigma^L \ \ \ \forall \rho \in (0, \overline{\rho}] \\ \sigma_2^* = \sigma^S \ \forall \rho \in (\hat{\rho}, \infty). \end{cases}$$

Furthermore, we have that $\hat{\rho} < \overline{\rho}$.

From Proposition 6, we notice that joining the longer queue can be an equilibrium strategy when the waiting cost, c, is not too high. Proposition 6 is a markedly different result from the results in the previous section, with homogeneous information, in which customers do never join the longest queue. Thus, heterogeneity in the signal quality is a key determinant of the equilibrium queue joining behavior. Interestingly, only when the arrival rate is low compared to the service rates will joining the longest queue be an equilibrium strategy even when there are no waiting costs ($c = 0$). Recall that when $N = \infty$ and $c = 0$ (Proposition 5), joining the longest queue was an equilibrium for *any* arrival rate. The reason is that as the buffer space is very restricted, high arrival rates make the system always full. As a result, not much information can be gleaned from a longer queue. In contrast, when the arrival rate is very low, there is a high probability that the customer in the longer queue is an informed one and hence joining the longer queue is rational for uninformed customers. Hence, the buffer is a 'damper' on the customer learning ability from queues.

4.4.4 Equilibrium Strategies: Numerical Examples with $N = 25$

In this section, we explore which characteristics identified in the previous sections for either $N = 2$ or $N = \infty$, which are amenable for analysis, are robust. For intermediate values of N, we rely on computations to determine the equilibrium strategy.

The computed equilibrium strategy can be surprisingly complex. Yet some key feature identified in the $c = 0$ and $N = \infty$ and in the $c > 0$ and $N = 2$ case remains persistent. In Figure 4.1, we show the computed equilibrium strategy for $N = 25$, $c > 0$, and $K = 2$ and different parameter settings in the $\mathcal{N}$ space. The white area indicates that the equilibrium action is to follow the signal. A horizontal bar when $n_1 > n_2$ indicates that the equilibrium action is to join the longer queue (i.e., n_1) at **n**. A vertical bar indicates that the equilibrium action is to join the shortest queue at **n**. From comparing the subplots in Figure 4.1, we obtain the following insights:

- As the signals get stronger, the customers follow their private signals more often (i.e., at more arrival states).
- As the fraction of more informed customers in the market increases, the less informed customers join longer queues at more states.
- The longer queue joining behavior is more pronounced when the arrival rates are low. As the arrival rates increase, the customers follow their private signals at more states.

The above insights are expected and hence confirm the confidence in our model. There are few other interesting observations that our model can further explain:

- When one queue is empty, the customers join the other non-empty queue even though they incur higher waiting costs. This may be expected when the waiting costs are zero (see Veeraraghavan and Debo 2008a). It is intriguing that the effect persists when the waiting costs are strictly positive. As long as the market contains more informed customers, the less informed customers reason out that empty queue is more likely to be worse, since no informed customers are currently in that queue. Given that there are informed customers in the market, what inference does an arriving customer make from an empty queue? The *only* way an empty queue would happen at a better server is if there are no informed customers in the customer base. If there is a fully informed customer in the market currently, clearly he is at the non-empty queue and then the non-empty queue would be surely better. Therefore, when one queue is empty, the information content in the non-empty queue gets stronger as the non-empty queue gets longer (since the conditional probability that there are no informed customers in the market decreases, the number of customers in the market increases). This explains often-found observations of customers choosing busier restaurants over empty restaurants.
- However, the behavior described above changes immediately off the boundary states. Customers might join the shorter queue immediately of the boundary. Less informed customers may join the shorter queue when the shorter queue contains a single customer. This is the effect of dissenting actions of 'informed minority.' The shorter queue possibly points to the one lone dissenting outlier which indicates to the arriving customers that the shorter queue is better. What does an arriving customer infer? Given that there are perfectly informed customers in the market, as long as the longer queue is too long, there could be *one* informed customer in the market who chose to dissent with the 'herding' majority. Note

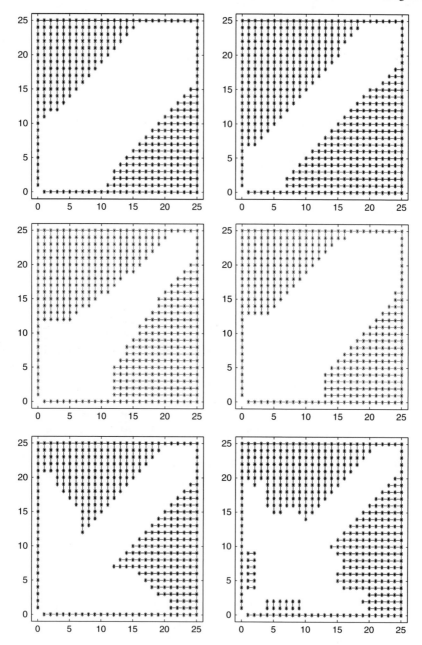

Fig. 4.1 Equilibrium strategy in the $\mathcal{N}$ space for $N = 25$, $c > 0$, $K = 2$, and $\rho = 0.9$. On the *top* row, *left* (*right*) panel, $g = 0.99$ (0.99) and $\alpha = 0.6$. On the *middle* row, *left* (*right*) panel, $g = 0.75$ (0.99) and $\alpha = 0.6$ (0.2). On the *bottom* row, *left* (*right*) panel, $g = 0.90$ (0.75) and $\alpha = 0.2$. The empty/blank area indicates that at these queue lengths, join the longest queue is the equilibrium action at $\mathbf{n}$, a horizontal bar when $n_1 > n_2$ indicates that joint the longer queue is the equilibrium action at $\mathbf{n}$ and a vertical bar indicates that join the shorter queue is the equilibrium action at $\mathbf{n}$.

that this shorter queue joining occurs when the longer queue is not sufficiently long: Queue lengths at such states point more to decisions made by arriving customers (buffer size effects are minimal).

- As the longer queue gets sufficiently congested, but not too long, customers' private information outweighs information gleaned from a lone dissenting minority. Since the longer queue is not too long, the information from the long queue is insufficient to overcome the strength of the private signal. Thus, the less informed customers follow their own private signals.
- When the queue difference is large, the value from customers' private information and the notion that the shorter queue points to a dissenting informed customer are both weak. First, long queues are more likely to have perfectly informed customers, and shorter queues might have some customers, because few customers chose an inferior alternative after being blocked at the longer queue. Under both perspectives, the longer queues provide sufficiently strong, quality information for less informed customers to overcome their private information. Then, the customers join the longer queue ignoring their private information.

In the following sections, we revert to $N = 2$ and study the aggregate performance measure of each service facility, assuming that customers make equilibrium queue selection decisions.

4.4.5 The Effect of Herding on the Market Share and Blocking Probability of Service Providers with Small Buffers

In this section, we compare the performance measures of different forms of market heterogeneity for $N = 2$ and $K = 2$. Let M represent the market heterogeneity $\{(\alpha_k, q_k)_{k \in K}\}$. Assume without loss of generality that service facility 1 is better than service facility 2. When the customers select a service facility based on their private information only,[9] the potential demand rate of service facility 1 is $\lambda \sum_{k \in K} \alpha_k q_k$ and the potential demand rate for service facility 2 is $\lambda \sum_{k \in K} \alpha_k (1 - q_k)$. As a result, all customer bases for which $\sum_{k \in K} \alpha_k q_k = m$ will generate the same potential demand rate $m\lambda$ for service facility 1 and $(1 - m)\lambda$ for service facility 2. In particular, having $m = \alpha + \frac{1}{2}(1 - \alpha) = q$ should lead to the same potential demand rate in the customer bases $M_a = \{(\alpha, \frac{1}{2}), (1 - \alpha, 1)\}$ and $M_b = \{(1, q)\}$. Now, we compare the loss rate, market share, and net arrival rate of service provider 1 for M_a and M_b. With queuing externalities, two effects will be introduced. First, the finite capacity will force some overflow and cause some spillover. Second, the strategic customer behavior will make customers deviate from following their private signal.

---

[9] Even if $g = \frac{1}{2}$ and the signal is uninformative, after observing the signal, the customers remain indifferent. We assume that they join with equal probability any queue. This is the same as assuming that the customers follow their signal, even if it is uninformative.

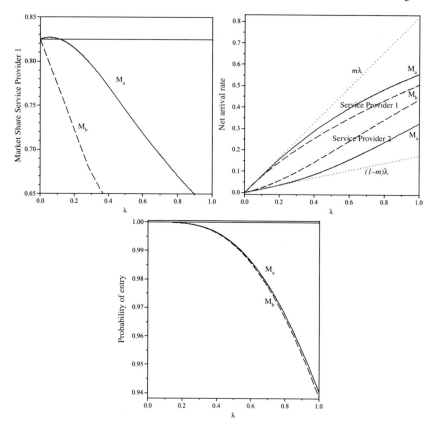

Fig. 4.2 Market share, net arrival rate, and probability of entry as a function of the arrival rate for both M_a with $\sigma_1^* = \sigma^F$, $\sigma_2^* = \sigma^L$ and M_b with $\sigma^* = \sigma^F$. The *thick curves* indicate market $M_a = \{(\alpha, \frac{1}{2}), (1 - \alpha, 1)\}$ and *dotted curves* indicate market $M_b = \{(1, g)\}$ The parameters are $m = \alpha + \frac{1}{2}(1 - \alpha) = q = 0.825$ and $c = 0$. In the *right panel* the probability of entry (not getting blocked) is shown as a function of the arrival rate for both M_a with $\sigma_1^* = \sigma^F$, $\sigma_2^* = \sigma^L$ and M_b with $\sigma^* = \sigma^F$.

Let $\lambda_1^*(M)$ be the equilibrium arrival rate to the better service facility, then we plot in Figure 4.2.

Market Share

The left frame in Figure 4.2 shows

$$\frac{\lambda_1^*(M_a)}{\lambda_1^*(M_a) + \lambda_2^*(M_a)} \quad \text{versus} \quad \frac{\lambda_1^*(M_b)}{\lambda_1^*(M_b) + \lambda_2^*(M_b)},$$

i.e., the market share of the better service facility for each of the market compositions.

For low arrival rates, the market share of the high-quality service facility increases first and then decreases for M_a but always decreases for M_b. Also note that the market share of the better service facility in a market with queueing delays can exceed its market share in a market without any such delays. This is the first result to our knowledge that shows the market share of a service facility improving in a market with congestion externalities. Intuitively, as $\lambda \to \infty$, the market share tends to $1/2$ for both market compositions.

Effective Arrival Rate

In the middle frame of Figure 4.2 the effective arrival rates to each firm in both the customer bases are provided. In particular $\lambda_1^*(M_a)$ versus $\lambda_1^*(M_b)$ provides the effective arrival rate to the service facility.

For low arrival rates, the demand rates for the high- and low-quality service facilities are close to $m\lambda$ and $(1-m)\lambda$, respectively. Note the effect of increased arrival rate: The net demand at the worse service facility improves directly at the expense of the better service facility. Even though the potential arrival rates with heterogeneous and homogeneous signal qualities are the same, the latter effect is mitigated when customers have heterogeneous qualities of their signal strengths. In other words, a high-quality service facility prefers a heterogeneous customer base composition, while a low-quality service facility prefers a homogeneous customer base composition. As long as there are limited buffer spaces, and some positive valuation from the worse server, customers might be forced to choose their 'second-best' option. Therefore the spillover effect increases with higher traffic intensity. Intuitively, as $\lambda \to \infty$, the demand rate tends to μ for both customer base compositions.

Entry Probability

The right frame of Figure 4.2 shows the probability of an arriving customer entering the system, i.e., probability of not being blocked, in each market. Recall that a customer is blocked when there is no waiting space available. She enters the better service facility with probability

$$\frac{\lambda_1^*(M_a) + \lambda_2^*(M_a)}{\lambda} \quad \text{versus} \quad \frac{\lambda_1^*(M_b) + \lambda_2^*(M_b)}{\lambda},$$

in each of the customer base compositions.

For a low arrival rate, notice that the loss due to blocking for customer base composition M_a is lower than for M_b. Thus when arrivals are sparse more customers enter the heterogeneous customer base compared to a comparable homogeneous customer base. Therefore, heterogeneity in market information allows for more customers to join the market (but the difference is small). Intuitively, as $\lambda \to \infty$, the entry probability at the service facilities tends to 0 for both customer base compositions.

4.4.6 Herding and Co-location of Service Facilities with Small Buffers

In this section, we explore possible motivations for service facilities with a hetero-geneous customer base ($K = 2$) to co-locate. This can be geographical co-location as well as virtual co-location (i.e., making congestion levels visible on-line, e.g., via a third-party website such as opentable.com). In the service industry, supply motiva-tions (labor pooling, knowledge spillovers or proximity to a natural resource) have been studied as determinants for geographical co-location (Kolko, 2007, Kimes and Fitzsimmons 1990).

Spillovers between the service facilities provide another congestion-driven moti-vation to co-locate. In this section, we study the role of strategic customer behavior as a determinant for co-location. To that end, we compare the net arrival rates in our model with the net arrival rates that would be obtained if the customers were to make first a service facility choice and then either join the facility or balk if there is no waiting space. This model is equivalent to one in which the switching costs from one facility to another one are infinitely high. The net arrival rate to the high (low) quality service facility is $m\lambda$ $((1 - m)\lambda)$. Each facility is modeled as a single queue with two waiting spaces. Note that in general, when signals are somewhat in-formative, more customers arrive at the better service provider. As the arrival rates increase, the better service facility is generally full, and blocked customers choose their second alternatives. Thus, a poorer quality service facility survives by attract-ing spillover demand by locating close to the high-quality service facility. However, do better service facilities have an incentive to be co-located with worse service facilities? Our answer critically depends on the customer equilibrium: Using the ex-ample in Figure 4.3, we discuss the effect of service facilities locating close to each other. On the left panel, we demonstrate the increase in entry probability (to any of the two service facilities) with co-location. Note that when the firms are co-located the customers are more likely to be served due to the reduced probability of being blocked. However, the increased net demand in the customer base does not neces-sarily assist both the firms under all arrival rates. On the right panel, we demonstrate how the increase is split between the high- and low-quality firms. When arrival rates are low, longer queue joining is in equilibrium. Because of this positive externality, more customers who would choose low-quality service join the high-quality ser-vice. The high-quality service provider always gains from co-locating, but the low-quality service provider does not always improve its throughput. When the arrival rates are high, joining the shorter queue is in equilibrium. Under this equilibrium, an opposite effect is observed: The low-quality service provider improves its net de-mand by co-locating, but the high-quality firm increases its throughput only when the arrival rates are sufficiently high. As $\lambda \to \infty$ the service providers are almost always full and the number of customers served at each firm remains the same ($1/\tau$) whether co-located or not. In summary, in the presence of waiting costs, at low ar-rival rates information externalities help high-quality service providers and at high arrival rates, spillover externalities assist low-quality service providers. Depending on the customers' waiting costs and their arrival rates, both the firms in the market

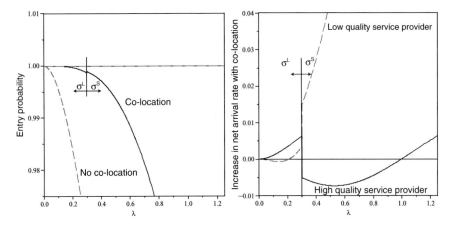

Fig. 4.3 Comparison of the net arrival rate changes (*right panel*) and entry probability (*left panel*) for the service firms by co-locating adjacent to each other. In the example, we examine an M_a market with parameters $\tau = 1, c = 0.56, \Delta = 1$ and $m = 0.755$. At low arrival rates (when $\rho < 0.3$), σ^L is in equilibrium (customers join the longer queue).

could improve their demands. When one firm is better off (and the other firm is hurt) by co-locating, a financial arrangement (transfer payment, etc.) that benefits both firms could be worked out.

Hence the high-quality service facility gains at low arrival rates. As arrival rate increases, the better service provider is more likely to be full.

The better service facility gains from locating closer to the worse service facility, when joining the longer queue behavior is observed in equilibrium. The latter occurs when the waiting costs are low and the market is heterogeneous.

4.5 Discussion and Further Research Opportunities

In this chapter we have discussed how customers infer information about the quality of a product or service from typical operational variables like queue lengths. We believe that this research is important to understand better how demand is generated for goods with considerable uncertainty about the quality. A first step is to understand the equilibrium demand. What did we learn from the analyses above? At the highest level, we think that the following features are interesting:

1. Positive information externalities create cyclic behavior. We have seen that for the single- and two-queue systems.
2. Positive information externalites combined with negative waiting externalities result in complex equilibrium strategies that are not of the threshold type.
3. Heterogeneity as well as sufficient queue buffer space is potential triggers 'herding.'

4. In the single queue, increasing the service rate (keeping the potential arrival rate constant) may lead to lower total welfare, even when the waiting costs are positive. In the two-queue case, increasing the service rates (keeping the potential arrival rate constant) may lead to more herding (i.e., joining the longer queue behavior).

It will occur to the reader that even though our model is very sparse (it can be described with only a few parameters), they are quite rich descriptively. Obviously, we have omitted a large number of factors that we conjecture may play a role in the real world. Nevertheless, we think that our model provides a useful 'first' step by combining the insights from two literatures: the herding and the queueing literature. Our results suggest that the insights into the respective literatures cannot be simply 'superposed' but that new phenomena emerge.

Our models can be extended in at least four important ways. We consider those extensions in the following sections.

4.5.1 Introducing Asymmetry

Many analytical results in the two-queue setting hinge on the symmetry assumption: service rates, prior beliefs that customers possess, arrival rates, etc. This assumption allowed us to demonstrate that following the longest queue behavior was driven by the quality uncertainty and not by any other factor. Obviously, when the quality is perfectly known, a faster service rate of higher expected quality may be very compelling reasons to join the longest queue. Hence, it is interesting to study the queue joining behavior in asymmetric settings in the presence of quality uncertainty (see also Veeraraghavan and Debo, 2008a). For instance, customers may *always* join the longer queues if there is uncertainty about service rates. A firm that provides slower service may gain market share in such scenarios. Moreover, such a model would be an important intermediate block when studying competitive setting, .e.g., service rates or prices, as will be discussed in the next point.

4.5.2 Introducing Capacity Decisions of Firms

The most important decisions that have been fixed in our models are the pricing and service rate decisions. A myriad of new issues arise when considering these. First, one needs to be careful about what exactly the service firms know. Do they know the quality of their own product or service? If so, consumers will glean information not only from the queue length upon arrival but also from the prices! Whenever firms can signal quality with their prices, the queue length information and herding behavior may become irrelevant. Hence, the question is what the complementary value of queue length are to firms that cannot signal quality through prices. If the firm does not know the quality of its own product (which may well be the case), then the firm can set prices that eliminate the herding behavior. When will that be the case? Finally, firms can set prices flexibly, incorporating congestion information and/or learning from past customer purchasing behavior. Besides pricing, capacity selection or competition is a major interesting firm decision that needs to be analyzed further. Debo et al. (2008b) showed that the social welfare can be increased when the capacity is decreased, even when waiting is expensive. How can optimal capacity strategies be determined? How do service firms compete with each other in capacity when positive and negative congestion externalities exist? We believe that there are many open and interesting questions that emerge from our framework and are not yet answered. For instance, consider the question of service delays. Afeche (2006) shows that a service provider could strategically delay services when customers belong to various priority classes. Debo et al. (2008a) show such service delays could occur in queues where the server provides *credence* goods. Anand et al. (2008) show that in *labor-intensive* services, a high-quality service provider might *slow down* on the provision of service *and* charge higher prices at the same time. So, would a service provider strategically delay services, if customers herd? How would the customers' herding behavior change when the service provider delays service? Such questions remain open. Tractable characterization and approximations developed in Maglaras and Zeevi (2003) appear to be a promising avenue that could yield analytical characterizations of the equilibrium behavior, as well as the optimal pricing and capacity decisions in the cases where service value is uncertain.

4.5.3 Empirical and Laboratory Testing of Herd Behavior in Queues

There are many factors that need to be understood in order to pave the way for empirical verification of the impact of congestion on real-life customer choice. Our modeling framework would suggest the following important ones:

1. Uncertainty about the service rates impact the inference from queue lengths in a way that can reinforce or annihilate the in–out result. Hence this internal uncertainty about service value needs to be appropriately constructed in empirical models.
2. Waiting costs significantly complicate the customer's value assessment. We find that some cycling still exists but is less pronounced than without waiting costs. It is therefore important to correctly estimate decision maker's waiting costs.
3. Heterogeneity in terms of the preference for each of the service choices, in terms of signal strength, in terms of prior belief about the service providers, etc. significantly impacts the information that can be derived from the congestion levels.
4. Asymmetric priors about the service quality of both firms; one firm could have a strong reputation for quality, while the other firm has a weak reputation.
5. Bounded rationality. Customers may follow some heuristic instead of Bayes' rule. What heuristic rules customers might follow itself is quite unknown. Decision analysis has some research devoted to understanding and estimating

irrational herding. (See, for example, Simonsohn and Ariely (2008), which discusses how rational sellers behave when selling to non-rational customers.)

Finally, we would like to point out that empirical verification of such phenomena is challenging. It has been a consideration of many experimental economists recently. Manski (2000) discusses many identification problems that need to be overcome for a rigorous empirical verification of the interaction effects similar to those noted in Becker's (1991) model. The problem continues to remain challenging from empirical verification point of view. The marketing literature and some literature on social networks have been currently exploring ideas set forth by Becker and other social economists. Many of the results require data acquired from both primary and secondary sources.

4.5.4 Herding on Other Operational Information

Herding does not necessarily have to be triggered by queue length or congestion information. The underlying key idea is that information about the quality of a product diffuses not only via 'social' word-of-mouth processes but may also via indicators that are typically studied in operations management and operations research. Our contribution lies in identifying the co-existence of public information (like queue lengths) together with private information that impacts the consumer purchasing decision. Debo and van Ryzin (2008) study herding behavior triggered by information about stock-outs. In their paper, stock-outs are a signal of high demand for a product, and hence an indication that many customers received information that the quality of the product is high. Hence, stock-outs may increase the willingness to buy.

However, somewhat unfortunately, the willingness to buy is the highest when it is the most difficult for the customers to obtain the product. Hence, it is not sure that herding behavior increases the *realized* sales.

Finally, a recent set of models analyze stock-out-related behavior. There is rich potential for future work that examines herding behavior with customer response to stock-outs, especially in newsvendor-type settings. Stock and Balachander (2005) show that stock-outs might be used as instruments to signal quality to consumers. Of course, the question whether such signals can increase sales is still an interesting unexplored research question. In a recent paper, Tereyagoglu et al. (2008) discuss how a newsvendor can increase profits by limiting production quantities, when a fraction of consumers are strategic and exhibit conspicuous consumption. Profits can be improved by pricing some of the hard-to-obtain goods higher. Swinney (2008) considers the pricing and quantity decisions of a monopolist selling to a market of strategic customers who have ex ante uncertain about the value of the product being sold.

In conclusion, we believe that through our models, we provide an initial step in understanding how consumers internalize both positive and negative congestion externalities. We think that our framework may be a rich one for further research. Really!

References

Adamy J (2006) Starbucks earnings rise; Wait time curbs sales growth. Wall Street Journal, August 3, B2

Adamy J (2008) McDonald's takes on a weakened starbucks – food giant to install specialty coffee bars, sees $1 billion business. Wall Street Journal, January 7

Afeche P (2006) Incentive-compatible revenue management in queueing systems: Optimal strategic delay and other delay tactics. University of Toronto working paper.

Anand K, Pac FM, Veeraraghavan S (2008) Quality-speed condundrum: Tradeoffs in labor-intensive services. Wharton Working paper

Banerjee A (1992) A simple model of herd behavior. Quarterly Journal of Economics 107:797–818

Banerjee A, Fudenberg D (2004) Word-of-mouth learning. Games and Economic Behavior 46(1):1–22

Becker G (1991) A note on restaurant pricing and other examples of social influences on price. Journal of Political Economy 99(5):1109–1116

Bikhchandani S, Hirshleifer D, Welch I (1992) A theory of fads, fashion, custom and cultural change as information cascades. Journal of Political Economy 100:992–1026

Boldt D (2006) Hybrid waiting list tips, Yahoo! Autos.

Callander S, Horner J (2006) The wisdom of the minority. Northwestern University, Working paper

Chamley CP (2004) Rational Herds: Economic Models of Social Learning, Cambridge University Press, Cambridge, UK

Debo LG, Toktay LB, Van Wassenhove LN (2008a) Queuing for expert services. Management Science 54(8):1497–1512

Debo L, Parlour C, Rajan U (2008b) The value of congestion. Tepper School of Business, Working paper 2005-E21

Debo L, van Ryzin G (2008) Customer search behavior when quality is uncertain. University of Chicago, Working paper

edmunds.com (2006) Top 10 Best-Selling Hybrids of 2006

Gans N (2002) Customer loyalty and supplier quality competition. Management Science 48:207–221

Hassin R, Haviv M (2003) To Queue or not to Queue: Equilibrium Behavior in Queuing Systems. Kluwer Academic Publishers, Norwell, MA

Hill J (2007) Interview: Penn's provost. Penn Current, Philadelphia, PA

hybridcars.com (2008) Price Pulse – Buying guide for hybrid cars

Johari R, Kumar S (2008) Externalities in services. Stanford Working Paper

Kingman JFC (1961) Two similar queues in parallel. Annals of Mathematical Statistics 32:1314–1323

Kimes SE, Fitzsimmons JA (1990) Selecting profitable hotel sites. Interfaces 20(2):12–20

Kolko J (2007) Agglomeration and co-agglomeration of services industries. Public Policy Institute of California, Working Paper

Kumar S, Parlakturk A (2004) Self-interested routing in queuing networks. Management Science 50(7):949–966

Lariviere MA, van Mieghem JA (2004) Strategically seeking service: How competition can generate poisson arrivals. Manufacturing and Service Operations Management 6(1): 23–40

Lewis G (2008) iPhone launch day arrives: A report from (near) the front of a line of buyers. ABC News, Technology and Science, June 29

Libert B, Spector J, Tapscott D (2007) We are Smarter than Me: How to Unleash the Power of Crowds in Your Business. Wharton School Publishing, Philadelphia, PA

Maglaras C, Zeevi A (2003) Pricing and capacity sizing for systems with shared resources: Approximate solutions and scaling relations. Management Science 49(8):1018–1038

Manski C (2000) Economic analysis of social interactions. Journal of Economic Perspectives 14(3):115–136

Mendelson H (1985) Pricing computer services: Queueing effects. Communications of the ACM 28:312–321

Mendelson H, Whang S (1990) Optimal incentive-compatible priority pricing for the M/M/1 queue. Operations Research 38:870–883

Naor P (1969) The regulation of queue size by levying tolls. Econometrica 37:15–24

Pullen D (2007) Queues form for Playstation 3 launch. The Inquirer. June 29

Saporito B, Marchant V, Rawe J (2001) Getting queued in. Time, 2001, May 28

Simonsohn U, Ariely D (2008) When rational sellers face nonrational buyers: Evidence from herding on eBay. Management Science 54(9):1624–1637

Smith L, Sorensen P (1998) Rational social learning with random sampling. University of Michigan working paper.

Stock A, Balachander S (2005) The making of a hot product: A signaling explanation of marketer's scarcity strategy. Management Science 51(8):1181–1192

Su X, Zenios SA (2005) Patient choice in kidney allocation: a sequential stochastic assignment model. Operations Research 53(3):443–455

Su X, Zenios SA (2004) Patient choice in kidney allocation: the role of the queueing discipline. Manufacturing and Service Operations Management 6(4):280–301

Surowiecki J (2005) The Wisdom of Crowds. Anchor Publishing, USA

Swinney R (2008) Selling to strategic consumers when product value is uncertain: The value of matching supply and demand. Stanford working paper

Tereyagoglu N, Veeraraghavan S (2008) Selling strategies under conspicuous consumption. Wharton Working Paper, Philadelphia, PA

Veeraraghavan S, Debo L (2008a) Joining longer queues: Information externalities in queue choice. Manufacturing and Service Operations Management. Forthcoming

Veeraraghavan S, Debo L (2008b) Is it worth the wait? Service choice when waiting is expensive. Wharton working paper

WardsAuto Database (2006) North American light hybrid car sales data

Whinston W (1977) The optimality of joining the shortest queue discipline. Journal of Applied Probability 14:181–189

Whitt W (1986) Deciding which queue to join: Some counterexamples. Operations Research 34(1):55–62

Wolff RW (1982) Poisson arrivals see time averages. Operations Research 30(2):223–231

Woodyard C (2006) Prius finally available without a wait, USA Today. November 5

Zhang J (2008) The sound of silence – evidence of observational learning from the U.S. kidney market. MIT working paper

Part II
Organizational Strategies for Managing Rational/Strategic Consumer Behavior

Chapter 5
Internet-Based Distribution Channel for Product Diversion with Potential Manufacturer's Intervention

Barchi Gillai and Hau L. Lee

Abstract We study a setting in which two channels of distribution are used by retailers for selling their merchandise. The first is the traditional channel of retail
stores, which the retailers use early in the product lifecycle, and the second is an
Internet-based channel, which is used by the retailers later on to reach new market
segments for disposing of their excess inventories. In addition, we investigate the
implications of the manufacturer's decision to intervene by offering additional units
for sale through the online channel. It is assumed that demand in the secondary
market[1]– the market that the retailers and manufacturer reach through the online
channel of distribution – is mainly price driven and that the equilibrium unit price in
this market is determined endogenously so as to equal demand and supply and clear
the market. Thus, through their inventory replenishment decisions, the retailers and
manufacturer can collectively influence future demand level and the equilibrium unit
price in the secondary market. We assume a large number of retailers, an assumption that is appropriate for an Internet-based market. To simplify the analysis, we
further assume that all retailers are identical. We derive the retailers' optimal order
quantity, the manufacturer's optimal number of units to offer for sale in the secondary market, and the resulting secondary market equilibrium unit price. We show
that when the retailers are the only ones to use the online channel, all entities along
the supply chain benefit, including the retailers, manufacturer, and primary- and

Barchi Gillai
Global Supply Chain Management Forum, Stanford University, Graduate School of Business, 518
Memorial Way, Room S398, Stanford, CA 94305-5015, USA,
e-mail: barchi@stanford.edu

Hau L. Lee
Stanford University, Graduate School of Business, Littlefield 253, Stanford University, Stanford,
CA 94305-5015, USA,
e-mail: haulee@stanford.edu

[1] The term "secondary market" is used to describe a market that is used for the disposal of excess
inventories.

S. Netessine, C.S. Tang (eds.), *Consumer-Driven Demand and Operations Management*
Models, International Series in Operations Research & Management Science 131,
DOI 10.1007/978-0-387-98026-3_5, © Springer Science+Business Media, LLC 2009

secondary-market customers. Intervention in the secondary market will not always be in the manufacturer's best interest, as it may reduce her total expected profits. Furthermore, the retailers as well as primary-market customers will always be worse off from the manufacturer's intervention, while the secondary-market customers will always benefit from this move.

5.1 Introduction

E-marketplaces, Internet destinations that bring diverse companies together to conduct electronic commerce on a secure business platform, are becoming a popular way for companies to conduct business and are available in a variety of forms. For example, these e-marketplaces can be private, characterized by a one-to-many type of relationship; public, involving multiple buyers and multiple sellers who use the Internet as a hub for their business transactions; or virtual private, – used by multiple buyers and multiple sellers but do not involve any interaction among buyers, so that each of them sees the system as a private e-marketplace. E-marketplaces may also differ in their target industry: some focus on a single industry, such as apparel or electronics, while others are more diverse, offering a wide variety of product categories. Furthermore, e-marketplaces may be used by companies for trading primary materials for production or for trading indirect materials for business operations. Finally, e-marketplaces can serve as the primary market, that is, as a main channel of distribution; as the secondary market, for the disposal of excess inventories; or as both. In this chapter we focus on the impacts of e-marketplaces that serve as secondary markets.

There seem to be several business models that companies can follow when using the Internet for disposal of their excess inventories. The first model is based on sellers offering their excess inventory directly to potential buyers through online websites that provide a meeting place for multiple buyers and sellers. Items in these sites are oftentimes sold via auctions. One example of such an online auction marketplace is Liquidation.com (http://www.liquidation.com/). EBay (http://www.ebay.com), the online auction and shopping website which started as a marketplace for individuals and small businesses to buy and sell goods and services online, launched in 2005 its business and industrial category, breaking into the industrial surplus business. A second model relies on companies that serve as middlemen: they buy the excess inventory from manufacturers, OEMs, or anyone else that has excess inventory and then offer it for sale online at discount prices. Examples of companies that provide such services include 4 Star Electronics (http://www.4starelectronics.com/) – a leading supplier of obsolete or discontinued electronic components; Freelance Electronics (http://www.rcfreelance.com/) – a distributor of obsolete and hard-to-find military and commercial electronic components; and WholesaleApparelSource (http://www.appareloverstock.com/) – which purchases over-stock and shelf-pulled apparel in large volumes from large department stores, U.S.-based brand representatives, and industry suppliers and offers them for sale to small-to-mid-sized apparel retailers and other businesses. While the second model is likely to be more convenient for organizations, requiring them to spend less time and effort on selling their excess inventories, the price they receive for their over-stock goods may be lower compared to the alternative of online auctions.

While in all the examples mentioned above each of the websites chose a single business model to follow, some online retailers offer both options. For example, Overstock (http://www.overstock.com/) offers for sale surplus tech products that it buys at liquidation prices and sells to consumers at an average 60% of retail price (Taylor, 2001). In addition to its direct retail sales, Overstock has also offered online auctions on its website since September 2004.[2]

A hybrid of the two business models described above is offered by companies such as Part-Miner (http://www.partminer.com), which launched in September 2007 its online ChipMarket trading platform (http://www.chipmarket.com) for selling and sourcing excess electronic component inventories. While they do not purchase any excess inventory themselves, they do more than just providing companies with a platform for online auctions. Rather, ChipMarket provides potential sellers with a number of services to help them price their goods according to up-to-date market conditions and reach a large number of potential buyers. In parallel, potential buyers can submit requests for quotes (RFQs), which are matched by ChipMarket with items available for sale. Virtual Chip Exchange (http://www.virtualchip.com/), a private marketplace for buyers and sellers of computer chips and semiconductors, operates under a business model similar to that of ChipMarket and also provides a number of value-added services to their members.

Another business model involves websites that simply provide a platform for companies to advertise and offer for sale their refurbished and over-stocked items. One such example is the Clearance Center of Cnet (http://clearance.cnet.com/), which lists items available for sale at clearance price. Those interested in buying are directed to the site of the manufacturer (or another organization) that offers these items for sale.

There are a variety of reasons for companies to use e-marketplaces as secondary markets. For example, when a company introduces new products, its old products may become obsolete and need to be phased out. Oftentimes the product life cycles of the old and new products overlap, and so the company must take steps to assure that sales of the old products do not interfere with the new product introduction. One such strategy is to introduce the new products first in a few targeted channels and use secondary markets to sell off the old ones to channels that focus on more mature products (Billington et al., 1998). Another potential use of secondary markets is for the disposal of excess inventories, which are usually a result of inaccurate demand forecast. One industry that can substantially benefit from such use of secondary markets is apparel goods. Due to the long lead times for design, order, and production, which can reach up to 9 months, orders must be based on early estimates of expected demand, which can vary dramatically from actual demand. In addition, for both apparel retailers and vendors the cost of under-stocking

---

[2] Source: http://en.wikipedia.org/wiki/Overstock.com

substantially exceeds the cost of over-stocking, inciting them to carry generous safety stocks. Finally, tight space constraints force retailers and vendors to quickly dispose of surplus merchandise at the end of each season (Doctorow and Saloner, 2000). Off-price or off-style retailers such as TJ MAXX or Burlington Coat Factory can then be used for selling excess inventories to other, more price-conscious, segments of the market. B2B and B2C e-markets, such as QRS and BlueFly, provide another means for selling off excess inventories to wholesalers or end consumers. Secondary markets are also commonly used for sale of older models of consumer electronic goods, since due to their short life cycle and the proliferation of product options manufacturers and retailers in this industry are likely to be left with excess inventories of some models. Secondary markets such as Virtual Chip Exchange may also provide a platform for spot markets, allowing companies with over-stock to sell their excess inventories to companies that have under-forecasted their demands. Such spot markets are quite common for semiconductors and electronic components.

Companies prefer to sell their excess inventories through Internet-based secondary markets so as to avoid polluting their normal sales channel. Furthermore, companies may prefer to use the services of online retailers such as Overstock despite the extremely low price they are likely to obtain for their excess inventories in order to better maintain their brand image and distance themselves from the sale of low-demand or returned items.

While retailers who use secondary markets to sell off their excess inventories clearly benefit since these markets provide an additional source of profit, it is not clear how the secondary markets affect the retailers' suppliers and primary-market customers. One of the goals of this chapter is to investigate the impacts of secondary markets on the entire supply chain.

Furthermore, Internet-based secondary markets can be easily accessed by other players along the supply chain. In particular, once the e-marketplace is established, the manufacturer that builds and supplies the goods to the retailers might adopt it as an additional channel of distribution, for directly reaching the secondary-market customers. But will it be in the manufacturer's best interest to take such an action? To participate in the secondary market the manufacturer must build additional goods, increasing her total production costs. Moreover, it is assumed that the secondary-market equilibrium unit price is endogenously determined to equal supply and demand and clear the market. Thus, if the equilibrium unit price is relatively low, the revenues generated from it might not be sufficient to cover the manufacturer's additional production cost. In addition, assuming that the retailers are aware of the manufacturer's decision to take part in the secondary market, they might decide to lower their initial order quantity, thus leading to a reduction in the manufacturer's profit from her sales to the retailers. Suppose the manufacturer decides to participate in the secondary market; how will it impact the retailers' expected profits? And how will the customers in both the primary and secondary markets be affected? In this chapter we try to provide answers to these questions. We study the conditions under which the manufacturer is most likely to benefit from participation in the secondary market and show how her participation will impact the expected profits to the retailers, as well as the expected service level in the primary and secondary markets.

The remainder of this chapter is organized as follows. Section 5.2 reviews the relevant literature. In Section 5.3 we describe the problem in detail. Section 5.4 analyzes the equilibrium of the model given that a secondary market is used only by the retailers and studies its impacts. Section 5.5 assumes that the manufacturer decides to take part in the secondary market and studies the potential impacts of that decision on the retailers and the primary and secondary-market customers. Section 5.6 concludes the chapter, discusses the limitations of the model, and includes some promising directions for future research. All proofs are in the Appendix.

5.2 Literature Review

There are several areas of research related to the use of Internet-based marketplaces for adjusting inventory levels. One such line of research studies auctions, which are commonly used as the mechanism for conducting business in online markets. There has been extensive research in economics on the theory of auctions. For overviews of auction literature, see, for example, McAfee and McMillan (1987), Klemperer (1999), and Elmaghraby (2000). Some papers, such as Vakrat (2000) and Wurman et al. (1998), focus on online auctions and study their optimal design and expected behavior. In this chapter we do not strive to study the mechanism of online secondary markets, but rather we focus on the impacts of using such a distribution channel on manufacturers, retailers, and consumers.

A number of studies focus on the use of spot markets to complement bilateral, fixed-price contracts with suppliers. The combination of bilateral contracts and spot markets allows supply chain participants to simultaneously realize the benefits of both relationship-based and market-based coordination (Grey et al., 2005). One example of this line of research is Mendelson and Tunca (2007), who examine the case where manufacturers first contract with the supplier to purchase commodities at a fixed price and then trade on a spot market, which is open to all, when more information about market demand and production costs is available. Kleindorfer and Wu (2003) survey the underlying theory and practice in the use of options, which play an important role in integrating long-and short-term contracting between multiple buyers and sellers, in support of emerging B2B markets. The paper focuses on capital-intensive industries and reviews economic and managerial frameworks that have been proposed to explain the structure of contracting in these markets. Some papers, such as Rudi et al. (2001), Axsäter (2003), and Sosic (2006), consider the use of lateral transshipments, rather than online auctions, for rebalancing inventories.

Our model differs from earlier work, in that it does not consider the e-marketplace as a mechanism for rebalancing inventories among manufacturers, but rather as a means – especially for retailers or distributors – to reach new market segments, usually more price sensitive, for selling off their excess inventories. Nike's product rollovers are a good example when such an assumption is most appropriate: when new shoe models are introduced the company first displays them at premium retailers like Footlocker or Niketown, while it uses discounters and outlets to sell its older shoe models (Billington et al., 1998). Many apparel companies have adopted such a strategy and use B2C solutions for selling off their excess inventories. One paper that studies the subject of channel diversion is Eppen and Iyer (1997), who analyze the problem of a catalogue merchandiser that also owns outlet stores, which provide her with the opportunity, as the season evolves, to divert inventory originally purchased for the "big book" to the outlet store. Kouvelis and Gutierrez (1997) study a similar topic while focusing on some of the special opportunities and challenges imposed by global markets, which offer a "style goods" producer more selling opportunities by exploiting the difference in timing of the selling season of geographically disperse markets. Rosenfield (1989) does not specify the means for disposing of excess inventory. Rather, he assumes a fixed salvage value for each unit of inventory and determines the optimal number of slow-moving units to keep in stock. Our model differs from the above-mentioned research work in several aspects, one of the major ones being their assumption of an exogenously determined unit salvage value. Such an assumption does not accurately represent online secondary markets, where oftentimes prices are determined endogenously to equal total supply and demand and clear the market. Modifying this assumption substantially changes the expected impacts of the secondary market on the various players within the supply chain.

Another difference between our model and some of the earlier related work mentioned above is that some of these studies consider a limited number of participants in the secondary market, whereas we assume a large number of participants. Such an assumption more accurately represents many of the Internet-based markets. Milner and Kouvelis (2007) justify their assumption of a limited number of suppliers and buyers by focusing on markets for industrial goods with some degree of design specification, as opposed to undifferentiated commodities. Lee and Whang (2002), who are the first to focus on the use of online secondary markets as a tool for improving inventory management, do consider a large number of participants in the secondary market and endogenously derive the optimal decisions for the retailers, along with the equilibrium market price of the secondary market. But, unlike our model, they assume that the secondary market is used for rebalancing inventories among a group of retailers. Some aspects of this research work can be viewed as an extension to the line of research which studies the impacts of inventory centralization by a group of retailers on the manufacturer whose goods the retailers stock. The first attempt to study this topic was made by Anupindi and Bassok (1999).

Another difference between our model and Lee and Whang (2002) is that they assume that trading in the secondary market is conducted solely by the retailers, while we allow the manufacturer to take action and intervene in the secondary market by releasing a quantity which was built in advance for sale in that market. We then determine the conditions under which taking such action would be in the manufacturer's best interest and study the potential impacts of this decision on the retailers as well as on the primary and secondary-market customers.

Other related research work includes Tunca and Zenios (2006), who study the competition between procurement auctions, which are used for the purchase of low-quality parts, and long-term relational contracts, which can ensure the quality of the procured products or services and therefore are used for high-quality parts. Peleg et al. (2002) consider a setting with both long-term and auction-based purchases and determine conditions under which each strategy is expected to yield better results. Their model assumes that both sources are used by the manufacturer to purchase commodities from her supplier. Choi et al. (2004) consider the use of Internet-based secondary markets for selling off excess inventory, but under a different setting compared with our model. They consider a supply chain which is integrated by a returns policy. With the advance of e-commerce, the returned products can be sold by the manufacturer on the e-marketplace, most likely with a higher price compared to their salvage value. Esteban and Shum (2007) focus on the automobile industry, where it is the consumers, rather than retailers or manufacturers, who trade in the secondary market, and the goods traded are used cars, which differ in value based on their age and model.

5.3 Problem Description

We consider n identical retailers who use a traditional distribution channel, such as retail stores, for reaching their primary market customers. We focus our attention on one type of product, which is ordered from a single manufacturer. It is assumed that products in the primary market are sold during a single season. This assumption is appropriate for many products in the high-tech and fashion industries, which are characterized by relatively short product life cycles that may not allow the retailers to resupply stocks from the manufacturer after their initial purchase. Unit production cost to the manufacturer equals c, and each unit is sold to the retailers at a unit price p_1 and by the retailers to their primary-market customers at a unit price r_1, where $r_1 > p_1 > c$ holds. D_1, the demand faced by each retailer in the primary market, is uncertain with a known distribution function $F(\cdot)$ and a finite mean $E(D_1) = \mu$. $F(\cdot)$ is differentiable over $[0, \infty)$, with $F'(\cdot) = f(\cdot)$. In addition, the retailers may use an Internet-based distribution channel to reach other, more price-sensitive segments of the market, for selling off their excess inventories at the end of the selling season. Retailers choose their replenishment strategy so as to maximize their expected profits. To study the impacts of the Internet-based secondary market and the manufacturer's potential intervention in that market we analyze the following three models:

1. **No secondary market.** Under this scenario, products are sold only to the primary-market customers. The sequence of events is as follows: prior to the beginning of period 1, each retailer places with the manufacturer an order for Q units. After the orders are shipped to the retailers, demand x_i is realized for each retailer i, where x_i is independently drawn from $F(\cdot)$ and is satisfied as much as possible from the retailers' existing inventory. Any unfilled demand is lost forever, and the salvage value of the units left unsold by the end of the period is zero. This is the standard setting of the newsvendor problem. Under this scenario, each

retailer determines her initial order quantity Q by solving the following optimization problem:

$$\max_{Q\geq 0}\left\{\Pi_R^I = r_1 E_x \min(Q,x) - p_1 Q\right\}$$

The optimal stock level that maximizes Π_R^I satisfies

$$F(Q^I) = (r_1 - p_1)/r_1 \qquad (5.1)$$

2. **Retailers-only secondary market.** This model extends the previous setting and provides the retailers with the opportunity to use an Internet-based distribution channel to access a secondary market at the end of the first period for disposing of their excess inventory. It is assumed that the secondary market is mainly cost driven. That is, the demand faced by each retailer in that market is characterized by a deterministic function of the form $a(1 - p_2/b)$, where p_2 is the secondary-market unit price and a and b are known and strictly positive constants. It is further assumed that the customers served in the secondary market belong to a different market segment than the primary-market customers, and so secondary-market demand level is independent of primary-market demand realization. One example that fits well with this assumption is the apparel industry. Places that offer branded and fashion merchandise, such as Macy's and Bloomingdale chains or Levi's stores, tend to have customers with much different characteristics compared to those who shop at retailers such as Ross or TJ MAXX, which offer off-price and off-style merchandise. Price in the secondary market is determined endogenously so as to equal demand and supply and clear the market. Thus, the retailers' decision regarding their order quantity Q will ultimately have an impact on demand level and the equilibrium unit price in the secondary market. The sequence of events is as follows: prior to the beginning of period 1 each retailer i places an order for Q units with the manufacturer. After the units are delivered, demand x_i is realized and satisfied as much as possible from the retailers' existing inventory. Any unfilled demand is lost. At the end of the first period the retailers sell their excess inventory in the secondary market, which is characterized by an aggregated demand that satisfies $D_2 = na(1 - p_2/b)$ and an equilibrium unit price p_2 that is endogenously determined to clear the market. We investigate the resulting impacts of the existence of the secondary market on the optimal strategy chosen by the retailers as well as the expected profits for the manufacturer and retailers, and the expected supply chain performance in the primary market.

3. **Manufacturer's intervention.** Under this scenario, the manufacturer may choose to take part in the secondary market and use it as an additional channel of distribution so as to increase her total sales level and profitability. The term "Intervention" used throughout the chapter does not intend to imply that the manufacturer uses any type of manipulation to discourage the retailers from participating in the secondary market. Rather, it refers only to the manufacturer's decision to participate in that market by offering additional quantity for sale. The sequence of events is as follows: prior to the beginning of period 1 each retailer i places an

order for Q units with the manufacturer. It is assumed that the manufacturer has a single production opportunity; thus after Q becomes known the manufacturer decides on nK, the additional quantity to build for the secondary market, and runs a production cycle of $n(Q+K)$ units. The manufacturer then delivers Q units to each retailer and keeps the nK units in inventory to be sold later in the secondary market together with the retailers' excess inventory. The progression of events is the same as the previous case. We study the conditions under which participating in the secondary market will be in the manufacturer's best interest, and the expected impact of the manufacturer's intervention on the retailers' profits as well as the supply chain performance in both the primary and the secondary markets.

It is assumed that all units are sold in the secondary market at the same unit price p_2 and that no transaction fees or transportation costs are incurred. In addition, we restrict p_2 from taking on negative values; thus whenever total supply in the secondary market exceeds na, p_2 is forced to equal zero. Given the assumption of a short selling season, the majority of the inventory holding costs incurred can most likely be attributed to the fixed cost of holding and operating a warehouse, or other storage space. Inventory holding cost will therefore not impact the optimal solution and thus is omitted from the mathematical model.

Sections 5.4 and 5.5 study in detail the two models described above that involve the sale of goods in a secondary market. The analysis is conducted under the assumption that all retailers are identical and equally smart, that is, each of them can assume that all other retailers will follow the same logic when choosing their replenishment strategy. Throughout the chapter, a boldface better denotes the n-vector of corresponding variables, e.g., $\mathbf{Q} = (Q_1, Q_2, \ldots, Q_n)$.

5.4 Retailer-Only Secondary Market

When the retailers are the only ones to use the Internet-based distribution channel for disposing of their excess inventories, each retailer chooses her initial order quantity Q based on the following optimization problem:

$$\max_{Q \geq 0} \left\{ \Pi_R^{II} = r_1 E_x \min(Q, x) - p_1 Q + p_2^{II} E_x (Q - x)^+ \right\} \qquad (5.2)$$

s.t. $\quad p_2^{II}$ is endogenously determined to clear the market

Moving backward in time, the symmetric equilibrium $\mathbf{Q}$ is defined in the following way:

1. Given $\mathbf{Q}$ and $\mathbf{x}$, unit price for the secondary market p_2^{II} is determined so as to equal supply and demand and clear the market.
2. Based on the expected secondary-market unit price, each retailer chooses Q^{II} so as to maximize her expected profit over the two periods.

We next determine the equilibrium unit price p_2^{II} and the optimal inventory level Q^{II}.

Secondary Market Unit Price

Given any Q and $\mathbf{x}$, total demand in the secondary market as a function of p_2 is given by $na(1 - p_2/b)$ whereas total supply is $\sum_{i=1}^{n}(Q - x_i)^+$. The secondary market unit price p_2 is determined by equating total supply and demand, so that in market equilibrium

$$p_2 = b - (b/na)\sum_{i=1}^{n}(Q - x_i)^+ \tag{5.3}$$

In an Internet-based market, it is typically the case that the number of retailers is relatively large, usually in the order of hundreds. Indeed, this expanded reach is considered to be one of the key powers of the Internet. In this case, we can use the law of large numbers to find the limiting value of $\sum_{i=1}^{n}(Q - x_i)^+$:

$$\lim_{n\to\infty}\frac{1}{n}\sum_{i=1}^{n}(Q - x_i)^+ = E(Q - x)^+ = \int_{x=0}^{Q}(Q - x)f(x)dx = \int_{x=0}^{Q}F(x)dx \triangleq \Gamma(Q)$$

For convenience, we denote $\Gamma(Q) \triangleq \int_{x=0}^{Q}(Q - x)f(x)\,dx$ throughout the chapter.

Thus, for a large enough n, and given that the equilibrium secondary-market unit price cannot take on negative values, p_2 can be simplified to

$$p_2^{II} = \lim_{n\to\infty}p_2 = b[1 - \Gamma(Q)/a]^+ \tag{5.4}$$

Primary Market Order Quantity

The solution to the optimization problem stated in (5.2) will satisfy

$$F(Q) = \frac{r_1 - p_1 + (dp_2^{II}/dQ)\,\Gamma(Q)}{r_1 - p_2^{II}} \tag{5.5}$$

Given the assumption of a sufficiently large n, each retailer is a price-taker in the secondary market, i.e., $dp_2^{II}/dQ = 0$. Consequently, the above result can be simplified to

$$F(Q) = \frac{r_1 - p_1}{r_1 - p_2^{II}} \tag{5.6}$$

Let Q^{ii} be the quantity that satisfies (5.6). Q^{ii} has a newsvendor-type solution, where $r_1 - p_1$ represents the cost of under-stocking and $p_1 - p_2^{II}$ represents the cost of over-stocking. Plugging the limiting value of p_2^{II} as given in (5.4) into (5.6), we obtain

$$F(Q^{ii}) = \frac{r_1 - p_1}{r_1 - b + (b/a)\Gamma(Q^{ii})} \tag{5.7}$$

Since both $F(Q^{ii})$ and $\Gamma(Q^{ii})$ increase in Q^{ii}, the right-hand side of (5.7) decreases in Q^{ii} while its left-hand side increases in Q^{ii}. Therefore, (5.7) will have at most a single unique solution.

The order quantity Q^{ii} as specified in (5.7) will be optimal only as long as it results in a non-negative equilibrium unit price p_2^{II}. Let $\overline{Q}$ be the value of Q that satisfies $\Gamma(Q) = a$, which, based on (5.4), yields $p_2^{II} = 0$. If we denote Q^{II} as the optimal order quantity, then Q^{II} will be equal to Q^{ii} only as long as $Q^{ii} \leq \overline{Q}$. Otherwise, if $Q^{ii} > \overline{Q}$, the retailers will prefer not to use the Internet-based channel as it will yield an equilibrium unit price equal to zero (since it is assumed that the secondary-market equilibrium unit price cannot take on negative values). Consequently, the retailers will prefer to set Q^{II} equal to Q^{I}, the optimal order quantity with no secondary market. In summary, Q^{II}, the optimal order quantity given a retailers-only secondary market, will satisfy

$$Q^{II} = \begin{cases} Q^{ii} & \text{if } Q^{ii} \leq \overline{Q} \\ Q^{I} & \text{if } Q^{ii} > \overline{Q} \end{cases} \qquad (5.8)$$

5.4.1 The Impacts of the Secondary Market

We next study the potential impacts of the secondary market on the manufacturer, each of the retailers, and the primary-market customers.

Impact on Optimal Order Quantity

By comparing (5.6) with (5.1), and given that the secondary-market unit price p_2^{II} cannot take on negative values, it is clear that the introduction of the secondary market will always lead the retailers to increase their initial order quantity Q.

Theorem 1. *In equilibrium, the retailers' use of a secondary market for disposing of excess inventory will always lead the retailers to increase their initial order quantity.*

With the introduction of the secondary market, the salvage value of any unsold units remaining at the end of the first period is increased from zero to p_2^{II}. Consequently, the retailers face lower average cost, which provides an incentive for them to increase their initial order quantity Q.

Impact on Expected Profits

Profits to the manufacturer are determined by her sales level to the retailers at the beginning of period 1. Thus, based on Theorem 1, it can be easily verified that the introduction of the secondary market will always increase the manufacturer's total profit, as summarized in Lemma 1.

Lemma 1. *In equilibrium, the secondary market will always increase the manufacturer's profits.*

As for the retailers, as stated in Lemma 2, they will never be worse off by participating in the secondary market since it provides them an additional source of profit.

Lemma 2. *In the presence of the secondary market the retailers will always increase their expected profits.*

Impact on Supply Chain Performance

We next study how the retailers' use of the Internet-based distribution channel impacts the performance of the supply chain in the primary market. We focus our attention on two supply chain measures, namely consumer sales and stockout level. It can be verified that the retailers' higher order quantity will improve both these performance indicators, as summarized in Lemma 3.

Lemma 3. *In equilibrium, the introduction of a secondary market will always result in a higher sales level and a lower stockout level in the primary market.*

In summary, we can conclude that the retailers' use of a second distribution channel to reach new market segments and dispose of their excess inventory will benefit all entities along the supply chain: the manufacturer, retailers, primary-market customers, and secondary-market customers.

Impact of Secondary-Market Characteristics

We next study how the characteristics of the secondary-market demand function affect the expected profits for the manufacturer and the retailers. Theorem 2 summarizes the impact of the secondary-market demand characteristics on the retailers' expected profits.

Theorem 2. Π_R^{II}, *the expected profit for each retailer, increases in a, the upper limit on secondary-market demand observed by each retailer, and in b, which reflects the sensitivity of secondary-market customers to changes in unit price and also represents the upper limit on the secondary-market unit price.*

For any value of Q, an increase in either a or b increases total demand in the secondary market, and consequently the secondary-market equilibrium unit price p_2. Thus, it results in higher profits for the retailers from the secondary market while not affecting their profits associated with sales in the primary market. By adjusting their initial order quantity based on the new values of a or b, the retailers can only further improve their expected profits.

As for the manufacturer, she too will benefit from a higher value of a or b.

Theorem 3. *The manufacturer's profit Π_M^{II} increases in a, the upper limit on the secondary-market demand observed by each retailer, and in b, the upper limit on the secondary-market unit price.*

The profits to the manufacturer are a linear function of the retailers' initial order quantity Q^{II}. Since a higher value of a or b means an increase in the maximum potential market size and/or in the equilibrium secondary-market unit price, as well as lower sensitivity of secondary-market demand to changes in unit price, it will always result in the retailers increasing their initial order quantity. And a higher order quantity Q will necessarily translate into higher revenues and profits for the manufacturer.

In summary, we can conclude that the larger the potential size of the market the retailers can access through the Internet-based distribution channel is, and the less sensitive customers in this secondary market are to changes in unit price, the more beneficial the secondary market will be for the retailers and the manufacturer.

While the Internet provides a relatively easy way for retailers to reach a large number of potential customers, oftentimes these customers may be quite price sensitive. Thus, it can be a mixed blessing for the retailers. While the advantages of the Internet as a channel of distribution for selling off excess inventory are clear, the retailers (as well as the manufacturer) will benefit the most if they are able to attract somewhat less price-sensitive market segments.

5.5 Manufacturer's Intervention

While originally the manufacturer may prefer to sell her products only through the retailers' main channel of distribution to ensure high product positioning, once a secondary market is established the manufacturer may decide to take part in it as a means for improving her profitability. To do so, the manufacturer may produce some additional quantity nK to be sold through the online channel together with the excess inventory sold by the retailers. It is assumed that if the manufacturer decides to intervene in the secondary market, the retailers will be aware of that decision ahead of time. In this section we analyze how the manufacturer's intervention in the secondary market will impact her expected profits and determine the conditions under which it is beneficial for her to take such action. In addition, we analyze the impacts of the manufacturer's decision to intervene in the secondary market on the retailers' actions and their expected profits, as well as on the overall supply chain performance in both the primary and the secondary markets. Given the detailed problem description specified in Section 5.3, for any value of Q the manufacturer will determine $K(Q)$ as follows:

$$K(Q) = \arg\max \left\{ \Pi_M^{III} = n \left[-[Q + K(Q)]c + p_1 Q + p_2^{III} K(Q) \right] \right\} \quad (5.9)$$

s.t. p_2^{III} is endogenously determined to clear the market

The retailers choose their order quantity Q based on the following optimization problem:

$$\max_{Q \geq 0} \left\{ \Pi_R^{III} = r_1 E_x \min(Q, x) - p_1 Q + p_2^{III} E_x (Q - x)^+ \right\} \quad (5.10)$$

s.t. $\begin{cases} p_2^{III} \text{ is endogenously determined to clear the market} \\ K(Q) \text{ satisfies (5.9)} \end{cases}$

One should note that for the retailers to be able to solve the optimization problem as specified in (5.10) they should be able to determine the value of K as a function of their order quantity Q. In particular, the retailers will need to have visibility to the value of the manufacturer's unit production cost c. Assuming that the retailers have access to such information is quite unrealistic; however, we make this assumption in order to simplify the problem and allow us to focus our attention on the secondary market, the effects its existence has on the behavior of the retailers and the manufacturer, and the resulting impacts on the entire supply chain.

Moving backward in time, the symmetric equilibrium order quantity $\mathbf{Q}$ and the production level K are defined in the following way:

1. Given $K, \mathbf{Q}$, and $\mathbf{x}$, unit price for the secondary market p_2^{III} is determined so as to equal supply and demand and clear the market.
2. Given $\mathbf{Q}$, the manufacturer chooses K so as to maximize her profits.
3. Based on the expected secondary-market unit price and the expected value of K, each retailer chooses Q^{III} so as to maximize her expected profit over the two periods.

Secondary-Market Unit Price

The secondary market unit price p_2 is determined by equating total supply and demand, so that in market equilibrium

$$p_2 = b - \frac{b}{a} \left(K + \frac{1}{n} \sum_{i=1}^{n} (Q - x_i)^+ \right) \quad (5.11)$$

As in Section 5.4, for a large enough n, and given that p_2 cannot take on negative values, we can use the law of large numbers to simplify p_2 and obtain

$$p_2^{III} = \lim_{n \to \infty} p_2 = b \left[1 - \frac{K + \Gamma(Q)}{a} \right]^+ \quad (5.12)$$

Comparing (5.4) with (5.12) we can verify that as expected, for any given Q the participation of the manufacturer in the secondary market reduces the equilibrium unit price p_2.

Secondary-Market Production Level

For any given Q, the optimal production level for the secondary market $K^{III}(Q)$ is obtained based on (5.9), where p_2^{III} satisfies (5.12). Since $K^{III}(Q)$ cannot take on negative values, the resulting optimal production level for the secondary market is

$$K^{III}(Q) = [a(b-c)/(2b) - \Gamma(Q)/2]^+ \tag{5.13}$$

Let $\widehat{Q}$ be the value of Q that satisfies $\Gamma(\widehat{Q}) = a(b-c)/b$. Then for all $Q > \widehat{Q}$, $K^{III}(Q)$ should be set equal to zero. That is, even if the manufacturer considers initially to potentially take part in the secondary market – a decision made before the retailers place their orders – it will not always be in her best interest to actually build some $nK > 0$ units to be sold in the secondary market. Rather, when the retailers' initial order quantity is relatively large, the level of excess inventory remaining for sale in the secondary market is also expected to be high. Consequently, the secondary market equilibrium unit price will be so low that it will result in the manufacturer losing money for each unit she builds for sale in that market.

Based on (5.12) it can be verified that for all $Q \leq \widehat{Q}$ the resulting value of p_2^{III} is strictly positive and satisfies $p_2^{III} > c$.

Primary-Market Order Quantity

The initial order quantity to maximize the retailers' optimization problem as stated in (5.10) is

$$F(Q) = \frac{r_1 - p_1 + \left(dp_2^{III}/dQ\right)\Gamma(Q)}{r_1 - p_2^{III}} \tag{5.14}$$

As in the previous section, given a sufficiently large n, each of the retailers is price-taker in the secondary market, i.e., $dp_2^{III}/dQ = 0$. Consequently, the above result can be simplified to

$$F(Q) = \frac{r_1 - p_1}{r_1 - p_2^{III}} \tag{5.15}$$

Let Q^{iii} be the quantity that satisfies (5.15). Based on the limiting value of p_2^{III} as given in (5.12) and assuming that $K^{III}(Q)$ is strictly positive, (5.15) can be simplified to

$$F(Q^{iii}) = \frac{r_1 - p_1}{r_1 - [a(b+c) - b\Gamma(Q^{iii})]/2a} \tag{5.16}$$

Since both $F(Q^{iii})$ and $\Gamma(Q^{iii})$ increase in Q^{iii}, the left-hand side of (5.16) is an increasing function of Q^{iii} while its right-hand side decreases in Q^{iii}. Therefore, there can be at most a single value of Q^{iii} that satisfies (5.16).

The order quantity Q^{iii} as specified in (5.16) will be feasible and thus optimal only as long as it results in non-negative equilibrium unit price p_2^{III} and production quantity $nK(Q^{iii})$.

Consider first those cases where $Q^{iii} > \widehat{Q}$ holds. To analyze the optimal solution under these circumstances, we would first like to study the relationship between Q^{ii} and Q^{iii}. As noted earlier, for any given Q, $p_2^{III}(Q) < p_2^{II}(Q)$ will always hold. Therefore, and by comparing (5.6) and (5.15), we can conclude that $Q^{iii} < Q^{ii}$ always holds (for a formal proof of this result, see Theorem 4). Therefore, for all those cases in which $Q^{iii} > \widehat{Q}$, necessarily $Q^{ii} > \widehat{Q}$ will hold as well. Thus, since the manufacturer will not participate in the secondary market for any $Q > \widehat{Q}$, if $Q^{iii} > \widehat{Q}$ holds, it will be optimal for each retailer to place with the manufacturer an order for Q^{ii} units, the optimal order quantity for a retailers-only secondary market. This, however, will be true only as long as Q^{ii} is feasible, that is, as long as $Q^{ii} \leq \overline{Q}$, where $\Gamma(\overline{Q}) = a$. Otherwise, if initially the secondary market provided no value to the retailers, it will continue to be of no value after the manufacturer's decision to consider participation in that market. Thus, it will be optimal for the retailers to not use the Internet-based channel of distribution, and consequently, their optimal order quantity will be equal to Q^I. It can be verified (see the proof of Lemma 4) that in this case $Q^I > \widehat{Q}$ will hold, which means that by placing an order for Q^I units, the retailers will not change the manufacturer's decision to not participate in the secondary market. Thus, we can conclude that if initially the secondary was of no value to the retailers, it will be of no value to the manufacturer as well.

We next focus our attention on those cases where $Q^{iii} \leq \widehat{Q}$ holds. In this case the optimal number of units nK to be built by the manufacturer for sale in the secondary market will be strictly positive, and by placing an order for Q^{iii} units, each of the retailers will optimize his expected profits given the manufacturer's intervention in the secondary market.

However, one must keep in mind that the retailers are the ones to take the first step by placing their orders with the manufacturer, and only then will the manufacturer decide how many additional units nK to build for sale in the secondary market. What, then, if Q^{iii} is smaller than $\widehat{Q}$, but Q^{ii}, the optimal order quantity with no manufacturer's intervention, is larger than $\widehat{Q}$? It can be proved (see Theorem 5) that the manufacturer's intervention in the secondary market will always reduce the retailers' expected profits. Therefore, whenever $Q^{iii} \leq \widehat{Q}$ but $Q^{ii} > \widehat{Q}$ holds, it will be optimal for each of the retailers to place an order for Q^{ii} units, which will force the manufacturer to stay out of the secondary market and will result in higher expected profits for the retailers compared to the outcome when they each place an order for Q^{iii} units.

Let Q^{III} be the optimal order quantity given the manufacturer's potential intervention in the secondary market. Lemma 4 summarizes the discussion above and lists the optimal value of Q^{III} under the different scenarios, while Figure 5.1 displays these results graphically.

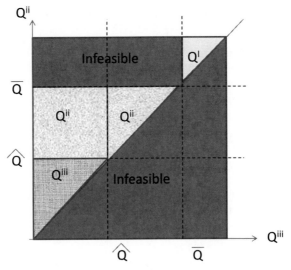

Fig. 5.1 Optimal order quantity Q^{III}.

Lemma 4. Q^{III}, *the optimal order quantity given the manufacturer's intervention in the secondary market, will satisfy*

$$Q^{III} = \begin{cases} Q^{iii} & \text{if} \quad Q^{ii} \leq \widehat{Q} \\ Q^{ii} & \text{if} \quad \widehat{Q} < Q^{ii} \leq \overline{Q} \\ Q^I & \text{if} \quad Q^{ii} > \overline{Q} \end{cases}$$

Consequently, and based on (5.12) and (5.13) as well as on the results obtained in Section 5.4, and since $\widehat{Q} < \overline{Q}$ always holds, we can derive the value of the secondary market equilibrium unit price, as summarized in Figure 5.2.

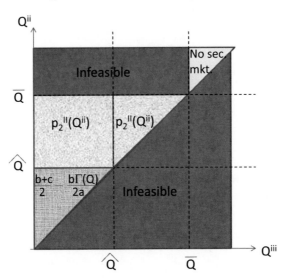

Fig. 5.2 Secondary-market equilibrium unit price p_2^{III}.

5.5.1 The Impacts of the Manufacturer's Intervention

We next study the impacts of the manufacturer's intervention in the secondary market on the expected profits for the manufacturer and the retailers, as well as the performance of the supply chain in both the primary and the secondary markets. To do that, we first study the impact of the manufacturer's intervention on the optimal order quantity Q.

Impact on Optimal Order Quantity

It turned out, as summarized in Theorem 4, that each retailer's optimal order quantity given the manufacturer's decision to participate in the secondary market will always be smaller than or equal to the retailers' optimal order quantity given a retailers-only secondary market.

Theorem 4. *In equilibrium, $Q^{III} \leq Q^{II}$ will always hold.*

The manufacturer's decision to offer additional units for sale in the secondary market will necessarily drive this market's equilibrium unit price down, which will make any excess inventory remaining at the end of the first period of less value for the retailers. Consequently, it will become optimal for the retails to reduce their initial order quantity.

Furthermore, under those scenarios where ordering Q^{ii} units will force the manufacturer out of the secondary market, or when initially a retailers-only secondary market was of no value to the retailers, the manufacturer's decision to consider participation in the secondary market should have no impact on the retailers' optimal replenishment strategy, since the manufacturer will in practice not intervene in the secondary market.

Impact on Expected Profits

We next want to determine under what conditions the manufacturer will benefit from taking part in the secondary market. The secondary market clearly provides an additional source of revenue for the manufacturer. However, it also leads to additional production costs for building the goods to be sold in the secondary market. In addition, once the retailers become aware of the manufacturer's intention to take part in the secondary market, it will become optimal for them to adjust their initial order quantity downward, as shown in Theorem 4, thus lowering the manufacturer's profit from her sale to the retailers. Overall, the manufacturer will benefit from her decision to intervene in the secondary market if and only if

$$\Pi_M^{III} - \Pi_M^{II} = n \left[(p_1 - c) \left(Q^{III} - Q^{II} \right) + K^{III}(p_2^{III} - c) \right] > 0 \qquad (5.17)$$

Unfortunately, due to the complexity of the solutions for Q^{II} and Q^{III}, (5.17) cannot be simplified any further and should be checked numerically for each situation to determine whether or not it is in the manufacturer's best interest to consider intervention in the secondary market.

To gain some insights into the conditions under which the manufacturer is most likely to benefit from participating in the secondary market, we have conducted a small numerical analysis, based on the parameter values given in Table 5.1, and under the assumption that D_1 is exponentially distributed with mean 1.

Table 5.1 Parameter values for numerical analysis.

$n = 100$	$c = 0.5$	$p_1 = 2, 2.5, 3$ (3 scenarios)	$r_1 = 5$	$a = 3.5$	$b = 1$

In particular, the numerical analysis provides us with a better understanding of the impacts of the secondary-market demand characteristics on the value of this market for the manufacturer. In addition, we gain insights into the impact of the ratio between the manufacturer's and the retailers' initial profit margins, measured by $p_1 - c$ and $r_1 - p_1$, respectively, on the manufacturer's likelihood of benefiting from intervening in the secondary market. The complete results of the numerical analysis are available in the Appendix.

As described in Section 5.3, the secondary-market aggregated demand function satisfies $D_2 = na(1 - p_2/b)$. Figure 5.3 shows how the gap between Π_M^{III} and Π_M^{II} changes as a function of a, while Figure 5.6 shows the change in value of $\Pi_M^{III} - \Pi_M^{II}$ as a function of b. Both figures were constructed based on three values of p_1, the price charged by the manufacturer for each unit sold to the retailers. Since the manufacturer's unit production cost c and the retailers' primary-market unit price r_1

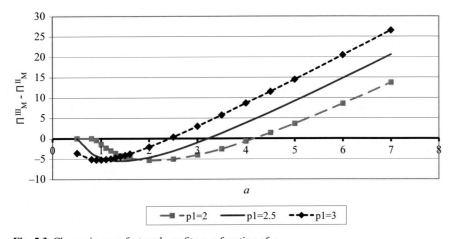

Fig. 5.3 Change in manufacturer's profits as a function of a.

remain unchanged in this numeric example, a higher value of p_1 corresponds with a higher profit margin for the manufacturer and a smaller profit margin for the retailers. Figures 5.4 and 5.7 show how each retailer's initial order quantity Q and the manufacturer's proportional quantity offered for sale in the secondary market K change as a function of a and b, respectively, to help us interpret the results presented in Figures 5.3 and 5.6.

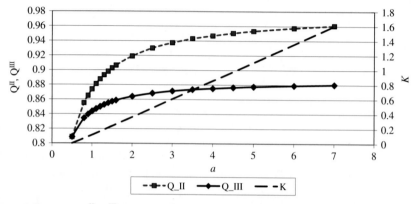

Fig. 5.4 Change in Q^{II}, Q^{III}, and K as a function of a ($p_1 = 2.5$).

Figures 5.3 and 5.4 study the impacts of a, the potential size of the secondary market, on the decisions made by the retailers and manufacturer, as well as the change in the manufacturer's expected profits. For extremely low values of a, the size of the secondary market is so small that it will result in an equilibrium unit price p_2 smaller in value compared with the manufacturer's unit production cost c. Thus, it will be optimal for the manufacturer to set $K = 0$, and for the retailers to order Q^{II} units, the optimal order quantity given no manufacturer's intervention. As a increases, so will the secondary-market equilibrium unit price, thus making it optimal for both the manufacturer and the retailers to have more units available for sale in the secondary market. However, the manufacturer's participation in the secondary market will lead the retailers to increase their initial order quantity more gradually, shrinking the manufacturer's profit from sales to the retailers. For intermediate values of a, the manufacturer's profits from the secondary market will not be sufficient to compensate for the reduction in profits from her sales to the retailers, and consequently, her decision to intervene in the secondary market will reduce the manufacturer's expected profits. Only for sufficiently high values of a, when the secondary-market equilibrium unit price p_2 is sufficiently high, and the gap between Q^{II} and Q^{III} becomes relatively stable even as the manufacturer increases her product offering in the secondary market, will the manufacturer be able to increase her total expected profits through participation in the secondary market.

As for the impact of the unit price p_1 on the retailers' behavior and the manufacturer's profitability, a smaller p_1 means that the retailers' profit from sales in the primary market is higher, which makes the secondary market relatively less attractive. Consequently, as can be seen in Figure 5.5, with smaller values of p_1 the manufacturer's intervention in the secondary market will result in a more drastic decline in the retailers' optimal order quantity Q. Going back to Figure 5.3, we see that for small values of a, which translate into a small size of the secondary market, the expected profits in the primary market are the main driver behind the retailers' behavior, and consequently the intervention of the manufacturer in the secondary market will have less impact on their initial order quantity Q. Therefore, for small values of p_1 the value of $\Pi_M^{III} - \Pi_M^{II}$ will be "less negative." However, the steeper decline in the retailers' initial order quantity for smaller values of p_1 will also lead to a more gradual increase in the manufacturer's total profits as a function of a.

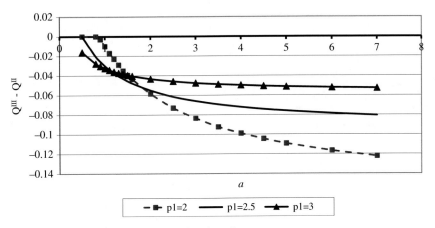

Fig. 5.5 Change in order quantity Q as a function of a.

Next, consider the impacts of b, which represents the sensitivity of the secondary-market customers to unit price, on the market behavior.

When the value of b is extremely low, any small change in the secondary-market unit price will have a big impact on total demand of this market's customers. This means that when supply is constant, any small increase in the value of b will lead to a significant increase in the value of the equilibrium unit price p_2. Even when the retailers and the manufacturer offer more units for sale in the secondary market, by increasing the value of Q and K, respectively, the impact on p_2 would be relatively minor, thus allowing them to reap a significant amount of profit from the secondary market. While the manufacturer's intervention will still result in the retailers increasing their initial order quantity Q more gradually, the difference between Q^{II} and Q^{III} will be relatively small, due to the huge potential for profits in the secondary market. Thus, as is demonstrated in Figure 5.6, the net effect of an increase in the value of b when its original value is very small will be a significant increase in the manufacturer's expected profits.

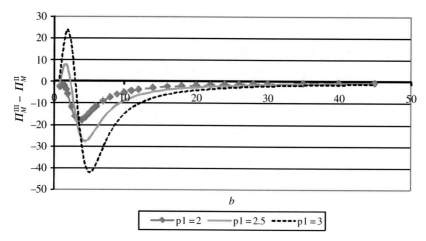

Fig. 5.6 Change in manufacturer's profits as a function of b.

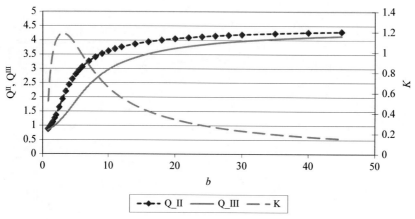

Fig. 5.7 Change in Q^{II}, Q^{III}, and K as a function of b ($p_1 = 2.5$).

As the value of b increases, any change in the total quantity offered for sale in the secondary market will have a more significant impact on the equilibrium unit price. Consequently, for intermediate values of b both the retailers and the manufacturer will increase their product offering to the secondary market more gradually. Furthermore, as the manufacturer's participation in the secondary market has a larger impact on the equilibrium unit price, the retailers will be more cautious in increasing their initial order quantity, resulting in a growing gap between Q^{II} and Q^{III} (see Figure 5.7). Overall, the manufacturer will see a decline in her total expected profits from sales to the retailers and the secondary-market customers.

As the value of b further increases, it becomes of less value for the manufacturer to participate in the secondary market due to the more significant impact any additional unit offered for sale will have on the equilibrium unit price in this market. Consequently, it will become optimal for the manufacturer to gradually reduce nK, the total number of units she offers for sale in the secondary market, as a means to avoid both a very low equilibrium unit price in the secondary market and a steep reduction in Q, the initial order quantity placed by the retailers (see Figure 5.8). With the value of K declining, so will the impact of the manufacturer's participation in the secondary market on the retailers' initial order quantity Q (see Figure 5.9). It is interesting to note that for high values of b, while the gap between the manufacturer's expected profits with and without intervention in the secondary market decreases in b, even for very high values of b the net effect of the manufacturer's intervention in the secondary market is a reduction in her total expected profits.

As for the impact of the unit price p_1 on the retailers' behavior and the manufacturer's profitability: for very low values of b, with a retailers-only secondary market the retailers' initial order quantity Q^{II} is much higher for smaller values of p_1 due to the retailers' higher profit margin associated with such scenarios. Once the manufacturer decides to intervene in the secondary market, the retailers will reduce their initial order quantity by a larger amount (in absolute terms, due to the higher value of Q for lower values of p_1). And since for small values of b the secondary-market equilibrium unit price p_2^{III} is very low (closer in value to c, the unit production cost), most of the manufacturer's profits come from her sales to the retailers. Therefore, for lower values of p_1, and for small values of b, the manufacturer's intervention in the secondary market will result in a more gradual increase in her profitability. For very low values of p_1, the manufacturer's intervention may even reduce her total profits compared with a retailers-only secondary market.

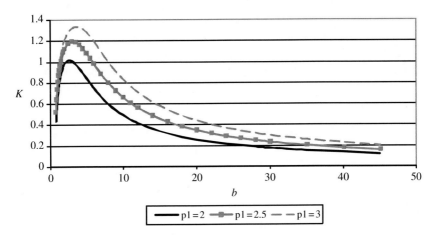

Fig. 5.8 Change in K as a function of b.

As b increases and the size of the secondary market becomes more stable, the retailers' focus shifts back to the primary market. And since a smaller value of p_1 means higher profit margins for the retailers from sales to the primary market, the

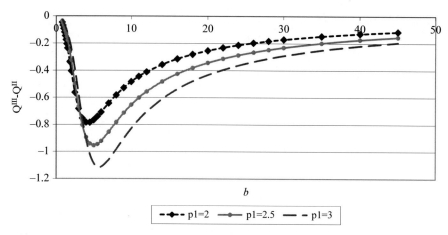

Fig. 5.9 Change in order quantity Q as a function of b.

manufacturer's intervention will lead to more gradual decline in their optimal order quantity Q (see Figure 5.9). Another contributor to the more gradual decline in the value of Q with the manufacturer's intervention is the smaller quantity K offered by the manufacturer for sale in the secondary market for lower values of p_1: smaller p_1 means higher profit margins for the retailers and therefore a higher order quantity Q. This will result in the retailers having a larger leftover quantity to be sold in the secondary market, which will make this market less attractive for the manufacturer due to the resulting lower equilibrium unit price p_2 and will therefore result in a lower K (see Figure 5.8). The more gradual decline in the retailers' order quantity is translated into a more gradual decline in the manufacturer's profitability for lower values of p_1 and higher values of b, as demonstrated in Figure 5.6.

Suppose that the manufacturer decides to take part in the secondary market. How will her intervention affect the retailers' expected profits? It turns out the retailers will always experience a decline in their expected profits due to the manufacturer's intervention, as summarized in Theorem 5.

Theorem 5. *In equilibrium, the manufacturer's intervention in the secondary market will always lead to lower expected profits for the retailers compared to a retailers-only secondary market.*

While the retailers may adjust their initial inventory level to mitigate the impact of the manufacturer's intervention on their profitability, it will never be sufficient for increasing their total profit to a level higher than their expected profit prior to the manufacturer's intervention in the secondary market.

Thus, the manufacturer's intervention takes away from the retailers some of the value the Internet-based distribution channel provided them with. However, as summarized in Theorem 6, the manufacturer's intervention will never reduce the retailers' expected profits to a level lower than in the absence of the secondary market. We can therefore conclude that the retailers will always benefit from establishing the

Internet-based distribution channel for disposing of their excess inventory, despite the possibility of the manufacturer's intervention in that channel.

Theorem 6. *In equilibrium, the manufacturer's intervention in the secondary market will never reduce the retailers' expected profits to a level lower than Π_R^I, their expected profits given no secondary market.*

As for the total supply chain profits, the way they are affected by the manufacturer's intervention in the Internet-based channel of distribution is indeterminate. The results of the numerical analysis demonstrate that the expected profits of the manufacturer and all retailers combined can either increase or decrease as a result of the manufacturer's intervention (see Figures 5.10 and 5.11). No simple conditions could be obtained to determine when expected supply chain profits are to increase.

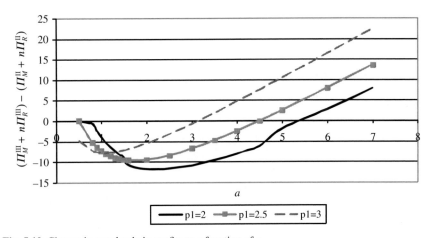

Fig. 5.10 Change in supply chain profits as a function of a.

Impact on Supply Chain Performance

We next study how the manufacturer's intervention in the secondary market will impact the supply chain performance in the primary and secondary markets, measured by consumer sales and stockout levels. Consider first the primary market: since the manufacturer's intervention will always lower the retailers' initial order quantity Q, this will have a negative impact on supply chain performance in this market, as summarized in Theorem 7.

Theorem 7. *In equilibrium, the manufacturer's intervention in the secondary market will always reduce sales level and increase stockout level in the primary market.*

As for the secondary-market customers, they always benefit from the manufacturer's intervention, as summarized in Theorem 8.

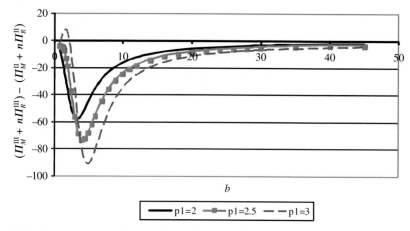

Fig. 5.11 Change in supply chain profits as a function of b.

Theorem 8. *In equilibrium, the manufacturer's intervention in the secondary market will always increase the total number of units offered for sale through this channel and reduce its equilibrium unit price.*

Finally, since both the manufacturer and the retailers completely clear off their inventories through the secondary market, the manufacturer's intervention in the secondary market increases the combined sales level in the primary and secondary markets, thus increasing the manufacturer's total market share if and only if

$$Q^{II} < Q^{III} + K^{III} \qquad (5.18)$$

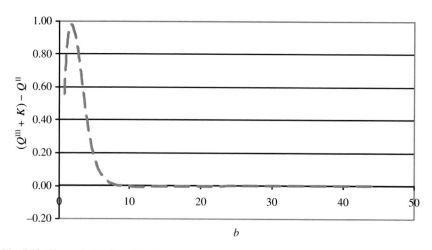

Fig. 5.12 Change in total market share.

Our numerical analysis illustrates that the manufacturer's intervention in the secondary market will not necessarily increase her total market share (see Figure 5.12, which is based on the following parameter values: $n = 100$, $c = 0.5$, $p_1 = 3$, $r_1 = 5$, $a = 3.5$). In this example the manufacturer is able to increase her total market share most of the time, and in those instances where the manufacturer's intervention results in a lower market share, the decline is very small. However, there may be other instances where the manufacturer's intervention in the secondary market will result in a more significant reduction in her total market share.

5.6 Discussion and Conclusion

In this chapter we study a setting in which a group of identical retailers may use a second, Internet-based, channel of distribution for disposing of their excess inventories. We assume that demand in the Internet-based secondary market is mainly price driven and that the equilibrium unit price is endogenously determined so as to equal supply and demand and clear the market. We investigate how the use of the Internet-based distribution channel impacts all players along the supply chain. We further study the impacts of the manufacturer's decision to intervene in the secondary market by offering additional units for sale. We show that all parties along the supply chain, including the manufacturer, retailers, and customers in both the primary and secondary markets, benefit from the retailers' decision to use the second distribution channel for selling off their excess inventories. Furthermore, we show that it is not always in the manufacturer's best interest to intervene in the secondary market, due to the negative impact such a decision will have on the retailers' initial order quantity, and given that the equilibrium unit price in the secondary market may end up being lower than the manufacturer's unit production cost. Moreover, the reduction in the retailers' initial order quantity may be so significant that even with the additional quantity offered for sale by the manufacturer, her total market share may be reduced. Thus, the manufacturer should carefully study the characteristics of the markets before announcing her intention to participate in the secondary market. As for the retailers, they will always be worse off from the manufacturer's decision to intervene in the secondary market. However, even with the manufacturer's intervention, their profits are still expected to be higher compared to the case where they do not make any use of the Internet-based channel of distribution. Therefore it is in the retailers' best interest to use the Internet for reaching new market segments for disposing of their excess inventories, even if they suspect that the manufacturer may later decide to intervene in that market. Primary market customers will also be worse off from the manufacturer's decision to intervene in the secondary market, due to the reduction in the retailers' initial order quantity, which will have a negative impact on expected stockouts and service level in the primary market. On the other hand, secondary market customers will benefit from the manufacturer's intervention since it will increase the total number of units offered for sale and reduce the equilibrium unit price in that market.

The model is built on several strong assumptions. One of them is the assumption that the retailers are aware of the manufacturer's unit production cost c when making their decision regarding their initial order quantity Q in the case of a secondary market with a manufacturer's intervention. A more realistic assumption would be to assume that the retailers assign some probability distribution function to c, with a mean value of $\tilde{c}$. Thus, and based on (5.12) and (5.13), the retailers will assume that for any order quantity Q, the manufacturer will build a total of $n\tilde{K}$ units for sale where $\tilde{K}(Q) = [a(b-\tilde{c})/(2b) - \Gamma(Q)/2]^+$, which will result in a secondary-market equilibrium unit price $\tilde{p}_2 = b[1 - (\tilde{K} + \Gamma(Q))/a]^+$. Based on (5.15) and (5.16), each of the retailers will then place an order for $\tilde{Q}$ units, where $\tilde{Q}$ satisfies

$$F(\tilde{Q}) = \frac{r_1 - p_1}{r_1 - \tilde{p}_2^{III}} = \frac{r_1 - p_1}{r_1 - [a(b+\tilde{c}) - b\Gamma(\tilde{Q})]/2a}$$

The manufacturer, however, will still base her decisions on the true value of c, and so the total number of units she will build for sale in the secondary market will be equal to $nK(\tilde{Q}) = n[a(b-c)/(2b) - \Gamma(\tilde{Q})/2]^+$. Consequently, the secondary-market equilibrium unit price will satisfy $p_2(\tilde{Q}) = b[1 - (K(\tilde{Q}) + \Gamma(\tilde{Q}))/a]^+$. In this case, the impact of the manufacturer's intervention in the secondary market will be based in part on the level of accuracy of the retailers' assumption regarding the value of c. The analysis will be further complicated if the different retailers have different levels of information or make different assumptions regarding the value of the unit production cost c.

Another restrictive assumption of the model is the independence of demand between the primary and secondary markets. While this assumption may hold in some situations, in many instances there may be some form of correlation between demand levels in the primary and secondary markets. For example, in the hi-tech industry, if the performance of a product is lower than expected, it is likely to lead to relatively low demand levels in both markets. Another example might come from the fashion industry: an item which was very popular in the primary market is likely to have high demand in the secondary market as well. One way to modify the model to include such correlation is to make a, the maximum size of the secondary market, a function of $\sum_{i=1}^{n} x_i$, the total demand in the primary market. For example, a positive correlation between the markets may be modeled by setting

$$a' = a\left[\beta + (1-\beta)\left(\sum_{i=1}^{n} x_i\right)\bigg/n\mu\right]$$

where a is the maximal size of the secondary market with no correlation and a' replaces a in our model as the upper limit on the size of the secondary market. $\beta \in [0,1]$ represents the degree of correlation between the primary and secondary markets: when $\beta = 1$ the two markets are uncorrelated; as β gets closer to zero the secondary-market demand function becomes more positively correlated with the actual primary-market demand. The fraction $(\sum_{i=1}^{n} x_i)/n\mu$ compares the demand realization in the primary market with the expected primary-market demand. As the average demand realization in the primary market increases compared to its expected level μ, so will the value of a', the potential size of the secondary market. Similarly, a negative correlation between the two markets may be modeled by setting

$$a' = a\left[\beta + (1-\beta)\left(1 - \left(\sum_{i=1}^{n} x_i\right)\Big/n\mu\right)\right]$$

Given a secondary market with no manufacturer's intervention, retailer i will then choose her initial order quantity Q to maximize

$$\max_{Q\geq 0}\left\{\Pi_R^{II} = r_1 E_{x_i}\min(Q,x_i) - p_1 Q + E_{x_j,j\neq i}\left[\int_{x_i=0}^{Q} p_2^{II}(Q - x_i)f(x_i)dx_i\right]\right\}$$

where

$$p_2^{II} = \lim_{n\to\infty}\left[b - (b/na')\sum_{i=1}^{n}(Q - x_i)^+\right] = b - (b/a')\,\Gamma(Q)$$

Similar modifications should be made to Π_R^{III}, for the case where the manufacturer decides to intervene in the secondary market.

Our model also assumes that all information is available to all decision makers at the point in time when decisions are made. Specifically, we assume that both the retailers and the manufacturer know the exact characteristics of the secondary-market demand function at the beginning of the first period. Since the characteristics of any market tend to change over time, in reality it is more likely that the exact demand information for the secondary market is revealed closer to the beginning of the second period, while at the beginning of the first period the manufacturer and the retailers only have some early signal of the secondary-market characteristics. In that case, the potential impacts of the secondary market will be a function of the accuracy of the secondary-market initial demand signal.

We also assume that the retailers and the manufacturer are the only potential sources of supply for the secondary market. It is possible though that the secondary market already exists and can be characterized by some demand and supply curves. The decision of the retailers or the manufacturer to use the Internet-based channel of distribution for reaching this market will then lead to a shift in the secondary market supply curve. For example, if the original cumulative supply curve in the secondary market is characterized by a linear function of the form

$$S = n[u + vp_2]$$

then the retailers' decision to offer their remaining inventories for sale in that market will change the total supply curve for the secondary market to satisfy

$$S' = n[u + vp_2] + \sum_{i=1}^{n}(Q - x_i)^+$$

Assuming that demand in the secondary market is still given by the function $D_2 = na(1 - p_2/b)$ then given an initial order quantity of Q, and assuming that n is sufficiently high, the limiting equilibrium unit price p_2 will satisfy

$$p_2^{II} = \frac{a - [u + \Gamma(Q)]}{v + (a/b)}$$

Similar modifications should be made to the model, given the manufacturer's decision to intervene in the secondary market.

Finally, to simplify the model we assume that secondary-market demand is characterized by a linear and deterministic function of the secondary-market unit price. One implication of this assumption is the need to modify the optimal decisions of the manufacturer and retailers so as to guarantee a non-negative equilibrium unit price. One way to overcome this problem is by using a different function for D_2, the cumulative demand in the secondary market, such as

$$D_2 = na/p_2$$

where a is some positive constant. Clearly, such a demand structure will guarantee a non-negative equilibrium unit price in the secondary market. A more realistic assumption would be to characterize the demand in the secondary market by some stochastic distribution function. However, making such an assumption substantially complicates the analysis.

5.7 Appendix

Proof of Lemma 1. Let Π_M be the manufacturer's profit. Then based on Theorem 1

$$\Pi_M^{II} = nQ^{II}(p_1 - c) \geq nQ^I(p_1 - c) = \Pi_M^I$$

Proof of Lemma 2. Given no secondary market, the expected profits to each retailer satisfy

$$\Pi_R^I(Q^I) = r_1 E_x \min(Q^I, x) - p_1 Q^I$$

Next, suppose that the retailers decide to use the Internet-based distribution channel to access the secondary market for selling off their excess inventory, but choose to leave the initial order quantity equal to Q^I. In that case the secondary market will provide an additional source of profit for the retailers while not affecting their expected profit from the primary market. That is, $\Pi_R^{II}(Q^I) = r_1 E_x \min(Q^I, x) - p_1 Q^I + p_2^{II}(Q^I) E_x(Q^I - x)^+ \geq \Pi^I R(Q^I)$.

Ordering the optimal order quantity Q^{II} instead of Q^I can only further increase the retailers' expected profits. That is, by definition, $\Pi_R^{II}(Q^{II}) \geq \Pi_R^{II}(Q^I)$ will always hold. Combining the two results we obtain that $\Pi_R^{II}(Q^{II}) \geq \Pi_R^{II}(Q^I) \geq \Pi_R^I(Q^I)$; thus we can conclude that by accessing the secondary market the retailers will always increase their total expected profits.

Proof of Lemma 3. Expected sales level by each retailer in the primary market is equal to $E_x \min(Q, x)$, which is an increasing function of Q; expected stockout level in the primary market is equal to $E_x(x - Q)^+$, which is a decreasing function of Q. Based on Theorem 1, the introduction of the secondary market will always increase the retailers' optimal order quantity, which will consequently lead to higher expected sales level and lower expected stockout level in the primary market.

Proof of Theorem 2. Each retailer's expected profit satisfies

$$\Pi_R^{II} = r_1 E_x \min(Q,x) - p_1 Q + p_2^{II}\Gamma(Q)$$

Differentiating Π_R^{II} with respect to a, and based on the value of p_2^{II} as given in (5.4), we obtain

$$\frac{d\Pi_R^{II}}{da} = \frac{d\Pi_R^{II}}{dQ}\bigg|_{Q=Q^{II}} \frac{dQ^{II}}{da} + (b/a^2)\Gamma^2(Q^{II})$$

We next determine the value of $(d\Pi_R^{II}/dQ)|_{Q=Q^{II}}$ and dQ^{II}/da:

$$
\begin{aligned}
\frac{d\Pi_R^{II}}{dQ}\bigg|_{Q=Q^{II}} &= r_1 Q^{II} f(Q^{II}) + r_1\left[1 - F(Q^{II})\right] - r_1 Q^{II} f(Q^{II}) \\
&\quad - p_1 + \frac{dp_2^{II}}{dQ}\Gamma(Q^{II}) + p_2^{II}\frac{d\Gamma(Q^{II})}{dQ} \\
&= r_1\left[1 - F(Q^{II})\right] - p_1 - \frac{b}{a}F(Q^{II})\Gamma(Q^{II}) + p_2^{II}F(Q^{II}) \\
&= -\frac{b}{a}F(Q^{II})\Gamma(Q^{II})
\end{aligned}
$$

To obtain the value of dQ^{II}/da we differentiate both sides of (5.7) with respect to a:

$$f(Q^{II})\frac{dQ^{II}}{da} = -\frac{r_1 - p_1}{[r_1 - b + (b/a)\Gamma(Q^{II})]^2}\left[-\frac{b}{a^2}\Gamma(Q^{II}) + \frac{b}{a}F(Q^{II})\frac{dQ^{II}}{da}\right]$$

After rearranging terms, and using the limiting value of p_2^{II} as given in (5.4), we obtain

$$\frac{dQ^{II}}{da} = \Gamma(Q^{II})\frac{b(r_1 - p_1)}{a\left[af(Q^{II})(r_1 - p_2^{II})^2 + b(r_1 - p_1)F(Q^{II})\right]}$$

Based on the above results we obtain

$$
\begin{aligned}
\frac{d\Pi_R^{II}}{da} &= \frac{d\Pi_R^{II}}{dQ}\bigg|_{Q=Q^{II}}\frac{dQ^{II}}{da} + (b/a^2)\Gamma^2(Q^{II}) \\
&= -\frac{b}{a}F(Q^{II})\Gamma^2(Q^{II})\frac{b(r_1 - p_1)}{a\left[af(Q^{II})(r_1 - p_2^{II})^2 + b(r_1 - p_1)F(Q^{II})\right]} \\
&\quad + \frac{b}{a^2}\Gamma^2(Q^{II}) \\
&= \frac{b}{a}\left[\frac{f(Q^{II})(r_1 - p_2^{II})^2}{af(Q^{II})(r_1 - p_2^{II})^2 + b(r_1 - p_1)F(Q^{II})}\right]\Gamma^2(Q^{II})
\end{aligned}
$$

To determine whether $f(Q^{II})$ is positive or negative, we differentiate (5.7) with respect to Q:

$$f(Q^{II}) = \frac{r_1 - p_1}{a(r_1 - p_2^{II})^2} F(Q^{II}) > 0$$

Thus we can conclude that $d\Pi_R^{II}/da > 0$.

Next, we study how each retailer's expected profit function changes in b:

$$\frac{d\Pi_R^{II}}{db} = \frac{d\Pi_R^{II}}{dQ}\bigg|_{Q=Q^{II}} \frac{dQ^{II}}{db} + \left[1 - \Gamma(Q^{II})/a\right]\Gamma(Q^{II})$$

To obtain the value of dQ^{II}/db we differentiate both sides of (5.7) with respect to b:

$$f(Q^{II})\frac{dQ^{II}}{db} = \frac{r_1 - p_1}{[r_1 - b + (b/a)\Gamma(Q^{II})]^2}\left[-1 + \frac{1}{a}\Gamma(Q^{II}) + \frac{b}{a}F(Q^{II})\frac{dQ^{II}}{db}\right]$$

After rearranging terms, and using the limiting value of p_2^{II} as given in (5.4), we obtain

$$\frac{dQ^{II}}{db} = \frac{(r_1 - p_1)[a - \Gamma(Q^{II})]}{a\left[f(Q^{II})(r_1 - p_2^{II})^2 + (b/a)(r_1 - p_1)F(Q^{II})\right]}$$

Based on the above results we obtain

$$\begin{aligned}
\frac{d\Pi_R^{II}}{db} &= -\frac{b}{a}F(Q^{II})\Gamma(Q^{II})\frac{(r_1 - p_1)[a - \Gamma(Q^{II})]}{a\left[f(Q^{II})(r_1 - p_2^{II})^2 + (b/a)(r_1 - p_1)F(Q^{II})\right]} \\
&\quad + \left[1 - \Gamma(Q^{II})/a\right]\Gamma(Q^{II}) \\
&= \frac{[a - \Gamma(Q^{II})]}{a}\Gamma(Q^{II})\left[\frac{f(Q^{II})(r_1 - p_2^{II})^2}{f(Q^{II})(r_1 - p_2^{II})^2 + (b/a)(r_1 - p_1)F(Q^{II})}\right] \\
&= \frac{p_2^{II}(r_1 - p_2^{II})^2 f(Q^{II})\Gamma(Q^{II})}{b\left[f(Q^{II})(r_1 - p_2^{II})^2 + (b/a)(r_1 - p_1)F(Q^{II})\right]}
\end{aligned}$$

Since, as shown earlier, $f(Q^{II}) > 0$, we can conclude that $d\Pi_R^{II}/db > 0$.

Proof of Theorem 3. The manufacturer's profit function satisfies $\Pi_M^{II} = nQ^{II}(p_1 - c)$. Differentiating Π_M^{II} with respect to a yields

$$\frac{d\Pi_M^{II}}{da} = n(p_1 - c)\frac{dQ^{II}}{da}$$

Based on the proof of Theorem 2, dQ^{II}/da satisfies

$$\frac{dQ^{II}}{da} = \Gamma(Q^{II})\frac{b(r_1 - p_1)}{a\left[af(Q^{II})(r_1 - p_2^{II})^2 + b(r_1 - p_1)F(Q^{II})\right]}$$

Because $f(Q^{II}) > 0$, as shown in the same proof, we obtain that $dQ^{II}/da > 0$ and consequently $d\Pi_M^{II}/da > 0$.

Next we study the behavior of the manufacturer's profit function with respect to b. Differentiating Π_M^{II} with respect to b yields $d\Pi_M^{II}/db = n(p_1 - c)(dQ^{II}/db)$. Based on the proof of Theorem 2, dQ^{II}/db satisfies

$$\frac{dQ^{II}}{db} = \frac{(r_1 - p_1)p_2^{II}}{b\left[f(Q^{II})(r_1 - p_2^{II})^2 + (b/a)(r_1 - p_1)F(Q^{II})\right]}$$

Again, since $f(Q^{II}) > 0$, we obtain that $dQ^{II}/db > 0$ and consequently $d\Pi_M^{II}/db > 0$.

Proof of Lemma 4.

Scenario 1: $Q^{ii} \leq \widehat{Q}$ and $Q^{iii} \leq \widehat{Q}$: in this case, it will be beneficial for the manufacturer to participate in the secondary market, and therefore the retailers' optimal order quantity is equal to Q^{iii}.

Scenario 2: $Q^{iii} \leq \widehat{Q}$ and $\widehat{Q} \leq Q^{ii} \leq \overline{Q}$: based on Theorem 5, the manufacturer's intervention in the secondary market will always reduce the retailers' expected profits. Therefore the optimal behavior for the retailers would be to each order Q^{ii} units and force the manufacturer out of the secondary market.

Scenario 3: $Q^{iii} > \widehat{Q}$ and $\widehat{Q} \leq Q^{ii} \leq \overline{Q}$: with Q^{iii} being greater than $\widehat{Q}$, the manufacturer will be better off by not participating in the secondary market, which brings us back to the scenario of a retailers-only secondary market. In this case, the retailers' optimal order quantity will be equal to Q^{ii}.

Scenario 4: $Q^{iii} \leq \widehat{Q}$ and $Q^{ii} > \overline{Q}$: this scenario is infeasible. When $Q^{ii} > \overline{Q}$ holds, it will result in a negative unit price $p_2^{II}(Q^{ii})$. Based on (5.1) and (5.6), this will in turn lead to $Q^{ii} < Q^I$ to be true. At the same time, if $Q^{iii} \leq \widehat{Q}$ then $p_2^{III}(Q^{iii}) \geq 0$ holds. Therefore, and based on (5.1) and (5.15), $Q^{iii} \geq Q^I$ will hold. Combining these results, and given that $\widehat{Q} \leq \overline{Q}$ will always hold, we obtain $\overline{Q} < Q^{ii} < Q^I \leq Q^{iii} \leq \widehat{Q} \leq \overline{Q}$, which is infeasible.

Scenario 5: $\widehat{Q} < Q^{iii} \leq \overline{Q}$ and $Q^{ii} > \overline{Q}$: this scenario is infeasible. Under this scenario,

$$K^{III}(Q^{iii}) < \left[\frac{a(b-c)}{2b} - \frac{\Gamma(\widehat{Q})}{2}\right] = 0$$

and

$$p_2^{III}(Q^{iii}) = b\left[1 - \frac{(K + \Gamma(Q^{iii}))}{a}\right] > b\left[1 - \frac{\Gamma(Q^{iii})}{a}\right] > b\frac{1 - \Gamma(\overline{Q})}{a} = 0$$

Thus, similar to the proof of Scenario 4 above, we can obtain that $Q^{iii} \geq Q^I$ will hold, while at the same time $Q^{ii} < Q^I$ will hold as well. Combining all these results we obtain $\overline{Q} < Q^{ii} < Q^I \leq Q^{iii} \leq \overline{Q}$, which is infeasible.

Scenario 6: $Q^{iii} > \overline{Q}$ and $Q^{ii} > \overline{Q}$: with $Q^{iii} > \overline{Q} > \widehat{Q}$, it is of no value for the manufacturer to participate in the secondary market. And since $Q^{ii} > \overline{Q}$ holds, the secondary market does not bring any value to the retailers either. Consequently, each retailer should place with the manufacturer an order for Q^I units and not make any use of the second, Internet-based, channel of distribution. Since $p_2^{II}(Q^{iii}) < 0$ for all $Q^{iii} > \overline{Q}$, which results in $Q^{iii} < Q^I$ to hold, this means that placing an order for Q^I units will not change the manufacturer's decision to not use herself the Internet-based distribution channel.

Proof of Theorem 4.

Scenario 1: $Q^{ii} \le \widehat{Q}$ and $Q^{iii} \le \widehat{Q}$. In this case $Q^{II} = Q^{ii}$ and $Q^{III} = Q^{iii}$. Based on (5.4) and (5.12), it can be verified that for any Q, $p_2^{II}(Q) > p_2^{III}(Q)$ will always hold. In particular, $p_2^{II}(Q^{ii}) > p_2^{III}(Q^{ii})$ will always be true. Consequently,

$$F^{II}(Q^{ii}) = \frac{r_1 - p_1}{r_1 - p_2^{II}(Q^{ii})} > \frac{r_1 - p_1}{r_1 - p_2^{III}(Q^{ii})}$$

will hold as well. Next suppose that $Q^{iii} > Q^{ii}$ holds. Since p_2^{III} decreases in Q, assuming that $Q^{iii} > Q^{ii}$ holds will result in $(r_1 - p_1)/(r_1 - p_2^{III}(Q^{ii}))$ being greater than $(r_1 - p_1)/(r_1 - p_2^{III}(Q^{iii}))$. Combining the two results we obtain

$$F^{II}(Q^{ii}) = \frac{r_1 - p_1}{r_1 - p_2^{II}(Q^{ii})} > \frac{r_1 - p_1}{r_1 - p_2^{III}(Q^{ii})} > \frac{r_1 - p_1}{r_1 - p_2^{III}(Q^{iii})} = F^{III}(Q^{iii})$$

Since $F(Q)$ is an increasing function of Q, we obtain from the above results that necessarily $Q^{ii} > Q^{iii}$ holds. But this contradicts our initial assumption that Q^{ii} is smaller than Q^{iii}. Thus, we can conclude that in equilibrium Q^{iii} must take on a value smaller than Q^{ii}.

Scenario 2: $\widehat{Q} < Q^{ii} < \overline{Q}$. In this case $Q^{II} = Q^{III} = Q^{ii}$.

Scenario 3: $Q^{ii} \ge \overline{Q}$ and $Q^{iii} \ge \overline{Q}$. In this case $Q^{II} = Q^{III} = Q^I$.

Proof of Theorem 5. When the manufacturer does not take part in the secondary market, total profit to each retailer satisfies $\Pi_R^{II} = r_1 E \min\left(Q^{II}, x\right) - p_1 Q^{II} + p_2^{II} E(Q^{II} - x)^+$, where $p_2^{II} = b - (b/a)\Gamma(Q^{II})$.

When the manufacturer participates in the secondary market, each retailer's expected profit is $\Pi_R^{III} = r_1 E \min\left(Q^{III}, x\right) - p_1 Q^{III} + p_2^{III} E(Q^{III} - x)^+$, where $p_2^{III} = b - (b/a)(K^{III} + \Gamma(Q^{III}))$. Then

$$\Pi_R^{II} = r_1 E \min\left(Q^{II}, x\right) - p_1 Q^{II} + \left[b - \frac{b}{a}\Gamma(Q^{II})\right] E(Q^{II} - x)^+$$

$$\ge r_1 E \min\left(Q^{III}, x\right) - p_1 Q^{III} + \left[b - \frac{b}{a}\Gamma(Q^{III})\right] E(Q^{III} - x)^+$$

$$\ge r_1 E \min\left(Q^{III}, x\right) - p_1 Q^{III} + \left[b - \frac{b}{a}\Gamma(Q^{III}) - \frac{b}{a}K^{III}\right] E(Q^{III} - x)^+ = \Pi_R^{III}$$

Proof of Theorem 6. Given no secondary market, total profit to each retailer satisfies $\Pi_R^I = r_1 E \min\left(Q^I, x\right) - p_1 Q^I$. Given the manufacturer's intervention in the secondary market, each retailer's expected profit satisfies $\Pi_R^{III} = r_1 E \min\left(Q^{III}, x\right) - p_1 Q^{III} + p_2^{III}(Q^{III}) E(Q^{III} - x)^+$. Then

$$\Pi_R^{III} = r_1 E \min(Q^{III}, x) - p_1 Q^{III} + p_2^{III}(Q^{III}) E(Q^{III} - x)^+$$
$$\geq r_1 E \min(Q^I, x) - p_1 Q^I + p_2^{III}(Q^I) E(Q^I - x)^+$$
$$\geq r_1 E \min(Q^I, x) - p_1 Q^I = \Pi_R^I$$

Proof of Theorem 7. Sales level in the primary market, $E_x \min(Q, x)$, increases in Q, while stockout level in the primary market, $E_x(x - Q)^+$, decreases in Q. Based on Theorem 4, the manufacturer's intervention in the secondary market will always reduce the retailers' initial order quantity Q. Consequently, expected sales level in the primary market will necessarily go down while expected stockout level will go up.

Proof of Theorem 8. We focus our attention in this proof only on those cases where $Q^{ii} \leq \hat{Q}$, since this is the only case in which Q^{II} and Q^{III} are not equal in value.

When the secondary market is only used by the retailers to dispose of their excess inventory, then the expected size of the secondary market is $n\Gamma(Q^{II})$. When the manufacturer takes part in the secondary market, its expected size is $n\left[\Gamma(Q^{III}) + K^{III}\right]$. For simplicity, we denote $y^{II} := \Gamma(Q^{II})$ and $y^{III} := \Gamma(Q^{III}) + K^{III}$; thus, we would like to prove that $y^{III} \geq y^{II}$ always holds.

Based on (5.6) and (5.15),

$$F(Q^{II}) = \frac{r_1 - p_1}{r_1 - p_2^{II}} \quad \text{and} \quad F(Q^{III}) = \frac{r_1 - p_1}{r_1 - p_2^{III}}$$

As shown in Theorem 4, the manufacturer's intervention will always reduce the retailers' initial order quantity; thus $F(Q^{II}) \geq F(Q^{III})$ or

$$\frac{r_1 - p_1}{r_1 - p_2^{II}} \geq \frac{r_1 - p_1}{r_1 - p_2^{III}}$$

After rearranging terms, we obtain that $p_2^{II} \geq p_2^{III}$.

Based on (5.4) and (5.12), the secondary market equilibrium unit price for a retailers-only secondary market will equal $p_2^{II} = b\left[1 - \Gamma(Q^{II})/a\right] = b\left(1 - y^{II}/a\right)$, while the secondary market equilibrium unit price for a secondary market with manufacturer's intervention will satisfy $p_2^{III} = b\left[1 - \left[K^{III} + \Gamma(Q^{III})\right]/a\right] = b\left(1 - y^{III}/a\right)$. Since the manufacturer's intervention will reduce the equilibrium unit price, we obtain that $b\left(1 - y^{II}/a\right) \geq b\left(1 - y^{III}/a\right)$ or $y^{III} \geq y^{II}$.

Results of Numerical Analysis

The numerical analysis was conducted with the following parameter values:
$$n = 100 \qquad c = 0.5 \qquad r_1 = 5.$$

1. **No secondary market:** Table 5.2 summarizes the numerical results for the three values of p_1, given the use of a single, traditional channel of distribution, with no secondary market.

Table 5.2 Numerical results given no secondary market.

	No Secondary Market		
p1	Q_I	PI_I_R	PI_I_M
2	0.916	1.167	137.444
2.5	0.693	0.767	138.629
3	0.511	0.468	127.706

Table 5.3 Numerical results for a variable a, given $p_1 = 2$.

	Retailers-Only Secondary Market				Manufacturer's Intervention				
a	Q_II	p_II	PI_II_R	PI_II_M	Q_III	K_(Q_III)	P2_III	PI_III_R	PI_III_M
0.8	1.086	0.471	1.339	162.900	1.086	0.000	0.471	1.339	162.900
0.9	1.105	0.515	1.359	165.788	1.102	0.008	0.509	1.356	165.359
1.0	1.122	0.552	1.375	168.338	1.112	0.030	0.530	1.365	166.858
1.1	1.137	0.584	1.389	170.573	1.120	0.052	0.547	1.373	168.230
1.2	1.150	0.611	1.402	172.553	1.127	0.075	0.562	1.379	169.498
1.3	1.162	0.635	1.413	174.323	1.133	0.097	0.575	1.385	170.674
1.4	1.173	0.656	1.423	175.913	1.138	0.121	0.586	1.390	171.785
1.5	1.182	0.674	1.432	177.353	1.143	0.144	0.596	1.395	172.841
1.6	1.191	0.691	1.440	178.665	1.147	0.168	0.605	1.399	173.851
2.0	1.219	0.743	1.466	182.918	1.161	0.263	0.632	1.412	177.550
2.5	1.245	0.787	1.490	186.728	1.172	0.384	0.654	1.422	181.674
3.0	1.263	0.818	1.506	189.510	1.180	0.506	0.669	1.430	185.498
3.5	1.278	0.841	1.519	191.640	1.185	0.629	0.680	1.435	189.132
4.0	1.289	0.859	1.529	193.320	1.190	0.753	0.688	1.439	192.651
4.5	1.298	0.873	1.537	194.685	1.193	0.877	0.695	1.442	196.083
5.0	1.305	0.885	1.544	195.818	1.196	1.001	0.700	1.445	199.459
6.0	1.317	0.902	1.554	197.580	1.201	1.249	0.708	1.449	206.091
7.0	1.326	0.916	1.562	198.885	1.204	1.498	0.714	1.452	212.617
8.0	1.333	0.925	1.568	199.905	1.206	1.747	0.718	1.454	219.077

Table 5.4 Numerical results for a variable a, given $p_1 = 2.5$.

	Retailers-Only Secondary Market				Manufacturer's Intervention				
a	Q_II	p_II	PI_II_R	PI_II_M	Q_III	K_(Q_III)	P2_III	PI_III_R	PI_III_M
0.5	0.809	0.492	0.876	161.740	0.809	0.000	0.492	0.876	161.740
0.8	0.855	0.650	0.918	171.000	0.834	0.066	0.582	0.900	167.420
0.9	0.865	0.682	0.927	173.000	0.840	0.089	0.599	0.904	168.786
1.0	0.874	0.709	0.935	174.740	0.844	0.113	0.613	0.908	170.019
1.1	0.881	0.731	0.942	176.200	0.847	0.137	0.625	0.911	171.110
1.2	0.888	0.751	0.947	177.500	0.850	0.161	0.634	0.914	172.168
1.3	0.893	0.767	0.952	178.640	0.853	0.186	0.643	0.916	173.187
1.4	0.898	0.782	0.957	179.600	0.855	0.210	0.650	0.918	174.146
1.5	0.903	0.795	0.961	180.520	0.857	0.234	0.656	0.920	175.059
1.6	0.907	0.806	0.964	181.300	0.859	0.259	0.662	0.922	175.926
2.0	0.919	0.841	0.975	183.800	0.864	0.357	0.679	0.926	179.182
2.5	0.930	0.870	0.985	186.000	0.868	0.481	0.692	0.930	182.934
3.0	0.937	0.890	0.991	187.460	0.871	0.605	0.702	0.933	186.486
3.5	0.943	0.905	0.996	188.600	0.874	0.729	0.708	0.935	189.924
4.0	0.947	0.916	1.000	189.400	0.875	0.854	0.714	0.936	193.236
4.5	0.951	0.925	1.003	190.120	0.876	0.979	0.717	0.938	196.564
5.0	0.953	0.932	1.005	190.670	0.878	1.103	0.721	0.939	199.847
6.0	0.958	0.943	1.009	191.520	0.879	1.353	0.725	0.940	206.315
7.0	0.961	0.951	1.012	192.150	0.880	1.603	0.729	0.941	212.728
8.0	0.963	0.957	1.014	192.620	0.881	1.852	0.732	0.942	219.098
10.0	0.967	0.965	1.017	193.300	0.882	2.352	0.735	0.943	231.767
15.0	0.971	0.977	1.021	194.220	0.884	3.601	0.740	0.944	263.250
20.0	0.973	0.982	1.023	194.690	0.885	4.851	0.743	0.945	294.612
25.0	0.975	0.986	1.024	194.980	0.885	6.101	0.744	0.945	325.933
30.0	0.976	0.988	1.025	195.170	0.886	7.351	0.745	0.946	357.233

Table 5.5 Numerical results for a variable a, given $p_1 = 3$.

	Retailers-Only Secondary Market				Manufacturer's Intervention				
a	Q_II	p_II	PI_II_R	PI_II_M	Q_III	K_(Q_III)	P2_III	PI_III_R	PI_III_M
0.5	0.622	0.682	0.558	155.525	0.606	0.049	0.599	0.545	151.960
0.8	0.644	0.789	0.575	161.000	0.616	0.122	0.652	0.553	155.908
0.9	0.649	0.810	0.579	162.175	0.618	0.146	0.663	0.555	156.957
1.0	0.653	0.827	0.582	163.125	0.620	0.171	0.671	0.556	157.925
1.1	0.656	0.841	0.585	163.900	0.621	0.196	0.678	0.557	158.808
1.2	0.658	0.853	0.587	164.600	0.622	0.220	0.684	0.558	159.651
1.3	0.661	0.864	0.588	165.175	0.623	0.245	0.689	0.559	160.476
1.4	0.663	0.873	0.590	165.700	0.624	0.270	0.693	0.560	161.283
1.5	0.665	0.881	0.592	166.150	0.625	0.295	0.697	0.560	162.047
1.6	0.666	0.888	0.593	166.550	0.626	0.320	0.700	0.561	162.813
2.0	0.671	0.909	0.597	167.775	0.628	0.419	0.710	0.562	165.713
2.5	0.675	0.926	0.600	168.800	0.629	0.544	0.718	0.564	169.157
3.0	0.678	0.938	0.602	169.500	0.630	0.669	0.723	0.565	172.501
3.5	0.680	0.947	0.604	170.025	0.631	0.793	0.727	0.565	175.762
4.0	0.682	0.953	0.605	170.400	0.632	0.918	0.730	0.566	179.031
4.5	0.683	0.958	0.606	170.725	0.632	1.043	0.732	0.566	182.233
5.0	0.684	0.962	0.607	170.950	0.633	1.168	0.734	0.566	185.415
6.0	0.685	0.968	0.608	171.325	0.633	1.418	0.736	0.567	191.774
7.0	0.686	0.973	0.609	171.588	0.634	1.668	0.738	0.567	198.116
8.0	0.687	0.976	0.609	171.800	0.634	1.918	0.740	0.567	204.425

Table 5.6 Numerical results for a variable b, given $p_1 = 2$.

	Retailers-Only Secondary Market				Manufacturer's Intervention				
b	Q_II	p_II	PI_II_R	PI_II_M	Q_III	K_(Q_III)	P2_III	PI_III_R	PI_III_M
0.8	1.189	0.687	1.439	178.365	1.144	0.425	0.597	1.396	175.656
0.9	1.232	0.765	1.478	184.830	1.164	0.540	0.639	1.415	182.103
1.0	1.278	0.841	1.519	191.625	1.185	0.630	0.680	1.435	189.118
1.1	1.325	0.914	1.561	198.780	1.207	0.701	0.720	1.455	196.556
1.2	1.375	0.985	1.604	206.220	1.230	0.760	0.761	1.476	204.232
1.3	1.427	1.052	1.648	214.005	1.253	0.808	0.800	1.497	212.134
1.4	1.481	1.117	1.692	222.098	1.276	0.847	0.839	1.518	220.160
1.5	1.536	1.178	1.737	230.468	1.301	0.880	0.877	1.540	228.290
1.8	1.713	1.340	1.870	256.995	1.377	0.949	0.988	1.606	252.920
2.0	1.836	1.431	1.955	275.415	1.432	0.977	1.058	1.652	269.332
2.5	2.142	1.601	2.145	321.225	1.578	1.008	1.220	1.769	309.248
3.0	2.419	1.707	2.291	362.903	1.737	1.002	1.359	1.886	346.539
3.5	2.656	1.774	2.398	398.430	1.903	0.974	1.474	1.999	380.276
4.0	2.853	1.816	2.476	427.935	2.070	0.933	1.567	2.103	409.995
4.5	3.016	1.845	2.534	452.340	2.232	0.886	1.639	2.195	435.681
5.0	3.151	1.866	2.577	472.665	2.384	0.837	1.696	2.274	457.664
5.5	3.265	1.881	2.611	489.720	2.525	0.788	1.739	2.341	476.417
6.0	3.362	1.892	2.638	504.225	2.653	0.742	1.773	2.397	492.446
7.0	3.516	1.908	2.677	527.430	2.873	0.660	1.820	2.484	518.135
8.0	3.634	1.919	2.704	545.130	3.052	0.591	1.851	2.546	537.627
9.0	3.727	1.926	2.724	559.035	3.197	0.534	1.872	2.591	552.838
10.0	3.802	1.932	2.740	570.240	3.318	0.486	1.887	2.626	565.010
11.0	3.863	1.936	2.751	579.465	3.418	0.445	1.898	2.653	574.958
12.0	3.915	1.939	2.761	587.175	3.503	0.410	1.907	2.674	583.237
14.0	3.996	1.944	2.775	599.355	3.639	0.355	1.919	2.705	596.223
16.0	4.057	1.947	2.786	608.513	3.743	0.312	1.927	2.728	605.936
18.0	4.104	1.950	2.793	615.660	3.824	0.279	1.933	2.744	613.476
20.0	4.143	1.952	2.799	621.390	3.889	0.252	1.937	2.756	619.499
22.0	4.174	1.953	2.804	626.085	3.943	0.229	1.941	2.766	624.420
24.0	4.200	1.954	2.808	630.000	3.988	0.210	1.943	2.774	628.515
26.0	4.222	1.955	2.812	633.315	4.026	0.195	1.945	2.780	631.978
28.0	4.241	1.956	2.814	636.165	4.058	0.181	1.947	2.786	634.943
30.0	4.258	1.957	2.816	638.633	4.087	0.169	1.949	2.791	637.512
35.0	4.291	1.958	2.820	643.575	4.144	0.145	1.952	2.800	642.644
40.0	4.315	1.959	2.824	647.280	4.187	0.127	1.953	2.805	646.490
45.0	4.334	1.960	2.827	650.168	4.220	0.113	1.955	2.810	649.478

Table 5.7 Numerical results for a variable b, given $p_1 = 2.5$.

b	Retailers-Only Secondary Market				Manufacturer's Intervention				
	Q_II	p_II	PI_II_R	PI_II_M	Q_III	K_(Q_III)	P2_III	PI_III_R	PI_III_M
0.8	0.881	0.732	0.942	176.260	0.845	0.519	0.619	0.910	175.195
0.9	0.911	0.819	0.968	182.220	0.859	0.636	0.664	0.922	182.236
1.0	0.943	0.905	0.996	188.540	0.873	0.730	0.708	0.935	189.886
1.1	0.976	0.989	1.025	195.220	0.888	0.805	0.753	0.948	197.975
1.2	1.011	1.071	1.055	202.280	0.903	0.867	0.797	0.962	206.407
1.3	1.049	1.152	1.086	209.720	0.919	0.918	0.841	0.975	215.081
1.4	1.088	1.230	1.118	217.580	0.935	0.961	0.884	0.989	223.939
1.5	1.129	1.306	1.152	225.840	0.951	0.998	0.928	1.004	232.954
1.8	1.266	1.518	1.257	253.140	1.004	1.079	1.055	1.049	260.640
2.0	1.367	1.645	1.331	273.320	1.042	1.115	1.137	1.080	279.410
2.5	1.644	1.902	1.516	328.860	1.146	1.168	1.334	1.165	326.581
3.0	1.932	2.077	1.682	386.440	1.264	1.185	1.516	1.256	373.164
3.5	2.200	2.189	1.815	440.080	1.396	1.178	1.678	1.352	418.051
4.0	2.435	2.260	1.916	486.940	1.541	1.154	1.819	1.450	460.270
4.5	2.634	2.307	1.991	526.800	1.693	1.117	1.936	1.546	499.005
5.0	2.802	2.339	2.048	560.440	1.847	1.073	2.032	1.636	533.788
5.5	2.945	2.361	2.092	588.940	1.999	1.024	2.109	1.717	564.477
6.0	3.066	2.378	2.126	613.240	2.145	0.973	2.169	1.789	591.314
7.0	3.261	2.401	2.175	652.280	2.407	0.876	2.253	1.905	635.044
8.0	3.411	2.415	2.209	682.100	2.629	0.790	2.306	1.989	668.469
9.0	3.528	2.424	2.233	705.560	2.814	0.716	2.341	2.052	694.548
10.0	3.622	2.431	2.251	724.460	2.968	0.653	2.365	2.098	715.362
11.0	3.700	2.437	2.265	740.000	3.098	0.599	2.382	2.134	732.327
12.0	3.765	2.441	2.277	752.980	3.208	0.553	2.395	2.163	746.405
14.0	3.867	2.447	2.294	773.480	3.385	0.478	2.412	2.204	768.415
16.0	3.945	2.450	2.305	788.920	3.519	0.421	2.424	2.232	784.828
18.0	4.005	2.454	2.314	800.940	3.625	0.376	2.432	2.252	797.538
20.0	4.053	2.456	2.320	810.580	3.710	0.339	2.437	2.268	807.672
22.0	4.092	2.458	2.327	818.460	3.780	0.309	2.442	2.280	815.943
24.0	4.125	2.459	2.329	825.060	3.838	0.284	2.445	2.289	822.821
26.0	4.153	2.460	2.335	830.620	3.888	0.262	2.448	2.297	828.631
28.0	4.177	2.461	2.338	835.400	3.930	0.244	2.450	2.303	833.604
30.0	4.198	2.461	2.339	839.560	3.967	0.228	2.452	2.309	837.909
35.0	4.239	2.463	2.343	847.860	4.041	0.196	2.455	2.319	846.506
40.0	4.270	2.464	2.348	854.080	4.097	0.171	2.458	2.327	852.941
45.0	4.295	2.465	2.352	858.920	4.140	0.152	2.459	2.332	857.941

2. **Secondary market, variable a:** For this part of the numerical analysis, the value of b was set to equal $b = 1$. Tables 5.3, 5.4, and 5.5 summarize the numerical results for $p_1 = 2$, $p_1 = 2.5$, and $p_1 = 3$, respectively, given a secondary market – either with or without the manufacturer's intervention.

3. **Secondary market, variable b:** For this part of the numerical analysis, the value of a was set to equal $a = 3.5$. Tables 5.6, 5.7, and 5.8 summarize the numerical results for $p_1 = 2$, $p_1 = 2.5$, and $p_1 = 3$, respectively, given a secondary market – either with or without the manufacturer's intervention.

Table 5.8 Numerical results for a variable b, given $p_1 = 3$.

	Retailers-Only Secondary Market				Manufacturer's Intervention				
b	Q_II	p_II	PI_II_R	PI_II_M	Q_III	K_(Q_III)	P2_III	PI_III_R	PI_III_M
0.8	0.638	0.762	0.571	159.613	0.612	0.579	0.632	0.550	160.739
0.9	0.659	0.855	0.587	164.675	0.622	0.698	0.680	0.558	167.944
1.0	0.680	0.947	0.604	170.025	0.631	0.793	0.727	0.565	175.762
1.1	0.703	1.038	0.621	175.675	0.641	0.871	0.774	0.573	184.051
1.2	0.727	1.128	0.639	181.675	0.651	0.935	0.820	0.581	192.719
1.3	0.752	1.217	0.659	188.038	0.661	0.988	0.867	0.589	201.618
1.4	0.779	1.305	0.679	194.800	0.672	1.034	0.913	0.597	210.784
1.5	0.808	1.391	0.700	201.963	0.683	1.073	0.960	0.606	220.103
1.8	0.905	1.641	0.770	226.200	0.718	1.161	1.097	0.633	248.891
2.0	0.979	1.797	0.822	244.825	0.744	1.203	1.187	0.652	268.576
2.5	1.202	2.141	0.967	300.563	0.814	1.272	1.408	0.705	318.932
3.0	1.468	2.401	1.121	367.000	0.896	1.306	1.620	0.764	370.176
3.5	1.748	2.578	1.263	436.900	0.991	1.319	1.819	0.830	421.666
4.0	2.011	2.691	1.379	502.863	1.100	1.315	2.003	0.902	472.600
4.5	2.245	2.763	1.468	561.250	1.224	1.297	2.167	0.980	522.121
5.0	2.446	2.810	1.536	611.525	1.360	1.267	2.310	1.061	569.207
5.5	2.618	2.843	1.588	654.525	1.505	1.228	2.429	1.141	612.948
6.0	2.765	2.866	1.629	691.350	1.653	1.182	2.526	1.217	652.711
7.0	3.003	2.895	1.686	750.650	1.942	1.083	2.665	1.350	719.739
8.0	3.184	2.914	1.725	795.975	2.201	0.985	2.751	1.452	771.909
9.0	3.326	2.925	1.752	831.600	2.424	0.897	2.806	1.529	812.654
10.0	3.441	2.934	1.773	860.275	2.612	0.820	2.842	1.586	845.038
11.0	3.535	2.940	1.788	883.850	2.772	0.753	2.867	1.630	871.299
12.0	3.614	2.945	1.800	903.550	2.909	0.696	2.885	1.664	893.000
14.0	3.738	2.951	1.818	934.600	3.127	0.602	2.908	1.713	926.748
16.0	3.832	2.956	1.830	957.950	3.294	0.530	2.923	1.746	951.787
18.0	3.905	2.959	1.840	976.125	3.424	0.473	2.933	1.769	971.111
20.0	3.963	2.961	1.846	990.700	3.529	0.427	2.940	1.787	986.482
22.0	4.011	2.963	1.851	1002.625	3.616	0.389	2.945	1.800	999.006
24.0	4.050	2.964	1.855	1012.575	3.688	0.357	2.949	1.810	1009.407
26.0	4.084	2.965	1.858	1021.000	3.749	0.330	2.952	1.819	1018.185
28.0	4.113	2.967	1.863	1028.200	3.802	0.307	2.954	1.826	1025.692
30.0	4.138	2.967	1.865	1034.462	3.847	0.287	2.956	1.832	1032.187
35.0	4.188	2.969	1.871	1046.975	3.938	0.246	2.960	1.844	1045.146
40.0	4.225	2.970	1.874	1056.375	4.007	0.216	2.963	1.851	1054.840
45.0	4.255	2.971	1.876	1063.687	4.060	0.192	2.965	1.857	1062.366

References

Anupindi R, Bassok Y (1999) Centralization of stocks: Retailers vs. manufacturer. Management Science 45(2):178–191

Axsäter S (2003) A new decision rule for lateral transshipments in inventory systems. Management Science 49(9):1168–1179

Billington C, Lee HL, Tang CS (1998) Successful strategies for product rollovers. Sloan Management Review 39(3):23–30

Choi TM, Li D, Yan H (2004) Optimal returns policy for supply chain with e-marketplace. International Journal of Production Economics 88(2):205–227

Doctorow D, Saloner G (2000) QRS corporation. A case study. Graduate School of Business, Stanford University, EC-14

Elmaghraby W (2000) Supply contract competition and sourcing policies. Manufacturing and Service Operations Management 2(4):350–371

Eppen GD, Iyer AV (1997) Improved fashion buying with Bayesian updates. Operations Research 45(6):805–819

Esteban S, Shum M (2007) Durable-goods oligopoly with secondary markets: The case of auto-mobiles. The RAND Journal of Economics 38(2):332–354

Grey W, Olavson T, Shi D (2005) The role of e-marketplaces in relationship-based supply chains: A survey. IBM Systems Journal 44(1):109–123

Kleindorfer PR, Wu DJ (2003) Integrating long- and short-term contracting via business-to-business exchanges for capital-intensive industries. Management Science 49(11):1597–1615

Klemperer P (1999) Auction theory: A guide to the literature. Journal of Economic Surveys 13(3):227–286

Kouvelis P, Gutierrez GJ (1997) The newsvendor problem in a global market: Optimal centralized and decentralized control policies for a two-market stochastic inventory system. Management Science 43(5):571–585

Lee HL, Whang S (2002) The impact of the secondary market on the supply chain. Management Science 48(6):719–731

McAfee R, McMillan J (1987) Auctions and bidding. Journal of Economic Literature 25:699–738

Mendelson H, Tunca TI (2007) Strategic spot trading in supply chains. Management Science 53(5):742–759

Milner JM, Kouvelis P (2007) Inventory, speculation, and sourcing strategies in the presence of online exchanges. Manufacturing and Service Operations Management 9(3):312–331

Peleg B, Lee HL, Hausman WH (2002) Short-term e-procurement strategies vs. long-term contracts. Production and Operations Management 11(4):458–479

Rosenfield DB (1989) Disposal of excess inventory. Operations Research 37(3):404–409

Rudi N, Kapur S, Pyke DF (2001) A two-location inventory model with transshipment and local decision making. Management Science 47(12):1668–1680

Sosic G (2006) Transshipment of inventories among retailers: Myopic vs. farsighted stability. Management Science 52(10):1493–1508

Taylor C (2001) They love the slump. Time Global Business B24–B25, June

Tunca TI, Zenios SA (2006) Supply auctions and relational contracts for procurement. Manufacturing and Service Operations Management 8(1):43–67

Vakrat Y (2000) Online auctions. PhD dissertation, University of Rochester

Wurman PR, Walsh WE, Wellman MP (1998) Flexible double auctions for electronic commerce: theory and implementation. Decision Support Systems 24(1):17–27

Chapter 6
Managing Client Portfolio in a Two-Tier Supply Chain

Basak Kalkanci and Seungjin Whang

Abstract Suppliers in a variety of industries today face the challenge of managing their business where the utilization of their capacities fluctuates dramatically over time. The fluctuations can be attributed to the business cycle of the economy, as well as to the amplification of demand variability as one moves upstream (i.e., the bull-whip effect). In this chapter, we investigate the source of the fluctuations by analyz-ing a two-tier supply chain where the supplier serves many clients whose demands are subject to individual trends and the business cycle of the general economy. We present conditions under which the bullwhip effect or the stabilizing effect of the clients' orders is felt by the supplier. We also analyze how the supplier can build an efficient client portfolio by analyzing the impact of a new client on the expected profit of the supplier in a newsvendor setting. We derive the key performance indi-cators that can guide a supplier in the right direction of the client portfolio. Thus, by understanding the clients' ordering behaviors and its impact on capacity deci-sions, the supplier can strategically select an efficient client portfolio, so that the risk-neutral supplier would maximize the expected long-term profit.

6.1 Introduction

Consider a supplier who has made a large investment in capacity in expectation of future demands. The supplier would face the challenge of managing the business if the economy slows down and the expectations do not materialize. Examples of such a business pattern would include semiconductor foundries (e.g., TSMC and UMC), manufacturing service providers (e.g., Foxconn and Flextronics), industrial parts

Basak Kalkanci
Stanford University, 380 Panama Way, Stanford, CA 94305, USA,
e-mail: kalkanci@stanford.edu

Seungjin Whang
Stanford University, 518 Memorial Way, Stanford, CA 94022, USA,
e-mail: whang_jin@gsb.stanford.edu

S. Netessine, C.S. Tang (eds.), *Consumer-Driven Demand and Operations Management*
Models, International Series in Operations Research & Management Science 131,
DOI 10.1007/978-0-387-98026-3_6, © Springer Science+Business Media, LLC 2009

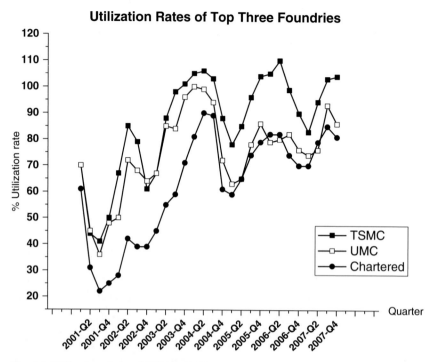

Fig. 6.1 Utilization chart of TSMC, UMC and Chartered (http://www.icknowledge.com/our_products/utilization.html).

manufacturers (e.g., Intel and LG–Phillips LCD), and equipment manufacturers (e.g., Cisco and Applied Materials). See, for example, Figure 6.1 that plots quarterly utilization rates of top three pure-play foundries – TSMC, UMC, and Chartered – in 2001–2007. The utilization significantly fluctuates over the years, ranging between 41 and 108% of its nominal capacity. The average utilization is, respectively, 85.85, 74.57, and 62.07% at these firms, with standard deviation (coefficient of variation) 19.68% (22.93%), 16.27% (21.81%), and 20.68% (33.32%). Also we observe that fluctuations at these three foundries are exposed to the same cycle, i.e., the economy's business cycle, far from meeting the usual independent and identically distributed (iid) demand assumption. This chapter attempts to answer two questions: Why do we see such fluctuations of utilization at the upstream sector? Is it all attributed to the business cycle or is the bullwhip effect also responsible? And, how can the supplier alleviate the exposure to the congestion–starvation cycles by building an efficient client portfolio?

In order to answer the questions, we develop a two-tier supply chain model (see Figure 6.2) in which one supplier serves multiple long-term industrial *clients* who themselves face stochastic demands from their respective *consumers.* Foundries, for example, face a diverse set of clients selling in different end-consumer sectors like computers, medical equipment, consumer electronic devices, and telecommunication gears. The demands in different sectors are subject to individual market trends

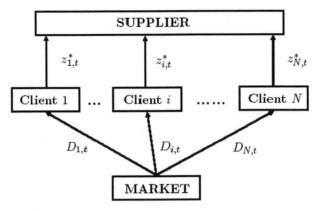

Fig. 6.2 Supply chain structure.

and fluctuations, as well as to the business cycles of the general economy. To capture this, we assume that consumer demands arriving to a client are correlated over time, and that consumer demands facing different clients are also correlated with each other.

In this "doubly correlated demands" setting, the first question revisits the bullwhip effect that refers to the phenomenon where "*orders* to the supplier tend to have larger variance than *sales* to the buyer" in a supply chain (Lee et al. 1997). One of the four causes of the bullwhip effect is demand signal processing which relates to how the firms update their forecast based on the observed demand. In a multiperiod inventory control setting where demands are serially correlated in time, a downstream firm would rightfully update demand forecasts based on the observed demand. If the observed demand is larger than expected, the firm would place an even larger order with its supplier. This is to raise the inventory to account for the adjustment of expected demand based on new information, as well as the one-for-one replacement of the last-period demand. A symmetric phenomenon – placing a smaller order than actual demand – happens when the downstream firm observes a lower-than-expected demand. Lee et al. (1997) offer a proof of the bullwhip effect in a model with one supplier and one buyer, but it is not clear if the effect will continue to exist in the presence of multiple buyers where the inventory risk pooling effect coexist with the bullwhip effect. Indeed, Baganha and Cohen (1998) report the opposite of the bullwhip (a stabilizing effect) at the macroeconomic level at the distribution center in a three-tier supply chain and present a model to explain this situation. We also present the conditions under which the bullwhip effect or the stabilizing effect arises in a multibuyer context where customer demands are correlated.

To answer the second question of client portfolio design, we analyze the impact of a new additional client on the expected profit to the supplier. The marginal impact is assessed in terms of the mean and variance of the demand portfolio. The traditional approach to portfolio design is mean–variance analysis in investment theory; a risk-averse investor would design a portfolio of stocks in consideration of the trade-off between the mean return and the variance. The result of the analysis is the efficient frontier. There exists a continuum of viable mean–variance pairs on the efficient frontier that are not dominated by other pairs attainable within a given budget constraint. One mean–variance pair on the frontier may be optimal to an investor with a specific utility function, but not necessarily so to another investor. This is the approach taken by Carr and Lovejoy (2000) in their analysis of demand portfolio. By contrast, we follow an alternative route of portfolio design where a risk-neutral supplier would maximize the expected profit by choosing the right level of capacity. In so doing, the supplier faces the newsvendor type of trade-off between overage and underage costs. Too much capacity will lead to idle capacity and wasted investment, while too little capacity results in loss of goodwill with her valued clients. Under normal demands, the optimal capacity decision would lead to an expected profit that increases in the mean demand and decreases in its variance. Thus, when a new client is added, the new demand stream could increase the volatility, as well as the mean, of total demand, so it may more than offset the gain in the expected revenue. Note that this approach is possible due to the unique nature of inventory management settings where both mean and variance endogenously affect the expected profit objective, without invoking the usual risk-averse utility assumption.

Our marginal analysis approach, as opposed to the usual optimization approach, seems reasonable in the context of client portfolio, since unlike the stock portfolio problem, no supplier is likely to enjoy full degrees of freedom in choosing the entire portfolio of clients for her convenience. Hence, we instead highlight the right KPIs (key performance indicators) that would guide a supplier in the right "direction" of the portfolio. The supplier can strategically use it to assess the current position of the firm, as well as to recruit the best available client.

The rest of this chapter is organized in five sections as follows. The next section briefly reviews the literature related to this work. In Section 6.3 we develop the basic model of doubly correlated supply chain and derive some preliminary results for later sections. Sections 6.4 and 6.5 form the core of the work. Section 6.4 derives the conditions for the bullwhip effect or the stabilizing effect in the two-tier supply chain. Section 6.5 offers the marginal analysis when a new client is added to the existing portfolio. The last section provides limitations of the model and directions of further research, followed by concluding remarks.

6.2 Literature Review

This work falls into the general field of *demand management* that studies a broad class of demand-side controls. Examples of demand-side controls include pricing and tariff structures (Wilson 1993), priority assignment (Mendelson and Whang 1989), seat protection levels (Brumelle and McGill 1993), admissions policy (Kelly et al. 1998), and others. For an excellent overview of revenue management (a substantial subset of demand management), readers are referred to the book

The Theory and Practice of Revenue Management (2004) by Talluri and van Ryzin. Our work follows the earlier work by Carr and Lovejoy (2000) that studies an optimal demand portfolio. They consider a supplier who has fixed capacity but faces a random yield. On the demand side, the supplier has a set of "raw" correlated random demands to choose from. The supplier's opportunity set is general, including a linear combination of raw demands and priority-based customer selection rules, each of which can be ultimately translated to demand distributions. The authors ask, "What is an optimal demand distribution with fixed capacity?" They offer mean–variance analysis and characterize the efficient frontier.

This work follows their work by extending the analysis to a multiperiod setting with serially correlated demand streams. The model assumes double correlation of demands in time and client demands. For the sake of exposition, however, we restrict the supplier's opportunity set to Boolean (accept/reject) choices under fixed capacity. Another key difference between the two works is the supply chain structure. Their supply chain has a single tier represented by a supplier selling to multiple end-consumers, while ours consists of two tiers: a supplier and multiple industrial clients serving end-consumers. By including the customer's customers in our model, we can better capture the specific nature of the business environment of the industrial sector (i.e., pure foundry or manufacturing service) we analyze. In particular, this enables us to endogenize the potential bullwhip effect in this supply chain, thereby allowing us to discuss broader issues of variance analysis.

Another stream of research that is relevant to this work is the bullwhip literature led by Forrester (1961), Sterman (1989), and Lee et al. (1997). More recently, Baganha and Cohen (1998) present a three-tier supply chain model (a supplier, distributor, and multiple retailers) in which they study the potential role of the distributor as a "stabilizer" of order flows in the supply chain. They identify a chain of factors – cost structure, inventory policy, and order patterns - that drive the bullwhip or the stabilizing effect at the distribution center. That is, the fixed cost of ordering leads to the optimality of an (s, S) policy to the retailer, which in return results in negative serial correlation in each retailer's orders. The authors observe that the variance of each retailer's orders is higher than the variance of the market demand. This implies that the aggregate market demand has a lower variance than the aggregate orders at the distribution center. However, under certain conditions, the optimal order policy (that happens to be a myopic one) by the distributor would reduce the variability of the demand faced by the supplier. A general lesson is that correlation over time matters to bullwhip and stabilization effects. Positive (or negative) correlation is associated with higher (or lower) variability on upstream orders. In our study, we restrict our attention to how the variability is propagated by the retailers and we observe that under a general forecasting model and correlation among retailers, it is possible to observe bullwhip or stabilization effect. We show similar results to Baganha and Cohen (1998) on serial correlation in a slightly different framework. In addition, we show that correlation among *clients* is a driver to accelerate or ameliorate the bullwhip.

6.3 The Basic Model

We closely follow the setup and notation of Lee et al. (1997) and extend it to a multi-client setting. Suppose there are N clients (he) who order from the same supplier (she) at each period. To client i, there is a delay of v_i periods between ordering and receiving the goods. We let $v^N = (v_1, v_2, \cdots, v_N)$. The timing of the events in a typical period (or period 1) is as follows: At the beginning of period t, a decision to order a quantity z_t from the supplier is made and executed. Next, the goods ordered v_i periods ago arrive. Lastly, demand is realized, and the available inventory is used to meet the demand. Excess demand is backlogged. We assume that excess inventory can be returned without cost. Let h_i, π_i, and c_i denote the unit holding cost, the unit shortage penalty cost, and the unit ordering cost for client i, respectively. Also, let γ be the cost discount factor per period.

Each client i faces serially correlated demands following the first-order autoregressive process $(AR(1))$

$$D_{i,t} = d_i + \rho_i D_{i,t-1} + u_{i,t}, \quad \text{for } 1 \le i \le N, \tag{6.1}$$

where $D_{i,t}$ is the demand arriving to client i in period t. We define

$$\rho^N := [\rho_1, \rho_2, ..., \rho_N],$$

where each element, ρ_i, is a constant that satisfies $-1 < \rho_i < 1$. Likewise, we let $d^N := [d_1, d_2, ..., d_N]$. $AR(p)$ for some integer p or its variation (e.g., $MS\text{-}AR(p)$) is widely used to describe economic cycles. Our formulation of demands as $AR(1)$ attempts to emulate economic cycles with a minimum burden on mathematics and notation.

Also, we define U_t as

$$U_t := [u_{1,t}, u_{2,t}, ..., u_{N,t}],$$

and assume that it is independently and identically distributed with a multivariate normal distribution $N(0, \Sigma^N)$ for each t. The covariance matrix of U_t, Σ^N, is given by $\Sigma_{ii}^N = \text{Var}(u_{i,t}) = \sigma_i^2$ and $\Sigma_{ij}^N = \text{Cov}(u_{i,t}, u_{j,t}) = \sigma_{ij}$, for $i \ne j$. Thus, our model allows double correlation across time periods and across clients' markets. d_i is a positive constant that is assumed to be significantly greater than σ_i, so the probability of a negative demand is negligible. We also assume that the covariance between any $D_{i,t}$ and $D_{j,t}$ (where $i \ne j$) is constant with respect to t. For simpler notation, we omit the superscripts on v^N, ρ^N, d^N, and Σ^N whenever we can avoid any confusion.

Optimal order-up-to quantity for client i is given by

$$S_{i,1}^* = d_i \sum_{k=1}^{v_i+1} \frac{1-\rho_i^k}{1-\rho_i} + \frac{\rho_i(1-\rho_i^{v_i+1})}{1-\rho_i} D_{i,0} + K_i^* \sigma_i \sqrt{\sum_{l=1}^{v_i+1} \left(\sum_{k=l}^{v_i+1} \rho_i^{k-l}\right)^2}, \tag{6.2}$$

where

$$K_i^* = \Phi^{-1}\left(\frac{\pi_i - c_i(1-\gamma)/\gamma^{v_i}}{h_i + \pi_i}\right).$$

Therefore, the optimal order amount $z_{i,1}^*$ for client i is given by

$$z_{i,1}^* = \frac{\rho_i(1-\rho_i^{v_i+1})}{1-\rho_i}(D_{i,0} - D_{i,-1}) + D_{i,0}. \qquad (6.3)$$

The supplier receives orders from N clients that add up to $\sum_{i=1}^{N} z_{i,1}^*$ in period 1. We first study the properties of $\sum_{i=1}^{N} z_{i,1}^*$ in the following lemma. Define $\Delta(\rho, \Sigma, v)$ as

$$\Delta(\rho, \Sigma, v) = \sum_{i=1}^{N} \alpha_i(\rho, v)\sigma_i^2 + 2\sum_{i=1}^{N}\sum_{j>i}^{N} \beta_{ij}(\rho, v)\sigma_{ij},$$

where

$$\alpha_i(\rho, v) := \frac{2\rho_i(1-\rho_i^{v_i+1})(1-\rho_i^{v_i+2})}{(1+\rho_i)(1-\rho_i)^2}$$

and

$$\beta_{ij}(\rho, v) := \frac{(1-\rho_i^{v_i+1})(1-\rho_j^{v_j+2})\rho_i(1-\rho_j) + (1-\rho_j^{v_j+1})(1-\rho_i^{v_i+2})\rho_j(1-\rho_i)}{(1-\rho_i)(1-\rho_j)(1-\rho_i\rho_j)}.$$

Lemma 1. *Letting $Z_N := \sum_{i=1}^{N} z_{i,1}^*$, we have*

(a) $E[Z_N] = \sum_{i=1}^{N} E[D_{i,0}] = \sum_{i=1}^{N} \frac{d_i}{1-\rho_i}$

(b) $\mathrm{Var}(Z_N) = \Delta(\rho, \Sigma, v) + \mathrm{Var}(\sum_{i=1}^{N} D_{i,0}) = \Delta(\rho, \Sigma, v) + \sum_{i=1}^{N} \frac{\sigma_i^2}{1-\rho_i^2}$

$+ 2\sum_{i=1}^{N}\sum_{j>i}^{N} \frac{\sigma_{ij}}{1-\rho_i\rho_j}$

(c) $\mathrm{Cov}(z_{i,1}^*, z_{j,1}^*) = \sigma_{ij}\left[\frac{1}{1-\rho_i\rho_j}\right.$

$\left. + \frac{(1-\rho_i^{v_i+1})(1-\rho_j^{v_j+2})\rho_i(1-\rho_j) + (1-\rho_j^{v_j+1})(1-\rho_i^{v_i+2})\rho_j(1-\rho_i)}{(1-\rho_i)(1-\rho_j)(1-\rho_i\rho_j)}\right]$

6.4 The Bullwhip Effect with Multiple Clients

Suppose that the client portfolio of the supplier consists of N clients whose individual demands follow an $AR(1)$ process as (6.1) for $i = 1, 2, \cdots, N$. Then, we can define the current *client portfolio* of the firm as

$$P^N := [D_{1,t}, D_{2,t}, ..., D_{N,t}],$$

whose process can be parameterized by (ρ, Σ, v, d). We use $\Delta(P^N)$ interchangeably with $\Delta(\rho, \Sigma, v)$. From Lemma 1(b), we find that the variance of total orders to the supplier comprises of two terms: the variance of consumer demand and $\Delta(P^N)$. Hence, $\Delta(P^N)$ is the determinant of the bullwhip effect or the stabilizing effect, as reported in the following proposition.

Proposition 1. *If $\Delta(P^N) > 0$ $(\Delta(P^N) < 0)$, the variance of total client orders is strictly larger (smaller) than that of total client demand.*

The proposition demonstrates that the supply chain may potentially experience either the bullwhip effect or the stabilizing effect depending on $\Delta(P^N)$. Note that $\Delta(P^N)$ is the result of using the middle tier of clients and would not exist if the supplier sells directly to end-consumers (bypassing the clients). Thus, we call $\Delta(P^N)$ "the middle-tier factor." If all ρ_i's are positive and client demands are independent or uncorrelated (i.e., $\sigma_{ij} = 0$ if $i \neq j$), the second term will equal zero, so the supply chain will always experience the bullwhip effect. Even when some pairs of demands are negatively correlated, the bullwhip effect will prevail if total covariance is negative and small in absolute value. Only when there exists strong negative correlation among client demands enough to offset the variance terms, the stabilizing effect will be at work. Note that as the number N of clients increases, the sum of $N(N-1)$ pair-wise covariance terms will dominate the sum of N individual variance terms. Thus, the correlation factor will mostly determine the presence of the bullwhip effect or the stabilizing effect. Given that demands in an industrial sector are more or less subject to the same business cycle, demands are more likely to be strongly positively correlated, hence the bullwhip effect would be the likely outcome. We conclude that fluctuations facing the upstream supplier will be driven by both the intrinsic volatility in the consumer market and the bullwhip effect within the supply chain.

To see if inventory risk pooling could mitigate the bullwhip effect, consider the variance of the average order size (i.e., $\text{Var}(\sum_{i=1}^{N} z_i^* / N)$). From Lemma 1(b), we see that the first term of the middle-tier factor divided by N^2 decreases as N grows, but even for a large N, the factor does not converge to zero. Instead, it approaches the average covariance of the portfolio. Thus, pooling helps, only in a minor form, to mitigate the bullwhip.

Pooling is also at work when the supplier forecasts the aggregate demand. Aggregate orders arriving to the supplier enable the supplier to access more data and more accurately observe the economic trend than any individual client. But unfortunately, this advantage is significantly eroded since the supplier reads the market signals one period later than her clients. In summary, the supplier may be in a good position to pool inventory risk as well as demand signals, so she may better detect the market trend, but her signals may arrive distorted, and one period too late.

Indeed, this is what might have happened at Cisco in 2001 when it announced a $2.69 billion loss, including a $2.25-billion write-off of obsolete excess inventories. In his *CIO* Magazine article, Berinato (2001) discusses how such a sophisticated manufacturer like Cisco could completely miss the sign of bubble burst that most others had detected. See Lee and Whang (2005) for more detailed discussions.

6.5 Client Portfolio

We now study the impact of a client newly added to an existing client portfolio. For the analysis, we consider the following scenario. In period 1, the supplier finds the opportunity of serving client $N + 1$ to its existing portfolio P^N to form a new portfolio P^{N+1}. Next, the supplier can adjust its capacity K to maximize her profit by serving the new portfolio of clients. Capacity cost $C(K)$ per period is linearly increasing; i.e., $C(K) = cK$ for some $c > 0$. Capacity is normalized so that one unit is required to produce one unit of the goods ordered by any client. After the capacity is installed, stochastic orders from the clients are realized, which is repeated each period for a long time. In order to facilitate our analysis, we assume that $v_i = 1$ for all i, implying that it takes one period to fulfill the order.

The order fulfillment process in each period is as follows. Each client places an order with the supplier at the beginning of any period t. The supplier accepts the orders up to the capacity, and the orders beyond the capacity are turned down and forever lost. The supplier starts production of the orders (to be completed and delivered in period $t + 1$). Next, the client receives the goods ordered in period $t - 1$. The supplier earns r per unit of capacity utilized, but if she fails to serve the orders of the portfolio, she incurs the cost p per unit for loss of goodwill, in addition to the lost revenue r. Denoting the sum of orders from the clients by Z, we solve the following newsvendor-type problem in order to find the optimal capacity K:

$$\Pi(Z) := \max_K rE(Z) - (p+r) \int_K^\infty (Z - K) dF(Z) - cK.$$

Here, $F(\cdot)$ represents the distribution function of Z.

Since this is a newsvendor-type problem, the optimal capacity K^* is given by the critical fractile solution $K^* = F^{-1}((p+r-c)/(p+r))$. In particular, if F is given by $N(\mu, s^2)$, we have $K^* = \mu + ks$ with $k = \Phi^{-1}((p+r-c)/(p+r))$, where $\Phi(\cdot)$ is the cumulative density function of standard normal distribution. In this case, the expected profit is $\Pi(Z) = (r-c)\mu - s(p+r)\phi(k)$, where $\phi(\cdot)$ is the standard normal density function (Porteus 2002).

As it turns out, Z_N (defined in Lemma 1) is indeed normally distributed as the following lemma reports.

Lemma 2. Z_N follows $N(\mu, s^2)$, where $\mu = \sum_{i=1}^N d_i/(1 - \rho_i)$ and

$$s^2 = \Delta(P^N) + \sum_{i=1}^N \frac{\sigma_i^2}{1 - \rho_i^2} + 2 \sum_{i=1}^N \sum_{j>i}^N \frac{\sigma_{ij}}{1 - \rho_i \rho_j}.$$

Lemma 2 implies that Z_{N+1} is also normally distributed. In order to evaluate the net worth of a new client, the supplier computes the difference in the optimal value of the objective between $Z = Z_N$ and $Z = Z_{N+1}$ (defined as in Lemma 1). The following proposition reports the impact of the new client on the key metrics of the portfolio.

Proposition 2. *The impact of the new client on the mean, variance, and expected profit of the portfolio is given as follows:*

(a) $E[Z_{N+1}] - E[Z_N] = E[D_{N+1,0}] = \dfrac{d_{N+1}}{1 - \rho_{N+1}}.$

(b) $\mathrm{Var}(Z_{N+1}) - \mathrm{Var}(Z_N) = \Delta(P^{N+1}) - \Delta(P^N) + \mathrm{Var}\left(\sum_{i=1}^{N+1} D_{i,0}\right) - \mathrm{Var}\left(\sum_{i=1}^{N} D_{i,0}\right)$

$$= \frac{2\rho_{N+1}(1 + \rho_{N+1})(1 - \rho_{N+1}^3) + 1}{1 - \rho_{N+1}^2}\sigma_{N+1}^2$$

$$+ 2\sum_{i=1}^{N}\left[\rho_{N+1}^2(1 + \rho_i) + (1 + \rho_{N+1})(1 + \rho_i + \rho_i^2) + \frac{\rho_i^2\rho_{N+1}^2}{1 - \rho_i\rho_{N+1}}\right]\sigma_{i,N+1}.$$

(c) $\Pi(Z_{N+1}) - \Pi(Z_N) = (r - c)\dfrac{d_{N+1}}{1 - \rho_{N+1}}$

$- (p + r)\phi(k)$

$$\cdot\left[\sqrt{\mathrm{Var}(Z_N) + \Delta(P^{N+1}) - \Delta(P^N) + \mathrm{Var}\left(\sum_{i=1}^{N+1} D_{i,0}\right) - \mathrm{Var}\left(\sum_{i=1}^{N} D_{i,0}\right)} - \sqrt{\mathrm{Var}(Z_N)}\right].$$

The proposition offers specific metrics for evaluating the impact of a new client. In particular, adding a new client does not necessarily increase the profit to the supplier. Even if the mean always increases, its variance may also increase more than enough to offset the mean increase. For instance, a client with a demand stream that is positively correlated with the other clients will definitely increase the variance of the orders since the coefficients of σ_{N+1}^2 and $\sigma_{i,N+1}$ are both nonnegative in part (b) of the proposition. Hence, if the increase in the mean demand is not very high, the profits of the supplier can actually decrease by adding the new client to the portfolio.

The increase in the variance to the supplier has two sources: end-consumers and the clients in the middle tier. An inefficient middle-tier company, as well as the volatile market, contributes to the poor performance to the supplier. By contrast, a client who brings complementary demands and is capable of controlling the bullwhip phenomenon represents a *hedging* opportunity to the supplier. His business volume will move in the reverse direction to the business cycle, so it will positively contribute to both the mean and variance of the portfolio.

6.6 Conclusion

In this chapter, we have analyzed upstream volatility in a two-tier supply chain with a supplier serving many clients whose demands are stochastic and are subject to individual trends as well as to the business cycle of the economy. To capture such a demand structure, we have assumed that consumer demands arriving to a client are serially correlated, and that consumer demands facing different clients are also correlated.

In the first part of this chapter, we look at the source of the fluctuation felt by the supplier by analyzing how the volatility is propagated to the upstream through the clients' orders. We observe that the variance of the orders consists of the variance of the total demand of the clients and an additional term that occurs solely due to the first tier of clients, which we call the "middle-tier factor." Hence, depending on the correlation structure, lead times and the clients' individual trends, the middle-tier effect may lead to the bullwhip or the stabilizing effect in this supply chain. Moreover, as the number of clients increases, the correlation structure will be dominant in determining which effect will be present. We see that our results may differ from Lee et al. (1997) due to the correlationship among many clients in the system. As an example, when all clients adjust the order-up-to levels to the observed demand, the stabilizing effect can occur if the client demands are strongly and negatively correlated. However, given that the clients tend to be in the same industrial sector, they are usually subject to the same business cycle and have positively correlated demands. Hence, the bullwhip effect is likely to occur in this supply chain.

In the second part of this chapter, we study how the supplier can build an efficient client portfolio by analyzing the impact of a new client on the expected profit of the supplier in a newsvendor setting. We use this setting due to its natural representation of the trade-off between the mean and variance of the total orders from the clients. We observe that although a new client always increases the mean of the total orders, he may also increase the variance of the orders substantially and actually lead to a decrease in the expected profits of the supplier.

In order to help the supplier in the evaluation of a new client, we provide specific metrics. These metrics point out that the new client's mean demand, his impact on the variance of the existing clients' total demand and his middle-tier factor are important factors to consider for the supplier. The change in the variance of the total demand is governed by the volatility of the new client's consumer market as well as how it is correlated with other clients. Therefore, a large and stable consumer market, a complementary demand pattern to the current client portfolio, and efficient operations to mitigate the bullwhip are the desired attributes for a new client.

Some factors in the model, such as the new client's mean demand and his impact on the variance of the total demand, are static and are largely determined by the nature of the client's business. Others, however, provide opportunities for improvement through the collaboration between the client and the supplier. For example, the middle-tier effect can be reduced by practices such as Vendor-Managed-Inventory (VMI) and Continuous Replenishment Programs (CRP), which eliminate the middle-tier, and information sharing of sell-through and inventory status data, which prevents losing sight of the true demand in the marketplace (Lee et al. 1997). Therefore, the attitude of the potential client toward working closely with the supplier is also an important factor and must be considered by the supplier during the evaluation process.

Appendix

Proof of Lemma 1

Clients' aggregate order is given by

$$\sum_{i=1}^{N} z_{i,1}^* = \sum_{i=1}^{N} \left[\frac{\rho_i(1-\rho_i^{v_i+1})}{1-\rho_i}(D_{i,0} - D_{i,-1}) + D_{i,0} \right]. \tag{6.4}$$

Since $D_{i,t}$ follows an AR(1) process and $-1 < \rho_i < 1$ (which implies that the demand process is weakly stationary (Hamilton 1994)), $E[D_{i,0}] = E[D_{i,-1}] = d_i/(1-\rho_i)$. Therefore,

$$E\left[\sum_{i=1}^{N} z_{i,1}^*\right] = \sum_{i=1}^{N} E[D_{i,0}] = \sum_{i=1}^{N} \frac{d_i}{1-\rho_i}. \tag{6.5}$$

This establishes the first part of the lemma.

Since

$$\begin{aligned}
D_{i,0} - D_{i,-1} &= D_{i,0} - \frac{D_{i,0} - d_i - u_{i,0}}{\rho_i} \\
&= -\left(\frac{1-\rho_i}{\rho_i}\right)D_{i,0} + \frac{d_i + u_{i,0}}{\rho_i},
\end{aligned} \tag{6.6}$$

the variance of both sides of (6.4) can be rewritten as

$$\begin{aligned}
&\mathrm{Var}\left(\sum_{i=1}^{N} z_{i,1}^*\right) \\
&= \mathrm{Var}\left(\sum_{i=1}^{N}\left[-(1-\rho_i^{v_i+1})D_{i,0} + \frac{1-\rho_i^{v_i+1}}{1-\rho_i}d_i + \frac{1-\rho_i^{v_i+1}}{1-\rho_i}u_{i,0} + D_{i,0}\right]\right). \tag{6.7}
\end{aligned}$$

The term $[(1-\rho_i^{v_i+1})/(1-\rho_i)]d_i$ is constant, so it will be omitted in the following steps. This means that the variance of Z_N is independent of the mean of clients' demands (which equals $d_i/(1-\rho_i)$) as long as ρ_i's stay constant.

Expanding (6.7), we get

$$\begin{aligned}
\mathrm{Var}\left(\sum_{i=1}^{N} z_{i,1}^*\right) = &\sum_{i=1}^{N}(1-\rho_i^{v_i+1})^2\,\mathrm{Var}(D_{i,0}) \\
&+ 2\sum_{i=1}^{N}\sum_{j>i}^{N}(1-\rho_i^{v_i+1})(1-\rho_j^{v_j+1})\,\mathrm{Cov}(D_{i,0},D_{j,0}) \\
&- 2\sum_{i=1}^{N}(1-\rho_i^{v_i+1})\frac{1-\rho_i^{v_i+1}}{1-\rho_i}\,\mathrm{Cov}(D_{i,0},u_{i,0})
\end{aligned}$$

$$-2\sum_{i=1}^{N}\sum_{j=1,j\neq i}^{N}(1-\rho_i^{v_i+1})\frac{1-\rho_j^{v_j+1}}{1-\rho_j}\operatorname{Cov}(D_{i,0},u_{j,0})$$

$$-2\sum_{i=1}^{N}(1-\rho_i^{v_i+1})\operatorname{Var}(D_{i,0})$$

$$-2\sum_{i=1}^{N}\sum_{j=1,j\neq i}^{N}(1-\rho_i^{v_i+1})\operatorname{Cov}(D_{i,0},D_{j,0})$$

$$+\sum_{i=1}^{N}\left(\frac{1-\rho_i^{v_i+1}}{1-\rho_i}\right)^2\sigma_i^2$$

$$+2\sum_{i=1}^{N}\sum_{j>i}\left(\frac{1-\rho_i^{v_i+1}}{1-\rho_i}\right)\left(\frac{1-\rho_j^{v_j+1}}{1-\rho_j}\right)\operatorname{Cov}(u_{i,0},u_{j,0})$$

$$+2\sum_{i=1}^{N}\frac{1-\rho_i^{v_i+1}}{1-\rho_i}\operatorname{Cov}(u_{i,0},D_{i,0})$$

$$+2\sum_{i=1}^{N}\sum_{j=1,j\neq i}^{N}\frac{1-\rho_i^{v_i+1}}{1-\rho_i}\operatorname{Cov}(u_{i,0},D_{j,0})+\operatorname{Var}\left(\sum_{i=1}^{N}D_{i,0}\right). \tag{6.8}$$

We divide this expression into three parts, A_N, B_N, and C_N. They are defined as

$$A_N=\sum_{i=1}^{N}(1-\rho_i^{v_i+1})^2\operatorname{Var}(D_{i,0})-2\sum_{i=1}^{N}(1-\rho_i^{v_i+1})\frac{1-\rho_i^{v_i+1}}{1-\rho_i}\operatorname{Cov}(D_{i,0},u_{i,0})$$

$$-2\sum_{i=1}^{N}(1-\rho_i^{v_i+1})\operatorname{Var}(D_{i,0})+\sum_{i=1}^{N}\left(\frac{1-\rho_i^{v_i+1}}{1-\rho_i}\right)^2\sigma_i^2$$

$$+2\sum_{i=1}^{N}\frac{1-\rho_i^{v_i+1}}{1-\rho_i}\operatorname{Cov}(u_{i,0},D_{i,0})+\operatorname{Var}\left(\sum_{i=1}^{N}D_{i,0}\right), \tag{6.9}$$

$$B_N=-2\sum_{i=1}^{N}\sum_{j=1,j\neq i}^{N}(1-\rho_i^{v_i+1})\frac{1-\rho_j^{v_j+1}}{1-\rho_j}\operatorname{Cov}(D_{i,0},u_{j,0})$$

$$+2\sum_{i=1}^{N}\sum_{j>i}\left(\frac{1-\rho_i^{v_i+1}}{1-\rho_i}\right)\left(\frac{1-\rho_j^{v_j+1}}{1-\rho_j}\right)\operatorname{Cov}(u_{i,0},u_{j,0})$$

$$+2\sum_{i=1}^{N}\sum_{j=1,j\neq i}^{N}\frac{1-\rho_i^{v_i+1}}{1-\rho_i}\operatorname{Cov}(u_{i,0},D_{j,0}), \tag{6.10}$$

$$C_N=2\sum_{i=1}^{N}\sum_{j>i}^{N}(1-\rho_i^{v_i+1})(1-\rho_j^{v_j+1})\operatorname{Cov}(D_{i,0},D_{j,0})$$

$$-2\sum_{i=1}^{N}\sum_{j=1,j\neq i}^{N}(1-\rho_i^{v_i+1})\operatorname{Cov}(D_{i,0},D_{j,0}). \tag{6.11}$$

We first simplify A_N, which excludes covariance terms across different clients. Since the process $D_{i,t}$ is weakly stationary, $\mathrm{Var}(D_{i,0}) = \mathrm{Var}(D_{i,-1}) = \sigma_i^2/(1-\rho_i^2)$. Since $D_{i,0} - u_{i,0} = d_i + \rho_i D_{i,-1}$ by (6.1) and we have

$$\mathrm{Var}(D_{i,0} - u_{i,0}) = \mathrm{Var}(D_{i,0}) + \mathrm{Var}(u_{i,0}) - 2\mathrm{Cov}(D_{i,0}, u_{i,0})$$
$$\mathrm{Var}(d_i + \rho_i D_{i,-1}) = \rho_i^2 \mathrm{Var}(D_{i,-1}),$$

$\mathrm{Cov}(D_{i,0}, u_{i,0})$ can be found by equating the right-hand sides of the last two equations given above and equals σ_i^2.

We rewrite (6.9) as

$$A_N = \sum_{i=1}^{N} (1 - \rho_i^{v_i+1})^2 \frac{\sigma_i^2}{1-\rho_i^2} - 2\sum_{i=1}^{N} (1 - \rho_i^{v_i+1}) \frac{1 - \rho_i^{v_i+1}}{1-\rho_i} \sigma_i^2$$
$$- 2\sum_{i=1}^{N} (1 - \rho_i^{v_i+1}) \frac{\sigma_i^2}{1-\rho_i^2} + \sum_{i=1}^{N} \left(\frac{1 - \rho_i^{v_i+1}}{1-\rho_i} \right)^2 \sigma_i^2 + 2\sum_{i=1}^{N} \frac{1 - \rho_i^{v_i+1}}{1-\rho_i} \sigma_i^2$$
$$+ \mathrm{Var}\left(\sum_{i=1}^{N} D_{i,0} \right).$$

We collect the terms involving σ_i^2 in the equation above and obtain

$$\sum_{i=1}^{N} \frac{1 - \rho_i^{v_i+1}}{1-\rho_i} \left[\frac{1 - \rho_i^{v_i+1}}{1+\rho_i} - 2(1 - \rho_i^{v_i+1}) - \frac{2}{1+\rho_i} + \frac{1 - \rho_i^{v_i+1}}{1-\rho_i} + 2 \right] \sigma_i^2$$
$$+ \mathrm{Var}\left(\sum_{i=1}^{N} D_{i,0} \right)$$

$$= \sum_{i=1}^{N} \frac{1 - \rho_i^{v_i+1}}{1-\rho_i} \cdot \frac{1}{1-\rho_i^2} [(1 - \rho_i^{v_i+1})(1 - \rho_i) - 2(1 - \rho_i^{v_i+1})(1 - \rho_i^2)$$
$$- 2(1 - \rho_i) + (1 - \rho_i^{v_i+1})(1 + \rho_i) + 2(1 - \rho_i^2)] \sigma_i^2 + \mathrm{Var}\left(\sum_{i=1}^{N} D_{i,0} \right)$$

$$= \sum_{i=1}^{N} \frac{2\rho_i(1 - \rho_i^{v_i+1})(1 - \rho_i^{v_i+2})}{(1+\rho_i)(1-\rho_i)^2} \sigma_i^2 + \mathrm{Var}\left(\sum_{i=1}^{N} D_{i,0} \right).$$

Now, we simplify B_N. First, we find the value of $\mathrm{Cov}(u_{i,0}, D_{j,0})$. Note that $D_{j,0} = d_j + \rho_j D_{j,-1} + u_{j,0}$ by (6.1) and we have

$$\mathrm{Var}(D_{j,0} + u_{i,0}) = \mathrm{Var}(D_{j,0}) + \mathrm{Var}(u_{i,0}) + 2\mathrm{Cov}(D_{j,0}, u_{i,0})$$
$$= \frac{\sigma_j^2}{1-\rho_j^2} + \sigma_i^2 + 2\mathrm{Cov}(D_{j,0}, u_{i,0})$$

$$\mathrm{Var}(d_j + \rho_j D_{j,-1} + u_{j,0} + u_{i,0}) = \rho_j^2 \frac{\sigma_j^2}{1-\rho_j^2} + \sigma_j^2 + \sigma_i^2 + 2\mathrm{Cov}(u_{j,0}, u_{i,0}).$$

$\text{Cov}(u_{i,0}, D_{j,0})$ can be found by equating the right-hand sides of the last two equations given above and noting that $\text{Cov}(u_{j,0}, u_{i,0}) = \text{Cov}(u_{i,0}, u_{j,0}) = \sigma_{ij}$. Therefore, $\text{Cov}(u_{i,0}, D_{j,0}) = \text{Cov}(D_{j,0}, u_{i,0}) = \text{Cov}(u_{j,0}, u_{i,0}) = \sigma_{ij}$. This also implies that $\text{Cov}(D_{i,0}, u_{j,0}) = \sigma_{ij}$. Then, we rewrite B_N as

$$
\begin{aligned}
B_N = & -2\sum_{i=1}^{N}\sum_{j>i}^{N}\left((1-\rho_i^{v_i+1})\frac{1-\rho_j^{v_j+1}}{1-\rho_j} + (1-\rho_j^{v_j+1})\frac{1-\rho_i^{v_i+1}}{1-\rho_i}\right)\sigma_{ij} \\
& +2\sum_{i=1}^{N}\sum_{j>i}^{N}\left(\frac{1-\rho_i^{v_i+1}}{1-\rho_i}\right)\left(\frac{1-\rho_j^{v_j+1}}{1-\rho_j}\right)\sigma_{ij} \\
& +2\sum_{i=1}^{N}\sum_{j>i}^{N}\left(\frac{1-\rho_i^{v_i+1}}{1-\rho_i} + \frac{1-\rho_j^{v_j+1}}{1-\rho_j}\right)\sigma_{ij} \\
= & 2\sum_{i=1}^{N}\sum_{j>i}^{N}\left[-\frac{1-\rho_i^{v_i+1}}{1-\rho_i}\frac{1-\rho_j^{v_j+1}}{1-\rho_j}(1-\rho_i-\rho_j)\right. \\
& \left. +\frac{1-\rho_i^{v_i+1}}{1-\rho_i} + \frac{1-\rho_j^{v_j+1}}{1-\rho_j}\right]\sigma_{ij}.
\end{aligned}
\tag{6.12}
$$

Finally, we consider C_N. Due to $\text{Cov}(D_{i,0}, D_{j,0}) = \text{Cov}(D_{j,0}, D_{i,0})$,

$$
\begin{aligned}
\sum_{i=1}^{N}\sum_{j=1, j\neq i}^{N}(1-\rho_i^{v_i+1})\text{Cov}(D_{i,0}, D_{j,0}) \\
= \sum_{i=1}^{N}\sum_{j>i}^{N}[(1-\rho_i^{v_i+1}) + (1-\rho_j^{v_j+1})]\text{Cov}(D_{i,0}, D_{j,0}).
\end{aligned}
$$

As a result, we can simplify C_N as

$$
\begin{aligned}
C_N = & 2\sum_{i=1}^{N}\sum_{j>i}^{N}(1-\rho_i^{v_i+1})(1-\rho_j^{v_j+1})\text{Cov}(D_{i,0}, D_{j,0}) \\
& -2\sum_{i=1}^{N}\sum_{j=1, j\neq i}^{N}(1-\rho_i^{v_i+1})\text{Cov}(D_{i,0}, D_{j,0}) \\
= & 2\sum_{i=1}^{N}\sum_{j>i}^{N}\left[(1-\rho_i^{v_i+1})(1-\rho_j^{v_j+1}) - (1-\rho_i^{v_i+1}) - (1-\rho_j^{v_j+1})\right] \\
& \cdot \text{Cov}(D_{i,0}, D_{j,0}).
\end{aligned}
\tag{6.13}
$$

Our stationarity assumption on the covariances of $D_{i,t}$ and $D_{j,t}$ implies that $\text{Cov}(D_{i,0}, D_{j,0}) = \sigma_{ij}/(1-\rho_i\rho_j)$. This can be derived from the relations

$$
\text{Var}(D_{i,0}+D_{j,0}) = \text{Var}(D_{i,0}) + \text{Var}(D_{j,0}) + 2\text{Cov}(D_{i,0}, D_{j,0})
$$

and

$$\mathrm{Var}(D_{i,0}+D_{j,0}) = \mathrm{Var}(\rho_i D_{i,-1}+\rho_j D_{j,-1}+u_{i,0}+u_{j,0})$$
$$= \rho_i^2\,\mathrm{Var}(D_{i,-1})+\rho_j^2\,\mathrm{Var}(D_{j,-1})+\sigma_i^2+\sigma_j^2+2\rho_i\rho_j\,\mathrm{Cov}(D_{i,-1},D_{j,-1})+2\sigma_{ij}.$$

Since last parts of the equalities above must be equal and we have $\mathrm{Cov}(D_{i,0},D_{j,0})=\mathrm{Cov}(D_{i,-1},D_{j,-1})$, $\mathrm{Cov}(D_{i,0},D_{j,0})=\sigma_{ij}/(1-\rho_i\rho_j)$. Therefore,

$$C_N = 2\sum_{i=1}^{N}\sum_{j>i}^{N}\left[(1-\rho_i^{v_i+1})(1-\rho_j^{v_j+1})-(1-\rho_i^{v_i+1})-(1-\rho_j^{v_j+1})\right]$$
$$\cdot\frac{\sigma_{ij}}{1-\rho_i\rho_j}. \tag{6.14}$$

Combining A_N, B_N, and C_N, we get

$$\mathrm{Var}\left(\sum_{i=1}^{N}z_{i,1}^{*}\right) = \sum_{i=1}^{N}\frac{2\rho_i(1-\rho_i^{v_i+1})(1-\rho_i^{v_i+2})}{(1+\rho_i)(1-\rho_i)^2}\sigma_i^2$$
$$+2\sum_{i=1}^{N}\sum_{j>i}^{N}\left[-\frac{1-\rho_i^{v_i+1}}{1-\rho_i}\frac{1-\rho_j^{v_j+1}}{1-\rho_j}(1-\rho_i-\rho_j)+\frac{1-\rho_i^{v_i+1}}{1-\rho_i}\right.$$
$$+\frac{1-\rho_j^{v_j+1}}{1-\rho_j}+\frac{(1-\rho_i^{v_i+1})(1-\rho_j^{v_j+1})}{1-\rho_i\rho_j}$$
$$\left.-\frac{1-\rho_i^{v_i+1}}{1-\rho_i\rho_j}-\frac{1-\rho_j^{v_j+1}}{1-\rho_i\rho_j}\right]\sigma_{ij}+\mathrm{Var}\left(\sum_{i=1}^{N}D_{i,0}\right). \tag{6.15}$$

We can simplify the second term on the right-hand side of the equation above. Subtracting $(1-\rho_i^{v_i+1})/(1-\rho_i\rho_j)$ from $(1-\rho_i^{v_i+1})/(1-\rho_i)$, we get

$$\frac{1-\rho_i^{v_i+1}}{1-\rho_i}-\frac{1-\rho_i^{v_i+1}}{1-\rho_i\rho_j}=(1-\rho_i^{v_i+1})\left(\frac{1}{1-\rho_i}-\frac{1}{1-\rho_i\rho_j}\right)=\frac{(1-\rho_i^{v_i+1})\rho_i(1-\rho_j)}{(1-\rho_i)(1-\rho_i\rho_j)}.$$

Similarly,

$$\frac{1-\rho_j^{v_j+1}}{1-\rho_j}-\frac{1-\rho_j^{v_j+1}}{1-\rho_i\rho_j}=\frac{(1-\rho_j^{v_j+1})\rho_j(1-\rho_i)}{(1-\rho_j)(1-\rho_i\rho_j)}.$$

We can also rewrite

$$-\frac{1-\rho_i^{v_i+1}}{1-\rho_i}\frac{1-\rho_j^{v_j+1}}{1-\rho_j}(1-\rho_i-\rho_j)+\frac{(1-\rho_i^{v_i+1})(1-\rho_j^{v_j+1})}{1-\rho_i\rho_j}$$

as

$$(1-\rho_i^{v_i+1})(1-\rho_j^{v_j+1})\left(-\frac{1-\rho_i-\rho_j}{(1-\rho_i)(1-\rho_j)}+\frac{1}{1-\rho_i\rho_j}\right)$$

$$=(1-\rho_i^{v_i+1})(1-\rho_j^{v_j+1})\frac{-(1-\rho_i-\rho_j)(1-\rho_i\rho_j)+1-\rho_i-\rho_j+\rho_i\rho_j}{(1-\rho_i)(1-\rho_j)(1-\rho_i\rho_j)}$$

$$=(1-\rho_i^{v_i+1})(1-\rho_j^{v_j+1})\frac{\rho_i\rho_j((1-\rho_i)+(1-\rho_j))}{(1-\rho_i)(1-\rho_j)(1-\rho_i\rho_j)}.$$

Then, $\mathrm{Var}(\sum_{i=1}^{N}z_{i,1}^{*})$ can be further simplified as

$$\mathrm{Var}\left(\sum_{i=1}^{N}z_{i,1}^{*}\right)=\sum_{i=1}^{N}\frac{2\rho_i(1-\rho_i^{v_i+1})(1-\rho_i^{v_i+2})}{(1+\rho_i)(1-\rho_i)^2}\sigma_i^2 \tag{6.16}$$

$$+2\sum_{i=1}^{N}\sum_{j>i}^{N}\frac{1}{(1-\rho_i)(1-\rho_j)(1-\rho_i\rho_j)}$$

$$\cdot\Big[(1-\rho_i^{v_i+1})(1-\rho_j^{v_j+1})\rho_i\rho_j((1-\rho_i)+(1-\rho_j))$$

$$+(1-\rho_i^{v_i+1})\rho_i(1-\rho_j)^2+(1-\rho_j^{v_j+1})\rho_j(1-\rho_i)^2\Big]\sigma_{ij}$$

$$+\mathrm{Var}\left(\sum_{i=1}^{N}D_{i,0}\right). \tag{6.17}$$

Since

$$(1-\rho_i^{v_i+1})(1-\rho_j^{v_j+1})\rho_i\rho_j(1-\rho_j)+(1-\rho_i^{v_i+1})\rho_i(1-\rho_j)^2$$

$$=(1-\rho_i^{v_i+1})(1-\rho_j)\rho_i((1-\rho_j^{v_j+1})\rho_j+1-\rho_j)$$

$$=(1-\rho_i^{v_i+1})(1-\rho_j^{v_j+2})\rho_i(1-\rho_j)$$

and, by symmetry,

$$(1-\rho_i^{v_i+1})(1-\rho_j^{v_j+1})\rho_i\rho_j(1-\rho_i)+(1-\rho_j^{v_j+1})\rho_j(1-\rho_i)^2$$

$$=(1-\rho_j^{v_j+1})(1-\rho_i^{v_i+2})\rho_j(1-\rho_i),$$

$\mathrm{Var}(\sum_{i=1}^{N}z_{i,1}^{*})$ is given by

$$\mathrm{Var}\left(\sum_{i=1}^{N}z_{i,1}^{*}\right)=\sum_{i=1}^{N}\frac{2\rho_i(1-\rho_i^{v_i+1})(1-\rho_i^{v_i+2})}{(1+\rho_i)(1-\rho_i)^2}\sigma_i^2$$

$$+2\sum_{i=1}^{N}\sum_{j>i}^{N}\frac{1}{(1-\rho_i)(1-\rho_j)(1-\rho_i\rho_j)}$$

$$\cdot\Big[(1-\rho_i^{v_i+1})(1-\rho_j^{v_j+2})\rho_i(1-\rho_j)$$

$$+(1-\rho_j^{v_j+1})(1-\rho_i^{v_i+2})\rho_j(1-\rho_i)\Big]\sigma_{ij}$$

$$+ \text{Var}\left(\sum_{i=1}^{N} D_{i,0}\right). \tag{6.18}$$

The sum of the first two terms equal to $\Delta(\rho, \Sigma, v)$ and is the difference between $\text{Var}(\sum_{i=1}^{N} z_{i,1}^*)$ and $\text{Var}(\sum_{i=1}^{N} D_{i,0})$. Also,

$$\text{Var}\left(\sum_{i=1}^{N} D_{i,0}\right) = \sum_{i=1}^{N} \frac{\sigma_i^2}{1-\rho_i^2} + 2\sum_{i=1}^{N}\sum_{j>i}^{N} \frac{\sigma_{ij}}{1-\rho_i\rho_j}.$$

This completes the second part of the lemma.

We use (6.18) to find $\text{Cov}(z_{i,1}^*, z_{j,1}^*)$. By (6.16), $\text{Var}(z_{i,1}^* + z_{j,1}^*)$ equals

$$\text{Var}(z_{i,1}^* + z_{j,1}^*) = \frac{2\rho_i(1-\rho_i^{v_i+1})(1-\rho_i^{v_i+2})}{(1+\rho_i)(1-\rho_i)^2}\sigma_i^2 + \frac{2\rho_j(1-\rho_j^{v_j+1})(1-\rho_j^{v_j+2})}{(1+\rho_j)(1-\rho_j)^2}\sigma_j^2$$

$$+2\frac{1}{(1-\rho_i)(1-\rho_j)(1-\rho_i\rho_j)}\left[(1-\rho_i^{v_i+1})(1-\rho_j^{v_j+2})\rho_i(1-\rho_j)\right.$$

$$\left. +(1-\rho_j^{v_j+1})(1-\rho_i^{v_i+2})\rho_j(1-\rho_i)\right]\sigma_{ij}$$

$$+\frac{\sigma_i^2}{1-\rho_i^2} + \frac{\sigma_j^2}{1-\rho_j^2} + 2\frac{\sigma_{ij}}{1-\rho_i\rho_j}. \tag{6.19}$$

$\text{Var}(z_{i,1}^* + z_{j,1}^*)$ also equals

$$\text{Var}(z_{i,1}^* + z_{j,1}^*) = \text{Var}(z_{i,1}^*) + \text{Var}(z_{j,1}^*) + 2\,\text{Cov}(z_{i,1}^*, z_{j,1}^*). \tag{6.20}$$

Noting that

$$\text{Var}(z_{i,1}^*) = \frac{2\rho_i(1-\rho_i^{v_i+1})(1-\rho_i^{v_i+2})}{(1+\rho_i)(1-\rho_i)^2}\sigma_i^2 + \text{Var}(D_{i,0})$$

and equating (6.19) and (6.20), we get

$$\text{Cov}(z_{i,1}^*, z_{j,1}^*) = \sigma_{ij}\left[\frac{1}{1-\rho_i\rho_j}\right.$$

$$\left. +\frac{(1-\rho_i^{v_i+1})(1-\rho_j^{v_j+2})\rho_i(1-\rho_j)+(1-\rho_j^{v_j+1})(1-\rho_i^{v_i+2})\rho_j(1-\rho_i)}{(1-\rho_i)(1-\rho_j)(1-\rho_i\rho_j)}\right]. \tag{6.21}$$

Proof of Lemma 2

Using (6.3) and (6.6) and noting that $V_i = 1$ for all i, we can write $z_{i,1}^*$ as

$$z_{i,1}^* = \rho_i^2 D_{i,0} + (1+\rho_i)d_i + (1+\rho_i)u_{i,0} \tag{6.22}$$

Following the notation in Hamilton (1994), we expand $D_{i,0}$ in terms of $u_{i,t}$ as

$$D_{i,0} = \frac{d_i}{1-\rho_i} + \sum_{k=0}^{\infty} \rho_i^k u_{i,-k}.$$

Therefore,

$$z_{i,1}^* = \rho_i^2 \frac{d_i}{1-\rho_i} + \rho_i^2 \sum_{k=0}^{\infty} \rho_i^k u_{i,-k} + (1+\rho_i)d_i + (1+\rho_i)u_{i,0}$$

$$= \frac{d_i}{1-\rho_i} + \sum_{k=1}^{\infty} \rho_i^{k+2} u_{i,-k} + (1+\rho_i+\rho_i^2)u_{i,0}.$$

Since $Z_N = \sum_{i=1}^{N} z_{i,1}^*$, we can write Z_N as

$$Z_N = \sum_{i=1}^{N} \left[\frac{d_i}{1-\rho_i} + \sum_{k=1}^{\infty} \rho_i^{k+2} u_{i,-k} + (1+\rho_i+\rho_i^2)u_{i,0} \right]$$

$$= \sum_{i=1}^{N} \frac{d_i}{1-\rho_i} + \sum_{k=1}^{\infty} \sum_{i=1}^{N} \rho_i^{k+2} u_{i,-k} + \sum_{i=1}^{N} (1+\rho_i+\rho_i^2)u_{i,0}. \tag{6.23}$$

Define S_k as

$$S_k = \begin{cases} \sum_{i=1}^{N}(1+\rho_i+\rho_i^2)u_{i,0} & \text{if } k=0 \\ \sum_{i=1}^{N} \rho_i^{k+2} u_{i,-k} & \text{if } k>0. \end{cases}$$

S_k follows a normal distribution since U_t follows a multivariate normal distribution and therefore, any linear combination of its components must also be normally distributed. Hence, the sum of S_k's are also normally distributed since U_t at each t is independent from each other. This proves that Z_N is normally distributed with $N(\mu, s^2)$.

The mean and the variance of Z_N are provided in Lemma 1. Therefore,

$$\mu = E[Z_N] = \sum_{i=1}^{N} \frac{d_i}{1-\rho_i} \quad \text{and}$$

$$s^2 = \text{Var}(Z_N) = \Delta(P^N) + \sum_{i=1}^{N} \frac{\sigma_i^2}{1-\rho_i^2} + 2\sum_{i=1}^{N}\sum_{j>i}^{N} \frac{\sigma_{ij}}{1-\rho_i\rho_j}.$$

Proof of Proposition 2

By Part 1 of Lemma 1, $E[Z_N] = \sum_{i=1}^{N} E[D_{i,0}]$ and $E[Z_{N+1}] = \sum_{i=1}^{N+1} E[D_{i,0}]$. Then, it is straightforward to show that

$$E[Z_{N+1}] - E[Z_N] = E[D_{N+1,0}] = \frac{d_{N+1}}{1 - \rho_{N+1}}.$$

The difference of the variance between old and new client portfolios is given by

$$\text{Var}\left(\sum_{i=1}^{N+1} z_{i,1}^*\right) - \text{Var}\left(\sum_{i=1}^{N} z_{i,1}^*\right)$$

$$= \Delta(P^{N+1}) - \Delta(P^N) + \text{Var}\left(\sum_{i=1}^{N+1} D_{i,0}\right) - \text{Var}\left(\sum_{i=1}^{N} D_{i,0}\right)$$

$$= \Delta(P^{N+1}) - \Delta(P^N) + \text{Var}(D_{N+1,0}) + 2\sum_{i=1}^{N} \text{Cov}(D_{i,0}, D_{N+1,0}).$$

$\text{Cov}(D_{i,0}, D_{j,0}) = \sigma_{ij}/(1 - \rho_i\rho_j)$ as demonstrated in Lemma 1. Then,

$$\text{Var}(D_{N+1,0}) + 2\sum_{i=1}^{N} \text{Cov}(D_{i,0}, D_{N+1,0}) = \frac{\sigma_{N+1}^2}{1 - \rho_{N+1}^2} + 2\sum_{i=1}^{N} \frac{\sigma_{i,N+1}}{1 - \rho_i\rho_{N+1}}. \quad (6.24)$$

We use (6.15) in order to simplify $\Delta(P^N)$ when all lead times are equal to 1:

$$\Delta(P^N) = \text{Var}\left(\sum_{i=1}^{N} z_{i,1}^*\right) - \text{Var}\left(\sum_{i=1}^{N} D_{i,0}\right) = \sum_{i=1}^{N} \frac{2\rho_i(1 - \rho_i^2)(1 - \rho_i^3)}{(1 + \rho_i)(1 - \rho_i)^2}\sigma_i^2$$

$$+ 2\sum_{i=1}^{N}\sum_{j>i}^{N}\left[-(1 + \rho_i)(1 + \rho_j)(1 - \rho_i - \rho_j) + (1 + \rho_i) + (1 + \rho_j)\right.$$

$$\left. + \frac{(1 - \rho_i^2)(1 - \rho_j^2)}{1 - \rho_i\rho_j} - \frac{1 - \rho_i^2}{1 - \rho_i\rho_j} - \frac{1 - \rho_j^2}{1 - \rho_i\rho_j}\right]\sigma_{ij}.$$

The second part of the above expression can be rewritten as

$$\left[-(1 + \rho_i)(1 + \rho_j)(1 - \rho_i - \rho_j) + (1 + \rho_i) + (1 + \rho_j)\right.$$

$$\left. + \frac{(1 - \rho_i^2)(1 - \rho_j^2)}{1 - \rho_i\rho_j} - \frac{1 - \rho_i^2}{1 - \rho_i\rho_j} - \frac{1 - \rho_j^2}{1 - \rho_i\rho_j}\right]\sigma_{ij}$$

$$= \left[(1 + \rho_i)\left(1 - (1 + \rho_j)(1 - \rho_i - \rho_j)\right) + (1 + \rho_j) - \frac{1 - \rho_i^2\rho_j^2}{1 - \rho_i\rho_j}\right]\sigma_{ij}$$

$$= \left[(1 + \rho_i)\left(1 - (1 - \rho_j^2) + \rho_i(1 + \rho_j)\right) + (1 + \rho_j) - \frac{1 - \rho_i^2\rho_j^2}{1 - \rho_i\rho_j}\right]\sigma_{ij}$$

$$= \left[(1 + \rho_i)\rho_j^2 + (1 + \rho_i)\rho_i(1 + \rho_j) + (1 + \rho_j) - \frac{1 - \rho_i^2\rho_j^2}{1 - \rho_i\rho_j}\right]\sigma_{ij}$$

$$= \left[\rho_j^2(1 + \rho_i) + (1 + \rho_j)(1 + \rho_i + \rho_i^2) - \frac{1 - \rho_i^2\rho_j^2}{1 - \rho_i\rho_j}\right]\sigma_{ij}.$$

Therefore,

$$\Delta(P^N) = \sum_{i=1}^{N} \frac{2\rho_i(1-\rho_i^2)(1-\rho_i^3)}{(1+\rho_i)(1-\rho_i)^2}\sigma_i^2$$

$$+2\sum_{i=1}^{N}\sum_{j>i}^{N}\left[\rho_j^2(1+\rho_i)+(1+\rho_j)(1+\rho_i+\rho_i^2)-\frac{1-\rho_i^2\rho_j^2}{1-\rho_i\rho_j}\right]\sigma_{ij}. \quad (6.25)$$

That gives

$$\Delta(P^{N+1}) - \Delta(P^N) = \frac{2\rho_{N+1}(1-\rho_{N+1}^2)(1-\rho_{N+1}^3)}{(1+\rho_{N+1})(1-\rho_{N+1})^2}\sigma_{N+1}^2$$

$$+2\sum_{i=1}^{N}\left[\rho_{N+1}^2(1+\rho_i)+(1+\rho_{N+1})(1+\rho_i+\rho_i^2)-\frac{1-\rho_i^2\rho_{N+1}^2}{1-\rho_i\rho_{N+1}}\right]\sigma_{i,N+1}.$$

Combining $\Delta(P^{N+1}) - \Delta(P^N)$ with (6.24), we get

$$\text{Var}\left(\sum_{i=1}^{N+1} z_{i,1}^*\right) - \text{Var}\left(\sum_{i=1}^{N} z_{i,1}^*\right) = \frac{2\rho_{N+1}(1+\rho_{N+1})(1-\rho_{N+1}^3)+1}{1-\rho_{N+1}^2}\sigma_{N+1}^2$$

$$+2\sum_{i=1}^{N}\left[\rho_{N+1}^2(1+\rho_i)+(1+\rho_{N+1})(1+\rho_i+\rho_i^2)+\frac{\rho_i^2\rho_{N+1}^2}{1-\rho_i\rho_{N+1}}\right]\sigma_{i,N+1}.$$

This completes the second part of the proposition. One point to note is that the coefficients of σ_{N+1}^2 and $\sigma_{i,N+1}$ are both nonnegative. It is straightforward to show that the coefficient of $\sigma_{i,N+1}$ is nonnegative. The fact that the coefficient of σ_{N+1}^2 is also nonnegative can be best seen from

$$2\rho_{N+1}(1+\rho_{N+1})(1-\rho_{N+1}^3)+1 = 2\rho_{N+1}(1-\rho_{N+1}^2)(1+\rho_{N+1}+\rho_{N+1}^2)+1$$

$$= 2\rho_{N+1}(1-\rho_{N+1}^2)+2\rho_{N+1}^2(1-\rho_{N+1}^2)(1+\rho_{N+1})+1.$$

The second term in the last equality is nonnegative. The first term, $2\rho_{N+1} \cdot (1-\rho_{N+1}^2)$ is minimized at $\rho_{N+1} = -1/\sqrt{3}$ and equals $-4/(3\sqrt{3})$ at this point. Since $1 - 4/(3\sqrt{3})$ is positive, the coefficient of σ_i^2 must be nonnegative.

Since Z_N and Z_{N+1} are normally distributed,

$$\Pi(Z_N) = (r-c)E[Z_N] - \sqrt{\text{Var}(Z_N)}(p+r)\phi(k) \quad \text{and}$$

$$\Pi(Z_N) = (r-c)E[Z_{N+1}] - \sqrt{\text{Var}(Z_{N+1})}(p+r)\phi(k)$$

where $k = \Phi^{-1}((p+r-c)/(p+r))$. Using the formulas we found in parts (a) and (b), we see that

$$\Pi(Z_{N+1}) - \Pi(Z_N) = (r-c)\frac{d_{N+1}}{1-\rho_{N+1}} - (p+r)\phi(k)$$

$$\cdot \left[\sqrt{\text{Var}(Z_N) + \Delta(P^{N+1}) - \Delta(P^N) + \text{Var}\left(\sum_{i=1}^{N+1} D_{i,0}\right) - \text{Var}\left(\sum_{i=1}^{N} D_{i,0}\right)} - \sqrt{\text{Var}(Z_N)} \right].$$

References

Baganha MP, Cohen MA (1998) The stabilizing effect of inventory in supply chains. Operations Research 46(3):72–83

Berinato S (2001) What Went Wrong at Cisco? CIO Magazine, August 1

Brumelle SL, McGill JI (1993) Airline seat allocation with multiple nested fare classes. Operations Research 41(1):127–137

Forrester JW (1961) Industrial Dynamics. MIT Press, Cambridge, MA

Hamilton JD (1994) Time Series Analysis. Princeton University Press, Princeton

Kelly K, Maulloo AK, Tan DKH (1998) Rate control in communication networks: Shadow prices, proportional fairness, and stability. Journal of the Operational Research Society 49:237–252

Lee H, Padmanabhan V, Whang S (1997) Information distortion in a supply chain: The bullwhip effect. Management Science 43(4):546–558

Lee H, Whang S (2005) The bullwhip effect: A review of field study. In O. Carranza Torres and F. Villegas Moran, eds. The Bullwhip Effect in Supply Chains: A Review of Methods, Components and Cases. Palgrave Macmillan, New York

Porteus EL (2002) Foundations of Stochastic Inventory Theory. Stanford University Press, California

Carr S, Lovejoy W (2000) The inverse newsvendor problem: choosing an optimal demand portfolio for capacitated resources. Management Science 46(7):912–927

Sterman J (1989) Modeling managerial behavior: Misperception of feedback in a dynamic decision making experiment. Management Science 35:321–339

Talluri KT, van Ryzin G (2004) The Theory and Practice of Revenue Management. Kluwer Academic Publishers, Norwell

Wilson RB (1993) Nonlinear Pricing. Oxford University Press, Oxford

Chapter 7
Strategic Customer Behavior and the Benefit of Decentralization

Xuanming Su and Fuqiang Zhang

Abstract In the operations management literature, decentralization is often associated with the double marginalization problem. However, in this chapter, we review several existing papers that demonstrate how decentralization can be beneficial to supply chain performance. A key premise in this literature is that consumers are *strategic*: They rationally anticipate and respond to future market conditions. We consider two broad classes of products, durable goods and perishable goods. In both cases, when facing strategic consumers, firms are typically better off if they can commit to future actions. When operating in a decentralized supply chain, contractual mechanisms can help firms achieve commitment power and increase profits. In this way, decentralized systems can outperform a centralized organization.

7.1 Introduction

Conventional wisdom in the operations management literature suggests that decentralized supply chains are inefficient. Under decentralization, individual firms in the supply chain (such as manufacturers, distributors, wholesalers, and retailers) make operational decisions with different and possibly conflicting objectives. In particular, double marginalization is a well-known problem that arises in decentralized supply chains. Much work has been done to rectify the double marginalization problem and to "coordinate" the supply chain. One major goal of contemporary

Xuanming Su
The Haas School of Business, University of California, Berkeley, Berkeley, CA 94720, USA,
e-mail: xuanming@haas.berkeley.edu, faculty.haas.berkeley.edu/xuanming/

Fuqiang Zhang
Olin Business School, Washington University in St. Louis, St. Louis, MO 63130, USA,
e-mail: fzhang22@wustl.edu, www.olin.wustl.edu/faculty/zhang/

S. Netessine, C.S. Tang (eds.), *Consumer-Driven Demand and Operations Management*   177
Models, International Series in Operations Research & Management Science 131,
DOI 10.1007/978-0-387-98026-3_7, © Springer Science+Business Media, LLC 2009

supply chain research has been to design economic mechanisms in order to achieve the benchmark performance of a centralized system. When all decision rights are concentrated in the hands of a single party, there is no incentive misalignment, and economic inefficiencies can be reduced or even eliminated. It is thus no wonder that centralized systems have served as gold standard for many research studies, while decentralization has been associated with a myriad of coordination problems. In this chapter, we wish to present a different perspective. We will show, through some specific settings, that decentralization can sometimes enhance supply chain performance.

One fundamental premise in this chapter is that consumers are strategic. In particular, we will consider dynamic settings (in their simplest form, two-period models) where consumers are capable of rationally anticipating future market conditions, such as prices. Interestingly, modeling such strategic consumer behavior often adds a novel twist to existing operations models. These new models generate new insights – specifically, in this chapter, we will see that decentralization (such as selling through an intermediary) can be beneficial when facing strategic consumers.

We will focus on two broad classes of products: durable goods and perishable goods. Durable goods refer to products whose consumption value persists over long time horizons. Examples include automobiles, furniture, and TV sets. In some cases, there are well-established secondary markets with used products that compete with the supply chain's new products. Such cannibalization is particularly severe when consumers are strategic and can optimally choose whether to purchase a new product or to wait for a used product from the secondary market. We shall see in this chapter that for durable goods, decentralization can be a useful supply chain strategy.

The second class of products that we will consider is perishable goods. They refer to items that have a short product life cycle and have little to no value afterward. Examples include fashion items (which become out of date quickly) as well as hi-tech products (which become obsolete quickly). In these cases, retailers and manufacturers have an incentive to offer deep discounts toward the end of the selling season in order to sell off excess inventory. While perfectly legitimate from an operational standpoint, price markdowns inevitably train consumers to wait for sales and have a negative impact on demand. When facing such strategic consumer behavior, decentralization again serves a useful purpose that we shall explore in this chapter.

In today's markets, durable goods and perishable goods are everywhere. Further, consumers are becoming increasingly sophisticated as they enjoy access to better information and decision aids over the Internet. In such settings, strategic decentralization will be a useful concept for operations management.

7.2 Durable Goods

The essence of most durable goods models can be captured using a simple two-period model. The analysis in this section is based on the papers by Bulow (1982), Desai et al. (2004) and Arya and Mittendorf (2006), which also contain some generalizations and more details. Here we make a number of simplifying assumptions to make the key insights more transparent. We begin with a centralized system before moving on to consider a decentralized system consisting of a manufacturer and a retailer.

7.2.1 Centralized System

7.2.1.1 Benchmark Model

Consider a centralized seller who operates over two time periods. The seller sells a durable good over both periods. The durable good lasts for both periods and provides consumption value in both periods. In each period $t = 1, 2$, the consumption value (for that period) is given by the following linear demand curve:

$$V_t = \alpha - \beta Q_t, \tag{7.1}$$

where Q_t is the total available quantity in that period. There is a perfect secondary market. We assume that old products are indistinguishable from and thus compete perfectly with new products. We use q_t to denote the number of new units produced in period t, so the cumulative available quantities Q_t satisfies $Q_1 = q_1$ and $Q_2 = q_1 + q_2$. In other words, the consumer who buys the product in period 2 earns utility V_2 and is thus willing to pay $p_2 = V_2$ as given by

$$p_2 = \alpha - \beta(q_1 + q_2), \tag{7.2}$$

while the consumer who buys in period 1 earns total utility $V_1 + V_2$ and is thus willing to pay $p_1 = V_1 + V_2$ as given by

$$p_1 = [\alpha - \beta q_1] + [\alpha - \beta(q_1 + q_2)]. \tag{7.3}$$

Then, normalizing production costs to zero, the seller's profit function can be written as

$$\Pi(q_1, q_2) = p_1 q_1 + p_2 q_2 \tag{7.4}$$
$$= \{[\alpha - \beta q_1] + [\alpha - \beta(q_1 + q_2)]\}q_1 + [\alpha - \beta(q_1 + q_2)]q_2, \tag{7.5}$$

which attains the maximum at

$$q_1^* = \frac{\alpha}{2\beta}, \qquad q_2^* = 0. \tag{7.6}$$

In this benchmark scenario, the centralized seller's optimal profit is

$$\Pi^* = \frac{\alpha^2}{2\beta}. \tag{7.7}$$

7.2.1.2 Strategic Consumers and the Lack of Commitment

Unfortunately, in the presence of so-called strategic consumers, the benchmark profit level above cannot be attained. This is because consumers are able to look ahead and anticipate all occurrences on the equilibrium path. We first explain why the benchmark solution above is not subgame perfect and then proceed to derive the subgame perfect outcome.

In the benchmark scenario above, the seller maximizes total profit $\Pi(q_1, q_2)$ by setting $q_1^* = \alpha/(2\beta)$ and $q_2^* = 0$. However, these actions are not subgame perfect. At the end of period 1, if q_1^* units have indeed been sold, then the seller's period 2 profit function becomes

$$\Pi_2(q_2) = [\alpha - \beta(q_1^* + q_2)]q_2, \tag{7.8}$$

which is maximized at $q_2 = (\alpha)/(2\beta) - (q_1^*)/2 = \alpha/(4\beta) > 0$. In other words, when period 2 arrives, the seller has the incentive to sell additional units, which decreases the consumption value in period 2. Recognizing such behavior, consumers' willingness to pay in period 1 will be decreased. The benchmark outcome is thus not attainable.

However, if the seller were able to commit to period 2 production quantity q_2 in advance (i.e., in period 1), then the analysis in the previous subsection holds and the benchmark profit is attainable. For this reason, we may also refer to the benchmark scenario as the "commitment scenario".

Next, we proceed to analyze the subgame perfect equilibrium when the seller is unable to commit and consumers are strategic. We use backward induction. Suppose that q_1 units were sold in period 1. Then, following the logic leading to the profit function in (7.8), we know that the seller's optimal period 2 response is to sell

$$q_2(q_1) = \frac{\alpha}{2\beta} - \frac{q_1}{2}. \tag{7.9}$$

Along the equilibrium path, q_1 and q_2 cannot be chosen freely; rather, choosing q_1 necessarily leads to $q_2(q_1)$ in period 2. Therefore, the seller's profit function (7.5) can be written in terms of q_1 only. After some calculations, we obtain the subgame perfect equilibrium

$$q_1^* = \frac{2\alpha}{5\beta}, \qquad q_2^* = \frac{3\alpha}{10\beta}. \tag{7.10}$$

In this case, the seller's total equilibrium profit is

$$\Pi^* = \frac{9\alpha^2}{20\beta}. \tag{7.11}$$

Notice that this equilibrium profit is lower than the benchmark case where either the seller can commit or consumers are not strategic. This is precisely the durability problem first discussed by Coase (1972), who observed that durable goods monopolies, through competition with their future selves, lose market power and may even be forced to price at marginal cost in some extreme cases.

7.2.2 Decentralized System

7.2.2.1 Wholesale Price Contract

Next, we turn attention to a decentralized system consisting of a manufacturer and a retailer. As in the previous case, we assume that consumers are strategic and firms are unable to commit to future actions. Our goal is to set up the analytical framework to study equilibrium actions of all players over the two time periods. Here, we first focus on the wholesale price contract. That is, the manufacturer sells to the retailer at a per unit wholesale price, and the retailer then sells to consumers. As before, the manufacturer's production cost is normalized to zero.

To use the backward-induction approach, we first suppose that q_1 units were produced in period 1 and the manufacturer sets the period 2 wholesale price to be w_2. Given these inputs, the retailer chooses quantity q_2 to maximize his period 2 profits

$$\Pi_2(q_2) = [\alpha - \beta(q_1 + q_2)]q_2 - w_2 q_2. \tag{7.12}$$

The optimal choice of q_2 is

$$q_2(q_1, w_2) = \frac{\alpha}{2\beta} - \frac{q_1}{2} - \frac{w_2}{2\beta}. \tag{7.13}$$

Anticipating this response, the manufacturer chooses the period 2 wholesale price w_2 to maximize his own period 2 profits $w_2 \cdot q_2(q_1, w_2)$. The manufacturer's optimal wholesale price w_2 and the retailer's corresponding production quantity q_2 in period 2, given q_1, turn out to be

$$w_2(q_1) = \frac{\alpha}{2} - \frac{\beta q_1}{2}, \qquad q_2(q_1) = \frac{\alpha}{4\beta} - \frac{q_1}{4}. \tag{7.14}$$

Next, we consider period 1. Suppose the manufacturer sets the wholesale price w_1. Then, the retailer's total profit function, similar to (7.5), is

$$\Pi(q_1) = \{[\alpha - \beta q_1] + [\alpha - \beta(q_1 + q_2)]\}q_1$$
$$+ [\alpha - \beta(q_1 + q_2)]q_2 - w_1 q_1 - w_2 q_2, \tag{7.15}$$

where q_2 and w_2 depend on q_1 as given above. The retailer's optimal period 1 response is

$$q_1(w_1) = \frac{13\alpha}{27\beta} - \frac{8w_1}{27\beta}. \tag{7.16}$$

Anticipating this response, the manufacturer sets the optimal w_1 to maximize his total profits $w_1q_1 + w_2q_2$. It can be shown that the equilibrium wholesale prices and production quantities are

$$q_1^* = \frac{11\alpha}{52\beta}, \qquad q_2^* = \frac{41\alpha}{208\beta}, \tag{7.17}$$

$$w_1^* = \frac{379\alpha}{416}, \qquad w_2^* = \frac{41\alpha}{104}. \tag{7.18}$$

The corresponding total supply chain profit is

$$\Pi^* = \frac{17,671\alpha^2}{43,264\beta} \approx 0.408\frac{\alpha^2}{\beta}. \tag{7.19}$$

Notice that the total system profit here is lower compared to that of the centralized case, even when the seller is unable to commit. In other words, the double marginalization problem is in effect here. For the case of durable goods, under a simple wholesale price contract, decentralization involves economic inefficiencies.

7.2.2.2 Two-Part Tariffs

It is well known that two-part tariffs can rectify the double marginalization problem. Now, we consider the same decentralized system as above, but we allow the manufacturer to charge the retailer a two-part tariff. In other words, apart from a fixed fee, the manufacturer also charges the retailer a fixed per unit wholesale price.

We first consider period 2. Suppose that q_1 units were already sold in period 1. Let us denote the wholesale price by w_2 and the fixed fee by F_2. Since the fixed fee does not influence the retailer's actions, the retailer's optimal choice of $q_2 = \alpha/(2\beta) - q_1/2 - w_2/(2\beta)$ remains unchanged, as given in (7.13). Now, the manufacturer can set the fixed fee high enough to extract the entire channel profit. In other words, the manufacturer would like to set w_2 to maximize

$$\Pi_2(w_2) = [\alpha - \beta(q_1 + q_2)]q_2. \tag{7.20}$$

The total channel profits for period 2 is maximized when the retailer is induced to choose $q_2 = \alpha/(2\beta) - q_1/2$. This corresponds to $w_2 = 0$, which is thus the manufacturer's optimal choice.

Next, we consider period 1. Suppose the manufacturer offers a wholesale price w_1 and fixed fee F_1 to the retailer. Since the retailer anticipates zero period 2 surplus, he will choose q_1 to maximize his period 1 profit given by

$$\Pi_1(q_1) = \{[\alpha - \beta q_1] + [\alpha - \beta(q_1 + q_2)]\}q_1 - w_1q_1. \tag{7.21}$$

The optimal choice of q_1 is $q_1(w_1) = \alpha/(2\beta) - w_1/(3\beta)$. Recognizing this response and using the fixed fee to extract the total supply chain profit in both periods, the manufacturer will then choose the wholesale price w_1 to maximize

$$\Pi(w_1) = \{[\alpha - \beta q_1] + [\alpha - \beta(q_1 + q_2)]\}q_1 + [\alpha - \beta(q_1 + q_2)]q_2. \qquad (7.22)$$

Since $q_2 = \alpha/(2\beta) - q_1/2$, this becomes

$$\Pi(w_1) = \frac{3}{2}(\alpha - \beta q_1)q_1 + \frac{1}{4\beta}(\alpha - \beta q_1)^2, \qquad (7.23)$$

where $q_1(w_1) = \alpha/(2\beta) - w_1/(3\beta)$. Consistent with (7.10), this is maximized at $q_1 = (2\alpha)/(5\beta)$, which corresponds to an optimal period 1 wholesale price of $w_1 = (3\alpha)/10$. In summary, with two-part tariffs, the equilibrium wholesale prices and quantities are

$$q_1^* = \frac{2\alpha}{5\beta}, \qquad q_2^* = \frac{3\alpha}{10\beta}, \qquad (7.24)$$

$$w_1^* = \frac{3\alpha}{10}, \qquad w_2^* = 0. \qquad (7.25)$$

The total supply chain profit is given by

$$\Pi^* = \frac{9\alpha^2}{20\beta}.$$

This analysis shows that with two-part tariffs, a decentralized system can attain the performance of a centralized system, as in (7.11). In familiar terminology, the system is coordinated. However, since the equilibrium profit is still below the benchmark profit (7.7), we conclude that two-part tariffs do not solve durability problem (Coase problem). In other words, when firms face strategic consumers and are unable to commit to future courses of action, two-part tariffs are inadequate. More needs to be done to solve the durability problem and achieve the benchmark profit.

7.2.2.3 Two-Part Tariffs: Long-Term Contracts

We now show that the key to solving both the coordination problem and the durability problem is to establish long-term contracts. Specifically, we consider a long-term two-part tariff between the manufacturer and the retailer. That is, the manufacturer specifies the wholesale prices w_1, w_2 for both periods as well as a fixed fee F at the start of the game.

Under the long-term contract, the retailer's optimal period 2 choices remain unchanged since he still wishes to maximize period 2 profit then. This optimal choice, as given above, is $q_2 = \alpha/(2\beta) - q_1/2 - w_2/(2\beta)$. In period 1, however, the retailer wishes to maximize his total profit given by

$$\Pi(q_1) = \{[\alpha - \beta q_1] + [\alpha - \beta(q_1 + q_2)]\}q_1$$
$$+ [\alpha - \beta(q_1 + q_2)]q_2 - w_1 q_1 - w_2 q_2, \tag{7.26}$$

where q_2 depends on q_1 as above. With some manipulation, the retailer's optimal choice is $q_1 = 2\alpha/(5\beta) - 2w_1/(5\beta) + 2w_2/(5\beta)$.

Now, we consider the manufacturer's optimal choice of wholesale prices. Since he can extract the entire profit share using the fixed fee, the manufacturer will choose w_1, w_2 such that the induced actions (by the retailer) will maximize total supply chain profit given by

$$\Pi(q_1, q_2) = \{[\alpha - \beta q_1] + [\alpha - \beta(q_1 + q_2)]\}q_1$$
$$+ [\alpha - \beta(q_1 + q_2)]q_2. \tag{7.27}$$

Similar to the calculations in the benchmark case, the manufacturer wishes the retailer to choose $q_1 = \alpha/(2\beta)$ and $q_2 = 0$, as in (7.6). Observe that these actions can be induced using the wholesale prices $w_1 = \alpha/4$ and $w_2 = \alpha/2$. In summary, with a long-term contract of two-part tariffs, the equilibrium wholesale prices and quantities are

$$q_1^* = \frac{\alpha}{2\beta}, \qquad q_2^* = 0, \tag{7.28}$$

$$w_1^* = \frac{\alpha}{4}, \qquad w_2^* = \frac{\alpha}{2}. \tag{7.29}$$

The total supply chain profit is then

$$\Pi^* = \frac{\alpha^2}{2\beta}.$$

Since this matches the optimal centralized benchmark profit (7.7), we conclude that a long-term two-part tariff can solve both the coordination problem and the durability problem.

This analysis highlights the strategic role of decentralization. A centralized seller that is unable to commit to future actions will be plagued by the Coase problem, as shown in Section 7.2.1.2. The highest possible benchmark profit cannot be attained. On the other hand, the situation is different under decentralization. Although the introduction of an intermediary may generate double marginalization problems as in Section 7.2.2.1, standard contractual mechanisms (such as a two-part tariff) can resolve coordination issues easily, as shown in Section 7.2.2.2. Further, when long-term contracts are feasible, a decentralized system can even attain the benchmark profit, as shown in Section 7.2.2.3. This is an important message to supply chain managers. While firms often find it difficult to commit to consumers in the market, it may be feasible for them to commit to other firms within the supply chain (through appropriate contractual mechanisms). Bringing into the supply chain an intermediary to whom one can commit to is thus a useful strategy to adopt. Such strategic decentralization effectively solves the Coase problem that is central to many durable goods markets.

7.2.3 Longer Time Horizons

Although we have so far focussed on two-period models, similar reasoning also applies to longer time horizons. With three or even more time periods, the same backward-induction approach can be used to derive the subgame perfect equilibrium. One can then obtain the equilibrium quantities and prices.

For a three-period model, Arya and Mittendorf (2006) analyze the centralized system as well as a decentralized system operating under the simple wholesale price contract. In other words, they provide analysis analogous to Sections 7.2.1.2 and 7.2.2.1. They obtain the following results. Details are omitted.

For the centralized seller who is unable to commit to future actions, the equilibrium production quantities are

$$q_1^* = \frac{10\alpha}{29\beta}, \qquad q_2^* = \frac{38\alpha}{145\beta}, \qquad q_3^* = \frac{57\alpha}{290\beta}, \qquad (7.30)$$

and total equilibrium profit level is

$$\Pi^* = \frac{361\alpha^2}{580\beta} \approx 0.622\frac{\alpha^2}{\beta}. \qquad (7.31)$$

For the decentralized system operating under a wholesale price contract, the equilibrium wholesale prices and quantities are

$$q_1^* \approx 0.19\frac{\alpha}{\beta}, \qquad q_2^* \approx 0.17\frac{\alpha}{\beta}, \qquad q_3^* \approx 0.16\frac{\alpha}{\beta}, \qquad (7.32)$$

$$w_1^* \approx 1.27\alpha, \qquad w_2^* \approx 0.74\alpha, \qquad w_3^* \approx 0.32\alpha. \qquad (7.33)$$

The total system profit, in equilibrium, is

$$\Pi^* \approx 0.631\frac{\alpha^2}{\beta}. \qquad (7.34)$$

The key observation here is that, with a longer time horizon, a decentralized channel may perform better than a centralized channel. Observe that the three-period decentralized profit (7.34) exceeds the three-period centralized profit (7.31). Recall that the decentralized system is operating under the simple per unit wholesale price contract. This suggests that even in the absence of complex contractual arrangements (such as long-term contracts), decentralization can be a useful strategy in its own right. With longer time horizons, simply introducing an intermediary into the supply chain can improve system performance.

Before concluding this section, we emphasize two points concerning time horizons.

1. We first clarify the interpretation of longer time horizons. Moving away from a two-period model, what does three time periods mean? One interpretation is that, longer time horizons implies higher durability. With two periods, the durable

good lasts for two periods. With three periods, the durable good lasts for three periods. In fact, in the classic model of Coase (1972), there are infinitely many periods, so the good is infinitely durable. In such cases, the durability problem is at its extreme severity and the monopoly seller makes zero profit. Therefore, longer time horizons are more applicable to goods that have higher durability. Next, a second interpretation is that time periods refer to time points during which the seller can change prices. With two time periods, the seller can change prices once during the season; with three time periods, the seller can change prices twice. In our opinion, with improving technology and increasing industry clockspeed, longer time horizons will become more and more relevant.

2. An implicit assumption in many durable goods models is that all consumers are present at the start of the time horizon. In the models discussed above, whether we have two, three, or even more time periods, the consumer pool is exogenously fixed at the outset. This is not an innocuous assumption. In many practical settings, new consumers may arrive to the market within the selling season, so longer time horizons may imply higher customer traffic. An influx of strategic consumers during the selling season creates analytical difficulties that require different solution approaches. Such problems have recently been addressed in the revenue management literature; see Shen and Su (2007) for a review. In this chapter, we focus on a static consumer pool and short time horizons (e.g., two or three periods), and discuss the benefits of decentralization in such settings. More generally, with longer time horizons and dynamic consumer arrivals, the effect of decentralization on supply chain performance remains an open question.

7.3 Perishable Goods

We proceed in this section to study the second class of products: perishable goods. In contrast to durable goods, perishable goods exhibit characteristics on the other extreme: the life cycle is relatively short either due to the perishability of the goods in nature (e.g., food and newspaper) or due to frequent new product introductions (e.g., fashion and hi-tech goods). Since most perishable goods possess more or less innovative elements and they are valuable only for a single, short selling season, market demand for perishable goods is usually highly uncertain. For these reasons, sellers of perishable goods face a remarkable challenge of matching their supply to market demand. Although many sellers have adopted various operational strategies (e.g., collaborative forecasting and quick response), completely eliminating the mismatch between supply and demand is not feasible. Therefore, perishable goods sellers actively seek remedies to minimize the consequences of demand–supply imbalances. A commonly used strategy is price markdown in which a seller clears excess inventory and garner additional revenue by dramatically dropping the product price at the end of a selling season. According to recent media reports, such a practice has been increasingly used both in terms of broadness and depth (see Merrick, 2001 and Byrnes and Zellner, 2004). However, this strategy trains consumers to wait for the after-season sales, which may affect the seller's profit in the regular season. How should a seller deal with this kind of strategic consumer behavior? Does strategic decentralization help as in the case of durable goods? In this section we present a modeling framework to investigate the role of strategic consumer behavior in supply chain management for perishable goods.

7.3.1 Model Setting

Consider a seller who sells a product in a single selling season. Demand for this product is uncertain and is denoted by a random variable X. One may interpret X as the total mass of infinitesimal consumers in the market. Let F and f denote the distribution and density functions of X. For technical reasons, we assume that f is continuous, $f(0) > 0$, and F has an increasing failure rate (i.e., $f(x)/(1 - F(x))$ is increasing in x). Most of the commonly used distributions satisfy this assumption. Each unit of the product costs c and has a salvage value of s at the end of the selling season. All consumers value the product at v, which is equivalent to the maximal willingness to pay. To avoid trivial solutions, assume $s < c < v$.

The above setup is exactly the classic newsvendor problem. Given a price p and a stocking quantity Q, we know the newsvendor profit is given by

$$\Pi(Q,p) = (p - s)E(X \wedge Q) - (c - s)Q, \qquad (7.35)$$

where $\wedge$ represents the minimum operation. The newsvendor model has been widely studied in the operations management literature and regarded as a building block for supply chain management research. The twist we add here is strategic consumer behavior. To explain, each consumer may choose to either buy the product during the regular selling season (i.e., pay a full price) or wait for sales till the end of the season (i.e., pay a lower price). However, there is a risk associated with waiting because the product may not be available anymore. Basically, each consumer needs to weigh the two options and choose the timing of purchase accordingly. In particular, the consumers can observe the price announced by the seller, but not the stocking quantity.

The seller's decisions include stocking quantity Q and price p for the selling season, whereas the consumers choose to buy immediately or wait. From the seller's standpoint, this setting resembles the newsvendor model with pricing (see Petruzzi and Dada, 1999). Further, to study the interaction between the seller and the consumers, we need to examine the beliefs formed by the two parties: First, the seller has to form expectations about the consumers' reservation prices in the regular season (i.e., the maximum price at which the consumers are willing to buy immediately). Second, since the consumers cannot observe the actual stocking quantity at the seller, they need to form expectations about the likelihood of product availability at the end of the season. To maintain tractability and make explicit the deliberations of the two parties, we utilize the rational expectations (RE) equilibrium concept to characterize the outcome of the game between the sellers and the consumers. The rational expectations hypothesis, first proposed by Muth (1961), states that economic outcomes do not differ systematically from what people expect them to be.

This model is identical to the RE game studied in Su and Zhang (2008). For consistency, we follow their notations as well. We briefly outline the equilibrium analysis and highlight the major insights in this chapter. More details can be found in Su and Zhang, where they also check the robustness of results in several extensions of the basic model.

For ease of exposition, we adopt the following sequence of events. First, the seller forms a belief ξ_r of the consumers' reservation price, and then choose the optimal price p and quantity Q to maximize the newsvendor profit $\Pi(Q,p)$. Then, the consumers privately form a belief ξ_{prob} over the availability probability in the salvage market, and determine a reservation price r for immediate purchase. Next, the random demand X is realized. Then sales occur at the full price p in the regular season, provided that p does not exceed r. Finally, unsold units are salvaged at price s after the selling season ends. Two additional assumptions are made in the basic model to facilitate analysis. First, we consider equilibrium outcomes where all consumers share the same belief ξ_{prob} and the same reservation price r. Second, all parties are risk neutral and there is no discounting of money over time. The following definition introduces the RE equilibrium concept.

Definition 1. A rational-expectations (RE) equilibrium (p,Q,r,ξ_{prob},ξ_r) must satisfy the following five conditions: (i) $r = v - (v-s)\xi_{prob}$, (ii) $p = \xi_r$, (iii) $Q = \arg\max_Q \Pi(Q,p)$, (iv) $\xi_{prob} = F(Q)$, (v) $\xi_r = r$.

The above equilibrium conditions deserve some explanation. A consumer's surplus is $v - p$ if she buys immediately, and the expected surplus is $(v-s)\xi_{prob}$ if she waits. Thus the maximal price a consumer is willing to pay in the regular season is $r = p = v - (v-s)\xi_{prob}$, which is condition (i). Conditions (ii) and (iii) assert that under expectations ξ_{prob} and ξ_r, the seller will take the profit-maximizing actions. The last two conditions require that expectations must be consistent with outcomes. Condition (iv) is about the consistence on the availability probability. We know ξ_{prob} is the belief on availability probability. The actual probability can be calculated as follows. In equilibrium, the seller prices the product at consumers' reservation price, so all consumers will buy the product. Consider an individual consumer who deviates and waits instead. Since this customer is infinitesimally small, the mass of remaining consumers is X. Hence, this individual will face a stockout later if $X > Q$. On the other hand, if $X \leq Q$, this individual consumer will get the product at the salvage price. Therefore, when an individual consumer waits, she will obtain the product with probability $F(Q)$, which must be consistent with her beliefs ξ_{prob}, as shown in (iv). An implicit assumption here is that consumers who wait for the sale have the highest priority to receive the product in the salvage market. This is reasonable because consumers who are interested in a particular product and eagerly waiting for a sale are also the ones who are more likely to get the product when the sale actually takes place. Finally, in (v), the seller's belief over the reservation price should be consistent with the consumers' actual reservation price.

7.3.2 Centralized System

7.3.2.1 RE Equilibrium Outcome

We first present the outcome of the RE equilibrium. Manipulation of the five conditions shows that the RE equilibrium in Definition 1 can be characterized by a pair of equations in p and Q only: $p = v - (v - s)F(Q)$ and $Q = \arg\max_Q \Pi(Q, p)$. Thus we have the following result.

Proposition 1. *There is a unique RE equilibrium. In the equilibrium, the seller's price p and quantity Q are characterized by*

$$p_c = s + \sqrt{(v - s)(c - s)} \text{ and } \bar{F}(Q_c) = \sqrt{\frac{c - s}{v - s}},$$

and all consumers will buy immediately.

We use subscript c for a centralized seller (later, we will consider a decentralized supply chain with a manufacturer and a retailer). For concision, we use $\bar{F}$ for $1 - F$. The proofs are presented in the appendix at the end of the chapter. Under such an RE equilibrium, the centralized seller's profit can be written as

$$\Pi_c = (p_c - s)E(X \wedge Q_c) - (c - s)Q_c, \tag{7.36}$$

which will serve as a benchmark in future comparisons.

7.3.2.2 Two Types of Commitment

The seller receives a profit Π_c in the RE equilibrium. In this subsection we show that the seller's profit can be improved with two types of commitments: quantity commitment (keeping quantities low) and price commitment (keeping prices high). The rationale under both strategies is to guarantee customers that the product is sufficiently exclusive: it is not available in large quantities and it cannot be purchased at low prices. Practical examples of quantity commitment include limited editions of cars, furniture, and collectors' items, while price commitment may arise in the form of "one-price" or "no-haggle" policies.

We begin with quantity commitment. Suppose the seller is able to convince the consumers that exactly Q units of the product will be available for the entire problem horizon. Or equivalently, the customers can observe the actual stocking quantity. Knowing the stocking quantity Q, customers no longer need to form rational expectations ξ_{prob} because if they wait for the sale (while all other customers buy), their chances of getting the product on the salvage market is $\Pr(X \leq Q) = F(Q)$. In other words, when the seller commits to sell Q units, customers are willing to pay (and the seller also charges) price $p(Q) = v - (v - s)F(Q)$. The seller's profits, as a function of price p and quantity Q, is

$$\Pi_q(Q) = (p(Q) - s)E(X \wedge Q) - (c - s)Q,$$

$$= (v - s)\overline{F}(Q)E(X \wedge Q) - (c - s)Q.$$

We use the subscript q for quantity commitment. Let $Q_q^* = \arg\max_Q \Pi_q(Q)$ be the seller's optimal quantity he will commit to. Then the seller charges price $p_q^* = v - (v - s)F(Q_q^*)$. Denote the corresponding optimal profit level under quantity commitment by Π_q^*. Essentially, quantity commitment allows the seller to manipulate the selling price $p(Q)$ as a function of the chosen quantity Q; on the other hand, in the absence of quantity commitment, the price p is determined by the RE equilibrium. We next compare the optimal outcome under quantity commitment with the RE equilibrium outcome.

Proposition 2. $\Pi_q(Q)$ *has a unique maximizer* Q_q^*. *In addition,* $Q_q^* \leq Q_c$ *and* $\Pi_q^* \geq \Pi_c$.

Proposition 2 confirms that the seller can obtain a higher profit ($\Pi_q^* \geq \Pi_c$) by committing to a lower quantity ($Q_q^* \leq Q_c$). The practice of artificially creating the impression of shortages is not uncommon. Zara, one of the largest Spanish fashion retailers, is well known for limiting production quantities to induce customers to make quick purchases (Ferdows et al. 2004). Now, why cannot the seller achieve Q_q^* in the RE equilibrium? It is because an external commitment device is critical in realizing the quantity Q_q^*. To see this, recall from Definition 1 that in order to sustain Q_q^* in equilibrium, the required expectations are $\xi_{prob} = F(Q_q^*)$ and $\xi_r = r$, and the required selling price is $p = r = v - (v - s)F(Q_q^*)$. It can be verified that these values satisfy conditions (i), (ii), (iv), and (v) in Definition 1, but the definition of Q_q^* contradicts condition (iii). Intuitively, under the expectations that only Q_q^* is available, consumers would be willing to pay $p(Q_q^*)$; but once customers are willing to pay this much, the seller has an incentive to raise the stocking quantity above Q_q^* to make higher profit, so the initial expectations of Q_q^* would not have be formed in the first place. Therefore, Q_q^* cannot be sustained in the RE equilibrium. However, this problem vanishes if the seller possesses some external commitment device.

Next we discuss price commitment. Suppose the seller can credibly commit to a high price throughout the entire horizon. It is sufficient to consider the case in which the seller commits to $p = v$ (any other price would not be optimal for the seller). Note that committing to maintain prices at v is equivalent to eliminating the markdown opportunity provided by the salvage market. Given that the price commitment is credible, consumers will be willing to pay v at the start. It can be shown that under price commitment, we have a standard newsvendor model with zero salvage value. The seller sets $p_p^* = v$ and his profit function is given by

$$\Pi_p(Q) = vE(X \wedge Q) - cQ. \tag{7.37}$$

The seller's optimal stocking quantity is $Q_p^* = \arg\max_Q \Pi_p(Q)$ with a profit level Π_p^*. The subscript p stands for price commitment. The following result compares the performance of price commitment to the RE equilibrium outcome.

Proposition 3. *(i) Given s and v, there exists a threshold value c_l such that $\Pi_p^* \geq \Pi_c$ for $c \leq c_l$ and a threshold value c_h such that $\Pi_p^* \leq \Pi_c$ for $c \geq c_h$.*

(ii) Given c and s, there exists a threshold v_l such that $\Pi_p^* \leq \Pi_c$ for $v \leq v_l$ and a threshold value v_h such that $\Pi_p^* \geq \Pi_c$ for $v \geq v_h$.

Proposition 3 shows that under certain conditions, price commitment may increase the seller's profits above the RE equilibrium level. In particular, the relationship $\Pi_p^* \geq \Pi_c$ holds when the production cost c is relatively low and when the valuation v is relatively high. However, unlike quantity commitment, price commitment is not unambiguously beneficial: We have identified examples in which the inequality $\Pi_p^* < \Pi_c$ holds. Proposition 3 also sheds light on when price commitment is valuable: Price commitment tends to be more valuable when the product becomes more profitable (either c decreases or v increases).

From the above analysis, we can see that quantity commitment and price commitment are both effective strategies in dealing with strategic consumers. The problem is, in most situations, the seller lacks an appropriate commitment device and the implementation of the strategies is not feasible. If this is indeed the case, our analysis suggests that the seller would have to contend with the RE equilibrium outcome. What can the seller do? Fortunately, this may be true in a centralized system (single seller), but not for decentralized systems. In the following sections, we focus on decentralized supply chains consisting of two independent firms. We examine different contractual arrangements between supply chain parties. It will be shown that these contractual arrangements can serve as a surrogate commitment device, and enable the supply chain to attain the optimal profit benchmarks Π_q^* and Π_p^* with commitment. Therefore, again we can see that a decentralized supply chain may yield higher profits than a centralized supply chain.

7.3.3 Decentralized System

In the previous analysis, customers purchase the product from a centralized seller. This section extends the newsvendor model to a supply chain setting. Specifically, we consider a manufacturer distributing a product through a retailer. The model setting is the same as before, except that now we interpret c as the manufacturer's production cost. The timing of the model is as follows: First, the contractual agreements between the manufacturer and the retailer are exogenously established; then, the retailer and customers make their pricing, stocking, and purchase decisions according to a RE equilibrium; finally, demand is realized during the selling season and unsold products are salvaged. In this decentralized setting, we assume that the manufacturer and the retailer are risk neutral, independent firms aiming at maximizing their own profits.

7.3.3.1 Wholesale Price Contracts

We first consider contracts with the simplest form: wholesale price contracts. In a wholesale price contract, the manufacturer specifies a unit price w ($w \geq c$) for the retailer. Under this contract, the retailer's profit function can be written as

$$\Pi_w^r(Q, p) = (p - s)E(X \wedge Q) - (w - s)Q. \tag{7.38}$$

Here, the subscript w stands for wholesale price and the superscript r stands for retailer. Later we will use the superscript m to refer to the manufacturer's profit function. The equilibrium analysis under the wholesale price contract can be derived similarly as before. Following the argument of Proposition 1, the retailer's order quantity Q_w and retail price p_w in RE equilibrium are given by

$$\overline{F}(Q_w) = \frac{w - s}{p_w - s} = \sqrt{\frac{w - s}{v - s}}, \tag{7.39}$$

$$p_w = s + (v - s)\overline{F}(Q_w) = s + \sqrt{(v - s)(w - s)}. \tag{7.40}$$

In this RE equilibrium, the profits to the retailer, the manufacturer, and the supply chain are given by

$$\begin{aligned}
\Pi_w^r &= (p_w - s)E(X \wedge Q_w) - (w - s)Q_w \\
&= (v - s)\overline{F}(Q_w)E(X \wedge Q_w) - (v - s)\overline{F}^2(Q_w)Q_w, \tag{7.41}
\end{aligned}$$

$$\Pi_w^m = Q_w(w - c) = Q_w[(v - s)\overline{F}^2(Q_w) - (c - s)], \tag{7.42}$$

$$\Pi_w \equiv \Pi_w^r + \Pi_w^m = (v - s)\overline{F}(Q_w)E(X \wedge Q_w) - (c - s)Q_w, \tag{7.43}$$

respectively.

It is worth noting that the wholesale price w can be used as a control lever for the supply chain to induce a particular equilibrium stocking quantity. The explanation is as follows. First, there is a one-to-one relationship between $Q_w \in [0, Q_c]$ and $w \in [c, v]$, since the equilibrium quantity Q_w is monotonically decreasing in w. (To highlight the dependence of the equilibrium quantities on the wholesale price w, later we write $Q_w(w)$, and similarly for $p_w(w), \Pi_w^r(w), \Pi_w^m(w)$, and $\Pi_w(w)$). Second, recall that Q_c is the RE equilibrium quantity in the centralized system. Then, by varying w between c and v, the supply chain can realize any equilibrium quantity within the range $[Q_w(v), Q_w(c)]$. Therefore, it is as if the supply chain could choose a desired quantity at the outset (though this particular quantity has to conform to the requirements of an RE equilibrium). In this sense, a pure wholesale price contract provides the supply chain with certain degree of quantity-commitment power. Actually, it turns out that quantity-commitment power can significantly enhance supply chain profits. The next proposition formalizes this observation.

Proposition 4. *There exists a $w^* \in (c, v)$ such that*
(i) $\Pi_w(w) \geq \Pi_c$ for every $w \in (c, w^*]$, i.e., the equilibrium profit in the decentralized system under the wholesale price contract w exceeds the equilibrium profit in the centralized system.

(ii) The decentralized system achieves the optimal profit Π_q^* under quantity commitment at $w = w^*$.

Proposition 4(i) states that the profit of a centralized supply chain is dominated by the profit of a decentralized supply chain, under an array of wholesale price contracts. This is a surprising result. A customary practice in operations management research is to use the centralized scheme as a benchmark to study supply chain efficiency. Proposition 4(i) delivers a message that the centralized optimal profit may not always be the highest possible profit that a supply chain can achieve. In particular, there have been numerous studies addressing the inefficiency caused by double marginalization. That is, when $w > c$, the retailer orders less than the optimal quantity for the entire supply chain. In contrast, here we show that increasing the wholesale price beyond c actually improves the supply chain's profit. The reason is that a higher wholesale price will enable the retailer to credibly stock a lower quantity (recall $Q_w(w)$ is a decreasing function of w), and hence charge a higher retail price to forward-looking consumers in equilibrium. Meanwhile, varying the wholesale price would not affect the supply chain profit since it only alters the transfer payment between the two parties.

Proposition 4(ii) further states that a decentralized supply chain can achieve Π_q^*, the optimal profit under the quantity commitment, by using a wholesale price contract $w = w^*$. That is, the wholesale price induces the optimal quantity Q_q^* in equilibrium and "coordinates" the supply chain. A similar situation where a wholesale price contract can coordinate a supply chain is when horizontal competition is present. For example, Netessine and Zhang (2005) demonstrate that in a distribution channel with a manufacturer and multiple retailers, the substitution effect among the retailers can offset the double marginalization effect and thus retain the supply chain optimal outcome. But here the underlying reason is different: There are strategic consumers on top of double marginalization, and therefore a wholesale price contract can serve as a coordination device to balance these two opposite forces.

We proceed by asking the following two questions. First, if given the choice, what wholesale price would the retailer and the manufacturer select? In other words, how are the quantities $w^r \in \arg\max_w \Pi_w^r(w)$ and $w^m \in \arg\max_w \Pi_w^m(w)$ characterized, and are they unique? Second, how do these unilaterally preferred wholesale prices w^r and w^m compare with the system-optimal wholesale price w^*? These questions are important, since although the wholesale price w^* allows the supply chain to attain the profit benchmark Π_q^*, it specifies a particular division of profits between the retailer and the manufacturer (their shares are $\Pi_w^r(w^*)$ and $\Pi_w^m(w^*)$, respectively). However, each individual party may prefer some wholesale price other than w^* and may negotiate for their preferences. The following proposition deals with these questions.

Proposition 5. *The profit maximizers w^r (for the retailer) and w^m (for the manufacturer) are unique. Moreover, they satisfy $w^r < w^* < w^m$.*

To further understand each party's preferences over wholesale prices, it would be useful to characterize the set of Pareto-optimal wholesale price contracts. A contract is Pareto optimal if there exists no alternative such that some firm is strictly better off and no firm is worse off. Any wholesale price in the Pareto set is a possible choice both parties agree upon. The next proposition presents the set of Pareto wholesale price contracts.

Proposition 6. *The Pareto-optimal wholesale price set is given by $w \in [w^r, w^m]$. In particular, if $w^r > c$, then the wholesale price $w = c$ is Pareto dominated by any $w \in [c, w^r]$.*

From the above two propositions we can see how the allocation of bargaining power affects supply chain efficiency (one may view the wholesale price as a proxy of the bargaining power of the two parties): Since $w^r < w^* < w^m$, the supply chain achieves its optimum when the wholesale price lies in the middle. This suggests that an extreme allocation of bargaining power may reduce the supply chain profit. Now, consider the retailer's profit. Intuitively, a retailer would prefer to have a lower wholesale price. But this is not necessarily true in our problem setting. In fact, even if the retailer has absolute bargaining power, it may not ask for a wholesale price $w = c$ to squeeze the manufacturer's profit to zero. The explanation is as follows. Note that the problem of choosing the wholesale price w faced by the retailer is equivalent to the problem of choosing the production cost c faced by the single seller in Section 7.3.2. In other words, one may view the seller's profit Π_c as a function of c, and then w^r is essentially the production cost that maximizes the seller's profit. Therefore, if $w^r > c$ (i.e., the profit-maximizing production cost is greater than the actual cost), then according to Proposition 6, the contract with $w = c$ is Pareto dominated by any $w \in [c, w^r]$. That is, under certain conditions, both the retailer and the manufacturer prefer a wholesale price higher than the production cost c. This is an interesting result because it implies that the retailer may increase his own profit by voluntarily inviting a higher wholesale price.

7.3.3.2 Buyback Contracts

So far we have explained that wholesale price contracts can achieve quantity commitment for a decentralized supply chain. Next, we show that decentralized supply chains can attain the price-commitment benchmark profit Π_p^* using buyback contracts. In a buyback contract, the manufacturer sells to the retailer at wholesale price w_b and agrees to buy back unsold items at b per unit after demand is realized. There are two separate cases to consider. When $b < s$, the retailer would prefer to salvage the excess inventory rather than selling them back to the manufacturer. The (w_b, b) contract essentially reduces to a pure wholesale price contract, which has already been studied above. For this reason, we will focus on the case $b \geq s$. In this case, the option of selling excess inventory back to the manufacturer becomes more attractive than marking down the price. More importantly, this buyback arrangement eliminates the salvage market, thereby inducing all customers to pay the maximum regular price $p = v$. We emphasize that the buyback contract requires the retailer to physically return the unsold products to the manufacturer (or the retailer "destroys" the leftover inventory by himself). Mere monetary transfers are insufficient because the retailer has to "burn his own bridge" in order to convince consumers that he is unable to activate the salvage market after all intra-supply chain transactions have occurred.

We start the analysis by assuming that a buyback contract (w_b, b) with $b \geq s$ has been established at the outset. In this environment, the RE equilibrium (between the retailer and the strategic customers) dictates that prices (selling price, reservation price, and anticipated reservation price) are all $p = r = \xi_r = v$ and the anticipated probability of low-price availability is $\xi_{prob} = 0$. Then, the retailer has a profit function

$$\Pi_b^r(Q) = (v - b)E(X \wedge Q) - (w_b - b)Q, \qquad (7.44)$$

and chooses the quantity Q_b^r characterized by $\overline{F}(Q_b^r) = (w_b - b)/(v - b)$. We use the subscript b for buyback. We also define $\Pi_b^m(Q)$ and $\Pi_b(Q) = \Pi_b^r(Q) + \Pi_b^m(Q)$ as the manufacturer's profits and total supply chain profits (under the buyback contract), as a function of the retailer's order quantity Q. These profit functions, respectively, can be written as

$$\Pi_b^m(Q) = bE(X \wedge Q) + (w_b - c - b)Q, \qquad (7.45)$$

and

$$\Pi_b(Q) = vE(X \wedge Q) - cQ. \qquad (7.46)$$

Total supply chain profit $\Pi_b(Q)$ is maximized at Q_b satisfying $\overline{F}(Q_b) = c/v$. Observe that total supply chain profit under the buyback contract $\Pi_b(Q)$ coincides with the profit function of the centralized system with price commitment, $\Pi_p(Q)$, so their maximizers also coincide. Therefore, if the supply chain can be coordinated to produce and stock the optimal quantity Q_b, the price-commitment profit benchmark Π_p^* can be attained. The next proposition shows that this can indeed be done, but only for a certain range of profit allocations.

Proposition 7. *Let $\lambda \in [0, 1 - s/v]$ be the retailer's profit share in a buyback contract. Then under the parameter values $w_b = \lambda c + (1 - \lambda)v$ and $b = (1 - \lambda)v$, the RE equilibrium outcome attains the price-commitment profit benchmark Π_p^* for the system. The retailer's and the manufacturer's profits are, respectively, $\lambda \Pi_p^*$ and $(1 - \lambda)\Pi_p^*$.*

It is well known that buyback contracts can coordinate a decentralized supply chain and arbitrarily divide the profit between supply chain members (see Cachon, 2003). Our results identify a new role that buyback contracts play when customers are strategic: They serve as a commitment device. The ability to commit to strategic customers, combined with the ability to coordinate on mutually beneficial actions, allows supply chains to attain the profit levels of a centralized system with price commitment. This may not even be an alternative when a centralized seller operates in isolation. Industry evidence seems to be consistent with the above analysis. For example, buyback or return policies are widely used in the book industry. Instead of marking down prices, major retailers such as Barnes & Noble return the unsold books to their publishers when the selling season ends. The returned copies are then sold to companies specializing in bargain books or books that cannot be sold are simply pulped for a total loss. There is an ongoing debate in the book industry over whether returns should be eliminated: while some retailers claim that they are willing to mark down books and sell them on spot, most publishers are leery of the change (see Trachtenberg, 2005). In fact, one major concern is that readers may learn to wait until books are cheaper. We suspect that the book industry, in spite of losses due to returns, may still be using such a practice as a price-commitment device in order to extract higher profits.

Another observation from Proposition 7 is that there is an upper bound $1 - s/v$ on the retailer's profit share λ. In general, the ability to allocate profits arbitrarily between parties is a desirable property in evaluating different contractual formats. This is because with such a property, we can separate the coordination process from the allocation process: The supply chain can concentrate on maximizing the size of the pie before negotiating over individual shares. In the current situation, the upper bound on retailer share may create problems, especially when the retailer is powerful relative to the manufacturer. This suggests that using buyback contracts as a price-commitment device may face implementation challenges. Note that $\lambda \leq 1 - s/v$ follows directly from the condition $b \geq s$. Thus, ironically, it is precisely these profit caps (due to the upper bound on profit share) that make buybacks effective in providing price commitment. This is different from the situations without the presence of strategic consumers, where buyback contracts can achieve arbitrary profit allocation through the manipulation of the contract parameters, w_b and b.

7.4 Conclusion and Future Research

The main theme of this chapter is to demonstrate that decentralized supply chains may perform better than centralized systems. This claim may appear to challenge conventional wisdom in operations management since decentralization is often associated with double marginalization problems. However, in this chapter, we first show that decentralization can indeed be a beneficial strategy in durable goods supply chains. Decentralization can be particularly useful in durable goods supply chains in the following two scenarios:

1. The first scenario is when firms are able to write long-term contracts. In such cases, long-term contracts allow firms to commit to one another, and this serves as a proxy for commitment to consumers (which firms are unable to achieve). Thus, through long-term contracts, durable goods supply chains are able to mitigate the Coase problem and improve profits.
2. The second scenario is when firms are selling over long time horizons. In such cases, we see that even in the absence of complex contractual arrangements, simply introducing an intermediary can increase supply chain profits. This is because double marginalization leads to lower future quantities and higher consumer willingness to pay. In this sense, double marginalization is no longer a

"problem" but rather, it helps to sustain higher prices over longer time horizons for durable goods.

We also show that decentralization can be beneficial to perishable goods supply chains since it can serve as a commitment device to convince consumers of certain actions taken by firms. Two types of commitment that may help enhance a seller's profit have been studied:

1. The first type is quantity commitment. In quantity commitment, the seller promises that the quantity will be low and thus induces the consumers to buy at a relatively high price in the regular season. While a centralized system may lack such a commitment power, a decentralized system under the simplest wholesale price contracts can credibly commit to a desirable quantity due to the double marginalization effect.
2. The second type is price commitment. A consumer may choose to wait simply because she anticipates a lower price in the salvage market. This opportunistic behavior will not exist anymore if a seller can credibly commit to a high price throughout the entire horizon. A buyback contract, which removes any leftover inventory of the product from the market, can clearly achieve the effect of price commitment.

It can be seen in this chapter that for both durable goods and perishable goods models, commitment power is the key. Essentially, both models involve the dynamic inconsistency (also known as time inconsistency) problem recognized in the economics literature. That is, a firm competes against his future self when making managerial decisions at multiple time points. (The only exception is the model of quantity commitment for perishable goods supply chains, where the seller makes a single-shot decision at the beginning of the selling season.) Under these circumstances, a firm may be better off if he possesses commitment power to convince other game players that certain actions will be taken.

We emphasize that strategic consumers are also critical for the results. We believe that modeling individual consumer behavior in various operations problems is a fruitful topic for future research. The majority of supply chain management literature study isolated operational systems by treating the demand as an exogenous random variable or a fixed downward-sloping curve. However, individual consumers may take strategic actions that in turn affect the performance of the operational system. In fact, modeling customer behavior explicitly has been quite common in service contexts (e.g., queueing analysis and revenue management), probably because consumers are more tangible in service than in other settings. Nevertheless, we hope this chapter can inspire more research in different operational settings.

All the analysis in this chapter requires that consumers act perfectly rational in response to firms' strategies and market conditions. That is, consumers are not myopic and possess unlimited information processing capability. Although this assumption is understandable from a research point of view, apparently, it may not hold in reality. Consumers are human beings and they are not necessarily always, perfectly rational. Thus another direction for future research is to investigate the impact of bounded rationality in consumer behavior on firms' operational strategies.

Finally, the message that strategic decentralization could benefit a firm has been reported in other studies. In these studies, a firm competes against other independent competitors rather than his future self. McGuire and Staelin (1983) consider two manufacturers selling substitutable products. Each manufacturer may sell his product through a manufacturer-owned outlet or an independent retailer. They find that both manufacturers may choose to distribute the products through a decentralized channel in equilibrium, depending on product substitutability. Cachon and Harker (2002) study two competitive service providers that have the option to outsource the service to a third party. It has been shown that both firms outsourcing could be an equilibrium since adding an upstream stage in the service supply chain can reduce the intensity of competition at the downstream stage. A recent paper by Liu and Tyagi (2007) shows that strategic decentralization could also be useful when two firms compete on horizontally differentiated products. Since production/service outsourcing is an important operational strategy that has gained tremendous popularity, it would be interesting to identify new driving forces underlying the industry trend.

Appendix

Proof of Proposition 1

The RE equilibrium conditions

$$p = v - (v - s)F(Q),\tag{7.47}$$
$$Q = \arg\max_{Q} \Pi(Q, p),\tag{7.48}$$

reduce to

$$p = s + (v - s)\overline{F}(Q),\tag{7.49}$$
$$\overline{F}(Q) = \frac{c - s}{p - s},\tag{7.50}$$

respectively. Solving these equations yields the desired results. □

Proof of Proposition 2

The first-order condition $\Pi_q'(Q) = 0$ yields

$$\frac{c - s}{\overline{F}(Q)} + (v - s)\frac{f(Q)}{\overline{F}(Q)}E(X \wedge Q) = (v - s)\overline{F}(Q).\tag{7.51}$$

The left-hand side is increasing (because F has an increasing failure rate), and the right-hand side is decreasing in Q, so the first-order condition has a unique solution.

Further, we know that $\Pi_q'(0) = v - c > 0$ and $\lim_{Q \to \infty} \Pi_q'(Q) = -(c-s) < 0$. Therefore, $\Pi_q(Q)$ is quasi-concave and has a unique maximizer.

The derivative of $\Pi_q(Q)$ at $Q = Q_c$ is

$$\begin{aligned}
\Pi_q'(Q_c) &= (v-s)\overline{F}^2(Q_c) - (c-s) - (v-s)E(X \wedge Q_c)f(Q_c) \\
&= -(v-s)E(X \wedge Q_c)f(Q_c) \\
&< 0,
\end{aligned}$$

where the second equality follows from $(v-s)\overline{F}^2(Q) - (c-s) = 0$. From the previous proposition we know that $\Pi_q(Q)$ is increasing first and then decreasing in Q. Hence there must be $Q_q^* < Q_c$ and $\Pi_q^* \geq \Pi_c$. $\square$

Proof of Proposition 3

The proof is similar to that of Proposition 2 and omitted. $\square$

Proof of Proposition 4

The proof follows directly from Proposition 2. $\square$

Proof of Proposition 5

Consider the equilibrium profits $\Pi_w^r(Q)$ and $\Pi_w^m(Q)$ as a function of equilibrium quantities Q. Denote the maximizers of these functions $Q_w^r \in \arg\max_Q \Pi_w^r(Q)$ and $Q_w^m \in \arg\max_Q \Pi_w^m(Q)$. It suffices to show that (i) Q_w^r and Q_w^m are unique and (ii) $Q_w^m < Q_q^* < Q_w^r$.

(i) Taking derivative of $\Pi_w^r(Q)$ gives

$$\frac{d}{dQ}\Pi_w^r(Q) = (v-s)f(Q)[-E(X \wedge Q) + 2Q\overline{F}(Q)]. \tag{7.52}$$

Let

$$g(Q) = -E(X \wedge Q) + 2Q\overline{F}(Q) = -\int_0^Q xf(x)dx + Q\overline{F}(Q), \tag{7.53}$$

then

$$g'(Q) = \overline{F}(Q) - 2Qf(Q). \tag{7.54}$$

Since F has an increasing failure rate, we know $g'(Q)$ starts at $g'(0) = 1$ and then decreases to the negative domain. Thus, $g(Q)$ starts at $g(0) = 0$, increases first, and then decreases to the negative domain. Let Q_w^r be the unique solution to $g(Q) = 0$, then $\Pi_w^r(Q)$ is increasing for $Q < Q_w^r$ and decreasing for $Q > Q_w^r$. That is, $\Pi_w^r(Q)$ is quasi-concave and has a unique maximizer.

The proof for $\Pi_w^m(Q)$ is similar and omitted.

(ii) Consider the first-order conditions for Q_w^r, Q_w^m, and Q_q^*:

$$Q_w^r : \frac{d}{dQ}\Pi_w^r(Q) = (v-s)f(Q)[E(X \wedge Q) - 2Q\overline{F}(Q)] = 0, \tag{7.55}$$

$$Q_w^m : \frac{d}{dQ}\Pi_w^m(Q) = (v-s)\overline{F}^2(Q) - (c-s) - (v-s)2Q\overline{F}(Q)f(Q) = 0, \tag{7.56}$$

$$Q_q^* : \frac{d}{dQ}\Pi_q(Q) = (v-s)\overline{F}^2(Q) - (c-s) - (v-s)E(X \wedge Q)f(Q) = 0. \tag{7.57}$$

Since $E(X \wedge Q_w^r) = 2Q_w^r\overline{F}(Q_w^r)$ and $\Pi_w^r(Q)$ is quasi-concave, we have

$$\frac{d}{dQ}\Pi_w^m(Q) \le \frac{d}{dQ}\Pi_q(Q),$$

for $Q < Q_w^r$ and the opposite holds for $Q > Q_w^r$. Therefore, the only possible orderings for Q_w^r, Q_w^m, Q_q^* are $Q_w^r < Q_q^* < Q_w^m$ and $Q_w^m < Q_q^* < Q_w^r$.

Next we show $Q_q^* < Q_w^r$. The retailer's optimal quantity Q_w^r is given by $E(X \wedge Q_w^r) = 2Q_w^r\overline{F}(Q_w^r)$ and is determined only by the distribution function. Define $\beta \equiv (c-s)/(v-s)$ $(0 < \beta < 1)$. Then, the first-order condition for Q_q^* can be written as

$$\beta + f(Q)E(X \wedge Q) = \overline{F}^2(Q). \tag{7.58}$$

If $\beta + f(Q_w^r)E(X \wedge Q_w^r) > \overline{F}^2(Q_w^r)$, then we know $Q_q^* < Q_w^r$. Since $\beta > 0$, it suffices to show $f(Q_w^r)E(X \wedge Q_w^r) > \overline{F}^2(Q_w^r)$. Plugging $E(X \wedge Q_w^r) = 2Q_w^r\overline{F}(Q_w^r)$ into the inequality, we only need to show

$$\overline{F}(Q_w^r) - 2Q_w^r f(Q_w^r) < 0. \tag{7.59}$$

Recall from (i) that $g'(Q) = \overline{F}(Q) - 2Qf(Q) = 0$ has a unique solution. Let $\hat{Q}$ be this solution. In addition, Q_w^r is the unique solution to $g(Q) = 0$. This implies that $\hat{Q} < Q_w^r$, so we have

$$g'(Q_w^r) = \overline{F}(Q_w^r) - 2Q_w^r f(Q_w^r) < g'(\hat{Q}) = 0. \tag{7.60}$$

The desired result follows. □

Proof of Proposition 6

The proof follows directly from Proposition 2 and Proposition 5. □

Proof of Proposition 7

Recall that the retailer faces the profit function

$$\Pi_b^r(Q) = (v-b)E(X \wedge Q) - (w_b - b)Q, \tag{7.61}$$

so the optimal stocking quantity is

$$\overline{F}(Q_b^r) = (w_b - b)/(v - b). \tag{7.62}$$

Recall also that the supply chain profit function is

$$\Pi_b(Q) = vE(X \wedge Q) - cQ, \tag{7.63}$$

which is maximized at Q_b, as characterized by

$$\overline{F}(Q_b) = c/v. \tag{7.64}$$

The proof follows the standard approach in the supply chain contracting literature, so we shall keep it brief. The appropriate buyback contract has two objectives: (i) to induce $Q_b^r = Q_b$ (coordination) and (ii) to yield a $(\lambda, 1 - \lambda)$ division of profits (allocation). The two conditions $v - b = \lambda v$ and $w_b - b = \lambda c$ together achieve both objectives because (i) $(w_b - b)/(v - b) = (\lambda c)/(\lambda v) = c/v$, so from (7.62) and (7.64), we have $Q_b^r = Q_b$, and (ii) from (7.61) and (7.63), we have $\Pi_b^r(Q) = (v - b)E(X \wedge Q) - (w_b - b)Q = \lambda vE(X \wedge Q) - \lambda cQ = \lambda \Pi_b(Q)$. Solving these two equations yields the desired contract parameters. Finally, since $b = (1 - \lambda)v$, the condition $b \geq s$ yields the upper bound of $1 - s/v$ on the retailer's share λ.   □

References

Arya A, Mittendorf B (2006) Benefits of channel discord in the sale of durable goods. Marketing Science 25(1):91–96

Bulow JI (1982) Durable-goods monopolists. Journal of Political Economy 90(2):314–332

Byrnes N, Zellner W (2004) Playing the discount game. Business Week. Dec 13

Cachon G (2003) Supply Chain Coordination with Contracts. Handbooks in OR&MS. Graves, de Kok, eds

Cachon G, Harker P (2002) Competition and outsourcing with scale economies. Management Science 48(10):1314–1333

Coase RH (1972) Durability and monopoly. Journal of Law and Economics 15(1):143–149

Desai P, Koenigsberg O, Purohit D (2004) Strategic decentralization and channel coordination. Quantitative Marketing and Economics 2:5–22

Ferdows K, Lewis MA, Machuca JAD (2004) Rapid-fire fulfillment. Harvard Business Review 82(11): 104–110

Liu Y, Tyagi RK (2007) The benefits of upward channel decentralization. Working paper

McGuire TW, Staelin R (1983) An industry equilibrium analysis of downstream vertical integration. Marketing Science 2(2):161–191

Merrick A (2001) Retailers attempt to get a leg up on markdowns with new software. Wall Street Journal, August 7

Netessine S, Zhang F (2005) Positive vs. negative externalities in inventory management: Implications for supply chain design. M&SOM 7(1):58–73

Petruzzi N, Dada M (1999) Pricing and the newsvendor problem: A review extensions. Operations Research 47:183–194

Shen ZJ, Su X (2007) Customer behavior modeling in revenue management and auctions: a review and new research opportunities. Production & Operations Management 16(6): 713–728

Su X, Zhang F (2008) Strategic customer behavior, commitment, and supply chain performance. Management Science. 54(10): 1759–1773.

Trachtenberg JA (2005) Shelf life: Quest for best seller creates a pileup of returned books. WSJ. Jun 3

Part III
Product Strategies for Managing Rational/Strategic Consumer Behavior

Chapter 8
Is Assortment Selection a Popularity Contest?
A Study of Assortment, Return Policy, and Pricing Decisions of a Retailer

Aydın Alptekinoğlu, Alex Grasas, and Elif Akçalı

Abstract Should retailers take product returns into account when choosing their assortments? And, when doing so, should they consider assortment selection as a *popularity contest* – by carrying products that they think will be popular among consumers? Or, is there ever a case for carrying *eccentric* products – those that are least likely to be purchased by a typical consumer? In search of answers to these questions, we explore in this chapter the interactions between product assortment, return policy, and pricing decisions of a retailer. We consider a category of horizontally differentiated products delivered in two alternative supply modes: make-to-order (MTO) and make-to-stock (MTS). In the MTO mode, products are supplied after demand materializes, whereas in the MTS mode, the retailer stocks products prior to the selling season. Underlying our demand model, consumer choice behavior follows a nested multinomial logit model, with the first stage involving a product choice, and the second stage involving a keep-or-return decision. We show that the structure of the optimal assortment strongly depends on both the return policy, which we parameterize by refund fraction (percentage of price refunded upon return) and the supply mode (MTO vs. MTS). For relatively *strict* return policies with a sufficiently low refund fraction, it is optimal for the retailer to offer most eccentric products in the MTO mode, and a mix of most popular and most eccentric products in the MTS mode. For relatively *lenient* return policies, on the other hand, conventional thinking applies: the retailer selects most popular products. We also

Aydın Alptekinoğlu
SMU Cox School of Business, Dallas, Texas, USA, e-mail: aalp@cox.smu.edu

Alex Grasas
Economics and Business, Universitat Pompeu Fabra, Barcelona, SPAIN,
e-mail: alex.grasas@upf.edu

Elif Akçalı
Industrial and Systems Engineering, University of Florida, Gainesville, FL, USA,
e-mail: akcali@ufl.edu

S. Netessine, C.S. Tang (eds.), *Consumer-Driven Demand and Operations Management Models*, International Series in Operations Research & Management Science 131, DOI 10.1007/978-0-387-98026-3_8, © Springer Science+Business Media, LLC 2009

numerically study three extensions of our base model to incorporate: (1) endogenous price, (2) endogenous refund fraction, and (3) multiple periods. We demonstrate that interesting aspects of our results regarding strict return policies prevail under all of these extensions.

8.1 Introduction

Financial impact of return policies can be quite large for a retailer. Overall customer returns are estimated to be 6% of sales in the United States, and may run as high as 15% for mass merchandisers and up to 35% for catalog and e-commerce retailers (Rogers and Tibben-Lembke, 1998, pp. 6–8). The annual value of returned goods in the United States is approximately $100 billion, and companies spend more than $40 billion annually on their reverse logistics processes for handling and disposition of returns (Blanchard, 2005, Enright, 2003).

Given their financial importance, should retailers take product returns into account when merchandising (choosing their product assortments)? Return policies are usually thought of as micro and more operational, whereas product assortment is usually thought of as strategic and more marketing related. Therefore, decisions associated with each are often made separately (see Stock et al., 2006, and Olavson and Fry, 2006). Our theoretical model counters this conventional thinking by showing that optimal assortment decisions fundamentally change in the presence of returns.

Is assortment selection a popularity contest? When choosing their product assortments for a particular category, say different colors and styles of a golf shirt, should retailers always prefer what they think will be popular among consumers? Or, is there ever a case for carrying eccentric products? In this chapter, we argue that relatively strict return policies (with less than full refunds) can render eccentric products more profitable than popular ones. Our argument is moderated by the retailer's basic operational mode: make-to-order (MTO – the retailer does not keep its own inventory but rather buys and delivers the product after a consumer places an order) versus make-to-stock (MTS – the retailer keeps the product in stock). When refunds are sufficiently low, it is optimal for retailers to carry nothing but most eccentric products in the MTO case, and a mix of most popular and most eccentric products in the MTS case. We also find that more lenient return policies (higher refunds) may sometimes require deeper assortments (larger variety of products). In view of our analytical results and numerical observations, we conclude that retailers should not only carefully consider their return policy in assortment planning, but also take their basic operational mode (MTO versus MTS) into account.

The rest of this chapter begins with an abridged version of a model that we developed and analyzed in a recent working paper (Grasas et al., 2008). We then describe three specific extensions of this model. The main purpose of the chapter is to demonstrate (by numerical experimentation) that the analytical results of our working paper, which we summarize above and in greater detail in Section 8.4.1, are robust to these extensions. That is, interesting aspects of our results regarding when a retailer should carry eccentric products survive these extensions, which – we have good reasons to believe – are analytically intractable.

8.2 Literature Review

Product assortment planning or product variety management has attracted considerable interest in the literature from various different angles: strategic/competitive aspects of product variety (e.g., Cachon and Kök, 2007, Alptekinoğlu and Corbett, 2008b); impact of product variety on consumer behavior (e.g., Kim et al., 2002, Borle et al., 2005); and interactions between product variety and operational considerations such as inventory and leadtime (e.g., van Ryzin and Mahajan, 1999, Smith and Agrawal, 2000, Aydin and Ryan, 2000, Cachon et al., 2005, Hopp and Xu, 2005, Gaur and Honhon, 2006, Li, 2007, Maddah and Bish, 2007, and Alptekinoğlu and Corbett, 2008a). The presence of product returns obviously complicates assortment planning further, yet it has not been addressed in this literature so far. We demonstrate a specific setting when returns make a fundamental difference for assortment decisions – beyond just complicating them.

Although operational, tactical, and strategic decisions associated with used product returns have been well studied in the closed-loop supply chain management literature (for an overview, see Dekker et al., 2004), research on resalable product returns has been somewhat limited. Arguing that returns need to be taken into account in inventory management, since they can act as a supplementary source to satisfy demand, the existing research focuses on characterizing the optimal ordering policy of a retailer (e.g., Mostard and Teunter, 2006). Guide et al. (2006) note the value that can be recovered from returns is time sensitive and focus on identifying the preferred reverse supply chain structure for a manufacturer. This entire line of work exclusively treats single product systems. Therefore, by considering assortment planning, we tackle a host of issues that have been ignored by the current literature on operations management of returns.

Another line of research that is closely related to our work pertains to product return policies. While a stream of research focuses on return policies between a manufacturer and a retailer (e.g., Pasternack, 1985, Emmons and Gilbert, 1998), another stream concentrates on the influence of a retailer's return policy on consumers (e.g., Yalabik et al., 2005, Shulman et al., 2008). Our work is similar to some of the work in the latter stream in that we have an explicit model of consumer choice, and limit attention to a single aspect of return policies: refund amount. The difference is that we explore how return policy interacts with product assortment, an issue none of these papers address.

8.3 Models

We first provide a compact description of our base model. For a more complete discussion of the key features and assumptions, we refer the reader to our working paper (Grasas et al., 2008).

8.3.1 Base Model: Assortment Decision for Exogenous Price and Return Policy

Motivated with the question of whether retailers should consider returns when merchandising (as they compose their product assortments), we explore in our working paper the interactions between product assortment decision and return policy of a price-taking retailer under both make-to-order (MTO) and make-to-stock (MTS) environments. These two basic operational modes, MTO and MTS, allow us to draw a distinction between cases where supply decision is made after and before the demand materializes, respectively. In the MTO case, the retailer procures the product after consumers make their purchase decisions (e.g., many of the sports gears sold online at REI.com are drop-shipped directly from a third-party supplier). Whereas in the MTS case, the reverse happens (e.g., backcountry.com, a retailer specialized in high-end gear and apparel for outdoors, carries all of its products in inventory at its central warehouse in Utah).

8.3.1.1 Product Assortment and Return Policy

When choosing its product assortment, we assume that the retailer exclusively considers an exogenous set of potential product designs; this set may represent a supplier's catalog of different variants in a given product line. Let $N = \{1, 2, ..., n\}$ denote the set of all products that the retailer can potentially offer, and let S be the subset of products actually offered by the retailer ($S \subseteq N$), termed *assortment*.

The assortment decision (S) considered here is for a narrow category of products, which are horizontally differentiated along a taste attribute such as color or some other component of fashion. All products in N are assumed to have the same unit production cost c, the same retail price p, and the same salvage value v. There is only one difference among the products in question: their *attractiveness* (a's introduced below). Following standard practice, we assume that $v < c < p$. The latter inequality, $c < p$, is necessary for the market to be profitable. The former inequality, $v < c$, says that any amount of leftovers can be sold below cost in a secondary market for v per unit; if $v \geq c$ were to hold true, the retailer's quantity decision would be riskless and thus uninteresting.

We assume exogenous prices. In some product categories, or with particular brands, many retailers do not dictate prices, but rather sell their products at MSRP, *manufacturer suggested retail price* (e.g., backcountry.com sells many of its products at MSRP; Crocs Shoes, a manufacturer and online retailer of shoes and other footwear, exercises a very high degree of control over the retail price of its products available in many online and brick-and-mortar retailers). Allowing prices to be decision variables would be clearly useful, but also analytically very difficult (see Maddah and Bish, 2007, for an attempt at endogenizing price in an MNL-choice-based assortment problem that also considers inventories but omits product returns). Yet, as pointed out by van Ryzin and Mahajan (1999) in the context of a closely related model, there are "realistic cases in which a retailer's pricing flexibility is quite limited" (p. 1498). We limit our analysis to such a case, as they also do, with the retailer exercising little or no control over prices, e.g., it sells the product line in question at MSRP. (We discuss in Sections 8.4.2 and 8.5 potential implications of endogenizing price.)

The types of returns we consider involve products returned in resalable condition. We exclusively focus on one aspect of return policies: refund amount, which we parameterize by *refund fraction*, the percentage of price refunded in the event of a return. Like price, we assume refund fraction to be exogenous, possibly driven by a category- or store-wide analysis (beyond the scope of ours, which focuses on a single horizontally differentiated product line), or dictated by common industry practice. (We discuss in Sections 8.4.3 and 8.5 potential implications of endogenizing refund fraction.) While it is common to offer refunds for the full purchase price in some settings (e.g., backcountry.com allows customers to send products back for a full refund with no questions asked) offering partial refunds and retaining some portion of the price in restocking fees is common in others (e.g., buydig.com, a retailer of consumer electronics, charges a processing fee of 10% of the value of all merchandise returned for a refund).[1] Let α denote the refund fraction ($0 \leq \alpha \leq 1$), which makes the refund amount per unit return αp. We assume that this single refund fraction applies to all products in S, which is how almost all retailers operate in practice (especially within a given narrow product category, as in our model). The retailer incurs a reverse logistics cost l for each unit of returned products. This figure includes such cost items as sorting, repackaging, and restocking.

Finally, consistent with common practice in retailing, we omit the possibility of product exchange. Many retailers, including backcountry.com (sports gear), Lids.com (baseball caps), Steve Madden (shoes), and buydig.com (consumer electronics), allow returns and ask consumers to place a new order if they want to do an exchange even for another product in the same product line. Excluding exchanges from consideration is not without loss of generality, of course, because those new orders would go to subsequent periods, which we do not model. (We discuss the implications of extending our model to multiple periods in Sections 8.4.4 and 8.5.) Allowing exchanges is akin to dynamic substitution, which is known to pose great difficulties in assortment optimization (more about this in the discussion of MTS environment).

---

[1] Newegg.com charges 15% for all returned items. Best Buy and Target charge 15% for many consumer electronics items. Returning a home theater set to Circuit City open box, even if not used at all, incurs 25% restocking fee. See van Riper and Nolan (2008) for more examples.

8.3.1.2 Individual Consumer Choice Behavior and Aggregate Demand

Any given consumer's consideration set comprises all the products in S offered by the retailer and the possibility of not purchasing any of those products, termed the *outside option*, which we denote by 0. We conceptualize the consumers' choice among $S \cup \{0\}$ and their subsequent decision to keep or return the purchased product by a two-stage nested multinomial logit (N-MNL) model. The nests are products, and they each contain two post-purchase alternatives: keep and return.

Stage 2. Conditional on purchasing product $i \in S$ in the first stage, we model the consumer's post-purchase decision to keep or return the product by utility maximization. Let the *attractiveness* of product i be a_i, which may differ across the products but not across consumers. Without loss of generality, we sort products in N in non-increasing order of attractiveness levels, i.e., $a_1 \geq a_2 \geq \cdots \geq a_n$. Thus, lower indexed products are more popular, and higher indexed products are more eccentric.

Suppose the utilities associated with purchasing product i and keeping or returning it are given by $u_{i,\text{keep}} = a_i - p + \varepsilon_{i,\text{keep}}$, and $u_{i,\text{return}} = -(1-\alpha)p + \varepsilon_{i,\text{return}}$, where $\varepsilon_{i,\text{keep}}$ and $\varepsilon_{i,\text{return}}$ are independent and identically distributed (*iid*) Gumbel random variables with mean zero and scale $1/\mu_2$ ($\mu_2 > 0$).[2] Note that the deterministic portion of $u_{i,\text{keep}}$ is the attractiveness minus the price; and the deterministic portion of $u_{i,\text{return}}$ is the negative of the dollar amount not refunded by the retailer. (If returns involve a fixed cost or disutility for the consumer, we could incorporate a deterministic parameter in $u_{i,\text{return}}$ to account for that; none of our findings would change as a result.)

By the principle of utility maximization, the probability that a typical consumer chooses the return option in the second stage is then $P_{\text{return}|i} \equiv \Pr\left\{u_{i,\text{return}} > u_{i,\text{keep}}\right\}$, which yields the following formula:[3]

$$P_{\text{return}|i} = \frac{1}{1 + \exp[(a_i - \alpha p)/\mu_2]}$$

And, of course, $P_{\text{keep}|i} = 1 - P_{\text{return}|i}$. Should the consumer choose the outside option in the first stage, there is no further choice to make in the second stage. Note that $P_{\text{return}|i}$ is non-zero even if the retailer offers no refund ($\alpha = 0$). This is largely a matter of scaling; the model should be calibrated such that $P_{\text{return}|i}$ is negligibly small when $\alpha = 0$, because most consumers would probably not return the product for no refund.

Stage 1. For a consumer who is grappling with the first stage decision of which product to purchase (if any), the *expected utility* of product $i \in S$ (or nest i) is $A_i \equiv$

---

[2] The cumulative distribution function (*cdf*) of a Gumbel random variable X with mean zero and scale $1/\mu$ is given by $P(X \leq x) = \exp[-\exp(-x/\mu - \gamma)]$, and has a variance of $\mu^2 \pi^2/6$, where γ is Euler's constant ($\gamma \approx 0.5772$) and μ is a positive constant. Gumbel distribution is also known as double-exponential distribution.

[3] We use the fact that the difference of two Gumbel random variables, ε_1 and ε_2, with scale $1/\mu$ follows a logistic distribution with *cdf* given by $\Pr\{\varepsilon_2 - \varepsilon_1 \leq x\} = [1 + \exp(-x/\mu)]^{-1}$.

$E\left[\max\left(u_{i,\text{keep}}, u_{i,\text{return}}\right)\right]$, which can be derived as

$$A_i = \mu_2 \ln\left[\exp\left(\frac{a_i}{\mu_2}\right) + \exp\left(\frac{\alpha p}{\mu_2}\right)\right] - p.$$

Furthermore, we assume without loss of generality that the outside option is a nest with zero expected utility, that is, $A_0 = 0$.

We model the consumer's purchase decision also by utility maximization. Suppose the utility of choosing nest $i \in S \cup \{0\}$ is given by $U_i = A_i + \varepsilon_i$, where ε_i are *iid* Gumbel random variables with mean zero and scale $1/\mu_1$ ($\mu_1 > 0$). (ε_i are also independent of $\varepsilon_{j,\text{keep}}$ and $\varepsilon_{j,\text{return}}$ for all $i, j \in N$.) Again by the principle of utility maximization, the probability that nest $i \in S \cup \{0\}$ is chosen in the first stage is $P_i^S \equiv \Pr\left\{U_i = \max_{j \in S \cup \{0\}} U_j\right\}$, which yields the following logit formula:[4]

$$P_i^S = \frac{\exp(A_i/\mu_1)}{\sum\limits_{j \in S \cup \{0\}} \exp(A_j/\mu_1)}$$

where P_0^S denotes the probability of choosing the outside option or not buying. Note that while the conditional probability of return $P_{\text{return}|i}$ only depends on a_i (i.e., it is independent of the rest of the products in S), the unconditional probability of return $P_{\text{return}} = \sum_{j \in S} P_{\text{return}|j} P_j^S$ does depend on the retailer's assortment S.

In sum, we represent consumers' choice process with a two-stage random utility model. Consumers are a priori homogeneous, but ex post heterogeneous on their tastes, preferences, and outside factors that may shape their pre- and post-purchase decisions. The random terms capture this heterogeneity. In particular, ε_i reflect consumers' diverse preferences for products and return policies, their diverse circumstances in which they need this product, their diverse information states, etc. They also differ in their post-purchase inclinations, as summed up in $\varepsilon_{i,\text{keep}}$ and $\varepsilon_{i,\text{return}}$. Heterogeneity at this stage stems from how different consumers deal with keep and return options given a purchase decision in the first stage. For instance, among two consumers who are considering to keep an apparel item, their spouses may give them different feedback. And, among two consumers who are considering to return a pair of hiking shoes, their experience with the product may differ due to their different backgrounds (or lack thereof) in hiking. Larger μ_1 and μ_2 mean higher variance for the random terms and thus higher heterogeneity. For the N-MNL model to be technically consistent, we require $\mu_1 \geq \mu_2$ (McFadden, 1978), which is plausible in our context. Consumers' pre-purchase heterogeneity is generally higher than their post-purchase heterogeneity, because presumably those who buy the same product will know more about what they want (or do not want) based on first-hand experience with a given product, and will differ less from each other due to this common experience.

---

[4] This is a standard result that comes from the fact that maximum of Gumbel random variables has a Gumbel distribution (see Anderson et al., 1992, for a proof).

We will make a semantic distinction between products with high and low values of attractiveness. The higher the attractiveness of a product, the higher the expected utility of consuming it (i.e., buying and keeping it), and thus higher the probability of purchase. In view of utility maximization behavior described above, every consumer buys what they consider to be the best or most "attractive" product. So, the magnitude of a_i does not so much reflect the attractiveness of a product in the common sense of the word, but rather determines the likelihood of purchase for product i. We will thus refer to products with high attractiveness values as *popular* products (in the sense that a typical consumer is more likely to buy them); and, those with low attractiveness values as *eccentric* products (in the sense that consumers with rare tastes will buy them).

We now specify how individual consumer choice behavior described above translates into aggregate demand for each product in S. Let λ denote the average number of consumers going through this choice process. Assuming that the consumers' product choice is purely governed by the set S and not influenced at all by the details of the retailer's fulfillment process (e.g., MTO versus MTS, inventory status, etc.), we model the demand for product $i \in S$ by a normal random variable D_i with mean λP_i^S and standard deviation $\sigma(\lambda P_i^S)^\beta$, where $\sigma > 0$ and $0 \le \beta < 1$. (This model of aggregate demand, dubbed the Independent Population Model, has been first proposed by van Ryzin and Mahajan (1999), and later used by Maddah and Bish (2007), Li (2007) and others.) Furthermore, we model the returns of product i by a normal random variable R_i with mean $\lambda P_{i,\text{return}}^S$ and standard deviation $\sigma(\lambda P_{i,\text{return}}^S)^\beta$. Note that the coefficient of variation (defined as standard deviation divided by mean) for D_i and R_i are decreasing in P_i^S and $P_{i,\text{return}}^S$, respectively. Also, Poisson demands and returns constitute a natural special case of our aggregate demand model (i.e., set $\sigma = 1$ and $\beta = 1/2$, and use normal approximation of Poisson).

8.3.1.3 Supply Process and the Timing of Events

We consider two alternative modes of supply: MTO and MTS. In either case, we assume away capacity limitations: the retailer can order as many units as desired of each item in S.

MTO Environment

Under MTO, ordering takes place after demand is realized. Therefore, demand for a given product never goes unsatisfied, which reduces the risk of the supply decision. In fact, in the case of MTO, the supply decision becomes trivial: the order quantity must be equal to the realized demand, because any inventory in excess of demand would certainly not be sold but rather salvaged for a unit loss of $(c - v)$. Nevertheless, due to the presence of returns, the quantity risk does not completely vanish; some products may be returned, and will need to be salvaged, which may involve a net loss (recall that $v < c$).

The expected profit in this case can be expressed as follows:

$$\Pi_{MTO}(S) = \sum_{j \in S} E\left[(p-c)D_j - (\alpha p + l - v)R_j\right] \tag{8.1}$$

The first term within expectation is the revenue, net of procurement costs. The second term is the net cost of handling returns: for each unit of returned product, the retailer refunds αp, pays l for reverse logistics activities, and eventually salvages it for v (e.g., sells it in a secondary market, such as a clearance store). We assume that returned items can only be salvaged (sold at a secondary market for a reduced price). A more general model of handling returns would allow resale of returned products in the store (possibly for full price), requiring a multiple-period planning horizon. We discuss the implications of this in Sections 8.4.4 and 8.5.

MTS Environment

Under MTS, the retailer takes an ordering decision for each product prior to the selling season, before demands realize. The supply decision under MTS is therefore riskier (than that under MTO): there is a chance that the retailer may over- or under-stock each and every product. Let x_j be the quantity of product j ordered and stocked in advance of the selling season.

In the event of a stock-out, the retailer places an emergency order at a unit cost of e ($v < c < e < p$), and we assume that the consumer is willing to wait for the delivery of her most preferred item and does not substitute for another item that happens to be in stock. Emergency orders are common in retailing. For instance, Express (apparel) and Famous Footwear both have written promises in their Web sites that if they happen not to have the right size or color of a particular product in their store, they would find and ship it for free. There is no guarantee of course that every consumer would take up this offer. So, we are clearly making a simplifying assumption, which helps us focus on the interaction between the retailer's assortment decision and the return policy in effect. If consumers were allowed to switch from their most preferred product that is out of stock to a different product that is in stock, the model would be significantly more complicated, and quite likely, analytically intractable. Assortment and inventory management under stock-out-based substitution (also called dynamic substitution in the literature) is by itself a difficult problem, even if product returns were ignored (see, for instance, Gaur and Honhon (2006) for a near-optimal heuristic approach).

The expected profit under MTS can be expressed as follows:[5]

$$\Pi_{MTS}(S) = \sum_{j \in S} \max_{x_j \geq 0} \left\{ E\left[pD_j - cx_j - e(D_j - x_j)^+ \right. \right.$$
$$\left. \left. - (\alpha p + l - v)R_j + v(x_j - D_j)^+ \right] \right\} \tag{8.2}$$

---

[5] For any real number y, let $(y)^+$ be equal to y if $y > 0$, and to 0 otherwise.

where x_j is the regular (non-emergency) order quantity for product j. The first term within expectation is the revenue; sales equals demand because, by assumption, the retailer can backlog excess demand and satisfy it with emergency orders. The second term is the cost of regular supply; and the third term is the cost of emergency supply. The fourth term is the cost of having to deal with returned items (consistent with the MTO case, returned items are salvaged). The last term is the salvage revenue from excess inventory, items that have never been sold.

Timing of Events

To sum up, events in our base model unfold as follows. With a given return policy – defined by refund fraction α – in effect, the assortment decision (S) is taken at the beginning of the period to maximize expected profit, $\Pi_{\text{MTO}}(S)$ or $\Pi_{\text{MTS}}(S)$. Then, in the case of MTO, random demands realize and the retailer orders the quantity demanded of each product. In the case of MTS, order quantity decisions (x_j for all $j \in S$) are taken first, and then demands realize. Consumers' random choice behavior in the first stage of the N-MNL model (described above) is what drives the realization of demands. Next, consumers who purchase their product of choice decide to keep or return it (following the behavior described in the second stage of the N-MNL model). Finally, the retailer salvages any returned or excess items at the end of the period.

8.3.2 Extension 1: Assortment and Price Decisions for Exogenous Return Policy

In this extension we drop the assumption of exogenous price. So, everything remains the same as in the base model, except now price is also a decision taken by the retailer, simultaneous with the assortment decision (with return fraction still fixed).

8.3.3 Extension 2: Assortment and Return Policy Decisions for Exogenous Price

In this extension we drop the assumption of exogenous refund fraction. So, everything remains the same as in the base model, except now return fraction is also a decision taken by the retailer, simultaneous with the assortment decision (with price still fixed).

8.3.4 Extension 3: Assortment Decision for Multiple Periods

Finally, we take the base model and assume a multiple-period planning horizon. As in the base model, product assortment is decided at the very beginning – the beginning of the first period. To simplify the inventory management problem, and to amplify the impact of inventory on assortment over multiple periods, we assume that returned items are not salvaged until the end of the last period, i.e., they are always re-stocked and possibly used in succeeding periods.

8.4 Analytical Results and Numerical Observations

8.4.1 Optimal Assortment in the Base Model

In this section we seek to optimize the retailer's assortment decision for a given retail price and return policy. This is generally a difficult task as there are 2^n different possibilities. We provide structural results that significantly reduce the search space for accomplishing this task.

8.4.1.1 MTO Model with Returns

To lay the groundwork for discovering the structure of the optimal assortment, we first conduct a thought experiment. Suppose the current assortment is some proper subset S of N. Consider adding a product with a certain attractiveness to the current assortment. How does the new expected profit behave as a function of the attractiveness of the "new" product? Does adding this particular product to the assortment improve the profit? These two questions are resolved in two lemmas reported in our working paper, and they provide building blocks for proving the structure of the optimal assortment.

Theorem 1 (Grasas et al., 2008).
(a) For a sufficiently lenient return policy with return fraction $\alpha \geq (v-l)/p$, the optimal assortment under the MTO environment is composed of some number of most popular products from N.
(b) For a sufficiently strict return policy with return fraction $\alpha < (v-l)/p$, the optimal assortment under the MTO environment is composed of some number of most eccentric products from N.

The presence of returns clearly changes the structure of the optimal assortment. If the refund fraction is sufficiently large, reflecting a lenient return policy, carrying only the most popular products is optimal. This result agrees with common intuition, previous results in the literature (e.g., van Ryzin and Mahajan, 1999, Aydin and Ryan, 2000, Hopp and Xu, 2005, Maddah and Bish, 2007, Li, 2007, and Cachon and Kök, 2007), and some industry practice (e.g., Cargille et al., 2005, and Olavson and Fry, 2006). Since high refund fractions are costly, they induce the retailer to be more selective when deciding on variety, and thus to offer products with less chances of being returned, i.e., the popular products.

However, if the refund fraction is low, reflecting a strict return policy, then it is optimal to carry only the most eccentric products. The intuitive reason is that the retailer makes more money from an item that is sold and returned than an item that is sold and not returned. In the former case, net unit profit is $(p - c - \alpha p - l + v)$; whereas in the latter case, it is $(p - c)$. This is akin to the "service escape" model of Xie and Gerstner (2007), in which a firm profits from service cancellations. Other factors that favor popular products, such as higher probability of purchase, seem to be dominated. We note that it can be best to add to an existing assortment the most popular (remaining) product. Even though this is true for incremental additions to an assortment, Theorem 1b establishes most eccentric assortments as optimal for strict return policies.

8.4.1.2 MTS Model with Returns

The analysis proceeds similarly; as in the MTO case, we first consider the question of which product (if any) should be added to an existing assortment. Based on this finding (reported in our working paper), we establish the following result regarding the structure of the optimal assortment.

Theorem 2 (Grasas et al., 2008).
For a sufficiently strict return policy with return fraction $\alpha < (v - l)/p$, the optimal assortment under the MTS environment is composed of some number of most popular and some number of most eccentric products from N. There exist problem instances where the optimal assortment is composed of: (1) most popular products only, (2) most eccentric products only, or (3) some most popular and some most eccentric products.

This result paves the way to showing that the structure of the optimal assortment is fundamentally different under MTS than under MTO. In the MTS case, it is possible to have – unlike the MTO case – an optimal assortment with a strictly positive number of most popular products only, or a strictly positive number of most popular products and a strictly positive number of most eccentric products. Such an example is illustrated in Table 8.1; details of the example are described in Section 8.4.1.4.

The key reason behind this counterintuitive result is the operational mode itself. Under the MTS environment, the ordering decision for each and every product in the assortment carries risks of over- and under-stocking. As usual with newsvendor costs, the burden of these risks is proportional to the standard deviation of demand. Normalizing by demand size, coefficient of variation (defined as standard deviation divided by mean) as a measure of relative demand variability is generally a good indicator of how risky a product is – operationally speaking. In our model, products with higher attractiveness enjoy a larger probability of purchase and a smaller coefficient of variation. Hence, for strict return policies, the retailer has two opposing goals: (1) choose eccentric products to benefit from their resale (much like in the MTO case); and (2) choose popular products to take advantage of their lower relative demand variability and therefore reduce operational risks. The structure of the optimal assortment reflects both of these goals.

Table 8.1 Optimal assortment S^*, composed of products that correspond to shaded cells, for the problem instance in Table 8.2 with threshold refund fraction, $(v-l)/p = 0.825$.

	i	α 0.0	0.1	0.2	0.3	0.4	0.5	0.6	0.7	0.8	0.9	1.0
MTO	1	▓								▓	▓	▓
	2	▓								▓	▓	
	3	▓								▓	▓	
	4	▓	▓							▓		
	5	▓	▓						▓	▓		
	6	▓	▓	▓					▓	▓		
	7	▓	▓	▓	▓	▓	▓	▓	▓			
	8	▓	▓	▓	▓	▓	▓	▓	▓			
	9	▓	▓	▓	▓	▓	▓	▓	▓			
	10	▓	▓	▓	▓	▓	▓	▓	▓			
MTS	1	▓								▓	▓	▓
	2	▓								▓	▓	▓
	3	▓								▓		▓
	4	▓								▓		
	5	▓	▓	▓						▓		
	6	▓	▓	▓						▓		
	7	▓	▓	▓	▓	▓	▓	▓	▓			
	8	▓	▓	▓	▓	▓	▓	▓	▓			
	9	▓	▓	▓	▓	▓	▓	▓				
	10	▓	▓	▓	▓	▓	▓	▓				

Clearly, our analytical results in the MTS case are limited to the strict return policy case only. Although we are unable to prove this, based on extensive numerical studies (only a subset of which is presented in our working paper), we conjecture that the lenient return policy case requires the optimal assortment to include some number of most popular products, just as in the MTO environment. The intuition given above for Theorem 2 also supports our claim because for lenient return policies the retailer finds popular products more desirable on both counts. They not only have less relative demand variability but also a smaller chance of return.

8.4.1.3 MTO and MTS Models without Returns

Both our MTO and MTS models include as a special case the possibility of the retailer disallowing returns. By a slight abuse of model definition, we can analyze this case by setting $\alpha = -\infty$, which implies that the consumers will choose the "keep" option with probability 1 in the second stage of our N-MNL model regardless of which product they choose in the first stage (i.e., they never return products). In fact, the N-MNL model reduces to a standard MNL model. The optimal assortment would then be comprised of some number of most popular products under both

MTO and MTS environments. (We omit the proof; same result was obtained by van Ryzin and Mahajan (1999) in an MTS model with lost sales and without returns.)

Therefore, by contrasting this result with Theorems 1 and 2, we conclude that if retailers were to ignore product returns when merchandising, they might easily run the risk of composing suboptimal assortments. This is especially true if they have relatively strict return policies.

8.4.1.4 A Numerical Example

We conclude our analysis of the base model with a numerical example that illustrates the different kinds of solutions that arise under MTO/MTS environments with strict/lenient return policies. Table 8.1 displays the optimal assortment out of a given set of 10 potential products (sorted in decreasing order of attractiveness levels) for different values of refund fraction α and for both MTO and MTS models. The optimal assortment in each of these instances is computed by complete enumeration. Note that the threshold refund fraction that separates strict and lenient return policies in this example is $(v - l)/p = 0.825$. As expected, optimal variety (number of products in the optimal assortment) is lower under MTS.

Our working paper (Grasas et al., 2008) contains an extensive numerical study section that explores the following research questions. We provide a brief summary of our most interesting findings here, and refer the reader to the paper for a full exposition.

- If a retailer ignored the presence of product returns when composing its assortment, or it assumed that the best assortment is always composed of most popular products, what would be the magnitude of its profit loss relative to the optimal profit?
- How is the *depth* of the optimal assortment, number of products offered, influenced by changes in refund fraction? Is it necessarily the case that more lenient return policies imply less variety? We find that the answer is no. More lenient return policies may sometimes call for deeper assortments with higher variety. This happens especially when the refund fraction is at neither extreme (0% or 100%), but just below a certain threshold $((v - l)/p)$.
- How does the degree of differentiation among the potential products considered by the retailer (spread of a-values for products in N) influence its profit and depth of assortment? If the retailer had any influence over this degree of differentiation, would it prefer higher or lower differentiation? From a managerial point of view, a retailer moving from an MTO to an MTS environment should seek higher product differentiation in its consideration set (N), because it will matter more. That effort is even more worthwhile when the retailer's return policy is more lenient.
- What is the effect of post-purchase heterogeneity (μ_2) on the optimal profit for a given refund fraction? Can more heterogeneity be ever beneficial for the retailer? Somewhat surprisingly, yes. The reasonable presumption that higher heterogeneity about consumers' keep/return decisions will lead to lower profits is wrong for strict return policies.

- How does the optimal refund fraction depend on the structure of the assortment? We find that sometimes higher variety requires a higher refund fraction. This essentially complements our observation earlier that moving toward more lenient return policies and deeper assortments simultaneously can be optimal.

In the rest of this section, we report results from our numerical study of the three extensions of the base model. Unless we state otherwise, in all experiments we use a set of base parameter values displayed in Table 8.2. Also, we report only the MTO case (the MTS case does not reveal any notably different insight).

Table 8.2 Base parameter values.

Parameter	Value	Product, i	a_i
λ	100	1	4.00
p	2	2	3.72
e	1.9	3	3.44
c	1.8	4	3.17
v	1.7	5	2.89
l	0.05	6	2.61
μ_1	1	7	2.33
μ_2	0.5	8	2.06
σ	1	9	1.78
β	0.5	10	1.50

8.4.2 Optimal Assortment and Price in Extension 1

In this subsection, allowing price to be a decision variable, we explore how pricing decisions interact with the optimal assortment and the return policy in effect. As in the base model, return fraction is considered exogenous.

8.4.2.1 Variety Versus Price

Does higher price lead to more or less variety? The answer depends on the refund fraction. For two values of refund fraction, $\alpha = 0.5$ and $\alpha = 0.8$, we compute the optimal assortment while varying price from 2 to 3 (see Figure 8.1). For $\alpha = 0.5$, and all prices within the range considered (from 2 to 3), we are in the strict return policy region, i.e., $\alpha < (v - l)/p$. As price increases, the unit cost of returns $(\alpha p + l - v)$ approaches to 0, and that makes all products more similar in terms of their profitability. The retailer then opts to offer full assortment to capture more demand. For $\alpha = 0.8$, the effect is opposite and more interesting. Increasing price increases the probability of return. Since we are in the lenient return policy region ($\alpha \geq (v - l)/p$) for all price points except $p = 2$, and the unit cost of returns $(\alpha p + l - v)$ increases in price, returns become increasingly more costly. The retailer then reduces its assortment by offering less number of most popular products, which effectively reduces

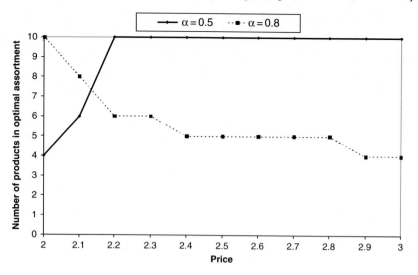

Fig. 8.1 Variety versus price: Number of products in the optimal assortment ($|S^*|$) as price (p) varies for different values of refund fraction (α).

the likelihood of return. It is interesting that, in a monopoly setting, lower variety can coincide with higher prices. This is not uncommon in competitive environments (e.g., Alptekinoğlu and Corbett, 2008b), but in monopoly environments price and variety are usually positively related (in fact, we do not know of a counterexample to this rule, besides the one caused by product returns in this work).

8.4.2.2 Behavior of Expected Profit with Respect to Price

We now study the behavior of the expected profit with respect to price. Among other things, we want to understand if the expected profit is generally unimodal, which would make numerical optimization of price relatively easy.

For different values of refund fraction, Figure 8.2 plots the expected profit as price varies from 2 to 6. For every data point shown in the chart, the assortment is optimized. We observe that the expected profit is unimodal for these problem instances. In fact, we have not seen any problem instance to the contrary. Note also from the graph that the optimal price increases as refund fraction decreases. We examine this in more detail in the next subsection.

8.4.2.3 Optimal Price with Respect to Refund Fraction

Figure 8.3 shows how optimal price changes as refund fraction (α) varies between 0 and 1 by increments of 0.1. A dashed line separates the strict return policy region ($\alpha p < v - l$) from the lenient return policy region ($\alpha p \geq v - l$).

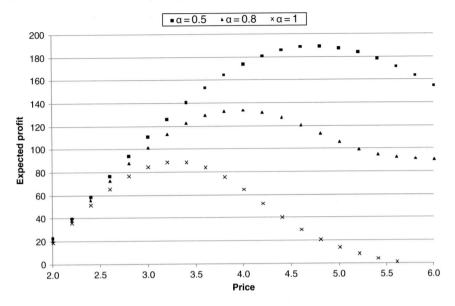

Fig. 8.2 Profit versus price: Expected profit as price (p) varies for different refund fractions (α) under optimal assortment (S^*).

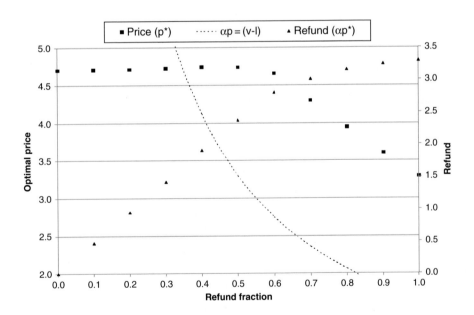

Fig. 8.3 Price versus refund: Optimal price (p^*) and refund (αp^*) for different values of refund fraction (α) under optimal assortment (S^*).

Again, the optimal assortment is computed for every data point. The optimization over S takes advantage of structural results presented earlier for the base model, whereas the optimization over p is done numerically by line search. For all problem instances that we have seen, we observe that the expected profit is generally unimodal in p, which makes the line search easy.

The optimal price increases very slightly for strict return policies, and then suddenly drops for lenient return policies as refund fraction approaches to 1. This is because the retailer tries to reduce the probability of return by lowering the price. With a lenient policy, the retailer would rather charge less and obtain a final sale than salvage a product for a lower revenue. It is surprising that optimal price would drop for increasingly more lenient return policies (higher α). Even from the perspective of absolute refund amount, the consumer enjoys a more favorable return policy as α increases, because αp^* also keeps increasing, albeit at a diminishing rate.

8.4.3 Optimal Assortment and Refund Policy in Extension 2

In this subsection, we investigate how endogenizing refund fraction (α) influences our assortment problem. As in the base model, price is considered exogenous.

8.4.3.1 Behavior of Expected Profit with Respect to Refund Fraction

Figure 8.4 plots the expected profit for several α values from 0 to 1 (with 0.05 increments) at three different price points. For every data point we optimize the assortment, therefore different data points may correspond to different product assortments. At $p = 2$ the optimal refund fraction is $\alpha^* = 0.55$; at $p = 2.25$, $\alpha^* = 0.5$; and at $p = 2.5$, $\alpha^* = 0.45$. So, for the three price points considered in this experiment, the optimal refund fraction is lower for higher prices. This result, which we further explore in the next subsection, complements the price versus refund analysis in Section 8.4.2.3.

8.4.3.2 Optimal Refund with Respect to Price

In this subsection, we study how optimal refund fraction is affected by changes in price. We vary the price from 2 to 6, and compute the optimal refund fraction and optimal assortment. The optimization over S takes advantage of structural results presented earlier for the base model, whereas the optimization over α is done numerically by line search. For all problem instances that we have seen, we observe that the expected profit is generally unimodal in α, which makes the line search easy.

Does higher price imply higher refund fraction? The answer is not necessarily. As seen in Figure 8.5, the optimal refund fraction represented by square dots, first

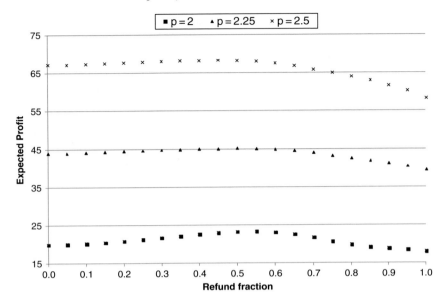

Fig. 8.4 Profit versus refund fraction: Expected profit as refund fraction (α) varies for different prices (p) under optimal assortment (S^*).

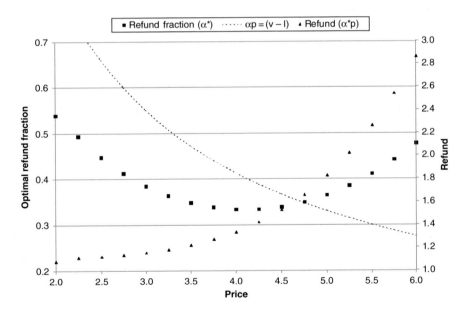

Fig. 8.5 Refund versus price: Optimal refund fraction (α^*) and refund ($\alpha^* p$) for different prices (p) under optimal assortment (S^*).

decreases and then increases in price. The intuition is the following. Starting from a low price, an increase in price raises the probability of return, forcing the retailer to reduce α to discourage returns. For low values of p, the expected profit margin per unit sales, $p - c - (\alpha p + l - v)P_{\text{return}|i}$, is more sensitive to returns since $(p - c)$ is small relative to the cost of returns term. As we keep increasing price, $(p - c)$ increases and returns become less relevant for the profit margin. Since the retailer is extracting enough profit from $(p - c)$, it can afford increasing α to make its value proposition more attractive. Note that a dashed line separates the strict return policy region ($\alpha p < v - l$) from the lenient return policy region ($\alpha p \geq v - l$) in the graph. Also note that refund amount, $\alpha^* p$, does consistently increase in price; thus at higher prices the retailer is effectively charging more for a more generous return policy.

8.4.4 Optimal Assortment for Multiple Periods in Extension 3

In this subsection, we extend the problem to a multiple-period setting. We assume that all returns are kept in inventory to satisfy future demand. Only returns from the last period (and any remaining inventory) are salvaged at the very end. Using the same base parameters shown in Table 8.2, we compute the optimal assortment for different values of α as we did in Table 8.1. We use an inventory cost of 0.05 per period for the returns kept in stock. In order to compute the expected profit for multiple periods, we use Monte Carlo simulation methods. The procedure is as follows: for every product in the assortment we generate random demand and return strings of size T, the length of the planning horizon. With known demands and returns, we easily compute the actual profit. We then estimate the expected profit by averaging the profits at a sufficiently large sample of realizations, $1,000$ in our case (Robert and Casella, 1999, p. 208). By the Law of Large Numbers, this estimation converges with probability 1 to the expected profit as the sample size goes to infinity. For every possible assortment (i.e., $2^{10} - 1 = 1023$), we compute the approximate expected profit and choose the one that yields the maximum.

We observe that the assortments that yield maximum expected profit have the same structures found to be optimal in the single-period setting (see Theorems 1 and 2). Tables 8.3 and 8.4 show the optimal assortment for MTO and MTS cases for the multiple-period problem with $T = 3$ and $T = 10$, respectively.

An interesting question that arises in a multiple-period context is whether the retailer includes more products as the length of the planning horizon T increases. Tables 8.3 and 8.4 suggest that the longer planning horizon (and multiple re-selling opportunities it brings) changes neither the structure of the assortment nor the composition in any significant fashion.

Table 8.3 Optimal assortment S^*, composed of products that correspond to shaded cells, for a multiple-period problem with three-period planning horizon.

	i	α										
		0.0	0.1	0.2	0.3	0.4	0.5	0.6	0.7	0.8	0.9	1.0
MTO	1											
	2											
	3											
	4											
	5											
	6											
	7											
	8											
	9											
	10											
MTS	1											
	2											
	3											
	4											
	5											
	6											
	7											
	8											
	9											
	10											

Table 8.4 Optimal assortment S^*, composed of products that correspond to shaded cells, for a multiple-period problem with ten-period planning horizon.

	i	α										
		0.0	0.1	0.2	0.3	0.4	0.5	0.6	0.7	0.8	0.9	1.0
MTO	1											
	2											
	3											
	4											
	5											
	6											
	7											
	8											
	9											
	10											
MTS	1											
	2											
	3											
	4											
	5											
	6											
	7											
	8											
	9											
	10											

8.5 Concluding Remarks

Motivated with the question of whether retailers should consider product returns when merchandising (as they compose their product assortments), we first explore in our base model the interactions between product assortment decision and return policy of a price-taking retailer under two basic operational modes, make-to-order (MTO) and make-to-stock (MTS). We have a demand model grounded on individual consumer behavior. Consumers decide which product to buy in the first stage of a nested multinomial logit model, and then decide to keep or return the item in the second stage. In their purchase and keep/return decisions, consumers take both the assortment and refund fraction, the percentage of price refunded upon return, into account. The retailer, an expected profit maximizer, makes its assortment decision from an exogenous set of potential products that are horizontally differentiated. We call products with high (low) attractiveness *popular* (*eccentric*), because they are more (less) likely to be purchased by a typical consumer. In the MTS case, the retailer also makes an inventory decision for each product offered.

Our main finding from the base model is that the structure of the optimal assortment critically depends on the refund fraction and whether the products are supplied on an MTO or MTS basis. More specifically, we have two major analytical results:

- For a strict return policy (with a sufficiently low refund fraction), the optimal assortment has a counterintuitive structure. In the MTO case, it is composed of some number of most eccentric products; whereas, in the MTS case, some number of most popular and some number of most eccentric products.
- For a lenient return policy (with a sufficiently high refund fraction), the optimal assortment is composed of some number of most popular products in the MTO case. Although we could not analytically prove that the same structure is optimal for the MTS case as well, our extensive numerical experiments confirm this. Including only the most popular products in an assortment agrees with common intuition, previous results in the literature (e.g., van Ryzin and Mahajan, 1999, Aydin and Ryan, 2000, Hopp and Xu, 2005, Maddah and Bish, 2007, Li, 2007, and Cachon and Kök, 2007), and some industry practice (e.g., Cargille et al., 2005, and Olavson and Fry, 2006). As indicated above, we show that the presence of returns can reverse this intuitive result.

The basic rationale for including an eccentric product in the optimal assortment is to benefit from the processing and resale of returned items. This benefit is higher for low refund fractions, and eccentric products have a higher likelihood of being returned. (We argue by numerical examples in this chapter that this logic would likely survive extensions of our base model to endogenous price, endogenous refund fraction, and multiple resale opportunities.) The case for popular products, on the other hand, is twofold. If returns are a net loss to the retailer, popular products become desirable because they minimize the likelihood of return. If the retailer is operating in an MTS mode, popular products also have the advantage of lower relative demand variability (measured by coefficient of variation) and therefore reduced operational risks.

Our analytical and numerical results so far amply illustrate that assortment and refund fraction can exhibit interactions that are not easily predictable. Therefore, endogenizing the return policy decision analytically would be a worthwhile extension of our work. An equally important direction would be to endogenize the pricing decision. Nevertheless, price and refund fraction simultaneously influence the purchase and return probabilities in a complex way, which proves to be quite challenging to investigate analytically. Our numerical study in this chapter demonstrates that the strict return policy region, where most of the interesting interactions occur, is still prominent after endogenizing either of these variables.

Another extension would be to consider multiple periods, which may allow richer inventory management issues and more sophisticated return behavior. Even in the simplest possible case, if assortment decision was to be made for once at the beginning of a finite planning horizon, the question of optimal assortment becomes analytically intractable. On a positive note, extending our model to multiple periods can only strengthen our result about strict return policies. Having multiple resale opportunities can only increase the resale value of returned products; therefore, the basic rationale for carrying eccentric products would actually be even more prominent over a multiple-period planning horizon. We indeed demonstrate this in our numerical studies: the strict return policy region remains to be highly salient.

In light of our analytical results and numerical observations, we conclude that retailers should not only carefully consider their return policy when merchandising, but also take their basic operational mode (MTO versus MTS) into account.

References

Alptekinoğlu A, Corbett CJ (2008a) Leadtime – variety tradeoff in product differentiation. Working paper, SMU, Dallas, Texas

Alptekinoğlu A, Corbett CJ (2008b) Mass customization vs. mass production: Variety and price competition. Manufacturing Service Operating Management 10(2):204–217

Anderson SP, de Palma A, Thisse JF (1992) Discrete choice theory of product differentiation. MIT Press, Cambridge, Massachusetts

Aydin G, Ryan JK (2000) Product line selection and pricing under the multinomial logit choice model. Working paper, Purdue University, West Lafayette, Indiana

Blanchard D (2005) Moving forward in reverse. Logistics Today 46(7):7–8

Borle S, Boatwright P, Kadane JB, Nunes JC, Shmueli G (2005) The effect of product assortment changes on customer retention. Marketing Science 24(4):616–622

Cachon GP, Kök AG (2007) Category management and coordination in retail assortment planning in the presence of basket shopping consumers. Management Science 53(6):934–951

Cachon GP, Terwiesch C, Xu Y (2005) Retail assortment planning in the presence of consumer search. Manufacturing Service Operating Management 7(4):330–346

Cargille B, Fry C, Raphel A (2005) Managing product line complexity. OR/MS Today 32(3):34–41

Dekker R, Fleischmann M, Inderfurth K, van Wassenhove LN (2004) Reverse logistics: Quantitative models for closed-loop supply chains. Springer-Verlag, New York

Emmons H, Gilbert SM (1998) The role of returns policies in pricing and inventory decisions for catalogue goods. Management Science 44(2):276–283

Enright T (2003) Post-holiday logistics. trafficWORLD, January 20

Gaur V, Honhon D (2006) Product variety and inventory decisions under a locational consumer choice model. Management Science 52(10):1528–1546

Grasas A, Alptekinoğlu A, Akçalı E (2008) When to carry eccentric products? Optimal assortment under product returns. Working paper, University of Florida, Gainesville, Florida

Guide VDR, Jr, Souza GC, van Wassenhove LN, Blackburn JD (2006) Time value of commercial product returns. Management Science 52(8):1200–1214

Hopp WJ, Xu X (2005) Product line selection and pricing with modularity in design. Manufacturing Service Operating Management 7(3):172–187

Kim J, Allenby GM, Rossi PE (2002) Modeling consumer demand for variety. Marketing Science 21(3):229–250

Li Z (2007) A single-period assortment optimization model. Production Operating Management 16(3):369–380

Maddah B, Bish EK (2007) Joint pricing, assortment, and inventory decisions for a retailer's product line. Naval Research Logistics 54(3):315–330

McFadden D (1978) Modelling the choice of residential location. North-Holland Publishing Company, Amsterdam

Mostard J, Teunter R (2006) The newsboy problem with resalable returns: a single period model and case study. European Journal of Operational Research 169(1):81–96

Olavson T, Fry C (2006) Understanding the dynamics of value-driven variety management. MIT Sloan Management Review 48(1):63–69

Pasternack BA (1985) Optimal pricing and return policies for perishable commodities. Marketing Science 4(2):166–176

Robert CP, Casella G (1999) Monte Carlo statistical methods. Springer-Verlag, New York

Rogers DS, Tibben-Lembke RS (1998) Going backwards: Reverse logistics trends and practices. University of Nevada report, Center for Logistics Management. Reverse Logistics Executive Council. URL http://www.rlec.org/reverse.pdf

Shulman JD, Coughlan AT, Savaskan RC (2008) Optimal restocking fees and information provision in an integrated demand-supply model of product returns. Working paper, University of Washington, Seattle, Washington

Smith S, Agrawal N (2000) Management of multi-item retail inventory systems with demand substitution. Operations Research 48(1):50–64

Stock J, Speh T, Shear H (2006) Managing product returns for competitive advantage. MIT Sloan Management Review 48(1):57–62

van Riper T, Nolan K (2008) The toughest holiday returns. Forbes, January 14. URL http://www.forbes.com

van Ryzin G, Mahajan S (1999) On the relationship between inventory costs and variety benefits in retail assortments. Management Science 45(11):1496–1509

Xie J, Gerstner E (2007) Service escape: Profiting from customer cancellations. Marketing Science 26(1):18–30

Yalabik B, Petruzzi NC, Chhajed D (2005) An integrated product returns model with logistics and marketing coordination. European Journal of Operational Research 161(1):162–182

Chapter 9
Product Design, Pricing, and Capacity Investment in a Congested Production System

Sergio Chayet, Panos Kouvelis, and Dennis Z. Yu

Abstract We investigate a firm's product positioning and capacity investment problem for a product that is vertically differentiated according to its design quality level. Customers arrive according to a Poisson process and are heterogeneous in the marginal valuation of the product's quality level, making product choices to maximize a linear utility function of price and quality level. Resulting product demands are met through capacity investments in a production process, which is modeled as a queuing system. Capacity investment and variable production costs are functions of the processed product's quality. We develop an integrated marketing-operations model that provides insights into the factors determining the right positioning of the product in terms of quality and pricing, the resulting market coverage, and the effects on production costs and congestion levels of the production process.

9.1 Introduction

For the fast-paced competitive environments of today, a frequent challenge for firms is to decide product design and prices of their products. Higher design quality products are more costly to produce and even though they can be priced at a premium, demand for them is relatively lower because fewer customers have the higher reservation prices. Production systems are expensive to build, with the required

Sergio Chayet
Olin Business School, Washington University in St. Louis, St. Louis, MO 63130-4899, USA,
e-mail: chayet@wustl.edu

Panos Kouvelis
Olin Business School, Washington University in St. Louis, St. Louis, MO 63130-4899, USA,
e-mail: kouvelis@wustl.edu

Dennis Z. Yu
School of Business, Clarkson University, Potsdam, NY 13699-5790, USA,
e-mail: dyu@clarkson.edu

S. Netessine, C.S. Tang (eds.), *Consumer-Driven Demand and Operations Management Models*, International Series in Operations Research & Management Science 131, DOI 10.1007/978-0-387-98026-3_9, © Springer Science+Business Media, LLC 2009

investments dependent on the design quality of the products to be produced, and often exhibit congestion. Such congestion results in long lead times and inventory stockpiles, not only adding to the variable product costs but also subtracting from the customer service experience. Even though the above tradeoffs are well understood at the conceptual level, they are often hard to quantify and be effectively captured as part of an optimal product design decision. Figuring out the right design quality and price often remains elusive issues for most firms, frequently decided in ad hoc and myopic ways.

The clearly cross-functional nature of product design decisions amplifies their difficulty, as different functional areas bring to the table different interests and managerial measures of success. From a marketing perspective, product design quality is key to revenue growth. From an operations perspective, increasing the product design quality level increases production capacity investment and affects production system congestion and thereby lead times and the costs for matching supply with demand. While both functions have sound arguments to make in support of their views, their answers in terms of an optimal product design are inconsistent and are not helping the overall business decision. The lack of integrated decision frameworks to capture and quantify all relevant tradeoffs on determining optimal product design and the appropriate price is further contributing to the confusion on the issue. Our research attempts to offer such an integrated decision framework and within a stylized model outlines the factors that affect product design for a given market and production environment. It also suggests how to position and price the product for profit maximization. Furthermore, it explicitly captures implications for capacity investments and the right utilization of production resources to effectively match supply and demand.

The study of product design and pricing has been a major research area in industrial organization and marketing science for decades. The main focus of this research stream has been the revenue optimization through careful pricing and the effective matching of customer preferences and product design attributes. However, such research models overemphasize the accuracy of depiction of customer choice along dimensions of price and product quality, at the expense of an oversimplified representation of the capacity investment, variable production, and congestion-related costs of the production and supply system. On the other hand, a rich operations management literature has been building detailed cost and congestion-level models of production systems under the assumption of given price and product segmentation. Recent research efforts have come closer to closing the gap between the front-end customer choice representation and the back-end operational implications of product design but, as we will argue, have so far remained short in effectively capturing capacity investment and congestion implications of product design for the production system.

In this chapter, we investigate a firm's product design and capacity investment decisions for a single product. The customer population is heterogeneous in the marginal valuation of the design quality level. Utility maximizing customers make choices using a linear utility function of both price and quality level. The customer heterogeneity of quality preferences is captured via a parameter assumed to have a uniform distribution over the range $[0, 1]$. The customer arrival process follows a Poisson process with a fixed rate. After making utility maximizing choices for a given product line, arriving customers decide whether or not to purchase the product, which results in a covered market segment as actual customer demand. This product demand has to be met through investment in a production facility. We use a simple queuing process to capture the relevant congestion effects in the production process. Capacity investment cost of a production technology is defined as a function of the design quality level that the facility is able to produce.

The firm is a make-to-order producer. An arriving customer order (all of them of size one) is released to the production facility for processing. The variable production cost of the product is a function of its design quality level. A heavily utilized production system suffers the consequences of its congestion via elongated lead time and high work-in-process inventory level. Appropriate congestion penalties account for such costs via holding costs per unit per unit time attributed to all orders waiting in the system. The offered design quality level and pricing influence the customer arrival rate to the production facility, and an appropriate capacity investment decision has to be made to fully reflect tradeoffs in capacity investment costs and congestion penalties. Thus, a profit maximizing firm has to simultaneously optimize its product design (along a quality dimension) and pricing, in addition to capacity investment, which indirectly affects congestion levels and together with the variable production costs determine its profit margins.

9.2 Literature Review

Product design and pricing issues have been extensively studied in economics/ industrial organization, marketing and operations management literatures. Marketing and industrial organization research emphasizes product design and associated pricing decisions to extract value from a heterogeneous population of customers via effective price discrimination. In their seminal work on vertical differentiation via product quality, Mussa and Rosen (1978) derive the monopolist's optimal price–quality schedule offered to a heterogeneous customer population with continuous preference parameter along the quality dimension over a bounded range. They assume that the variable cost of quality is a convex increasing function of the quality level. Moorthy (1984) substantiates the benefits of market segmentation through product design when customers have discrete types. In this work, the monopolist offers a menu of products, with higher quality products priced higher. Choudhary et al. (2005) utilize vertical differentiation models to study the effect of personalized pricing on the firm's choices over quality. By using personalized pricing, the firm can charge different prices to different consumers based on their willingness to pay, assuming the firm can implement a pricing policy based on complete knowledge of the customer's willingness to pay (first-degree price discrimination). In all of the above literature there is usually no explicit consideration of relevant operational costs beyond variable production costs (even those are typically simplified to a constant or a quadratic function of quality). Such relevant operational costs will capture inherent economies of scale in production systems through fixed costs of production and/or important non-linear congestion phenomena and associated costs due to the uncertain nature of order arrivals and processing times of the production system.

In the operations management literature on product design, the design attribute is commonly predetermined, and customer choice and associated pricing decisions are usually not considered in these models. With the assumption of given number of products and customer demands, Benjaafar and Gupta (1998) study the effect of scheduling and batch sizing policies on the choices of product mix and capacity of flexible and dedicated production facilities. By considering an un-capacitated multi-product lot-sizing problem, de Groote (1994) analyzes the monopolist's problem of selecting product line breadth and production flexibility. Netessine and Taylor (2007) study the impact of production technology on the firm's product line design strategies with an economic order quantity (EOQ) type economies of scale (fixed cost vs. linear variable and holding costs) production model. Our model differs from the Netessine and Taylor (2007) work in that it captures operational (back end) details via a queuing model of the production system, thus emphasizing non-linear congestion effects in capacity investments instead of fixed cost-driven economies of scale.

The main focus of our study is to understand the factors that impact the monopolist's choice of optimal design quality level in the presence of a heterogeneous customer population of utility maximizers, with utility functions linear in price and product quality, uncertain demand, and the associated implications for capacity investments to a production system that is subject to congestion effects as in common queuing models. Furthermore, we are explicitly asking the question of how the offered product partitions the market via its quality–price choice and what the resulting product quality is and what factors affect it. Our model includes reasonable details in its representation of both market coverage and operational decisions. Following the rich tradition of marketing science models, we carefully capture the heterogeneous customer preferences for product quality and the way utility maximizing customers are affected by product design. Our model of the operational structure is a queuing system that captures congestion phenomena and inventory implications of the product design decisions. Our results contribute to the existing literature through analytical clarity on factors affecting product design quality for congested production systems and insightful answers on the profit maximizing market coverage and product positioning of a monopolist's product for uncertain and heterogeneous consumer markets. Furthermore, we offer insights into the needed capacity investments to produce the right design quality product.

The rest of the chapter is organized as follows. We first introduce the basic model and assumptions in Section 9.3. We then consider variable costs as function of the design quality level that can be either quadratic (in Section 9.4) or more general power cost functions (in Section 9.5). We conclude with the summary of our results and managerial insights in Section 9.6.

9.3 Basic Model and Assumptions

To study the interactions between market positioning decisions in product design and congestion effects in capacity planning, we formulate an integrated model with both product design quality and capacity variables as endogenous choices. Such a model allows us to better understand important interactions previously ignored as independent choices of these variables. Many of the insights we obtain on the effects of factors such as variable production costs, market size, and congestion levels on product design and capacity could not have been predicted via models that treated either the marketing (product design) or the operational (capacity) variables as exogenous.

We consider the case in which the firm produces a single product using a single production facility. The firm's decisions are the product design quality level, the selling price, and the capacity of the production facility. Customers arrive according to a Poisson process with rate λ and have no obligation to purchase the product. The customers are heterogeneous in their marginal valuation of the product quality level. Each customer has a utility function $u(p,q) = \tilde{\theta}q - p$, where p is the price and q the quality level. Any customer who has a non-negative utility of consumption is willing to buy the product. The parameter $\tilde{\theta}$ captures the customer's valuation of the quality level, and it is uniformly distributed on $[0,1]$. For a given quality level, a higher $\tilde{\theta}$ represents a higher willingness to pay. Without loss of generality we assume the quality level is bounded, i.e., $q \in [0, q_{max}]$.

The production system is make-to-order and each customer arrival triggers a size-one production order. There is a capacity investment cost incurred when the firm sets up the facility, and production capacity refers to the system's processing rate. We assume the marginal capacity investment cost per unit time $b(q)$ is a sufficiently smooth, strictly increasing, and convex function of the quality level, hence $b'(\cdot) > 0$, $b''(\cdot) > 0$, and $b(0) = 0$. There is also a variable production cost $c(q)$ with analogous properties, i.e., $c'(\cdot) > 0$, $c''(\cdot) > 0$, and $c(0) = 0$.

For a given product with quality level q there exists a unique $\theta \in (0,1)$ such that the selling price $p = \theta q$. Hence, the effective customer arrival rate $\lambda_p = (1 - \theta)\lambda$ is the arrival rate of customers who buy the product. The firm's revenue is thus

$$\pi_S(p,q) = [p - c(q)]\lambda_p = [\theta q - c(q)](1 - \theta)\lambda. \tag{9.1}$$

Revenue function (9.1) is widely used in the economics and marketing literature. However, it does not include any relevant production costs, such as capacity investment or congestion costs. In our model, we represent the production system as an M/M/1 queuing system, with both the optimal quality level q and capacity (processing rate) μ as relevant decision variables, and incorporate the economic consequences of the production system's congestion (elongated lead times and work-in-process inventory) via a constant marginal holding cost per unit time h.

The firm's objective is to maximize the profit

$$\max_{p,q,\mu} \Pi_S(p,q,\mu) = \pi_S(p,q) - h\frac{\lambda_p}{\mu - \lambda_p} - b(q)\mu. \tag{9.2}$$

The second term in the above expression is the average holding cost of work-in-process orders in the M/M/1 system and the third term is the capacity investment cost.

We have chosen this stylized model for the production system for consistency with the operational detail available during the product design stage. Modern plant management practices (such as just-in-time) recognize the critical roles that congestion and inventory levels play in fostering smoother, more controllable systems and improved levels of conformance quality. Therefore, beyond holding costs, h is meant to represent the manager's level of concern in keeping low work-in-process levels relative to revenues and capacity costs. Observe that in our model customer preferences do not include disutilities of expected delays, and including them would imply customers are willing to pay premiums for speedy delivery and expect price cuts for delays. However, our modeled customers are not cycle time insensitive, since we can still assume they use delivery time as an order qualifier in their purchasing decision process. Thus, in setting h, among other considerations the plant manager also makes certain that cycle times will meet customer expectations.

Notice that only two terms in (9.2) depend on the processing rate μ, and it is straightforward to show they are strictly concave in μ. The optimal capacity is given by $\mu^*(\lambda_p) = \lambda_p + \sqrt{h\lambda_p/b(q)}$. Substitution of $\mu^*(\lambda_p)$ into (9.2) yields the following maximization problem:

$$\max_{p,q} \Pi_S(p,q) = \{p - [b(q) + c(q)]\}\lambda_p - 2\sqrt{h\lambda_p b(q)}. \tag{9.3}$$

We consider two different functional forms for capacity investment cost $b(q)$ and unit production cost $c(q)$. We assume both are quadratic functions in Section 9.4, and general power functions in Section 9.5.

9.4 Quadratic Cost Functions

We first assume that both $b(q)$ and $c(q)$ are quadratic functions of the quality level, i.e., $b(q) = \beta q^2$ and $c(q) = \alpha q^2$, with $\alpha, \beta > 0$. We can then rewrite optimization problem (9.3) with θ and q as decision variables, i.e.,

$$\max_{\theta,q} \Pi_S(\theta,q) = [\theta q - (\alpha + \beta)q^2](1 - \theta)\lambda - 2q\sqrt{\beta h(1 - \theta)\lambda}. \tag{9.4}$$

Given θ, $\Pi_S(\theta,q)$ is concave in q. Using the first-order condition $\partial \Pi_S(\theta,q)/\partial q = 0$ yields the optimal quality level

$$q^*(\theta) = \frac{1}{\alpha+\beta}\left(\frac{\theta}{2} - \sqrt{\frac{\beta h}{(1-\theta)\lambda}}\right),$$

and the optimization problem can be formulated in terms of the single decision variable θ:

$$\max_{\theta\in(0,1)} \Pi_S(\theta) = \frac{\lambda}{4(\alpha+\beta)}\left(\theta\sqrt{1-\theta} - M\right)^2$$

$$\text{s.t.} \quad \theta\sqrt{1-\theta} > M, \quad \text{where } M = 2\sqrt{\frac{\beta h}{\lambda}},$$

and the constraint is needed to ensure $q^*(\theta) > 0$. We provide the optimal decision variables in the following theorem.

Theorem 1. *When $0 \leq M < 2/(3\sqrt{3})$, the optimal product positioning θ^*, quality level q^*, production capacity μ^*, and profit Π_S^* are given by*

$$\theta^* = \frac{2}{3}, \quad q^* = \frac{1}{\alpha+\beta}\left(\frac{1}{3} - \sqrt{\frac{3\beta h}{\lambda}}\right), \quad \mu^* = \frac{\lambda}{3} + \frac{\lambda(\alpha+\beta)\sqrt{3h}}{\sqrt{\beta\lambda} - 3\beta\sqrt{3h}},$$

and $\quad \Pi_S^* = \frac{1}{27(\alpha+\beta)}\left(\sqrt{\lambda} - 3\sqrt{3\beta h}\right)^2.$

The system's utilization level is given by $\rho^* = (\sqrt{\beta\lambda} - 3\beta\sqrt{3h})/(\sqrt{\beta\lambda} + 3\alpha\sqrt{3h})$. When $M \geq 2/(3\sqrt{3})$, the firm's profit is non-positive and the optimal choice is not to produce any product.

Recall that the optimal price $p^* = \theta^*q^*$, which follows the behavior of q^* since θ^* is constant. The solution has the following properties.

Proposition 1. *(i) The optimal quality level q^* increases in λ and decreases in β, α, and h; (ii) the optimal profit function Π_S^* increases in λ and decreases in β, α, and h.*

Observe that because the market coverage $1 - \theta^*$ is constant, the effective arrival rate $\lambda_p = (1 - \theta^*)\lambda$ is only sensitive to changes in the arrival rate λ. Therefore, when production costs α or capacity costs β increase, the firm has no other option but to lower the quality level to control capacity investment costs. We establish the monotonic effect on the optimal quality level of changes in either congestion cost h or the arrival rate λ. But even more insightful, and counterintuitive in their nature, are the effects of such factors on the behavior of the optimal capacity level μ^*, which we present in the following comparative statics.

Proposition 2. *(i) We define $M_r(\omega) := 2[1 - \omega + \sqrt{1 + \omega + \omega^2}]/9\sqrt{3}$, where $\omega = 27\alpha h/\lambda$. There exists a unique $\hat{\lambda}_S$ that solves $M = M_r(\omega)$, and the optimal production capacity μ^* has the following properties:*

$$\mu^* : \begin{cases} decreases\ in\ \lambda, & 0 < \lambda < \hat{\lambda}_S \\ increases\ in\ \lambda, & \lambda \geq \hat{\lambda}_S, \end{cases}$$

and

$$\mu^* : \begin{cases} is\ concave\ in\ \lambda, & 27\beta h < \lambda < 243\beta h \\ is\ convex\ in\ \lambda, & \lambda \geq 243\beta h. \end{cases}$$

(ii)   *If $\alpha = 0$ or $\beta \geq \alpha$, μ^* increases in β. If $\alpha > 0$ and $\beta < \alpha$,*

$$\mu^* : \begin{cases} decreases\ in\ \beta, & 0 < \beta < \hat{\beta}_S \\ increases\ in\ \beta, & \beta \geq \hat{\beta}_S, \end{cases}$$

where $\hat{\beta}_S = \alpha \left(\sqrt{27\alpha h + \lambda} - 3\sqrt{3\alpha h} \right)^2 \Big/ \lambda$. Furthermore, if $\alpha = 0$,

$$\mu^* : \begin{cases} is\ concave\ increasing\ in\ \beta, & 0 < \beta < \frac{\lambda}{243h} \\ is\ convex\ increasing\ in\ \beta, & \frac{\lambda}{243h} \leq \beta < \frac{\lambda}{27h}. \end{cases}$$

If $\alpha > 0$, we define

$$\hat{\beta}_C = \left[\frac{\lambda - 216\alpha h + \sqrt{(216\alpha h + \lambda)^2 + 1323\alpha h\lambda}}{27\sqrt{3h\lambda}} \right]^2$$

and

$$\Delta(\hat{\beta}_C) = 27 \left[\lambda\hat{\beta}_C \left(\sqrt{\frac{h\hat{\beta}_C}{\lambda}} - \frac{1}{9\sqrt{3}} \right) + \alpha \left(\frac{\lambda}{3\sqrt{3}} - 3\sqrt{h\lambda\hat{\beta}_C} + \frac{8h\hat{\beta}_C}{27\sqrt{3}} \right) \right].$$

When $\Delta(\hat{\beta}_C) \geq 0$, μ^* is convex in β. When $\Delta(\hat{\beta}_C) < 0$ there exist $\hat{\eta}_1 \in (0, \hat{\beta}_C)$ and $\hat{\eta}_2 > \hat{\beta}_C$ such that

$$\mu^* : \begin{cases} is\ convex\ in\ \beta, & 0 < \beta < \hat{\eta}_1 \\ is\ concave\ in\ \beta, & \hat{\eta}_1 \leq \beta < \hat{\eta}_2 \\ is\ convex\ in\ \beta, & \beta \geq \hat{\eta}_2. \end{cases}$$

(iii)   *The optimal capacity μ^* is linearly increasing in α and*

$$\mu^* : \begin{cases} is\ concave\ increasing\ in\ h, & 0 < h < \frac{\lambda}{243\beta} \\ is\ convex\ increasing\ in\ h, & \frac{\lambda}{243\beta} \leq h < \frac{\lambda}{27\beta}. \end{cases}$$

The optimal capacity μ^* increases in h because with no change in the effective arrival rate λ_p, the firm can only control costs by reducing congestion through increased capacity. Hence, because production and capacity costs are convex in the quality level, lowering quality allows the firm to control both the increased capacity costs and margins, by reducing variable costs to compensate for the price reduction from $p^* = \theta^* q^*$. Analogously, when α increases, the resulting lower quality level decreases the cost of capacity, which the firm increases in order to relieve congestion and its associated costs.

At first glance, one might expect the optimal capacity μ^* to be decreasing in the marginal capacity investment cost β. However, as Proposition 2 shows, the response of μ^* to changes in β (though λ_p^* is independent of it) depends on the relative magnitudes of α and β. If β dominates α (i.e., $\beta > \alpha$ or $\alpha = 0$), μ^* is increasing in β. To understand this result it is sufficient to consider the effect of β on q^*, and the convexity in q^* of capacity costs: For relatively large β, q^* is low and marginal capacity investment cost is low and relatively insensitive to changes in β; therefore, as β increases, the firm resorts to increasing its capacity investments in order to reduce congestion costs. The following result shows that for this case ($\alpha = 0$ or $\beta \geq \alpha$), the total operations costs (congestion plus capacity investment) decrease in β, supporting the assertion that μ^* increasing in β is an effective way to manage the system.

Proposition 3. *If $\alpha = 0$ or $\beta \geq \alpha$, the sum of congestion and capacity financing costs decreases in β.*

If variable production costs dominate (i.e., $\alpha > \beta$), the above result no longer holds. For low levels of β ($\beta < \hat{\beta}_S$), q^* is high, and the marginal capacity investment cost is high and highly sensitive to changes in β; therefore, as β increases the firm tightens its capacity. When β increases past a critical value ($\beta \geq \hat{\beta}_S$), q^* becomes sufficiently low for the marginal capacity cost to be relatively low and insensitive to changes in β. Hence capacity investment costs are dominated by congestion costs, which the firm controls by increasing capacity.

Even though θ^* is constant, the effective arrival rate λ_p is increasing in λ. Therefore, an increase in λ generates higher congestion, which can be relieved through capacity investments whose cost can in turn be controlled by reducing the quality level. However, the directional change in margins cannot be unequivocally determined at first glance because profits are also affected by the increase in λ_p. But from Proposition 1 it follows that as λ increases, optimal profits increase in q^* and outweigh the associated increase in marginal capacity costs and costlier congestion management. The lack of monotonicity of μ^* in λ can be explained similarly to that in β. Notice that $M_r(\omega)$ is decreasing in ω, which in turn is linearly increasing in α, and recall that $M = 2\sqrt{\beta h/\lambda}$. When β is relatively low, M is small, and the firm handles an increase in customer arrival rate by raising production capacity to reduce congestion. In contrast, when capacity investment costs are high, M is large, and the high quality level makes adding capacity expensive; therefore, the savings from reducing capacity outweigh the increase in congestion costs and μ^* becomes decreasing in λ.

Because θ^* is constant, the comparative statics of the utilization level ρ^* follow directly from those of μ^*.

Corollary 1. *(i) The optimal utilization level ρ^* is concave increasing in λ and convex decreasing in both α and h; (ii) if $\alpha = 0$ or $\beta \geq \alpha$, ρ^* decreases in β. If*

$\alpha > 0$ and $\beta < \alpha$, there exists a unique $\hat{\beta}_S = (\alpha/\lambda)\left(\sqrt{27\alpha h + \lambda} - 3\sqrt{3\alpha h}\right)^2$ such that

$$\rho^* : \begin{cases} \text{increases in } \beta, & \text{for } \beta \leq \hat{\beta}_S \\ \text{decreases in } \beta, & \text{for } \beta > \hat{\beta}_S. \end{cases}$$

Furthermore, ρ^* is convex decreasing in β when $\alpha = 0$. If $\alpha > 0$, there exists a unique $\hat{\beta}_A$ satisfying

$$\alpha = \frac{9\hat{\beta}_A\sqrt{h} - \sqrt{3\hat{\beta}_A\lambda} + \sqrt{\hat{\beta}_A\left(81\hat{\beta}_A h + 3\lambda - 14\sqrt{3h\hat{\beta}_A\lambda}\right)}}{6\sqrt{h}}.$$

Therefore,

$$\rho^* : \begin{cases} \text{is convex in } \beta, & \text{when } 0 \leq \beta < \hat{\beta}_A \\ \text{is concave in } \beta, & \text{when } \beta \geq \hat{\beta}_A. \end{cases}$$

As we have shown in this section, the correct product positioning is a challenging decision with unanticipated operational implications. According to our stylized model, such product positioning targets the top one-third of the market, with product quality that is increasing in market size, and decreasing in capacity investment, variable production, and congestion (holding) costs per unit of met demand. However, the total capacity and its resulting utilization for meeting the demand of the optimal product positioning have far from immediately intuitive comparative statics, especially with respect to market size and capacity investment cost per unit. The invested optimal capacity is non-monotonic to increased market size, first decreasing and then increasing, while the utilization level stays increasing in it. When the capacity investment costs per unit are dominant relative to the variable production costs, the capacity and its utilization are increasing in these costs; however, this effect becomes non-monotonic when such dominance is not present. These results emphasize the importance of capturing the queuing-related implications of product positioning decisions on the operational processes that will meet the resulting demand and how such effects lead to counterintuitive insights.

9.5 General Power Cost Functions

We now consider the case in which both capacity investment and variable production costs are general power functions of the product quality level, i.e., $b(q) = \beta q^\gamma$ and $c(q) = \alpha q^\gamma$, where $\gamma > 2$ and $\alpha, \beta > 0$. An increase in γ models a production technology that becomes more expensive in both capacity investment and production costs for a given quality level. The firm's profit function becomes

$$\max_{p,q,\mu} \Pi_G(p, q, \mu) = (p - \alpha q^\gamma)\lambda_p - \frac{h\lambda_p}{\mu - \lambda_p} - \beta q^\gamma \mu. \tag{9.5}$$

We obtain the optimal product positioning θ^* and the optimal quality level q^* using the same solution approach as for the quadratic cost functions case.

Theorem 2. *Consider a single product offering with $q \in [q_{min}, q_{max}]$ for any $q_{min} > 0$ and $b(q) = \beta q^{\gamma}$, $c(q) = \alpha q^{\gamma}$ where $\alpha, \beta > 0$ and $\gamma > 2$. For*

$$0 \leq M < 2\sqrt{\frac{\gamma-1}{2\gamma-1}} \left[\frac{1}{(2\gamma-1)q_{min}^{\gamma/2-1}} - (\alpha+\beta)q_{min}^{\frac{\gamma}{2}} \right],$$

the firm's optimal product positioning decision is given by $\theta^* = \gamma/(2\gamma-1)$. The optimal quality level q^* is the solution to

$$[\theta^* - \gamma(\alpha+\beta)q^{\gamma-1}](1-\theta^*)\lambda - \gamma q^{\gamma/2-1}\sqrt{h\beta(1-\theta^*)\lambda} = 0, \qquad (9.6)$$

and the optimal capacity and system's utilization are given by

$$\mu^* = (1-\theta^*)\lambda + \frac{1}{(q^*)^{\gamma/2}}\sqrt{\frac{h(1-\theta^*)\lambda}{\beta}}$$

and

$$\rho^* = \left[1 + \frac{1}{(q^*)^{\gamma/2}}\sqrt{\frac{h}{\beta(1-\theta^*)\lambda}} \right]^{-1},$$

respectively.
When

$$M \geq 2\sqrt{\frac{\gamma-1}{2\gamma-1}} \left[\frac{1}{(2\gamma-1)q_{min}^{\gamma/2-1}} - (\alpha+\beta)q_{min}^{\frac{\gamma}{2}} \right],$$

the firm's profit is non-positive and the optimal choice is not to produce any product.

Notice that Theorem 2 holds for any $\alpha, \beta > 0$. Similarly to the quadratic cost functions case, the optimal product positioning decision θ^* is constant and depends only on γ. It is straightforward to show that $\theta^* > 1/2$ for all $\gamma > 2$ and $\theta^* \to 1/2$ as $\gamma \to \infty$. Hence, the firm responds to higher capacity costs by expanding the market coverage.

The comparative statics of the optimal solution are similar to the case of quadratic cost functions. From the optimal product positioning θ^* and the optimal quality level q^*, we derive the following properties of the optimal solution for the case with general power cost functions.

Proposition 4. *(i) The optimal quality level q^* is increasing in λ and decreasing in α, β, and h, (ii) the optimal capacity level μ^* is increasing in α and h, (iii) μ^* is decreasing in β if $\beta < \hat{\beta}_G$ and increasing in β otherwise, where*

$$\hat{\beta}_G = \frac{(2\gamma-1)}{2\lambda(\gamma-1)} \left\{ \sqrt{h[\alpha\gamma(2\gamma-1)]^{-\frac{\gamma-2}{2(\gamma-1)}} + \frac{4\alpha\lambda(\gamma-1)^2}{2\gamma-1}}} \right.$$
$$\left. - \sqrt{h}[\alpha\gamma(2\gamma-1)]^{\frac{\gamma}{2(\gamma-1)}} \right\}^2.$$

(iv) Let

$$\mathscr{G}(\lambda;q) = q^{\frac{\gamma}{2}-1}\sqrt{h\beta} + \beta q^{\gamma-1}\sqrt{\lambda}\sqrt{\frac{\gamma-1}{2\gamma-1}} \quad and$$

$$\mathscr{H}(q) = \sqrt{\lambda}\sqrt{\frac{\gamma-1}{2\gamma-1}}\left(\frac{1}{2\gamma-1} - \alpha q^{\gamma-1}\right).$$

There exist a unique pair of $\hat{\lambda}_G$ and $\hat{q}$ which solve both $\mathscr{G}(\hat{\lambda}_G;\hat{q}) = \mathscr{H}(\hat{q})$ and

$$\frac{\gamma-2}{2(2\gamma-1)}\hat{q}^{\frac{\gamma}{2}}\sqrt{\beta\hat{\lambda}_G} + (\alpha+\beta)\hat{q}^{\frac{3}{2}\gamma-1}\sqrt{\beta\hat{\lambda}_G} + (\alpha+\beta)\hat{q}^{\gamma-1}\sqrt{h}\sqrt{\frac{2\gamma-1}{\gamma-1}}$$

$$= \frac{\sqrt{h}}{\gamma\sqrt{(\gamma-1)(2\gamma-1)}},$$

such that μ^* is decreasing in λ if $\lambda < \hat{\lambda}_G$ and increasing in λ otherwise. (v) The optimal utilization level ρ^* is increasing in λ and decreasing in α and h. In addition, ρ^* is increasing in λ if $\lambda < \hat{\lambda}_G$ and decreasing in λ otherwise.

To investigate the role of the degree of the variable costs' convexity, in the following result we analyze the effect of γ on the firm's optimal choices, imposing $q_{min} \geq 1$ to ensure variable costs are increasing in γ for any fixed $q \in [q_{min}, q_{max}]$.

Proposition 5. *For general power cost functions, with $\gamma > 2$ and $q_{min} \geq 1$, both the optimal design quality q^* and optimal utilization ρ^* are decreasing in γ, while the optimal capacity μ^* is increasing in γ.*

Therefore, as γ increases, the firm expands market coverage and lowers the quality level, thus reducing capacity costs, which leads it to increase capacity and thereby lessen congestion costs.

Our analysis with generalized power cost functions shows that expensive technologies in both capacity investment and variable production costs favor higher quality products and the careful targeting of the high-end market segments.

To illustrate the previous results, in Figure 9.1 we include plots for specific examples of the optimal design quality level q^* as a function of β and λ for several power cost functions characterized by different values of γ. In Figure 9.2 we include the corresponding plots for the optimal capacity level μ^* ($h = 0.05$, $\alpha = 0.06$, $\lambda = 1$ in Figures 9.1(a) and 9.2(a), and $h = 0.05$, $\alpha = 0.06$, $\beta = 0.03$ in Figures 9.1(b) and 9.2(b)). Observe that for all of these instances $q^* \geq 1$, and as shown in Propositions 1, 4, and 5, q^* is decreasing in β and γ and increasing in λ. Moreover, μ^* is increasing in γ, and as both β and λ increase, μ^* decreases up to a critical value and increases thereafter.

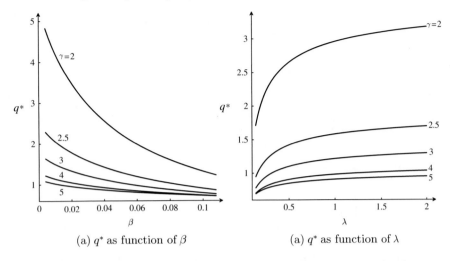

(a) q^* as function of β (a) q^* as function of λ

Fig. 9.1 Illustration of properties of optimal quality levels for different power cost functions.

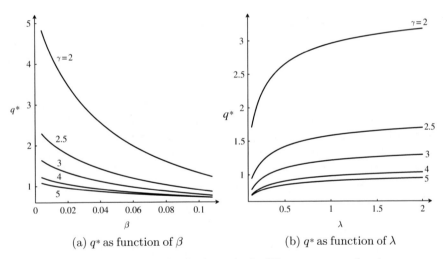

(a) q^* as function of β (b) q^* as function of λ

Fig. 9.2 Illustration of properties of optimal capacity for different power cost functions.

9.6 Conclusions and Current Research

Decisions on how to choose the product positioning in terms of offered quality and price are important and challenging decisions for all firms. Frequently such decisions are made with a sales and revenue growth mindset, with increased product quality allowing to price in a way that extracts higher rents from consumers. However, such decisions have serious implications for the operational investments and variable production costs in meeting customer demand. Often such considerations become afterthoughts of an already made product design decision, mostly based on market growth and desirable market coverage issues. The typical outcome of this traditional sequential nature product development approach is that the bottom-line implications of product design quality are exaggerated on revenue growth and underestimated on capacity investments and production expenses. In this chapter we provide an integrated marketing-operations decision model that depicts relevant tradeoffs on both the revenue and cost sides of the product design debate and offers insights into the factors that determine the right level of design quality to be offered. We provided useful insights into the positioning of the offered product, the resulting market coverage, and the product design effects on production costs and the operational investments, especially on congestion measures of the supporting processes (utilization, work-in-process inventories, etc.).

As it becomes apparent from our discussions in Sections 9.4 and 9.5, the correct product positioning is a challenging decision with unanticipated operational implications. According to our stylized model, such product positioning targets a constant top segment of the market, with product quality that is increasing in market size and decreasing in capacity investment, variable production, and congestion (holding) costs per unit of met demand. However, the total capacity and its resulting utilization in meeting the demand of the optimal product positioning have far from immediately intuitive comparative statics, especially with respect to market size and capacity investment cost per unit. The invested optimal capacity is non-monotonic to increased market size, first decreasing and then increasing, while the utilization level stays increasing in it. When the capacity investment costs per unit are dominant relative to the variable production costs, the capacity and its utilization are increasing in these costs; however, this effect becomes non-monotonic when such dominance is not present. These early results emphasize the importance of capturing the queuing-related implications of product positioning decisions on the operational processes that will meet the resulting demand and how such effects lead to counterintuitive insights. Our analysis with the use of generalized power cost functions allows us to observe that expensive technologies in both capacity investment and variable production costs favor higher quality products and the careful targeting of the high-end market segments.

Our current research builds on this work in several ways. First, we are now able to analyze the design of product lines with multiple products and understand how product variety affects the above insights. Second, we offer insights into the optimal variety to offer and explain why limited variety is optimal even in the absence of fixed costs. We emphasize the system's congestion effects on optimal variety in contrast to economies of scale and fixed costs considerations in other work. Finally, we have also incorporated a more detailed representation of different types of production technologies into the model and are able to study how they affect the product line design decisions. In particular, we explore how dedicated versus flexible production technologies affect the optimal product variety offerings. For these and other enhancements of the work presented in this chapter please see Chayet et al. (2008).

The current research is a definite first step in addressing in an integrated way the optimal product design and capacity investments questions for a monopolist firm. More research is needed in understanding the impacts of different competitive environments in both number of players and dimensions of competition. Furthermore, more detailed accounting of combined economies of scale (both fixed costs and congestion phenomena) and economies of scope (non-linear complexity costs of product variety affecting both capacity investment and variable production costs) of production facilities can lead to new theories and operational measures in describing the economics of production systems supporting product line in the marketplace.

Appendix

Proofs

Proof of Theorem 1

Substituting $q^*(\theta)$ into the firm's profit function, we have

$$\max_\theta \; \Pi_S(\theta, q^*(\theta)) = [\theta q^*(\theta) - (\alpha + \beta)q^{*2}(\theta)](1-\theta)\lambda - 2q^*(\theta)\sqrt{\beta h(1-\theta)\lambda}$$

$$= \frac{\theta^2}{4(\alpha+\beta)}(1-\theta)\lambda - \frac{\theta}{\alpha+\beta}\sqrt{h\beta(1-\theta)\lambda} + \frac{\beta h}{\alpha+\beta}$$

$$= \frac{\lambda}{4(\alpha+\beta)}\left(\theta\sqrt{1-\theta} - M\right)^2$$

$$\text{s.t.} \quad \theta\sqrt{1-\theta} > M, \quad \text{where } M = 2\sqrt{\frac{\beta h}{\lambda}}.$$

Therefore, the problem can be recast as that of maximizing $\theta\sqrt{1-\theta}$ such that $\theta\sqrt{1-\theta} > M$. Since $\theta\sqrt{1-\theta}$ is strictly concave in θ, the optimal θ^* can be obtained by letting

$$(\theta\sqrt{1-\theta})' = \sqrt{1-\theta} - \frac{\theta}{2\sqrt{1-\theta}} = 0,$$

which yields $\theta^* = 2/3$. To ensure positive profits, the condition $M < 2/(3\sqrt{3})$ must be imposed. Finally, the expressions for $q^*(\theta^*)$, $\mu^*(\theta^*, q^*)$, and $\Pi_S^*(\theta^*, q^*)$ follow directly from using $\theta^* = 2/3$. □

Proof of Proposition 1

By Theorem 1, it is straightforward to show that $dq^*/d\lambda > 0$ and $dq^*/d\beta$, $dq^*/d\alpha, dq^*/dh < 0$. The properties of Π_S^* follow directly once the optimal profit function is rewritten as $\Pi_S^* = \left(\sqrt{\lambda} - 3\sqrt{3\beta h}\right)^2/[27(\alpha+\beta)]$. □

Proof of Proposition 2

From Theorem 1,

$$\frac{d\mu^*}{d\lambda} = \frac{\beta\left[\lambda(2\sqrt{\beta\lambda} - 9\beta\sqrt{3h}) + \alpha(3\lambda\sqrt{3h} - 54h\sqrt{\beta\lambda})\right]}{6\sqrt{\beta\lambda}(\sqrt{\beta\lambda} - 3\beta\sqrt{3h})^2}.$$

To obtain the derivative's sign, it suffices to consider the numerator, which can be written as

$$\frac{\lambda^2}{\sqrt{h}}\left\{M\left[1 - \frac{9\sqrt{3}}{4}M\right] + \omega[3\sqrt{3} - 27M]\right\} = \frac{\lambda^2}{\sqrt{h}}\varphi(M;\omega),$$

where $M = 2\sqrt{h\beta/\lambda}$ and $\omega = 27\alpha h/\lambda$. $\varphi(M;\omega)$ is a quadratic function of M, with $\varphi(0;\omega) = 3\sqrt{3}\omega$ and $\varphi\left(2/(3\sqrt{3});\omega\right) = -3\sqrt{3}\omega - 1/(3\sqrt{3}) < 0$. The unique positive root of $\varphi(M;\omega) = 0$ is

$$M_r(\omega) := \frac{2}{9\sqrt{3}}[1 - \omega + \sqrt{1 + \omega + \omega^2}].$$

$M_r(\omega)$ decreases in ω since $M_r'(\omega) < 0$ and then $M_r(\omega) \leq 4/(9\sqrt{3}) < 2/(3\sqrt{3})$.

Therefore, M decreases in λ while $M_r(\omega)$ increases in λ. For $0 \leq M < 2/(3\sqrt{3})$, there exists a unique $\hat{\lambda}_S$ such that $M = M_r(\omega)$ where $\lambda = \hat{\lambda}_S$. But

$$\varphi(M;\omega) : \begin{cases} > 0, & \text{for } \lambda > \hat{\lambda}_S \\ = 0, & \text{for } \lambda = \hat{\lambda}_S \\ < 0, & \text{for } \lambda < \hat{\lambda}_S. \end{cases}$$

The second-order derivative of μ^* with respect to λ is

$$\frac{d^2\mu^*}{d\lambda^2} = \frac{\beta(\alpha+\beta)\sqrt{h}(\sqrt{3\beta\lambda} - 27\beta\sqrt{h})}{6\sqrt{\beta\lambda}(\sqrt{\beta\lambda} - 3\beta\sqrt{3h})^3},$$

which vanishes when $\lambda = 243\beta h$. Since $M < 2/(3\sqrt{3})$, we need $\lambda > 27\beta h$.

Similarly,

$$\frac{d\mu^*}{d\beta} = \frac{\lambda^2\sqrt{3h}\left[\beta + \alpha\left((9/\sqrt{3})M - 1\right)\right]}{2\beta\sqrt{\beta\lambda}(\sqrt{\lambda} - 3\sqrt{3\beta h})^2}.$$

When $\alpha = 0$, $d\mu^*/d\beta > 0$. If $\alpha > 0$, then

$$M \geq \frac{1}{3\sqrt{3}}\left(1 - \frac{\beta}{\alpha}\right), \quad \frac{\beta}{\alpha} + \frac{9}{\sqrt{3}}M - 1 \geq 0.$$

Therefore, if $\alpha = 0$ or $\beta \geq \alpha$, $d\mu^*/d\beta > 0$. If $\alpha > 0$ and $\beta < \alpha$, there exists a unique $\hat{\beta}_S$ such that

$$\frac{\hat{\beta}_S}{\alpha} + \frac{6\sqrt{3h\hat{\beta}_S}}{\sqrt{\lambda}} - 1 = 0,$$

where

$$\hat{\beta}_S = \frac{\alpha}{\lambda}\left(\sqrt{27\alpha h + \lambda} - 3\sqrt{3\alpha h}\right)^2.$$

Then, $d\mu^*/d\beta > 0$ when $\beta > \hat{\beta}_S$; for $\beta = \hat{\beta}_S$, $d\mu^*/d\beta = 0$; and, when $\beta < \hat{\beta}_S$, $d\mu^*/d\beta < 0$.

The second-order derivative of μ^* with respect to β is

$$\frac{d^2\mu^*}{d\beta^2} = \frac{\lambda^2\sqrt{h\beta\lambda}\left[\lambda\beta\left(27\sqrt{h\beta/\lambda} - \sqrt{3}\right) + 3\alpha(\sqrt{3}\lambda - 27\sqrt{h\beta\lambda} + 72\sqrt{3}h\beta)\right]}{4(\beta\lambda)^{3/2}(\sqrt{\beta\lambda} - 3\beta\sqrt{3h})^3}.$$

When $\alpha = 0$, $d^2\mu^*/d\beta^2 = 0$ when $\beta = \lambda/(243h)$. If $\alpha > 0$, let $x = \sqrt{\beta}$, and

$$\phi(x) = \lambda x^2\left(27\sqrt{\frac{h}{\lambda}}x - \sqrt{3}\right) + 3\alpha(\sqrt{3}\lambda - 27\sqrt{h\lambda}x + 72\sqrt{3}hx^2).$$

When $\beta = 0$, $\phi(x) = 3\sqrt{3}\alpha\lambda > 0$:

$$\phi'(x) = \lambda x\left(81\sqrt{\frac{h}{\lambda}}x - 2\sqrt{3}\right) + \alpha(432\sqrt{3}hx - 81\sqrt{h\lambda}).$$

The positive root of $\phi'(x) = 0$ is

$$x^* = \frac{\lambda - 216\alpha h + \sqrt{(216\alpha h + \lambda)^2 + 1323\alpha h\lambda}}{27\sqrt{3h\lambda}}.$$

$\phi'(x) < 0$ as $0 < x < x^*$, and $\phi'(x) > 0$ when $x > x^*$. Let $x^* = \sqrt{\hat{\beta}_C}$. Then, the minimum of $d^2\mu^*/d\beta^2$ is attained at $\hat{\beta}_C$. $d^2\mu^*/d\beta^2$ decreases in β as $0 < \beta < \hat{\beta}_C$, and $d^2\mu^*/d\beta^2$ increases when $\beta > \hat{\beta}_C$. Denote $\Delta(\hat{\beta}_C) = \phi(x^*)$. Therefore, $d^2\mu^*/d\beta^2 > 0$ for all β if $\Delta(\hat{\beta}_C) > 0$. When $\Delta(\hat{\beta}_C) < 0$, there are two positive roots of $d^2\mu^*/d\beta^2 = 0$ denoted by $\hat{\eta}_1$ and $\hat{\eta}_2$, in which $0 < \hat{\eta}_1 < \hat{\beta}_C$ and $\hat{\eta}_2 > \hat{\beta}_C$.

It is straightforward to show that $d\mu^*/d\alpha, d\mu^*/dh > 0$. The result follows from

$$\frac{d^2\mu^*}{d\alpha^2} = \frac{\lambda\sqrt{3h}}{\sqrt{\beta\lambda} - 3\beta\sqrt{3h}}$$

and

$$\frac{d^2\mu^*}{dh^2} = \frac{\lambda\beta(\alpha + \beta)(27\sqrt{h\beta\lambda} - \sqrt{3}\lambda)}{4h^{3/2}(\sqrt{\beta\lambda} - 3\beta\sqrt{3h})^3}. \qquad \square$$

Proof of Proposition 3

Let C denote the operations costs, defined as the sum of congestion and capacity investment costs. Then,

$$C = 2q^* \sqrt{\beta h \lambda/3} + \beta(q^*)^2 \lambda/3$$

$$= \frac{1}{(\alpha+\beta)^2} \left(\frac{1}{27} \beta\lambda + \frac{2}{3\sqrt{3}} \alpha \sqrt{\beta h \lambda} - \beta^2 h + 2\alpha\beta h \right).$$

$$\frac{dC}{d\beta} = \frac{1}{(\alpha+\beta)^3} \left[\frac{\lambda(\alpha-\beta)}{27} + \frac{\alpha\sqrt{h\lambda}(\alpha-3\beta)}{3\sqrt{3\beta}} + 2\alpha h(\alpha-\beta) \right].$$

When $\alpha = 0$ or $\beta \geq \alpha$, $dC/d\beta < 0$. $\square$

Proof of Corollary 1

Since $\theta^* = 2/3$, $\rho^* = \lambda/(3\mu^*)$. It follows from Proposition 2 that ρ^* is decreasing in α and h. It is straightforward to show that

$$\frac{d\rho^*}{d\lambda} = \frac{3\sqrt{3h}\beta(\alpha+\beta)}{2\sqrt{\beta\lambda}(3\sqrt{3h}+\sqrt{\beta\lambda})^2} > 0,$$

so ρ^* increases in λ. The proof of *(ii)* follows directly from the properties of $d\mu^*/d\beta$.

The second-order derivatives of utilization level ρ^* follow from Theorem 1:

$$\frac{d^2\rho^*}{d\alpha^2} = \frac{54h\sqrt{\beta\lambda}(1-3\sqrt{3}\sqrt{\beta h/\lambda})}{(3\alpha\sqrt{3h}+\sqrt{\beta\lambda})^3} > 0,$$

$$\frac{d^2\rho^*}{dh^2} = \frac{3(\alpha+\beta)\sqrt{\beta\lambda}(\sqrt{3\beta\lambda}+27\alpha\sqrt{h})}{4h^{3/2}(3\alpha\sqrt{3h}+\sqrt{\beta\lambda})^3} > 0,$$

$$\frac{d^2\rho^*}{d\lambda^2} = -\frac{9\beta^2(\alpha+\beta)\sqrt{h}(3\alpha\sqrt{h}+\sqrt{3\beta\lambda})}{4(\beta\lambda)^{3/2}(3\alpha\sqrt{3h}+\sqrt{\beta\lambda})^3} < 0,$$

$$\frac{d^2\rho^*}{d\beta^2} = \frac{3\sqrt{3}\lambda^2\sqrt{h}[\beta\sqrt{\beta\lambda}-3\alpha(\sqrt{\beta\lambda}+\alpha\sqrt{3h}-3\beta\sqrt{3h})]}{4(\beta\lambda)^{3/2}(3\alpha\sqrt{3h}+\sqrt{\beta\lambda})^3}.$$

If $\alpha = 0$, $d^2\rho^*/d\beta^2 > 0$. If $\alpha > 0$, let $\beta\sqrt{\beta\lambda}-3\alpha(\sqrt{\beta\lambda}+\alpha\sqrt{3h}-3\beta\sqrt{3h}) = 0$, which implies

$$\alpha = \frac{9\beta\sqrt{h} - \sqrt{3\beta\lambda} \pm \sqrt{\beta(81\beta h+3\lambda-14\sqrt{3h\beta\lambda})}}{6\sqrt{h}}.$$

Since

$$9\beta\sqrt{h} - \sqrt{3\beta\lambda} - \sqrt{\beta(81\beta h+3\lambda-14\sqrt{3h\beta\lambda})} < 0,$$

there exists a unique $\hat{\beta}_A$ satisfying

$$\alpha = \frac{9\hat{\beta}_A\sqrt{h} - \sqrt{3\hat{\beta}_A\lambda} + \sqrt{\hat{\beta}_A(81\hat{\beta}_A h + 3\lambda - 14\sqrt{3h\hat{\beta}_A\lambda})}}{6\sqrt{h}}. \qquad \square$$

Proof of Theorem 2

Given θ and q, the optimal capacity is

$$\mu^*(\theta,q) = (1-\theta)\lambda + \frac{1}{q^{\gamma/2}}\sqrt{\frac{h(1-\theta)\lambda}{\beta}}.$$

We can rewrite the firm's problem as

$$\max_{\theta,q} \Pi_G(\theta,q) = [\theta q - (\alpha+\beta)q^\gamma](1-\theta)\lambda - 2q^{\gamma/2}\sqrt{h\beta(1-\theta)\lambda}.$$

The profit function $\Pi_G(\theta,q)$ is strictly concave in q for every θ. Then, the optimal quality level $q^*(\theta)$ in terms of θ is given by the solution of

$$\{\theta - \gamma(\alpha+\beta)[q^*(\theta)]^{\gamma-1}\}(1-\theta)\lambda - \gamma[q^*(\theta)]^{\gamma/2-1}\sqrt{h\beta(1-\theta)\lambda} = 0. \quad (9.7)$$

Since $q \geq q_{\min}$, to ensure that (9.7) yields a solution with a positive quality level, we need

$$q_{\min}^{\gamma/2-1}\sqrt{h\beta(1-\theta^*)\lambda} + (\alpha+\beta)(1-\theta^*)\lambda q_{\min}^{\gamma-1} < \frac{\theta^*(1-\theta^*)\lambda}{\gamma}.$$

Therefore, the profitability condition becomes

$$M < 2\sqrt{\frac{\gamma-1}{2\gamma-1}}\left[\frac{1}{(2\gamma-1)q_{\min}^{\gamma/2-1}} - (\alpha+\beta)q_{\min}^{\gamma/2}\right].$$

Applying the implicit function theorem to (9.7) yields

$$\frac{dq^*(\theta)}{d\theta} = \frac{(1-\theta)\lambda q/\gamma - \frac{q^{\gamma/2}}{2}\sqrt{\frac{h\beta\lambda}{1-\theta}}}{\theta(1-\theta)\lambda\left(1-\frac{1}{\gamma}\right) - \frac{\gamma}{2}q^{\gamma/2-1}\sqrt{h\beta(1-\theta)\lambda}}.$$

Substitution of $q^*(\theta)$ into the firm's profit function yields the single variable function $\Pi_G(\theta,q^*(\theta))$. Therefore,

$$\frac{d\Pi_G(\theta,q^*(\theta))}{d\theta} = \lambda q^*(\theta)\left[1-\theta\left(2-\frac{1}{\gamma}\right)\right].$$

For $\theta \in (0,1)$, $1 - \theta(2 - 1/\gamma)$ is linear in θ. Then, there exists a θ^* such that $1 - \theta^*(2 - 1/\gamma) = 0$, i.e., $\theta^* = \gamma/(2\gamma - 1)$. Since $q^*(\theta) > 0$, $\Pi_G(\theta, q^*(\theta))$ increases in θ when $\theta \in (0, \theta^*)$ and $\Pi_G(\theta, q^*(\theta))$ decreases in θ when $\theta \in (\theta^*, 1)$. By direct substitution $\Pi_G(\theta, q^*(\theta))|_{\theta=0} = 0$ and $\Pi_G(\theta, q^*(\theta))|_{\theta=1} = 0$. Therefore, $\Pi_G(\theta, q^*(\theta))$ is unimodal in θ. The maximum is attained when $\theta = \theta^*$. The optimal quality level q^* follows from solving the first-order optimality condition (9.6). $\qquad \square$

Proof of Proposition 4

The optimal quality level q^* is the root of

$$\sqrt{\frac{\gamma-1}{2\gamma-1}} \left[\frac{1}{2\gamma-1} - (\alpha+\beta)(q^*)^{\gamma-1} \right] = (q^*)^{\gamma/2-1} \sqrt{\frac{h\beta}{\lambda}}.$$

Define

$$G(\lambda, \alpha, \beta, h; q) = \sqrt{\lambda} \sqrt{\frac{\gamma-1}{2\gamma-1}} \left[\frac{1}{2\gamma-1} - (\alpha+\beta)q^{\gamma-1} \right] - q^{\gamma/2-1} \sqrt{h\beta}.$$

Clearly, $G(\lambda, \alpha, \beta, h; 0) > 0$. For any $\lambda_1 > \lambda_2 > 0$, let q_1 and q_2 be roots of $G(\lambda_1, \alpha, \beta, h; q) = 0$ and $G(\lambda_2, \alpha, \beta, h; q) = 0$, respectively. For any $q > 0$ such that $1/(2\gamma-1) - (\alpha+\beta)q^{\gamma-1} > 0$, it follows that $G(\lambda_1, \alpha, \beta, h; q) > G(\lambda_2, \alpha, \beta, h; q)$, and thus $q_1 > q_2$. Therefore, the optimal quality level q^* is increasing in λ. It is straightforward to show that q^* is decreasing in α, β, and h by showing that $dG(\alpha)/d\alpha, dG(\beta)/d\beta, dG(h)/dh < 0$.

The optimal quality level q^* satisfies

$$\mathscr{F}(\lambda, \alpha, \beta, h; q^*) = \sqrt{\lambda} \sqrt{\frac{\gamma-1}{2\gamma-1}} \left[\frac{1}{2\gamma-1} - (\alpha+\beta)(q^*)^{\gamma-1} \right] - (q^*)^{\gamma/2-1} \sqrt{h\beta} = 0,$$

and by the implicit function theorem

$$\frac{dq^*(h)}{dh} = -\frac{\partial \mathscr{F}}{\partial h} \Big/ \frac{\partial \mathscr{F}}{\partial q^*}.$$

The optimal capacity is

$$\mu^*(\lambda, \beta, h; q^*) = \frac{\lambda(\gamma-1)}{2\gamma-1} + \frac{1}{(q^*)^{\gamma/2}} \sqrt{\frac{h\lambda(\gamma-1)}{\beta(2\gamma-1)}}.$$

Therefore

$$\frac{d\mu^*}{dh} = \frac{\partial \mu^*(\lambda, \beta, h; q^*)}{\partial h} + \frac{\partial \mu^*(\lambda, \beta, h; q^*)}{\partial q^*} \frac{dq^*(h)}{dh} > 0,$$

so μ^* is increasing in h. Similarly, we show that μ^* is increasing in α by showing that $d\mu^*(\alpha)/d\alpha > 0$.

In contrast to the above results, μ^* does not change monotonically in β. We have

$$\frac{d\mu^*}{d\beta} = \frac{\lambda(\gamma-1)\sqrt{h}\left[\frac{1}{2\gamma-1} - \alpha\gamma(q^*)^{\gamma-1}\right]}{2(2\gamma-1)(q^*)^{\gamma-1}\beta\sqrt{\beta}\left[(\gamma-1)(\alpha+\beta)(q^*)^{\frac{\gamma}{2}}\sqrt{\frac{\lambda(\gamma-1)}{2\gamma-1}} + \left(\frac{\gamma}{2}-1\right)\sqrt{h\beta}\right]}.$$

The first-order condition

$$[\theta^* - \gamma(\alpha+\beta)q^{\gamma-1}](1-\theta^*)\lambda - \gamma q^{\gamma/2-1}\sqrt{h\beta(1-\theta^*)\lambda} = 0$$

can be written as

$$q^{\gamma/2-1}\sqrt{h\beta} + \beta q^{\gamma-1}\sqrt{\lambda}\sqrt{\frac{\gamma-1}{2\gamma-1}} = \sqrt{\lambda}\sqrt{\frac{\gamma-1}{2\gamma-1}}\left(\frac{1}{2\gamma-1} - \alpha q^{\gamma-1}\right).$$

Let

$$\mathcal{G}(\beta;q) = q^{\frac{\gamma}{2}-1}\sqrt{h\beta} + \beta q^{\gamma-1}\sqrt{\lambda}\sqrt{\frac{\gamma-1}{2\gamma-1}}$$

and

$$\mathcal{H}(q) = \sqrt{\lambda}\sqrt{\frac{\gamma-1}{2\gamma-1}}\left(\frac{1}{2\gamma-1} - \alpha q^{\gamma-1}\right).$$

It is straightforward to show that $\mathcal{G}(\beta;q)$ is increasing in β, $\mathcal{G}(\beta;0) = 0$, $\mathcal{H}(q)$ is decreasing in q, and $\mathcal{H}(0) = \sqrt{\lambda}\sqrt{(\gamma-1)/(2\gamma-1)} > 0$. Define q_0 and q_1 such that $\mathcal{H}(q_0) = 0$ and $1/(2\gamma-1) - \alpha\gamma q_1^{\gamma-1} = 0$. Then,

$$q_0 = \left[\frac{1}{\alpha(2\gamma-1)}\right]^{1/(\gamma-1)}, \quad q_1 = \left[\frac{1}{\alpha\gamma(2\gamma-1)}\right]^{1/(\gamma-1)},$$

and $q_0 > q_1$. Let q^* be the root of $\mathcal{G}(\beta;q^*) = \mathcal{H}(q^*)$. It follows that $q^*(\beta)$ is decreasing in β and $q^* \in (0, q_0)$. Moreover, $q^* \to q_0$ as $\beta \to 0$ and $q^* \to 0$ as $\beta \to \infty$. Let $\hat{\beta}_G$ solve $\mathcal{G}(\hat{\beta}_G;q_1) = \mathcal{H}(q_1)$, then

$$\hat{\beta}_G = \frac{2\gamma-1}{2\lambda(\gamma-1)}$$
$$\cdot\left\{\sqrt{h\left[\frac{1}{\alpha\gamma(2\gamma-1)}\right]^{\frac{\gamma-2}{2(\gamma-1)}} + \frac{4\alpha\lambda(\gamma-1)^2}{2\gamma-1}} - \sqrt{h}[\alpha\gamma(2\gamma-1)]^{\frac{\gamma}{2(\gamma-1)}}\right\}^2.$$

Therefore, $d\mu^*/d\beta$ is negative when $\beta < \hat{\beta}_G$, zero when $\beta = \hat{\beta}_G$, and positive when $\beta > \hat{\beta}_G$. Similarly,

$$\frac{d\mu^*(\lambda)}{d\lambda} = (\gamma-1)\left[\frac{\gamma-2}{2(2\gamma-1)}\sqrt{\beta\lambda}q^{\gamma/2} + (\alpha+\beta)\sqrt{\beta\lambda}q^{(3/2)\gamma-1}\right.$$

$$\left. + \sqrt{h}\sqrt{\frac{2\gamma-1}{\gamma-1}}(\alpha+\beta)q^{\gamma-1} - \frac{\sqrt{h}}{\gamma\sqrt{(\gamma-1)(2\gamma-1)}}\right]$$

$$\cdot\left\{(2\gamma-1)q^{\gamma/2}\sqrt{\beta\lambda}\left[\frac{\gamma-2}{2(2\gamma-1)} + (\alpha+\beta)q^{\gamma-1}\right]\right\}^{-1}.$$

There exist $\hat{\lambda}_G$ and q_2 which solve both $\mathscr{G}(\hat{\lambda}_G;q_2) = \mathscr{H}(q_2)$ and

$$\frac{\gamma-2}{2(2\gamma-1)}q_2^{\gamma/2}\sqrt{\beta\hat{\lambda}_G} + (\alpha+\beta)q_2^{(3/2)\gamma-1}\sqrt{\beta\hat{\lambda}_G} + (\alpha+\beta)q_2^{\gamma-1}\sqrt{h}\sqrt{\frac{2\gamma-1}{\gamma-1}}$$

$$= \frac{\sqrt{h}}{\gamma\sqrt{(\gamma-1)(2\gamma-1)}},$$

and it follows that $d\mu^*/d\lambda$ is negative, zero, and positive when $\lambda < \hat{\lambda}_G$, $\lambda = \hat{\lambda}_G$, and $\lambda > \hat{\lambda}_G$, respectively. Notice that

$$\rho^* = \left[1 + \frac{1}{(q^*)^{\gamma/2}}\sqrt{\frac{h(2\gamma-1)}{\beta\lambda(\gamma-1)}}\right]^{-1}.$$

Since q^* is increasing in λ and decreasing in α and h, ρ^* is increasing in λ and decreasing in α and h. Finally, from

$$\frac{d\mu^*}{d\beta} = \frac{d\mathscr{A}(\beta)}{d\beta}\left[\lambda\left(\frac{\gamma-1}{2\gamma-1}\right)\right]^{-1},$$

where

$$\mathscr{A}(\beta) = \frac{1}{(q^*)^{\gamma/2}}\sqrt{\frac{h(2\gamma-1)}{\beta\lambda(\gamma-1)}}.$$

The comparative statics for ρ^* follow from those of μ^*.   □

Proof of Proposition 5

Applying the implicit function theorem to (9.7),

$$\frac{dq^*(\gamma)}{d\gamma} = \frac{-\dfrac{4\gamma-5}{2(\gamma-1)(2\gamma-1)^2} - \dfrac{(\alpha+\beta)q^{\gamma-1}}{2(\gamma-1)(2\gamma-1)} - \dfrac{(\alpha+\beta)q^{\gamma-1}\log q}{2} - \dfrac{\log q}{2(2\gamma-1)}}{\dfrac{(\alpha+\beta)q^{\gamma-2}(3\gamma-2)}{4} + \dfrac{\gamma-2}{4(\gamma-1)q}},$$

and since $q \geq q_{\min} \geq 1$, $dq^*(\gamma)/d\gamma < 0$.

Let $C = \sqrt{h\lambda/\beta}$. From

$$\mu^* = \lambda \left[\frac{\gamma - 1}{2\gamma - 1} + \frac{C}{(q^*)^{\gamma/2}} \sqrt{\frac{\gamma - 1}{2\gamma - 1}} \right]$$

it follows that

$$\frac{d\mu^*(\gamma)}{d\gamma} = \frac{1}{(2\gamma - 1)^2} + \frac{C}{2(q^*)^{\gamma/2}(2\gamma - 1)^2} \sqrt{\frac{\gamma - 1}{2\gamma - 1}}$$

$$- \frac{C}{2(q^*)^{\gamma/2}} \sqrt{\frac{\gamma - 1}{2\gamma - 1}} \left(\log q^* + \frac{\gamma}{q^*} \frac{dq^*(\gamma)}{d\gamma} \right).$$

It is straightforward to show that $d\mu^*(\gamma)/d\gamma > 0$.

Notice that

$$\rho^* = \left[1 + \frac{1}{(q^*)^{\gamma/2}} \sqrt{\frac{h(2\gamma - 1)}{\beta\lambda(\gamma - 1)}} \right]^{-1}.$$

Let

$$\mathscr{B}(\gamma) = \frac{1}{(q^*)^{\gamma/2}} \sqrt{\frac{h(2\gamma - 1)}{\beta\lambda(\gamma - 1)}}.$$

It is straightforward to show that $d\mathscr{B}(\gamma)/d\gamma > 0$, so $\mathscr{B}(\gamma)$ increases in γ, which implies ρ^* is decreasing in γ. □

References

Benjaafar S, Gupta D (1998) Scope versus focus: Issues of flexibility, capacity, and number of production facilities. IIE Trans 30(5):413–425

Chayet S, Kouvelis P, Yu DZ (2008) Product Variety and Capacity Investments in Congested Production Systems. Working Paper, Olin Business School, Washington University in St. Louis

Choudhary V, Ghose A, Mukhopadhyay T, Uday R (2005) Personalized pricing and quality differentiation. Management Sci 51(7):1120–1130

de Groote X (1994) The flexibility of production processes: A general framework. Management Sci 40(7):933–945

Moorthy KS (1984) Market segmentation, self-selection, and product line design. Marketing Sci 3(4):288–305

Mussa M, Rosen S (1978) Monopoly and product quality. J Econom Theory 18:301–317

Netessine S, Taylor TA (2007) Product line design and production technology. Marketing Sci 26(1):101–117

Chapter 10
Selling to Strategic Customers: Opaque Selling Strategies

Kinshuk Jerath, Serguei Netessine, and Senthil K. Veeraraghavan

Abstract Over the past few years, firms in the travel and entertainment industries have begun using novel sales strategies for revenue management. In this chapter, we study a selling strategy called opaque selling, in which firms guarantee one of several fully specified products, but hide the identity of the product that the consumer will actually obtain until after the purchase is completed. Several firms such as Hotwire, Priceline, and Mystery Flights engage in opaque selling of travel products. The academic literature in this area is recent and evolving. We first survey the nascent literature on opaque selling strategies. After presenting the current state of theory and practice, we analyze in-depth a model of competing firms selling horizontally differentiated products through an opaque channel. Consumers strategically time their purchases by developing rational expectations about future availability in the opaque market, keeping in mind that demand is uncertain and product supply could be limited. This model helps illustrate the conditions under which opaque selling can increase firm profits. We conclude the chapter by discussing ongoing research and charting out future research directions.

10.1 Introduction

The emergence of electronic commerce has had a massive impact on the travel industry. In just over a decade after online ticket sales were introduced in the travel

Kinshuk Jerath
Tepper School of Business, Carnegie Mellon University, Pittsburgh, PA, USA,
e-mail: kinshuk@cmu.edu

Serguei Netessine
The Wharton School, University of Pennsylvania, Philadelphia, PA, USA,
e-mail: netessine@wharton.upenn.edu

Senthil K. Veeraraghavan
The Wharton School, University of Pennsylvania, Philadelphia, PA, USA,
e-mail: senthilv@wharton.upenn.edu.

S. Netessine, C.S. Tang (eds.), *Consumer-Driven Demand and Operations Management Models*, International Series in Operations Research & Management Science 131, DOI 10.1007/978-0-387-98026-3_10, © Springer Science+Business Media, LLC 2009

industry, more than 50% of airline tickets are sold online (SITA 2007), and this proportion is increasing at a fast rate – from 2001 to 2003, online leisure travel bookings in the United States more than tripled (Tedeschi 2005). The major players in the online travel market are Expedia, Travelocity, Orbitz, Hotwire, and Priceline. The first three companies sell regular or *transparent* tickets: consumers see a posted price against each ticket that is available and make their purchase decisions. In addition, technological advancements brought about by electronic commerce have also enabled firms to employ other creative selling strategies. For instance, Hotwire and Priceline offer opaque tickets, whereby consumers are not given the full details of the ticket (e.g., specific airline, time of departure, number of stops) until after they have purchased it, but they do often pay a much lower price because of this uncertainty. The consumers are guaranteed that the ticket they receive will meet certain conditions (e.g., the range of departure and arrival times might be guaranteed), but they can receive one of several tickets from a host of carriers that meet these conditions. A particular consumer might prefer one of the tickets over the other, and there is a possibility that she will receive this preferred ticket. However, she also runs the risk of receiving a ticket she does not prefer.

There are several examples of firms engaging in opaque selling. For instance, several airlines (e.g., Delta, Northwest Airlines, United Airlines, and US Airways) supply tickets to an intermediary Hotwire which sells them as opaque tickets at discounted prices. A potential customer at Hotwire keys in the details of the route she wants to fly and the time frame. In response, Hotwire provides the option to purchase an opaque ticket at a discounted price in which it does not reveal the name of the airline and the exact itinerary[1] along with several options for transparent tickets. The consumer then makes her purchase or no-purchase decision. Likewise, Priceline sells opaque tickets but with one major difference – it asks the user to bid the price that she wants to pay, which is known as Name-Your-Own-Price strategy. Besides airline tickets, Hotwire and Priceline also use opaque selling for hotel rooms and rental cars, in both cases again partnering with major companies in these businesses. Beyond Hotwire and Priceline, firms such as Norwegian cruise lines sell opaque tickets for cruises, whereby a customer pays a discounted price which guarantees a minimum class of cabin and is promised an upgrade (if available), but the details of the upgrade or the exact location of the cabin are revealed later based on availability. Mystery Flights, a firm in Australia, sells opaque tickets in which the starting and ending times of the itinerary are specified, but the destination is not revealed and it can be one of several pre-specified destinations. In this case, the opacity is with respect to a different aspect of the ticket attribute as compared to Hotwire, i.e., the destination is opaque, rather than the flight time.

An essential feature of opaque selling is that it requires at least two differentiated products to credibly hide the identity of the final product the consumer will receive. A monopolist selling several differentiated products can therefore choose to sell opaque products (e.g., a day ticket or a night ticket on the same route) but competing firms can also sell opaque products through intermediaries. Under the

---

[1] It is typically possible to determine the name of the airline from the exact itinerary and vice versa, so that opaque sellers hide both of these details.

latter arrangement, an intermediary, such as Hotwire, is authorized to sell an opaque ticket with the final service delivered by one of the participating firms, such as US Airways or United Airlines. A salient feature of opaque products in the travel industry is that they are only available late in the selling horizon. In other words, for a particular route, typically only transparent tickets (with full product information) are available several weeks before the date of the flight, but a few days before the flight one can observe opaque sales as well. This observation indicates that the opaque selling strategy is often used as a mechanism to sell capacity that could not be sold at higher prices, which is consistent with opinions of several industry experts we communicated with. Thus, the opaque selling strategy is an important tool for clearing unsold inventory of seats/rooms.

The practice of selling opaque products has generated a lot of debate in the industry. Travel companies are always on the lookout for innovative revenue management strategies and companies practicing opaque selling strategies argue that they augment revenues because they "enable airlines to generate incremental revenue by selling distressed inventory cheaply without disrupting existing distribution channels or retail pricing structures" (Smith et al. 2007). However, other experts argue that selling cheaper opaque tickets amounts to introducing another channel that competes with the full-price channel, which is harmful for the industry since it "starts a cycle of price degradation that will eventually lead to ... destroying the airlines" (Sviokla 2004). The argument for price degradation is captured in Figure 10.1.

To explain the picture, traditionally the revenue management literature as well as many real-life revenue optimization engines make simplistic assumptions regarding customer arrival patterns. Namely, customers are assumed to be passive to the different pricing strategies used by firms and their propensity to buy tickets is traditionally described by the exogenously specified stochastic arrival process. However, there is growing evidence that customers are strategic and, realizing that prices

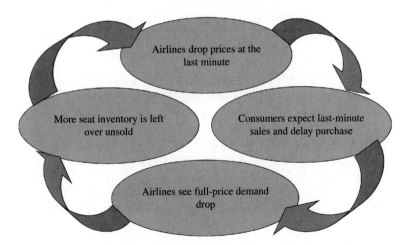

Fig. 10.1 Last-minute price discounting hurts airline revenues as more leisure customers continue to anticipate last-minute sales.

can decrease over time if there is unsold capacity late in the selling horizon, they learn to wait for these low prices. If a lot of customers wait in this manner, there will be excess unsold capacity close to flight departure and this can become a self-fulfilling cycle: more and more capacity will remain unsold at the full price, causing more discounts, which causes more customers to wait for discounts, etc. This is the "cycle of price degradation" referred to in the picture above, and an argument can be made that opaque selling is one way of giving such last-minute discounts. However, the argument can also be made that opaque selling strategies help break the cycle of degradation because the consumer has to anticipate which company will be the ultimate service provider. Thus, opaqueness introduces the additional level of price discrimination and makes last-minute discounts harder to exploit by strategic consumers.

The academic study of this novel selling strategy is nascent but growing. This stream of literature lies at the intersection of the study of revenue management strategies and the study of strategic consumer behavior. Currently most papers appear in the marketing domain and all of these papers are very recent. Formal research is needed to understand the impact of opaque selling strategies on strategic consumer behavior, as well as to compare effectiveness of opaque selling relative to other selling strategies. In this chapter, we survey the papers in the academic literature that study this phenomenon and we attempt to answer the question: Under what conditions, and why, is opaque selling attractive to firms? Broadly speaking, at least three different explanations emerge: (1) A monopolist using opaque selling can weakly improve profits by using opaque selling as a price discrimination strategy. (2) Under competition, when opaque selling is introduced simultaneously with transparent selling, it is profitable only if there is a large-enough class of brand-loyal consumers for each airline. (3) Under competition, even if the assumption of brand loyalty is not relied upon, opaque sales can still be profitable when introduced late in the selling horizon as a mechanism to sell off distressed inventory, and this happens without disrupting sales in the regular transparent channels. Overall, our chapter suggests that there are reasons to believe in viability of opaque selling strategies but it is also evident that this literature is just beginning to emerge and much more research is needed in this area. We discuss directions of potential future avenues of research in this chapter.

The rest of the chapter proceeds as follows. In Section 10.2, we place the literature on opaque selling within the related literature in Economics, Marketing, and Operations Management. The focus of this section is on discussing five recent papers on opaque selling (Jiang 2007, Fay and Xie 2008, Fay 2008, Shapiro and Shi 2008, and Jerath et al. 2008). We then provide extensive coverage of the model in Jerath et al. 2008 with deterministic (Section 10.3) and stochastic (Section 10.4) demand. With the help of this model, we uncover the mechanism behind the opaque selling strategy and show how the profitability of opaque sales varies with demand uncertainty and customer valuation for the product. In Section 10.5, we summarize our conclusions from the current literature and provide directions for future work.

10.2 Literature Review

In this section, we survey the recent literature on opaque selling strategies as well as related work in other areas. We focus on papers that model opaque products as sold by Hotwire, so that a price for the opaque product is posted and consumers decide whether to make the purchase or not, rather than as sold by Priceline, which asks consumers to bid the price they want to pay and their bids can be accepted or rejected.[2] This helps us to narrow our focus down to five papers that we will discuss: Jiang (2007), Fay and Xie (2008), Fay 2008, Shapiro and Shi (2008), and Jerath et al. (2008). But first we place the literature on opaque selling strategies within the larger literature in Economics, Marketing, and Operations Management and only then review the papers above in greater detail.

The study of opaque selling strategies is closely related to the literature on price discrimination (e.g., Narasimhan 1984) and market self-segmentation (e.g., Moorthy 1984). In these settings, firms offer a menu of products and customers self-select into classes based on their product preference. Since opaque sales also have a temporal aspect to them, as in the model in Jerath et al. (2008), they are related to the literature on inter-temporal pricing. The seminal work on inter-temporal sales is Coase (1972) which demonstrates that, given a durable product with an infinite number of selling opportunities over time, a monopolist will eventually decrease a product's price to its marginal cost because consumers will anticipate this decrease and will wait for discounts (the famous Coase conjecture). Numerous papers that followed laid out conditions in which the Coase conjecture may not hold (Stokey 1979, Besanko and Winston 1990, and DeGraba 1995). In particular, DeGraba (1995) showed that under uncertain demand and capacity constraints, there is a threat of unavailability in the future and all consumers will not wait so higher prices can be charged. Note that both uncertain demand and limited short-term capacity are features of the travel industry.

The strategy of selling products both directly and through an opaque channel is related to the "damaged goods" literature (Deneckere and McAfee 1996) in which a high-quality product is sold with different options by disabling (or "damaging") some of its features. This is similar to versioning (Varian 2000) in which the same product is sold in different versions. While these are related to opaque selling, the main difference is that here the consumer knows that she is obtaining a lower-quality product and she knows exactly what is wrong with the product. On the other hand, with opaque selling the consumer can obtain her preferred product with a positive probability. In other words, opaque selling introduces "buyer uncertainty" in terms of product assignment. In that vein, opaque selling is related to the strategy of advance selling (Xie and Shugan 2001) which utilizes a different kind of buyer uncertainty by selling to consumers before they learn their valuations. Finally, opaque selling is related to the literature on revenue management (Talluri and van Ryzin

---

[2] There is a rich literature studying the Name-Your-Own-Price selling format, e.g., Terwiesch et al. (2005). The reader is referred to this paper for references.

2004) and it is also related to the strategic consumer behavior literature in operations management strategies which is described elsewhere in this book.

We now proceed to review the five papers on opaque selling mentioned earlier. All of these papers use economic modeling to study opaque sales. We first classify them according to their modeling framework. The main dimension of differentiation is monopoly versus competition models: while a majority of opaque sales currently happen under competition between service providers (e.g., Hotwire sells air tickets from competing airlines), there are also cases like Norwegian cruise lines such that a single firm sells several of its own products as opaque. Papers by Jiang (2007) and Fay and Xie (2008) model a monopolist selling opaque products while Fay (2008), Shapiro and Shi (2008), and Jerath et al. (2008) model competing firms selling opaque products through an intermediary. The second dimension is demand uncertainty. In practice, demand for travel services is highly uncertain and, as a result, supply may not always match the demand. The uncertainty in demand and capacity constraints are reflected in models of Fay and Xie (2008) and Jerath et al. (2008). The third dimension is whether the model is dynamic (multi-period) or static (single-period). Only work of Jerath et al. (2008) incorporates dynamic considerations: the two competing firms first sell transparent tickets at full prices and then they may sell leftover capacity through the opaque intermediary. This modeling approach is meant to reflect an often-observed practice of selling opaque tickets only close to the date of travel service occurrence. Finally, in cases when there is an intermediary selling opaque tickets (i.e., when firms compete), the intermediary can be strategic (i.e., it makes pricing decisions) or passive. Works of Fay (2008) and Jerath et al. (2008) model strategic intermediaries. The classification in the previous discussion is summarized in Table 10.1. We now proceed to analyze opaque literature by discussing each paper in detail.

In the monopoly setting, Jiang (2007) uses a single-period model with horizontally differentiated products and deterministic demand. The motivation is that the firm sells a morning flight (M) and an afternoon or night flight (N) on the same route. Even though the customer buying the opaque ticket knows the firm that is selling him the ticket, he does not know the departure time. The customers are uniformly distributed along the Hotelling line with each flight (M and N) located at the end points of the line. The monopolist can sell both transparent and opaque tickets. The main assumption made in the paper is that, although the flight information is not revealed for the opaque tickets, consumers expect an equal probability of obtaining

Table 10.1 Taxonomy of papers on opaque selling.

	Competition	Demand Uncertainty	Single Period	Strategic Intermediary
Jiang (2007)	No	No	Yes	–
Fay and Xie (2008)	No	Yes	Yes	–
Shapiro and Shi (2008)	Yes	No	Yes	No
Fay (2008)	Yes	No	Yes	Yes
Jerath et al. (2008)	Yes	Yes	No	Yes

M or N ticket independent of the actual allocation made by the firm. In other words, equal availability is assumed (i.e., there is equal number morning and afternoon flights sold in the opaque market). This is a common assumption in this stream of literature that is largely driven by the absence of capacity constraints and the absence of demand uncertainty which, if present, could lead to different proportions of M and N tickets sold as opaque.

Jiang shows that, since the seller imposes consumption uncertainty on the buyers, the buyers trade off consumption values for price savings (i.e., opaque tickets are priced lower, which is consistent with business reality). Due to buyer heterogeneity, some buyers believe that the difference between two product groups (opaque and transparent) is significant while others do not. Opaque selling can therefore help the monopolist increase profits by discriminating among these groups. Jiang (2007) also conducts welfare analysis of the effect of selling opaque tickets in the market and shows that, when buyer heterogeneity is high enough, selling opaque products can improve social welfare. Both the firm and the customers can benefit from the dual-market strategy such that the firm sells both opaque and transparent tickets, so Pareto improvements are achieved. On the other hand, when very few customers in the market differentiate strongly between opaque tickets and transparent tickets, the firm might choose to sell only transparent tickets and serve only the high-value customers in the market.

Fay and Xie (2008) refer to opaque selling as "probabilistic selling." They begin by considering a monopolist offering two products with consumers distributed on a Hotelling line as in Jiang (2007). The products have identical production costs. The seller considers two selling strategies: *traditional* selling (TS) and *probabilistic* selling (PS). Under traditional selling each good is offered at a certain price. Under probabilistic selling, the seller offers one *probabilistic* good, which has a chance to be one of the two traditional goods. PS is essentially the same strategy as opaque selling, since the customer does not know the actual product until it is purchased. The traditional products are located at each end of the Hotelling line of unit length with the utilities normalized to one and all consumers have the same travel cost t. A customer located at x receives utility $1 - xt$ from buying product 1, and he receives utility $1 - (1 - x)t$ from buying product 2. Each customer needs only one good and chooses the good that maximizes his or her expected surplus based on the prices of those goods. Thus, each customer can buy either of the traditional goods, or the probabilistic good, or not buy at all. An important feature of their model is that the consumers are rational and forward looking (see Muth 1961). In other words, consumers form expectations about each product's allocation to the opaque channel by the monopolist, and these expectations are consistent in equilibrium.

Fay and Xie (2008) find that opaque selling strictly improves the monopolist's profit if production costs are sufficiently low. However, the advantage from opaque selling depends strongly on the magnitude of travel costs. When the travel costs are very small, the products are essentially substitutes and the equilibrium prices are very similar. Therefore, in this case probabilistic selling does not help improve profits since the opportunity to price discriminate is very limited. On the other hand, when there is significant differentiation between two products on the Hotelling line, (i.e., when t is high) no customer wants to risk buying the probabilistic good. Thus, probabilistic or opaque selling does not add much profit when there is high differentiation between the two traditional goods. In summary, Fay and Xie (2008) show that profit advantage from opaque selling is highest when the horizontal differentiation of the products is at the intermediate level. Interestingly, Fay and Xie (2008) show that advantages of opaque selling do not depend so much on standard assumptions behind the classical Hotelling model. For instance, the demand distribution need not be uniform, and the preferences of the consumer population as a whole need not be symmetric. For example, when market demand for one product is more than for the other, the results continue to hold. They also extend the model to a special case of information uncertainty when the firm does not know which product has more demand than the other and all results still continue to hold. Finally, the authors confirm their results by considering a Salop circle (i.e., all customers are distributed along the circumference of a unit radius) while the seller offers N goods located equidistantly along the circumference. They show that offering probabilistic goods can reduce the seller's information disadvantage and lessen the negative effect of demand uncertainty on profit by significantly reducing the problem of mismatch between capacity and demand.

Shapiro and Shi (2008) model a circle-shaped city (Salop's circle) with N firms located equidistantly (similar to the aforementioned extension considered in Fay and Xie 2008). The market size is fixed (i.e., the demand is deterministic) so the firms cannot attract more customers by lowering prices. Furthermore, all the firms are endowed with ample capacity so that each firm has enough capacity to supply the entire market. The customers are typified by two parameters: their location and their travel (transportation) cost. The location of the customer is specified by the standard Hotelling model. The travel cost is a binary variable. There are some customers of the high type (with high travel cost, e.g., business travelers), and the rest have the low type (with low travel cost, e.g., leisure travelers). The number of customers in each class can be unequal.

The competing firms can sell through their own channels or through an opaque intermediary. The intermediary is passive, i.e., if a firm decides to participate in the opaque channel, it dictates the opaque price to the intermediary. The intermediary posts prices from the different firms but hides the identity of the firm. In their model with the opaque intermediary, the customers can make reservations either through the direct channels or they could use the opaque travel agency. In the former case, customers can choose a specific hotel, and, other things being equal, they would like to stay at the hotel that is closest to their preferred location. When customers make their reservations in the opaque market, they do not know the hotel's location and they simply prefer the hotel with the lowest price. The authors focus on the equilibria in which all N firms participate in the opaque market. Clearly, as N becomes larger, there is more uncertainty with respect to the ultimate product that the customer receives in the opaque channel. In theory, there could be several opaque and transparent prices but the authors restrict their attention to the symmetric equilibria in which prices, both transparent and opaque, are equal across all firms. Furthermore, the authors assume that the probability of receiving a product from any one firm is the same and equal to $1/N$ (N is assumed to be an even number). These assumptions significantly reduce the complexity of the analysis since a customer's location becomes immaterial if he makes a reservation with the opaque intermediary.

There are many possible candidates for the equilibria and some further restrictions are needed to analyze the problem. The authors assume that it is never the case that all customers buy only opaque products and the authors also do not consider the case in which no customer buys opaque products. Thereafter, the authors show an interesting result regarding the effect of the number of competitors on the opaque selling. (To our knowledge, this is the only known result regarding dependency of opaque selling on the number of competing firms). In particular, they show that, when $N \geq 4$, the high-type customers strictly prefer to use the non-opaque product. Thus, if too many firms sell in the opaque market, the high-type customers are too uncertain about the good they receive through the opaque channel, and hence they choose to buy in the regular transparent market instead. Thus, the rest of the analysis is restricted to equilibria in which the high-type customers only buy in the regular (transparent) market.

Subject to the aforementioned conditions, Shapiro and Shi (2008) focus on two possible equilibrium types. In the *Full Separation* equilibrium all the high-type customers use the transparent channel and all the low-type customers use the opaque channel because intense competition for opaque sales drives prices down. In the *Partial Separation* equilibrium some low-type customers might use the transparent channel to buy tickets. There exists some minimal distance S to the nearest product such that all the low-type customers buy from the firm directly, and the rest of the customers buy in the opaque channel. Shapiro and Shi (2008) conclude that, although the opaque feature virtually erases product differentiation and intensifies competition, service providers can differentiate between those customers who are sensitive to service characteristics and those who are not. As a result, competition intensifies for low-type customers, and it reduces for high-type customers. Reduced competition for more valuable customers enables providers to commit to a higher price for this lucrative segment which leads to higher profits overall.

Fay (2008) constructs a model of an opaque selling in which channel considerations are investigated in richer details by considering a wide variety of contracts between service providers and an opaque intermediary, including simultaneous contract offers by the participants, sequential offers by the intermediary, sequential offers by the firms, etc. This is the only paper we are aware of that investigates in detail the contracting decisions made by the product sellers and the opaque intermediary. There are three firms in the model – two symmetric competing firms at the two ends of a Hotelling line of unit length and an intermediary that sells opaque tickets. The consumers in the market are divided into three classes: those loyal to one firm, those loyal to the other firm, and those who are willing to buy from both firms. The latter consumers are distributed uniformly on the Hotelling line. The first two consumer classes are equal in size and may be thought of as being collocated with the firm and/or having infinite travel costs. Essentially, they buy from their preferred firm or they do not buy at all. Such customers are called *brand loyals* and form fraction ρ of the population. The rest of the customers (i.e., fraction $(1 - \rho)$) are called *searchers*. The total demand in the market is assumed to be fixed and deterministic.

Initially, both firms allocate some tickets to sell through the opaque intermediary in return for a lumpsum payment. Then, they set prices for their transparent tickets and the intermediary observes these prices and sets its own price in the opaque channel. From the intermediary's perspective, the products from both firms are perfect substitutes. As a result, equilibrium wholesale prices are equal and they cannot exceed marginal costs or else the intermediary would only buy from one firm. Effectively, the intermediary sets its own profit margin through its pricing ability in the opaque market. The *searchers* observe the prices charged by the firms and by the opaque intermediary and make their purchase decisions. An important assumption in the model is that, although the consumers cannot observe the number of tickets initially allocated by each firm to the opaque channel, when purchasing an opaque ticket they expect to obtain it from either firm with equal probability. This assumption, again, is due to absence of the capacity constraints as well as absence of demand uncertainty. Fay (2008) finds that a monopolist can improve profits by introducing an opaque good at a small discount and by raising the prices of the traditional goods. However, if there is competition between the selling firms then the dynamics are different. In case when there is little brand loyalty, an opaque product intensifies price competition and thus reduces industry profits. On the other hand, if there is a significant amount of brand loyalty, an opaque good curtails price competition and thus increases industry profits. As a result, Fay finds that, with sufficient brand loyalty, opaque sales help reduce price rivalry in the market and increase industry profits.

Jerath et al. (2008) analyze opaque selling in a two-period model with demand uncertainty. They assume that two symmetric firms are located at the ends of a Hotelling line and offer horizontally differentiated products. Firms have limited capacities. An intermediary offers an opaque product. The market demand can be high with a certain probability and low with the remaining probability. The consumers are distributed uniformly over the Hotelling line. If demand turns out to be high, the firms run out of capacity, while if demand turns out to be low, the firms are left with excess capacity. In the first period, the distribution of demand is known to every player but the realization is not known. Both firms only sell transparent tickets in this period and declare to sell opaque tickets through the intermediary in the second period if any tickets are left over. Consumers make their purchase or no-purchase decisions keeping in mind two factors: (1) they might be able to obtain cheap opaque tickets in the second period and (2) if demand turns out to be high and enough others purchase transparent tickets in the first period, a consumer buying in the second period might not be able to obtain the ticket. Keeping in mind these factors, consumers develop rational expectations about future product availability on which they base their decisions, and these expectations are consistent in equilibrium.

Note that the model of demand uncertainty which is a feature of travel industries is a significant differentiator in the model of Jerath et al. (2008) compared to the models in Shapiro and Shi (2008) and Fay (2008). Furthermore, tickets are not assumed to be allocated to the opaque channel a priori, but only if they are leftover late in the selling horizon. Of course, the firms can also sell transparent tickets in the second period through their own channels. Jerath et al. (2008) consider this strategy as well and compare the profits from both strategies to determine which strategy is more profitable under different conditions of demand uncertainty and customer valuations. They find that opaque selling does not distort sales in the regular channels but helps increase profits by inducing consumers who would otherwise not purchase at all to purchase in the second period. This happens because, by creating uncertainty regarding which product a consumer will obtain in the opaque channel, the ex ante utility of purchasing the product is higher than with the transparent sales. Hence, the opaque channel acts as a distress-selling mechanism without disrupting sales in the regular channels. In comparison with the last-minute transparent sales strategy, the authors find that opaque selling is a more profitable strategy when the probability of high demand is significant, the customer valuation for the product is low, and/or customers have a high fit/travel cost. In the next section, we delve deeper into the phenomenon of opaque selling by developing a simple economic model based on Jerath et al. (2008).

10.3 Firm's Selling Strategies Under Deterministic Demand

In this section, we explore the strategies of the firms when demand is deterministic. The firms can sell through their own channels and they have the option of offering different prices in each period of sale. The firms can also choose to sell opaque products in the second period, after sales in the first period have ended. We consider two possible scenarios for each strategy: low-demand scenario ($J < K$) and high-demand scenario ($J > K$). The deterministic-demand model helps us gain insights into the players' decisions when demand is lower/higher than capacity and serves as a logical building block for the more complex model with demand uncertainty (Section 10.4).

10.3.1 Selling Through Firms' Direct Channels

The demand is deterministic and equals J. The firms and all consumers know J. Assume that firm i (where $i \in \{A, B\}$) charges p_i^1 in the first period and p_i^2 in the second period. Each consumer buys a product, if available, from the firm that provides him with the highest net utility (conditional on it being positive), either in the first period or the second period. In this case, we find that each firm charges the same price in the two periods.[3] This is formalized in the following lemma.

---

[3] Prices would not be identical across periods if consumers discounted their second period utility. However, the *discount-adjusted* prices would be identical across periods. Introducing discounting makes the analysis more tedious, while all the insights continue to hold.

Lemma 1. *When customers are rational, the equilibrium prices are such that* $p_i^1 = p_i^2 = p_i, i \in \{A, B\}$.

Intuitively, if the firms were to try and charge a higher price in the first period and a lower price in the second period, the consumers, being strategic and having full information about demand, would wait to buy products until the prices were lowered. (In case of the uncertain demand, we will see that this result changes.) Employing this result ($p_A^1 = p_A^2 = p_A$ and $p_B^1 = p_B^2 = p_B$), we now analyze the cases of low and high demand.

10.3.1.1 Low Demand ($J < K$)

Firms A and B set revenue maximizing prices p_A and p_B and accrue profits $\pi_A = p_A x_A J$ and $\pi_B = p_B(1 - x_B)J$, where x_A and x_B represent the locations of the farthest consumers who bought products from firms A and B, respectively, on the Hotelling line. The solution to the game is formalized in Proposition 1.

Proposition 1. *When demand is deterministic, there is ample capacity ($J < K$) and firms sell only through their own channels, the optimal prices, market coverage, and profits in the equilibrium are as follow:*

$\dfrac{V}{t}$	Prices p_A, p_B	Market Coverage $x_A, 1 - x_B$	Profits π_A, π_B
$\dfrac{1}{2} \leq \dfrac{V}{t} < 1$	$\dfrac{V}{2}$	$\dfrac{V}{2t}$	$\dfrac{V^2}{4t}J$
$1 \leq \dfrac{V}{t} < \dfrac{3}{2}$	$V - \dfrac{t}{2}$	$\dfrac{1}{2}$	$\left(V - \dfrac{t}{2}\right)\dfrac{J}{2}$
$\dfrac{V}{t} \geq \dfrac{3}{2}$	t	$\dfrac{1}{2}$	$\dfrac{t}{2}J$

When $1/2 \leq V/t < 1$, each firm finds it optimal to cover less than $1/2$ of the market (Hotelling line) and there are some leftover products. When $1 \leq V/t < 3/2$, each firm finds it optimal to cover exactly $1/2$ of the market at the price $V - t/2$. In both of these cases, the firms act as local monopolies. In the third case, when $V/t > 3/2$, the competitive equilibrium emerges. Hence, as V/t increases, the prices, market coverage, and firm revenues increase up to the point where the market becomes competitive.

10.3.1.2 High Demand ($J > K$)

Since demand is larger than capacity available in this scenario, full market coverage cannot occur. To maximize revenues, each firm will then cover the $K/2$ consumers located closest to it. The location of the farthest consumer covered by firm A (when valuation is high enough) is, therefore, $x_A = K/(2J) < 1/2$. (Similarly, $x_B = 1 - K/(2J) > 1/2$.) The following proposition lays out the solution to the game.

Proposition 2. *When demand is deterministic, capacity is a constraint $(J > K)$, and firms sell only through their own channels, the optimal prices, market coverage, and profits in the equilibrium are as follow:*

$\dfrac{V}{t}$	Prices p_A, p_B	Market Coverage $x_A, 1 - x_B$	Profits π_A, π_B
$\dfrac{1}{2} \leq \dfrac{V}{t} < \dfrac{K}{J}$	$\dfrac{V}{2}$	$\dfrac{V}{2t}$	$\dfrac{V^2}{4t} J$
$\dfrac{K}{J} \leq \dfrac{V}{t}$	$V - \dfrac{K}{2J} t$	$\dfrac{K}{2J}$	$\left(V - \dfrac{K}{2J} t \right) \dfrac{K}{2}$

When $1/2 \leq V/t < K/J$, the optimal price charged by the firm is such that not all $K/2$ closest consumers have positive valuation to buy from the firm, and there are some leftover products. When $V/t \geq K/J$, each firm has more than $K/2$ consumers who are willing to buy the products. Hence, the firm sells all its inventory at a high price $(V - Kt/(2J))$, and the farthest consumer who buys a product is located at $K/(2J)$.

10.3.2 Opaque Selling

As we described in the introduction, firms often sell products/services through opaque intermediaries (such as hotwire.com and priceline.com in the travel industry). Further, opaque products typically go on sale only very close to the terminal time, i.e., after consumers have bought in the transparent channel but the firms still have some inventory of products leftover. In the model described, after sales have been resolved in the transparent channel, the firms can accomplish opaque selling through an intermediary I that obtains products from the firms and sells them to maximize its own profits. For every product that the intermediary sells at price p_I, the airline receives δp_I.

Before purchasing an opaque product, a consumer does not know which firm will eventually provide it. However, every consumer develops expectations about the probability of obtaining the product from firm A or B. Since the opaque sales are based on remaining capacity, the expectations are regarding the leftover capacity after transparent sales have concluded. Therefore, the probabilities of obtaining products from each firm develop *endogenously* in the game according to the following sequence of events.

1. Firms A and B set prices p_A and p_B in the direct-to-consumers channel and declare that they might sell through an opaque channel later in the selling horizon (e.g., hotwire.com lists all airlines that sell products through its web site). Firms will engage in opaque selling only if there are products that are left unsold through their own direct channels.
2. Given prices p_A and p_B and his expectations about future availability from both firms, every consumer makes a purchase decision in the transparent channel.

3. After the transparent channel sales are over, the leftover products are made available to the opaque intermediary I by both firms. The opaque intermediary sets a price p_I for the opaque product. Consumers who did not buy in the transparent channel now make their buying decisions in the opaque channel. A consumer may not obtain an opaque product if the number of leftover products is less than the number of consumers who are willing to buy at price p_I. We denote the probability that the consumer can obtain an opaque product by β so that each consumer desiring a product is equally likely to obtain it. Consumers considering the opaque channel form expectations about the probabilities that the product they will obtain will be from firm A (denoted by γ_A^e) or firm B (denoted by γ_B^e). Hence, any consumer who is considering buying an opaque product has an ex ante expected utility given by

$$\beta \left(V - p_I - \gamma_A^e t x - \gamma_B^e t (1-x) \right).$$

Based on the price p_I, the probabilities γ_A^e and γ_B^e, and position x on the line, each consumer decides whether to purchase a product from the opaque channel or not.

4. The opaque intermediary keeps a fraction $1 - \delta$ of the revenues from the opaque channel. The remaining fraction δ is distributed between firms A and B in proportion to the products sold for each firm, i.e., firm A obtains a fraction $\delta \gamma_A$ and firm B obtains a fraction $\delta \gamma_B$ of the total opaque channel revenues.[4]

We now discuss how consumers purchasing in the opaque channel form their expectations. Let x_A^e and x_B^e denote the points on the Hotelling line such that every consumer believes that, in the transparent channel, the consumers in the interval $[0, x_A^e]$ bought products from A and the consumers in the interval $[x_B^e, 1]$ bought products from B. Thus, every consumer believes that the number of products leftover for firm A to sell in the opaque channel is $l_A^e = \max\{K/2 - x_A^e J, 0\}$ and the number of products leftover for firm B is $l_B^e = \max\{K/2 - (1 - x_B^e)J, 0\}$. In line with these expectations, consumers perceive that, if they buy in the opaque channel, they will obtain a product from firm A with probability $\gamma_A^e = l_A^e / (l_A^e + l_B^e)$ and from firm B with probability $\gamma_B^e = 1 - \gamma_A^e = l_B^e / (l_A^e + l_B^e)$. Consequently, for the consumer at x_A who is indifferent between buying from firm A and buying in the opaque channel, the following condition holds:

$$V - p_A - t x_A = \beta \left(V - p_I^e - \gamma_A^e t x_A - \gamma_B^e t (1 - x_A) \right).$$

Note that p_I^e is a function of γ_A^e and γ_B^e, and the consumers rational beliefs are imposed on availabilities. To solve for the rational expectations equilibria under high and low demand, we first characterize the equilibrium beliefs of the consumers by the following lemma. Recall that, in equilibrium, the profit maximizing prices set by the firms are expected rationally by consumers. Further, in equilibrium, expectations of all consumers regarding the number of consumers that buy in the first (and

---

[4] This revenue sharing contract with opaque intermediaries is consistent with observations and industry practice (see Phillips 2005).

second) period, are consistent, i.e., it should match the actual number of consumers buying in both periods.

Lemma 2. *When the capacities of the firms are equal, the equilibrium expectations of the fraction of opaque products from each firm are* $\gamma_A = \gamma_A^e = 1/2 = \gamma_B = \gamma_B^e = 1/2$.

Lemma 2 is a significant result. It shows that, if the firms have equal capacities, then it is rational for consumers to expect that, in the opaque channel, half of the products come from one firm and the other half from the other. Furthermore, the lemma also specifies that any other expectations about product availability are either irrational or inconsistent or both. Conditional on the event that a consumer has received an opaque product, we allow for asymmetric consumer expectations about its source, but they are not sustained in equilibrium when the firms are identical. Suppose that the customers have asymmetric expectations about the product availability. For such asymmetric availability to be an equilibrium (the realization of) second-period leftover inventory from both the firms must be unequal. This in turn implies that one of the firms had poorer market coverage in the first period. Therefore, the prices were asymmetric in the first period. However, in such a case, the firm charging the higher price would unilaterally deviate to a lower price to increase its coverage in the market. The equilibrium occurs at symmetric prices.

This result implies that, in the equilibrium, at price p_I the expected utility of each consumer from buying in the opaque channel is $V - p_I - t/2$. Without loss of generality, we focus on $\delta = 1$; any $\delta \in [0, 1]$ yields same insights.

10.3.2.1 Low Demand ($J < K$)

Suppose that the prices p_A and p_B in the transparent channels are such that consumers located in the interval $[0, x_A]$ buy from firm A and consumers in $[x_B, 1]$ buy from firm B. After the firms have sold through their direct channels, the intermediary has access to consumers in the range $[x_A, x_B]$ as shown in Figure 10.2. Note that the opaque market will exist only if there are some products leftover after sales in the transparent channel have concluded. Since demand is low, there will be enough units in the opaque channel to cover the remaining market so that each consumer in the opaque channel will definitely obtain the product (i.e., $\beta = 1$). If the intermediary charges a price p_I, the total revenue from the opaque channel is $\pi_I = p_I(x_B - x_A)J$, and each firm obtains a part of it.

Since the firms now have the opaque channel to "clear up" the remaining market in the second period, they can raise prices in the first period (sell to fewer consumers at higher prices) which can lead to higher profits.

Note, however, that consumers are strategic. They recognize that the firms could rely upon the opaque channel and increase prices in the transparent channels. Further, consumers know that they can prevent the firms from implementing the opaque channel if they delay their purchases (in the extreme, delay purchases until right before the selling horizon ends). Effectively, through this strategic behavior, the

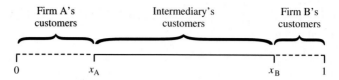

Fig. 10.2 Consumers to the left of x_A buy from firm A and consumers to the right of x_B buy from firm B. x_A denotes the location of the consumer indifferent to buying from firm A or from the opaque channel. x_B denotes the location of the consumer indifferent to buying from firm B or the opaque channel. Consumers between x_A and x_B are the target consumers for the intermediary.

consumers will make the firms charge a price no higher than the price in the direct channel equilibrium (Section 10.3.1.1). In this equilibrium, however, the firms can still use the opaque channel when $1/2 \leq V/t < 1$ since the market is not covered with transparent prices. In the equilibrium, the firms will charge a price $V - t/2$ in the opaque channel to all remaining consumers, who will all buy products. The following proposition characterizes the equilibrium in this case.

Proposition 3. *When demand is deterministic, there is ample capacity ($J < K$) and firms can utilize the opaque channel, the equilibrium prices charged in the first period by the firms, the price charged in the opaque channel by the intermediary, and the opaque market coverage in the equilibrium are as follow:*

$\dfrac{V}{t}$	First-Period Prices p_A, p_B	Opaque Prices p_I	Opaque Coverage $x_B - x_A$
$\dfrac{1}{2} \leq \dfrac{V}{t} < 1$	$\dfrac{V}{2}$	$V - \dfrac{t}{2}$	$1 - \dfrac{V}{t}$
$1 \leq \dfrac{V}{t} < \dfrac{3}{2}$	$V - \dfrac{t}{2}$	—	—
$\dfrac{3}{2} \leq \dfrac{V}{t}$	t	—	—

Proposition 3 shows that (compared to Proposition 1) using the opaque channel increases the total market coverage (and profits) given the same valuation V and strength of brand preferences t when the ratio V/t is small ($1/2 \leq V/t < 1$). For higher V/t, the firms cover the full market through the transparent channel and there is no leftover capacity for the opaque channel.

10.3.2.2 High Demand ($J > K$)

When demand is deterministic and higher than available capacity, some consumers do not obtain products. The right-most consumer that firm A can cover through its own channel is located at $K/(2J) < 1/2$. Similarly, the left-most consumer that firm B can cover is located at $1 - K/(2J) > 1/2$. Further, the insight that the firms will not be able to leverage the opaque channel to increase prices in the first period holds in the high-demand case also. Hence, as before, the equilibrium in this case will be similar to that in Section 10.3.1.2, except that when the firms do not cover the full market in the first period they resort to opaque sales in the second period to clear up remaining inventory.

Proposition 4. *When demand is deterministic, capacity is a constraint ($J > K$) and firms can utilize the opaque channel, the equilibrium prices charged in the first period by the firms, the price charged in the opaque channel by the intermediary, and the opaque market coverage in the equilibrium are as follow:*

$\dfrac{V}{t}$	First-Period Prices p_A, p_B	Opaque Prices p_I	Opaque Coverage $x_B - x_A$
$\dfrac{1}{2} \leq \dfrac{V}{t} \leq \dfrac{K}{J}$	$\dfrac{V}{2}$	$V - \dfrac{t}{2}$	$K - J\dfrac{V}{t}$
$\dfrac{K}{J} \leq \dfrac{V}{t}$	$V - \dfrac{t}{2}$	—	—

10.3.3 Comparison of Strategies Under Deterministic Demand

We now compare the profits that the firms make with and without the opaque channel. Note that in both high- and low-demand scenarios, the opaque channel acts as a "clean up" mechanism to dispose of unsold products, without disturbing the pattern of sales in the transparent channels. Hence, if the opaque channel exists (when the market is not fully covered by the transparent channels), it will strictly improve firm profits (as in Fay 2008). We demonstrate this observation in Figures 10.3a, b.

In the opaque channel, the ex ante expected utility from buying a product is zero for all consumers. To see this, consider a consumer who is located at x. His net expected utility from buying in the opaque channel is

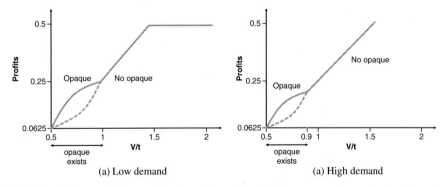

(a) Low demand   (a) High demand

Fig. 10.3 (a) The equilibrium profits of one firm with and without opaque channels when demand is deterministic and lower than capacity are shown. In this figure $\delta = 1, t = 1, J = 1, K > J$. (b) The equilibrium profits of a firm with and without opaque channels when demand is deterministic and higher than capacity are shown. In this figure $\delta = 1, t = 1, J = 1, K = 0.9$.

$$V - p_I - \gamma_A^e tx - \gamma_B^e t(1-x),$$

which is zero in equilibrium (in equilibrium, $\gamma_A^e = \gamma_B^e = 1/2$ and $p_I = V - t/2$).
Therefore, all consumers who have not yet purchased a product and find one available do purchase it. In other words, by hiding the identity of the product, the opaque channel helps sell products at lower prices to the consumers who are not willing to buy directly from the firms because direct prices are too high.

Ex post, however, under the assumption that products in the opaque channel are allocated randomly, half the consumers obtain positive valuations from the products they bought (since they obtain a product from the firm they prefer more), and the other half obtain negative valuations (since they obtain a product from the firm they prefer less). This is consistent with the practical observation that although consumers pay lower prices when they buy opaque products, sometimes they experience dissatisfaction because the product does not meet their preferences.

Figure 10.4 depicts the optimal strategies for the firms given different values of consumer valuations (the ratio V/t) and inventory availability relative to demand (the ratio K/J). As we discussed earlier, as V/t increases, the market becomes more competitive because either the consumers' valuations (V) for flying are high, or the strength of brand preference in the market (t) is low, or both.

Under both high and low demand, firms sell products through the opaque channel only if V/t is small enough because in this case the firms do not cover the full market in the transparent channels and use opacity as a mechanism to dispose of unsold products. As the ratio V/t increases above a threshold, the firms have the option of using an opaque channel, but price in the transparent channels to cover the market anyway, and do not need to resort to selling cheaper opaque products. Figure 10.4 also shows that if demand is high, opaque sales will be seen less frequently (for a smaller range of V/t), than if demand is low. This is consistent with the

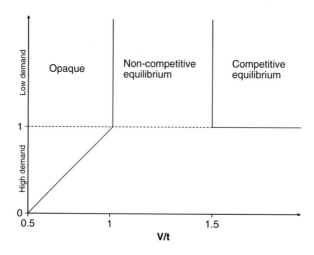

Fig. 10.4 Strategy space for different valuations and capacity/demand scenarios.

notion that the opaque channel is used to dispose off distressed inventory (Harrison 2006). Finally, as we argued in Sections 10.3.2.1 and 10.3.2.2, when demand is deterministic, strategic consumer behavior prevents the firms from leveraging the opaque channel to increase prices in the transparent channel by adopting a strategy of waiting. This is consistent with the Coase conjecture.

10.4 Modeling Uncertain Demand: The Effect of Uncertainty on Opaque Selling Strategies

Uncertainty in demand volume is a pervasive feature in the travel industry. Firms usually can estimate the demand distribution for a given airline route or hotel using historical records but the precision of such estimates is quite limited (see Talluri and van Ryzin 2004). As the departure date approaches, the firms can improve the forecast and therefore project with a higher degree of confidence whether the demand for the route is higher or lower than the available capacity. Building on the analysis in previous sections, this section extends our model to incorporate demand uncertainty.

Due to the presence of demand uncertainty, consumers cannot always adopt a strategy of waiting in the early stages of the game because market demand could be high and tickets could be unavailable later. However, a consumer can form rational expectations about future availability and buy early if the expected utility from doing so is higher than the expected utility from waiting. These dynamics capture the practical consideration that not all consumers wait for last-minute discounts and allow us to derive several insights beyond the model with deterministic demand. As mentioned in the introductory sections, the possibility of capacity shortage is one of the counter arguments to the Coase conjecture.

The specifications of the model remain the same, except that the level of demand is now variable. We assume that, with probability α the total number of consumers in the market is $H(> K)$ and, with probability $1 - \alpha$ the total number of consumers in the market is $L(< K)$. As before, each firm has capacity $K/2$. The parameters α, L, H, and K are common knowledge. The selling horizon is divided into two periods. In the first period, the firms and the consumers know the distribution of demand, but do not know the state of nature (whether demand is H or L). At the end of the first period, but before the second period begins, the realization of demand is observed by the firms and the consumers. This assumption is clearly a simplification of reality. In practice, some residual uncertainty in demand would remain. There are also several ways to extend this assumption. We discuss some future research prospects in our concluding section.

We assume that, in any selling period, if the number of consumers who are willing to buy a seat is higher than the capacity available, tickets are allocated randomly to the consumers. In other words, if a certain number of consumers desire tickets at the announced price but the number of tickets available is lower than the number of tickets demanded (which can be the case if demand is high), it is possible that consumers with a lower expected (but positive) surplus obtain tickets at the expense of consumers with a higher expected surplus. In the following sections, we analyze the two strategies of selling through the firms' direct channels ("last-minute sales" strategy, or LMSS) and opaque selling ("opaque sales" strategy, or OpSS).

We consider the following two selling strategies of the firms:

1. "Last-minute sales" strategy (LMSS): In the first period, firms sell tickets at prices p_A^1 and p_B^1. In the second period, they sell the leftover tickets at the "last-minute" prices based on the demand realization. If the demand is high, they sell the unsold seats at prices p_A^{2H} and p_B^{2H} and at prices p_A^{2L} and p_B^{2L} if the demand is low.

2. "Opaque sales" strategy (OpSS): In the first period, firms sell tickets using their own channels at prices p_A and p_B. In the second period, the firms provide access to the unsold tickets to an intermediary, I, who sells opaque tickets at price p_I^H if the demand is high and at price p_I^L if the demand is low.

Under each strategy, consumers might postpone their purchase based on prices in the first period and their expectations for availability and prices in the second period, which in turn are influenced by the fraction of consumers who postpone the purchase. In equilibrium, the fraction of consumers who postpone should be consistent with the belief that each consumer has about the fraction of consumers who have postponed purchasing their ticket. We ensure this by solving for the rational expectations equilibrium.

In the first period, the firms and the consumers know the distribution of demand, but do not know the state of nature (whether demand is H or L). At the beginning of the first period, the firms announce their first period prices and their second period selling strategies.[5] The consumers strategically decide whether to buy in the first period itself or postpone their purchase to the later period. For consumers who postpone the purchase, there is a possibility that they may not be able to obtain tickets in the second period if the demand turns out to be high, or if the firms charge a very high price. At the end of the first period, but before the second period starts, the realization of demand is observed. During the second period, the demand realization is known to the firms and the consumers. Depending on their strategies, the leftover tickets are sold by the firms through their own channels at "last-minute" prices (which can be high or low) or through an opaque intermediary. The consumers obtain tickets at the prices offered only if available.

10.4.1 Selling Though Firms' Direct Channels

The following is the order of events in the game when firms adopt a LMSS.

1. In the first period, firm A prices its tickets at p_A^1 and firm B prices its tickets at p_B^1 and both firms declare that there might be last-minute sales.

---

[5] Both firms announce the same strategy. This is imperative if they want to sell through an opaque intermediary.

2. All consumers form expectations about the number of consumers purchasing in the first period (and therefore the corresponding future prices and availability) and strategically make or postpone their purchase.
3. At the end of period 1 and before period 2 begins, demand uncertainty is fully resolved. The level of demand is determined as H or L and is observed by both the firms and the consumers.
4. The firms then set their prices (e.g., firm A sets price p_A^{2L} if demand is low and p_A^{2H} if demand is high, and similarly for firm B).
5. The consumers who postponed their purchase in the first period decide to purchase or not in the second period at the announced prices.

The rational expectations equilibrium solution for the above game is provided in the following proposition.

Proposition 5. *When the firms sell products through their own channels, the following equilibrium always exists: In the first period both firms set prices to cover* $x_A = 1 - x_B = K/(2H)$ *of the market. If demand is high, no products are sold in the second period since the firms stock out in the first period. If demand is low, consumers located between* $x_A = K/(2H)$ *and* $x_B = 1 - K/(2H)$ *buy in the second period. The first-period and second-period prices are as follow:*

$\dfrac{V}{t}$	First-Period Prices $(p_A^1 = p_B^1)$	Second-Period Prices When Demand is Low $(p_A^{2L} = p_B^{2L})$
$\dfrac{1}{2} \leq \dfrac{V}{t} < 1 - \dfrac{K}{2H}$	$\left(\dfrac{1+\alpha}{2}\right)\left(V - \dfrac{K}{2H}t\right)$	$\dfrac{1}{2}\left(V - \dfrac{K}{2H}t\right)$
$1 - \dfrac{K}{2H} \leq \dfrac{V}{t} < \dfrac{3}{2}$	$\alpha\left(V - \dfrac{K}{2H}t\right) + (1-\alpha)\left(V - \dfrac{t}{2}\right)$	$V - \dfrac{t}{2}$
$\dfrac{V}{t} \geq \dfrac{3}{2}$	$\alpha\left(V - \dfrac{K}{2H}t\right) + (1-\alpha)t$	t

In the equilibrium, all consumers who attempt to buy a ticket in the first period obtain a ticket, but pay the high price $V - Kt/(2H)$. If demand is high, firm A sells to $K/(2H) \cdot H(= K/2)$ consumers in the first period and thus exhausts its capacity so there are no tickets sold in the second period through last-minute sales. If demand is low, firm A sells to $K/(2H) \cdot L(< K/2)$ in the first period and will have some seats leftover. (The situation is symmetric for firm B.) Moreover, there are more of these leftover seats than the number of unserved consumers in the market in the second period. Therefore, the consumers who waited for the "last-minute" tickets obtain them at lower prices only if demand is lower than capacity.

To summarize, in the first period all consumers with "high brand preference" (locate in the interval $[0, K/(2H)]$) buy at a high price from firm A. If there are any leftover tickets, the consumers with "low brand preference" (located in the interval $[K/(2H), 1/2]$) buy from firm A during the last-minute sales at lower prices. If there are no leftover tickets, there are no sales in the second period. In effect, the firms are separating out consumers who are ready to pay a higher price under the threat of stockout and making most of their profits from the high prices charged to the high-preference consumers in the first period.

10.4.2 Opaque Selling

The following is the order of events in the game when the firms adopt an opaque sales strategy.

1. In the first period, firm A prices its tickets at p_A^1 and firm B prices its tickets at p_B^1 and both firms declare intention of sales through an opaque channel.
2. Consumers develop expectations about availability in the second period and the firm they will probably obtain a ticket from in the opaque channel and strategically purchase or postpone purchasing a ticket.
3. At the end of period 1 and before period 2 begins, demand uncertainty is resolved, the level of demand is determined as H or L and is observed by the firm and the consumers.
4. The leftover seats, if any, are made available to the opaque intermediary I, who then sets a price p_I^H if the demand realization is H or a price p_I^L if the demand realization is L.
5. Consumers who have not purchased in the transparent channel now make their buying decision in the opaque channel.
6. For every ticket sold, the opaque intermediary keeps a fraction $1 - \delta$ of the revenue accrued from the opaque channel. The intermediary commits to a credible opaque strategy and sells tickets from both firms at price p_I with equal preference. It distributes the remaining fraction δ to firm A or B whose ticket it sold.

We now discuss how consumers purchasing in the opaque channel form their expectations about the probabilities of ticket availability. The consumers do not know which firm will ultimately provide the service, but they form expectations about the locations of the right-most and left-most consumers on the Hotelling line who buy tickets from A and B, respectively, in the transparent channel.

1. If the level of demand is low, then leftover seats for firm A must be $l_A^{L,e} = \max\{K/2 - x_A^e L, 0\}$ and leftover seats for firm B must be $l_B^{L,e} = \max\{K/2 - (1 - x_B^e)L, 0\}$. In line with these expectations, consumers perceive that if they buy in the opaque channel then they will obtain a ticket from A with probability $\gamma_A^{L,e} = l_A^{L,e}/(l_A^{L,e} + l_B^{L,e})$ and from B with probability $\gamma_B^{L,e} = l_B^{L,e}/(l_A^{L,e} + l_B^{L,e})$.
2. If the level of demand is high, then the expected leftover for firm A must be $l_A^{H,e} = \max\{K/2 - x_A^e H, 0\}$ and the expected leftover for firm B must be $l_B^{H,e} = \max\{K/2 - (1 - x_B^e)H, 0\}$. In line with these expectations, $\gamma_A^{H,e} = l_A^{H,e}/(l_A^{H,e} + l_B^{H,e})$ and from B with probability $\gamma_B^{H,e} = l_B^{H,e}/(l_A^{H,e} + l_B^{H,e})$.

Based on the price p_I, the expectation probabilities $\gamma_A^{,e}$ and $\gamma_B^{,e}$, and his position x on the line, every consumer decides whether to purchase a ticket or not. In equilibrium, for all consumers the outcomes γ_A and γ_B must be consistent with their beliefs

$\gamma_A^{;e}$ and $\gamma_B^{;e}$. The equilibrium prices in the rational expectations equilibrium of the above game are provided in Proposition 6. (To keep results simple, we present the case with $\delta = 1$. The analysis for any $\delta \in [0,1]$ yields similar insights.)

Proposition 6. *When the firms sell tickets through the opaque intermediary, the following equilibrium always exists:*

$\dfrac{V}{t}$	First-Period Prices p_A, p_B	Opaque Prices p_I^L, p_I^H
$\dfrac{1}{2} \le \dfrac{V}{t} \le \dfrac{K}{H}$	$\dfrac{V}{2}$	$V - \dfrac{t}{2}, V - \dfrac{t}{2}$
$\dfrac{K}{H} < \dfrac{V}{t} \le \dfrac{K}{H} + \left(\dfrac{\alpha}{1-\alpha}\right)\dfrac{K}{2L}$	$V - \dfrac{K}{2H}t$	$V - \dfrac{t}{2}, -$
$\dfrac{K}{H} + \left(\dfrac{\alpha}{1-\alpha}\right)\dfrac{K}{2L} < \dfrac{V}{t} < 1 + \left(\dfrac{\alpha}{1-\alpha}\right)\dfrac{K}{2L}$	$\dfrac{V}{2} + \left(\dfrac{\alpha}{1-\alpha}\right)\dfrac{K}{4L}t$	$V - \dfrac{t}{2}, -$
$1 + \left(\dfrac{\alpha}{1-\alpha}\right)\dfrac{K}{2L} \le \dfrac{V}{t} < \dfrac{3}{2} + \left(\dfrac{\alpha}{1-\alpha}\right)\dfrac{K}{L}$	$V - \dfrac{t}{2}$	$-, -$
$\dfrac{V}{t} \ge \dfrac{3}{2} + \left(\dfrac{\alpha}{1-\alpha}\right)\dfrac{K}{L}$	$\left(1 + \left(\dfrac{\alpha}{1-\alpha}\right)\dfrac{K}{L}\right)t$	$-, -$

Under deterministic demand we saw that the opaque channel was primarily a clearance mechanism when the entire market could not be covered by the firms using transparent prices. However, in the deterministic demand case, the consumers know the state of demand and adopt a strategy of waiting if the firms charge high prices. In contrast, when demand is uncertain, the consumers do not know the state of demand in the first period and therefore may not wait because of the imminent possibility of the firms stocking out if demand is high. In other words, if a consumer has positive utility in the first period at the price offered by a firm, then he will purchase the ticket, inferring that he might not obtain it at all if the demand turns out to be high. This consideration allows the firms to charge higher prices in the first period. Consequently, if demand is low, only a few tickets will be sold in the first period. However, in this eventuality, the firms can use the opaque channel to "clean up" the leftover seats if any. Selling to a smaller population at higher prices in the first period helps the firms to increase the expected profit across two periods.

The above argument naturally leads to the interesting insight that, as the probability of high demand increases, the firms will rely more and more on the opaque channel. The reason is that, if there is a greater chance that demand is high, the "competition for tickets" among consumers in the first period will be higher, which means that the firms will be able to raise the first-period prices. If demand turns out to be high, the firms will exhaust their capacities. On the other hand, even if demand turns out to be low, there will still be some consumers left in the market because of high first-period prices. Consequently, there will be some leftover tickets, and the firms will sell them through the opaque channel.

10.4.3 A Comparison of Two Selling Strategies

We saw in the previous two sections that both LMSS and OpSS can increase the firms' profits. In this section, we seek to answer the question: When should firms employ LMSS versus OpSS? For expositional simplicity, we provide a graphical illustration of the profits of the firms for these two strategies for a representative set of parameter values ($\alpha = 1/2, K = 1, L = 1/2, H = 3/2, t = 1$) in Figure 10.5. If V is low, the profits from OpSS are higher than the profits from LMSS. However, as V increases, the profits from OpSS flatten out, while the profits from LMSS keep increasing. Above a certain threshold for V, LMSS profits become higher than OpSS profits.

To see why the above result holds, note that under LMSS the bulk of a firm's profits comes from tickets sold in the first period to the consumers that are closer to the firm on the Hotelling line. If the valuation for flying in the market is high (i.e., V is high), this price $(V - tK/(2H))$ is high. However, if the valuation for flying is low, the first-period prices are very low, the second-period prices are even lower, and hence profits from LMSS are low. In OpSS, on the other hand, the first-period prices are higher than in LMSS for low V because each firm is choosing to cover only a small portion of the market in the transparent channel and the rest using the opaque channel. Moreover, note that the second-period prices in the opaque channel (if opaque sales are present) are higher than the second-period prices for LMSS because the firms collude via the intermediary to sustain these higher second-period prices.

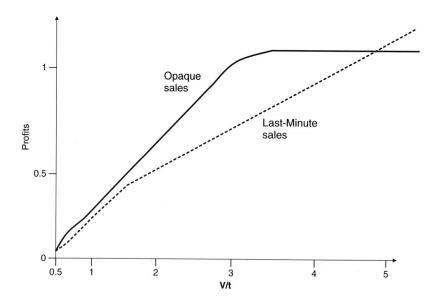

Fig. 10.5 Profits accrued by a firm under uncertain demand, when the firm employs the last-minute sales strategy and the opaque sales strategy. For the figure, we use $\alpha = \frac{1}{2}$, $K = 1$, $L = \frac{1}{2}$, $H = \frac{3}{2}$, $t = 1$, $\delta = 1$.

As V increases, the revenue from LMSS increases faster, because the firms are able to separate out the consumers with a high preference for a particular firm and charge these consumers higher prices even if demand is low. In OpSS, on the other hand, prices are such that the firms cover a large portion of the market at lower prices if demand is low. In fact, if V is high enough, the firms are in a competitive equilibrium under OpSS when demand is low, so that prices are very low. (In Figure 10.5, this is the region where the OpSS profits level off.) Hence, when V is high, LMSS yields higher profits because it allows the firms to "milk" the high-preference consumers in the first period, even if it has to charge lower prices in the second period when demand turns out to be low.

We now investigate the effect of increasing probability of high-demand realization. As we discussed earlier for OpSS, as the probability of high-demand realization increases, consumers are under a higher threat of stockout in the first period. Thus, many more consumers prefer to buy in the first period and therefore the firms increase prices. In other words, not only is there a higher chance that demand is high, the prices are high also. If demand turns out to be low, the first-period sales suffer, but the leftover capacity is cleared through the opaque channel. Over the two periods, expected profits increase. In LMSS, however, the firms charge a first-period price $V - Kt/(2H)$ irrespective of the probability of high demand. Further, consumers with low firm preferences buy only if demand is low, which now happens with lower probability. Hence, even though expected profits increase (because there is a higher chance of high demand) the increase is slower than in OpSS. Figure 10.6 summarizes the comparison between the opaque strategy and the last-minute direct sales strategy for various probabilities of high demand ($\alpha \in [0, 1)$ on the y-axis) and consumer valuations (V on the x-axis). The shaded area denotes the region where the opaque selling market exists for deterministic low demand (i.e., when $V/t \leq 1$).

10.4.4 Concluding Discussion

When product/service demand is uncertain and available capacity cannot be changed easily in the short term, companies often end up with one of the two extremes – a shortfall of capacity due to high demand or leftover unused (and expensive) capacity due to low demand. To deal with the mismatch between demand and supply, firms have implemented a variety of strategies, and two of the most prominent strategies are direct last-minute sales at reduced prices and sales through an opaque intermediary. However, consumers are becoming more and more strategic – they have learned to anticipate this last-minute distress selling and might decide to postpone their purchase in expectation of future lower prices. The risk the consumers face while making this decision is of not being able to obtain a product if demand turns out to be high.

Several papers have tried to model this strategic interaction between competing firms and consumers to understand different selling mechanisms. The key question that we posed to address is: when should firms offer last-minute sales through an

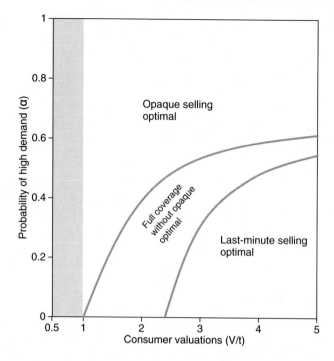

Fig. 10.6 Strategies the firm should adopt for different consumer valuations ($\frac{V}{t}$) and various probabilities of high demand (α). In the intermediate region, the firm is able to cover the entire market without actually selling opaque tickets, even though it declares opaque sales as its strategy. For the figure, we use $K = 1, L = \frac{1}{2}, H = \frac{3}{2}, t = 1, \delta = 1$.

opaque intermediary? In this chapter we presented a model that helps answer this question and which compares opaque selling with direct-to-consumer selling. We find that the answer depends on at least three factors: (1) the valuations that consumers have for the service, (2) the strength of brand preference that consumers have for competing firms (alternatively, the extent of service differentiation between competing firms), and (3) the probability that demand in the market exceeds capacity. If consumer valuation for product is high and/or the strength of brand preference of the consumers in the market is low, firms prefer direct last-minute sales over opaque sales. Furthermore, as the probability of high demand increases, firms start to prefer opaque sales over direct last-minute sales. At the extreme, if market demand is deterministic, direct last-minute sales are never offered while opaque sales can be offered if consumer valuations for travel are very low. These findings immediately translate into empirically testable hypotheses.

The dynamics underlying the functioning of opaque selling strategy are intriguing. In general, each firm prices in the earlier periods so that only consumers with high preference for the firm buy the product. Thus, each firm derives the bulk of its profits primarily by charging high prices to these consumers, while second-period prices are very low (however, these cheap products are available only if demand turns out to be lower than capacity). Quite differently, in the opaque selling strategy, if the consumer valuations are very low, the firms set first-period prices to extract maximum profits from consumers and then clear any remaining products through the opaque channel. When valuations are high, the firms price in the first period to ensure that the number of consumers who want to buy products exceeds supply, introducing clamor for the limited number of products and leveraging the risk of product shortage to charge higher first-period prices. To summarize, the direct last-minute sales strategy can be construed as extracting profits from high-preference consumers, while the opaque sales strategy can be thought of as creating a frenzy for products to raise prices. Clearly, opaque selling is far from a simple "inventory clearance mechanism" – such strategies are indeed responses by the firms to consumers making strategic purchasing decisions.

10.5 Other Related Considerations and Future Research

Opaque sales and last-minute sales are encountered in a variety of practical situations, many of which are not fully reflected in the stylized model described above. Below we outline some of the interesting modeling considerations that are quite promising to be considered by future research in this area.

Different selling mechanisms: In our model, we assume that the opaque intermediary operates using a posted-price regime. This assumption quite accurately reflects the way hotwire.com conducts business but it is not reflective of NYOP price regime of priceline.com. The reason different opaque intermediaries utilize different pricing strategies is probably to avoid direct competition with each other. Nevertheless, we expect that NYOP selling has a potential to further increase attractiveness of opaque selling because it allows for finer price discrimination among consumers as compared to last-minute selling.

Heterogeneous values for the core product: In our model, consumers are homogeneous in their preference for the core product, i.e., value V does not vary by consumer. In practice, some companies (e.g., airlines) derive significant profits by discriminating between "business" and "leisure" travelers who typically have drastically different travel requirements, time preferences, attitudes toward risk of not getting a ticket, or all of them together. This is the subject of voluminous revenue management literature in operations (Talluri and van Ryzin 2004), which often models consumer preferences as evolving over time. We ignore such considerations since consumers with high utility for product consumption are likely to purchase the product at a full price and would not participate in either opaque or last-minute sales channels. Thus, our model focuses exclusively on price-conscious consumers with relatively low value for the product itself. It is, however, straightforward to incorporate into our model consumers that differ in their core value for the product. For example, we could introduce a second Hotelling line with a much higher core value V representing consumers with high valuation for the product. Since these consumers have high willingness to pay, the firms will allocate capacity to satisfy these consumers first, and then sell to consumers with lower V. Essentially, demand from high-valuation consumers can be subtracted from firms' capacities and the remaining problem is solved as described above with insights unchanged. An even more realistic model would incorporate a continuous distribution of values of V. In this case our results above indicate that higher values of V make last-minute sales preferable over opaque sales. Therefore, depending on the distribution of values of V, we expect that opaque selling will be preferred when there are more consumers with low valuations and direct last-minute selling will be preferred when there are more consumers with high valuations. In either case, our insights will remain qualitatively unchanged.

Concentrated versus monopolistic markets: In our model, there is competition in the transparent market but the opaque intermediary is a monopoly. In practice this may or may not be true. For example, for several years priceline.com enjoyed near monopoly in selling opaque products but recently it has experienced competition from other opaque intermediaries such as hotwire.com. It is possible to have situations in which both transparent and opaque markets are either monopolistic or competitive. For example, Norwegian Cruise Lines offer both specific staterooms on their ships as well as opaque staterooms which guarantee certain minimal amenities but not specific location on the ship. To analyze the impact of market competitiveness in the transparent market on our findings, we considered a situation in which both transparent products A and B are managed by the same firm which maximizes the total profit. We find that the monopoly firm is able to derive higher profit from direct last-minute sales due to its ability to charge higher prices. Thus, without competition, the last-minute direct sales strategy becomes preferred over opaque selling for a larger range of problem parameters.

Multiple hidden product attributes: In the opaque literature the products are characterized by a single attribute. In practice, however, products may differ in multiple dimensions. Hotel rooms purchased on hotwire.com differ in size, location, and amenities. Airline tickets differ in the number of stops, departure times, and trip lengths. All these different attributes can be hidden from or revealed to consumers in the opaque selling channel. Some opaque intermediaries allow consumers to select the level of opacity: e.g., priceline.com lets its consumers specify whether a "red eye" flight is acceptable and also allows to set the upper bound on the number of stops. The issue of selecting the optimal level of opacity and the right attributes to hide provides potential for future research but is outside the scope of this study.

Vertical product differentiation: In the literature we have surveyed, the consumers are certain that the firms are selling products of identical valuations in both the channels. However, if there is additional uncertainty about exact features of the product purchased from the opaque channel, then the consumers will be more likely to purchase directly from the firms.

Queueing for semi-opaque products: In practice, we often encounter examples of semi-opaque products. For example, theaters in New York's Broadway area sell leftover tickets on the day of the show through a service run by an intermediary called TKTS. The decision-making process of theater customers is somewhat different from the model considered in this chapter, but has strong similarities to it as well. Local customers who are keen on seeing a particular performance will buy directly from the theaters. However, leisure customers, say tourists visiting New York for a weekend, might consider buying at TKTS, because they are fine with watching one of several shows. This is not to say that those customers have no preferences between the shows, but as long as they can purchase one of the shows they would like to see, the customers receive a positive value. TKTS sells mainly unsold (and some rationed tickets) on the last day of the show. The customers have to queue up, based on their ex ante expectations of getting a ticket for one of their preferred shows. The queues are generally quite long, and therefore represent a significant waiting cost for an unclear final outcome. However, at the end of the queue, the customers get to *choose* the show they would like to see, as long as tickets for the show are available. In this sense, the products sold by TKTS are only semi-opaque. Clearly, there are some dynamic issues involved here and the customer may not always get the show they lined up for. In fact, sometimes none of the shows a customer stood in line for might be available. In such cases, they might have to just quit at (or close to) the head of the line.

Dynamic pricing decisions: In all the models that we surveyed, the pricing decisions made by the firms are simplified. There are only two selling opportunities: one "regular" and one "sales." In practice, for example, airlines offer many fares, and prices tend to increase until the very last moment when last-minute sales are announced. Incorporating such considerations into modern decision support systems, while simultaneously integrating them with selling strategies such as opaque selling remains a challenge and is an exciting avenue for dynamic pricing research.

Empirical work: Finally, we note the existence of rich opportunities for empirical modeling in the airline revenue management literature. Although numerous studies have modeled airline revenue management decisions, there have been very few attempts to verify these findings empirically. See Koenigsberg et al. (2008) for an exception which analyzes the pricing strategy employed by Easy-Jet, which is based on the idea of increasing prices as the selling horizon matures. They find that the last-minute sales are likely to be offered when the capacity levels are intermediate (i.e., not too high or low relative to demand) and when there are many flight segments. Cho et al. (2008) is another example, our perception is that empirical studies in the revenue management area tend to be limited by data availability. Although airlines share lots of data with regulatory authorities (Federal Aviation Administration and the Department of Transportation), these data are not precise enough to rigorously study specific pricing strategies employed by an airline. Neverthless, this an area where tremendous program can be made.

10.6 Appendix A: Deterministic Demand

10.6.1 Proof of Lemma 1

Proof. We begin the proof by observing that the two periods are identical in the information all the players (firms and consumers) have and there is no stochastic component in demand or utilities. Further, there is no discounting.

Consider the case of firm A. First, consider the case when demand is low ($J < K$). Suppose, in equilibrium, the consumer located at x_A is indifferent between buying from firm A in the first period at price p_A^1 and in the second period at price p_A^2. For this consumer, the following indifference condition holds when he is making his purchase or postpones his decision in the first period ($p_A^{2,e}$ is his first-period expectation of the second-period price):

$$V - p_A^1 - tx_A = V - p_A^{2,e} - tx_A,$$

which implies that $p_A^1 = p_A^{2,e}$ in equilibrium, regardless of the location of the indifferent customer. Further, in any rational expectations equilibrium, the expectations will be correct, i.e., $p_A^{2,e} = p_A^2$. Therefore, firm A will offer the same price ($p_A^1 = p_A^2 = p_A$) in both periods.

When demand is high ($J > K$), there are two kinds of consumers based on their locations – those who will obtain firm A's product (located in the region $[0, K/(2J)]$) and those who will not obtain firm A's product (located to the right of $K/(2J)$). When demand is high, firm A maximizes revenues by selling to the consumers located to the left of $K/(2J)$. The second kind of consumers therefore would be unable to buy products in the high-demand scenario. For the first set of consumers, the indifference condition above again holds and we have $p_A^1 = p_A^2$. Further, firm A sets these prices so that the consumer at $K/(2J)$ is indifferent between purchasing and not purchasing a ticket, i.e., $V - p_A^1 - tK/(2J) = V - p_A^2 - tK/(2J) = 0$, which yields $p_A^1 = p_A^2 = V - K/(2J)$.

Similar arguments apply for prices offered by firm B.

10.6.2 Proof of Proposition 1

Proof. We prove the proposition for low demand. Note that the total capacity of the two firms (K) is more than the total demand (J). Let $V/t \geq 1/2$ as described in the chapter.

First, consider the case in which the firms are acting as local monopolies. We consider the decision of firm A in detail, and the analysis will be identical for firm B. If firm A chooses the price p_A, the right-most consumer to buy from the firm will be at x_A such that $V - tx_A - p_A = 0$, i.e., the utility of the consumer at x_A is zero. The price charged by the firm to all consumers will then be $p_A = V - tx_A$, and the demand will be $x_A J$. Thus, the profit for the firm will be $\pi_A = p_A x_A J = (V - t x_A) x_A J$. This profit is maximized at $x_A = V/(2t)$, and the maximized profit is given by $\pi_A = JV^2/(4t)$. However, to ensure that the firms are local monopolies, we need to ensure that at the optimum $x_A < 1/2$, which yields $V/t < 1$.

When $V/t \geq 1$, the above equilibrium does not hold, since the firms are not local monopolies (the optimal coverage for each firm will be $>1/2$). We propose that for $1 \leq V/t < 3/2$ both firms charge prices $p_A = p_B = V - t/2$ in equilibrium, cover half the market and make profits $\pi_A = \pi_B = (V - t/2)J/2$. We now show that this is the unique equilibrium. Suppose firm A raises its price and charges $p_A^+ = V - t/2 + \varepsilon t$ where $\varepsilon > 0$, while firm B still charges $p_B = V - t/2$. Then, firm A covers $x_A = 1/2 - \varepsilon$ and makes a profit $(1/2 - \varepsilon)(V - t/2 + \varepsilon t)J$. However, under the condition $V/t \geq 1$, this profit is lower than the equilibrium profit, so that the firm does not have an incentive to raise its price above the equilibrium price. Now, consider the case in which the firm lowers its price and charges $p_A^- = V - t/2 - \varepsilon t$. The point $\tilde{x}$ at which the indifferent consumer is located is then found by solving the condition $V - p_A^- - t\tilde{x} = V - p_B - t(1 - \tilde{x})$, which yields $\tilde{x} = (1 + \varepsilon)/2$, and the profit for firm A is given by $\frac{1}{2}(1 + \varepsilon)(V - t/2 - \varepsilon t)J$. However, under the condition $V/t < 3/2$, this profit is always lower than the equilibrium profit, so that the firm does not have an incentive to lower its price below the equilibrium price. Hence, the equilibrium proposed above is indeed an equilibrium for the range $1 \leq V/t < 3/2$.

Now consider the case in which the two firms are in direct competition. Firm A charges a price p_A and firm B charges a price p_B. Assume that the indifferent consumer is located at $\tilde{x}$. Since this consumer is indifferent to buying from A or B, the following condition holds for him: $V - p_A - t\tilde{x} = V - p_B - t(1 - \tilde{x})$, which gives $\tilde{x} = 1/2 + (p_B - p_A)/(2t)$. The profits for firms A and B are given, respectively, by $\pi_A = p_A \tilde{x} J$ and $\pi_B = p_B(1 - \tilde{x})J$. Maximizing the profits jointly, we obtain $p_A = p_B = t, \tilde{x} = 1/2$, and $\pi_A = \pi_B = Jt/2$. Under our assumption that the outside utility of a consumer is zero, we need to ensure that $V - p_A - t\tilde{x} = V - p_B - t(1 - \tilde{x}) \geq 0$, which gives the condition $V/t \geq 3/2$.

This specifies the equilibrium for all values of $V/t \geq 1/2$ and completes the proof.

10.6.3 Proof of Proposition 2

Proof. Note that $V/t \geq 1/2$. In this proposition, we analyze the high-demand case. The total capacity of the two firms (K) is less than the total demand (J) and firms will act as local monopolies. Again, we consider firm A and the analysis is identical for firm B. If firm A chooses the price p_A, the right-most consumer to buy from the firm will be at x_A such that $V - t x_A - p_A = 0$. The price charged by the firm to all consumers will then be $p_A = V - t x_A$, and the demand will be $x_A J$.

Thus, the profit for the firm will be $\pi_A = p_A x_A J = (V - t x_A) x_A J$. This profit is maximized at $x_A = V/(2t)$, and the maximized profit is given by $\pi_A = JV^2/(4t)$.

However, to ensure that the firms do not stockout, we need to ensure that at the optimum $x_A \leq K/(2J)$, which gives $V/t \leq K/J$.

For $V/t > K/J$ each firm will charge the price $p_A = p_B = V - tK/(2J)$, cover $x_A = 1 - x_B = K/(2J)$, and make profits $\pi_A = \pi_B = (V - Kt/(2J))(K/2)$. Note that the firm cannot lower its price below this level, since it does not have the capacity to serve the expanded market. It can be easily shown, using an ε-deviation argument as in the proof of proposition 1, that the firm does not have an incentive to lower its price below this level. This specifies equilibria for all values of $V/t \geq 1/2$ and completes the proof.

10.6.4 Proof of Lemma 2

Proof. We first prove that, when demand is deterministic, the rational expectations equilibrium does not exist for $\gamma_A^e \in [0,1] \setminus \{\frac{1}{2}\}$, and only $\gamma_A^e = \gamma_B^e = 1/2$ are supported in equilibrium. We first consider the deterministic low-demand case and then the high-demand case. In both cases, we establish the rational expectations equilibrium by first analyzing the second period and then the first period. In all cases, $V/t \geq 1/2$ as before.

Low demand: We consider the case in which the firms have ample capacity, i.e., $J < K$. Let us consider the *second* period. Without loss of generality, let x_A, x_B be the location of the consumers closest to the firm who did not buy in the first period. Hence interval $[x_A, x_B]$ denotes the location of all the consumers remaining in the second period. Consider any consumer located at $x \in [x_A, x_B]$. x_A and x_B are the left-most and right-most points on the line available to the intermediary to sell opaque products.

Since we are in the second period, demand realization has occurred, and opaque seller has announced price p_I. The consumer has expectations over availability. Upon buying the opaque product at price p_I, the surplus a consumer located at x expects to attain is

$$V - p_I - \gamma_A^e t x - \gamma_B^e t (1-x),$$

which, using $\gamma_B^e = 1 - \gamma_A^e$, can be written as

$$V - p_I - t(1 - \gamma_A^e) + (1 - 2\gamma_A^e) t x.$$

$0 < \gamma_A^e \leq 1/2:$ It suffices to consider $0 < \gamma_A^e \leq 1/2$ because, if $\gamma_A^e = 0$, the market is not opaque since the consumers believe that all the products in the opaque channel are coming from firm B. The analysis for $1/2 \leq \gamma_A^e < 1$ is identical to the analysis for $0 < \gamma_B^e \leq 1/2$ (which is the same as the analysis below by symmetry). For a given p_I, the surplus for a consumer purchasing in the opaque market is increasing in his location x, as long as $\gamma_A^e < 1/2$. In other words, the minimum surplus is obtained by the consumer located at x_A. We consider two cases, namely, when the intermediary wants to cover the full market from x_A to x_B and when the intermediary considers covering this interval partially.

The intermediary may not necessarily cover the full market $[x_A, x_B]$ available to him. Suppose that the intermediary only aims to cover the market $[x', x_B]$, where $x' > x_A$. Note that the surplus of a consumer is increasing in his location x. Therefore, the opaque intermediary will price such that $p_I = V - (1 - \gamma_A^e)t + (1 - 2\gamma_A^e)tx'$, $x_A < x' < x_B$. Then the consumers in the interval $[x_A, x')$ (which is defined to be null if $x' < x_A$) do not buy because they have negative utility. The consumers in the interval $[x', x_B]$ buy in the opaque channel because they have non-negative utility. The profit of the intermediary is then $\pi_I = (V - (1 - \gamma_A^e)t + (1 - 2\gamma_A^e)tx')(x_B - x')J$. To maximize this profit the intermediary sells to the market $[x'^*, x_B]$ where

$$x'^* = \frac{(1 - \gamma_A^e)t - V + (1 - 2\gamma_A^e)tx_B}{2(1 - 2\gamma_A^e)t}.$$

This implies that $p_I = \frac{1}{2}(V - (1 - \gamma_A^e)t + (1 - 2\gamma_A^e)tx_B)$.

Now consider the analysis for firm A selling in the transparent channel. The person located at x_A has negative utility in the opaque channel. Thus, to this consumer, firm A selling in the transparent channel can charge $p_A = V - x_A t$ and make him indifferent between buying and not buying. This gives firm A a profit of $\pi_A = (V - tx_A)x_A J + \delta\gamma_A^e(V - (1 - \gamma_A^e)t + (1 - 2\gamma_A^e)tx_B)(x_B - x')$.

Now consider firm B. The consumer at x_B has to be indifferent between purchasing in the first period and in the second period. The consumer at x_B solves $V - p_B - t(1 - x_B) = V - p_I - \gamma_A^e tx_B - (1 - \gamma_A^e)t(1 - x_B)$, which, using the value of p_I from above, gives $p_B = \frac{1}{2}(V + t(-1 + x_B - \gamma_A^e + 2x_B\gamma_A^e))$. The profit for firm B is $\pi_B = p_B(1 - x_B)J + \delta(1 - \gamma_A e)p_I(x_B - x')J$. Maximizing π_A and π_B w.r.t. x_A and x_B simultaneously, we obtain

$$x_A = \frac{V}{2t} \quad \text{and} \quad x_B = \frac{V(1 + (-1 + \gamma_A^e)\delta) + t(-2 + \delta + (\gamma_A^e)^2\delta - \gamma_A^e(3 + 2\delta))}{t(-2 + \delta + 2(\gamma_A^e)^2\delta - \gamma_A^e(4 + 3\delta))}.$$

Using these values of x_A and x_B, we obtain

$$\gamma_A^{\text{realized}} = \frac{K/2 - x_A J}{K/2 - x_A J + K/2 - (1 - x_B)J}.$$

In the rational expectations equilibrium, the beliefs have to be consistent with the outcome. It must be that $\gamma_A^{\text{realized}} = \gamma_A^e$. Imposing this condition we solve for $\gamma_A^{\text{realized}} = \gamma_A^e = \gamma_A^e(V, t, J, K, \delta)$. The value of $\gamma_A(V, t, J, K, \delta)$ is algebraically complicated and we do not present it here. However, we check that imposing the condition $0 < \gamma_A^e < 1/2$ implies $V/t < 1/2$, which is a contradiction. (Recall that we require $V/t \geq 1/2$ as a "sanity condition" to ensure that if the firms sell products for free, then everybody in the market will have positive evaluation to obtain the product from at least one of the firms. In other words the condition ensures some market coverage at zero prices.) Thus, when the intermediary sets prices such that the intermediary's market coverage is partial, then the rational expectations equilibrium does not exist.

Let us now analyze the case when the intermediary prices to cover the entire market $[x_A, x_B]$. If the intermediary wants to cover the full opaque market, he will price so as to make the surplus of the consumer at x_A equal to zero, i.e., $p_I = V - t(1 - \gamma_A^e) + x_A(1 - 2\gamma_A^e)t$.

Since the consumer x_A is indifferent between the opaque and first period market, firm A sets its price p_A by solving the following equation:

$$V - p_A - t x_A = V - p_I - \gamma_A^e t x_A - (1 - \gamma_A^e)t(1 - x_A).$$

To extract maximum revenues in the opaque market, the intermediary sets p_I such that the right-hand side of the above equation is zero. Therefore, the value that x_A receives is zero.

Therefore in the first period, if firm A covers the interval $[0, x_A]$, the price is $p_A = V - t x_A$. In the first period firm A then maximizes its profit $\pi_A = (V - t x_A) x_A J + \delta \gamma_A^e p_I (x_B - x_A) J$, where p_I is as above.

Firm B solves

$$V - p_B - t(1 - x_B) = V - p_I - \gamma_A^e t x_B - (1 - \gamma_A^e)t(1 - x_B).$$

Restricting to $\gamma_A^e \in (0, 1/2]$ and using p_I above, we obtain $p_B = V + t(-1 + x_A - 2x_A\gamma_A^e + 2x_B\gamma_A^e)$. The profit for firm B is given by $\pi_B = p_B(1 - x_B)J + \delta(1 - \gamma_A^e)p_I(x_B - x_A)J$.

Maximizing π_A and π_B simultaneously for the firms w.r.t. x_A and x_B gives

$$\begin{aligned}
x_A = &\left[V(4 - (1 + 2\gamma_A^e)\delta + (1 - 3\gamma_A^e + 2(\gamma_A^e)^2)\delta^2)\right. \\
&\left. + t\delta(1 - \delta + 2(\gamma_A^e)^3\delta + 4\gamma_A^e(1 + \delta) - (\gamma_A^e)^2(8 + 5\delta))\right] \\
&\cdot \left[t(8 + (1 + 4\gamma_A^e - 12(\gamma_A^e)^2)\delta + (1 - 2\gamma_A^e)^2(-1 + \gamma_A^e)\delta^2)\right]^{-1},
\end{aligned}$$

$$\begin{aligned}
x_B = &\left[t(2 - 2\delta + 2(\gamma_A^e)^4\delta^2 - 5(\gamma_A^e)^3\delta(2 + \delta) + (\gamma_A^e)^2\delta(1 + 4\delta)\right. \\
&\left. + \gamma_A^e(4 + 5\delta - \delta^2)) + V(3(-1 + \delta) + (\gamma_A^e)^2(4 - 3\delta)\delta\right. \\
&\left. + 2(\gamma_A^e)^3\delta^2 + \gamma_A^e(2 - 6\delta + \delta^2))\right] \\
&\cdot \left[t\gamma_A^e(8 + (1 + 4\gamma_A^e - 12(\gamma_A^e)^2)\delta + (1 - 2\gamma_A^e)^2(-1 + \gamma_A^e)\delta^2)\right]^{-1}.
\end{aligned}$$

Using the above values, we obtain

$$\gamma_A^{\text{realized}} = \frac{K/2 - x_A J}{(K/2 - x_A J) + (K/2 - (1 - x_B)J)}.$$

In the rational expectations equilibrium, $\gamma_A^{\text{realized}} = \gamma_A^e$. Upon solving this, we obtain $\gamma_A^{\text{realized}} = \gamma_A^e = 1/2$ as the only real-valued solution. Hence, the equilibrium does not exist for $0 \le \gamma_A^e < 1/2$ when the intermediary wants to cover the full market between $[x_A, x_B]$. Only $\gamma_A^e = \gamma_B^e = 1/2$ can be supported in the equilibrium.

$1/2 < \gamma_A^e \leq 1$: When $1/2 < \gamma_A^e \leq 1$, for a given p_I, the surplus decreases with x. In other words, the minimum surplus is obtained by the consumer located at x_B. The analysis proceeds as above, except the subscripts A and B are suitably interchanged. Using identical arguments, we show that there is no equilibrium such that $1/2 < \gamma_A^e \leq 1$. Further, the analysis for $\gamma_A^e > 1/2$ is the same as the analysis for $\gamma_B^e < 1/2$.

In summary, all consumers develop rational expectations $\gamma_A^e = \gamma_B^e = 1/2$, which are realized in equilibrium.

In other words, the rational expectations equilibrium does not exist for $\gamma_A \in [0,1] \setminus \{\frac{1}{2}\}$ and only $\gamma_A^e = \gamma_B^e = 1/2$ are supported in the rational expectations equilibrium.

Since $\gamma_A^e = \gamma_A = 1/2$ for every consumer in the market and the probability of getting an opaque product $\beta = 1$ (since there is ample capacity), the ex ante expected surplus for each consumer buying from the opaque channel is simply $V - p_I - t/2$ and is independent of the location of the consumer. Therefore, intermediary prices at $p_I = V - t/2$ and attains the revenue $\pi_I = (1 - \delta)(V - t/2)(x_B - x_A)J$ by selling to the entire remaining market. Note that the revenue-maximizing action in the opaque channel is independent of the fraction of revenues $(1 - \delta)$ held by the intermediary.

Limited capacity/High demand: In the case in which the firms have limited capacity, i.e., $J > K$, we need to impose the conditions $x_A \leq K/(2J)$ and $1 - x_B \leq K/(2J)$ while optimizing the profits for firms A and B, respectively, which does not change the procedure of the preceding proof. We sketch the argument below.

Let us consider the second period when opaque products are being offered. WLOG, let x_A, x_B be the locations of the consumers who were indifferent between purchasing and not purchasing from the firms A and B in the first period, respectively. Hence $[x_A, x_B]$ denotes the interval of all the consumers remaining in the second period. Now, consider any consumer located at $x \in [x_A, x_B]$.

Since we are in the second period, demand realization has occurred, and opaque seller has announced price p_I. The consumer located at x has beliefs over availability. Upon buying the opaque product at price p_I, the surplus he expects to attain is

$$V - p_I - \gamma_A^e tx - \gamma_B^e t(1 - x),$$

which, using $\gamma_B^e = 1 - \gamma_A^e$, can be written as

$$V - p_I - t(1 - \gamma_A^e) + (1 - 2\gamma_A^e)tx.$$

If capacity is not binding, then the analysis is no different from the previous analysis of the low-demand case (i.e., in equilibrium, the expectations $\gamma_A = \gamma_B = 1/2$).

Suppose capacity is limited in the second period. In other words, the residual capacity in the second period is less than the unfulfilled demand in the second period, i.e., $(K - x_A J - (1 - x_B)J) < (x_B - x_A)J$. Let us assume that the opaque intermediary covers interval $[x', x'']$ where $x' > x_A$ and $x'' < x_B$.

Consider $0 < \gamma_A^e < 1/2$. p_I is obtained by solving $V - p_I - t(1 - \gamma_A^e) + (1 - 2\gamma_A^e) \cdot tx' = 0$. Since the indifferent consumer is located at $x_A < x'$, we have that the net valuation of the consumer purchasing from firm A is zero. (If the consumer has positive utility, then a consumer to the right of x_A would also buy with positive utility.) The optimal revenue of firm A is achieved by maximizing $\pi_A = (V - tx_A)x_A J + \delta\gamma_A^e p_I(x'' - x')J$ w.r.t. x_A. This implies $x_A^* = \min\{K/(2H), V/(2t)\}$.

Since capacity is binding, all the seats with the opaque intermediary are sold. Hence, $x'' < x_B$ is determined by $(K - x_A J - (1 - x_B)J) = (x'' - x')J$. Then firm B maximizes $\pi_B = (V - t(1 - x_B))(1 - x_B)J + \delta(1 - \gamma_A^e)p_I(x'' - x')J$ w.r.t. x_B. This implies $x_B = 1 - \min\{K/(2H), V/(2t)\}$. Hence $x_A = 1 - x_B$, and the rational expectations regarding the probabilities of availability of the leftover products from each firm will be symmetric. Hence only $\gamma_A = \gamma_B = 1/2$ is sustained in equilibrium in the high-demand environment.

10.6.5 Equilibrium Characterization for the Low-Demand Case (If Consumers Do Not Strategically Wait)

From proof of Lemma 2 in Appendix 10.6.4, we have $\gamma_A^e = \gamma_A = 1/2$ and $\beta = 1$ for all consumers in the market. The ex ante expected surplus for each consumer buying from the opaque channel is simply $V - p_I - t/2$ and is independent of the location of the consumer. Therefore, the intermediary prices at $p_I = V - t/2$ and attains the revenue $\pi_I = (V - t/2)(x_B - x_A)J$ by selling to the entire remaining market.

We now analyze the optimal choices of the firms in their own transparent channels before the opaque sales. The consumers located between x_A and x_B prefer to buy from the opaque channel. As before, for firm A the consumer located at x_A must be indifferent between buying from the firm now or in the opaque channel later. In a low-demand state, the leftover products are sufficient to cover all the remaining demand. Hence, we have

$$V - p_A - tx_A = V - p_I - \gamma_A^e tx_A - \gamma_B^e t(1 - x_A).$$

Since $\gamma_A^e = 1/2$ and $p_I = V - t/2$, the right-hand side of the equation above is zero. Hence, the price charged by firm A is $p_A = V - tx_A$. Firm A, which covers the market till x_A and charges price $p_A = V - tx_A$, makes a profit of

$$\pi_A = (V - tx_A)x_A J + \delta\gamma_A^e \left(V - \frac{t}{2}\right)(x_B - x_A)J.$$

The value of x_A that maximizes the profit for firm A is

$$x_A = \frac{V}{2t} - \frac{\delta}{4}\left(\frac{V}{t} - \frac{1}{2}\right),$$

which is decreasing in δ. As the ability to earn more revenues from the opaque channel increases, the firm chooses to cover less through its own channels. This does not imply that the firm is generating smaller revenue through its own channel. The corresponding optimal price $p_A = V - tx_A = V/2 + (\delta/4)(V/t - 1/2)t$ is increasing in δ. Because of the presence of the opaque channel, firms sell fewer products in their own channels at *higher* prices. Proceeding with a similar analysis for firm B, we obtain

$$x_B = 1 - \left(\frac{V}{2t} - \frac{\delta}{4}\left(\frac{V}{t} - \frac{1}{2}\right)\right).$$

Thus, the coverage by the intermediary is

$$x_B - x_A = 1 - \frac{V}{t} + \frac{\delta}{2}\left(\frac{V}{t} - \frac{1}{2}\right).$$

For the above expression, we need to ensure that

$$x_A \leq \frac{1}{2} \quad \Rightarrow \quad \frac{V}{t} \leq \frac{4 - \delta}{2(2 - \delta)}.$$

For $V/t \geq 3/2$, the competitive equilibrium holds, with both firms covering exactly half the market at prices $p_A = p_B = t$ and obtaining profits $\pi_A = \pi_B = tJ/2$ while $\pi_I = 0$. For $(4 - \delta)/[2(2 - \delta)] \leq V/t \leq 3/2$ we construct the non-competitive equilibrium as both firms charging $p_A = p_B = (V/t - 1/2)t$, covering exactly half the market, and therefore making profits $\pi_A = \pi_B = (V/t - 1/2)(t/2)J$ with $\pi_I = 0$ (see table below). Thus, for $V/t \geq (4 - \delta)/[2(2 - \delta)]$ it turns out that nothing is allocated to the opaque channel in equilibrium.

	Profit from the first period	Profit from opaque sales
$\frac{1}{2} \leq \frac{V}{t} \leq \frac{4 - \delta}{2(2 - \delta)}$	$\left(\frac{V}{2} + \frac{\delta}{4}\left(\frac{V}{t} - \frac{1}{2}\right)t\right)$ $\cdot\left(\frac{V}{2t} - \frac{\delta}{4}\left(\frac{V}{t} - \frac{1}{2}\right)\right)J$	$\delta\left(\frac{V}{t} - \frac{1}{2}\right)\left(1 - \frac{V}{t} + \frac{\delta}{2}\left(\frac{V}{t} - \frac{1}{2}\right)\right)\frac{t}{2}J$
$\frac{4 - \delta}{2(2 - \delta)} \leq \frac{V}{t} \leq \frac{3}{2}$	$\left(\frac{V}{t} - \frac{1}{2}\right)\frac{t}{2}J$	0
$\frac{3}{2} \leq \frac{V}{t}$	$\frac{t}{2}J$	0

The analysis above shows that (compared to the table in Proposition 1) using the opaque channel increases the total market coverage (and profits), given the same valuation V and strength of brand preferences t when the ratio V/t is small. However, the firms utilize the opaque channel only when the consumers' willingness to pay is low. For a higher willingness to pay, i.e., when $V/t \geq (4 - \delta)/[2(2 - \delta)]$, the firms price in the transparent channel so as to cover the entire market and there are no sales through the opaque channel. Note that, in the above case, when $V/t \geq (4 - \delta)/[2(2 - \delta)]$, the profits are identical to what a firm makes when it does not use an opaque channel and $V/t \geq 1$ (Proposition 1). Also, note that

$1 \leq (4-\delta)/[2(2-\delta)] \leq 3/2$ for all values of $\delta \in [0,1]$, which means that using the opaque channel increases profits in the non-competitive regime. Therefore, firms charge a higher price in the first period, cover less through their own channels after the introduction of the opaque channel, but "clear up" the remaining market using the opaque channel (albeit at a lower price), which leads to higher overall profits.

10.6.6 Proof of Proposition 3

Proof. When $1/2 \leq V/t < 1$, the firms find it optimal to charge a price $V/2$ and cover $V/(2t)$, which is less than $1/2$. The remaining $1-V/t$ portion of the market (between $V/(2t)$ and $1-V/(2t)$) is covered in the opaque channel by charging a price $V-t/2$. The proof is along the lines of the proof in Appendix 10.6.5. When $V/t \geq 1$, the full market is covered in the transparent channel in the first period itself, and there are no products left to be allocated to the opaque channel.

10.6.7 Equilibrium Characterization for the High-Demand Case (If Consumers Do Not Strategically Wait)

Consider a consumer at $x \in [x_A, x_B]$ and note that $K < J$. The probability this consumer obtains a product is

$$\beta = \frac{K - x_A J - (1-x_B)J}{(x_B - x_A)J}.$$

If this consumer obtains a product from the opaque seller at price p_I, the surplus he attains is

$$V - p_I - \gamma_A^e t x - \gamma_B^e t (1-x).$$

Again, using Lemma 2, $\gamma_A^e = 1/2$. In this case, the expected surplus in the equilibrium is simply $V - p_I - t/2$ and is independent of the location of the consumer. The opaque intermediary prices the products at $p_I = V - t/2$ and the total revenue accrued in the channel is $\pi_I = (V - t/2)(K/J - x_A - (1-x_B))J$. Note that the intermediary can sell to *any* consumer located between x_A and x_B even though he is unable to cover the full market between these two points due to constrained capacity.

Now consider firm A in the transparent channel. The consumer at x_A (the rightmost consumer that buys from A) solves

$$V - p_A - t x_A = \beta (V - p_I^e - \gamma_A^e t x_A - \gamma_B^e t (1-x_A)).$$

Since $\gamma_A^e = 1/2$ and $p_I^e = p_I = V - t/2$, the right-hand side of the equation above is zero.

The rest of the analysis proceeds exactly as above in the proof for Proposition 3, except that the firm stocks out if the optimal value of x_A is greater than $K/(2J)$. After imposing $x_A \leq K/(2J)$ in the solution above due to capacity constraints, we obtain

$$\frac{V}{2t} - \frac{\delta}{4}\left(\frac{V}{t} - \frac{1}{2}\right) < \frac{K}{2J} \Rightarrow \frac{V}{t} \leq \frac{4K/J - \delta}{2(2 - \delta)}.$$

Upon imposing the condition $V/t \geq 1/2$, we obtain a lower bound on K/J, i.e., $K/J > 1/2$. Thus, for

$$\frac{1}{2} \leq \frac{V}{t} \leq \frac{4K/J - \delta}{2(2 - \delta)}$$

(ensuring the firm does not stockout in the transparent channel) we obtain

$$\pi_A = \pi_B = \left(\frac{V}{2} + \frac{\delta}{4}\left(\frac{V}{t} - \frac{1}{2}\right)t\right)\left(\frac{V}{2t} - \frac{\delta}{4}\left(\frac{V}{t} - \frac{1}{2}\right)\right)J$$

$$+ \frac{\delta}{2}\left(\frac{V}{t} - \frac{1}{2}\right)\left(K - \left(\frac{V}{t} - \frac{\delta}{2}\left(\frac{V}{t} - \frac{1}{2}\right)\right)J\right)t,$$

$$\pi_I = (1 - \delta)\left(\frac{V}{t} - \frac{1}{2}\right)\left(K - \left(\frac{V}{t} - \frac{\delta}{2}\left(\frac{V}{t} - \frac{1}{2}\right)\right)J\right)t.$$

For the case in which $V/t \geq (4K/J - \delta)/[2(2 - \delta)]$, we construct the non-competitive equilibrium as follows: both firms charge a price $p_A = p_B = (V/t - K/(2J))t$ and cover $x_A = 1 - x_B = K/(2J)$. The profits are given by

$$\pi_A = \pi_B = \left(\frac{V}{t} - \frac{K}{2J}\right)\frac{K}{2}t \quad \text{and} \quad \pi_I = 0.$$

When demand is higher than capacity available, the profits accrued by the firms from the sales through their own channels and opaque channels are as follows:

V/t	Profit from the first period	Profit from opaque sales
$\frac{1}{2} \leq \frac{4K/J - \delta}{2(2 - \delta)}$	$\left(\frac{V}{2} + \frac{\delta}{4}\left(\frac{V}{t} - \frac{1}{2}\right)t\right)$ $\cdot \left(\frac{V}{2t} - \frac{\delta}{4}\left(\frac{V}{t} - \frac{1}{2}\right)\right)J$	$\delta t\left(\frac{V}{t} - \frac{1}{2}\right)\left(K - \left(\frac{V}{t} - \frac{\delta}{2}\left(\frac{V}{t} - \frac{1}{2}\right)\right)J\right)$
$\frac{4K/J - \delta}{2(2 - \delta)} \leq \frac{V}{t}$	$\left(\frac{V}{t} - \frac{K}{2J}\right)\frac{t}{2}J$	0

10.6.8 Proof of Proposition 4

Proof. When $1/2 \leq V/t < K/J$, the firms find it optimal to charge a price $V/2$ and cover $V/(2t)$, which is less than $1/2$. The remaining $K/2 - VJ/t$ portion of the market $\left((V/(2t), K/(2J))\right.$ and $\left.(1 - K/(2J), 1 - V/(2t))\right)$ is covered in the opaque channel by charging a price $V - t/2$. The proof is along the lines of the proof in Appendix 10.6.7.

When $V/t \geq K/J$, the full market is covered in the transparent channel in the first period itself (i.e., the firms sell all $K/2$ products), and there are no products left to be allocated to the opaque channel.

10.7 Appendix B: Uncertain Demand

10.7.1 Proof of Proposition 5

Proof. Consider any consumer at some position $x \leq 1/2$ who has the following beliefs about the location of the indifferent consumers: The consumer x believes that the consumer indifferent between buying in the first period from firm A and buying in the second period from firm A is located at x_A^e. Further, x believes the consumer indifferent between buying and not buying from A in the second period is located at $y_A^{H,e} \geq x_A^e$ when demand is high and at $y_A^{L,e} \geq x_A^e$ when demand is low.

Second Period: In the second period, if demand is high, the number of products available is $(K/2 - x_A^e H)^+$ and the number of products demanded is $(x_A^e H - K/2)^+ + (y_A^{H,e} - x_A^e)H$. Hence, the probability of obtaining a product is

$$\min\left\{1, \frac{\min\left\{(K/2 - x_A^e H)^+, (x_A^e H - K/2)^+ + (y_A^{H,e} - x_A^e)H\right\}}{(x_A^e H - K/2)^+ + (y_A^{H,e} - x_A^e)H}\right\}.$$

If demand is low, the number of products available is $(K/2 - x_A^e L)^+$ and the number of products demanded is $(x_A^e L - K/2)^+ + (y_A^{L,e} - x_A^e)L$ so that the probability of obtaining a product is $\min\left\{1, (K/2 - x_A^e L)^+ / ((x_A^e L - K/2)^+ + (y_A^{L,e} - x_A^e)L)\right\}$.

The expected surplus for the consumer at x for the second period is, therefore,

$$= \alpha \min\left\{1, \frac{\min\left\{(\frac{K}{2} - x_A^e H)^+, (x_A^e H - \frac{K}{2})^+ + (y_A^{H,e} - x_A^e)H\right\}}{(x_A^e H - \frac{K}{2})^+ + (y_A^{H,e} - x_A^e)H}\right\}(V - xt - p_A^{2H})$$

$$+ (1 - \alpha)\min\left\{1, \frac{(\frac{K}{2} - x_A^e L)^+}{(x_A^e L - \frac{K}{2})^+ + (y_A^{L,e} - x_A^e)L}\right\}(V - xt - p_A^{2L}).$$

First Period: In the first period, if demand is high, the probability that a consumer will obtain a product is $\left(\min\{\frac{K}{2}, x_A^e H\}/(x_A^e H)\right)$ and, if demand is low, the probability that this consumer will obtain a product is 1. Hence, the expected surplus for the consumer at x from buying in the first period is

$$[\alpha(\min\{K/2, x_A^e H\}/(x_A^e H)) + (1 - \alpha)](V - xt - p_A^1).$$

Let x_A be the actual location of the indifferent consumer in the first period. Therefore, in the equilibrium, let $x_A = x_A^e$ be the position of the indifferent consumer so we can write

$$\left(\alpha \left(\frac{\min\{\frac{K}{2}, x_A^e H\}}{x_A^e H} \right) + (1 - \alpha) \right) (V - x_A^e t - p_A^1)$$

$$= \alpha \min \left\{ 1, \frac{\min\left\{ \left(\frac{K}{2} - x_A^e H\right)^+, \left(x_A^e H - \frac{K}{2}\right)^+ + (y_A^{H,e} - x_A^e)H \right\}}{\left(x_A^e H - \frac{K}{2}\right)^+ + (y_A^{H,e} - x_A^e)H} \right\}$$

$$\cdot (V - x_A^e t - p_A^{2H})$$

$$+ (1 - \alpha) \min \left\{ 1, \frac{\left(\frac{K}{2} - x_A^e L\right)^+}{\left(x_A^e L - \frac{K}{2}\right)^+ + (y_A^{L,e} - x_A^e)L} \right\} (V - x_A^e t - p_A^{2L}). \quad (10.1)$$

Note that, trivially, we can ensure $y_A^{L,e} \geq x_A^e$ and $y_A^{H,e} \geq x_A^e$. The condition above looks quite imposing to solve, but we can simplify it considerably by dividing it into two cases: (1) when $x_A^e \leq K/(2H)$ and (2) when $x_A^e > K/(2H)$.

Assuming $x_A = x_A^e < K/(2H)$, the above simplifies to

$$V - x_A t - p_A^1 = \alpha(V - x_A t - p_A^{2H}) + (1 - \alpha)(V - x_A t - p_A^{2L}).$$

Assuming $x_A = x_A^e > K/(2H)$ (and $y_A^{L,e} L < K/2$, i.e., no stockout in the low-demand state), the above simplifies to

$$\left(\alpha \frac{K/2}{x_A H} + (1 - \alpha) \right) (V - x_A t - p_A^1) = (1 - \alpha)(V - x_A t - p_A^{2L}).$$

We analyze the above cases separately in the following subsections. We consider firm A but the analysis for firm B is identical.

- $x_A = x_A^e < K/(2H)$

  Suppose all consumers correctly believe that $x_A = x_A^e < K/(2H)$. In the first period, denote the price charged by firm A by p_A^1. In the second period, the firms know the state of demand to be high or low. Denote the prices charged by firm A in high- and low-demand states by p_A^{2H} and p_A^{2L}, respectively. Let the indifferent consumer be located at x_A. For this consumer, in the equilibrium and when expectations are consistent, we have

  $$V - p_A^1 - t x_A = \alpha(V - p_A^{2H} - t x_A) + (1 - \alpha)(V - p_A^{2L} - t x_A)$$

  $$\Rightarrow p_A^1 = \alpha p_A^{2H} + (1 - \alpha) p_A^{2L}.$$

  Now consider a consumer at $x_A + \delta$ where $\delta > 0$ and such that $x_A + \delta < K/(2H)$. This consumer has the same belief x_A^e, which is consistent. Moreover, for this consumer the net utility from buying a product in the first period is $U_1 = V - p_A^1 - t(x_A + \delta)$, and the net expected utility from waiting to buy in the second period is $U_2 = \alpha(V - p_A^{2H} - t(x_A + \delta)) + (1 - \alpha)(V - p_A^{2L} - t(x_A + \delta))$. Using the fact that $p_A^1 = \alpha p_A^{2H} + (1 - \alpha)p_A^{2L}$, these utilities are equal. Hence, the consumer at $x_A + \delta$ is also indifferent between buying in the first period or waiting to buy in the second period. This argument can be extended to any consumer in the range $[0, K/(2H))$, which means that the belief x_A^e is incorrect in the equilibrium. Hence, a rational expectations equilibrium with $x_A = x_A^e < K/(2H)$ does not exist.

- $x^A = x_A^e > K/(2H)$

The goal of this section is to show that this equilibrium does not exist for all values of the parameters $V, t, K, L, H,$ and α.

Consider the second period. Suppose demand is high. Then the firm stocks out in the first period, because the number of products is less than the demand in the first period $x^A H > HK/(2H) = K/2$. Now, suppose demand is low. We consider firm A and limit ourselves to the case when, even in low demand, it is a local monopoly and covers the line till $y_A^L \leq 1/2$. The firm charges a price $p_A^{2L} = V - y_A^L t$ where $y_A^L \leq 1/2$ and sells $(y_A^H - x_A)L$ products to make a profit of $\pi_A^{2L} = (V - y_A^L t)(y_A^L - x_A)H$, which is maximized at $y_A^L = (V + x_A t)/(2t)$, with $p_A^{2L} = (V - x_A t)/2$ and $\pi_A^{2L} = (V - x_A t)^2 L/(4t)$.

Next, consider the equation for the indifferent consumer. Under the assumption $x_A^e \geq K/(2H)$ and $y_A^{L,e} L < K/2$, i.e., no stockout in the low-demand state, the indifference condition is

$$p_A^1 = \frac{\alpha K/(x_A^e H) + (1 - \alpha)}{\alpha K(x_A^e H) + 2(1 - \alpha)}(V - x_A t).$$

Writing the expression for the total expected profit of firm A as

$$\pi_A = p_A^1(\alpha K/2 + (1 - \alpha)x_A L) + (1 - \alpha)\pi_A^{2L}$$

and differentiating w.r.t. to x_A, we obtain

$$x_A = \frac{\alpha K(VL(1 - \alpha) - \alpha K t - x_A^e H(1 - \alpha)t}{L(1 - \alpha)t(2H(1 - \alpha)x_A^e + 3K\alpha)}.$$

In the rational expectations equilibrium, we have $x_A^e = x_A$, which yields

$$x_A = x_A^e = \frac{\sqrt{\alpha K(\alpha K(H^2 + 9L^2 - 2HL) + 8(V/t)HL^2(1 - \alpha)) - \alpha K(H + 3L)}}{4HL(1 - \alpha)}.$$

Note that we need the following conditions to hold: $V/t \geq 1/2$, $x_A \geq K/(2H)$ and $y_A^L \leq 1/2 \Rightarrow V/t \leq 1 - x_A$. This equilibrium does not always exist. For instance, when $L = 1/2, K = 1, H = 3/2, \alpha = 1/2, t = 1,$ and $V = 2/3$, the equilibrium does not hold.

- $x^A = x_A^e = K/(2H)$

Suppose all consumers correctly hold the belief that $x^A = x_A^e = K/(2H)$. Consider the indifferent consumer at $x_A = K/(2H)$. In the first period, irrespective of demand being high or low, this consumer can obtain a product at price p_A^1. In the second period, if demand is high, no products are being sold. If demand is low, the consumer can obtain a product at price p_A^{2L}. For this consumer, we can therefore write

$$V - tx_A - p_A^1 = (1 - \alpha)(V - tx_A - p_A^{2L})$$
$$p_A^1 = \alpha(V - Kt/(2H)) + (1 - \alpha)p_A^{2L}.$$

Next, consider a consumer to the left of this indifferent consumer, at $x_A - \varepsilon$, $\varepsilon > 0$, who holds the belief $x_A = x_A^e = K/(2H)$. In the first period, this consumer can obtain a product irrespective of high or low demand at price p_A^1, which gives him net utility $U_1 = V - t(x_A - \varepsilon) - p_A^1$. If the consumer waits for the second period, he can obtain a product only in the case of low demand at price p_A^{2L}. His net expected utility from waiting is $U_2 = (1 - \alpha)(V - t(x_A - \varepsilon) - p_A^{2L})$. Then, $U_1 - U_2 = \alpha \varepsilon t > 0$, which means that this consumer prefers to buy in the first period rather than wait.

Next, consider a consumer to the right of the indifferent consumer, at $x_A + \varepsilon$, $\varepsilon > 0$ who holds the belief $x_A = x_A^e = K/(2H)$. In the first period, this consumer can obtain a product if demand is high. (In the case of high demand, $K/2$ products are being bought by $K/(2H) \cdot H = K/2$ consumers and if this consumer wants to buy a product, $K/2$ products will be bought by $K/2 + \varepsilon'$ consumers, and he will obtain a product with probability $\lim_{\varepsilon' \to 0}[(K/2)/(K/2 + \varepsilon')] = 1$.) The consumer can also obtain a product in the low-demand state. In other words, he can obtain a product in the first period irrespective of high or low demand at price p_A^1, which gives him net utility $U_1 = V - t(x_A + \varepsilon) - p_A^1$. If he waits for the second period, he can obtain a product only in the case of low demand at price p_A^{2L}. His net expected utility from waiting is $U_2 = (1 - \alpha)(V - t(x_A + \varepsilon) - p_A^{2L})$. Then, $U_1 - U_2 = -\alpha \varepsilon t < 0$, which means that this consumer prefers to wait and buy in the second period.

Hence, a consumer to the left of the indifferent consumer prefers to buy in the first period, and a consumer to the right of the indifferent consumer prefers to wait for the second period, which is consistent with equilibrium beliefs. Hence, this equilibrium always exists. It now remains to characterize the equilibrium. We first limit ourselves to the case in which, even in the low-demand state, each firm is a local monopoly. If demand is low, the firm charges a price $p_A^{2L} = V - y_A^L t$ where $y_A^L < 1/2$, and sells $(y_A^H - K/(2H))L$ products to make a profit of $\pi_A^{2L} = (V - y_A^L t)(y_A^L - K/(2H))H$. This profit is maximized at $y_A^L = [V + Kt/(2H)]/(2t)$, with $p_A^{2L} = (V - Kt/(2H))/2$ and gives $\pi_A^{2L} = [(V - Kt/(2H))^2/(4t)]L$. Using $p_A^1 = \alpha(V - Kt/(2H)t) + (1 - \alpha)p_A^{2L}$, we obtain $p_A^1 = ((1 + \alpha)/2)(V - Kt/(2H)t)$. The firm's first-period profit is given by $\pi_A^1 = p_A^1(\alpha H + (1 - \alpha)L)K/(2H)$, and total profit is given by $\pi_A = \pi_A^1 + \pi_A^{2L}$. However, we need to impose $y_A^{2L} \leq 1/2$, which gives the restriction $V/t < 1 - K/(2H)$.

For $1 - K/(2H) \leq V/t < 3/2$, $y_A^{2L} = 1/2$, $p_A^{2L} = V - t/2$, $p_A^1 = \alpha(V - Kt/(2H)) + (1 - \alpha)(V - t/2)$, $\pi_A^{2L} = (1 - \alpha)(V - t/2)(1 - K/H)L/2$, and $\pi_A^1 = p_A^1(\alpha H + (1 - \alpha)L)K/(2H)$. This is the non-competitive equilibrium with each firm covering exactly half the line.

For $V/t \geq 3/2$, $y_A^{2L} = 1/2$, $p_A^{2L} = t$, $p_A^1 = \alpha(V - Kt/(2H)) + (1 - \alpha)t$, $\pi_A^{2L} = (1 - \alpha)t(1 - K/H)L/2$, and $\pi_A^1 = p_A^1(\alpha H + (1 - \alpha)L)K/(2H)$. This is the competitive equilibrium with each firm covering half the line. This completely characterizes the equilibrium for all values of V/t.

10.7.2 Proof of Proposition 6

Proof. We characterize the equilibrium for the case $\delta = 1$; the intuition remains similar for all $\delta \in [0,1]$, because changing δ only changes the profits transferred from the opaque intermediary to the firms.

The analysis below is for $\gamma_A^{H,e} = \gamma_A^{L,e} = 1/2$, which are rational expectations in equilibrium. To see why this is the case, assume that $\gamma^{\cdot,e} = 1/2$. Consider the case when demand is low and consumers purchase in the opaque channel. Suppose that the intermediary has the market (x_A, x_B) available to it (and enough capacity to fulfill this demand) and offers a price p_I^L. For any customer at $x \in (x_A, x_B)$, the ex ante surplus from purchasing an opaque ticket is $V - p_I^L - \gamma_A^{L,e}tx - \gamma_B^{L,e}t(1 - x) = V - p_I^L - t/2$. This is independent of position x, or, stated differently, all consumers have the same ex ante utility from purchasing an opaque ticket. The intermediary will then price at $p_I^L = V - t/2$, since at this price all consumers will purchase.

Now, consider the case when demand is high and consumers purchase in the opaque channel. Suppose that the intermediary has the market (x_A, x_B) available to it (but not enough capacity to meet all this demand, so that a consumer who wants to purchase an opaque ticket will only get it with probability β) and offers a price p_I^H. For any customer at $x \in (x_A, x_B)$, the ex ante surplus from an opaque ticket is

$$\beta\left(V - p_I^L - \gamma_A^{L,e}tx - \gamma_B^{L,e}t(1 - x)\right) = \beta\left(V - p_I^L - t/2\right).$$

Once again, the intermediary will then price at $p_I^H = V - t/2$, since at this price all consumers will want to purchase (while only a fraction β of them will actually get tickets).

Now, using these expressions, we solve for firm prices p_A and p_B in the first period. Finally, to confirm that $\gamma^{\cdot,e} = 1/2$ are equilibrium expectations, in each of the cases below we will confirm that the realized probabilities of availability, γ, are all equal to $1/2$.

- $1/2 \leq V/t \leq K/H$
  The firms will not stockout even when demand is high. As in the deterministic demand case, consumers will not let the firms leverage the opaque channel to increase first-period prices, so that

$$\pi_A = p_A x_A(\alpha H + (1 - \alpha)L)$$
$$+ \delta\gamma_A\left(\alpha p_I^H\left(\frac{K}{2} - x_A H + \frac{K}{2} - (1 - x_B)H\right) + (1 - \alpha)p_I^L(x_B - x_A)L\right),$$

$$\pi_B = p_B(1-x_B)(\alpha H + (1-\alpha)L)$$
$$+ \delta\gamma_B\left(\alpha p_I^H\left(\frac{K}{2} - x_A H + \frac{K}{2} - (1-x_B)H\right) + (1-\alpha)p_I^L(x_B - x_A)L\right)$$
$$\pi_I = (1-\delta)\left(\alpha p_I^H\left(\frac{K}{2} - x_A H + \frac{K}{2} - (1-x_B)H\right) + (1-\alpha)p_I^L(x_B - x_A)L\right).$$

The profit π_I is shared by firms A and B in proportion to the products sold by each. The no-stockout situation implies $x_A \le K/(2H)$ and $x_B \ge 1 - K/(2H)$. Firm A sets $p_A = V - x_A t$ and firm B sets $p_B = V - (1-x_B)t$. Optimizing the above two expressions w.r.t. x_A and x_B, we obtain $x_A = 1 - x_B = V/(2t)$ and $p_A = p_B = V/2$. After imposing $x_A \le K/(2H)$ we obtain $V/t \le K/H$, which we have already assumed. Moreover, $1/2 \le V/t \Rightarrow 1/2 \le K/H \Rightarrow K/H \ge 1/2$, which is required, but is a mild assumption.[6]
Using these values of x_A and x_B, we obtain

$$\gamma_A^{L,\,\text{realized}} = \frac{K/2 - x_A L}{K/2 - x_A L + K/2 - (1-x_B)L} = \frac{1}{2} \quad \text{and}$$

$$\gamma_A^{H,\,\text{realized}} = \frac{K/2 - x_A H}{K/2 - x_A H + K/2 - (1-x_B)H} = \frac{1}{2}.$$

This confirms that $\gamma_{\cdot}^{\cdot,e} = 1/2$ are indeed equilibrium expectations.

If demand is high, the capacity sold in the opaque channel is the leftover from the transparent channel which is $K - VH/(2t)$, and if demand is low, the amount sold in the opaque channel is $L - VL/(2t)$. The prices in the opaque channel are $p_I^H = p_I^L = V - t/2$ and the profits are $\pi_I^H = (V/t - 1/2)(K - VH/(2t))t$ and $\pi_I^L = (V/t - 1/2)(1 - V/(2t))Lt$. In equilibrium, half of the above profits will be transferred to each firm. Hence, the profits for firms A and B are

$$\pi_A = \pi_B = \frac{V^2}{4t}(\alpha H + (1-\alpha)L)$$
$$+ \frac{1}{2}\left(\frac{V}{t} - \frac{1}{2}\right)\left(\alpha\left(K - \frac{V}{2t}H\right) + (1-\alpha)\left(1 - \frac{V}{2t}\right)L\right)t.$$

In the cases that follow, we construct the equilibria and it can be shown using an ε-deviation argument that these are indeed equilibria. Further, we do not explicitly show that $\gamma_{\cdot}^{\cdot,\,\text{realized}} = \gamma_{\cdot}^{\cdot,e}$ in all these cases; the reader can, however, check that this always holds.

- $\dfrac{K}{H} < \dfrac{V}{t} \le \dfrac{K}{H} + \left(\dfrac{\alpha}{1-\alpha}\right)\dfrac{K}{2L}$

Here, we construct the equilibrium as follows: both firms charge $p_A = p_B = V - Kt/(2H)$ and cover exactly $x_A = 1 - x_B = K/(2H)$ in both high and low demand. In high demand there is no leftover for the opaque channel, while in

---

low demand the total leftover is $(x_B - x_A)L = (1 - K/H)L$. In high demand the opaque channel profit is zero (since nothing is leftover to be allocated to it). In low demand the opaque channel price is $p_I^L = V - t/2$ and the profit is $\pi_I = (V/t - 1/2)(1 - K/H)Lt$. The profit for firms A and B is therefore

$$\pi_A = \pi_B = \left(V - \frac{K}{2H}t\right)\left(\alpha\frac{K}{2} + (1-\alpha)\frac{K}{2H}L\right)$$
$$+ \frac{1}{2}(1-\alpha)\left(\frac{V}{t} - \frac{1}{2}\right)\left(1 - \frac{K}{H}\right)Lt.$$

- $\frac{K}{H} + \left(\frac{\alpha}{1-\alpha}\right)\frac{K}{2L} < \frac{V}{t} < 1 + \left(\frac{\alpha}{1-\alpha}\right)\frac{K}{2L}$

Here, we construct the equilibrium as follows: both firms charge

$$p_A = p_B = \frac{V}{2} + \left(\frac{\alpha}{1-\alpha}\right)\frac{K}{4L}t$$

and cover exactly $K/(2H)$ when demand is high and

$$\frac{V}{2t} - \left(\frac{\alpha}{1-\alpha}\right)\frac{K}{4L}$$

when demand is low. (For $V/t < 1 + (\alpha/(1-\alpha))K/(2L)$ this is $\leq 1/2$.) In the high-demand state there is no leftover capacity for the opaque channel, while in the low-demand state the total uncovered market is

$$1 - \frac{V}{t} + \left(\frac{\alpha}{1-\alpha}\right)\frac{K}{2L}.$$

Thus, in the high-demand state the profit from opaque channel is zero. In the low-demand state the opaque channel price is $p_I^L = V - t/2$ and the profit is

$$\pi_I = \left(\frac{V}{t} - \frac{1}{2}\right)\left(1 - \frac{V}{t} + \left(\frac{\alpha}{1-\alpha}\right)\frac{K}{2L}\right)Lt.$$

The profit for firms A and B is therefore

$$\pi_A = \pi_B = \left(\frac{V}{2} + \left(\frac{\alpha}{1-\alpha}\right)\frac{K}{4L}t\right)\left(\alpha\frac{K}{2} + (1-\alpha)\left(\frac{V}{2t} - \left(\frac{\alpha}{1-\alpha}\right)\frac{K}{4L}\right)\right)$$
$$+ \frac{1}{2}(1-\alpha)\left(\frac{V}{t} - \frac{1}{2}\right)\left(1 - \frac{V}{t} + \left(\frac{\alpha}{1-\alpha}\right)\frac{K}{2L}\right)Lt.$$

- $1 + \left(\frac{\alpha}{1-\alpha}\right)\frac{K}{2L} \leq \frac{V}{t} < \frac{3}{2} + \left(\frac{\alpha}{1-\alpha}\right)\frac{K}{L}$

We construct the equilibrium as follows: both firms charge $p_A = p_B = V - t/2$ and cover exactly $K/(2H)$ in the high-demand state and $1/2$ in the low-demand state. In both high- and low-demand cases, there is no leftover for the opaque channel and the opaque channel profit is zero. The profit for firms A and B is therefore

$$\pi_A = \pi_B = \left(\frac{V}{t} - \frac{1}{2}\right)\left(\alpha\frac{K}{2} + (1 - \alpha)\frac{L}{2}\right)t.$$

- $\dfrac{V}{t} \geq \dfrac{3}{2} + \left(\dfrac{\alpha}{1-\alpha}\right)\dfrac{K}{L}$

We begin by assuming that the firms cover $K/(2H)$ each in the high-demand state but are in the "competitive equilibrium" in the low-demand state. Thus, for prices p_A and p_B, $x_A = 1/2 + (p_B - p_A)/(2t)$ in the low-demand state. In either demand state, nothing is leftover for the opaque channel. Thus, the firms' profits are

$$\pi_A = p_A\left(\alpha\frac{K}{2} + (1 - \alpha)\left(\frac{1}{2} + \frac{p_B - p_A}{2t}\right)\right) \quad \text{and}$$

$$\pi_B = p_B\left(\alpha\frac{K}{2} + (1 - \alpha)\left(\frac{1}{2} + \frac{p_A - p_B}{2t}\right)\right).$$

Optimizing the above expressions simultaneously w.r.t. p_A and p_B, we obtain $p_A = p_B = (1 + (\alpha/(1 - \alpha))(K/L))t$, $x_A = x_B = 1/2$, and the optimal profits are

$$\pi_A = \pi_B = \left(1 + \left(\frac{\alpha}{1 - \alpha}\right)\frac{K}{L}\right)\left(\alpha\frac{K}{2} + (1 - \alpha)\frac{L}{2}\right)t.$$

For the equilibrium to exist, the consumer located at $1/2$ should have a non-negative utility. Mathematically,

$$V - p_A - \frac{t}{2} \geq 0 \Rightarrow \frac{V}{t} \geq \frac{3}{2} + \left(\frac{\alpha}{1 - \alpha}\right)\frac{K}{L},$$

which we have already assumed.

The above analysis characterizes the equilibria for the full range of $V/t \geq 1/2$.

References

Besanko D, Winston WL (1990) Optimal price skimming by a monopolist facing rational consumers. Management Science 36(5):555–567

Cho M, Fan M, Zhu Y-P (2008) An empirical study of revenue management practices in the airline industry. University of Washington, working paper

Coase RH (1972) Durability and monopoly. Journal of Law and Economics 15(1):143–149

DeGraba P (1995) Buying frenzies and seller-induced excess demand. Rand Journal of Economics 26(2):331–342

Deneckere RJ, McAfee RP (1996) Damaged goods. Journal of Economics & Management Strategy 5(2):149–174

Fay S (2008) Selling an opaque product through an intermediary: a case of disguising one's product. Journal of Retailing 84(1):59–75

Fay S, Xie J (2008) Probabilistic goods: a creative way of selling products and services. Marketing Science 27(4):674–690

Harrison J (2006) Traveling 'blind'. The Ottawa Citizen, September 26

Jerath K, Netessine S, Veeraraghavan SK (2008) Revenue management with strategic customers: last-minute selling and opaque selling. Carnegie Mellon University, working paper

Jiang Y (2007) Price discrimination with opaque products. Journal of Revenue and Pricing Management 6(2):118–134

Koenigsberg O, Muller E, Vilcassim NJ (2008) EasyJet pricing strategy: Should low-fare airlines offer last-minute deals? Quantitative Marketing and Economics 6(3):279–297

Moorthy KS (1984) Market segmentation, self selection, and product-line design. Marketing Science 3(4):288–307

Muth JF (1961) Rational expectations and the theory of price movements. Econometrica 29(3):315–335

Narasimhan C (1984) A price discrimination theory of coupons. Marketing Science 3(2):128–147

Phillips RL (2005) Pricing and revenue optimization. Stanford Business Books, Stanford, CA

Shapiro D, Shi X (2008) Market segmentation: The role of opaque travel agencies. University of North Carolina, working paper

SITA (2007) Airline IT Trends Survey 2007
    http://www.sita.aero/News_Centre/Industry_surveys_and_trends/default/default.htm

Smith BC, Darrow R, Elieson J, Gunther D, Rao BV, Zouaoui F (2007) Travelocity becomes a travel retailer. Interfaces 27(1):68–81

Stokey N (1979) Intertemporal price discrimination. Quarterly Journal of Economics 93(3):355–371

Sviokla J (2004) Value poaching. Conference Board Review, June

Talluri K, van Ryzin G (2004) The theory and practice of revenue management. Kluwer Academic Press, Boston, MA

Tedeschi B (2005) Online travel industry tries to adjust to maturity. New York Times, May 30

Terwiesch C, Savin S, Hann I (2005) Online haggling at a name-your-own-price retailer: theory and application. Management Science 51(3):339–351

Varian H (2000) Versioning information goods. In: Internet publishing and beyond: The economics of digital information and intellectual property. MIT Press, Cambridge, MA. 190–202

Xie J, Shugan SM (2001) Electronic products, smart cards and online prepayments: When and how to advance sell. Marketing Science 20(3):219–243

Chapter 11
Competing Through Mass Customization

Ali K. Parlaktürk

Abstract We consider a market with heterogeneous customer tastes served by a duopoly. In our base model the firms first decide whether to adopt MC, which enables a firm to provide each customer her ideal product configuration. A firm that chooses not to invest in MC serves a standard product. Following investment decisions, the firms competitively price their products. A customer evaluates a product alternative considering its price and misfit relative to her ideal point (and delay in our extended model). We solve for the resulting equilibrium and study its characteristics. We then study the competition between a firm that adopted MC and a firm that continues to sell standard products in more detail extending our base model to account for some key operational differences between these two firms: While the firm selling standard products usually carries product inventories, the firm selling custom products does not carry inventory, it makes-to-order and its customers incur waiting costs until they receive their orders. Our results are useful for characterizing conditions that favor custom and standard products under competition. We find that the value of mass customization critically depends on the firm's competitive position, determined by its cost efficiency and perceived quality vis-à-vis its competitor: It may not be desirable even at zero cost due to its negative effect on price competition. A firm with an overall cost and quality disadvantage never adopts mass customization. We show that allowing firms to set custom prices for each product configuration leads to a broader adoption of mass customization compared to when they are restricted to uniform prices. Furthermore, we find that a customizing firm's profit is *not* monotone in the market size and its ease of customization when competing against a firm selling standard products. We show that its competitive position crucially affects its ideal market size and its returns from improving the ease of customization.

Ali K. Parlaktürk
Kenan-Flagler Business School, University of North Carolina, Chapel Hill, NC 27599, USA,
e-mail: pturk@unc.edu

S. Netessine, C.S. Tang (eds.), *Consumer-Driven Demand and Operations Management* 301
Models, International Series in Operations Research & Management Science 131,
DOI 10.1007/978-0-387-98026-3_11, © Springer Science+Business Media, LLC 2009

11.1 Introduction

Following the shift of power to consumers, they are increasingly demanding products that closely match their individual preferences (Frazier 2001). We are far from one color only Ford Model T; the number of vehicle models increased from 140 to 260 between the early 1970s and late 1990s where each model was offered in numerous styles and colors (Cox and Alm 1998). Indeed, selection has increased significantly over time for a variety of products. For example, the number of distinct breakfast cereals increased from 160 to 340, the number of soft drink brands from 20 to 87, and the number of running shoe styles increased from 5 to 285 during the same time period. With the advances in manufacturing and information technologies, rather than keep increasing their number of product variants, many firms are adopting an alternative approach based on *mass customization* (MC) (Pine 1993; Feitzinger and Lee 1997; Zipkin 2001), whereby they attempt to give each customer exactly what she asked for by offering individually customized products. Lands' End (Piccoli et al. 2003), mi adidas (Seifert 2002), Dell (Dell and Fredman 2000), and NikeID are some well known working examples.[1]

Anecdotal examples show that MC enables a firm to increase its unit selling price about 50% (Mirapaul 2001; Keenan and Crockett 2002), and empirical studies show that customers may be willing to pay as much as 150% more for a product that fits better to their needs than the second best solution available (Piller 2004). It is suggested that MC can help a variety of domestic industries fight the outsourcing of production to low-cost overseas manufacturers (Keenan et al. 2004; Schuler and Buehlmann 2003; Karnes and Karnes 2000). The US furniture industry is one example: US manufacturers are more successful against imports in market sectors where they offer more customization (Lihra et al. 2005). Keenan et al. (2004) argue that MC can give competitive advantage to the domestic EU apparel industry against mass production alternatives in developing countries. Indeed, MC is not conducive to outsourcing as standard mass production since it requires promptness, higher skilled labor, specialized business processes, and machinery. Anderson (2004) argues that "outsourcing is at odds with the inventory-less aspect of build-to-order & MC, since outsourcing is usually a batch operation."

The literature recognizes that MC is no panacea on the other hand (Zipkin 2001; Agrawal et al. 2001; Ahlström and Westbrook 1999). Zipkin (2001) points out that many product markets are not attractive for MC. Pine (1993) identifies conditions under which MC is attractive vis-à-vis mass production. Indeed, there are many recent examples of firms that abandoned MC initiatives or had gone out of business selling customized products (e.g., Levi Strauss, Reflect.com, Mattel, CMax.com), and in many markets firms following MC are competing against firms that continue to offer standard products. Thus, it is important to identify the conditions that make MC an attractive strategy vis-à-vis selling standard products.

---

[1] Other examples can be found in Moser and Piller (2006), which are a collection of MC case studies.

It has been suggested that the most advanced forms of MC will combine product customization with price customization (cf. Piller and Stotko 2002) and perhaps other dimensions of the marketing mix (Wind 2001). Riemer and Totz (2003) discuss how MC can be used to combat uniform pricing through the individualization of both products and prices. Indeed, firms selling customized information goods often resort to price differentiation (Shapiro and Varian 1998). Whether more firms will adopt such practices depends on the value of customized prices for firms that offer customized products.

We consider a market with heterogeneous customer tastes served by a duopoly. In our base model, each firm decides whether to adopt MC, which enables the firm providing each customer her ideal product configuration. A firm may also choose not to invest in MC and sell a standard product. Following investment decisions, the firms competitively price their products. A customer takes into account price and misfit relative to her ideal point (and delay in our extended model) to evaluate a product offer. We consider two scenarios with regard to customizing firms' pricing policies: They may be restricted to a uniform price, or they may set a different price for each customized product configuration.

We extend our base model in Sections 11.5 and 11.6. Here, we assume that the production technology investments are already made and we study the competition between a *customizing* firm that adopted MC and a *traditional* firm that continues to sell standard products. We explicitly model some important differences between the operations of customizing and traditional firms: A traditional firm usually carries inventory and fulfills customer demand from stock. In contrast, a customizing firm does not carry finished goods inventory as it customizes to order. There is a trade-off, however, as customers need to wait for custom orders, whereas a traditional seller can make the product immediately available from inventory.[2]

Our analysis enables us to study the attractiveness of MC in a competitive context. We address questions like: When should (not) a firm adopt MC? What will be the structure of markets where competing firm can adopt MC? How do the answers to these questions depend on MC firm's ability to customize prices? What market conditions make the MC or the traditional approach more profitable? How do these depend on the firms' competitive positions?

We find that firms considering MC should carefully assess their competitive positions before jumping on the MC bandwagon. MC may not be desirable in a competitive market even at zero cost due to its adverse effect on price competition; this is in contrast to a monopoly who always benefits from zero cost MC. Specifically, MC is beneficial only for a firm with a sufficiently strong competitive position, determined by its perceived quality and cost efficiency vis-à-vis its competitor. We show that in equilibrium, a firm with an overall cost/quality disadvantage never adopts MC. In addition, comparing equilibrium outcomes when firms set uniform prices and price menus, we show that allowing price menus leads to a wider adoption of MC.

We characterize the conditions in terms of market size, ease of customization, cost efficiency, and quality, which make MC more attractive for competing against

---

[2] This delay is, for example, one of the main reasons for few US consumers (7% in 2000) to order custom cars (Agrawal et al. 2001).

standard products. For example, we find that the relationship between the profitability of MC and market size is not monotone: A larger market can make MC less profitable due to the traditional competitor's scale economies. This relationship again critically depends on the customizing firm's perceived quality and cost efficiency vis-à-vis its competitor. When a customizing firm has a large cost/quality disadvantage, it may be better off in a smaller market where a traditional opponent cannot compete effectively due to its high inventory costs. Furthermore, contrary to one's basic intuition, we show that shorter customization times can make the customizing firm worse off due to its competitor's response. This is because customization delays create a degree of separation between customized and standard products, which softens price competition. When the customizing firm has a weak cost/quality position, speeding customization up reduces this separation, and this in turn reduces its profit.

MC is a growing area of research. This chapter is based on the research presented in Mendelson and Parlaktürk (2008a,b).[3] Here, we briefly point to the other work in this area that also considers MC in competitive contexts.[4] Alptekinoğlu and Corbett (2008) study duopoly competition between a traditional firm and a customizing firm, finding that the traditional firm can attain positive profit even with a cost disadvantage. Alptekinoğlu and Corbett (2008) assume production technology choices as given whereas in this chapter we study when competing firms choose to adopt MC. Dewan et al. (2003) consider two symmetric firms offering a standard product and a range of customized products. They show that a firm can deter entry by over-customizing its product in a sequential entry game. Syam et al. (2005) also consider two symmetric firms that can customize two attributes and they study which attributes are customized in equilibrium, finding that both firms either choose not to customize any attribute or they both customize one (the same) attribute. The assumption of equal (zero) unit costs in Dewan et al. (2003) and Syam et al. (2005) is critical, as the firms always choose symmetric strategies (when they move simultaneously). In contrast, the margin differences between the firms are key drivers of our results and we identify equilibria where only one firm chooses to sell customized products. Similarly, Syam and Kumar (2006) consider two symmetric firms and two consumer segments with different "transportation" cost parameters, i.e., sensitivities to product misfit, and they study the firms' choice of customization level. They find that the firms choose the same customization level unless the gap between the two consumer segments is sufficiently large. In our model, all consumers have the same transportation cost parameter, but the firms make asymmetric choices (i.e., only one firm choosing to offer customized products). Clearly, when the drivers of MC are differences between the firms, these drivers cannot be identified when the firms are completely symmetric.

---

[3] Specifically, we consider a special case of Mendelson and Parlaktürk (2008a) in this chapter. An MC firm chooses its desired customization level in Mendelson and Parlaktürk (2008a) that determines its ability to reduce product misfit for each customer while we restrict the firm to one of the two extremes, none vs. perfect customization, in this chapter.

[4] A related paper that considers MC in a monopoly context is Jiang et al. (2006).

The above literature focuses on the firm's product variety and pricing decisions and – with the exception of Mendelson and Parlaktürk (2008b) – it does not consider the roles of inventory fulfillment and queuing delays, which are important operational characteristics of the problem. In this chapter, we also explicitly model these operational features, incorporating the stocking of standard products and the make-to-order nature of customized products (with its associated queuing delay), in addition to product variety and pricing. For a monopoly, Alptekinoglu and Corbett (2007) also incorporate these operational elements, and they study which customer segments are served with standard and custom products under more general demand functions. Xia and Rajagopalan (2006) study duopoly competition where each firm can choose to sell either standard or custom products and they also incorporate customization delay in their model. However, the customization delay in Xia and Rajagopalan (2006) is deterministic (there is no capacity constraint), so it does not depend on the congestion or utilization of the customizing firm. Furthermore, they do not model fulfillment of standard products, e.g., the standard products do not incur holding costs.

In the remainder of the chapter, we describe our base model in Section 11.2. We characterize the pricing equilibrium in Section 11.3. We discuss the competitive value of MC and characterize when firms adopt it in Section 11.4. Then we focus on the competition between a firm selling mass-customized products and a firm selling standard products and we extend our base model to account for some key operational differences between these two approaches in Section 11.5. We then discuss how some market and operating characteristics affect the profitability of MC under competition in Section 11.6. Our concluding remarks are in Section 11.7. The proofs of all results can be found in Mendelson and Parlaktürk (2008a,b).

11.2 Model

We consider a market with two firms and customers who have heterogenous preferences for product attributes. Similar to Chen et al. (1998), we model these preferences along the Hotelling Line (Hotelling 1929): Each customer's ideal product θ is represented by the customer's location on the unit interval $[0, 1]$. This can represent, for example, preferences for the size or color of a piece of apparel. Each firm has a single product ζ and the firms' products are located at the opposite ends of the unit interval, $\zeta_1 = 0, \zeta_2 = 1$, a standard assumption in Hotelling-based competition models (see e.g., Tirole (1988), Chapter 7).[5] Later on, we study what happens when a firm can offer multiple standard products in Section 11.5. The distance between a customer and the firm's product position results in customer sacrifice relative to her

---

[5] Indeed, locating its product maximally differentiated from the competitor is optimal for each firm in most cases (d'Aspremont et al. 1979) as it avoids unbridled price competition. However, this may not be true when the firms are sufficiently asymmetric. Dewan et al. (2003), Syam et al. (2005) and Syam and Kumar (2006) also assume duopoly firms with single standard products and maximal differentiation for studying MC.

ideal product. However, a firm can eliminate the customer sacrifice by customizing its product to the customer's liking. In the remainder of this section, we specify our demand model and describe the firms' decisions and operations.

Customer Choice:

Customers trade off price and disutility of sacrifice from their ideal product in their decision making. When a type-θ customer buys Firm i's standard product, her utility is equal to

$$U(\theta, \zeta_i, w_i, p_i) = w_i - p_i - r|\theta - \zeta_i|, \qquad (11.1)$$

where the reservation value w_i is the customer's willingness to pay for her ideal product, and each firm can have a different reservation value due to difference in the perceived product quality. The customer utility decreases by $r|\theta - \zeta_i|$, the disutility of misfit, where r shows the intensity of customer preferences and $|\theta - \zeta_i|$ is the distance from customer's ideal product. The customer can avoid this disutility by buying a product customized exactly for her ideal configuration, i.e., $\zeta = \theta$, if it is offered.[6]

Customers arrive to the market at rate, or demand intensity λ, and they differ only in their ideal product types θ which are uniformly distributed over $[0, 1]$. Each customer buys one unit of the product that gives her the highest utility. We assume that the reservation values w_i are sufficiently high so all customers derive nonnegative utility from buying a product.[7]

Firm's Decisions:

Each firm first decides whether to adopt MC. Adopting MC entails a fixed investment cost K. A firm that does not adopt MC is called a *traditional* firm (T). A traditional firm does not customize its product, it sells only a single product type and sets a uniform price. On the other hand, a firm that adopts MC is called a *customizing* firm (*CM* or *CU*). We consider two alternative scenarios with regard to customizing firm's pricing policy. In the uniform price scenario, a customizing firm (*CU*) is restricted to a uniform price whereas in the menu price scenario, a customizing firm (*CM*) can set a different price for each customized product configuration.

Each firm incurs a unit production cost c, which can be different across two firms due to differences in the efficiency of their processes. We assume that adopting MC entails only a fixed cost and it does not affect the firm's marginal cost. This is in line with the MC's premise of achieving mass-production efficiency (Tseng and Jiao

---

[6] Here, we assume that MC enables a firm to completely eliminate customers' sacrifice, however in practice this depends on the degree the firm chooses to customize its product, a higher degree of customization leading to a smaller customer sacrifice. This is explored in depth in Mendelson and Parlaktürk (2008a).

[7] This is standard in the literature (e.g., Syam et al. 2005; Dewan et al. 2003; Thisse and Vives 1988) and a sufficient condition in our context is to assume $w_1 + w_2 - (c_1 + c_2) > 3r$, where c_i is the unit cost of Firm i as described in the following.

2001; Pine 1993).[8] We define Firm i's *maximum margin* $m_i = w_i - c_i$ by the difference between its reservation value and its unit cost, and $m_i - m_j$ determines its competitive position vis-à-vis Firm j. We say that Firm i has a margin advantage (disadvantage) when $m_i > m_j$ ($m_i < m_j$). By definition, $m_i - m_j = (w_i - w_j) - (c_i - c_j)$, where the first term shows the quality differential and the second term shows the cost differential between the firms.

Following the firm's investment decisions (whether to adopt MC), the firms competitively price their products. We consider two alternative scenarios. Under uniform prices, the firms simultaneously set uniform prices for all of their product types, whereas under menu prices the firms first set the price of their standard products and then the customizing firms (if any) set the price premiums for their customized products. After the prices are set, customers make their purchasing decisions. So, a firm chooses either between T and CU or between T and CM. It is straightforward to show that CM always dominates CU if a firm is to choose between CU and CM.

We study the subgame perfect Nash equilibrium (SPNE) using backward induction. We consider two consecutive games: In the adoption game, firms decide whether to adopt MC; then in the pricing game, firms competitively set their prices. We begin by solving the pricing game for each outcome of the adoption game.

11.3 Pricing Game

After observing the firms' product prices, customers make their purchasing decisions. Specifically, a type-θ customer buys from Firm i if

$$U(\theta, p_i, \zeta_i) > \max(0, U(\theta, p_j, \zeta_j)).$$

We assume that customers break all ties in favor of the socially efficient outcome, choosing the firm with a larger profit margin. When every customer buys a product, the marginal customer θ^m is given by $U(\theta^m, p_1, \zeta_1) = U(\theta^m, p_2, \zeta_2)$, such that customers $\theta < \theta^m$ buy from Firm 1 and customers $\theta > \theta^m$ buy from Firm 2, leading to market shares θ^m and $1 - \theta^m$.

A firm sets its price policy to maximize its total profit. In particular, T- and CU-firms set their prices to maximize the product of their profit margin and market share. On the other hand, a CM-firm sets the maximum price for each configuration that leaves its customers indifferent to their next best alternative (either buying from the other firm or not buying at all), as long as this price is above its unit cost. When this price is below its unit cost, the price for that configuration is set equal to the unit cost.

---

[8] In some cases MC can lead to cost savings due to eliminating inventory risks and holding costs, while in some cases it can lead to additional costs due to the need for more sophisticated labor and machinery. Overall, if MC increases the firm's unit cost, this will only strengthen our key message while making the analysis cumbersome.

The following Lemma summarizes the firms' equilibrium prices and profits (i.e., their profits before subtracting investment costs) in the pricing games.

Lemma 1. *The firms' equilibrium prices and profits are as follows in each pricing game.*

Pricing Game	Region	Equilibrium prices and profits in the pricing game
(T,T)	$m_1 - m_2 \leq -3r$	$p_1 = c_1,\ p_2 = -m_1 + m_2 - r + c_2,$ $\Pi_1 = 0,\ \Pi_2 = \lambda(-m_1 + m_2 - r)$
	$-3r < m_1 - m_2 < 3r$	$p_1 = \dfrac{m_1 - m_2 + 3r}{3} + c_1,\ p_2 = \dfrac{m_2 - m_1 + 3r}{3} + c_2,$ $\Pi_1 = \dfrac{\lambda(m_1 - m_2 + 3r)^2}{18r},\ \Pi_2 = \dfrac{\lambda(m_2 - m_1 + 3r)^2}{18r}$
	$m_1 - m_2 \geq 3r$	$p_1 = m_1 - m_2 - r + c_1,\ p_2 = c_2,$ $\Pi_1 = \lambda(m_1 - m_2 - r),\ \Pi_2 = 0$
(CU,T)	$m_1 - m_2 \leq -2r$	$p_1 = c_1,\ p_2 = -m_1 + m_2 - r + c_2,$ $\Pi_1 = 0,\ \Pi_2 = \lambda(-m_1 + m_2 - r)$
	$-2r < m_1 - m_2 < r$	$p_1 = \dfrac{m_1 - m_2 + 2r}{3} + c_1,\ p_2 = \dfrac{m_2 - m_1 + r}{3} + c_2,$ $\Pi_1 = \dfrac{\lambda(m_1 - m_2 + 2r)^2}{9r},\ \Pi_2 = \dfrac{\lambda(m_2 - m_1 + r)^2}{9r}$
	$m_1 - m_2 \geq r$	$p_1 = m_1 - m_2 + c_1,\ p_2 = c_2,$ $\Pi_1 = \lambda(m_1 - m_2),\ \Pi_2 = 0$
(CM,T)	$m_1 - m_2 \leq -2r$	$p_1(\theta) = c_1,\ p_2 = -m_1 + m_2 - r + c_2,$ $\Pi_1 = 0,\ \Pi_2 = \lambda(-m_1 + m_2 - r)$
	$-2r < m_1 - m_2 < 0$	$p_1(\theta) = [m_1 - m_2 + r - \theta r]^+ + c_1,\ p_2 = \dfrac{m_2 - m_1}{2} + c_2,$ $\Pi_1 = \dfrac{\lambda(m_1 - m_2 + 2r)^2}{8r},\ \Pi_2 = \dfrac{\lambda(m_2 - m_1)^2}{4r}$
	$m_1 - m_2 \geq 0$	$p_1(\theta) = m_1 - m_2 + r - \theta r + c_1,\ p_2 = c_2,$ $\Pi_1 = \lambda(m_1 - m_2 + r/2),\ \Pi_2 = 0$
(CU,CU)	$m_1 - m_2 \leq 0$	$p_1 = c_1,\ p_2 = -m_1 + m_2 + c_2,$ $\Pi_1 = 0,\ \Pi_2 = \lambda(-m_1 + m_2)$
	$m_1 - m_2 > 0$	$p_1 = m_1 - m_2 + c_1,\ p_2 = c_2,$ $\Pi_1 = \lambda(m_1 - m_2),\ \Pi_2 = 0$
(CM,CM)	$m_1 - m_2 \leq 0$	$p_1(\theta) = c_1,\ p_2(\theta) = -m_1 + m_2 + c_2,$ $\Pi_1 = 0,\ \Pi_2 = \lambda(-m_1 + m_2)$
	$m_1 - m_2 > 0$	$p_1(\theta)1 = m_1 - m_2 + c_1,\ p_2(\theta) = c_2,$ $\Pi_1 = \lambda(m_1 - m_2),\ \Pi_2 = 0$

Notice that when a firm has a sufficiently large margin advantage it dominates the market, leaving zero market share for its competitor. Furthermore, when both firms adopt MC either in uniform or menu price scenario ((CU,CU) or (CM,CM)), horizontal differentiation between the firms disappears as each firm provides the same product type – her ideal product configuration – to each customer. This results in head-to-head Bertrand competition always leaving one of the firms with zero market share.

Lemma 1 shows that the competitor's price decreases, that is, the intensity of price competition increases as a firm moves from T, to CU and on to CM. Furthermore, the lemma shows that the region in which both firms have positive profits shrinks, that is, survival becomes harder as firms move from T, to CU and on to CM.

We next study the firms' investments in MC given the resulting payoffs in the pricing game.

11.4 The Adoption Game

In this section, we first discuss the competitive value of MC which helps forming the best responses in the adoption game. We then characterize and discuss the equilibrium of the adoption game.

Mass customization helps a firm create value for its customers, and it always helps a monopoly extract more surplus from its customers. However, when a firm adopts MC in duopoly competition, its competitor sets a more aggressive price in response, which limits the firm's gain from customizing its product.

We study the value of MC in two different settings, depending on the type of competitor, i.e., against a traditional or a customizing firm. Let $\Pi_i^{v,u}$ denote Firm i's payoff in the pricing game (profit before investment cost) when Firms i and j follow strategies v and u, respectively, where $v, u : T, CU, CM$.

The following propositions characterize when MC can yield positive returns showing the change in the firm's profit in the pricing game after it adopts MC.

Proposition 1. (i) $\Pi_1^{CU,T} \geq \Pi_1^{T,T}$ if and only if $m_1 - m_2 \geq (\sqrt{2}-1)r$.
(ii) $\Pi_1^{CM,T} \geq \Pi_1^{T,T}$ if and only if $m_1 - m_2 \geq 0$.

Proposition 1 shows that the adoption of MC does not necessarily yield higher profits; it can make the firm worse off because it intensifies price competition. In particular, Firm i cannot benefit from adopting MC even at zero cost unless the margin differential $m_i - m_j$ is sufficiently favorable which in turn depends on the quality and cost differential between the two firms as $m_i = w_i - c_i$. In other words, there is a quality/cost prerequisite (relative to the competitor) below which a firm never benefits from customizing its product. Furthermore, this threshold is lower when the firm is able to customize prices in addition to customizing the product.

The intuition behind this result is as follows. When a firm adopts MC, its traditional competitor drops its price to defend its turf. When the margin differential $m_i - m_j$ is sufficiently favorable for Firm i, it can make money while dropping its price in response to its traditional competitor. Therefore in this case, MC is profitable in spite of the competitor's price drop. On the other hand, when the margin differential $m_i - m_j$ is not sufficiently favorable for Firm i, its competitor's price response makes adopting MC a losing proposition.

The next proposition describes the value of adopting MC against a customizing competitor.

Proposition 2. *(i)* $\Pi_1^{CU,CU} \geq \Pi_1^{T,CU}$ *if and only if* $m_1 - m_2 \geq 0$. *(ii)* $\Pi_1^{CM,CM} \geq \Pi_1^{T,CM}$.

Proposition 2*(i)* shows that when the firms are restricted to a uniform price, a firm with a margin disadvantage (either due to low quality or high cost) does not benefit from adopting MC against a customizing competitor. On the other hand, when the firms set different prices for each product type, adopting MC always weakly increases a firm's payoff in the pricing game against a customizing competitor. However, a firm with a margin disadvantage does not get a positive market share in either case and it is better off staying as a traditional firm considering the cost of adopting MC technology.

It is interesting to consider the value of price customization in addition to product customization, which is given by $\Pi_1^{CM,T} - \Pi_1^{CU,T}$. For a monopoly, this is zero, as MC eliminates the differences in customers' willingness to pay by providing each customer her ideal product, the firm charges the same price, the reservation price which is the maximum price each customer is willing to pay. In contrast to the monopoly case, there is value to customizing prices in competition. This is because price flexibility enables the firm to set competitive prices for product configurations that are closer to the competitor's standard product while keeping higher prices for more remote products.

We are ready to characterize the equilibrium of the adoption game.

Proposition 3. *Let* $m_1 \geq m_2$. *The SPNE of the adoption game is as follows*

(i) For uniform prices:

    a. When $K < \lambda r/9$, equilibrium is (T,T) if $\lambda(m_1 - m_2 - r)^2/(18r) - \lambda r/9 < K$, (CU,T) otherwise.

    b. When $K \geq \lambda r/9$, equilibrium is (T,T) if $\lambda(m_1 - m_2)(12r - (m_1 - m_2))/(18r) - \lambda r/2 < K$, (CU,T) otherwise.

(ii) For menu prices: equilibrium is (T,T) *if* $\lambda(m_1 - m_2)(12r - (m_1 - m_2))/(18r) < K$, (CU,T) *otherwise.*

Proposition 3 shows that a firm with a margin disadvantage never unilaterally adopts MC in equilibrium even when the cost of technology is zero. The intuition for this result follows from Proposition 1: Contemplating that its competitor will drop its price to protect its turf, the firm needs to consider the value of MC in the face of such a price drop. When the firm has a sufficiently large margin advantage, it can make money while reducing its price in response to its traditional competitor. However, when the firm has a margin disadvantage, its competitor's price response always makes adopting MC unprofitable. As a special case, when the firms have symmetric margins, no firm adopts MC in equilibrium.

It is straightforward to show that the left-hand side in the condition in part *(ii)* of Proposition 3 is larger than those of part *(i)*. Thus, the proposition shows that allowing firms to set price menus for different configurations leads to a wider adoption of MC as the firms can better take advantage of their customized product lines.

In our model, both firms never adopt MC at the same time. This is because MC enables a firm provide each customer her ideal product configuration exactly and when both firms adopt MC, this eliminates the distance between them leading to Bertrand competition where one of the firms cannot get a positive market share. However, when MC does not eliminate customer sacrifice completely, both firms may adopt MC in equilibrium.[9] This is studied in Mendelson and Parlaktürk (2008a) where a customizing firm chooses its degree of customization which determines its ability to decrease a customer's sacrifice. With this extension, the firms with symmetric margins also adopt MC when the adoption cost is sufficiently small.

11.5 MC vs. Traditional Approach

So far we have discussed the firms' choice of production technology, that is the choice between MC vs. traditional approach of offering standard products, and we have characterized when firms adopt MC in duopoly. In this section, we assume that production technology decisions are already made and we study in more detail the duopoly competition between a customizing and a traditional firm. To this end, we extend our base model in various directions.

A traditional firm usually carries inventory and fulfills customer demand from stock. In contrast, a customizing firm does not carry finished good inventory as it customizes to order. However, customers need to wait for custom orders whereas a traditional firm can provide instant availability from inventory. We extend our base model to account for these key operational differences and we study their subsequent effects on the profitability of MC and traditional approach. Furthermore, we allow the traditional firm to offer more than one standard product configuration and determine the number of product variants it will carry considering its inventory holding and procurement costs. Here, we only consider the uniform price scenario, that is, each firm has to set a uniform price for all product configurations. The resulting insights also carry over to the menu price scenario as shown in Mendelson and Parlaktürk (2008b).

In the following, we first describe the model extensions then we state and discuss the resulting equilibrium. We extend the customer's utility function to account for disutility of delay. Thus, customers trade off price, disutility of product misfit, and delay in their decision making. Specifically, when a type-θ customer buys product ζ from Firm i, her utility is equal to

$$U(\theta, \zeta, w_i, p_i, W_i) = w_i - p_i - r|\theta - \zeta| - vW_i. \tag{11.2}$$

---

[9] A firm with a margin disadvantage still never unilaterally adopts MC.

Note that the only difference between (11.1) and (11.2) is the last term in (11.2), where W_i is the average delay for getting a product from Firm i and v is the customers' sensitivity to delay. Customers incur delay due to waiting either for a custom product or for a backordered standard product. We assume that customers do not observe the queue length of the customizing firm and inventory position of the traditional firm. Thus, they make their decisions based on the average delay to maximize their expected utility. We derive the average delays in the following.

We use index c to denote the customizing firm. The customizing firm does not carry inventory. It customizes to order fulfilling customer orders on a first-come-first-served basis. The customization times are exponentially distributed with rate μ which reflects the ease of customization and firm's customization capacity. We assume that customers arrive to the market according to a Poisson process, thus customers who buy custom products form a Poisson process and the customizing firm is characterized by an M/M/1 queue. Therefore, the average delay for a customized product is

$$W_c = 1/(\mu - \lambda_c). \tag{11.3}$$

We assume $\lambda < \mu$, so that $W_c(\lambda_c) < \infty$ for all $\lambda_c < \lambda$. The customization capacity μ is exogenous, i.e., it cannot be changed within the timescale of our model. Mendelson and Parlaktürk (2008b) study what happens when the customizing firm can choose its capacity endogenously.

We use index t to denote the traditional firm. In addition to its unit price p_t, now the traditional firm decides how many products to offer n and their configurations $\zeta_j \in \Theta$ for $j : 1, ..., n$. Once the firm determines its product offers, it outsources the production to a supplier with replenishment lead time l, and it replenishes its stocks at a fixed cost S per order at unit cost c_t. For each unit in stock, the firm also incurs inventory holding cost h per unit time. The traditional firm is considered to have unlimited supply. The firm follows a (Q,R) continuous review policy. The firm orders Q_j units whenever its inventory position of product variant j falls below $d_j + k\sigma_j$, where d_j and σ_j are the mean and the standard deviation of the lead time demand for that product variant and k is the *safety stock factor* (cf. Axsäter 1995). Our results are independent of the specific value of k. Mendelson and Parlaktürk (2008b) allow k to be chosen endogenously. The firm backorders any unmet demand which is fulfilled once the stocks for that variant become available. The delay due to backorders inflicts a cost on the firm's customers (see (11.2)) and affects their product choice.

It is straightforward to show that the demand for product variant j follows a Poisson process with mean λ_j, thus $d_j = \lambda_j l$ and $\sigma_j = \sqrt{\lambda_j l}$. We adopt the standard Normal approximation for Poisson demand (cf. Hadley and Whitin, 1963, Section 4.9) The firm's average number of backorders at any time for product variant j is

$$B(Q_j) = \sigma_j^2 \left[(1 + k^2)(1 - \Phi(k)) - k\phi(k) \right] / (2Q_j), \tag{11.4}$$

and its annual total inventory holding and fixed order cost are given by

$$C(\lambda_j, Q_j) = S\lambda_j / Q_j + h(Q_j/2 + \sigma_j k + B(Q_j)), \tag{11.5}$$

where $\Phi(\cdot)$ is the cumulative distribution and $\phi(\cdot)$ is the probability density function of a unit normal random variable. Thus, following Little's Law and (11.4), the average delay for standard product variant j due to backorders is

$$W_j = \left[(1+k^2)(1-\Phi(k)) - k\phi(k)\right]\sigma_j^2/(2Q_j\lambda_j), \qquad (11.6)$$

and following (11.5), the optimal order quantity for a standard product with demand rate λ_j is

$$Q^*(\lambda_j) = \sqrt{\lambda_j\left(\frac{2S}{h} + [(1+k^2)(1-\Phi(k)) - k\phi(k)]l\right)}. \qquad (11.7)$$

We make a few parametric assumptions in order to focus on more interesting scenarios. We continue to assume that the customers' reservation values w_i are high enough so the market is covered in equilibrium. In addition, we assume that the unit margin differential between standard and customized products $|m_t - m_c|$ is sufficiently small so both standard and customized products are offered in equilibrium, that is, customized products always have a positive market share and there is at least one standard product variant. This is determined by unit costs and reservation values since $m_i = w_i - c_i$. Specifically, we consider the case of $\underline{m} < m_t - m_c < \overline{m}$, where

$$\underline{m} = \left(2\gamma - \frac{1}{2}\right)r - \frac{v(\mu - \gamma\lambda)}{(\mu - \lambda(1-\gamma))^2} \text{ and } \overline{m} = \frac{3\gamma r}{2} - \frac{v(\mu-\lambda)}{\mu^2}, \qquad (11.8)$$

where

$$\gamma = \sqrt[3]{\frac{h}{\lambda r^2}\left(\frac{2S + l(v/2+h)[(1+k^2)(1-\Phi(k)) - k\phi(k)]}{\sqrt{2S + lh[(1+k^2)(1-\Phi(k)) - k\phi(k)]}} + k\sqrt{lh}\right)^2}, \qquad (11.9)$$

which happens to be optimal market share for a standard product variant as shown in Proposition 4 in the following.

The firms simultaneously determine their competitive product offerings to maximize their expected profits. They set prices p_t and p_c and the traditional firm also determines the number of its product variants n and their configurations $\zeta_j \in [0,1]$ for $j: 1,...,n$.[10] As they arrive, customers choose from the product offerings to maximize their utility. The following proposition characterizes the equilibrium.

Proposition 4. *When traditional Firm t competes with customizing Firm c, the firms set prices*

$$p_c = c_c + \frac{v\lambda_c}{(\mu - \lambda_c)^2} + \frac{\lambda_c\gamma r}{2(\lambda - \lambda_c)} \quad \text{and}$$

$$p_t = p_c - (w_c - w_t) + \frac{v}{\mu - \lambda_c} - \frac{\gamma r}{2} - \frac{lv[(1+k^2)(1-\Phi(k)) - k\phi(k)]}{2Q^*(\gamma\lambda)},$$

---

[10] In addition, the traditional firm also determines the optimal replenishment batch size Q_j for each product variant j, where its optimal batch size is specified in (11.7).

where $Q^*(\cdot)$ is given by (11.7) and λ_c is given by the solution of

$$\frac{v(\mu + \lambda_c - \lambda)}{(\mu - \lambda_c)^2} + \frac{\lambda_c \gamma r}{2(\lambda - \lambda_c)} = \frac{3\gamma r}{2} - (m_t - m_c). \tag{11.10}$$

The traditional firm offers

$$n = (1 - \lambda_c/\lambda)/\gamma \tag{11.11}$$

product variants, and chooses their positions $(\zeta_1, \zeta_2, ..., \zeta_n)$ so each has an equal market share. These result in profit rates

$$\Pi_t = \frac{v(\lambda - \lambda_c)^2}{(\mu - \lambda_c)^2} \ and \ \Pi_c = \frac{v\lambda_c^2}{(\mu - \lambda_c)^2} + \frac{\lambda_c^2 \gamma r}{2(\lambda - \lambda_c)}. \tag{11.12}$$

An explicit solution for λ_c in (11.10) is provided in Mendelson and Parlaktürk (2008b).

In the following section we discuss the effect of some operational and market parameters on the profitability of MC and traditional approach studying their impacts on the equilibrium profits stated in Proposition 4.

11.6 Comparative Statics: Conditions Favoring MC

Table 11.1 shows comparative statics for the effects of various market and operating characteristics in monopoly and duopoly. These help us understand how competitive considerations affect the attractiveness of MC. The table shows that in some cases competition can entirely reverse the monopoly results. For example, the changes in customization rate and market size can affect the customizing firm in diametrically opposite directions in monopoly and under competition. Similarly, improving the unit holding cost is always beneficial for a monopoly, whereas it may be harmful for a traditional firm under competition. Likewise, the changes in customers' preference intensity r and replenishment lead time of standard products l can have opposite effects in monopoly and duopoly. These are derived and discussed in Mendelson and Parlaktürk (2008b). Overall, it was shown that the margin differential $m_c - m_t$

Table 11.1 Comparative statics in monopoly and duopoly of traditional vs. customizing firms.

	Traditional monopoly	Traditional firm in duopoly	MC monopoly	MC firm in duopoly
$d\Pi/d\lambda$	+	+	+ or 0	+ or −
$d\Pi/dr$	−	+ or −	0	+
$d\Pi/d\mu$	N/A	−	+	+ or −
$d\Pi/dh$	−	+ or −	N/A	+
$d\Pi/dl$	−	+ or −	N/A	+

plays a critical role in determining the outcome of these changes.

In this section, we focus on the effects of market size λ and customization rate μ.

11.6.1 Market Size λ

An increase in market size has two effects. It increases the size of the "pie," so each firms worries less about its market share and more about its profit margin, potentially softening the competition. But it also helps the traditional competitor decrease its unit fulfillment cost as a result of scale economies that characterize its operations. Both effects favor the traditional firm, therefore its profit always increases in market size. On the other hand, they affect the customizing firm in opposite directions, and the following proposition shows that either effect can dominate and an increase in market size may increase or decrease the customizing firm's profit.

Proposition 5. (i) $d\Pi_t/d\lambda > 0$.
(ii.a) If $\gamma r \le 2v\lambda/\mu^2$ then $d\Pi_c/d\lambda > 0$.
(ii.b) If $\gamma r > 2v\lambda/\mu^2$, there exists $m^* \in (\underline{m},\overline{m})$ such that $d\Pi_c/d\lambda < 0$ for $m_t - m_c > m^*$.

One can show that the traditional firm's unit fulfillment cost (holding + ordering) is equal to γr and the Proposition shows that when this is small, there is not much to be gained from economies of scale, hence the larger pie effect dominates. However, when γr is large, the customizing firm's profit decreases in market size if its margin disadvantage $m_t - m_c$ is above a threshold (e.g., due to high cost or low quality). Figure 11.1(a) shows the regions in which the profit of the customizing firm increases or decreases due to a larger market size, and Figure 11.1(b) shows the firm's profit rate for various margin differentials. The figure shows that the customizing firm has an ideal market size when its margin disadvantage is large either due to high cost or

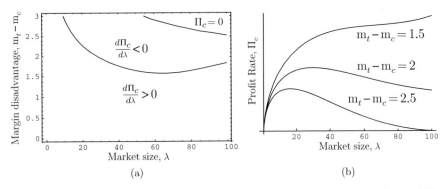

Fig. 11.1 Effect of market size ($S = 3$, $h = 0.15$, $k = 0.75$, $l = 6$, $v = 20$, $r = 80$, $\mu = 100$). (a) The regions in which the customizing firm's profit increases or decreases in market size. (b) The customizing firm's profit rate as a function of market size at various margin differentials.

low quality (recall that $m_t - m_c = w_t - w_c - (c_t - c_c)$). Furthermore, Figure 11.1(a) shows that this ideal market size decreases in the firm's margin disadvantage. This is because the traditional opponent cannot compete effectively in a small market due to its high unit holding and ordering cost. On the other hand, when the customizing firm's margin disadvantage is small, it can compete with the traditional firm head to head and it always prefers a larger market. Finally, when the customizing firm's margin disadvantage is in the middle in Figure 11.1(a), its profit decreases in market size unless the market is either sufficiently small or sufficiently large. This is because the traditional opponent cannot effectively compete in a small market, and the competition is mild in a large market.

11.6.2 Customization Rate μ

We now discuss the effect of improving the expected time needed to customize each unit, $1/\mu$, which reflects the capacity of the customizing firm as well as the difficulty or complexity of customization. Intuition suggests that customization should be more attractive when it takes less time. While this always holds for a monopoly, increasing μ may actually adversely affect the customizing firm in duopoly. The following proposition shows that the outcome critically depends on the firm's competitive position which is determined by the margin differential.

Proposition 6. *(i)* $d\Pi_t/d\mu < 0$.
(ii.a) If $\mu \geq 2\lambda$ then $d\Pi_c/d\mu > 0$.
(ii.b) If $\lambda < \mu < 2\lambda$ then there exist $m^* \in (\underline{m}, \overline{m})$ such that $d\Pi_c/d\mu < 0$ for $m_t - m_c > m^*$.

As might be expected, a shorter customization time always hurts the traditional firm. However, this can also be detrimental to the customizing firm itself. Specifically, when customization is not very fast and the customizing firm's margin advantage is below a threshold, improving its customization time hurts the customizing firm. Intuitively, longer customization delays create a degree of separation between customized and standard products, which softens the competition. When the customizing firm has a weak competitive position, it is not in its best interest to undermine this differentiation by speeding customization up through capacity expansion or design improvements even when these are free. Overall, the firm is more likely to benefit from a capacity expansion when it has a stronger competitive position.

11.7 Concluding Remarks

With this chapter we aim to contribute to the growing literature on the value and adoption of MC (Ahlström and Westbrook 1999; Agrawal et al. 2001; Zipkin 2001; Piller et al. 2004), studying how it relates to the firm's competitive position. We consider a market with heterogeneous customer tastes modeled by a location-based customer choice model. The market is served by two firms that differ in their cost efficiency and perceived quality, which determine their competitive positions. In our base model, the firms compete in a two-stage game: Firms first make their production technology decisions (i.e., whether to adopt MC) and then compete in prices. We consider two alternatives with regard to the customizing firms' price policies: When they can set a price menu for each configuration and when they have to set a uniform price. We solve for the resulting equilibrium and characterize when firms invest in MC under competition.

We find that the value of MC critically depends on the firm's competitive position. Ignoring competitive forces can lead to critically incorrect decisions for firms considering MC. While adopting MC always helps a monopolist extract more surplus from its customers, it may lead to a negative return (even before paying back the investment cost) in duopoly when the firm does not have a sufficiently strong competitive position. This is due to the adverse effect of MC on price competition. We show that a firm with an overall quality/cost disadvantage never adopts MC in equilibrium. Our results suggest that MC would be more suitable only for firms with sufficiently large quality or efficiency advantage. Furthermore, we find that ability to customize prices in conjunction with product customization would lead to a broader adoption of MC in the marketplace.

We then extend our base model to capture some key differences in the operations of a firm that follow MC: A customizing firm does not carry finished good inventories and it customizes to order resulting in customer waits. In contrast, a traditional firm usually fulfills customer demand using its inventories and it can provide instant availability from inventory. When the traditional firm backorders demand, this also results in customer waits. In our extended model, we assume that production technology decisions are already made and we study the competition between a customizing firm and a traditional firm.

Our results are useful for identifying how some market and operating characteristics affect profitability of MC when competing against a traditional firm. We find that a larger customization capacity does not always translate into higher profits under competition while it is always beneficial for a monopoly. Specifically, a larger capacity decreases the customizing firm's profit when the firm has a large margin disadvantage (either due to high cost or low quality). Intuitively, customization delays create a degree of separation between customized and standard products, which softens the price competition. When the firm has a weak competitive position, it is better off maintaining this separation. In addition, we show that a larger market does not necessarily increase the customizing firm's profit: When the customizing firm has a sufficiently large margin disadvantage, a larger market can hurt its profit. We find that in this case the customizing firm will be better off in a smaller market where the traditional competitor cannot compete effectively due to its scale economies. Overall, we find that the effects of both market size and customization rate on the profitability of the customizing firm are non-monotonic and their desirable levels depend on the firm's competitive position.

Our results may be extended in a number of ways. As is common in the literature that study MC (e.g., Mendelson and Parlaktürk 2008a; Alptekinoğlu and Corbett 2008; Syam and Kumar 2006; Jiang et al. 2006; Dewan et al. 2003), our product space is restricted to a single attribute. So adopting MC enables a firm offer product types same as or similar to that of its competitor which in turn intensifies the price competition. In contrast to our model, in a model with multiple product attributes a firm may benefit from adopting MC even with a margin disadvantage by customizing those attributes that will help distance itself from its competitor.

In practice, the firms not only decide whether to customize their products, but they also decide the degree of customization they will provide. For example, NikeID provides only style customization for its sneakers letting customers choose colors and imprint their names on the shoe, however it does not offer customized fit, whereas mi adidas offers customized fit in addition to customized colors and imprinted names. In Mendelson and Parlaktürk (2008b), the firms competitively choose their customization levels where a higher customization level requires a larger investment.

Allowing customers customize the product to their liking may have additional benefits beyond what is captured in our model, which would be fruitful to incorporate in further studies of MC. For example, MC may help a firm gain a better understanding of customer preferences and trends in the marketplace. The firm can then also improve configuration of its standard product offerings. For P&G, Reflect.com was reported to be one of its most efficient market research tools. Shoppers could create custom cosmetic products through Reflect.com. Data gathered provided valuable insights on customer needs and it also helped P&G improve its standard product line. Furthermore, offering a custom product allows a firm establish stronger ties with its customers. The customer invests in the customization process to communicate her preferences and that leads to higher switching cost. For example, in the case of Lands'End, the customer needs to provide numerous measurements for custom fit in addition to choosing her favorite style options. Lands'End stores this information making the repeat purchase more convenient for the customer compared to the hassle of describing her preferences again to another firm.

References

Agrawal M, Kumaresh TV, Mercer GA (2001) The false promise of mass customization. McKinsey Quarterly 3:62–71

Ahlström P, Westbrook R (1999) Implications of mass customization for operations management. International Journal of Operations Management 19(3):262–274

Alptekinoglu A, Corbett CJ (2007) Leadtime—variety tradeoff in product differentiation. Working Paper, University of Florida

Alptekinoğlu A, Corbett CJ (2008) Mass customization versus mass production: Variety and price competition. M&SOM 10:204–217

Anderson DM (2004) Build-to-order & mass customization. CIM Press, Los Angels, CA

Axsäter S, (1995) Inventory control. Kluwer Academic Publishers, Boston, MA

Chen F, Eliashberg J, Zipkin P (1998) Customer preferences, supply-chain costs, and product-line design, in TH Ho, CS Tang, eds., Product Variety Management. Kluwer Academic Publishers, Boston, 123–144

Cox MW, Alm R (1998) The right stuff: America's move to mass customization. Technical report, Federal Reserve Bank of Texas

d'Aspremont C, Gabszewicz J, Thisse JF (1979) On Hotelling's stability in competition. Econometrica 17:1145–1151

Dell M, Fredman C (2000) Direct from Dell: Strategies that revolutionized an industry. Harper-Collins Publishers, New York

Dewan R, Jing B, Seidmann A (2003) Product customization and price competition on the Internet. Management Sci 49(8):1055–1070

Feitzinger E, Lee HL (1997) Mass customization at Hewlett-Packard: The power of postponement. Harvard Business Review 75(1):116–121

Frazier C (2001) Swap meet: Consumers are willing to exchange personal information for personalized products. American Demographics 23(7):51–55

Hadley G, Whitin T (1963) Analysis of inventory systems. Prentice-Hall, Englewood Cliffs, NJ

Hotelling H (1929) Stability in competition. Economic Journal 39(1):41–57

Jiang K, Lee HL, Seifert RW (2006) Satisfying customer preferences via mass customization and mass production. IIE Transactions 38:25–38

Karnes CL, Karnes LP (2000) Ross controls: A case study in mass customization. Production and Inventory Management Journal 41(3):1–4

Keenan F, Greene J, Crockett RO (2002) A mass market of one. BusinessWeek, December 2

Keenan M, Saritas O, Kroener I (2004) A dying industry—or not? The future of the european textiles and clothing industry. Foresight 6(5):313–322

Lihra T, Buehlmann U, Beauregard R (2005) Mass customization of wood furniture: Literature review and application potential. Working Paper, CENTOR, Université Laval, Canada

Mendelson H, Parlaktürk AK (2008a) Competitive customization. M&SOM 10(3):377–390

Mendelson H, Parlaktürk AK (2008b) Product-line competition: Customization vs. proliferation. Management Science 54(12): 2039–2053

Mirapaul M (2001) Made especially for you, in industrial quantities. The New York Times, March 11

Moser K, Piller FT (2006) Integration challenges of mass customisation businesses: the case of steppenwolf. Internation Journal of Mass Customisation 1(4):507–522

Piccoli G, Bass B, Ives B (2003) Custom-made apparel at lands' end. MIS Quarterly Executive 2(2):74–84

Piller F (2004) Mass customization: Reflections on the state of the concept. The International Journal of Flexible Manufacturing Systems 16:313–334

Piller FT, Stotko CM (2002) Mass customization: four approaches to deliver customized products and services with mass production efficiency, in TS Durrani, ed., Proceedings of the IEEE International Engineering Management Conference (IEMC-2002). Cambridge University, UK, 773–778

Piller FT, Moeslein K, Stotko CM (2004) Does mass customization pay? An economic approach to evaluate customer integration. Production Planning and Control 15(4):435–444

Pine BJ (1993) Mass customization: The new frontier in business competition. Harvard Business School Press, Boston, MA

Riemer K, Totz C (2003) The many faces of personalization: An integrative economic overview of mass customization and personalization, in MM Tseng, FT Piller, eds., The customer centric enterprise: advances in mass customization and personalization. Springer Verlag, New York/Berlin, 35–50

Schuler A, Buehlmann U (2003) Identifying future competitive business strategies for the U.S. residential wood furniture industry: Benchmarking and paradigm shifts, Technical report, United States Department of Agriculture, Forest Service, Northeastern Research Station. Report NE-304

Seifert RW (2002) The "Mi Adidas" mass customization initiative. International Institute for Management Development Case Study POM 249

Shapiro C, Varian HR (1998) Information rules. Harvard Business School Press, Cambridge, MA

Syam B, Ruan R, Hess JD (2005) Customized products: A competitive analysis. Marketing Science 24(4):569–584

Syam NB, Kumar N (2006) On customized goods, standard goods and competition. Marketing Science 25(5):525–537

Thisse JF, Vives X (1988) On the strategic choice of spatial price policy. American Economic Review 78(1):122–137

Tirole J (1988) Theory of industrial organization. MIT Press, Cambridge, MA

Tseng M, Jiao J (2001) Mass customization, in G Salvendy, ed., Handbook of industrial engineering, 3rd edition. Wiley, New York, 684–709

Wind J (2001) The challenge of "customerization" in financial services. Communications of the ACM 44(6):39–44

Xia N, Rajagopalan S (2006) Standard versus custom products: Competitive analysis. Working Paper, University of Southern California

Zipkin P (2001) The limits of mass customization. MIT Sloan Man. Review 42(3):81–88

Part IV
Operational Strategies for Managing Rational/Strategic Consumer Behavior

Chapter 12
Counteracting Strategic Consumer Behavior in Dynamic Pricing Systems

Yossi Aviv, Yuri Levin, and Mikhail Nediak

Abstract Dynamic pricing and revenue management practices are gaining increasing popularity in the retail industry, and have engendered a large body of academic research in recent decades. When applying dynamic pricing systems, retailers must account for the fact that, often, strategic customers may time their purchases in anticipation of future discounts. Such strategic consumer behavior might lead to severe consequences on the retailers' revenues and profitability. Researchers have explored several approaches for mitigating the adverse impact of this phenomenon, such as rationing capacity, making price and capacity commitments, using internal price-matching policies, and limiting inventory information. In this chapter, we present and discuss some relevant theoretical contributions in the management science literature that help us understand the potential value of the above mitigating strategies.

12.1 Introduction

In the 30 years since the successes of revenue management systems in airlines were first reported, applications have spread steadily into other business areas. Revenue management is now common in such service businesses as passenger railways, cruise lines, hotel and motel accommodation, and car rentals. Other applications have been proposed in such diverse areas as broadcast advertising, sports and entertainment event management, medical services, real estate, freight transportation,

Yossi Aviv
Olin Business School, Washington University, St. Louis, MO, USA
e-mail: aviv@wustl.edu

Yuri Levin
School of Business, Queen's University, Kingston, ON, Canada
e-mail: ylevin@business.queensu.ca

Mikhail Nediak
School of Business, Queen's University, Kingston, ON, Canada
e-mail: mnediak@business.queensu.ca

S. Netessine, C.S. Tang (eds.), *Consumer-Driven Demand and Operations Management Models*, International Series in Operations Research & Management Science 131, DOI 10.1007/978-0-387-98026-3_12, © Springer Science+Business Media, LLC 2009

and manufacturing. Dynamic pricing and revenue management practices are also gaining increasing popularity in the retail industry, and have engendered a growing body of academic research in recent years. When applying dynamic pricing schemes, sellers need to account for key characteristics of the sales environment, including the scarcity of goods, demand uncertainty, and consumer behavior. In particular, sellers must account for the fact that, often, strategic customers may time their purchases in anticipation of future discounts. When supply is limited, strategic customers need to consider not only future prices, but also the likelihood of stockouts. And since the level of remaining inventory depends on the individual purchase decisions, each customer has to take into account the behavioral pattern of other customers. In recent years, a significant body of research on the topic of *strategic consumer behavior* has emerged in the management science literature.

Previous chapters in this book explain the notion of strategic waiting, and clearly articulate that it is present in many dynamic pricing environments, and that it has severe consequences on revenues and profitability. The purpose of this chapter, then, is to provide a framework for addressing the adverse impact of this phenomenon; namely, How could designers of dynamic pricing systems counteract strategic consumer behavior? To achieve this goal, we chose to focus on scientific models and emerging theoretical contributions in the management science literature. In fact, rather than providing a complete list of all relevant research, we chose to focus on a few papers with greater details. This allows us to present to the reader a meaningful description of modeling structures, different assumptions on system parameters, and ways in which equilibria settle in the dynamic pricing settings. Our research community has explored several approaches for dealing with strategic consumer behavior: (i) making credible price commitments (also known as "announced pricing schemes"); (ii) rationing capacity; (iii) making credible capacity commitments; (iv) using internal price-matching policies; and (v) limiting inventory information. All of these strategies can potentially be used to reduce the incentives of high-valuation customers to wait, and consequently mitigate the adverse impact of strategic waiting. Below, we provide a section-by-section description of some recent research papers that explore each of these strategies, and summarize and explain their findings.

12.2 The Effectiveness of Price Segmentation in Face of Strategic Customers

Research on price commitment goes back to the famous paper of Coase (1972), which considers a monopolist that sells a durable good to a large set of consumers with different valuations. Coase begins his paper with a qualitative discussion of how, ideally, the seller would want to price the product in a way that results in *perfect segmentation*. Namely, charge (initially) a high price from customers with high valuation, and then sequentially reduce the prices to capture customers with smaller valuations. Such strategy is called a *price-skimming strategy*, and if it works as planned, it results in extracting most or all of the consumer surplus. However, Coase argues that if high-valuation customers anticipate that prices will decline (in our terms – if customers behave strategically), they would wait for a price reduction rather than buy at premium costs. This, in equilibrium, will effectively lead the seller to offer the product at marginal cost.

Coase suggests a number of ways for the seller to avoid this result. For example, the seller can make a special contractual arrangement with the purchasers not to sell more than a given quantity of the product. In fact, this idea is close in spirit to the subject of *capacity rationing* we discuss in the next section. Alternatively, the seller could offer customers to buy back the product if it was offered in the future at a lower price. This idea is very similiar to the subject of *internal price guarantees* that we explore in a later section. The seller could also lease the product for relatively short periods of time and, e.g., announce that he would not change the rental price during the lease period.

Besanko and Winston (1990) introduce a game-theoretic model of a monopolistic seller facing a market of strategic consumers with heterogeneous valuations. The distribution of these valuations is uniform over the interval $[0, v^+]$. Customers know their individual valuations, but the monopolist is only privy to the statistical distribution characteristics. The population size is known and equal to N; in fact, all customers are present in the "store" from the beginning of the game. The monopolist has T periods of time to set the price, with p_t denoting the price in period t. It is assumed that the seller cannot make any price commitment (see extended discussion of this aspect later in this section), and thus the authors look for a subgame perfect equilibrium, in which the seller makes the optimal pricing decision in each given period. The seller's production capacity is unlimited, so any desired qauntity can be produced at any period, at a cost c per unit (where $c < v^+$). The monopolist and the seller are assumed to have the same discount factor δ.

The first observation made in the paper has to do with consumer behavior and the dynamics of information in the game. It is argued that if in period $t - 1$ it was optimal for a customer with valuation v to buy the product, then it means that all customers with valuations of v and above have also purchased the product by that time. As a consequence, it suffices to consider a *threshold value* at the end of each period: For instance, v_{t-1} means that all customers with valuations larger or equal to v_{t-1} have purchased the product, whereas all other customers (with valuations below v_{t-1}) are still in the market. Therefore, let $p_t^*(v_{t-1})$ be the seller's equilibrium pricing strategy at time t, when faced with the state v_{t-1}. Taking the customers' perspective now, let $v_t^*(p_t, v_{t-1})$ be the threshold value that sets their buying policy in period t. Besanko and Winston derive the following dynamic program that is based initially on a "guess" that prices and thresholds in subsequent periods are set in a way that makes a customer with valuation v_t indifferent about immediately purchasing the product (and gaining a surplus of $v_t - p_t$) and waiting for the next period, and gaining a *discounted* surplus (of $\delta \cdot (v_t - p_{t+1}^*(v_t))$). With this structural restriction in mind, they show that the seller's equilibrium discounted profit over periods t through T is given by the recursive scheme:

$$H_t^*(v_{t-1}) = \max_{p_t, v_t} \left\{ (p_t - c) \cdot \frac{v_t - v_t}{v^+} \cdot N + \delta H_{t+1}^*(v_t) \right\}$$

$$\text{s.t.} \quad v_t \leq v_{t-1},$$

$$v_t - p_t = \delta \cdot \left(v_t - p_{t+1}^* (v_t) \right)$$

with $v_0 = v^+$. Indeed, they prove that this dynamic program formulation can serve as a basis for calculating a subgame perfect Nash equilibrium for the game.

Proposition 1 of Besanko and Winston (1990). *A subgame perfect Nash equilibrium exists and can be described as follows.*

$$H_t^* (v_{t-1}) = A_t \cdot (\max \{v_{t-1} - c, 0\})^2 \cdot \frac{N}{v^+}, \qquad t = 1, \ldots, T$$

$$p_t^* (v_{t-1}) = \min \{2A_t v_{t-1} + (1 - 2A_t) c, v_{t-1}\}, \qquad t = 1, \ldots, T$$

$$v_t^* (v_{t-1}) = \min \{\lambda_t v_{t-1} + (1 - \lambda_t) c, v_{t-1}\} \qquad t = 1, \ldots, T$$

$$v_t^* (p_t, v_{t-1}) = \min \left\{ \frac{p_t - \delta (1 - 2A_{t+1}) c}{1 - \delta + 2A_{t+1}}, c \right\} \qquad t = 1, \ldots, T$$

where $\{A_t\}$ and $\{\lambda_t\}$ are sequences defined by the recursions specified in (8) and (9) in the paper.

The authors show that in the above type of equilibrium, prices monotonically decline over time; in other words, *price skimming* arises in equilibrium. Additionally, they develop a benchmark model in which all customers are myopic. Here, it is easy to see that the seller's optimal policy is provided by a solution to the dynamic program

$$H_t (v_{t-1}) = \max_{p_t : p_t \leq v_{t-1}} \left\{ (p_t - c) \cdot \frac{v_{t-1} - p_t}{v^+} \cdot N + \delta H_{t+1} (p_t) \right\}$$

Comparing the two models, Besanko and Winston show that with myopic consumers, the price is always higher in any *given* state than it is with strategic consumers. In other words, the *first-period price* with myopic consumers is higher than the first-period price with strategic consumers. It is noteworthy, however, that because the time paths of sales in the two cases differ, it is possible that the price with myopic consumers will fall below the price with strategic consumers in later periods. Two other interesting observations were made in the paper. First, the authors illustrate a situation in which a seller that commits to a price path that is based on the "myopic case," and use it when customers are actually strategic, might significantly hurt his expected profit. Second, the authors argue that for any v, $H_t^* (v)$ is *increasing* in t. In contrast, $\hat{H}_t (v)$ (the optimal expected profit in the myopic case) is *decreasing* in t. Consequently, starting in any state v, a monopolist prefers a *shorter* time horizon if faced with strategic consumers, but a *longer* time horizon if faced with myopic consumers. The intuition behind this is that the shorter is the time horizon, the smaller is the power of strategic consumers. In contrast, with myopic consumers, the monopolist prefers a longer time horizon because it gives him more flexibility in setting prices over time and hence extracting more revenues.

12.2.1 Models with Limited Inventories

Elmaghraby et al. (2007) consider a setting in which a seller uses a pre-announced markdown pricing mechanism, to sell a finite inventory of a product. Specifically, the seller's objective is to maximize expected revenues by optimally choosing the number of price steps over the season, and the price at each step. All potential buyers are present at the start of the selling period and remain until all the units have been sold or their demand has been satisfied. The buyers, who demand multiple units, may choose to wait and purchase at a lower price, but they must also consider a scarcity in supply. The authors study the potential benefits of segmentation; namely, the difference between the seller's profit under the optimal markdown mechanism and that under the optimal single price. They also provide a detailed discussion on the design of profitable markdown mechanisms.

Su (2007) presents a pricing control model in which consumers are infinitesimally small and arrive continuously according to a deterministic flow of constant rate. The customer population is heterogeneous along two dimensions: valuations and degree of patience (vis-à-vis waiting). The seller has to decide on pricing and a rationing policy which specifies the fraction of current market demand that is fulfilled. Given these retailer's choices, customers decide whether or not to purchase the product and whether to stay or leave the market. The paper shows how the seller can determine a revenue-maximizing selling policy in this game. Su demonstrates that the heterogeneity in valuation and degree of patience jointly influence the structure of optimal pricing policies. In particular, when high-valuation customers are proportionately less patient, markdown pricing policies are effective. On the other hand, when the high-valuation customers are more patient than the low-valuation customers, prices should increase over time in order to discourage waiting.

Aviv and Pazgal (2008) consider a seller that has Q units of an item available for sale during a sales horizon of length H. The sales season $[0, H]$ is split into two parts, $[0, T]$ and $[T, H]$, for a given fixed value T. During the first part of the season, a "premium" price p_1 applies, and during the second phase of the season a "discount" price p_2 is offered (where $p_2 \leq p_1$). The seller's objective is to set the premium and discount prices in order to maximize the expected total revenues collected during the sales horizon. An important feature of their model is that it includes two types of *demand uncertainty*: the total market size and the time of arrivals. Specifically, it is assumed that customers arrive to the store following a Poisson process with a rate of λ. Customers' valuations of the product vary across the population, and decline over the course of the season according to

$$V_j(t) = V_j \cdot e^{-\alpha t}$$

for every customer j. Specifically, customer j's *base valuation* V_j is drawn from a given continuous distribution form F. Then, depending on the particular time of purchase (t), the realized valuation is discounted appropriately by a known exponential decline factor $\alpha \geq 0$, fixed across the population. Customers that arrive prior to time T behave according to the following strategy: A given customer j, arriving at time t, will purchase immediately upon arrival (if there is inventory) if two conditions are satisfied about his current surplus $V_j e^{-\alpha t} - p_1$: (i) it is non-negative; and (ii) it is larger or equal to the *expected* surplus he can gain from a purchase at time T (when the price is changed to p_2). Of course, the latter expected surplus depends on the customer's belief about p_2 as well as the likelihood that a unit will be available to the customer. If the customer purchases a unit, he leaves the store immediately. Otherwise, the customer stays until time T. At time T, all existing customers take a look at the new price p_2 and if they can gain a non-negative surplus, they request a unit of the remaining items (if any). In case there are fewer units than the number of customers who wish to buy, the allocation is made randomly. After time T, new customers buy according to whether or not they can immediately gain a non-negative surplus. Clearly, it does not make sense for a customer to wait in the store after time T, since prices will not drop. The seller observes the purchases, or equivalently, his level of inventory. Hence, the discounted price p_2 depends on the remaining inventory at time T.

Aviv and Pazgal identify a subgame perfect Nash equilibrium for the game between the customers and the seller. Note that the seller's strategy is characterized by the initial premium price p_1 and the discounted price menu $\{p_2(q)\}_{q=1}^Q$. The customers' strategy is one that prescribes purchasing decisions for every possible pair of individual arrival time t and base valuation V.

They first study the best response of the customers to a given seller's *pure* strategy of the form $p_1, p_2(1), \ldots, p_2(Q)$. The response strategy is based on a competitive situation that exists among consumers, which arises due to the fact that an individual consumer's decision impacts the product availability for others. It is shown that a *time-dependent* threshold emerges, as follows.

Theorem 1 of Aviv and Pazgal (2008). *For any given pricing scheme* $\{p_1, p_2(1), \ldots, p_2(Q)\}$, *it is optimal for the customers to base their purchasing decisions on a threshold function* $\theta(t)$. *Specifically, a customer arriving at time* $t \in [0, H]$ *will purchase an available unit immediately upon arrival if* $V(t) \geq \theta(t)$. *Otherwise, if* $V(t) < \theta(t)$ *and* $t < T$, *the customer will revisit the store at time* T, *and purchase an available unit if* $V(T) \geq \theta(T)$. *The threshold function* $\theta(t)$ *is given by*

$$\theta(t) = \begin{cases} \psi(t) & 0 \leq t < T \\ p_2 & T \leq t \leq H \end{cases} \tag{12.1}$$

where $\psi(t)$ *is the unique solution to the implicit equation*

$$\psi - p_1 = E_{Q_T}\left[\max\{\psi e^{-\alpha(T-t)} - p_2(Q_T), 0\} \cdot \mathbf{1}\{\mathscr{A}|Q_T\}\right] \tag{12.2}$$

The random variable Q_T *represents the remaining inventory at time* T, *and the event* A *represents the allocation of a unit to the customer upon request.*

The function ψ hence defines the customers' purchasing strategy. The left-hand side of (12.2) represents the current surplus the customer can gain by purchasing a unit, whereas the right-hand side of the equation represents the expected surplus that will be gained by the customer if he postpones his purchase to time T. The latter expected value takes into account two conditions. The first condition is that the discounted price needs to leave the customer with a non-negative surplus. This is simply given by the condition $\psi e^{-\alpha(T-t)} - p_2(Q_T) \geq 0$, where Q_T is a random variable. The second condition is that in order to provide a surplus, a unit needs to be available and be allocated to the customer. Given a specific realization of Q_T, the allocation probability depends on the statistical distribution of the number of other customers that postpone their purchases to time T. This is taken into account by the indicator expression $\mathbf{1}\{\mathscr{A}|Q_T\}$. The strength of this theorem is that it demonstrates the optimality of a threshold-type policy for each individual customer, under *any arbitrary* purchasing strategies of the others. Using this result, Aviv and Pazgal argue that for any given pricing scheme $\{p_1, p_2(1), \ldots, p_2(Q)\}$, the equilibrium in the game between the customers is unique, and consists of symmetric strategies; i.e., ψ is the same for all customers. Additionally, they show that the threshold function $\psi(t) : [0, T) \rightarrow [p_1, \infty)$ is increasing in t.

Next, the seller's strategy is studied; namely, the best contingent pricing $\{p_2(1), \ldots, p_2(Q)\}$ in response to a given purchasing strategy ψ and a given initial premium price p_1. As a basis for the analysis, it is useful to distinguish between five types of customers, as illustrated in Figure 12.1.

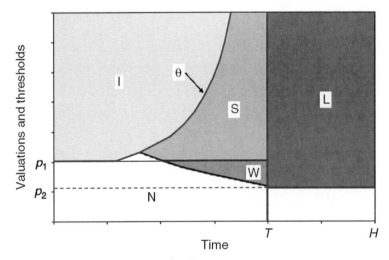

Fig. 12.1 For a given realized price path (p_1, p_2) and a customer threshold purchasing policy $\psi(t)$, the customer's space (arrival times and valuations) is split into five areas: (i) "I" = immediate buy at premium price; (ii) "S" = strategic wait and buy at discounted price; (iii) "W" = non-strategic wait and buy at discounted price; (iv) "L" = immediate purchasers at discounted price; and (v) 'N' = no buyers. In this context "buy" means a desire to buy.

The first group is of customers that arrive during $[0, T]$ and purchase[1] immediately at price p_1 (denoted by 'I'). It is easy to see that the expected number of
customers of this type is

$$\Lambda_I (\psi) \doteq \lambda \int_{t=0}^{T} \bar{F} \left(\psi (t) e^{\alpha t} \right) dt$$

We define the remaining four types of customers with respect to a *realized* value
of p_2 at time T. The second group of customers (denoted by "S") consists of those
who could get a non-negative surplus upon their arrival during $[0, T]$ but decided to
wait "strategically" (i.e., in anticipation of a better expected surplus at time T), and
indeed want to purchase a unit at the realized price p_2 (note that it may happen that
the actual surplus realized is lower than the original surplus a customer could gain
if purchased a unit immediately upon arrival). The number of customers that falls in
this category has a Poisson distribution with a mean

$$\Lambda_S (\psi, p_1, p_2)$$
$$\doteq \lambda \int_{t=0}^{T} \left[\bar{F} \left(\min \left\{ \max \left\{ p_1 e^{\alpha t}, p_2 e^{\alpha T} \right\}, \psi (t) e^{\alpha t} \right\} \right) - \bar{F} \left(\psi (t) e^{\alpha t} \right) \right] dt$$

The third group (denoted by "W") includes those customers who waited for time T
because their valuations upon arrival were below the premium price p_1, and want to
purchase a unit at the realized discount price p_2. The number of such customers is
Poisson distributed with a mean

$$\Lambda_W (p_1, p_2) \doteq \lambda \int_{t=0}^{T} \left[\bar{F} \left(\min \left\{ p_1 e^{\alpha t}, p_2 e^{\alpha T} \right\} \right) - \bar{F} \left(p_1 e^{\alpha t} \right) \right] dt$$

The fourth group of customers (denoted by "L" for "late") includes those who arrive at or after time T with a valuation higher than the posted discounted price p_2.
Clearly, the number of customers in this group is Poisson with a mean of

$$\Lambda_L (p_2) \doteq \lambda \int_{t=T}^{H} \bar{F} \left(p_2 e^{\alpha t} \right) dt$$

Finally, a fifth group (denoted by "N" in Figure 12.1) includes those customers who
do not wish to purchase a unit of the product at any point of time. Note that in
this group, we include customers who decided (strategically) to wait for time T in
anticipation of a better surplus, but then find out that the realized discounted price
p_2 is higher than their individual valuations.

It is instructive to note that the values of Λ_S, Λ_W, and Λ_L depend on the value
of p_2, which is generally unknown prior to time T. Therefore, such uncertainty
needs to be taken into account by customers who contemplate between an immediate
purchase and a strategic wait. For the seller, the above values play a key role in

---

[1] We use the term "purchase" to reflect a desire to purchase a unit. Clearly, when inventory is
depleted, we assume that the store closes and no further purchases are feasible.

setting the contingent pricing menu. Let $Q_T \in \{0,\ldots,Q\}$ be the current inventory at time T. Clearly, if $Q_T = 0$, then pricing is irrelevant. When Q_T is positive, the optimal discounted price $p_2(Q_T)$ is chosen so as to maximize the revenues collected from customers of types "S", "W", and "L". Specifically, for $Q_T \in \{1,\ldots,Q\}$, let

$$p_2(Q_T) \in \arg\max_{z \leq p_1} \{z \cdot N(Q_T, \Lambda_S(\psi, p_1, z) + \Lambda_W(p_1, z) + \Lambda_L(z))\} \qquad (12.3)$$

where $N(q, \Lambda) \doteq \sum_{x=0}^{\infty} \min(x, q) \cdot P(x|\Lambda)$ is the expected value of a Poisson random variable (with mean Λ) truncated at q.

Now, consider the subgame that begins after the premium price p_1 is set. A contingent pricing scheme $\{p_2(q)\}$ for the seller and a purchase strategy ψ for the consumers form a Nash equilibrium in the subgame, if the following conditions are satisfied. First, each price $p_2(q)$ needs to satisfy (12.3); i.e., it is a best response of the seller if all customers follow the equilibrium strategy ψ. Second, the strategy ψ needs to satisfy the conditions of theorem 1 stated above; i.e., it needs to be an optimal response to the contingent pricing scheme $\{p_2(q)\}$. For brevity of exposition, we refer the reader to Section 4.3 of the paper for a discussion of an iterative algorithm developed and employed by Aviv and Pazgal to find an equilibrium to the *subgame*. Finally, in search of maximizing the expected total revenue over the sales horizon, the seller needs to pick the best premium price p_1. This is done with the anticipation that a choice of p_1 will be followed by the subgame we described above. Given a Nash equilibrium $\psi^*(p_1)$ and $\{p_2^*(q|p_1)\}_{q=1}^{Q}$, the seller is faced with an optimization problem of the following type. Let $J(q|p_1)$ be the expected revenues collected during the second part of the season ($[T, H]$) given the subgame Nash equilibrium strategies:

$$J(q|p_1) = p_2^*(q|p_1)$$

$$\cdot N(q, \Lambda_S(\psi^*(p_1), p_1, p_2^*(q|p_1)) + \Lambda_W(p_1, p_2^*(q|p_1)) + \Lambda_L(p_2^*(q|p_1)))$$

Then, the seller's task is to maximize the expression

$$\pi_{C/S}^* \doteq \max_{p_1} \left\{ p_1 \cdot Q \cdot \left(1 - \sum_{x=0}^{Q-1} P(x \mid \Lambda_I(\psi^*(p_1)))\right) \right. \qquad (12.4)$$

$$\left. + \sum_{x=0}^{Q-1} (p_1 \cdot x + J(Q-x|p_1)) \cdot P(x|\Lambda_I(\psi^*(p_1))) \right\}$$

The subscript "C/S" denotes the case of contingent pricing policies with strategic customers.

In order to measure the effectiveness of price segmentation, Aviv and Pazgal consider the expected increase in revenues obtained by moving from an optimal *static-pricing* strategy (π_F^*) to a two-price strategy. In other words, they propose the metric $(\pi_{C/S}^* - \pi_F^*)/\pi_F^*$, where

$$\pi_F^* \doteq \max_p \left\{ p \cdot N \left(Q, \lambda \int_0^H \bar{F} \left(p \cdot e^{\alpha t} \right) dt \right) \right\}$$

Like Besanko and Winston (1990), they also consider benchmark models in which all customers are myopic. Their findings are summarized below.

In general, the benefits of using contingent pricing schemes appear to be very significant under the case of myopic customers. Unlike the case of myopic customers, they show that strategic customer behavior clearly interferes with the benefits of price segmentation to the retailer. Strategic consumer behavior suppresses the benefits of segmentation, under medium-to-high values of heterogeneity and modest rates of decline in valuations. An underlying reason for this is that when the rate of decline in valuation is small, customers are patient in waiting for the discount time. Not only that, but unlike the case of fixed-price strategies, customers rationally expect discounts to take place. However, when the level of consumer heterogeneity is small, the rate of decline is medium to high, and the time of discount can be optimally chosen (in advance) by the seller, segmentation can be used quite effectively even with strategic consumers. The rationale for the result is that under these conditions, there is typically a little difference in price valuations at the time of discount. Hence, the discount price is generally set in a way that does not offer a substantial surplus to consumers.

The seller cannot effectively avoid the adverse impact of strategic behavior even under low levels of initial inventory. When the initial inventory level is low, the seller expects customers to be more concerned about product availability at discount time, and thus act in a similar way to myopic customers. However, for myopic consumers the seller should benefit from *high-price experimentation*. In other words, the seller would set a high price for the initial period of time in order to bet on collecting large revenues, speculating that small number of unsold units can be easily sold at the end of the season. But high-price experimentations in the case of strategic consumers could drive customers to wait even if the availability probability is relatively low. Thus, high-price betting cannot be sustained in equilibrium and for more moderate prices customers are more inclined to purchase immediately than wait and take the risk of a stockout.

When the seller incorrectly assumes that strategic customers are myopic in their purchasing decisions, it can be quite costly, reaching up to 20% loss of potential revenues. When the level of heterogeneity is large, misclassification results in offering high discounts. Now, if valuations do not decline significantly during the horizon, strategic customers would most likely wait. The dependency of the sub-optimality gap on rate of decline in valuations works in two different ways. On one hand, when it is small, customers are typically more inclined to wait, but their valuations do not decline significantly. When the rate of decline is high, fewer customers will decide to wait, but the rapid decline in these customers' valuations would hurt the seller's ability to extract high revenues at the time of discount. Finally, when customers' valuations are homogeneous and the decline rate is large, strategic customers do not have a substantial incentive to wait, and so misclassification is not expected to lead to significant loss.

12.3 Price Commitments

In addition to the models described above, Aviv and Pazgal (2008) also consider a two-period pricing problem in which the seller commits *upfront* to a *fixed*-price path (p_1, p_2). Specifically, under this policy class, named "announced discount strategies," the discounted price p_2 is not contingent upon the remaining inventory at time T. Interestingly, sellers such as Filene's Basement (Bell and Starr 1994), Land's End, and Syms use this method for pricing some of their products. Consider for a moment the case of myopic customers. Clearly, in such settings, a fixed discount is generally not optimal. The seller could obviously increase his expected revenues by waiting until time T and *then* determine the best-price discount according to the remaining amount of inventory on hand. The same logic does not straightforwardly apply in face of strategic customers. In fact, under strategic consumer behavior there could be cases in which announced pricing schemes (denoted by "A/S") may perform better than contingent pricing policies (denoted by "C/S"). For the sake of illustration, let us consider the case of unlimited inventory ($Q = \infty$). In this case, it is easy to show that "A/S" is at least as good as "C/S". This is because the discounted price under "C/S" can be determined accurately in advance. Thus, that same discounted price could be used under "A/S", yielding the same expected revenues as in the best strategy under "C/S". But, of course, the seller could perhaps do even better by announcing (and committing to) a smaller discount in order to discourage strategic waiting. Indeed, game theory provides us with variety of examples in which limiting one's choices of future actions (burning the bridges) may put one in a better position at equilibrium. The following result is proven.

Theorem 2 of Aviv and Pazgal (2008). *Consider any given (and credible) announced pricing path $\{p_1, p_2\}$. Then, the threshold-type policy defined by the function θ below constitutes a Nash equilibrium in the customers' purchasing strategies. Let*

$$\theta(t) \doteq \begin{cases} \psi_A(t) \doteq \max\left\{ p_1, \dfrac{p_1 - w p_2}{1 - w e^{-\alpha(T-t)}} \right\} & 0 \le t < T \\ p_2 & T \le t \le H \end{cases} \tag{12.5}$$

where w is a solution to the equation:

$$w \doteq \sum_{x=0}^{Q-1} P(x | \Lambda_I(\psi_A)) \cdot A(Q - x | \Lambda_S(\psi_A, p_1, p_2) + \Lambda_W(p_1, p_2)) \tag{12.6}$$

(Note that ψ_A is dependent on w, as given in (12.5).) Specifically, a customer arriving at time $t \in [0, H]$ will purchase an available unit immediately upon arrival if $V(t) \ge \theta(t)$. Otherwise, if $V(t) < \theta(t)$ and $t < T$, the customer will revisit the store at time T, and purchase an available unit if $V(T) > \theta(T) = p_2$.

As in the case of contingent pricing policies, in equilibrium, every customer needs to take into account the behavior of the other customers. This is reflected by the parameter w which represents the likelihood of receiving a unit of the product at time T. Clearly, if Q is relatively large, the interaction between customers is negligible, and their optimal purchasing policy is given in (12.5), with $w \approx 1$.

It is easily seen that the game between the seller and the customers has a Stackelberg form, with the seller being the leader in his announcement of the strategy (p_1, p_2) and the customers following by selecting their strategy w. Given the seller's knowledge of the customers' response to any particular pair of prices, his task is to maximize the expected revenue[2]:

$$\pi_{A/S}(p_1, p_2) \doteq p_1 \cdot Q \cdot \left(1 - \sum_{x=0}^{Q-1} P(x|\Lambda_I)\right)$$

$$+ \sum_{x=0}^{Q-1} P(x|\Lambda_I) \cdot [p_1 \cdot x + p_2 \cdot N(Q - x, \Lambda_S + \Lambda_W + \Lambda_L)]$$

In other words, find the solution to $\pi_{A/S}^* = \max_{p_1, p_2 : p_2 \le p_1} \{\pi_{A/S}(p_1, p_2)\}$. Aviv and Pazgal find that announced fixed-discount strategies perform essentially the same as contingent pricing policies in the case of myopic consumers. However, they suggest caution in interpreting this result. First, they consider the *optimal* announced discount. If a seller picks an arbitrary discount level, the sub-performance with respect to contingent pricing can be very high. Second, announced discounts prevent the seller from acting upon *learning* about demand; see, e.g., Aviv and Pazgal (2005) and Mantrala and Rao (2001). Under strategic consumer behavior, they found that announced pricing policies can bring an advantage to the seller (up to 8.32% increase in expected revenues), compared to contingent pricing schemes. Particularly, they observed that announced pricing schemes are advantageous compared to contingent pricing schemes under the following conditions: (i) the number of units are sufficiently high; (ii) the level of heterogeneity in base valuations is high; (iii) the discounts are offered at a late part of the season; and (iv) the rate of decline in valuations is at a medium level. The underlying reason for the better performance of announced discount strategies is that a *credible* pre-commitment to a fixed-discount level removes the rational expectation of customers that at discount time the seller will optimally offer large discounts. Interestingly, they found that in those cases that announced discount strategies offer a significant advantage compared to contingent pricing policies, they appear to offer only a minimal advantage in comparison to fixed pricing policies.

12.4 Capacity Rationing

In order to mitigate the adverse impact of strategic consumer behavior, firms may consider the use of *capacity rationing strategies*. Under such strategies, a seller deliberately understocks a product, hence creating a shortage risk for customers.

---

[2] The functions Λ_I, Λ_S, Λ_W, and Λ_L stand for $\Lambda_I(\psi_A)$, $\Lambda_S(\psi_A, p_1, p_2)$, $\Lambda_W(p_1, p_2)$, and $\Lambda_L(p_2)$, respectively.

As a consequence, this motivates high-valuation customers to purchase early in the season at premium prices.

Liu and van Ryzin (2008) propose a model for examining the potential value of rationing strategies. In their model, a (monopoly) firm pre-announces a single markdown pricing policy over two periods: A premium price p_1 for the first period, and a *discounted* price, p_2, for the second period. Similarly to some of the models surveyed in the previous section, this situation represents a setting in which the seller is able to make a price commitment. The market size, denoted by N, is deterministic, and consists of strategic consumers that are present at the "store" from the beginning of the horizon. Consumers have heterogeneous valuations that are independently drawn from a known distribution $F(v)$, and they enjoy a utility of $u(v-p)$ when they have valuation v and purchase a unit at price p. The model assumes that the market size is large enough so that strategic interaction between customers can be ignored. The firm seeks to maximize profits by choosing its stocking quantity (capacity) at the beginning of the sales season.

When making their purchasing decisions, customers weigh the immediate utility $u(v-p_1)$ (reflecting a "buy now" choice) against the expected utility that they can gain in the second period. But to calculate the latter value, the customers need to multiply the utility $u(v-p_2)$ by the likelihood that a unit will be available. This probability, denoted by q, is assumed to be estimated exactly at the same value by all customers. It follows that, for any given q, the customers optimally follow a threshold policy with a parameter $v(q)$. This threshold value is implicitly defined by the equation:

$$u(v-p_1) = q \cdot u(v-p_2)$$

Consequently, customers with valuations larger than $v(q)$ buy in period 1; the other customers wait for period 2.

The firm needs to determine its optimal capacity C, by taking into account the per-unit procurement cost of α (assumed to be lower than p_2). But before we get into showing the formulation of the firm's decision problem, it is important to consider the connection between the capacity choice and the customers' behavior. Liu and van Ryzin show that under rational expectations[3]:

$$q = \frac{C - N \cdot \bar{F}(v(q))}{N \cdot (F(v(q) - F(p_2)))}$$

the probability q is referred to as the *fill rate*. Note that $N \cdot \bar{F}(v(q))$ represents the number of customers that purchases the product (or more precisely, attempt to) in period 1. The term $N \cdot (F(v(q) - F(p_2)))$ is equal to the number of customers that

---

[3] In fact, they use the equation

$$q = \min\left\{ \max\left(\frac{C - N \cdot \bar{F}(v(q))}{N \cdot (F(v(q) - F(p_2)))}, 0 \right), 1 \right\}$$

but argue that under all reasonable policies, the condition $\bar{F}(p_1) \leq C/N \leq \bar{F}(p_2)$ needs to be satisfied, and so the "min" and "max" operands are redundant.

is still in the market at the beginning of period 2, and has valuations that are at least as high as the discounted price p_2. The firm's profit maximization is given by

$$\max \ \{N \cdot (p_1 - p_2) \cdot \bar{F}(v) + (p_2 - \alpha) \cdot C\}$$
$$\text{s.t.} \quad u(v - p_1) = \frac{C - N \cdot \bar{F}(v(q))}{N \cdot (F(v(q) - F(p_2)))} \cdot u(v - p_2)$$
$$p_1 \leq v \leq \bar{U}$$

where $\bar{U}$ is an upper bound on the customers' valuations. Let us now follow the special case studied in that paper, where F is uniform over $[0, \bar{U}]$, and the utility function takes the form $u(x) = x^\gamma$ ($0 < \gamma < 1$). The parameter γ corresponds with the degree of *risk aversion* (lower values of γ correspond to more risk aversion). Under these assumptions, the authors show that the potential value of rationing depends on the number of high-valuation customers in the market (reflected by the parameter $\bar{U}$). Specifically, with a sufficiently large number of high-valuation customers in the market, it makes sense to adopt a rationing policy; otherwise, the firm should serve the entire market at the low price. The intuition behind this observation is simple. Note that by increasing the degree of rationing (i.e., less capacity brought to market), the firm induces higher demand in period 1 at the expense of missing the opportunity to serve some demand in period 2. Therefore, if the number of high-valuation customers in the market is small, the benefits gained in period 1 cannot justify the loss incurred in period 2. The authors find that when the firm can optimally select the prices, rationing is *always* an optimal strategy, for *any* value of $\bar{U}$. Liu and van Ryzin also explore the way in which the level of risk aversion (γ) influences the value of capacity rationing. They argue that when γ approaches 1 (i.e., customers becoming risk-neutral), the rationing risk that is needed in order to induce segmentation is very high. In other words, the planned leftover capacity level for period 2 should practically be set to 0 as γ approaches 1. Consequently, when the market consists of a sufficiently large number of high-valuation customers, it is optimal for the firm to serve the market only at the high price in period 1; otherwise, the firm serves the entire market at the low price only.

Liu and van Ryzin also study a model of oligopolistic competition. In sake of brevity, we refer the interested reader to their paper for technical details (see Section 4.4 there). They show that competition makes it more difficult to support segmentation using rationing, and explain this as follows. When competing against a large number of other firms, a focal firm is very limited in his ability to create a sense shortage risk. Thus, by reducing its capacity, a focal firm severely influences his own ability to serve demand, rather than drive high-valuation customers to buy at high prices. Particularly, the authors prove that there exists a critical number of firms beyond which creating rationing risk is never a sustainable equilibrium. Thus, rationing is more likely to be used in cases where a firm has some reasonable degree of market power.

Cachon and Swinney (2008) explore a two-period model that allows for dynamic planning of pricing and inventory. Recall, from our discussion in the previous section, that whether or not a retailer commits to a price path can significantly influence consumer behavior and retailer's performance. The key features of the model setup are as follows. A retailer sells a product over two periods. The price for the first period, p, is *exogenously* given. In the second period, the product is sold at a given markdown price s. The retailer's objective is to maximize his expected profit by selecting the optimal sale price and the initial level of inventory. The unit cost to the retailer is c.

The total number of customers that may purchase during the first period is random and denoted by D, having a distribution F. Customers are heterogeneous in terms of their behavior. A portion of the customers $(\alpha \cdot D)$ are strategic, and the remainder $((1-\alpha) \cdot D)$ are myopic consumers that exist in the market in the first period *only*. All customers have the same (known) valuation in the first period, equal to v_M ($v_M \geq p$). The valuations of strategic customers in the second period change in a random manner, assumed to be uniformly distributed between $[\underline{v}, \bar{v}]$ (where $\bar{v} \leq p$). It is assumed that strategic consumers know their individual second-period valuations in advance, from the beginning of period 1. In addition to the above mix of customers, the model introduces a third group of *bargain hunters*. These customers arrive only in period 2, and in large numbers; they are all assumed to share the same common valuation, v_B. The value of v_B is assumed to be lower than the cost c, meaning that targeting this set of customers could be used as a mechanism for salvaging unsold inventory.

The retailer's and customers' actions are driven by a rational expectation equilibrium in the game we will describe below. But let us dwell for a moment on the types of beliefs that drive actions. In contemplating a "buy now versus buy later" decision, a customer needs to assess the likelihood of getting a unit in period 2. Of course, this is influenced by the retailer's level of inventory, which is not directly observed. Hence, $\hat{q}$ is defined as the customers' (common) belief about the initial stocking level of the retailer. Similarly, in order for the retailer to set the optimal inventory quantity, he needs to be able to anticipate the way in which customers make their purchasing decisions. Let $\hat{v}$ represent this belief.[4] The authors identify a *subgame perfect Nash equilibrium* with *rational expectations* to the game. Such equilibrium is denoted by (q^*, v^*) and needs to satisfy a set of three conditions. First, the retailer is assumed to act optimally under his belief about the consumer behavior. In other words,

$$q^* \in \arg\max_{q \geq 0} \pi(q, \hat{v})$$

where $\pi(q, \hat{v})$ is equal to the retailer's expected profit under a given choice of initial inventory q, and if all customers behaved according to the purchasing threshold policy $\hat{v}$. Second, the consumers' purchasing policy should be optimal if the seller indeed sets the initial quantity to $\hat{q}$. Let $v^*(q)$ denote an optimal threshold policy for a known inventory q. Then this condition is reflected by

$$v^* \in v^*(\hat{q})$$

---

[4] The authors show that in equilibrium, there exists some $v^* \in [\underline{v}, \bar{v}]$ such that all strategic consumers with second-period valuation less than v^* purchase in period 1, and all consumers with valuation greater than v^* wait for period 2.

Third, the beliefs need to be consistent. In other words,

$$\hat{q} = q^*, \quad \hat{v} = v^*$$

Note that the retailer's expected profit under a belief $\hat{v}$ can be presented in a stochastic dynamic programming format, where the first action (at the beginning of period 1) is the initial level of inventory q, and the second action (at the beginning of period 2) is the markdown price s. The retailer knows that if indeed the customers' policy is $\hat{v}$, then the portion of strategic consumers that will purchase in period 1 is given by $(\hat{v} - \underline{v})/(\bar{v} - \underline{v})$. Together with the myopic customers who purchase in the first period, the demand in the first period sums up to

$$D_1(\hat{v}, D) \doteq \alpha \frac{\hat{v} - \underline{v}}{\bar{v} - \underline{v}} \cdot D + (1 - \alpha) \cdot D = \left(1 - \alpha \cdot \frac{\bar{v} - \hat{v}}{\bar{v} - \underline{v}}\right) \cdot D$$

The sales in period 1 are hence given by $S_1(\hat{v}, D) \doteq \min(q, D_1(\hat{v}, D))$, and the remaining level of inventory by the end of period 1 is

$$I(\hat{v}, D) \doteq \max(q - D_1(\hat{v}, D), 0)$$

With this, we get

$$\pi(q, \hat{v}) = -c \cdot q + E_D \left[p \cdot S_1(\hat{v}, D) + \max_s \{R(s, I(\hat{v}, D))\} \right] \qquad (12.7)$$

where the function $R(s, I)$ represents the expected revenues collected during the second period if the retailer has a residual capacity of I units, and sets the price to s; see paper for details.

Note that at the beginning of period 2, the retailer knows the actual value of D. Specifically, for a given $I > 0$, the retailers infer that $D_1 = q - I$, and so

$$D = (q - I) \cdot \left(1 - \alpha \cdot \frac{\bar{v} - \hat{v}}{\bar{v} - \underline{v}}\right)^{-1}$$

Cachon and Swinney now show that if demand D is sufficiently large (which also means that the residual inventory level I is relatively small), the retailer should set the highest price that clears the Inventory I. If the demand is in some medium level, the retailer needs to optimally pick a price that maximizes the revenues collected from the remaining *strategic* customers. Typically, this will result in partial sales of the inventory I. Finally, if the demand is at a relatively low level, the retailer then prices at an inventory clearance price of v_B (making the product attractive to the large set of bargain hunters). To find the optimal level of inventory (namely, the solution to $\max_{q \geq 0} \pi(q, \hat{v})$), the optimal sales price in period 2 is substituted into (12.7). The authors prove that the function $\pi(q, \hat{v})$ is quasi-concave in q, and that the optimal order quantity is determined by the unique solution to the first-order condition $d\pi(q, \hat{v})/dq = 0$.

Let us now examine how Cachon and Swinney analyze the customers' purchasing policy. As in most papers we previously discussed, strategic customers need to compare the current surplus (namely, $v_M - p_1$) with the expected surplus to be gained if they wait for period 2. Let us then consider a focal strategic customer with valuation equal to v^* (i.e., a valuation at the indifference point). A key technical observation in the analysis is that for such focal customer, the only scenario under which he can gain a positive surplus in period 2 is if the retailer sets the clearance price v_B. Recall, this event will happen if the demand D turns to be sufficiently small (say, below a given value D_l). Thus, the expected surplus for the focal consumer is

$$(v^*(\hat{q}) - v_B) \cdot \Pr\{D < D_l \text{ and the consumer receives a unit}\}$$

In sake of brevity, we refer the reader to Section 5 in the paper, which presents a rationing mechanism for allocating the inventory in case the demand in period 2 exceeds the residual quantity I.

Cachon and Swinney prove the following theorem.

Theorem 1 of Cachon and Swinney (2008). *There exists a subgame perfect Nash equilibrium with rational expectations (q^*, v^*) to the game between the retailer and strategic consumers, and any equilibrium satisfies $q^* \leq q^m$ and $\pi^* \leq \pi^m$.*

The superscript "m" refers to the *benchmark* case of myopic customers, reflected by the exact same model above, with α reset to 0. For example, we can learn from this theorem that the retailer orders less with strategic consumers compared to the case where he faces myopic customers only. In other words, this behavior can be viewed as an act of capacity rationing. It is noteworthy to consider the authors' statement vis-à-vis this result: *Other [researchers] have also found that the presence of strategic consumers causes a firm to lower its order quantity (e.g., Su and Zhang [2008a] and Liu and van Ryzin [2008]). However, the mechanism by which this result is obtained is different: they depend on rationing risk, whereas in our model the result is due to price risk – strategic consumers expect they will receive a unit in the markdown.* This observation is quite important in appreciating the value of the second model of Cachon and Swinney that we next present.

Consider now a situation in which the retailer can replenish his inventory at the beginning of period 2, *after* observing the demand D. Such type of replenishment option is generally feasible when the supply side (in terms of procurement, production, and delivery) is sufficiently responsive. Thus, the authors use the title *Quick Response* to reflect this situation. The analysis of the quick response setting appears to be very similar to that of the previous model. But, more importantly, the authors show that for a *given* value of $\hat{q}$, the customers' behavior does *not* change in comparison to the situation with no replenishment opportunity. The driver of this result is that in both cases (with or without quick response), strategic customers can gain positive surplus in period 2 only if the demand happens to be sufficiently low. If that happens, then the retailer will not exercise the quick response option anyway. But the reader should not be confused! As can be expected, the retailer will not order the same number of units (q) under both cases; we anticipate the initial order quantity to be lower with quick response, since the retailer can always order more later. In other words, the customers' behavior in equilibrium will be different (in general), depending on the feasibility of a quick response delivery. It is shown that

Theorem 2 of Cachon and Swinney (2008). *There exists a subgame perfect Nash equilibrium with rational expectations (q_r^*, v_r^*) to the game between the retailer with quick response and strategic consumers. It yields equilibrium expected profit π_r^* and satisfies $q_r^* \leq q^*$ and $\pi_r^* \geq \pi^*$. Furthermore, if*

$$\frac{v_M - p}{\bar{v} - v_B} \geq \frac{c_2 - c_1}{c_2 - v_B},$$

then in equilibrium all strategic consumers purchase in the first period (c_2 is the per-unit procurement cost in period 2).

The result $q_r^* \leq q^*$, together with the discussion above, means that quick response enables the retailer to increase the sense of rationing risk among strategic consumers, by ordering less. By driving strategic customers to purchase at the premium price p, the retailer gains an increased profit. Not only that, but with quick response, the retailer has an option to better match the supply with demand after observing D. Based on a numerical analysis, Cachon and Swinney note that the profit increase due to quick response can be dramatically higher when a retailer faces strategic consumers, than under settings with myopic customers only. This observation is key to the understanding of the potential benefits of quick response systems, and the ways in which it depends on consumer behavior.

Su and Zhang (2008a) propose an extension of the traditional "*newsvendor*" inventory model to incorporate the impact of strategic consumer behavior. In their setting, a single seller makes a choice of the capacity Q to bring to the market, as well as the price (p) to charge during the main season. Per-unit cost to the seller is c, and at the end of the season the seller must set the price to s (not a decision variable). Demand, denoted by X, is a random variable and is interpreted as the total mass of infinitesimal consumers in the market. The random variable X follows a distribution F. Consumers' valuations for the product are fixed at v. It is assumed that $s < c < v$. Customers' purchasing behavior is assumed to be governed by a threshold policy with a *reservation price* r. Specifically, if $r \geq p$, they all attempt to buy immediately at price p; otherwise, they all wait for the salvage price.

It is noteworthy that the level of inventory, picked by the seller, is not observable to the customers. Similarly, the reservation price r is known to the customers, but not directly observed by the seller. Thus, Su and Zhang propose to study a rational expectation equilibrium in which estimates of these values are formed by the seller and customers. Specifically, the seller forms a belief ξ_r about the customers' reservation price, while the customers form a belief ξ_{prob} about the probability of availability on the salvage market (which obviously depends on the seller's choice of Q). Based on these expectations, customers need to compare between the surplus gained by a "buy now" decision (i.e., $v - p$) and the expected surplus to be gained by waiting (i.e., $(v - s)\xi_{prob}$). Since r has an interpretation of an indifference point (between a "buy now" and "wait"), it is easy to see that

$$r\left(\xi_{\text{prob}}\right) = v - (v - s)\,\xi_{\text{prob}}$$

(where r is stated as a function of the customers' belief ξ_{prob}). From the seller's perspective, it is obviously optimal to set the price to be equal to the customers' reservation price. However, since this value is not observed, we can write, for the moment, $p = \xi_r$. The optimal quantity (for any given price p) is given by

$$Q(p) = \arg\max_{Q}\{\Pi(Q,p) = (p - s)\cdot E\left[\min\{X,Q\}\right] - (c - s)Q\}$$

The authors show that a rational expectation equilibrium is given by the solution to the equation $p = v - (v - s)\,F(Q(p))$. They further show that

Proposition 1 of Su and Zhang (2008a). *In the rational expectation equilibrium, all customers buy immediately, and the seller's price and quantity are characterized by* $p_c = s + \sqrt{(v - s)(c - s)}$ *and* $F(Q_c) = 1 - \sqrt{(c - s)/(v - s)}$.

(The subscript "c" is used to refer to a centralized setting with a single seller.) One of the lessons taken of this proposition is that the seller lowers his stocking quantity under strategic consumer behavior. We will get back to this paper in the next section, in which we discuss the topic of capacity commitment.

Su and Zhang (2008b) propose a similar "newsvendor"-type model as in the previous setting, but with a slightly different feature. Here, instead of strategic customers contemplating between a "buy now" versus a "wait" decision, they are contemplating whether to "go to the store," or not. A "go to the store" action involves a search cost of h, which could be justified if the surplus from a purchase exceeds this value. However, customers face uncertainty about product availability, and so they risk losing the search cost if they came to the store and did not find an item available. The authors explore the outcome of the rational expectation game. The setting of the game is very similar to the aforementioned framework: The seller announces a price and selects a capacity (not directly observed by customers), and customers form a belief about the likelihood of finding a product available (this likelihood is not directly observed by the seller).

Ovchinnikov and Milner (2005) consider a firm that offers last-minute discounts over a series of periods. Their model incorporates both stochastic demand and stochastic customer waiting behavior. Two waiting behaviors are considered in their paper. In the first, called "the smoothing case," customers interpolate between their previous waiting likelihood and their observation of the firm's policy. In the second, named "the self-regulating case," customers anticipate other customers' behavior and the likelihood that they will receive a unit on sale. They show that, under the self-regulating case, it is generally optimal for the firm to set some units on sale in each period and allow the customer behavior to limit the number of customers that enjoy the benefit of the reduced price. In contrast, in the smoothing case, the firm can increase its revenues by following a sales policy that regulates the number of customers waiting. The authors conduct numerical simulations to illustrate the value of making decisions optimally, as compared to a set of reasonable benchmark heuristics. They find that the revenues can increase by about 5–15%. The paper also discusses how these benefits are affected if overbooking is allowed, and show that the impact of overbooking is greatly dependent on the proportion of high-valuation customers in the market.

12.4.1 Capacity Commitments

In the last part of their paper, Cachon and Swinney (2008) report on some results related to the question of whether or not a price commitment can perform better than subgame perfect dynamic pricing. It is noteworthy that unlike the model of Aviv and Pazgal (2008) (who studied a similar type of question), the current model assumes that the initial price is set exogenously, and so commitment here is on the markdown price s *only*. Another important difference is that in the first period, all strategic and myopic customers share the *same valuation*, v_M. It is for these reasons that Cachon and Swinney could argue that if the retailer had to commit for a discount, it would be optimal to not markdown at all; in other words, the retailer should use a *static-pricing* policy, equal to the exogenously set price p. In settings with no quick response, making a "no markdown" commitment is beneficial *only* when the ratio between the margins in the first period ($p - c$) and the cost of leftover inventory ($p - v_B$) is sufficiently high. This is because the gain from inducing purchase during period 1 outweighs the loss due to the inability of the retailer to salvage inventory in case of a low-demand realization. When the retailer has quick response capability, static pricing tends to be more beneficial. The reason behind this is that quick response reduces the likelihood of having significant leftovers, and thus the loss due to price commitment (or, alternatively viewed – the likelihood of a need for inventory clearance) is not high.

We now get back to Su and Zhang (2008a). This paper considers two types of commitments that can be made by the seller: a capacity commitment and a price commitment. The first commitment represents a situation in which the seller can order Q units and convince customers that this is indeed the quantity level. In this case, there is no need for the customers to form a rational expectation about ξ_{prob}, as they can simply calculate the availability probability via $F(Q)$. The seller will then price

$$p_q(Q) = v - (v - s)F(Q)$$

Consequently, the seller's optimal quantity decision is given by Q_q^*, the maximizer of the expected profit

$$\Pi_q(Q) = (p(Q) - s)E[\min\{X,Q\}] - (c - s)Q$$
$$= (v - s)\bar{F}(Q)E[\min\{X,Q\}] - (c - s)Q$$

Let us now look at their model of *price commitment*. Here, it is easy to verify that the seller should commit not to reduce the price; i.e., use a static price of v. Given this commitment, all customers attempt to buy the product at price v, and hence the expected profit is given by $\Pi_p(Q) = vE[\min\{X,Q\}] - cQ$. Su and Zhang show that price commitment may increase the seller's profit when the production cost c is relatively low and when the valuation v is relatively high. However, there exist situations in which price commitments is not desirable. This happens when the valuation v is relatively small. The intuition behind this is similar in spirit to that argued by Cachon and Swinney (2008); see above.

Su and Zhang (2008b) also discuss two commitment strategies that the seller can use to improve expected profits. When capacity commitment can be made, it can be very valuable in that it encourages customers to spend the search cost and visit the store. This effect increases expected profit margins and leads the seller to set a higher capacity. As a consequence, with higher inventory, the customers indeed experience a higher level of product availability. A second type of mechanism studied in this paper is an *availability guarantee*. Here, the seller promises to compensate consumers, ex post, if the product is out of stock. They find that the seller has an incentive to over-compensate consumers during stockouts, relative to the benchmark case under which social welfare is maximized. Finally, the authors argue that first-best outcomes (i.e., those achieved under the benchmark case) do not arise in equilibrium, but can be achieved when the seller uses some combination of commitment and availability guarantees.

12.5 Internal Price-Matching Policies

In the retail industry, many companies offer some form of price guarantee to encourage customers not to delay their purchases; see Arbatskaya et al. (2004). One such offering, called an *internal*[5] price-matching guarantee, reflects a situation in which a retailer ensures that a customer will be reimbursed the difference between the current purchase price and any lower price the retailer might offer within a fixed *future time* period. The practice of internal price matching is very common in the retail industry and has been adopted (either formally or informally) by companies such as Amazon.com, Circuit City, and Gap. For example, if a product you purchased at Amazon.com within the last 30 days has dropped in price, they will typically credit you back the difference. In fact, a price-matching policy is effectively practiced by retailers who offer "free-return" policies. This is because customers who witness a price drop can simply return their purchased item for a full refund, and then immediately repurchase the same item at a lower price.

Obviously, in order to extract the maximum benefit from price matching, customers need to monitor the price constantly. From a retailer's perspective, a worst case refund scenario is one in which all customers are willing and able to monitor prices, and then exercise their right for a refund when applicable. In fact, with the evolution of technology and web-based services, this concern is becoming increasingly realistic. For example, Refundplease.com is a company that offers a web

---

[5] An alternative offering, called an *external* price-matching guarantee, is also popular in practice. Here, the retailer offers to match the price advertised by any *other* retailer at the time of purchase. Nonetheless, our focus in this section is on *internal* price-matching mechanism only.

service that simplifies the process for customers. Customers no longer need to keep track of the latest prices in order to get a credit. After a customer makes a purchase, he visits their web site and enters the purchase information. Refundplease.com will then check the prices everyday and send the customer a message if the price has dropped, and provide a link right to the place where the customer can claim a credit.

There are many possible variations of internal price-matching guarantees. One way is to offer a refund equal to the difference between what the customer paid and the marked down price (if such action took place within a specified time window); see, e.g., Debo et al. (2008). Another way is to compute a compensation (to customers) by taking the difference between the price of the product at some future point in time and the *strike price* offered at the time of purchase. There are several possibilities for the selection of the time when the price is compared to the strike price. One of them is to allow a customer to select it. Another is to let it be the time when the price is the lowest. Another set of the instrument's details is related to the notion of "similar product." In the case of airlines, for example, this could be "a ticket for the exact same flight," "a ticket for the same route by the same airline on the same date," or "a ticket on the same date by any airline with flights to this destination." Each definition of similarity will result in its own price for the service. For example, Levin et al. (2007) analyze the case of the same items and the comparison of the price with the strike price made at the time when the price is the lowest.

A limited amount of research on price matching has been done by economists and marketing scientists; see Hess and Gerstner (1991), Moorthy and Winter (2005), and Srivastava and Lurie (2001). These studies focus on the economics of price matching and do not involve revenue management practices. For example, Butz (1990) studies the impact of posterior price-matching policies in a setting with a durable goods sold over an infinite horizon. The seller is also a producer and can meet any demand quantity; i.e., unlike the situation in typical revenue management systems, there is no constraint on capacity (inventory). In his model, the seller offers a price-matching guarantee to buyers with a prespecified time window. Finally, this model assumes that demand is exogenous and free of strategic consumer behavior.

Levin et al. (2007) present a dynamic pricing model that includes an internal price guarantee instrument. Their paper considers a situation with *limited capacity*, reflective of revenue management settings. The internal price guarantee they consider provides a customer with compensation if the price of the product drops below a specified level (called the strike price). Customers have the choice of either buying or declining the guarantee; if they buy, then need to pay a fee. A price guarantee can increase the probability that customers will purchase at or near the time they first inquire about a product because it reduces their risk of future opportunity loss. For the company, an increased number of early purchases can reduce the uncertainty of late-purchasing "rushes" and last-minute price reductions, facilitate forecasting and capacity planning, and improve customer satisfaction and retention. Furthermore, the price guarantee itself constitutes a service provided for a fee in addition to the regular product price. Because this fee can be set by the seller so that it exceeds potential average losses from paying compensations, the collected fees provide an additional revenue stream. We elaborate below on some of the model details.

Assume that customers arrive according to a discrete-time counting process $N(t)$ with at most one arrival per time period and the probability of arrival is λ in each period. (The actual sales process is non-homogeneous in time in a manner described below.) The company has a total of Y items in inventory available for sale during T time periods. The company's policy is specified by a triple of values, representing the price, strike price (for the guarantee option), and the option purchase fee, given by the "quote": $\Pi(t) = (p(t), k(t), f(t))$, respectively. Thus, the quote is a three dimensional (stochastic) process. The guarantee is assumed to have a duration equal to D time periods, and the price guarantee *payments* are always made at the end of the planning period (i.e., at time T) regardless of the value of D. Specifically, if a customer bought an item with the price guarantee at time t, then the price guarantee payment to this customer will be equal to

$$\max\left\{\max\left(k(t) - p(\tau), 0\right) : t \le \tau \le \min\{t + D, T\}\right\}$$

Customers, who are assumed to be *myopic*, choose between not making a purchase, making a purchase without the price guarantee at price $p(t)$, or paying $p(t) + f(t)$ for the purchase with the guarantee. The consumer choice model is described by two probability functions. First, it is assumed that the probability that a customer makes either type of purchase upon arrival at time t is given by a function $u(p, k, f, t)$. Thus, the effective probability of sale at time t is $\lambda(\Pi(t), t) = u(\Pi(t), t) \cdot \lambda$. Second, the conditional probability that a customer also purchases the price guarantee (given that a purchase is made) is given by $\upsilon(\Pi(t), t)$. The sales process is a two-dimensional counting process $(N_1(t), N_2(t))$, where $N_1(t)$ specifies the number of sales without price guarantees and $N_2(t)$ specifies the number of sales with price guarantees.

The problem of identifying an optimal policy for the retailer is not simple! At any point in time, the state of information consists of the values $(N_1(t), N_2(t))$ and the history of the process Π. It is easy to verify that the retailer's dynamic planning problem does not possess a Markovian property with respect to $(N_1(t), N_2(t))$, and hence an optimal policy will need to get involved with a solution of a dynamic program with a prohibitively large state space. To tackle this technical problem, Levin et al. confine themselves to a policy class that prescribes the values $\Pi(t)$ on the basis of the values $(N_1(t), N_2(t), t)$. They propose a nonlinear programming (NLP) approach to identify the best policy within this class. This approach can be implemented in relatively small problems. For large-scale problems, the paper offers a computationally tractable heuristic.

12.5.1 Internal Price Guarantees Under Strategic Consumer Behavior

Png (1991) considers a monopolist that sells a limited capacity (of size k) to customers whose valuations are either low (v_l) or high (v_h; $v_h > v_l$). A random portion of the customers $x \in [0, 1]$ belongs to the high-valuation set; x follows a given statistical distribution Φ. There are two periods in the interaction between the seller and customers. If at any time there is excess demand, the available units are allocated at random. All customers are present at the "store" from the beginning of period 1. To study the equilibrium in the game, it is useful to begin from the second period, where it is clear that the price $p_2 = v_l$ should be set. Going back to the first period, we now consider the customers' choice. Suppose that a high-valuation customer decides to purchase in period 1. Then, the likelihood of getting a "unit" of the product is given by

$$\sigma_1(k) = \Phi(k) + \int_k^1 \frac{k}{x} d\Phi(x)$$

and therefore, the expected utility for buying in advance is $(v_h - p_1) \cdot \sigma_1(k)$. The latter value is based on an implicit assumption that all other high-valuation customers will act the same way as that of the "focal" customer. Now, let us consider the situation in which just the "focal" customer *deviates* from the buy now action, and decides to wait for period 2. In this case, he will receive the product in the second period with the probability

$$\sigma_2(k) = \int_0^k \frac{k-x}{1-x} d\Phi(x)$$

and hence his expected utility will be $(v_h - v_l) \cdot \sigma_2(k)$. Png argues that in order to maximize profit, the seller should set the first-period price p_1 so that each high-valuation customers will be indifferent between buying immediately and waiting. In other words,

$$p_1(k) = v_h - (v_h - v_l) \frac{\sigma_2(k)}{\sigma_1(k)}$$

The seller's expected revenues are given by

$$R(k) = v_l \cdot E[\max(k-x,0)] + p_1(k) \cdot E[\min(x,k)]$$

In his second model, Png (1991) considers a *most favorable customer* (MFC) protection plan. Under this policy, the seller promises customers who buy early that they will receive a refund to cover for any subsequent price cut. Let $\hat{p}_1$ and $\hat{p}_2$ denote the prices in the first and second periods, respectively. It is clear that for high-valuation customers, the best strategy is to purchase in the first period. This is because when customers buy early, they increase their likelihood of product availability and they have nothing to lose on price. Therefore, it is optimal for the seller to set $\hat{p}_1 = v_h$. Given this choice, the low-valuation customers will wait to period 2. Consequently, there are two cases that need to be analyzed: $x \geq k$ and $x < k$. The first case is simple, since all units are purchased by the high-valuation customers, and the seller's profit is given by $v_h \cdot x$. In the second case, the seller faces the following trade-off in setting $\hat{p}_2$. If $\hat{p}_2$ is set to v_l, the seller can extract a revenue of $v_l \cdot (k-x)$, but will need to refund the high-valuation customers. Or, more simply, the seller will effectively charge all customer the price v_l, and gain a revenue of $v_l \cdot k$. If $\hat{p}_2$ is set to v_h, then the seller's revenue is $v_h \cdot \min(k,x) = v_h \cdot x$ (in view of $x < k$). The seller's revenue under the second case is therefore $\max(v_l \cdot k, v_h \cdot x)$, and therefore the total expected revenue with an MFC provision is equal to

$$\hat{R}(k) = E[\max(v_l \cdot k, v_h \cdot \min(x, k))]$$

A key result in Png's paper is that the seller always (weakly) prefers to guarantee MFC treatment to first-period buyers and sell over two periods than to sell in one period only (see Proposition 1 in his paper). He explains the intuition behind this finding by arguing that selling over two periods enables the seller to collect and use information about the customer demand. Formally, this type of advantage is described in the following inequality:

$$\hat{R}(k) = E[\max(v_l \cdot k, v_h \cdot \min(x, k))] \geq \max(v_l \cdot k, E[v_h \cdot \min(x, k)])$$

with the right-hand side representing the maximal expected revenues that can be gained under a fixed-price policy. Another important observation made by Png has to do with the comparison of MFC to no-MFC policies. He finds that MFC protection is the favorable choice for the seller when the capacity is large. The logic behind this result is that when capacity is high, customers have a large confidence that waiting will not significantly harm their likelihood of receiving the product at v_l (under the no-MFC policy). Therefore, customers will wait for the second period, resulting in minimal expected revenues. Png also finds that when customers are more uncertain about the degree of excess demand in the first period, they tend to buy early at the high price. As a consequence, such customer base is a good candidate for price discrimination, and no-MFC is the right choice for the seller.

Xu (2008) studies the optimal choice of internal price-matching policies, to which she refer by the term *best-price policies* (BP). Unlike the previous paper, Xu characterizes the *best choice of policy parameters*; namely, the time window during which the BP applies and the portion of the price difference that is refunded (*refund scale*). The models of this paper are set on the basis of the following set of assumptions. A seller and customers interact over an infinite horizon, with the seller essentially able to continuously change prices.[6] Customers are either high valuation or low valuation, and they all have the same discount rate (the seller, too, share the same discount factor). At some point (and only one point) of time the valuations of all customers jump simultaneously into a lower state, according to some probabilistic mechanism. This *random-shock* phenomenon is embedded in the model in order to represent situations in practice where a product is going out of fashion, or become obsolete. The main model in the paper considers the case where the seller offers a BP policy, and cannot commit to prices. Two benchmark models are also analyzed: A case in which no BP is offered, but the seller can *commit to prices* (prices are contingent on the information history), and a case in which no BP is offered and the seller cannot make a price commitment. Xu finds that a *finite* and positive BP policy can be optimal for the seller, when the likelihood for a sharp drop in evalua-

---

[6] The paper assumes that the price-change points are confined to the time epochs $t = 0, \Delta, 2\Delta, \ldots$, but it then focuses on the limiting case $\Delta \to 0$.

tion can take place. In other words, BP policies can be effective for retailers whose products may go out of fashion or become obsolete. The seller's equilibrium profit under the optimal BP policy falls between the profits of the two benchmark models. In general, the optimal BP policy cannot achieve the profit that can be gained with full commitment because of the uncertainty in the time of demand drop, and the fact that a BP policy cannot be contingent on the event of demand drop (since such event is unverifiable and non-contractible).

Debo et al. (2008) consider a *posterior price-matching policy*, a marketing policy offered by a seller to match the lower prices if the seller marks down within a specified time. In their model, the market consists of high-end (valuation = V_H) and low-end (valuation = V_L; $V_L < V_H$) consumers. They assume that the number of low-end consumers in the market is infinite, and that there is a large volume of potential high-end consumers, such that an individual consumer has a negligible effect on demand. The total volume of high-end consumers, denoted by λ, is unknown in advance, but can be characterized by a known distribution F, with a mean μ and a standard deviation σ. Information about the actual value of λ is gained via sales observations during the first period. In the second period, the high-end customer's valuations decline from V_H to V_h (where $V_L \leq V_h \leq V_H$). In contrast, the low-end consumer's valuations remain constant over the two periods. Among the high-end consumers, a fraction ϕ is strategic, whereas the rest are myopic. Strategic customers always request a refund, whereas only a fraction (γ) of the myopic customers do so. The seller determines whether or not to offer a posterior price matching (denoted by a binary variable υ), sets the first-period price (p_1), and invests in inventory (Q). These decisions are made *before* the market volume is realized. The unit acquisition cost, c, satisfies the condition $V_L < c < V_H$.

Debo et al. use the following dynamic procedure to evaluate the outcome of the two-period interaction between the seller and customers. Considering the second period, the seller is equipped with the information (υ, p_1, Q, q_s, s); the first three values are the seller's actions in the first period, whereas the latter values are observed during period 1. Specifically, q_s is the seller's belief about the customers' purchasing probabilities q, and s is the realized amount of sales during the first period. The seller's best choice for the second period's price is given by

$$p_2^o \in \arg\max_{p_2} R_2\left(p_2; \upsilon, p_1, Q, q_s, s\right) \tag{12.8}$$

where R_2 is the seller's second-period profit. Going back to the first period, in which customers need to determine their purchasing parameter q, they do so by weighing the expected utilities gained from a purchase in each period (the functions u_1 and u_2), as follows:

$$q^o \in \arg\max_q \left\{(1-q) \cdot u_1\left(\upsilon, p_1, Q_c, q_c, p_2^o\right) + q \cdot u_1\left(\upsilon, p_1, Q_c, q_c, p_2^o\right)\right\}$$

where Q_c is the seller's level of inventory that the customers rationally expect. Getting one step back to the seller's initial decision, the authors consider a two-level optimization process. First, for any given choice of p_1, the seller determines the optimal quantity of inventory through

$$Q^o(v,p_1) \in \arg\max_Q \{\pi(Q;v,p_1,q_s,p_2^o)\}$$

Note that the q_s represents the seller's belief about the customers' purchasing policy parameter q. The function π represents the seller's two-period profit with p_2^o satisfying (12.8). Finally, the seller's first-period price is determined via

$$p_1^o(v) \in \arg\max_{p_1} \{\pi(Q^o(v,p_1);v,p_1,q^o,p_2^o)\}$$

Obviously, to establish a rational expectation equilibrium, we need to find a solution to the above system, in which $q_s = q_c = q^o$ and $Q_c = Q^o$.

We present below a part of the solution to the models, focusing on the second-period pricing and the customers' choices. This will be sufficient for the reader to develop a sense of the fundamental difference between the cases with and without posterior price matching. Of course, the interested reader is referred to the paper for complete details.

Consider first the model without posterior price matching. Here, it can be shown that the price p_2 can be restricted to the two values V_h and V_L (either sell exclusively to strategic customers, or mark down further and clear the inventory). To compute the function R_2, consider two cases: (i) if $p_2 = V_L$, all remaining $Q - s$ units will be purchased; (ii) if $p_2 = V_h$, then only strategic customers will purchase. In this case, the seller needs to infer the size of the market from the sales volume s (note that only the case $s < Q$ is of interest, since if there is no inventory left, the second price has no meaning). In this case, the authors argue that the size of the high-end market is given by $s/(1 - \phi q_s)$, and hence the number of high-end strategic customers that will purchase in period 2 is estimated by $q_s \phi s/(1 - \phi q_s)$. To summarize, we get

$$R_2 = \begin{cases} (Q-s) \cdot V_L & \text{if } p_2 = V_L \\ \min\{Q-s, q_s\phi s/(1-\phi q_s)\} \cdot V_h & \text{if } p_2 = V_h \end{cases}$$

As a consequence (see Proposition 1 in the paper), the seller's second-period price can be shown to satisfy

$$p_2^o = \begin{cases} V_L & \text{if } s/(1-\phi q_s) < \alpha(q_s)Q \\ V_h & \text{if } \alpha(q_s)Q \leq s/(1-\phi q_s) \leq Q/(1-\phi q_s) \\ \text{n/a} & \text{if } s = Q \end{cases}$$

where $\alpha(q) \doteq V_L/(V_L + q\phi(V_h - V_L))$. Let us now consider the strategic customers' decisions. If the customer purchases immediately (i.e., in period 1), he gains a surplus of $(V_H - p_1)$. However, a unit needs to be available. Clearly, if the total demand is given by a quantity $\lambda \leq Q_c/(1 - \phi q_c)$, a focal customer will be allocated a unit upon purchase. If, however, the latter inequality is reversed, the Q_c units will need to be allocated among the $(1 - \phi q_c) \lambda$ customers who decide to purchase immediately. Thus,

$$u_1 = \left[F\left(\frac{Q_c}{1 - \phi q_c} \right) + \int_{Q_c/(1 - \phi q_c)}^{\infty} \frac{Q_c}{(1 - \phi q_c) \lambda} f(\lambda) d\lambda \right] (V_H - p_1)$$

If a focal customer decides to postpone the purchase to the second period, then he expects the price p_2 to be either V_h (with probability $1 - F(\alpha(q_c) Q_c)$), or V_L with the complementary probability. Thus, we get

$$u_2 = F(\alpha(q_c) Q_c) \cdot (V_h - V_L)$$

Let us consider now the case in which a posterior price-matching policy is offered. Here, it is also useful to consider the values V_L or V_h for p_2. However, the seller may want to consider charging $p_2 > \max\{p_1, V_h\}$. The rational behind the last price possibility is as follows: if a price $p_2 > V_h$ is expected, then the no strategic customer is expected to wait for period 2. Then, setting the price below p_1 is ineffective since it will result in myopic high-end customers asking for refund. When the seller perception about the delay probability (i.e., q_s) is sufficiently small, the best pricing in period 2 is to either clear leftover inventory ($p_2 = V_L$) or price above $\max\{p_1, V_L\}$. It is only when q_s passes a certain threshold that it is worthwhile to consider the price $p_2 = V_h$; see Proposition 5 in the paper. Interestingly, when it comes to purchasing behavior of customers, the authors state (Lemma 4): The unique purchasing equilibrium is to buy immediately; i.e., $q^o = 0$. It is easy to see the reasoning behind this result. For a focal strategic customer, the posterior price-matching policy enables to obtain refund if prices decline. Furthermore, the likelihood of obtaining a unit can only decline from period 1 to period 2. As a consequence of this observation, it is easy to verify that the optimal first-period price is $p_1^o = V_H$. As can be seen, the seller's first-period price and the customers' waiting strategy are both independent of ϕ – the fraction of strategic customers. The fraction ϕ influences the salvage value of the leftover inventory in a monotonic way. The largest is ϕ, the larger are the refunds in case of inventory clearance. Consequently, the authors show that the seller's equilibrium inventory level Q^o and his optimal expected profit are both monotonically decreasing in ϕ; see Proposition 8 in the paper.

Based on the above analytical findings and further numerical analyses, the authors conclude that price-matching policies eliminate strategic consumers' waiting incentive and thus allows the seller to increase the price in the regular selling season. When the market consists of a sufficiently large fraction of strategic consumers with declining valuations (over time), the matching policy can be very effective. In contrast, price-matching policies can be detrimental when there are only a few strategic consumers in the market, or if the strategic consumers' valuations do not decline much during the sales horizon. Finally, they find that the ability to credibly commit to a fixed-price path is not very valuable when the seller can implement price matching.

12.6 Limiting Inventory Information

Recently, Yin et al. (2008) have proposed a game-theoretic model of a retailer who sells a limited inventory of a product over a finite selling season, using one of the two inventory display formats: Display All (DA) and Display One (DO). Under the DA format, the retailer displays all available units so that each arriving customer has perfect information about the actual inventory level. Under the DO format, the retailer displays only one unit at a time so that each customer knows about product availability but not the actual inventory level. Clearly, display formats can be used as a tool to influence customers' perceptions about the risk of stockouts if they decide to wait. Therefore, by optimally selecting the display format, a retailer could discourage high-valuation customers from waiting to the clearance sales. Focusing on price-commitment strategies, Yin et al. address the following questions: When considering the influence of the display formats on the level of inventory information conveyed to customers, which one of the two formats is better for the retailer? Furthermore, can a move from one display format to another be effective in mitigating the adverse impact of strategic consumer behavior? They find support to the hypothesis that the DO format could potentially create an increased perception of scarcity among customers, and hence it is better than the DA format. However, while potentially beneficial, the move from a DA to a DO format is very far from eliminating the adverse impact of strategic consumer behavior. Since this paper is surveyed in great detail on a separate chapter in this book, we omit the technical details.

References

Arbatskaya M, Hviid M, Shaffer G (2004) On the incidence and variety of low price guarantees. Journal of Law and Economics XLVII:307–332

Aviv Y, Pazgal A (2005) A partially observed Markov decision process for dynamic pricing. Management Science 51(9):1400–1416

Aviv Y, Pazgal A (2008) Optimal pricing of seasonal products in the presence of forward-looking consumers. Manufacturing & Service Operations Management 10(3):339–359

Bell DE, Starr D (1994) Filene's basement. Harvard Business School Case 9-594-018

Besanko D, Winston WL (1990) Optimal price skimming by a monopolist facing rational consumers. Management Science 36:555–567

Butz D (1990) Durable goods monopoly and best-price provisions. Amer Econ Rev 80(5):659–683

Cachon GP, Swinney R (2009) Purchasing, pricing, and quick response in the presence of strategic consumers. Management Science 55(3): 497–511

Coase RH (1972) Durability and monopoly. J Law Econom 15:143–149

Debo L, Lai G, Sycara K (2009) Buy now and match later: The impact of posterior price matching on profit with strategic consumers. Manufacturing & Service Operations Management, Published online in *Articles in Advance*, February 10, 2009 DOI: 10.1287/msom.1080.0248

Elmaghraby W, Gulcu A, Keskinocak P (2008) Designing optimal pre-announced markdowns in the presence of rational customers with multi-unit demands. Manufacturing and Service Operations Management 10(1): 126–148

Hess J, Gerstner E (1991) Price matching policies: An empirical case. Managerial Decision Economics 12:305–315

Levin Y, McGill J, Nediak M (2007) Price guarantees in dynamic pricing and revenue management. Operations Research 55(1):75–97

Liu Q, van Ryzin G (2008) Strategic capacity rationing to induce early purchases. Management Science 54(6):1115–1131

Mantrala MK, Rao S (2001) A decision-support system that helps retailers decide order quantities and markdowns for fashion goods. Interfaces 31(3 part 2):S146–S165

Moorthy S, Winter R (2006) Price-matching guarantees. RAND Journal of Economics 37(2): 449–465.

Ovchinnikov A, Milner JM (2005) Strategic response to wait-or-buy: Revenue management through last minute deals in the presence of customer leaning. University of Toronto. Working paper

Png IP (1991) Most-favored-customer protection vs price discrimination over time. Journal of Political Economy 99:1011–1028

Srivastava J, Lurie N (2001) A consumer perspective on price-matching refund policies: Effect on price perceptions and search behaviour. J Consumer Res 28(2):296–307

Su X (2007) Inter-temporal pricing with strategic customer behavior. Management Science 53(5):726–741

Su X, Zhang F (2008) Strategic customer behavior, commitment and supply chain performance. Management Science 54(10): 1759–1773

Su X, Zhang F (2009) On the value of commitment and availability guarantees when selling to strategic consumers. Management Science 55(5): 713–726

Xu Z (2008) Optimal best-price policy. Working paper

Yin R, Aviv Y, Pazgal A, Tang CS (2008) Optimal markdown pricing: Implications of inventory display formats in the presence of strategic customers. Management Science.

Chapter 13
Mitigating the Adverse Impact of Strategic Waiting in Dynamic Pricing Settings: A Study of Two Sales Mechanisms

Yossi Aviv, Christopher S. Tang, and Rui Yin

Abstract As post-season clearance sales become more prevalent, more customers postpone their purchases and wait for the clearance price. This form of strategic waiting can reduce retailers' revenue. As a way to mitigate the negative effect of strategic waiting, we analyze two sales mechanisms in this chapter. The first sales mechanism deals with the way inventory information is conveyed to customers. Specifically, we consider two types of inventory display formats under which the retailer can either display all (DA) available units to the customers or display one (DO) unit at a time so that customers have perfect (imperfect) information about the actual inventory level under the DA (DO) display format. The second sales mechanism involves an additional purchasing option that allows each customer to make a "non-withdrawable reservation." Specifically, if a customer reserves an item during the season and the reserved item remains unsold at the end of the season, then this customer is obligated to purchase the reserved item at the clearance price. In this chapter, we analyze the implications of these two sales mechanisms on the customers' strategic purchasing behavior, the retailer's optimal pricing and ordering decisions, and the retailer's expected profit.

13.1 Introduction

Many retailers use post-season clearance sales as a reactive response to dispose of unsold items at the end of a selling season. However, some retailers proactively pre-announce their price-markdown schedules at the beginning of the selling season.

Yossi Aviv
Olin Business School, Washington University in St. Louis, St. Louis, MO, USA
e-mail: aviv@wustl.edu

Christopher S. Tang
Anderson School of Management, University of California, Los Angeles, CA, USA
e-mail: ctang@anderson.ucla.edu

Rui Yin
W. P. Carey School of Business, Arizona State University, Tempe, AZ, USA
e-mail: rui.yin@asu.edu

S. Netessine, C.S. Tang (eds.), *Consumer-Driven Demand and Operations Management Models*, International Series in Operations Research & Management Science 131, DOI 10.1007/978-0-387-98026-3_13, © Springer Science+Business Media, LLC 2009

A well-known example of pre-announced markdown pricing strategy has been adopted by Filene's Basement since 1908. At the Filene's Basement Boston store, most unsold items after 2, 4, and 6 weeks will be sold at 25%, 50%, and 75% off the regular price, respectively. After 2 months, Filene's Basement donates all unsold items to charity; see Bell and Starr (1994) for more details. Lands' End Overstocks uses a similar pre-announced markdown pricing strategy to sell their leftover inventory via its "On the Counter" Web site. Other retailers such as Dress4less and Tuesday Morning adopt similar pre-announced markdown pricing strategies.

Pre-announced markdown pricing strategy is intended to segment customers with different valuations so that high (low) valuation customers will purchase the product at the regular (clearance) price; see Pashigian and Bowen (1991) and Smith and Achabal (1998) for comprehensive discussions. However, one of the drawbacks of pre-announced pricing schemes is that they cannot segment customers completely because they often lead to *strategic waiting*: a phenomenon in which some high-valuation customers postpone their purchases by waiting for the clearance price, even when there is a risk of not getting the product due to stockout at the end of the selling season (c.f., Phillips, 2005 and Fisher, 2006). Fisher (2006) commented that 26% of fashion goods are sold at markdown prices, and McWilliams (2004) lamented that approximately 20% of Best Buy's customers wait for markdowns.

In recent years, academic research on strategic customer purchasing behavior has gained considerable attention; e.g., Aviv and Pazgal (2008), Cachon and Swinney (2007), Elmaghraby et al. (2008), Jerath et al. (2007), Levin et al. (2006), Liu and van Ryzin (2008), Ovchinnikov and Milner (2005), Su (2007), and Yin and Tang (2006). Evidently, the existing literature varies substantially in terms of underlying assumptions, modeling approaches, and research objectives. Therefore, instead of providing a long and tedious description of these papers, we refer the reader to these papers for details. Nevertheless, when useful, we shall refer to some of these papers when we introduce certain features of our model throughout this chapter.

As strategic waiting reduces retailer's revenue, some researchers have analyzed ways to reduce this strategic waiting behavior. Besides corporate level strategy that calls for no markdown pricing (c.f., Aviv and Pazgal, 2008, Cachon and Swinney, 2007, and Su and Zhang, 2009), Liu and van Ryzin (2008) examine the use of limited supply as an operational strategy to entice high-valuation customers to purchase the product at the regular price instead of waiting for the clearance price.

In this chapter, we analyze two types of sales mechanisms that are intended to reduce the strategic waiting behavior. In the first mechanism, the retailer uses the *inventory display format* as a tool to influence customers' perceptions about the risk of stockouts if they decide to wait. Specifically, we consider two types of inventory display formats that are commonly seen in retailing. The first is called the *Display All* (DA) format under which the retailer displays all available units so that customers have *perfect* information about the actual inventory level. For example, since 2005, Expedia.com provides their customers with perfect information about the exact number of plane tickets available at a particular price for a particular flight. Similarly, Filene's Basement, Benetton, and Seven-Eleven adopt the DA format. The second display format is called the *Display One* (DO) format. Here, the retailer displays only one item at a time so that customers have *imperfect* information about the actual inventory level. For example, Lands' End Overstocks Web site provides each arriving customer information about the availability but not the actual inventory level of each product.

In the second mechanism, the retailer uses the number of purchasing options as a tool to increase competition among customers. We consider two regimes. The first regime is essentially the traditional sales format under which each customer has two purchasing options upon arrival: either "buy now" at the regular price or "wait" and attempt to purchase at the discount price at the end of the season. We call this regime the "No Reservation" (NR) regime. Our second regime is called the "With Reservation" (WR) regime under which each customer has an additional option to place a (non-withdrawable) reservation during the season. If he reserves an item, then he is obligated to purchase the item at the reduced price when the reserved item remains unsold at the end of the season.[1] As some customers may reserve some items, the likelihood for other customers to obtain the product at the clearance price if they decide to wait is reduced. As such, the WR regime could pressure more customers to purchase the product at the regular price.

In this chapter, we analyze the implications of these two sales mechanisms on the customers' strategic purchasing behavior, the retailer's optimal pricing and ordering decisions, and the retailer's expected profit. Hence, the primary contribution of this chapter is the comparison of the two display formats (DA vs. DO) and two operating regimes (NR vs. WR) in the presence of strategic consumers. The remainder of the chapter is organized as follows. In Section 13.2, we describe some model preliminaries. The two display formats and the two operating regimes are analyzed in Sections 13.3 and 13.4, respectively. We conclude the chapter in Section 13.5.

13.2 Model Preliminaries

Consider a retailer who orders Q units at a unit cost c, to be sold over a selling season $[0, T]$. Assume that the retailer can only place a single order prior to the start of the season, and that the order will be received and become available for sale at time 0. We consider the situation in which the retailer pre-announces two prices at

---

[1] The WR regime has been examined in two different settings. First, Biyalogorsky and Gerstner (2004) introduced the concept of "contingent pricing" in which a buyer has an option to "reserve" a product at a low price that will obligate him to buy the product if the seller is unable to sell the product at a high price during a specified period. They showed that the contingent pricing policy enables the seller to reduce the expected loss from price risks, and the contingent pricing policy benefits the buyers and the seller. Second, Gallego et al. (2008) and Phillips (2005) described the concept of "callable products" in the context of airline tickets. Essentially, a callable product is an item sold to a self-selected buyer who willingly grants the seller the option to 'call' the item (demand its return) at a pre-specified recall price. They developed conditions under which the seller can obtain a higher expected profit by offering callable airline tickets. The "callable" concept is akin to the reservation option under the WR regime in the sense that the seller reserves the right to 'call' a product and sell it to a different buyer at a higher price after the product has been reserved or sold under the "callable" agreement.

time 0: the *premium* price p_h (i.e., the selling price throughout the entire season), and the post-season clearance price p_l. Clearly, $p_h \geq p_l$. All units not sold at either prices can be salvaged at s per unit. For each sales mechanism, the objective of the retailer is to determine the optimal price path (p_h^*, p_l^*) and the optimal order quantity Q^* so as to maximize his expected profit.

Customers arrive at the store according to a Poisson process with rate λ. Upon arrival, each customer must take her own valuation as well as the announced price path into consideration when making her purchase decision. To capture market heterogeneity, customers are classified into two classes according to their valuations. Specifically, all customers that belong to class-0 have valuation of v_0 and all customers that belong to class-1 have valuation of v_1, where $v_0 < v_1$. We assume that the arrival process can be described as a combination of two independent Poisson processes associated with class-0 and class-1 customers. Specifically, we let α_0 be the portion of class-0 customers in the market, and $\alpha_1 = 1 - \alpha_0$ be the complementary portion of class-1 customers. Throughout the chapter, we assume the set of parameters $\{\alpha_0, \alpha_1, v_0, v_1, \lambda, T, c, s\}$ is a common knowledge. Furthermore, for $i = 0, 1$ and $t \in [0, T]$, let $B_i(t)$ and $A_i(t)$ be the number of class-i customers to arrive "before" and "after" time t so that $B_i(t)$ and $A_i(t)$ are independent Poisson random variables with parameters $\alpha_i \lambda t$ and $\alpha_i \lambda (T - t)$, respectively.

To ensure some potential sales at the premium price and to enable the retailer to facilitate effective price discrimination, it suffices to consider the case when the premium price p_h satisfies the inequality: $v_0 \leq p_h \leq v_1$. Because $p_l \leq p_h$, we need to consider two settings: (i) $v_0 < p_l \leq p_h \leq v_1$ and (ii) $p_l \leq v_0 \leq p_h \leq v_1$. The first case corresponds to a setting in which the retailer posts prices that exclude class-0 customers. Such strategy can be desirable especially when the market consists primarily of high-valuation customers or when v_1 is significantly larger than v_0. Obviously, if such exclusive-sales strategy is adopted, it is optimal for the retailer to set $p_l = p_h = v_1$ (i.e., no markdown). This way, class-1 customers will purchase the product at v_1, since they have no incentive to wait for the clearance price. Hence, regardless of the inventory display format or operating regime, the retailer's expected profit can be expressed similar to that in the "newsvendor" problem. We denote the retailer's expected profit associated with the first case as π^1 throughout this chapter. The second case (i.e., when $p_l \leq v_0 \leq p_h \leq v_1$) reflects a setting in which the retailer chooses to target both customer classes. This case, which is considerably harder to analyze, is treated extensively in the remainder of this chapter.

13.3 Two Inventory Display Formats

13.3.1 The "Display All" (DA) Format

In this section, we consider the case in which the retailer adopts the "Display All" (DA) format, so that each arriving customer has perfect information about the actual inventory level. We begin by studying the customers' subgame for any given price path (p_h, p_l), and then proceed to analyzing the retailer's problem.

13.3.1.1 Strategic Purchasing Under the Display All Format

Consider a given order quantity Q and a pre-announced price path (p_h, p_l) that satisfies $p_l \leq v_0 \leq p_h \leq v_1$. Because $v_0 \leq p_h$, all class-0 customers will wait for the clearance price p_l. For class-1, consider a customer who arrives at time t and observes k units available for sale. Associated with the state (k, t), let $H(k, t)$ be the perceived fill rate that represents the likelihood of getting the product at the post-season clearance price p_l if he decides to wait and returns to the store at the end of the season.[2] Hence, this customer will buy immediately at p_h if $H(k, t) \leq (v_1 - p_h)/(v_1 - p_l)$; otherwise, he will wait for the clearance price p_l.[3]

As customers may follow any arbitrary purchasing policy in general, the assessment of the fill rate by an individual customer is complex because it depends on many factors: the inventory level, the customer's arrival time, and the purchasing behavior of all other customers. To determine the customer's rational purchasing behavior, we first propose a purchasing rule and then we show that all customers will follow this purchasing rule in equilibrium. Let us begin by considering the following DA *threshold purchasing rule* that is based on a set of thresholds $\{t^*(k)\}$ such that for any class-1 customer who arrives at time t and observes k units available, he should (a) "buy now" at p_h if $t \leq t^*(k)$; and (b) "wait" if $t > t^*(k)$, where the threshold $t^*(k) = t(k)$ if $0 \leq t(k) \leq T$, $t^*(k) = 0$ if $t(k) < 0$ and $t^*(k) = T$ if $t(k) > T$, and $t(k)$ satisfies

$$H(k, t(k)) = \frac{v_1 - p_h}{v_1 - p_l}, \tag{13.1}$$

and $t(Q) < t(Q-1) < \cdots < t(1)$.

In general, the probability $H(k, t)$ associated with the DA threshold purchasing rule is a complex function. However, the probability $H(k, t)$ can be established for the case when $t = t(k)$. When $t = t(k)$, the DA threshold purchasing rule implies that, in order for a class-1 customer to observe k items available at time $t(k)$, no class-1 customers who arrived before $t(k)$ would observe k and wait, and all class-1 customers who arrive after $t(k)$ and observe k will wait. Therefore, all k units available at time $t(k)$ will still be available for sale at the reduced price p_l at time T. This observation enables us to determine the probability $H(k, t(k))$. In preparation, consider the case when there are k unsold units at time T. In this case, a class-1 customer who arrives at time $t(k)$, observes the actual inventory level k and decides to return to the store at time T, will compete with two groups of returning customers:

---

[2] The term $H(k, t)$ also captures the possibility of stockout so that no items will be available at the end of the season.

[3] For ease of exposition, we assume that all customers who decide to wait will return at the end of the season. Yin et al. (2008) analyze the case when the return rate is random.

$A_0(0)$ (i.e., the total number of class-0 customers who will return to the store at time T) and $A_1(t(k))$ (i.e., the number of class-1 customers who will return to the store at time T). Recall from above that $A_0(0)$ is a Poisson random variable with parameter $\alpha_0 \lambda T = (1 - \alpha_1)\lambda T$, and $A_1(t(k))$ is a Poisson random variable with parameter $\alpha_1 \lambda (T - t(k))$. Hence, we can conclude that $A_1(t(k)) + A_0(0)$ is a Poisson random variable with parameter $\alpha_1 \lambda (T - t(k)) + \alpha_0 \lambda T$.

Given $A_1(t(k)) + A_0(0)$, a class-1 customer who arrives at time $t(k)$, observes k units are available and decides to return to the store at time T, will get the item at the reduced price p_l with probability 1 when $A_1(t(k)) + A_0(0) \leq k - 1$ and with probability $k/[A_1(t(k)) + A_0(0) + 1]$ when $A_1(t(k)) + A_0 \geq k$. Combine this observation with the fact that $A_1(t(k)) + A_0(0)$ is a Poisson random variable with parameter $\alpha_1 \lambda (T - t(k)) + \alpha_0 \lambda T$, we can express the probability $H(k, t(k))$ as

$$H(k, t(k)) = \sum_{n=0}^{k-1} \text{Prob}(A_1(t(k)) + A_0(0) = n) \cdot 1$$

$$+ \sum_{n=k}^{\infty} \text{Prob}(A_1(t(k)) + A_0(0) = n) \cdot \frac{k}{n+1}. \qquad (13.2)$$

By using the above expression for the probability $H(k, t(k))$ and by showing that no customers can obtain a higher expected surplus when deviating from the threshold purchasing rule, Yin et al. (2009) show that

Theorem 1. *Under the DA format, an "always-wait" strategy for class-0 customers and a threshold-type policy (based on threshold values $\{t^*(k)\}$) for class-1 customers form the unique Nash equilibrium in the subgame among customers.*

Proposition 1. *The sequence $\{t^*(k)\}$ is unique and non-increasing in k. Also, the values $t^*(k)$ are increasing in λ, v_1, and p_l, and decreasing in p_h.*

13.3.1.2 The Retailer's Problem Under the Display All Format

Anticipating customers' purchasing behavior in equilibrium as prescribed in Theorem 1, the retailer needs to identify an order quantity Q and a pair of optimal prices (p_h, p_l) that maximize his expected profit. We first consider the case when $p_l \leq v_0 \leq p_h \leq v_1$. As it turns out, the computation of the retailer's expected payoff for any given values of p_h, p_l, and Q is not straightforward. However, it can be computed in a recursive manner as follows. The reader is referred to Yin and Tang (2006) for details.

Under the DA threshold policy, the retailer's revenue depends on the purchasing decisions made by the class-1 customers who arrive during different time intervals $(t^*(j), t^*(i)]$ for $1 \leq i < j \leq Q + 1$, where $t^*(Q + 1) \equiv 0$. To determine the retailer's revenue obtained within this time interval $(t^*(j), t^*(i)]$ for $1 \leq i < j \leq Q + 1$, let

$$f(j, i) = \text{the retailer's expected revenue to be obtained from } t^*(j) \text{ to } T$$

$$\text{when } i \text{ units are available for sale at time } t^*(j).$$

For $1 \leq i \leq Q$, let $f(i,i)$ be the retailer's expected revenue to be obtained from $t^*(i)$ to T when i units are available for sale at time $t^*(i)$. Since Q units are available for sale at time $t^*(Q+1) \equiv 0$, the function $f(Q+1,Q)$ corresponds to the retailer's expected revenue over the entire season. Hence, for any given values of p_h, p_ℓ, and Q, the retailer's expected profit under the Display All format can be expressed as

$$\pi^{DA}(Q,p_h,p_\ell) = f(Q+1,Q) - cQ. \tag{13.3}$$

To determine the retailer's expected profit $\pi^{DA}(Q,p_h,p_\ell)$ for any given Q, p_h, and p_l, it suffices to focus on the function $f(j,i)$ for $1 \leq i \leq j \leq Q+1$.

In preparation, let $N_1(j,i)$ be the number of class-1 customers who arrives within the time window $(t^*(j),t^*(i)]$, where $i < j$. Consider the following three mutually exclusive and exhaustive events associated with $N_1(j,i)$. First, when $N_1(j,i) = 0$, all i units available at time $t^*(j)$ will still be available at time $t^*(i)$. In this case, $f(j,i) = f(i,i)$. Second, when $N_1(j,i) \geq i$, all i units available at time $t^*(j)$ will be sold out by time $t^*(i)$. Hence, $f(j,i) = ip_h$. Third, when $0 < N_1(j,i) = k < i$, out of those i units available at time $t^*(j)$, k of them will be sold at p_h and $(i-k)$ units will be remained by time $t^*(i)$. Therefore, $f(j,i) = kp_h + f(i,i-k)$. By considering the probability associated with each of these three events, it is easy to show that

Proposition 2. For $1 \leq i \leq j \leq Q+1$, the recursive function $f(j,i)$ satisfy[4]:

1. When $i < j$, $f(j,i) = f(i,i)\,\mathrm{Prob}(N_1(j,i) = 0) + ip_h\sum_{k=i}^{\infty}\mathrm{Prob}(N_1(j,i) = k) + \sum_{k=1}^{i-1}(kp_h + f(i,i-k))\,\mathrm{Prob}(N_1(j,i) = k)$.
2. When $i = j$, $f(i,i) = ip_l - (p_l - s)\sum_{k=0}^{i-1}(i-k)\,\mathrm{Prob}(A_1(t^*(i)) + A_0(0) = k)$.

Since $N_1(j,i)$ is a Poisson random variable with parameter $\alpha_1\lambda(t^*(i) - t^*(j))$, we can determine the function $f(j,i)$ and then utilize the recursive function $f(j,i)$ to compute the retailer's expected profit $\pi^{DA}(Q,p_h,p_\ell)$ given in (13.3) accordingly.

In order to identify the optimal strategy for the retailer under the regime $p_l \leq v_0 \leq p_h \leq v_1$, we conduct a hierarchical search procedure that can be described as follows. To reduce the search effort for determining the optimal premium price p_h^* and the optimal order quantity Q^*, we show that it is sufficient to limit the search over certain pre-specified ranges. We sequentially examine a plausible set of values of the initial inventory level Q. Given each level of Q, Yin et al. (2009) show that it is optimal to prescribe the clearance price $p_l^* = v_0$.

Finally, in order to identify the overall optimal expected profit associated with the DA format denoted hereafter by Π^{DA}, we need to compare the retailer's optimal expected profit associated with the second setting (denoted by $\pi^{DA} = \max_{(Q,p_h,p_l)}\{\pi^{DA}(Q,p_h,p_l)\}$) with the retailer's optimal expected profit associated with the first setting (denoted by π^1) when $p_h = p_l = v_1$. Thus,

$$\Pi^{DA} \doteq \max\left\{\pi^{DA},\pi^1\right\}.$$

---

[4] We define $\sum_{k=1}^{0} \equiv 0$.

13.3.2 The "Display One" (DO) Format

Under the "Display One" (DO) format, the retailer displays only a single unit on the sales floor and keeps the rest in a "storeroom." Upon a sale, the retailer immediately retrieves a new unit from the storeroom and places it on display.[5] For any given price path (p_h, p_l) and order quantity Q, we first analyze the customer's optimal purchasing behavior and then we study the retailer's problem.

13.3.2.1 Strategic Purchasing Under the Display One Format

For any given price path (p_h, p_l) that satisfies $p_l \leq v_0 \leq p_h \leq v_1$, it is optimal for all class-0 customers to wait for the clearance price p_l. Similar to the DA format, the purchasing decision of class-1 customers would depend on the perceived fill rates. However, it is difficult to determine the perceived fill rate because, under the DO format, each customer knows his arrival time t and product availability, but not the actual inventory level k. From the customer's perspective, the perceived fill rate for any customer who arrives at time t is $\tilde{H}(t)$. When the actual inventory level is not observable, we use the following approach to determine the perceived fill rate.[6] Specifically, we assume that the initial order quantity Q is a common knowledge,[7] and we define $\tilde{H}_Q(t)$ as the fill rate assessed by a customer who arrives at time t when the initial inventory level is Q. Clearly, the fill rate $\tilde{H}_Q(t)$ depends on the customers' purchasing behavior in equilibrium. Yin et al. (2009) show that all the class-1 customers will follow a single-threshold purchasing rule in equilibrium.

Theorem 2. *For any purchasing policy to be sustained in equilibrium, it must possess the following properties: all class-0 customers must wait for the clearance price* p_l; *and all class-1 customers must follow a threshold policy. Specifically, all class-1 customers arriving prior to a threshold* τ *should purchase the product at* p_h *and all class-1 customers arriving after the threshold* τ *should wait for the clearance price* p_l.

By considering the single-threshold purchasing policy τ as stated in Theorem 2, we can use the same approach as in the DA case to determine the fill rate function at the threshold point (i.e., $\tilde{H}_Q(\tau)$) as follows:

---

[5] A situation like this is common in an e-tailing environment. For example, Lands' End Overstocks' Web site provides each arriving customer about product availability but not the actual inventory level. In our analysis, we do not include the additional handling costs associated with the DO format. These cost may include the labor cost for a staff member to retrieve and display a new item every time a display item is sold. However, certain cost factors can be incorporated in the model. See Yin et al. (2009) for details.

[6] The reader is referred to Yin et al. (2009) for a detailed discussion of other approaches.

[7] Several online retailers (especially liquidator such as PacificGeek.com) provide consumers with their initial level of inventory for a particular item but do not update it during the selling season.

$$\tilde{H}_Q(\tau) = \frac{\sum_{m=0}^{Q-1} \text{Prob}(B_1(\tau) = n) \cdot K(Q-m,\tau)}{\sum_{m=0}^{Q-1} \text{Prob}(B_1(\tau) = n)}, \tag{13.4}$$

where

$$K(Q-m,\tau) = \sum_{n=0}^{Q-m-1} \text{Prob}(A_1(\tau) + A_0(0) = n)$$

$$+ \sum_{n=Q-m}^{\infty} \text{Prob}(A_1(\tau) + A_0(0) = n) \frac{Q-m}{n+1}.$$

Yin et al. (2009) show that the function $\tilde{H}_Q(\tau)$ is continuous in τ; hence, there always exists an equilibrium (say τ_Q) in the customers' subgame. Specifically, there are three potential equilibria: (i) $\tau_Q = T$, if $\tilde{H}_Q(T) < (v_1 - p_h)/(v_1 - p_l)$; (ii) $\tau_Q = 0$, if $\tilde{H}_Q(0) > (v_1 - p_h)/(v_1 - p_l)$; and (iii) any solution τ_Q (if exists) that satisfies the equation:

$$\tilde{H}_Q(\tau_Q) = (v_1 - p_h)/(v_1 - p_l). \tag{13.5}$$

The existence of multiple equilibria can be established via the following theorem.

Theorem 3. *The function $\tilde{H}_Q(\tau)$ satisfies the following properties:*

(i) $\tilde{H}_1(\tau)$ *is strictly increasing in τ.*
(ii) *For all $Q \geq 2$, the function $\tilde{H}_Q(\tau)$ is unimodal (quasi-convex) in τ. Moreover, the function $\tilde{H}_Q(\tau)$ attains its unique minimum in the range $(0,T]$, and it is strictly decreasing (increasing) for all values of τ below (above) that minimum point.*
(iii) *For every $Q \geq 1$ and $\tau \in [0,T]$, $\tilde{H}_Q(\tau)$ is decreasing in λ.*

From the perspective of game theory, Theorem 3 is key to the characterization of the equilibrium in the customers' subgame. It implies that, when $Q = 1$, there is always a unique equilibrium in the game, and that the threshold in equilibrium is increasing in the ratio $(v_1 - p_h)/(v_1 - p_l)$. However, when $Q > 1$, the unimodality implies that there could be as many as three equilibrium points in the game. Specifically, this happens if

$$\min_{\tau \in [0,T]} \tilde{H}_Q(\tau) < (v_1 - p_h)/(v_1 - p_l) < \min\{\tilde{H}_Q(0), \tilde{H}_Q(T)\},$$

in which case the three equilibrium points are $\tau = 0$ as well as the only two solutions to the equation $\tilde{H}_Q(\tau) = (v_1 - p_h)/(v_1 - p_l)$. The theorem also implies that if $(v_1 - p_h)/(v_1 - p_l) > \tilde{H}_Q(0)$, the game has a unique equilibrium strategy that has a positive threshold (i.e., $0 < \tau \leq T$). Clearly, for $(v_1 - p_h)/(v_1 - p_l) < \min_{\tau \in [0,T]} \tilde{H}_Q(\tau)$, the unique equilibrium is $\tau_Q = 0$ (i.e., everyone waits).

Given any game, a prediction of players' behavior which is not a Nash equilibrium cannot be commonly believed. Hence, when we study a game that has only one equilibrium, it must be the only rational prediction of players' behavior. However, when a game possesses multiple Nash equilibria, Schelling (1960) suggests that one should focus on an equilibrium that offers the highest possible payoffs to all players (i.e., a Pareto-dominant equilibrium that one can assume that all players will focus on).[8] Our next Proposition shows that the customers' subgame has a unique equilibrium, that is, Pareto dominant.

Proposition 3. *Suppose that $Q \geq 2$ and that $(v_1 - p_h)/(v_1 - p_l) < \tilde{H}_Q(0)$. Then, among all possible existing equilibrium strategies, $\tau_Q = 0$ strictly dominates the others (if any) in terms of the expected surplus gained by class-1 customers.*

Proposition 3 enables us to determine the single threshold τ_Q^* as follows.

$$
\tau_Q^* \doteq
\begin{cases}
0 & \text{if } \dfrac{v_1 - p_h}{v_1 - p_l} \leq \tilde{H}_Q(0) \\[2ex]
\begin{array}{l}\text{The unique positive} \\ \text{solution to Eq. (13.5)}\end{array} & \text{if } \tilde{H}_Q(0) < \dfrac{v_1 - p_h}{v_1 - p_l} \leq \max\left\{\tilde{H}_Q(0), \tilde{H}_Q(T)\right\} \\[2ex]
T & \text{if } \dfrac{v_1 - p_h}{v_1 - p_l} > \max\left\{\tilde{H}_Q(0), \tilde{H}_Q(T)\right\}
\end{cases}.
$$

Proposition 4. *Under the DO format, the threshold τ_Q^* as defined above is increasing in λ, v_1 and p_l, and decreasing in p_h.*

Notice that the single threshold τ_Q^* possesses the same properties as those thresholds $\{t^*(k)\}$ for the DA case as in Proposition 1. By comparing τ_Q^* for the DO case with those thresholds $\{t^*(k)\}$, $k = 1, \ldots, Q$ for the DA case, we have

Proposition 5. *For any given inventory $Q \geq 1$ and for any price path (p_h, p_l) that satisfies $p_l \leq v_0 \leq p_h \leq v_1$,*

$$
t^*(Q) \leq \tau_Q^* \leq t^*(1).
$$

Proposition 5 can be interpreted as follows. Consider a situation in which the retailer is currently using a DA format that yields $\tau^*(Q) > 0$. Now, suppose that the retailer contemplates moving to a DO format without changing the price path. One of the concerns the retailer may have is that the DO format might lead all class-1 customers to wait. In other words, is it conceivable that τ_Q^* will settle at the value 0? Proposition 5 implies that this cannot happen because $\tau_Q^* \geq t^*(Q) > 0$.

Proposition 5 also suggests that by moving from a DA to DO while keeping the price path unchanged, the *volatility* of the retailer's profit under the DO model will be lower than that of the DA model. This is because the DO model appears to be less sensitive to the arrival time of the first class-1 customer than the DA model. To see this, note that if no arrival occurs prior to $t^*(Q)$, then no purchase at premium price will be made during the entire horizon under the DA model. However, purchases could still occur under the DO model until $\tau_Q^* \geq t^*(Q)$. Nonetheless, if sales are made early enough, and so the inventory declines, purchases under the DA model may still continue after τ_Q^*: the time at which class-1 customers begin to wait under the DO model.

---

[8] For further discussion, see Section 1.2.4 in Fudenberg and Tirole (1991).

13.3.2.2 The Retailer's Problem Under the Display One Format

Anticipating the threshold policy τ_Q^* adopted by all class-1 customers in equilibrium, the retailer's expected profit can be expressed as

$$\pi^{DO}(Q, p_h, p_l) = -(c-s)Q + (p_l - s) \cdot (B_0(T) + B_1(T)) + (p_h - p_l) \cdot B_1(\tau_Q^*).$$

The retailer's expected profit $\pi^{DO}(Q, p_h, p_l)$ can be interpreted as follows. The first term represents the loss incurred if no unit was sold during the season. By noting that the minimum price for all customers who arrives before T is p_l, the second term represents the "minimum profit" level generated from these customers (each of which has a margin of $(p_l - s)$). Next, by observing that all customers who arrive before τ_Q^* will purchase the product at p_h, the third term corresponds to the "additional profit" generated from these customers (each of which has an additional margin of $(p_h - p_l)$). Given $\pi^{DO}(Q, p_h, p_l)$, we use the same approach as in the DA case to determine Π^{DO}; i.e., the optimal expected profit associated with the DO. To do so, we compare the retailer's optimal expected profit associated with the second setting (denoted by $\pi^{DO} = \max_{(Q, p_h, p_l)}\{\pi^{DO}(Q, p_h, p_l)\}$) with the retailer's optimal expected profit associated with the first setting (denoted by π^1) when $p_h = p_l = v_1$. Thus,

$$\Pi^{DO} \doteq \max\{\pi^{DO}, \pi^1\}.$$

13.3.3 Summary of Numerical Results

Given (p_h, p_l) and Q, we have shown that, under both DA and DO display formats, all customers will follow a threshold-type purchasing rule in equilibrium. Anticipating this purchasing behavior, we have determined the retailer's profit function so that we can search for the optimal price path and the optimal order quantity for the retailer. We now summarize our findings based on extensive numerical experiments reported in Yin et al. (2009).

Our first set of numerical experiments is based on the case when the level of inventory Q is exogenously given so that it is sufficient to focus on the retailer's expected revenue. We found that, by changing from the DA format to the DO format even without changing the price path, the retailer is always better off under the DO format! This observation confirms our intuition that the DO format reduces the strategic waiting behavior by increasing the perceived level of product scarcity. Interestingly, we observed that while the DO format could be beneficial, it is far away from totally eliminating the strategic waiting behavior. Although the DO format increases a retailer's revenue slightly, it could generate a high impact on the retailer's profit.

Despite the DO display format yields a slightly higher profit, we have identified the following conditions under which the DO format can yield a significantly higher profit than the DA format. First, when the market is dominated by the high-valuation customers or when the store traffic is sufficiently high, the retailer should focus on the high-valuation customers only by setting the discount price $p_l > v_0$. In this case, the retailer can obtain a much higher revenue under the DO format than that of the DA format. Second, when the store traffic is in the medium range, the DO format can also yield a significant higher profit than the DA format when there is a significant spread in valuations $(v_1 - v_0)$.

In our second set of numerical experiments, we consider the case when the retailer selects both inventory (or order quantity) and pricing so as to optimize his expected profit. As articulated by Liu and van Ryzin (2008), the inventory level can be used as a lever to influence the customers' perception of product scarcity as well. Based on our extensive numerical analysis, we have observed a complementarity property between the optimal inventory and the optimal premium price: the optimal premium price decreases (increases) as the optimal inventory increases (decreases) when the retailer changes from the DA display format to the DO display format. However, the optimal inventory and pricing choices can settle in equilibrium in a couple of ways. In some cases, the retailer's optimal action is to increase the order quantity, but maintain the same premium price or decrease it. In other cases, the retailer's optimal action is to increase the premium price, along with a decrease or no change in the order quantity.

13.4 Two Operating Regimes

This section deals with a different mechanism that involves an additional purchasing option. Besides the two traditional options (buy now or wait), the retailer allows a customer to place a (non-withdrawable) reservation during the season so that he is obligated to purchase at the item at the reduced price when the reserved item remains unsold at the end of the season. For ease of exposition, we focus on the case when the inventory $Q = 1$ so that the DA and DO display formats are essentially the same.

13.4.1 No Reservation Regime

Consider the base case that we call the No Reservation (NR) regime. Under the NR regime, each arriving customer can either purchase the product at p_h or wait (i.e., join a lottery at the end of the season). Hence, the NR regime is equivalent to the case when $Q = 1$ under the DA display format. As such, Theorem 1 continues to hold. Specifically, this theorem stipulates that all class-0 customers will wait and all class-1 customers will follow a single-threshold policy $t^*(1)$ in equilibrium. For notational convenience, we denote this threshold under the NR regime as t^{NR}, where $t^{NR} = t^*(1)$.

Anticipating the customer's purchasing behavior in equilibrium, we can compute the retailer's expected profit and the customers' expected surplus for any given p_h

and p_l as follows. By noting that all class-1 customers follow the t^{NR} threshold rule in equilibrium, the retailer's payoff depends on the number of customers arriving before and after the threshold t^{NR} (i.e., $B_1(t^{NR})$ and $A_1(t^{NR})$). Consider the retailer's payoff associated with the following three mutually exclusive and exhaustive events. Specifically, the retailer's payoff is the salvage value s when $B_1(t^{NR}) + A_1(t^{NR}) + B_0(0) + A_0(0) = 0$ (i.e., no customers arrive during the season), the reduced price p_l when $B_1(t^{NR}) = 0$ and $A_1(t^{NR}) + B_0(0) + A_0(0) > 0$ (i.e., no class-1 customers arrive before t^{NR} and at least one customer arrives during the season), and the regular price p_h when $B_1(t^{NR}) > 0$ (i.e., at least one class-1 customer arrives before t^{NR}). Coupling these observations with the facts that $B_1(t)$, $A_1(t)$, $B_0(t)$, $and A_0(t)$ are independent Poisson random variables with parameters $\alpha_1 \lambda t$, $\alpha_1 \lambda (T - t)$, $\alpha_0 \lambda t$, and $\alpha_0 \lambda (T - t)$, respectively, we can compute π_r^{NR}, the retailer's expected payoff under the NR regime in equilibrium, where

$$\pi_r^{NR}(p_h, p_l) = p_h - e^{-\alpha_1 \lambda t^{NR}}(p_h - p_l) - e^{-\lambda T}(p_l - s).$$

Also, in equilibrium, the customers earn a surplus of $(v_1 - p_h)$ when $B_1(t^{NR}) > 0$, and earn a surplus of $(v_1 - p_l)$ when $B_1(t^{NR}) = 0$ and $A_1(t^{NR}) + B_0(0) + A_0(0) > 0$. Hence, the customers' expected surplus can be expressed as

$$\pi_c^{NR}(p_h, p_l) = (v_1 - p_h)(1 - e^{-\lambda \alpha_1 t^{NR}}) + \left[v_1 \frac{\alpha_1 \lambda (T - t^{NR})}{\lambda (T - \alpha t^{NR})} \right.$$
$$\left. + v_0 \left(1 - \frac{\alpha_1 \lambda (T - t^{NR})}{\lambda (T - \alpha_1 t^{NR})} \right) - p_l \right] (e^{-\lambda \alpha_1 t^{NR}} - e^{-\lambda T}).$$

13.4.2 With Reservation Regime

Under the With Reservation (WR) regime, each arriving customer has three options: purchase the item (if available) at p_h, wait, or reserve the product for purchase at the clearance price p_l. If the buyer reserves the product and if it remains unsold at the end of the selling season, then he is obligated to purchase it at price p_l (because $v_1 - p_l > 0$, the customer willingly fulfills his obligation). If the buyer waits and the product has not been sold or reserved by the end of the selling season, then all interested buyers enter a lottery in which the winner purchases at the reduced price p_l.

To analyze the customer's optimal purchasing behavior in equilibrium, we first show that the reservation option dominates the option of waiting when the customers are rational. First, as class-0 customers will never purchase at p_h (because $v_0 < p_h$), it is optimal for class-0 customers to reserve the product (if available) instead of waiting. Next, consider a class-1 customer who arrives at time t and the item is available and has not been reserved. If he chooses not to purchase the item at p_h, he either waits (joins the lottery) or reserves the item. Consider two scenarios: $A_1(t) = 0$ and $A_1(t) > 0$. In scenario 1, when no class-1 customers arrive after t, he purchases the item at p_l for sure if he reserves the item and purchases the item with probability less than or equal to 1 if he joins the lottery.[9] In scenario 2, he will not get the item if he reserves the item at time t because any rational class-1 customer arriving after t will purchase the item at p_h. However, if he joins the lottery at time t, he will not get the item either because at least one of the rational class-1 customers arriving after t, say, the last class-1 customer who arrives before T, will reserve the item. By using this argument, one can prove that the reservation option dominates the option of waiting . Hence, it is sufficient to conduct our analysis of the WR regime based on two options: purchase the item at p_h or reserve the item at p_l.

Because all class-0 customers will reserve the product in equilibrium, we now define a purchasing rule for class-1 customers based on a single threshold and then show that this threshold policy is a unique Nash equilibrium for the customers' sub-game. Specifically, a class-1 customer arriving at time t is said to follow the "WR-threshold" policy if he (a) purchases the product at p_h whenever it has already been reserved; (b) purchases the product at p_h if $t < t^{WR}$; and (c) reserves the product if $t \geq t^{WR}$, where the threshold t^{WR} is defined as the instant at which a customer arriving at t^{WR} is indifferent between purchasing the item at p_h and reserving the item at p_l. To understand the underlying logic of the WR-threshold policy, consider a class-1 customer arriving at time t. First, if the product was reserved earlier by another customer, then this focal customer arriving at time t should purchase the product at price p_h and earn a surplus of $(v_1 - p_h)$; otherwise, he will earn a surplus of 0. Second, if the product is available for purchase or reservation at time t, then he earns a surplus of $(v_1 - p_h)$ if he immediately purchases the product at price p_h. If instead he reserves the product, then he obtains a surplus of $(v_1 - p_l)$ if no class-1 customer arrives after time t and he obtains a surplus of 0 if one or more class-1 customers arrive after time t (because the next arriving class-1 customer will in fact purchase the reserved product). Combining these observations with the fact that $e^{-\alpha_1 \lambda (T-t)}$ is the probability that no class-1 customer arrives after t, the threshold t^{WR} that equalizes these two surpluses satisfies

$$v_1 - p_h = e^{-\alpha_1 \lambda (T-t^{WR})}(v_1 - p_\ell). \tag{13.6}$$

By considering (13.6), the WR threshold t^{WR} satisfies the following:

$$t^{WR} = \begin{cases} T - \dfrac{1}{\alpha_1 \lambda} \ln \dfrac{v_1 - p_l}{v_1 - p_h} & \text{if } \alpha_1 \geq \hat{c} \\ 0 & \text{if } \alpha_1 < \hat{c}, \end{cases} \tag{13.7}$$

where

$$\hat{c} = \frac{1}{\lambda T} \ln \frac{v_1 - p_l}{v_1 - p_h}.$$

Notice that $0 \leq \hat{c} \leq 1$ when $(1 - e^{-\lambda T})/(\lambda T) \leq (v_1 - p_h)/(v_1 - p_l)$, which holds when T is reasonably large.

---

[9] The winning probability is less than or equal to 1 because there could be other customers who arrived before t and joined the lottery.

By showing that no customer can obtain a higher surplus by deviating from the threshold purchasing policy, Elmaghraby et al. (2009) establish the following result:

Proposition 6. *Given p_h and p_l, all class-0 customers reserve the product and all class-1 customers follow the WR-threshold policy in equilibrium. The threshold t^{WR} has the following properties: (a) t^{WR} is increasing in λ, v_1, p_l, and α_1 and is decreasing in p_h; and (b) there exists a critical value c with $\hat{c} < c < 1$ such that $t^{WR} < t^{NR}$ when $\alpha_1 < c$ and $t^{WR} \geq t^{NR}$ when $\alpha_1 \geq c$.*

Proposition 6 indicates that as α_1 increases, the purchasing window for class-1 will be longer. In addition, when $\alpha_1 \geq c$, the purchasing window under the WR regime is longer than of the NR regime. Therefore, the WR regime reduces the strategic waiting behavior under the NR regime.

Computing the retailer's expected payoff under the WR regime, denoted by π_r^{WR}, is slightly more difficult than that of the NR regime described in Section 13.4.1 due to one additional mutually exclusive and exhaustive event E, where $E \equiv \{B_1(t^{WR}) = 0, A_1(t^{WR}) = 1, \text{ and } A_0(0) \geq 0\}$. When the customers follow the WR threshold and event E occurs, the retailer will earn p_h if at least one customer of class-0 arrives before the one arriving customer of class-1. This is because, under the WR-threshold policy, the first arriving customer of class-0 will reserve and the one arriving customer of class-1 will purchase the item at p_h. Also, the retailer will earn p_l if no customers of class-0 arrive before the one arriving customer of class-1 because under the WR-threshold policy, the one arriving customer of class-1 will reserve the item and all customers of class-0 who arrive after the one arriving customer of class-1 will get nothing. Define u to be the conditional probability that no customers of class-0 arrive before the class-1 customer arrives given that E occurs. Because there is exactly one class-1 customer arriving between t^{WR} and T, the distribution of the arrival time t for this class-1 customer is uniformly distributed between t^{WR} and T. Combining this observation with the fact that the number of class-0 customers arriving before t is a Poisson random variable with parameter $(1 - \alpha_1)\lambda t$, it follows that the retailer's expected payoff for this event equals $p_h(1 - u) + p_l u$, where

$$u \equiv \int_{t^{WR}}^{T} \frac{e^{-\alpha_0 \lambda t}}{T - t^{WR}} dt = \int_{t^{WR}}^{T} \frac{e^{-(1-\alpha_1)\lambda t}}{T - t^{WR}} dt = \frac{e^{-(1-\alpha_1)\lambda t^{WR}} - e^{-(1-\alpha_1)\lambda T}}{(1 - \alpha_1)\lambda(T - t^{WR})}.$$

Combining the retailer's expected payoff for this event E along with the other three events presented in Section 13.4.1, we can use the same approach as before to show that the retailer's expected payoff π_r^{WR} and the customers' expected surplus π_c^{WR} satisfy

$$\pi_r^{WR} = p_h - (p_l - s)e^{-\lambda T} - (p_h - p_l)e^{-\alpha_1 \lambda T}(1 + u \cdot \alpha_1 \lambda(T - t^{WR})),$$

$$\pi_c^{WR} = (1 - e^{-\alpha_1 \lambda T} - u\alpha_1 \lambda(T - t^{WR})e^{-\alpha_1 \lambda T})(v_1 - p_h)$$
$$+ u\alpha_1 \lambda(T - t^{WR})e^{-\alpha_1 \lambda T}(v_1 - p_l) + (e^{-\alpha_1 \lambda T} - e^{-\lambda T})(v_0 - p_l).$$

13.4.3 Comparison of Payoffs

When $\alpha_0 = 0$ (i.e., when the market consists of only class-1 customers), Elmaghraby et al. (2009) show that, for any given values of p_h and p_ℓ, the retailer's expected payoff is higher under the WR regime, whereas the customers expected payoff is larger under the NR regime. With two classes of customers, they obtain the following result:

Proposition 7. *Suppose $\alpha_0 > 0$ and $\alpha_1 > 0$. Then there exists a critical value c' such that the retailer's expected payoff under the WR regime is greater than the expected payoff under the NR regime when $\alpha_1 \geq c'$: $\pi_r^{WR} \geq \pi_r^{NR}$ when $\alpha_1 \geq c'$. Conversely, there is a critical number c'' such that the customers' expected payoff is greater under the NR regime when $\alpha_1 \geq c''$: $\pi_c^{WR} \leq \pi_c^{NR}$ when $\alpha_1 \geq c''$.*

Proposition 7 asserts that the retailer obtains a higher expected payoff and the customers obtain a lower expected surplus under the WR regime when α_1 is sufficiently large. We speculate the opposite is true when α_1 is sufficiently small. For example, if most Filene's Basement's shoppers are bargain hunters with the low valuation (i.e., α_1 is sufficiently small), then Proposition 7 suggests that the NR regime is more profitable for the retailer, which is consistent with the actual practice at the Filene's Basement. Hence, when choosing between the NR regime and the WR regime, it is important for the retailer to gain a clear understanding about the distribution of customer valuation.

13.4.4 Summary of Numerical Results

Anticipating the customers' purchasing behavior in equilibrium under the two operating regimes, the retailer needs to determine the optimal prices p_h and p_l to maximize his expected profits $\pi_r^{NR}(p_h, p_l)$ and $\pi_r^{WR}(p_h, p_l)$. Because there are no closed-form expressions for the optimal prices, Elmaghraby et al. (2009) conduct a numerical study to compare the retailer's optimal expected profits and the customers' optimal expected surpluses under both regimes. Specifically, they consider the case when the arrival rate is price dependent: $\lambda(p_h, p_l) = \alpha_0 - ap_h + b(p_h - p_l)$. Essentially, this functional form captures the increase in store traffic as a result of the pre-announced pricing strategy because one can interpret the term $b(p_h - p_l)$ as representing the increase in arrival rate due to the pre-announced markdown price p_l, where b represents customers' sensitivity toward the markdown price. Their numerical result indicates that, when there is a single class of customers with valuation $v_1 \geq p_h$, the WR regime can lead to a win–win situation for the retailer and the customers when b is sufficiently small. Also, their result suggests that, when there are two classes of customers, both the market composition, i.e., (α_0, α_1), and the customer's price sensitivity, i.e., b, have major impacts on the retailer's optimal expected profit and the customers' optimal expected surplus. (See Elmaghraby et al. (2009) for details.)

13.5 Conclusions

In this chapter, we have considered two add-on sales mechanisms that are intended to reduce the strategic waiting behavior. The first sales mechanism deals with the way inventory information is conveyed to customers. Specifically, we have presented two types of inventory display formats under which the retailer can either display all (DA) available units to the customers or display one (DO) unit at a time. As such, customers have perfect (imperfect) information about the actual inventory level under the DA (DO) display format. We have analyzed customers' strategic purchasing behavior in equilibrium. Then, in anticipation of such behavior, we have determined the optimal ordering and pricing decisions for maximizing the retailer's expected profit. Based on an extensive numerical study, we have shown that, for any initial order quantity, the retailer's optimal regular price and expected profit are higher under the DO format. When the retailer can optimally set the initial order quantity, we have found that a change from DA to DO would never lead to a simultaneous decline in inventory and pricing and consequentially never lowers the retailer's expected profits. We have also characterized the conditions under which the DO format performs best relative to the DA format. The second mechanism deals with the case when a retailer allows customers to "reserve" an item at the clearance price during the selling season. If a customer reserves an item and the reserved item remains unsold at the end of the season, then this customer has the right to purchase the reserved item at the clearance price. When customers are strategic, we have shown that the customers will be worse off when the retailer offers the option to reserve an item. While not without its limitations, we hope the models presented in this chapter can serve as a building block for examining other issues arising from the strategic purchasing behavior.

References

Aviv Y, Pazgal A (2008) Optimal pricing of seasonal products in the presence of forward-looking consumers. Manufacturing & Service Operations Management 10(3):339–359

Bell DE, Starr D (1994) Filene's basement. Harvard Business School Case 9-594-018

Biyalogorsky E, Gerstner E (2004) Note: Contingent pricing to reduce price risks. Marketing Science 23(1):146–155

Cachon GP, Swinney R (2007) Purchasing, pricing, and quick response in the presence of strategic consumers. University of Pennsylvania, working paper

Elmaghraby W, Gulcu A, Keskinocak P (2008) Designing optimal pre-announced markdowns in the presence of rational customers with multi-unit demands. Manufacturing & Service Operations Management 10(4):126–148

Elmaghraby W, Lippman SA, Tang CS, Yin R (2009) Will more purchasing options benefit customers? Production and Operations Management. Forthcoming

Fisher ML (2006) Rocket science retailing. INFORMS Annual Meeting, Pittsburgh, Nov 5–8

Fudenberg D, Tirole J (1991) Game theory. MIT Press, Cambridge, MA

Gallego G, Kou SG, Phillips R (2008) Revenue management of callable products. Management Science 54(3):550–564

Jerath K, Netessine S, Veeraraghavan SK (2007) Last-minute selling and opaque selling. University of Pennsylvania, working paper

Levin Y, McGill J, Nediak M (2006) Optimal dynamic pricing of perishable items by a monopolist facing strategic consumers. Queen's University, Kingston, Ontario, Canada, working paper

Liu Q, van Ryzin G (2008) Strategic capacity rationing to induce early purchases. Management Science 54(6):1115–1131

McWilliams G (2004) Minding the store: Analyzing customers, Best Buy decides not all are welcome. Wall Street Journal. Nov 8, A1

Ovchinnikov A, Milner JM (2005) Strategic response to wait-or-buy: Revenue management through last minute deals in the presence of customer leaning. University of Toronto, working paper

Pashigian BP, Bowen B (1991) Why are products sold on sale? explanations of pricing regularities. Quarterly Journal of Economics, 106:1015–1038

Phillips RL (2005) Pricing and revenue optimization. Stanford University Press, Palo Alto, USA

Schelling TC (1960) The strategy of conflict. Harvard University Press, Cambridge, MA

Smith SA, Achabal DD (1998) Clearance Pricing and Inventory Policies for Retail Chains. Management Science 44(3): 285–300

Su X (2007) Inter-temporal pricing with strategic customer behavior. Management Science 53(5):726–741

Su X, Zhang F (2009) Strategic customer behavior, commitment and supply chain performance. Management Science. Forthcoming

Yin R, Tang CS (2006) The implications of customer purchasing behavior and in-store display formats. UCLA Anderson School of Management, unpublished manuscript

Yin R, Aviv Y, Pazgal A, Tang CS (2009) Optimal markdown pricing: implications of inventory display formats in the presence of strategic customers. Management Science. Forthcoming.

Chapter 14
The Impact of Strategic Consumer Behavior on the Value of Operational Flexibility

Gérard P. Cachon and Robert Swinney

Abstract Increasingly sophisticated consumers have learned to anticipate future price reductions and forego purchasing products until such markdowns occur. Such forward-looking or strategic behavior on the part of consumers can have a significant impact on retail margins by shifting a large number of sales from higher, "full" prices to lower, "clearance" prices. Some firms, however, have become adept at dealing with the strategic consumer problem by implementing various forms of operational flexibility (for example, investing in faster supply chains capable of rapidly responding to changing demand conditions). A firm famous for this strategy is the Spanish fashion retailer Zara. In this chapter, we explore the strategic consumer purchasing phenomenon, and in particular address how the Zara model of operational flexibility impacts consumer behavior (and, conversely, how consumer behavior impacts the value of operational flexibility). We examine in detail the consequences of *volume flexibility* – the ability of a firm to adjust production or procurement levels to meet stochastic demand – and demonstrate that this type of flexibility can be highly effective at reducing the extent of strategic behavior. Indeed, we show that in many cases, the value of volume flexibility is greater when consumers are strategic than when they are not. We also show that volume flexibility is always socially optimal (i.e., it increases the total welfare of the firm and consumers) and may also improve consumer welfare (i.e., it can be a Pareto improving strategy). We also discuss the impact of other types of operational flexibility – *design flexibility*, in which a product's design can be modified to suit changing consumer tastes, and *mix flexibility*, in which production capacity can be dynamically allocated among several similar product variants – and argue that these types of flexibility are also effective at mitigating strategic customer purchasing behavior.

Gérard P. Cachon
The Wharton School, University of Pennsylvania, Philadelphia, PA 19104, USA,
e-mail: cachon@wharton.upenn.edu

Robert Swinney
Graduate School of Business, Stanford University, Stanford, CA 94305-5015, USA,
e-mail: swinney@stanford.edu

S. Netessine, C.S. Tang (eds.), *Consumer-Driven Demand and Operations Management Models*, International Series in Operations Research & Management Science 131, DOI 10.1007/978-0-387-98026-3_14, © Springer Science+Business Media, LLC 2009

14.1 Introduction

Accustomed to rigid seasonality and trained by years of predictable sale patterns, consumers have come to expect frequent and significant price reductions in the retail sector. As a result, many retailers suffer from eroded margins generated by customers intentionally waiting for markdowns before purchasing (Hurlbut 2004). Consumers expect deep end-of-season clearance sales, and firms, anxious to clear space for newer products, often oblige them. There is, however, at least one firm that has achieved success at managing and even preventing strategic customer purchasing behavior: the Spanish fashion retailer Zara. There are two key components to their strategy. First, they produce in small batches with fast replenishment lead times to their stores. Second, their initial price for an item at the start of a selling season is not outrageously high. Consequently, they rarely need to markdown merchandise (because they do not stock too much inventory) and when they do offer a discount, it is not particularly deep (because their initial price is reasonable). These factors combine to train Zara's customers to avoid the "wait for the discount" strategy – if a customer sees an item that she likes, she should purchase it now either because it will be sold at the same price later on or it will not even be available. As a result, compared to its chief competitors, consumers are much more likely to purchase an item at the full price at Zara (Ghemawat and Nueno 2003).

To achieve its operational flexibility, Zara produces locally (e.g., Spain, Eastern Europe or North Africa). As a result, Zara's leadtimes are typically less than 5 weeks for new designs and 2 weeks for the replenishment of existing designs (Ghemawat and Nueno 2003). This contrasts with their competitors who can incur average design and production leadtimes of 9 months. But Zara's operational flexibility comes with a cost (from, for example, higher labor costs and expedited shipping). Combined with Zara's lower initial prices, one might naturally be concerned that the company enjoys smaller gross margins per unit. However, as illustrated by Figure 14.1, Zara makes up for this deficit with volume: it typically sells a much higher percentage of its inventory at its full price than other retailers, which can result in superior overall financial performance.

The goal of this chapter is to study the Zara model to better understand its success. We begin with a model of consumer behavior first developed by Su and Zhang (2008). As in their model, we consider a single retailer who sets an initial price and makes a production decision before the realization of stochastic consumer demand. Each consumer decides whether to purchase at the initial (i.e., full) price or to wait for the discount period. The discount period offers a better deal (i.e., a lower price), but there may not be any inventory left to purchase. Hence, the scarcity of product at the discount price may make a consumer purchase at the full price.

We depart from Su and Zhang (2008) by introducing operational flexibility. With operational flexibility the firm can make a second production decision after observing demand, a system that is often called quick response (see, e.g., Fisher and Raman 1996). Of course, this second production opportunity is more expensive. However, in the absence of strategic consumer behavior, this operational flexibility is well known to benefit firms by allowing them to better match their supply to their

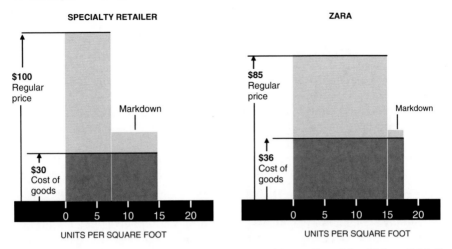

Fig. 14.1 Pricing patterns at Zara versus competing specialty retailers. Adapted from Grichnik et al. 2008.

demand. We want to assess the value of operational flexibility in the presence of strategic consumer behavior. In particular, relative to the value of matching supply with demand, does operational flexibility provide more or less value when consumers are strategic?

We find that operational flexibility is generally more valuable (but not always) when the retailer must sell to strategic consumers. Put another way, even though operational flexibility is known to increase profits considerably with non-strategic consumers (i.e., consumers that never wait for the discount no matter what prices are chosen) we show that it can be even more valuable when the firm must sell to strategic consumers, often substantially more valuable. Cachon and Swinney (2009) arrive at a similar conclusion, but with a significantly different model. Thus, here we provide further support for the conclusion that the presence of strategic consumers enhances the value of operational flexibility.

The remainder of this chapter is organized as follows. In Section 14.2 we describe our approach to modeling production flexibility, while in Section 14.3 we discuss modeling details of strategic customer purchasing. We then solve models of non-flexible and flexible supply chains with strategic customers in Section 14.4, and discuss the incremental value of flexibility in Section 14.5. Section 14.6 presents a discussion of complications and extensions to the basic setup, and Section 14.7 concludes the chapter with a discussion of the results.

14.2 Modeling Traditional and Flexible Production

We refer to our base model with non-flexible production as the *traditional replenishment* model. It is also known as a newsvendor model – a canonical model in operations management that is well suited to capture the supply – demand mismatch issues inherent in fashion retailing. This model consists of a single firm selling a single product with the following key features:

1. **Constant Selling Price During the Season:** The firm sells the product at a constant (full) price p throughout a short selling season.
2. **Demand Uncertainty:** The size of the market D (the number of consumers) is stochastic and initially unknown to the firm. The firm has prior beliefs that the market size follows distribution $F(\cdot)$.
3. **Inventory Production or Procurement:** Prior to learning the size of the market, the firm orders q units that will arrive, ready for sale, by the start of the selling season. Each unit in this order costs c, where $c < p$, and so the total purchase cost is cq.
4. **Supply – Demand Mismatches and End-of-Season Salvaging:** The firm sells the minimum of demand D and inventory q at the full price p, and all remaining inventory is salvaged at the markdown price $s < c$ at the end of the season.

We assume that a large salvage market is available at the end of the season, in which the firm may sell all remaining units at an exogenous price $s < c$ per unit. While such a market is commonly assumed in newsvendor models without further justification, in our model it may be useful to think of this market as representing a second consumer segment (beyond the initial D consumers), e.g., a large number of "bargain hunting" customers who possess very low valuations for the product. Cachon and Swinney (2009) also incorporate a bargain hunting segment into their model.

This traditional replenishment model mimics the production environment of the majority of Zara's competitors: long design and production leadtimes lead to inventory commitment far in advance of the selling season, when precise demand is still quite uncertain. As typically presented, the newsvendor model consists of an exogenous selling price p. However, we make this price endogenous – the firm sets the price p at the start of the selling season (after demand information is revealed but before any sales occur – see Figure 14.2). The newsvendor model with pricing is explored by, for example, Dada and Petruzzi (1999). The nature of the pricing decision in our context is discussed further in the next section.

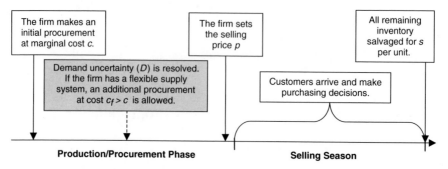

Fig. 14.2 The sequence of events.

In contrast to the traditional replenishment system, a *flexible replenishment* model represents the system employed by Zara: greatly reduced leadtimes resulting in some inventory decisions being made very near (or during) the selling season, when demand information is far more accurate. Typically, the model employed to analyze this sort of production flexibility is a *quick response* or *reactive capacity* model (see, e.g., Cachon and Terwiesch 2005). This model is identical to the traditional replenishment model described above, with one exception: an additional procurement opportunity is available after precise market size (D) is revealed to the firm. As with the firm's initial order, units in this second order arrive by the start of the selling season. Because this second order is placed much closer to the start of the selling season, each unit in this second order costs the firm c_f, where it is natural to assume that $c_f > c$ – it is cheaper to order units in advance of learning demand.[1] (The f subscript denotes the "flexible" replenishment model.) Furthermore, like the first order, there is no capacity constraint imposed on the quantity in this second order. The sequence of events in the two models is presented in Figure 14.2.

The quick response framework frequently assumes that demand uncertainty is completely eliminated by the time of the second procurement – a simplification, to be sure, but one that leads to clean analytical results. In reality, the firm may receive a series of forecast updates with each reducing (but not entirely eradicating) error in the forecasting process. For the sake of simplicity, we adopt the traditional assumption that uncertainty is completely resolved.[2]

14.3 Modeling Strategic Consumer Purchasing

To address the issue of strategic customer purchasing behavior, we modify the classic newsvendor and quick response settings by enriching the consumer demand model. Suppose that consumers are risk-neutral surplus maximizers and have homogeneous valuations for the product equal to v (constant over the entire season).[3] When customers arrive at the firm, they observe the selling price p and whether the product is currently in-stock. We consider two types of customers: myopic (or non-strategic) customers and forward-looking (or strategic) customers.

---

[1] We describe this model as if the second order is placed before the season starts but after some demand information is learned. In some cases, demand information is learned only at the start of the selling season and so the second order can only arrive at some point during the season. As long as initial season sales are highly informative, and the lead time to receive the second order is sufficiently short, our model can approximately represent that situation as well – the first order covers sales at the start of the season and the second order should arrive before inventory is depleted.

[2] We suspect that our results continue to hold even in a more complex setting with imperfect demand signals. In particular, even in that setting the optimal second-order quantity does not depend on the full price – it is a function of c, c_f, and s. Thus, our analysis would not require significant modification.

[3] We model risk-neutral consumers for simplicity. Risk-averse consumers behave similarly; see Liu and van Ryzin (2008).

Myopic consumers do not consider purchasing the product at the end of the season at the markdown price, s, possibly because they no longer value the product at the end of the season or because they do not anticipate the price reduction. Myopic consumers have zero reservation utility and hence purchase if their surplus is non-negative; in other words, myopic customers purchase at price p if the product is in-stock and if

$$v - p \geq 0. \tag{14.1}$$

Strategic customers, on the other hand, are forward-looking in the sense that they anticipate the opportunity to purchase the product at the sale price s.[4] (Implicit in this statement is the assumption that consumers are *capable* of obtaining a unit at the salvage price – i.e., excess inventory is cleared in a way that makes it available to the general population, as with end-of-season clearances at fashion retailers, rather than alternative methods of salvaging such as material recycling or industrial disposal.) Thus, these customers compare the surplus of an immediate purchase at the full price $(v - p)$ with the expected surplus of waiting for the sale. The value of waiting depends on the discount price, s, as well as the chance there will be inventory remaining to purchase at the discount price. Let ϕ be a consumer's expectation for the probability of being able to procure a unit at the clearance price (more on the nature of this expectation will be discussed momentarily). If consumers do not obtain the product at the sale price, they receive zero surplus. Expected surplus from waiting for the sale is thus $\phi(v - s)$. We assume that strategic customers purchase at the full price if they are indifferent between the two options; hence, strategic customers purchase at price p if the product is in-stock and

$$v - p \geq \phi(v - s). \tag{14.2}$$

Given these assumptions, with strategic consumers there are only two candidates for equilibrium purchasing behavior: either all consumers purchase early (at the higher price) or all purchase late (at the salvage price).[5] Because the salvage price is less than the production cost, it follows that an equilibrium with all consumers strategically waiting results in market failure – the firm does not produce at all. For the remainder of the chapter, we focus on the more interesting case in which positive production occurs, i.e., equilibria in which all strategic consumers attempt to purchase at the full price. This implies that (14.2) is satisfied in any relevant

---

[4] A wide variety of recent models address operational issues related to such forward-looking strategic consumers, including: intertemporal pricing with no capacity constraints in Besanko and Winston (1990), pricing policies with finite inventory in Aviv and Pazgal (2008), pricing policies for consumable goods with voluntary customer stockpiling in Su (2007), product display formats in Yin et al. (2007), and restaurant reservations in Alexandrov and Lariviere (2006), in addition to the previously cited papers.

[5] All consumers must have the same expectation, ϕ, value, v, and opportuntity to purchase early at the full price, p, or late at the discount price, s. Therefore either they all prefer to purchase early, $v - p \geq \phi(v - s)$, or they all prefer to wait. Here, we assume that a consumer indifferent between the two options chooses to purchase early. If the indifferent consumer chooses a mixed strategy, then the firm could shave its full price by an infinitesimal amount to make consumers strictly prefer purchasing early while not reducing revenue by a material amount.

equilibrium, and ϕ is the consumer belief of the probability of obtaining a unit at price s conditional on all other consumers purchasing at price p (i.e., $\phi(v-s)$ is the expected surplus resulting from a unilateral deviation from equilibrium by a single consumer).

Now we turn to the issue of how the ϕ expectation is set. Assuming arbitrary beliefs can lead to problems of consistency; consumers could expect ϕ to be the probability of obtaining a unit at the sale price but the firm may act in a way that leads to an entirely different probability of being able to purchase at the markdown price. While it may not always be desirable to rule out inconsistency on axiomatic grounds – inconsistent beliefs may be an entirely real phenomenon with important implications – such irregularities do not appear to be the norm in the sort of pre-dictable, seasonal industries (such as fashion apparel) that provide our prime moti-vation.

It is natural, then, to seek models of customer purchasing in which beliefs are consistent with reality: in other words, to specify that consumer *expectations* of firm behavior are *rational*. The idea of rational expectations – discussed in the context of financial markets by Muth (1961) – were first formally integrated in a game theoretic framework by Stokey (1981) and Bulow (1982) to explain the strategic consumer purchasing problem. In short, rational expectations imply that (a) consumers have expectations of future firm decisions, and (b) these expectations are rational and consistent with actual firm decisions. Such correct anticipation of firm actions may be thought of as the outcome of a series of repeated interactions in which consumers learn about firm policies, for instance, with regard to inventory availability (my size is never in-stock at the end of the season) or sale pricing patterns (this store never has deep discounts). Our analysis in this chapter – and a great deal of the literature on strategic consumer purchasing – makes use of the rational expectations paradigm.

We note here that while the term *rational expectations* is used to highlight the fact that consumers correctly anticipate firm actions and hence behave optimally given firm actions, this concept is inherent in the definition of a Nash equilibrium with full information. For example, in a two-player game a Nash equilibrium represents a pair of actions such that each player expects the other player to choose the equilibrium actions and in equilibrium it is optimal for each person to choose their equilibrium actions given their expectations. The same applies in our game – the firm chooses an optimal q given its belief regarding consumer actions and consumers choose optimal actions (buy now or later) given their expectations. The subtle difference has to do with what is assumed regarding what the players know. Suppose we were to define the game between the firm and consumers such that the firm chooses q and consumers choose whether to purchase at the full price or to wait for the dis-count. Let $G(q)$ be the probability that inventory is available for a consumer to purchase in the discount period, conditional that all other consumers purchase at the full price. Furthermore, assume consumers know the $G(q)$ function. A consumer's surplus from waiting to purchase at the discount price, assuming all other consumers purchase at the full price, is $G(q)(v-s)$. The consumer purchases at the full price if $v-p \geq G(q)(v-s)$. Note, to evaluate an equilibrium the consumer does not need to observe the actual q choice. Instead, the consumer infers q will be chosen because it is optimal for the firm given the consumers' equilibrium actions. In other words, consumers and the firm choose their actions simultaneously. In our model we merely replace $G(q)$ with ϕ, i.e., we assume consumers have an expectation for the probability inventory is available in the discount period without necessarily knowing the mapping between the firm's action, q, and that probability. To maintain consistency, we then require that in equilibrium $G(q) = \phi$. Therefore, the equilibrium in these two games is identical even if they make different assumptions regarding what consumers know. Put another way, the rational expectations terminology is technically unnecessary but we invoke this terminology for ease of exposition. (In addition, one may argue that it makes less stringent assumptions regarding consumer knowledge and analytical capabilities.)

Returning to our model, recall that rational expectations require ϕ is the *actual probability* that a strategic customer successfully obtains a unit if she waits for the sale. To calculate ϕ, we must provide some sort of *rationing rule* that specifies how inventory is allocated should demand exceed supply at the salvage price. We employ the same rule as Su and Zhang (2008): strategic consumers are "first in line" at the salvage price, followed by customers from the infinite pool that makes up the salvage market. This is an appealing choice for several reasons. First, customers who arrive early in the season and intentionally choose to delay purchasing until a price reduction may closely monitor the price of the product and "pounce" once a sale occurs. Second, if we consider the infinite salvage pool to be a large group of consumers with lower valuations (i.e., with valuations equal to s), then this allocation rule maximizes consumer welfare. Third, the rule is particularly amenable to analysis, yielding closed form equilibrium solutions to the game.[6]

Given this allocation rule, what is the resulting probability that a strategic consumer obtains a unit at price s if she unilaterally deviates from an equilibrium in which all consumers purchase at price p? Such a consumer will receive a unit at the lower price if and only if the firm has enough inventory (q) to satisfy all demands (D). In other words, the probability is $\Pr(q \geq D) = F(q)$. To connect this result with our earlier discussion, $F(q) = G(q)$, but as already mentioned, in a rational expectations framework, consumers need not be aware of the actual demand distribution function, $F(q)$.

Having described our firm and consumer models, we may now proceed to analyze the game between consumers and the firm in each of the two systems: traditional replenishment and flexible replenishment.

14.4 Equilibrium Analysis

This section evaluates the equilibrium choices and profits for the four models constructed from the two types of replenishment modes (traditional or flexible) and the two types of consumers (myopic or strategic). (We do not consider models with a

---

[6] Alternative allocation mechanisms do exist and do not appear to substantially alter qualitative results: see Cachon and Swinney (2009) and Swinney (2008) for random rationing rules.

mixture of consumer types.) To help keep track of notation, we use a "t" subscript to denote "traditional replenishment" (i.e., a single order), analogous to c_f, an "f" subscript to denote "flexible replenishment" (i.e., a second-order opportunity), an "m" subscript to denote "myopic consumers", and an "s" subscript to denote "strategic consumers". For example, p_{mf} will be the firm's optimal full price with myopic consumer and flexible replenishment.

14.4.1 Traditional Replenishment

With myopic consumers, the traditional model resembles a newsvendor model with endogenous pricing. With strategic consumers, the traditional model mirrors the model in Su and Zhang (2008). We replicate some of their results here to ease the comparison with the flexible replenishment model in the next section.

We first observe that given the sequence of events depicted in Figure 14.2, and because price is directly observed by consumers, the game is essentially one of two stages. In the first stage, the firm is a Stackelberg leader in price, and in the second-stage consumers and the firm play a simultaneous game in inventory and purchasing. Exploiting its status as a price leader, the firm sets the price that yields the greatest expected profit; since we focus on equilibria in which all strategic consumers purchase at the full price, this is clearly the greatest price such that either condition (14.1) or (14.2) holds, depending on whether consumers are myopic or strategic, respectively. In other words, the optimal price with myopic consumers is

$$p_{mt} = v, \tag{14.3}$$

while the optimal price with strategic customers is

$$p_{st} = v - \phi(v - s). \tag{14.4}$$

Note that $p_{st} \leq p_{mt}$, i.e., the firm must choose a more moderate full price when selling to strategic consumers because they will purchase early only if they enjoy a positive surplus with the full price.[7]

We are concerned only with equilibria in which all strategic customers purchase at the full price, so the firm's expected profit as a function of inventory (q) and the full price (p) is

$$\pi_t(q) = \mathbb{E}\left[p \min(q, D) - cq + s(q - D)^+\right],$$

---

[7] Recall, we assume that strategic consumers earn value v no matter when they make a purchase. Therefore, because the discount price, s, is lower than the full price, p, the strategic consumer strictly prefers to purchase at the discount price if the item is available. She will purchase at the full price when she earns some surplus from doing so and there is a sufficiently high risk that the item will not be available in the discount period.

where the expectation operator, $\mathbb{E}[\cdot]$, is taken over demand D, and $(x)^+ = \max(x,0)$. This expression provides the profit of the firm in both the myopic and strategic customer cases, with the only difference between the two being the optimal selling prices given by (14.3) and (14.4). For fixed p, this function is concave in q and possesses a unique optimum. Thus, we may immediately deduce that a firm maximizing profit in the inventory–purchasing subgame invests in an inventory level q that satisfies

$$1 - F(q) = \frac{c - s}{p - s}. \tag{14.5}$$

Combining (14.3) with (14.5) yields the optimal inventory level with myopic consumers, q_{mt}, which satisfies

$$1 - F(q_{mt}) = \frac{c - s}{v - s}. \tag{14.6}$$

In the case of strategic consumers, we note that a Nash equilibrium with rational expectations to the game between the firm and strategic consumers satisfies:

1. The firm prices optimally, $p_{st} = v - \phi(v - s)$;
2. The firm chooses an inventory level that maximizes expected profit, $1 - F(q_{st}) = (c - s)/(p - s)$;
3. Consumer expectations are rational, $\phi = F(q_{st})$.

Combining these three conditions, we see that the unique equilibrium inventory and price satisfy

$$1 - F(q_{st}) = \sqrt{\frac{c - s}{v - s}} \text{ and } p_{st} = s + \sqrt{(v - s)(c - s)}. \tag{14.7}$$

14.4.2 Flexible Replenishment

In this section, we address the case of flexible replenishment. Recall that the flexible replenishment model is identical to the traditional replenishment model analyzed in the previous section, with the following exception: after learning perfect demand information (i.e., market size D), the firm has the opportunity to procure additional inventory before the season begins at a higher marginal cost $c_f > c$. As in the previous section, q represents the quantity purchased or produced in the early stocking opportunity.

It remains true that the optimal prices with myopic and strategic consumers satisfy (14.3) and (14.4), respectively: acting as a Stackelberg leader in the price game, the firm sets the greatest possible price supported by the equilibrium. The optimal procurement at the second-order point is clear: if, after learning D, the firm has sufficient inventory to cover all demands ($q > D$), then the firm orders no additional inventory. On the other hand, if the firm has insufficient inventory to cover demand ($q < D$), then the firm orders precisely enough supply to perfectly match demand

$(D - q)$ as long as $c_f \leq p$, otherwise the firm again orders no additional inventory. Consequently, the firm's expected profit function – with either myopic or strategic consumers – is

$$\pi_f(q) = \mathbb{E}\left[p \min(q, D) - cq + s(q - D)^+ + (p - c_f)(D - q)^+\right].$$

Or, rearranging the terms of this expression,

$$\pi_f(q) = \mathbb{E}\left[pD - cq - c_f(D - q)^+ + s(q - D)^+\right].$$

As in the traditional replenishment case, the profit function is concave in q and possesses a unique optimal inventory quantity, given by the solution q to

$$1 - F(q) = \frac{c - s}{c_f - s}. \tag{14.8}$$

Note that this is independent of the full price p – consequently, the initial inventory procurement is *independent* of whether consumers are strategic or myopic. This is our first important result concerning the value of a flexible replenishment system. Flexibility simplifies the firm's inventory planning duties by proving to be robust to the presence of strategic customers: misjudging or ignoring the extent of strategic customer behavior can be far less costly in a flexible replenishment system.

From (14.8), we immediately deduce that with myopic customers, the optimal inventory level and price in a flexible replenishment system satisfy

$$1 - F(q_{mf}) = \frac{c - s}{c_f - s},$$

and $p_{mf} = v$, respectively. Recall that with strategic consumers, a Nash equilibrium satisfies:

1. The firm prices optimally, $p_{sf} = v - \phi(v - s)$;
2. The firm chooses an inventory level that maximizes expected profit, $1 - F(q_{sf}) = (c - s)/(c_f - s)$;
3. Consumer expectations are rational, $\phi = F(q_{sf})$.

The second condition becomes trivial in the flexible replenishment system, as the initial inventory procurement is independent of the full price. Thus, combining the first and third conditions yields an equilibrium full price

$$p_{sf} = v - \frac{c_f - c}{c_f - s}(v - s). \tag{14.9}$$

Again, the second term in (14.9) indicates that there is a "strategic consumer penalty." If consumers are non-strategic, the firm merely charges v; due to forward-looking behavior, the firm must reduce the price to induce early purchasing.

Note that p_{sf} is decreasing in c_f – as c_f increases, the firm purchases more in advance and so the firm needs to offer a lower full price to induce strategic consumers to purchase at the full price. In fact, when $c_f = s + \sqrt{(c-s)(v-s)}$, it follows that $p_{st} = p_{sf} = c_f$. For any greater c_f, the firm finds itself in a situation in which the second procurement opportunity is of no value because the full price, p_{sf}, is then *less* than the cost of procuring additional units. Therefore, in the strategic consumer model the firm uses flexible replenishments only when $c_f < s + \sqrt{(c-s)(v-s)}$ and does not use flexible replenishments when

$$s + \sqrt{(c-s)(v-s)} \le c_f \le v.$$

14.5 The Value of Flexibility

Armed with equilibrium results for both the traditional and flexible replenishment systems, we may now address the *value of flexibility* – that is, the increase (or decrease) in expected profit that a firm experiences when moving from a traditional to a flexible replenishment system. When discussing the value of flexibility, we have two choices for the unit of analysis: the *absolute* or the *relative* value. The absolute value refers to the incremental change in firm profit with either myopic consumers, Δ_m, or strategic consumers, Δ_s:

$$\Delta_m = \pi_{mf} - \pi_{mt},$$
$$\Delta_s = \pi_{sf} - \pi_{st}.$$

The relative value of flexibility, δ, on the other hand, refers to the percentage change in firm profit:

$$\delta_m = \frac{\pi_{mf} - \pi_{mt}}{\pi_{mt}},$$
$$\delta_s = \frac{\pi_{sf} - \pi_{st}}{\pi_{st}}.$$

Both measures can be important to a firm exploring the value of flexibility. In this section, we address both quantities, beginning with the relative value. Of primary interest are the following key questions: (1) How does the value of flexibility change when consumers are strategic, rather than myopic? and (2) What are the drivers of this change in value?

14.5.1 The Relative Value of Flexibility

To analyze the relative value of flexibility, we examine the behavior δ_m and δ_s as a function of c_f – the cost of a flexible replenishment. Focusing on the marginal cost of flexibility provides a natural starting point for the analysis; we intuitively expect that, either with myopic or strategic consumers, if c_f is very high, flexibility is not very valuable, while if c_f is very low, flexibility should hold more value. It is far less intuitive how the difference in relative value, $\delta_s - \delta_m$, changes with c_f.

From differentiation of δ_m we obtain

$$\frac{d\delta_m}{dc_f} = \frac{1}{\pi_{mt}} \frac{d\pi_{mf}}{dc_f} < 0 \quad \text{and} \quad \frac{d\delta_s}{dc_f} = \frac{1}{\pi_{st}} \frac{d\pi_{sf}}{dc_f} < 0,$$

where the inequality follows from

$$\frac{d\pi_{mf}}{dc_f} < 0 \quad \text{and} \quad \frac{d\pi_{sf}}{dc_f} < 0.$$

As we would expect, the relative value of flexibility decreases as the cost of flexibility increases – a natural result. Comparing this expression with strategic and myopic consumers, we have

$$\frac{d\delta_s}{dc_f} - \frac{d\delta_m}{dc_f} = \frac{1}{\pi_{st}} \frac{d\pi_{sf}}{dc_f} - \frac{1}{\pi_{mt}} \frac{d\pi_{mf}}{dc_f}.$$

Note that $\pi_{st} \leq \pi_{mt}$ implies

$$\frac{1}{\pi_{st}} \geq \frac{1}{\pi_{mt}} > 0.$$

Furthermore, from the Envelope theorem,

$$\frac{d\pi_{mf}}{dc_f} = -\frac{c_f - c}{c_f - s} < 0,$$

$$\frac{d\pi_{sf}}{dc_f} = -\frac{c_f - c}{c_f - s} - \mu(v - s) \frac{c - s}{(c_f - s)^2} < \frac{d\pi_{mf}}{dc_f}.$$

Therefore, the relative value of flexibility decreases faster with strategic consumers than with myopic consumers:

$$\frac{d\delta_s}{dc_f} - \frac{d\delta_m}{dc_f} < 0. \qquad (14.10)$$

The difference in the relative value of flexibility is

$$\delta_s - \delta_m = \left(\frac{\pi_{sf}}{\pi_{st}} - 1 \right) - \left(\frac{\pi_{mf}}{\pi_{mt}} - 1 \right).$$

Now consider a particular point, $c_f = c$, in which case $\pi_{sf} = \pi_{mf}$. Hence, for $c_f = c$, the difference in the relative value of flexibility can be written as

$$\delta_s - \delta_m = \left(\frac{\pi_{mf}}{\pi_{st}} - 1 \right) - \left(\frac{\pi_{mf}}{\pi_{mt}} - 1 \right) = \pi_{mf} \left(\frac{1}{\pi_{st}} - \frac{1}{\pi_{mt}} \right) > 0.$$

Therefore, when $c_f = c$, the relative value of flexibility is greater with strategic consumers than with myopic consumers ($\delta_s > \delta_m$), but (14.10) indicates that δ_s

decreases faster with c_f than δ_m does. This raises the possibility that for a large enough c_f, δ_s decreases to the point that it is less than δ_m. In fact, this occurs. Recall that flexible replenishment provides no value with strategic consumers when $c_f \geq s + \sqrt{(c-s)(v-s)}$. In that regime $\delta_s = 0$. On the other hand, $\delta_m > 0$ for all $c_f < v$. Consequently, there exists some $\hat{c}_f < s + \sqrt{(c-s)(v-s)}$ such that $\delta_s > \delta_m$ for all $c_f \in [c, \hat{c}_f)$ and $\delta_s \leq \delta_m$ for all $c_f \in [\hat{c}_f, v]$. In words, as long as the cost of the second replenishment is not too high (less than $\hat{c}_f$), flexible replenishment provides greater value with strategic consumers than it does with myopic consumers.

This result is depicted graphically in Figure 14.3. As the figure demonstrates, the relative value of flexibility with myopic consumers is rather flat, whereas the value with strategic consumers is strongly dependent on c_f. When c_f is small (in the figure, $c = 3$) then flexibility can offer an enormous advantage with strategic consumers, resulting in a profit increase of over 250% in the example.

The potentially large increase in the relative value of flexibility under strategic customer behavior has significant implications for how a firm evaluates a flexible supply chain. It is well established in the literature that flexible replenishment can provide significant value when consumers are myopic (see, e.g., Fisher and Raman 1996, Eppen and Iyer 1997, Iyer and Bergen 1997, and Fisher et al. 2001). Here, we find that flexible replenishment can provide substantially more value when consumers are strategic as long as the marginal cost of the second replenishment is not too high, $c_f < \hat{c}_f$. However, if the marginal cost is high ($\hat{c}_f \leq c_f$), then flexible replenishment provides little value in a market with strategic consumers. This occurs because strategic consumers require a lower full price than myopic consumers to induce them to purchase at the full price. If the flexible replenishment system cannot deliver goods at a cost lower than the full price, it provides no value. Referring to Figure 14.1, if the special retailer sells to myopic consumers at a price of \$100, then

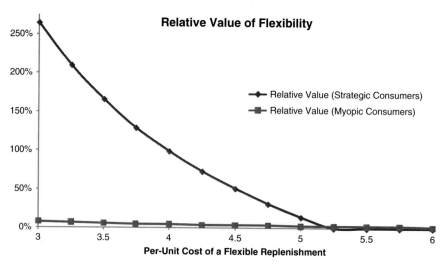

Fig. 14.3 The relative value of flexibility as a function of the unit cost of a flexible replenishment (c_f). In this example, demand is normally distributed with mean 50 and standard deviation 10, and $v = 10$, $c = 3$, and $s = 1$.

flexible replenishment is valuable to that retailer for any $c_f < \$100$. In contrast, Zara sells to strategic consumers for $85, so its flexible replenishment system provides value only if $c_f < \$85$.

14.5.2 The Absolute Value of Flexibility

Despite the fact that we have shown that flexibility possesses greater relative value if consumers are strategic and c_f is not too high, it need not be the case that the analogous result holds with absolute values. To see this, suppose $\pi_{st} = 10$ and $\pi_{sf} = 20$, yielding a relative value of 100% and an absolute value of 10 under strategic behavior. If, for example, $\pi_{mt} = 100$ and $\pi_{mf} = 150$, then with myopic customers the relative value is 50% (less than with strategic customers) while the absolute value is 50 (more than with strategic customers). Hence, in the following subsection we explicitly address the *absolute value* of flexibility.

To calculate this value, note that in general, the firm's expected profit equals the expected maximum profit (i.e., the profit if the firm produces exactly at the demand level and incurs no lost sales or excess inventory) minus the expected mismatch cost, i.e., the opportunity cost of lost sales ($p - c$ per unit) plus the cost of inventory that must be sold at the discount price ($c - s$ per unit) (see Cachon and Terwiesch 2005). Let M_Ω be the expected mismatch cost in one of our four models, $\Omega \in \{mt, mf, st, sf\}$:

$$M_\Omega = (c-s)\,\mathbb{E}\,(q_\Omega - D)^+ + \begin{cases} (p_\Omega - c)\,\mathbb{E}\,(D - q_\Omega)^+ & \Omega \in \{mt, st\} \\ (\min\{c_f, p_\Omega\} - c)\,\mathbb{E}\,(D - q_\Omega)^+ & \Omega \in \{mf, sf\} \end{cases},$$

where the first term is the cost of discounted inventory and the second term is the cost of lost sales with traditional replenishment and the cost of satisfying demand above the initial order quantity with flexible replenishment. Thus, expected profit in model Ω may be written as

$$\pi_\Omega = (p_\Omega - c)\,\mathbb{E}\,(D) - M_\Omega.$$

Using the expression for profit, the absolute value of flexibility with myopic consumers (Δ_m) is

$$\begin{aligned} \Delta_m &= (p_{mf} - c)\,\mathbb{E}\,(D) - M_{mf} - (p_{mt} - c)\,\mathbb{E}\,(D) + M_{mt} \\ &= (p_{mf} - p_{mt})\,\mathbb{E}\,(D) - M_{mf} + M_{mt} \\ &= M_{mt} - M_{mf}, \end{aligned}$$

where the latter follows from $p_{mf} = p_{mt} = v$. The absolute value of flexible replenishment with strategic consumers is

$$\begin{aligned} \Delta_s &= (p_{sf} - c)\,\mathbb{E}\,(D) - M_{sf} - (p_{st} - c)\,\mathbb{E}\,(D) + M_{st} \\ &= (p_{sf} - p_{st})\,\mathbb{E}\,(D) - M_{sf} + M_{st}. \end{aligned}$$

The difference in the absolute values of flexibility can now be expressed as

$$\Delta_s - \Delta_m = \left(p_{sf} - p_{st}\right)\mathbb{E}(D) - M_{sf} + M_{st} - M_{mt} + M_{mf}$$
$$= \left(p_{sf} - p_{st}\right)\mathbb{E}(D) + M_{st} - M_{mt},$$

where the latter follows from $q_{sf} = q_{mf}$, which in turn implies $M_{sf} = M_{mf}$. The first term reflects the use of flexible replenishment to increase its per-unit revenue: $p_{sf} \geq p_{st}$. This occurs because flexible replenishment lowers the initial-order quantity, thereby lowering the availability of inventory in the discount period, thereby allowing the firm to charge a higher full price (assuming $p_{sf} \geq c_f$). The second term reflects the differences in mismatch costs with traditional replenishment.

Consider the difference in the absolute value of flexibility when $c_f = c$. In this case $p_{sf} = v = p_{mt}$, which implies

$$\Delta_s - \Delta_m = \left(p_{mt} - p_{st}\right)\mathbb{E}(D) + M_{st} - M_{mt}$$
$$= \pi_{mt} - \pi_{st} > 0.$$

Hence, the absolute value of flexibility is greater with strategic consumers when flexibility is cheap (when $c_f = c$) and therefore highly effective. Furthermore,

$$\frac{d\left(\Delta_s - \Delta_m\right)}{dc_f} = \frac{dp_{sf}}{dc_f}\mathbb{E}(D) < 0,$$

and so the difference in absolute value of flexibility decreases as c_f increases. Thus, we have established the same pattern as with the relative value of flexibility: Δ_s is initially greater than Δ_m (for $c_f = c$) but decreases as flexibility becomes costlier. For large enough c_f, we have established that $\Delta_s = 0$ (because then $c_f > p_{sf}$) while Δ_m remains positive. Thus, for some value $\bar{c}_f$ we have $\Delta_s > \Delta_m$ for all $c_f < \bar{c}_f$ and otherwise $\Delta_s \leq \Delta_m$. This pattern is illustrated in Figure 14.4. In this example the absolute value of flexibility can be substantially greater with strategic consumers than with myopic consumers, upward of 10 times more valuable.

Figures 14.3 and 14.4 also illustrate that relative and absolute values need not correspond. For example, for the range $5 < c_f < 5.25$ we see that the relative value of flexibility is greater with strategic customers but the absolute value of flexibility is greater with myopic consumers. Nevertheless, in the range $c_f < 5$, both the relative and absolute values of flexibility are greater with strategic consumers.

To summarize, we find that not only does flexibility often provide greater *relative* value when consumers are strategic, it can also provide greater *absolute* value. This in an important result for firms considering to implement a flexible supply system: if their customer base is strategic, then flexibility can provide enormous additional benefits over the myopic customer case, giving greater justification to spending the high fixed costs associated with implementing a flexible system.

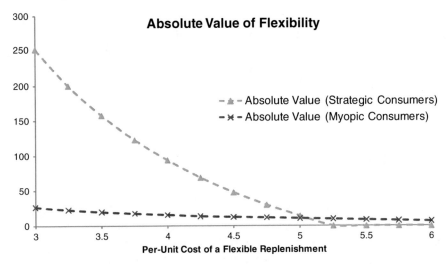

Fig. 14.4 The absolute value of flexibility as a function of the unit cost of a flexible replenishment (c_f). In this example, demand is normally distributed with mean 50 and standard deviation 10, and $v = 10$, $c = 3$, and $s = 1$.

14.5.3 Drivers of the Value of Flexibility

What causes the potentially large increase in the value – both relative and absolute – of flexibility under strategic customer behavior? The key lies in two distinct consequences of flexibility: matching supply with demand and reducing strategic behavior.

The value to the firm of better matching supply to demand is present regardless of the type of customer population it faces. Flexibility in our model eliminates lost sales (assuming $c_f \leq p$). Thus, the firm uses flexibility to lower its initial purchase quantity, which reduces the cost of excess inventory that needs to be marked down to the salvage price. However, the full price with strategic consumers is lower than the full price with myopic consumers. Hence, the value of eliminating lost sales is actually lower with strategic consumers than with myopic consumers. In other words, the value of better matching supply with demand is higher when the full price is higher. If only this effect were present, we would conclude that flexibility is more valuable with myopic consumers than with strategic consumers. But there is a second effect.

The full price with myopic consumers is independent of whether the firm possesses flexibility or not, i.e., $p_{mt} = p_{mf} = v$. However, with strategic consumers, adding flexibility allows the firm to increase the full price, $p_{st} < p_{sf}$, because flexibility reduces the initial order quantity, $q_{sf} < q_{st}$. With less initial inventory, the firm is less likely to sell any inventory at the salvage price and so strategic consumers are willing to pay a higher full price. Therefore, adding operational flexibility allows the firm to earn a higher price on *all* sales. This effect can dominate the former – while flexibility helps to reduce lost sales and excess inventory, it can be more valuable to use flexibility to increase revenue on all regular season sales. Our numerical studies indicate that not only can this effect dominate, it tends to dominate by a considerable amount over a large range of parameters. Therefore, while we cannot conclude that operational flexibility is always more valuable with strategic consumers, we find that operational flexibility is generally more valuable.

14.5.4 Consumer and Social Welfare

Flexibility results in higher prices when consumers are strategic, so an immediate concern is that operational flexibility results in decreased consumer (and possibly social) welfare. We define consumer welfare to be the total surplus of the customer population, i.e., the surplus of each individual who successfully obtains a unit times the expected number of sales. Observe that with myopic consumers, the firm extracts all surplus in either replenishment system, resulting in zero consumer surplus with either replenishment system.

With strategic consumers, however, this is not the case. The surplus of an individual consumer who obtains a unit is $v - p$, where p is the full price. In the traditional replenishment model, the resulting total equilibrium consumer surplus is

$$\left(v - s - \sqrt{(v-s)(c-s)}\right) \mathbb{E}\left(\min\left(q_{st}, D\right)\right).$$

In this system, consumers pay a low price (so individual surplus is high) but not all consumers are served. In the flexible replenishment model (again, assuming $c_f \leq p_{sf}$), total surplus is

$$\frac{c_f - c}{c_f - s}(v - s)\mathbb{E}(D).$$

With flexibility, consumers pay a higher price (so individual surplus is lower) but all consumers are ultimately served. Therefore, it is not clear whether flexibility increases or decreases consumer surplus.

Let $\eta = \mathbb{E}\left(\min\left(q_{st}, D\right)\right) / \mathbb{E}(D)$, which is the fill rate (fraction of demand that is fulfilled) with traditional replenishment. We can now write an expression for when consumer surplus is greater with flexible replenishment than with traditional replenishment:

$$\frac{c_f - c}{c_f - s} \geq \eta\left(1 - \sqrt{(c-s)/(v-s)}\right).$$

The left-hand side is increasing in c_f. If we let c_f equal its maximum feasible value, $c_f = s + \sqrt{(c-s)(v-s)}$, then the above expression can be written as

$$\left(v - s - \sqrt{(v-s)(c-s)}\right) \geq \eta\left(v - s - \sqrt{(v-s)(c-s)}\right),$$

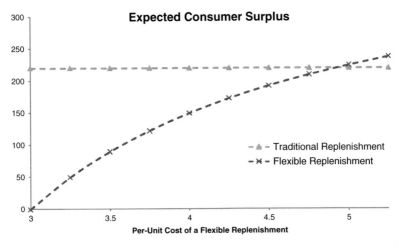

Fig. 14.5 Expected consumer surplus as a function of c_f. In this example, demand is normally distributed with mean 50 and standard deviation 10, and $v = 10$, $c = 3$, and $s = 1$.

which always holds (given that $\eta < 1$). Therefore, as long as c_f is sufficiently large, flexibility increases consumer surplus when selling to strategic consumers. This pattern is illustrated in Figure 14.5.

Also of interest is the impact of flexibility on *social* welfare, i.e., the sum of firm and consumer surplus. Combining consumer welfare with expected firm profit, we see that social welfare in the traditional system is

$$W_{st} = \mathbb{E}\left[v\min\left(q_{st}, D\right) - cq_{st} + s\left(q_{st} - D\right)^+\right],$$

while social welfare in the flexible system is

$$W_{sf} = \mathbb{E}\left[v\min\left(q_{sf}, D\right) - cq_{sf} + \left(v - c_f\right)\left(D - q_{sf}\right)^+ + s\left(q_{sf} - D\right)^+\right].$$

Note that if $c_f = c$,

$$W_{sf} = \mathbb{E}\left[(v - c)D\right] \geq \mathbb{E}\left[v\min\left(q_{st}, D\right) - cq_{st} + s\left(q_{st} - D\right)^+\right] = W_{st}.$$

Alternatively, if $c_f = v$, $q_{st} = q_{sf}$ and

$$W_{sf} = \mathbb{E}\left[v\min\left(q_{sf}, D\right) - cq_{sf} + s\left(q_{sf} - D\right)^+\right] = W_{st}.$$

Since $dW_{sf}/dc_f < 0$, it follows that $W_{sf} \geq W_{st}$, i.e., flexible replenishment is socially optimal for all viable c_f. Thus, flexibility never decreases social welfare – see Figure 14.6. We conclude that while flexibility may not always be in the best interests of the individual consumer, it is socially optimal (and may even be Pareto optimal).

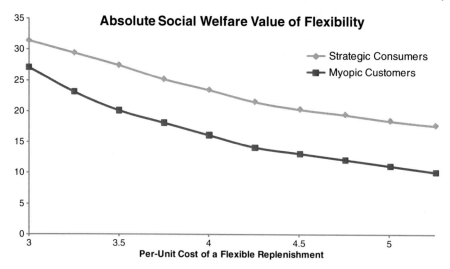

Fig. 14.6 The value of flexibility (in terms of social welfare) as a function of c_f. In this example, demand is normally distributed with mean 50 and standard deviation 10, and $v = 10$, $c = 3$, and $s = 1$.

14.6 Extensions and Complications

In this section, we discuss the impact of a variety of extensions and complications to the simple model analyzed thus far. In each of the three extensions, just as in the preceding model, the interaction of operational flexibility with strategic customer behavior is addressed. The first considers the impact of dynamic markdown pricing (rather than static pricing as we assume in our model) and consumers with heterogeneous valuations. The second explores the consequences of consumers that do not know (but learn) their valuations over time. The third discusses alternative forms of operational flexibility and considers their impact on strategic customer behavior.

14.6.1 Dynamic Sale Pricing and Consumer Heterogeneity

There are two key simplifications present in our model: the end-of-season clearance price is exogenously determined and *ex ante* fixed, and consumers are homogeneous both in the degree to which they are strategic (i.e., they are either all myopic or all strategic) and in their valuation for the good.

Suppose the firm is allowed at the end of the season to choose to keep the full price, p, or to lower the price to s to clear inventory in the infinite salvage market. This does not, in the context of homogeneous consumers, alter the analysis because all strategic consumers purchase early in equilibrium and so the firm always lowers the price to s at the end of the season to clear inventory. Hence, a consumer unilaterally deviating from equilibrium finds the product for sale at price s during the clearance period, precisely as she would in our static pricing model.

Imagine, however, that consumers are heterogeneous in their valuation for the product, possessing, for example, uniform valuations in a fixed interval. Because consumers are no longer homogeneous, it need not be the case that all consumers purchase at the full price in a viable equilibrium; indeed, it can be shown that in equilibrium, consumers with high valuations purchase early while consumers with low valuations purchase later. If the firm is free to set a clearance price, the equilibrium division of consumers according to valuations will induce the firm to *price skim* – set a high price for higher value customers that purchase earlier, and set a lower price for lower value customers who purchase later. If a large "bargain hunting" customer segment exists (e.g., the infinite salvage market) then the firm may still lower the price to *s* if inventory during the clearance phase is significant (i.e., if demand during the full price phase is low). Thus, a dynamic clearance price is a function of stochastic demand and the equilibrium number of consumers who purchase at the full price. When making their purchasing decision, consumers must consider all possible future sale prices to calculate their expected surplus of waiting until the clearance sale.

What is the impact of this richer model on our results concerning supply chain flexibility? Because flexibility lowers the amount of excess inventory, it decreases the chances that a firm will have to set a deep discount to clear inventory during the end-of-season sale. It also ensures that the firm has adequate inventory to cover demand if the product is a "hit" and prices are high. Flexibility thus has two effects: it *reduces supply – demand mismatch* (just as in our simple model) and it *increases the clearance price*. By increasing the expected clearance price, the firm is able to encourage more consumers to buy at the full price; why wait for a sale if the savings are not very significant? In turn, this allows the firm to set a higher full price and reap greater demand at the full price. The net result is that flexibility may possess even greater value when consumers have heterogenous valuations and sale prices are endogenously determined – in addition to the benefits discussed in our preceding analysis, the firm gains additional value from higher prices at the end of the season.

We might also imagine other models of consumer heterogeneity, for instance heterogeneous rates of consumption (e.g., different discount rates) or heterogeneous degrees of foresight (some myopic consumers mixed in with strategic consumers). The intuition in such models is similar: with dynamic pricing, flexibility helps to raise the average clearance price and thus encourage more consumers to purchase at the full price – see Cachon and Swinney (2009). This, in turn, enhances the value of flexibility beyond that which we derived in our simple model. We therefore conjecture that the benefits of flexibility in helping a firm cope with strategic behavior are robust to complications involving heterogeneous customer populations and various pricing schemes.

14.6.2 Uncertain Consumer Valuations and Learning

In the model analyzed in Sections 14.2–14.5, consumers are fully informed concerning their valuations at the start of the game. While this may be true for generic goods or products with relatively simple attributes that are easily analyzed (e.g., clothing), consumers may not initially know how much they value some products. Examples include innovative or complex products, products with long life cycles reliant on secondary goods of uncertain quality (e.g., video game systems), and even experience goods. With many of these products, information about value is disseminated over time to the customer population as, for example, expert product reviews are published, secondary goods are released, and consumers experience the product's features via units purchased by friends or in-store demonstrations. See Swinney (2008) for an analysis of this problem, the key results of which we summarize here.

With products of this type, consumers have an added benefit to delaying a purchase: to gather more information about the product's value to them. In such a setting, it is possible for a flexible supply chain to actually *decrease* a firm's profit (even in the absence of fixed costs to implement a flexible system) – by operating with an agile supply system capable of meeting future demand, the firm increases the overall availability of the product, thereby minimizing rationing risk and increasing consumer incentives to learn as much information about product value as possible before purchasing. This effect can be called *demand shifting* – by increasing availability, the firm causes customers to purchase later.

When this occurs, overall demand to the firm can actually decrease. This is because in selling to consumers before valuations are learned – also known as *advance selling*, see Xie and Shugan (2001) – the firm inevitably induces some consumers to purchase the product who ultimately will not value it. If customers are encouraged to delay their purchase, some of these "false positives" are eliminated from the firm's demand, thereby decreasing profit.

There are cases, however, in which shifting demand (and subsequently reducing advance selling) benefits the firm. If, for instance, prices increase over time (e.g., due to promotional discounts during new product introduction) or if unsatisfied customers are allowed to return products for full refunds, selling to many customers early (before value is fully learned) can actually harm the firm; in these cases, supply chain flexibility – which reduces the extent of advance selling – helps the firm by increasing the number of sales at a higher, later price or by decreasing the number of false positive purchases resulting in costly product returns.

These results imply that flexibility can provide both positive and negative values when a firm sells a product for which consumers have uncertain valuations. Thus, firms must carefully consider the nature of their product and the ease with which consumers can judge value when choosing their own supply chain structure. A key implication of this result is that it is critical for the operations side of the firm to work closely with marketing, design, and development groups to properly ascertain the characteristics of the consumer population and their interaction with the product.

14.6.3 Alternative Forms of Flexibility

This discussion has focused on a particular form of supply chain flexibility: the ability to rapidly procure additional inventory to meet demand, also known as volume flexibility or quick response. There are, however, other forms of operational flexibility that may be analyzed, two of which we discuss here: *design flexibility* and *mix flexibility* (also know as postponement).

Design flexibility refers to the ability to modify or create new product designs close to the start of the selling season in order to capture evolving and uncertain consumer trends. This type of flexibility is a crucial part of Zara's philosophy – by vastly reducing both design and production leadtimes, Zara can create styles that are more suited to consumer tastes *and* produce inventory that more closely matches its demand. Essentially, such practices serve to increase overall consumer value for a product, thereby increasing consumer willingness to pay. By giving consumers more valuable products, strategic behavior is lessened; customers are less willing to wait for a sale and risk a stock-out if they highly value the item. Furthermore, design flexibility and supply flexibility are complimentary in nature: higher value products increases the value of matching supply and demand, and less supply – demand mismatch increases the benefit of raising consumer value for a product. Thus, the combination of both types of flexibility – often referred to as a *fast fashion* system by Zara – results in a superadditive increase in firm profit. See Cachon and Swinney (2008) for more on the effect of design flexibility on strategic customer behavior.

Mix flexibility or postponement refers to the ability of a firm to dynamically allocate capacity between two or more different products. Suppose, for example, a firm sells to a market of fixed size N but with uncertain aggregate preferences between two product variants: a fraction β prefers variant 1 while a complementary fraction $1 - \beta$ prefers variant 2, where β is *ex ante* stochastic to the firm. Consumers know their private preference between variants, and just as in our previous models, the product is sold at a high price during the selling season and cleared at a low price at the end of the season. A firm without mix flexibility must make inventory decisions prior to the revelation of market preferences (β), essentially solving two (correlated) newsvendor problems, resulting in similar consumer incentives and strategic purchasing to the model we analyzed in this chapter.

A firm with mix flexibility, however, may pre-manufacture a common base product, while postponing final assembly into specific variants until after β is learned. If the firm has mix flexibility, then it will clearly be optimal to produce exactly N units of the base product and, after learning β, allocate final assembly such that the supply of each variant perfectly matches demand. Consequently, no sales occur at the salvage price, and there is no chance for consumers to obtain a unit at the clearance sale.[8] Strategic behavior is hence completely eliminated. While this simple model provides overly sharp results, the basic intuition supports our conclusions that operational flexibility in general benefits the firm by reducing strategic behavior.

---

[8] To be precise, this depends on whether consumers are atomistic. If consumers are atomistic (i.e., they do not consider the impact that their own behavior has on quantities like availability), then there is zero availability at the clearance price if they delay purchasing and the firm produces exactly to the level of demand. If consumers do consider their own impact on product availability, then this may not be true – however, in this case, the firm may react by reducing inventory by some small amount (e.g., one unit) thereby restoring zero availability at the clearance price.

14.7 Conclusions

In this chapter, we show how techniques for generating operational flexibility – long thought to be valuable solely by virtue of matching supply with uncertain demand – can have an enormous impact on customer purchasing behavior and pricing. This impact is almost always beneficial to the firm, and indeed can result in the value of flexibility being substantially greater when consumers are strategic relative to when they are non-strategic (i.e., myopic).

These results help to refine and strengthen our understanding of how "fast fashion" firms such as Zara have achieved so much success in an industry facing an increasingly savvy and strategic customer base. By producing inventory much closer to the start of the selling season, Zara is able to generate and utilize more precise demand forecasts than its competitors. Exploiting the increased precision of these demand forecasts, Zara is able to reduce the likelihood of drastically overproducing a given product, which in turn reduces the chance and magnitude of a potential markdown at the end of the season. In short, Zara exploits its "fashion on demand" capabilities to limit the extent of season-ending sales, thereby lowering the incentive for consumers to strategically delay purchases.

The key innovation in this work is to study the interaction between a firm's operational strategy and consumer behavior. This analysis leads to new insights into the value of operational flexibility as well as to insights on a firm's optimal pricing strategy. We feel there are many other opportunities to further explore and develop models that refine the dependency between consumer behavior and operations, not just in procurement and supply chain management but in all aspects of operations. By addressing such models, our hope is that a more complete picture of the impact of operating practices emerges, one that addresses not just firms and their suppliers, but also another crucial member of the supply chain – consumers.

References

Alexandrov A, Lariviere MA (2006) Are reservations recommended? Northwestern University. Working paper

Aviv Y, Pazgal A (2008) Optimal pricing of seasonal products in the presence of forward-looking consumers. Manufacturing Service Oper Management 10(3):339–359

Besanko D, Winston WL (1990) Optimal price skimming by a monopolist facing rational consumers. Management Sci 36(5):555–567

Bulow JI (1982) Durable-goods monopolists. The Journal of Political Economy 90(2):314–332

Cachon GP, Swinney R (2008) Using a fast fashion system for rapid product design with strategic consumers. University of Pennsylvania. Working paper

Cachon GP, Swinney R (2009) Purchasing, pricing, and quick response in the presence of strategic consumers. Management Sci. 55(3):497–511

Cachon GP, Terwiesch C (2005) Matching supply with demand: An introduction to operations management. McGraw-Hill/Irwin

Dada M, Petruzzi N (1999) Pricing and the newsvendor model: A review with extensions. Oper Res 47:183–194

Eppen GD, Iyer AV (1997) Improved fashion buying with Bayesian updating. Oper Res 45(6): 805–819

Fisher M, Rajaram K, Raman A (2001) Optimizing inventory replenishment of retail fashion products. Manufacturing Service Oper. Management 3(3):230–241

Fisher M, Raman A (1996) Reducing the cost of demand uncertainty through accurate response to early sales. Oper Res 44(1):87–99

Ghemawat P, Nueno JL (2003) ZARA: Fast Fashion. Case Study, Harvard Business School.

Grichnik K, Winkler C, Rothfeder J (2008) Make or break: How manufacturers can leap from decline to revitalization. McGraw-Hill

Hurlbut, T (2004) The markdown blues. Inc.com

Iyer AV, Bergen ME (1997) Quick response in manufacturer-retailer channels. Management Sci 43(4):559–570

Liu Q, van Ryzin G (2008) Strategic capacity rationing to induce early purchases. Management Sci 54(6):1115–1131

Muth JF (1961) Rational expectations and the theory of price movements. Econometrica 29(3):315–335

Stokey NL (1981) Rational expectations and durable goods pricing. The Bell Journal of Economics 12(1):112–128

Su X (2007) Inter-temporal pricing and consumer stockpiling. University of California, Berkeley. Working paper

Su X, Zhang F (2008) Strategic consumer behavior, commitment, and supply chain performance. Management Science. 54(10):1759–1773

Swinney R (2008) Selling to strategic consumers when product value is uncertain: The value of matching supply and demand. Stanford University. Working paper

Xie J, Shugan SM (2001) Electronic tickets, smart cards, and online prepayments: When and how to advance sell. Marketing Sci 20(3):219–243

Yin R, Aviv Y, Pazgal A, Tang CS (2007) Optimal markdown pricing: Implications of inventory display formats in the presence of strategic customers. Arizona State University. Working paper

Chapter 15
Capacity Rationing with Strategic Customers

Qian Liu and Garrett van Ryzin

Abstract Dynamic pricing offers the potential to increase revenues. At the same time, varying prices creates an incentive for customers to strategize over the timing of their purchases. How should a firm account for customer strategic behavior and profitably influence such behavior when making pricing and capacity decisions? One approach is to create rationing risk by deliberately understocking products. Then the resulting threat of shortages creates an incentive for customers to purchase early at higher prices. We develop a stylized capacity rationing model in which customers have heterogeneous valuations for the firm's product and face declining prices over two periods. Customers behave strategically and weigh the payoff of immediate purchases against the expected payoff of delaying their purchases. Via its capacity choice, the firm is able to influence the fill rate and hence the rationing risk faced by customers. We analyze the firm's optimal capacity choice in two different scenarios. In one case, customers can perfectly anticipate fill rates; in the other case, customers do not have fully rational expectations and they learn about availability through experience. We investigate, for both cases, when the rationing is optimal; if it is optimal, how it is affected by market characteristics and risk aversion of customers, etc. We also relate the results for each case together when the firm's discount factor approaches 1.

Qian Liu
Industrial Engineering and Logistics Management Department, Hong Kong University of Science and Technology, Kowloon, Hong Kong, e-mail: qianliu@ust.hk

Garrett van Ryzin
Graduate School of Business, Columbia University, New York, USA,
e-mail: gjv1@columbia.edu

S. Netessine, C.S. Tang (eds.), *Consumer-Driven Demand and Operations Management Models*, International Series in Operations Research & Management Science 131, DOI 10.1007/978-0-387-98026-3_15, © Springer Science+Business Media, LLC 2009

15.1 Introduction

Dynamic pricing is a common strategy for increasing revenues in response to uncertain and fluctuating market conditions: manufacturers will maintain full prices for the best-selling products in their line while discounting slow sellers; retailers change prices over time for seasonal products like apparel and sporting goods; airlines and hotels tactically change prices based on seasonal patterns and the real-time status of bookings on hand; and so on. Increasingly, such dynamic pricing is supported by sophisticated revenue management systems that use forecasting and optimization models to determine the most effective prices to use at each point in time. Yet faced with dynamic prices, savvy customers accelerate or postpone their purchases to game firms' dynamic pricing policies. Such behavior is pervasive. To give one example, executives at Macy's, America's largest operator of department stores, have lamented to us that the department store industry's habit of running frequent promotional sales has "trained our customers to only buy on sale."

What are the implications of such strategic customer behavior? For one, strategic behavior violates the assumptions of most revenue management systems, which model demand at each point in time as only a function of the price charged at that time; that is, customers are assumed to be *myopic* and buy if and only if the current price is less than their reservation price. This myopic customer assumption is quite reasonable when customers make impulse purchases, as in the case of small-ticket consumable goods such as food, beverages. However, for high-value purchases and/or more durable goods, customers are more likely to take the entire price path into account when making a purchase decision and try to get lower prices by strategizing over the timing of their purchases. This is after all, prima facie, how most of us shop for airline tickets, apparel, and large-ticket purchases like vacations, cars, and computers.

How should firms account for such strategic customer behavior when they make pricing and capacity decisions? Ideally, they should try to profitably influence such behavior by using appropriate pricing and capacity strategies. To thwart strategic purchase behavior, firms may attempt to create rationing risk by deliberately understocking products; the resulting threat of shortages creates an incentive for customers to purchase early at higher prices. Such strategies have been adopted by industrial practitioners. For example, Zara, one of the largest Spanish apparel retailers, is known for deliberately setting low stock levels for its products to encourage customers to buy when they first see products they like, rather than waiting for sales (Ferdows et al. 2005). Industry analysts estimate that unsold products at Zara represent less than 10% of stock, compared with the industry average of almost 20% as a result of this strategy (Ferdows et al. 2005).

As discussed by Cachon and Swinney earlier in this volume, there are many ways to profitably influence customer purchase behavior. Our particular focus in this chapter is on capacity decisions. We consider a model in which customers have heterogeneous valuations for the firm's product and face declining prices over a two-period selling season (the "full price" and "markdown" price seasons). Prices for each period are preannounced and the firm is assumed to be able to commit to the price path. Customers are strategic and weigh the payoff of immediate purchase against the expected payoff of postponing their purchase in the hope of getting lower prices. To discourage late purchases at a lower price, the firm can under-stock and create rationing risk, inducing more customers to buy early at full price. However, this happens at the cost of lost sales in the second period. Therefore, there is a trade-off between benefits of rationing and costs of lost sales. The central problem we analyze is whether it is optimal to create such rationing risk and if so, what level of rationing risk is optimal. We also analyze how these answers depend on character-istics of the market, and customers' risk preferences and incumbent expectations of availability.

This chapter is mainly based on two of our papers (Liu and van Ryzin 2007, 2008) and it is organized as follows.

In Section 15.2, we consider a single season (stage) model in which customers can perfectly anticipate fill rates in each period (i.e., they have fully rational ex-pectations about availability). Via its capacity choice, the firm controls the fill rate and hence the rationing risk faced by customers. We analyze the capacity choice that maximizes the firm's profits. First, we consider a monopoly market and characterize conditions under which rationing is optimal. We examine how the optimal amount of rationing is affected by the magnitude of price changes over time and the de-gree of risk aversion among customers. We then analyze an oligopoly version of the model and show that competition reduces the firms' ability to profit from rationing. Indeed, there exists a critical number of firms beyond which a rationing equilibrium cannot be supported.

Section 15.3 relaxes the assumption of fully rational expectations. Customers learn about availability through repeated purchases. Specifically, customers know the firm's capacity choices in the past, but do not observe its current capacity. They use a simple heuristic rule to integrate their beliefs and observed capaci-ties and thus form capacity expectations. Based on these expectations, customers decide to buy at either the full price or markdown price in each season. We imbed this customer learning process into a dynamic program of the firm's ca-pacity choices over time. One main result establishes the existence of a mono-tone optimal path of customers' expectations, which converges to either a ra-tioning equilibrium or a low-price-only equilibrium. Further, there exists a criti-cal value of customer expectation such that the market converges to a rationing equilibrium if customers' expectations are less than that critical value; otherwise, a low-price-only equilibrium is the limiting outcome. These results show why firms may be stuck with unprofitable selling strategies due to entrenched customer expectations.

In Section 15.4, we relate the equilibrium capacity under adaptive learning pro-cess to the optimal stocking quantity when customers have fully rational expecta-tions. We show that the equilibrium capacity under adaptive learning converges to that under fully rational expectations as the firm's discount factor approaches 1.

The final section summarizes the major insights generated from this work and provides guidance for future research.

15.2 Capacity Rationing Under Rational Expectations

15.2.1 Model Formulation

We first consider a monopoly firm which commits to a preannounced single mark-down pricing policy over two periods; the unit price in period 1, denoted p_1, is greater than the unit price in period 2, denoted p_2. The assumption of credible commitment to prices can be justified by the folk theorem of infinitely repeated games, implicit contracts between a firm and repeat customers, or due to advertising constraints and the desire to simplify administration of prices (see Liu and van Ryzin 2008 for detailed discussion). For example, Broadway theaters sell discounted tickets on the day of performance through TKTS outlets, where their "half-price tickets" policy is central to the concept. Filene's Basement has made a tradition of having automatic markdowns, in which products are marked down based on a preset schedule that begins with 25% off and drops to 75% off after 4 weeks. Standby airline fares at fixed discounts off full fares are yet another example of such price commitments.

The firm faces a market with a deterministic mass N consisting of a continuum of individual customers (e.g. a large market of infinitesimally small customers). This large-market assumption enables us to ignore strategic interactions among customers since one customer's behavior has a negligible impact on the outcomes experienced by others. Customers have heterogeneous valuations which we assume are distributed independently and identically with cumulative distribution function $F(v)$ and constant over time. Customers have identical utility functions, denoted $u(\cdot)$, which are time invariant, strictly increasing and concave. All customers are present when sales begin and remain in the market until their requests are satisfied or the sales season is over. Customers are strategic and they take both the current and the future prices and availability into consideration when deciding to buy early or late.

We assume the firm is risk neutral and customers are risk averse. Allowing customers to be risk averse is one distinct feature of our work and the assumption plays a key in the analysis. The firm seeks to maximize profits by choosing its stocking quantity at the beginning of the sales season. There is no replenishment opportunity once sales start.

15.2.1.1 The Customer's Decision

All purchase requests in period 1 are filled, while customers may face a rationing risk in period 2 due to insufficient supply. Let q denote the probability of obtaining a unit in period 2 (the *fill rate*). Random (parallel) rationing is assumed; that is, each customer attempting to purchase in period 2 has an equal chance of obtaining a unit. We assume customers can correctly anticipate the firm's fill rate; that is, customers have full information and rational expectations. As noted, we relax this assumption in Section 15.3.

In particular, a customer weighs the payoff of an immediate purchase at a high price against the expected payoff of a later purchase at a low price and buys one unit in period 1 if and only if: $u(v - p_1) \geq qu(v - p_2)$ and $v - p_1 \geq 0$. One can show that there exists a threshold value such that only customers with valuations greater than that will purchase early and otherwise wait to buy. Obviously, this threshold value depends on the firm's fill rate, and thus its capacity choice. Intuitively, a lower fill rate induces more customers to make early purchases. But this increase in early sales comes at the expense of lost sales due to rationing in period 2. This trade-off between the benefits of inducing early purchases and the costs of lost sales in period 2 is key to understanding the firm's optimal stocking decisions.

15.2.1.2 The Firm's Stocking Decision

Let C be the firm's stocking quantity before sales, and α be the unit procurement cost, $\alpha < p_2$. We assume the firm's cost function is linear, hence αC is the cost of stocking C units.

The fill rate in period 2 is given by the ratio of residual capacity to residual demand in period 2. Since the firm stocks at least enough to meet potential demand at the high price, $N\bar{F}(p_1)$, and never more than required to satisfy the potential demand at the low price, $N\bar{F}(p_2)$, the fill rate can be determined by

$$q = \frac{C - N\bar{F}(v(q))}{N(F(v(q)) - F(p_2))}. \tag{15.1}$$

Equation (15.1) shows how the firm is able to influence the fill rate via its capacity choice. The fill rate in turn influences customer behavior through the threshold function $v(q)$, defined (implicitly) by the indifference point:

$$u(v - p_1) = qu(v - p_2). \tag{15.2}$$

The firm would like to choose its capacity to induce the most profitable demand outcome.

We assume that customers' valuations are bounded above by $\bar{U}$. Then according to (15.2), the market can be segmented only if the fill rate is less than $\bar{q} = [u(\bar{U} - p_1)]/[u(\bar{U} - p_2)]$. Once the fill rate exceeds $\bar{q}$, no customer buys at the high price. In this case, the firm stocks $N\bar{F}(p_2)$ exactly serving the entire low-price market. Therefore, the firm's stocking decision problem is divided into two cases – a segmented market with rationing and a non-segmented market without rationing.

When the market is segmented, the firm's profit maximization problem can be expressed in terms of C and v as follows:

$$\max \quad N(p_1 - p_2)\bar{F}(v) + (p_2 - \alpha)C \tag{15.3}$$

$$\text{s.t.} \quad u(v - p_1) = \frac{C - N\bar{F}(v)}{N(F(v) - F(p_2))}u(v - p_2),$$

$$p_1 \leq v \leq \bar{U}.$$

Let (v^0, C^0) denote the optimal solution to (15.3) and Π^0 be the associated optimal profit for a segmented market.

When the market cannot be segmented, the maximal profit, denoted Π^{NS}, is obtained by serving the entire market at a low price; that is, $\Pi^{NS} = (p_2 - \alpha)N\bar{F}(p_2)$. So, the firm's optimal stocking quantity corresponds to the one that achieves the maximum of Π^0 and Π^{NS}. We denote the optimal cutoff value by v^*, the optimal fill rate by q^*, and the optimal stocking quantity by C^*.

15.2.2 Optimal Stocking Policy

We now answer the key question of whether it is optimal to create rationing risk or to simply serve the entire market at one price. If rationing is optimal, what level of rationing risk should be created?

To facilitate the analysis, we assume in the remainder of this chapter that customers' valuations are uniformly distributed over $[0, \bar{U}]$; and customers have a power utility function $u(x) = x^\gamma$ $(0 < \gamma < 1)$, which is a common form in the economics literature and corresponds to the case where customers have decreasing absolute risk aversion. [1] Lower values of γ correspond to more risk aversion. These assumptions greatly simplify the analysis.

15.2.2.1 The Optimal Stocking Quantity

Under these simplified assumptions, the firm's stocking decision for a segmented market given in (15.3) becomes

$$\max \quad \frac{N}{\bar{U}}(p_1 - p_2)(\bar{U} - v) + (p_2 - \alpha)C \tag{15.4}$$

$$\text{s.t.} \quad \left(\frac{v - p_1}{v - p_2}\right)^\gamma = \frac{(\bar{U}/N)C - \bar{U} + v}{v - p_2},$$

$$\bar{U} \geq v \geq p_1.$$

The profit can be further expressed only in terms of v as follows:

$$\max_{\bar{U} \geq v \geq p_1} \Pi(v) = \frac{N}{\bar{U}}\left((p_1 - \alpha)(\bar{U} - v) + (p_2 - \alpha)(v - p_2)\left(\frac{v - p_1}{v - p_2}\right)^\gamma\right). \tag{15.5}$$

The first-order conditions yield

---

[1] We numerically tested the model under more general forms of distributions for valuations such as normal and log-normal, and other utility functions including exponential and log utility functions. The main results still qualitatively hold. See Liu and van Ryzin (2008) for details.

$$\left(\frac{v-p_1}{v-p_2}\right)^{\gamma}\left(1+\frac{\gamma(p_1-p_2)}{v-p_1}\right)-\frac{p_1-\alpha}{p_2-\alpha}=0. \tag{15.6}$$

Using the fact that the profit function $\Pi(v)$ defined in (15.5) is strictly concave in $v \geq p_1$ and thus the maximizer of (15.5) is either the solution to (15.6) denoted by v^0 if $v^0 \leq \bar{U}$ or $\bar{U}$ otherwise, we can characterize the firm's optimal stocking quantity as follows (Liu and van Ryzin 2008):

Proposition 1. *Let v^0 be defined as the solution to (15.6), and denote*

$$U_c = \frac{(p_2+\gamma(p_1-\alpha))v^0 - p_2(p_1+\gamma(p_2-\alpha))}{v^0 - p_1 + \gamma(p_1-p_2)}. \tag{15.7}$$

If $\bar{U} \geq U_c$, the optimal stocking strategy is to induce segmentation by creating rationing risk. The optimal solution in this case is

$$v^* = v^0, \quad q^* = q^0 = \left(\frac{v^0-p_1}{v^0-p_2}\right)^{\gamma}, \quad and \quad C^* = C^0 = \frac{N}{\bar{U}}(\bar{U}-v^0+(v^0-p_2)q^0).$$

Otherwise, it is optimal to serve the entire market at the low price, namely, $v^* = \bar{U}$, $q^* = 1$, and $C^* = (N/\bar{U})(\bar{U}-p_2)$.

This result shows that whether it is optimal to create rationing risk or not depends on the number of high-value customers in the market. When there are a large number of high-value customers ($\bar{U} \geq U_c$), the incremental demand induced in period 1 more than compensates for the lost-sales cost of rationing in period 2. If there are relatively few high-value customers ($\bar{U} < U_c$), the opposite is true; the incremental demand induced in period 1 by creating rationing risk does not compensate for the lost sales in period 2. In fact, one direct result from Proposition 1 is the sufficient condition for creating rationing risk; that is, when $\bar{U} \geq p_1 + p_2 - \alpha$, creating rationing characterized by (v^0, q^0, C^0) is always optimal; when $\bar{U} \leq p_1 + \gamma(p_2-\alpha)$, the optimal strategy is to serve the entire market only at the low price.

15.2.2.2 Comparative Statics

We next examine how the firm's capacity decision is affected by prices for each period and the degree of risk aversion.

We can show (Liu and van Ryzin 2008) that the optimal fill rate decreases in the first period price while increases in the second period price as long as rationing is optimal. Figure 15.1a, b illustrates these results. Intuitively, as price differences over time decrease, the opportunity cost of rationing increases. On the other hand, a smaller price difference reduces customers' incentive to postpone their purchases. Both effects reduce the benefits of creating rationing in period 2 and drive fill rates up. Note that the optimal fill rate is not necessarily continuous in p_1 and p_2. At some level of p_1 (or p_2), the optimal fill rate jumps to one. This implies that inducing

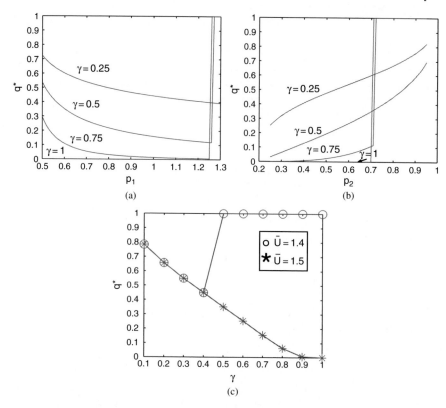

Fig. 15.1 Optimal fill rates versus prices for each period and degree of risk aversion.

segmentation cannot compensate for the lost-sales cost at that point and thus the firm would rather serve the entire market at the low price.

We also show that the optimal fill rate decreases in the degree of risk aversion (denoted γ). See Figure 15.1c for illustration. The formal proof is given in Liu and van Ryzin (2008). As customers become less risk averse, more rationing risk is needed to induce segmentation. However, at some point, the opportunity cost of rationing becomes too great and it is then optimal to serve the entire market at the low price. In fact, when γ approaches 1, customers become risk neutral. In this limiting case, the firm must create an extremely high rationing risk to induce early purchases. Again, whether rationing is optimal or not hinges on the market composition. Specifically, for risk-neutral customers, when the market consists of a sufficiently large number of high-value customers ($\bar{U} \geq p_1 + p_2 - \alpha$), it is optimal for the firm to serve the market only at the high price in period 1 (fill rate of 0); otherwise, the firm serves the entire market at the low price only (fill rate of 1).

15.2.3 Extensions to the Basic Model

Here we consider several extensions to the basic rationing model. First, suppose the firm optimizes over both prices and capacity and commits to both upfront. How does this change the outcome? Second, what if the firm and customers discount profits and utilities over time? Third, when there are several competitors in the market that offer the same product and customers assess the aggregate fill rate at the market level, how does this competition affect the firms' capacity strategy? Those questions are to be answered below.

15.2.3.1 Optimizing Over Both Prices and Capacity

When the firm has the ability to choose prices for each period, for an unsegmented market, one can easily show that the optimal single price is equal to $(\bar{U} + \alpha)/2$ and the associated profit is $[N(\bar{U} - \alpha)^2]/(4\bar{U})$. For a segmented market, the firm's optimal pricing and capacity decisions are determined by

$$\max_{\bar{U} \geq v \geq p_1 \geq p_2 \geq \alpha} \frac{N}{\bar{U}} \left((p_1 - \alpha)(\bar{U} - v) + (p_2 - \alpha)(v - p_2) \left(\frac{v - p_1}{v - p_2} \right)^\gamma \right). \quad (15.8)$$

With risk-averse customers, it turns out that rationing is always beneficial if the firm is able to use an optimal price schedule. This is established in Proposition 2 below (Liu and van Ryzin 2008):

Proposition 2. *The optimal value determined by (15.8) is strictly greater than the optimal revenue under a uniform pricing policy when $0 < \gamma < 1$. This implies with risk-averse customers, the optimal pricing strategy is a high $-$ low pricing policy $(p_1 > p_2)$ and the optimal stocking decision is to create a fill rate of strictly less than 1.*

This result implies that price flexibility and rationing enable the firm to price discriminate and capture surplus from customers who value the product more and prefer to pay to avoid the risk of rationing. It shows that prices can be designed such that the extra revenue from these high-value customers always offsets the cost of rationing. In this sense, this result shows rationing is a quite general strategy for extracting surplus and maximizing profits, provided prices can be chosen optimally.

15.2.3.2 Discounted Utility

Even without the risk of rationing, discounting of utilities over time creates an incentive for customers to buy early at high prices. Below we examine the case when both discounted utilities and rationing risk are considered.

We denote the discount factors for the firm and customers by δ_1 and δ_2. It is natural to assume that customers discount the value of products faster than the firm for seasonal, fashionable, and durable goods; that is, $\delta_1 \geq \delta_2$. To avoid trivialities, we assume $\delta_1 > \alpha/p_2$ to ensure a positive margin at the low price.

When the market cannot be segmented, the firm stocks $(N/\bar{U})(\bar{U} - p_2)$ to serve the entire market at one price p_2. When the market is segmented, the firm maximizes its total profit, composed of a base profit and an extra profit margin via sales at the high price:

$$\max \quad \frac{N}{\bar{U}}(p_1 - \delta_1 p_2)(\bar{U} - v) + (\delta_1 p_2 - \alpha)C \tag{15.9}$$

$$\text{s.t.} \quad (v - p_1)^\gamma = \delta_2 \frac{C - (N/\bar{U})(\bar{U} - v)}{(N/\bar{U})(v - p_2)}(v - p_2)^\gamma,$$

$$\bar{U} \geq v \geq p_1.$$

This optimization problem can be further written in terms of v as follows:

$$\max_{p_1 \leq v \leq \bar{U}} \Pi(v) = \frac{N}{\bar{U}}\left\{ (p_1 - \alpha)(\bar{U} - v) + \frac{1}{\delta_2}(\delta_1 p_2 - \alpha)(v - p_2)\left(\frac{v - p_1}{v - p_2}\right)^\gamma \right\}. \tag{15.10}$$

The first-order conditions yield:

$$\left(\frac{v - p_1}{v - p_2}\right)^\gamma \left(1 + \frac{\gamma(p_1 - p_2)}{v - p_1}\right) - \frac{\delta_2(p_1 - \alpha)}{\delta_1 p_2 - \alpha} = 0. \tag{15.11}$$

One can show that the profit function $\Pi(v)$ defined in (15.10) is strictly concave in $v \geq p_1$. Therefore, there exists a unique solution, denoted v^D, to (15.11).

The precise characterization of the optimal stocking decisions with discounts is shown in the following (Liu and van Ryzin 2008):

Proposition 3. *Let v^D be the solution to (15.11), and denote*

$$U_c^D = \left[(\gamma(p_1 - p_2)(p_1 - \alpha) + p_2(p_1 - \delta_1 p_2))v^D \right.$$
$$\left. - p_1 p_2 (p_1 - \delta_1 p_2) - \gamma p_2 (p_1 - p_2)(\delta_1 p_2 - \alpha) \right]$$
$$\cdot \left[(p_1 - \delta_1 p_2)v^D - (p_1 - \delta_1 p_2)(p_1 - \gamma(p_1 - p_2)) \right].$$

1. If $\bar{U} \geq \max\{v^D, U_c^D\}$, inducing segmentation is optimal, namely

$$v^* = v^D, \quad q^* = \frac{1}{\delta_2}\left(\frac{v^* - p_1}{v^* - p_2}\right)^\gamma, \quad \text{and} \quad C^* = \frac{N}{\bar{U}}(\bar{U} - v^* + (v^* - p_2)q^*);$$

2. Otherwise, a low-price-only solution is optimal, that is

$$v^* = \bar{U}, \quad q^* = 1 \quad \text{and} \quad C^* = \frac{N}{\bar{U}}(\bar{U} - p_2).$$

The results parallel the undiscounted case. For a large high-value segment, rationing is optimal; for a market with a small number of high-value customers, no rationing is optimal. We ignore discounting partly as a practical approximation, but more importantly to isolate and study the effect that rationing risk alone has on customer behavior.

15.2.4 Oligopolistic Competition

We now look at the case when multiple retailers carry the same product. Then it is natural to assume that customers base their strategic behavior on the product's availability across the entire market rather than in any one store. We, therefore, consider the aggregate supply and aggregate demand among all stores in the market to analyze this problem.

Specifically, an oligopoly market with n firms provides the same product. We assume customers exhibit no preference over the source of supply and, with equal probability, a customer buys a product from any firm as long as there is inventory. Capacity choice in the market is a vector, denoted by $C = (C_1, \cdots, C_i, \cdots, C_n)$. We assume all suppliers set the same prices for both periods and have the same unit of procurement cost. This obviously helps keep the model tractable, but is not unreasonable in a competitive retail market, where retailers frequently stock identical products and sell them at the same suggested retail prices but at nearly identical costs from manufacturers. The remaining notation is the same as in a monopoly case. Moreover, two additional assumptions are made to simplify the analysis of stocking decisions under competition: (i) sales in period 1 are equally shared by all firms; and (ii) a buyer will try other firms in period 2 if the firm he initially selects is out of stock until his request is accepted or the market supply is exhausted. Those assumptions are direct consequences of the assumption that customers randomly select suppliers and they have no preference of one specific supplier over another. These assumptions are, again, reasonable in a commodity-like market.

Under these assumptions, the aggregate equilibrium capacity is always greater than the potential demand at the high price, that is $N\bar{F}(p_1)$, and less than the potential demand at the low price equal to $N\bar{F}(p_2)$. Hence, the aggregate fill rate is determined by

$$q = \frac{\sum_{i=1}^{n} C_i - N\bar{F}(v)}{N(F(v) - F(p_2))}.$$

Note that each firm's capacity choice contributes to aggregate fill rate and thus impacts not only its own market share, but also that of all its competitors. This creates a strategic interaction between the stocking decisions of the n firms in the market. Determining optimal stocking quantities under competition therefore becomes a problem of finding equilibria in their capacity choices. Given the perfect symmetry among firms, in what follows we focus only on symmetric equilibria.

When the market can be segmented, given the capacity choices of other firms', denoted $C_{-i} = (C_1, \cdots, C_{i-1}, C_{i+1}, \cdots, C_n)$, firm i maximizes its total profit, which consists of an extra margin on an equal share $(1/n)$ of first period sales plus a base margin of $p_2 - \alpha$ on each unit, C_i, firm i stocks:

$$\max \quad \Pi_i(C_i, C_{-i}) = \frac{N}{n\bar{U}}(\bar{U} - v)(p_1 - p_2) + (p_2 - \alpha)C_i \quad (15.12)$$

$$\text{s.t.} \quad (v - p_1)^\gamma = \frac{\sum_{i=1}^n C_i - (N/\bar{U})(\bar{U} - v)}{(N/\bar{U})(v - p_2)}(v - p_2)^\gamma,$$

$$\bar{U} \geq v \geq p_1.$$

When the market cannot be segmented, the firms provide $\frac{N}{\bar{U}}(\bar{U} - p_2)$ to serve the entire market at the low price.

Given C_{-i}, the optimization problem for a segmented market (15.12) can be expressed only in terms of v:

$$\max_{\bar{U} \geq v \geq p_1} \Pi_i(v) = \left\{ \frac{N}{\bar{U}} \left(p_2 - \alpha + \frac{p_1 - p_2}{n} \right)(\bar{U} - v) \right.$$
$$\left. + \frac{N}{\bar{U}}(p_2 - \alpha)(v - p_2)\left(\frac{v - p_1}{v - p_2} \right)^\gamma - (p_2 - \alpha) \sum_{j=1, j \neq i}^n C_j \right\}.$$

Again, it is easy to show that firm $i's$ profit function, $\Pi_i(v)$, is strictly concave in $v \geq p_1$. The first-order conditions yield:

$$\left(1 + \frac{\gamma(p_1 - p_2)}{v - p_1} \right)\left(\frac{v - p_1}{v - p_2} \right)^\gamma - \left(1 + \frac{p_1 - p_2}{n(p_2 - \alpha)} \right) = 0. \quad (15.13)$$

There exists a unique solution $\bar{v}^0 > p_1$ to (15.13).

As in the monopoly case, the equilibrium involves rationing and segmentation if the market consists of a sufficiently large high-value population; while the equilibrium has no rationing or segmentation if the market has a small number of high-value customers. However, both equilibria may be supportable. The precise characterization of symmetric Nash equilibria is given as follows (Liu and van Ryzin 2008):

Proposition 4. *Let $\bar{v}^0$ be the solution to (15.13) and $\bar{q}^0 = [(\bar{v}^0 - p_1)/(\bar{v}^0 - p_2))]^\gamma$. Denote*

$$U_c^1 = \frac{n(p_2 - \alpha)(\bar{v}^0 - p_2)(1 - \bar{q}^0)}{p_1 - p_2} + \bar{v}^0, \quad U_c^2 = \frac{p_1 - \alpha}{1 - [(n-1)/n]^{1/\gamma}} + p_2 .$$

1. If $\bar{U} \geq U_c^1$, there exists a symmetric segmented Nash equilibrium, namely

$$v^* = \bar{v}^0, \quad q^* = \bar{q}^0 \quad and \quad C_i^* = \frac{N}{n\bar{U}}(\bar{U} - \bar{v}^0 + (\bar{v}^0 - p_2)q^0), \quad \forall i = 1, \ldots, n.$$

2. If $\bar{U} \leq U_c^1$, or $U_c^1 \leq \bar{U} \leq U_c^2$ and $\bar{q}^0 < 1 - 1/n$, there exists a symmetric low-price-only Nash equilibrium, namely

$$v^* = \bar{U}, \quad q^* = 1 \quad and \quad C_i^* = \frac{N}{n\bar{U}}(\bar{U} - p_2), \quad \forall i = 1, \ldots, n.$$

One sufficient condition for the symmetric equilibrium to exist uniquely is the following (Liu and van Ryzin 2008):

Corollary 1. *If $\bar{U} \geq p_1 + n(p_2 - \alpha)$ and $q^0 \geq 1 - 1/n$, the symmetric Nash equilibrium exists uniquely at a segmented market. If $\bar{U} \leq p_1 + n\gamma(p_2 - \alpha)$, the symmetric Nash equilibrium exists uniquely at a low-price-only solution.*

Intuitively, competition should make a segmentation strategy more difficult to sustain. This is because with large numbers of competitors, restricting supply has only a negligible impact on the overall market availability but the lost-sales cost of rationing is incurred entirely by firms that are restricting their supply. Indeed, there exists a critical number of firms ($n^* = (\bar{U} - p_1)/[\gamma(p_2 - \alpha)]$) beyond which creating rationing risk is never a sustainable equilibrium. This implies increased competition eventually eliminates the industry's ability to support segmentation via rationing.

We compare the outcomes of the oligopoly market with those in the monopoly market. The first difference is that more competition leads to higher aggregate capacity and higher fill rates relative to the monopoly case and these differences increase in the level of competition. However, firms generate lower aggregate profits compared to the monopoly market under more competition, and the difference increases in the level of competition as well. This is shown in Liu and van Ryzin (2008).

15.3 Capacity Rationing When Customers Learn

A key assumption made in Section 15.2 is that customers have rational expectations about the firm's capacity choice; that is, customers perfectly anticipate availability. It is arguably more realistic to assume that customers do not have perfect information on availability and rather learn about a firm's availability through repeated experience. In this section, we relax the rational expectation assumption and assume customers adaptively learn about the firm's capacity decisions over time. Our focus is how a firm should profitably influence customer learning behavior by its sequence of capacity choices.

15.3.1 Adaptive Learning Model

We look at an environment in which a firm sells products over repeated sales seasons to a fixed population of customers. Each season (also called a *stage*), indexed by t, consists of two selling periods – a full-price period and a markdown period – is the same as in the rational expectation model. The only difference is that customers do not perfectly know the firm's capacity (fill rate) in each stage. In other words, customers' estimate of capacity in season t, denoted $\hat{C}_t$, may differ from the actual capacity chosen by the firm, denoted C_t.

In each season t, customers decide when to buy as before. They either buy early at the full price and obtain the product for sure or they wait for the markdown price at the risk of being rationed out. Specifically, customers assess the fill rate in the markdown period of season t, denoted $\hat{q}_t$. Note that $\hat{q}_t$ is the customer's estimate of fill rate; the actual fill rate is denoted by q_t. They then weigh the payoff of purchasing immediately at full price versus the expected payoff of waiting for the markdown.

As argued in Section 15.2, for each fill rate there exists a unique cutoff value, denoted v_t, such that only customers with valuations greater than v_t purchase at the full price, while others wait for the markdown. The difference is that this threshold value v_t is now determined by a customer's estimate of fill rates rather than the actual fill rate in that period. The estimated fill rate is the ratio of residual capacity to residual demand in the markdown period given by

$$\hat{q}_t = \frac{\hat{C}_t - N\bar{F}(v_t)}{N(F(v_t) - F(p_2))},$$ (15.14)

and v_t is defined implicitly by

$$u(v_t - p_1) = \hat{q}_t u(v_t - p_2).$$ (15.15)

15.3.1.1 The Model of Customer Learning

Customers observe the capacity in each season and form their estimate of fill rates from this past history. We use adaptive expectation theory to model this learning process. Adaptive expectation theory assumes that customers employ simple heuristic estimates, e.g., an exponentially smoothed averages of current and past information, to update their estimates. For analytical tractability, we assume that customers learn about capacity instead of fill rates; that is, customers' estimate of the capacity at the start of season $t + 1$, $\hat{C}_{t+1}$, is a weighted average of the firm's capacity in season t, C_t, and customers' prior estimate, $\hat{C}_t$:

$$\hat{C}_{t+1} = \theta C_t + (1 - \theta)\hat{C}_t,$$ (15.16)

where θ is the learning speed, $0 \le \theta \le 1$. As θ increases, customers place more weight on new information and adjust their expectations more rapidly.

Although the main reason for using a capacity representation of the learning process is mathematical tractability, we justify the plausibility of this assumption as follows: note the update of capacity (15.16) is made ex post after season t is completed, and hence it would be influenced by a variety of information other than direct observation, including word of mouth, advertisements, Web sites, reports and surveys. These sources of information may compensate for the ability to observe capacity directly. Alternatively, one can view capacity updating as being a change of variable from fill rate updating since capacity and fill rate are directly related by the expression:

$$\hat{C}_t = N\bar{F}(v_t(\hat{q}_t)) + N(F(v_t(\hat{q}_t)) - F(p_2))\hat{q}_t,$$

so that knowing one variable is equivalent to knowing the other, provided that customers know the market size N, though admittedly this may be an equally unpalatable assumption. More importantly, we did numerical testing of the model under fill rate updates and found that the basic structural properties do not depend significantly on the capacity parameterization of the learning process. Collectively, this capacity learning model strikes a reasonable balance between model tractability and behavioral realism.

We also assume all customers have the same estimate of capacity; that is, $\hat{C}_t$ is a consensus and commonly held estimate among customers. Admittedly, it may be more realistic to allow customers to have heterogeneous estimates based on their own purchase histories and stock-out experiences. Still, this too is an extreme assumption, because it in effect posits that customers only obtain information from their immediate shopping experience, when in reality there is word of mouth, advertising, Web site, and other common information that contributes to a customer's expectation about stock availability at a particular retailer. Moreover, with such idiosyncratic information, we would have to track each individual customer's expectation of availability, which would require a state vector with large dimension, and this would likely make the problem intractable. The assumption of a common estimate for all customers is much simpler and roughly corresponds to a case where there is a free flow of information among customers and hence the entire market "learns" about the actual capacity at the end of each season and updates their beliefs identically.

Lastly, note that by combining (15.15) and (15.14), the cutoff value and the customers' estimate of capacity are related by

$$\hat{C}_t = N(F(v_t) - F(p_2))\frac{u(v_t - p_1)}{u(v_t - p_2)} + N\bar{F}(v_t). \qquad (15.17)$$

To facilitate further analysis, we again specialize the model by assuming that $F(\cdot)$ is uniformly distributed over $[0, \bar{U}]$ and that customers have a power utility function $u(\cdot) = (\cdot)^\gamma$, where $0 < \gamma < 1$.[2] The capacity estimate can then be expressed as

$$\hat{C}_t = \frac{N}{\bar{U}}\left(\bar{U} - v_t + (v_t - p_2)\left(\frac{v_t - p_1}{v_t - p_2}\right)^\gamma\right), \quad p_1 \leq v_t \leq \bar{U}. \qquad (15.18)$$

When customers estimate a large amount of capacity, they are more likely to postpone their purchases. Specifically, we define

$$C_s = \bar{C}\left(\frac{\bar{U} - p_1}{\bar{U} - p_2}\right)^\gamma, \qquad (15.19)$$

and call C_s a *segmentation threshold* capacity estimate. Such C_s has the property that if customers' expectation of capacity, $\hat{C}_t$, exceeds C_s, then all customers opt to buy

---

[2] We numerically find that the main results derived under those specialized assumptions remain qualitatively the same for more general distributions of valuation and utility functions. See Liu and van Ryzin [2007] for details.

in the markdown period; if $\hat{C}_t < C_s$, then the market is segmented and some positive fraction of customers buy at full price.

One can easily check that $\hat{C}_t(v_t)$ defined by (15.18) is strictly increasing and concave in $v_t \in [p_1, \bar{U}]$. This implies the inverse function of $\hat{C}_t(v_t)$, denoted $\tilde{v}(\hat{C}_t)$, exists; further, $\tilde{v}(\hat{C}_t)$ is strictly increasing and convex in $\hat{C}_t \in [\underline{C}, C_s]$. Therefore, the cutoff valuation v_t is uniquely characterized by $\tilde{v}(\hat{C}_t)$ when $\underline{C} \leq \hat{C}_t \leq C_s$. Once $\hat{C}_t$ exceeds C_s, customer purchase behavior changes fundamentally; all customers wait to buy in the markdown period and segmentation of customers is no longer attainable. Hence, we define v_t to be constant at $\bar{U}$ when $C_s \leq \hat{C}_t \leq \bar{C}$. Then, for any given expected capacity $\hat{C}_t \in [\underline{C}, \bar{C}]$, the cutoff value v_t is uniquely determined by

$$v(\hat{C}_t) = \begin{cases} \tilde{v}(\hat{C}_t) & \text{if } \underline{C} \leq \hat{C}_t \leq C_s, \\ \bar{U} & \text{if } C_s \leq \hat{C}_t \leq \bar{C}. \end{cases}$$

15.3.1.2 The Model of the Firm

The capacity learning model (15.16) links the firm's capacity decisions from one season to the next. The firm's capacity decision problem is then naturally modeled as a dynamic program. Let $V(\hat{C}_t)$ denote the maximum discounted profit given that customers' current estimate is $\hat{C}_t$. Future value is discounted by a discount factor δ per season, with $0 < \delta < 1$. $V(\hat{C}_t)$ satisfies the following Bellman equation:

$$V(\hat{C}_t) = \max_{C_t \in [\underline{C}, \bar{C}]} \left\{ \Pi(\hat{C}_t, C_t) + \delta V(\theta C_t + (1 - \theta)\hat{C}_t) \right\}, \qquad (15.20)$$

where $\Pi(\hat{C}_t, C_t)$ is the one-stage profit given that customers' expected capacity is $\hat{C}_t$ and the firm's capacity is C_t:

$$\Pi(\hat{C}_t, C_t) = \frac{N}{\bar{U}}(p_1 - p_2)(\bar{U} - v(\hat{C}_t)) + (p_2 - \alpha)C_t. \qquad (15.21)$$

As in the rational expectation case, the range of control constraints is defined by $\underline{C} = (N/\bar{U})(\bar{U} - p_1)$ and $\bar{C} = (N/\bar{U})(\bar{U} - p_2)$. These constraints ensure there is no shortage during the full-price period and no overage during the markdown period. Note that in some cases (e.g., see Greenleaf 1995, Byers and Huff 2005), it may be profitable to deliberately under-stock products in the full-price period in order to change expectations as quickly as possible. While potentially of interest, our control constraints rule out such extreme actions.

When the firm's optimal response to the state $\hat{C}_t$ is to choose $C_t^* = \hat{C}_t$, we call such capacity an *equilibrium* of the model (15.20). At the equilibrium, customers' estimates of capacity and the firm's decisions are constant over time and equal to each other; hence customers' expectations are consistent with the capacity choices of the firm. More precisely, let $C^*(\hat{C})$ denote the optimal solution to (15.20) given state $\hat{C}$. Then an equilibrium of (15.20) is a fixed point of the *state updating function*

$$f(\hat{C}) = \theta C^*(\hat{C}) + (1 - \theta)\hat{C}.$$

That is, $\hat{C}$ is an equilibrium if $f(\hat{C}) = \hat{C}$. At the equilibrium, $C^*(\hat{C}) = \hat{C}$. We henceforth do not differentiate the firm's capacity and customer expected capacity at the equilibrium, both of which we call the *equilibrium capacity*.

To understand the basic trade-off the firm faces, notice that customers' decisions about when to buy depend only on their estimate of capacity in season t, $\hat{C}_t$, and not on the firm's actual capacity choice C_t. Hence, if the firm were only interested in maximizing profits in season t, they would choose the maximum capacity $\bar{C}$, and satisfy all demand during both the full-price and markdown periods. But the firm's capacity choice also influences customers' future expectations; a larger capacity choice in season t increases customers' estimate of capacity in future seasons, which encourages them to wait for markdowns. This reduces future profits. So the key trade-off is between the short-term benefit of stocking amply to satisfy current demand versus the negative impact that such high stock levels have on customers' future expectations of availability. The firm's goal is to seek a sequence of capacity choices over time that optimally balances these effects and maximizes its discounted profit over time.

15.3.2 Optimal Capacity Decisions Over Time

We next derive the structural properties of the firm's optimal capacity choice over time. We show that the firm's optimal capacity choices converge to either a rationing equilibrium or a low-price-only equilibrium, depending on initial customer expectations. Indeed, we show that there exists a critical state of initial customer expectations that determines which of these equilibria is reached. When initial customer expectations are less than that of critical value, the rationing equilibrium is a sustainable outcome; otherwise, the low-price-only equilibrium is the optimal long-run outcome.

Since customers exhibit fundamentally different purchase behavior once their expectations of capacity exceed the segmentation threshold capacity estimate C_s, the direct analysis of the learning model (15.20) is quite complex. However, the problem can be easily solved as long as the state (i.e., customer estimates of capacity) does not cross the segmentation threshold capacity estimate. Therefore, we use a "separate-and-paste" approach to analyze the problem; we divide the entire state space into two subspaces, over which two isolated subproblems, called *the region 1 and region 2 problems*, are defined. Both the region 1 and region 2 problems are well behaved and can be completely analyzed using classical optimization techniques. Furthermore, we show that there always exists a monotone optimal state path for the original problem. Because of this important monotonicity property, the problem eventually remains in either region 1 or region 2. We can then "paste" the results of the region 1 and region 2 problems together to solve the original problem.

15.3.2.1 The Region 1 and Region 2 Problems

As discussed above, all customers wait to buy in the markdown period if their expectation of capacity is greater than the segmentation threshold capacity estimate C_s. The firm's best response is then to stock $\bar{C}$, which is strictly larger than C_s, to meet all the potential demand at the markdown price. Since the switch from a segmented market to a non-segmented market induces a jump of capacity, the value function $V(\hat{C}_t)$, unfortunately, is not well behaved. Nevertheless, the threshold function $v(\hat{C}_t)$ has special structure: it is convex in the range of $[\underline{C}, C_s]$ and constant at $\bar{C}$ afterward. As mentioned, this motivates us to "separate" the entire region of state space into two subspaces of $[\underline{C}, C_s]$ and $[C_s, \bar{C}]$, denoted, respectively, the region 1 and region 2 problems.

The region 1 problem is defined as follows:

$$V^1(\hat{C}_t) = \max_{C_t \in S^1(\hat{C}_t)} \left\{ \frac{N}{\bar{U}} (p_H - p_L)(\bar{U} - v(\hat{C}_t)) + (p_L - \alpha)C_t + \delta V^1(\theta C_t + (1-\theta)\hat{C}_t) \right\},$$

$$(15.22)$$

where

$$S^1(\hat{C}) = \left\{ C \,\middle|\, \underline{C} \leq C \leq \bar{C} \quad \text{and} \quad C \leq -\frac{1-\theta}{\theta}\hat{C} + \frac{C_s}{\theta} \right\}.$$

The region 2 problem is the following:

$$V^2(\hat{C}_t) = \max_{C_t \in S^2(\hat{C}_t)} \left\{ (p_L - \alpha)C_t + \delta V^2(\theta C_t + (1-\theta)\hat{C}_t) \right\}, \qquad (15.23)$$

where

$$S^2(\hat{C}) = \left\{ C \,\middle|\, \underline{C} \leq C \leq \bar{C} \quad \text{and} \quad C \geq -\frac{1-\theta}{\theta}\hat{C} + \frac{C_s}{\theta} \right\}.$$

We require $C_t \in S^1(\hat{C}_t)$ in the region 1 problem to ensure any state falls within $[\underline{C}, C_s]$; and $C_t \in S^2(\hat{C}_t)$ guarantees the state space of the region 2 problem is $[C_s, \bar{C}]$. There are no overlapping states between these two subproblems except state C_s.

We first explore the region 2 problem, which is quite simple to analyze. Since all customers delay purchases in this region, the firm stocks $\bar{C}$ to satisfy all the demand at the markdown price. The value function $V^2(\hat{C}_t)$ is then state independent and the equilibrium is trivially $\bar{C}$.

We then focus on the analysis of the region 1 problem. Since customers decide to buy early or late based on their expected capacity, the current profit will increase in the firm's capacity for the present. However, a large capacity leads to a high expectation for the future, thus reducing future profits. Hence, there is a trade-off between stocking more to increase the current profit and stocking less to reduce customer expectations and induce more early purchases in the future. We show that there exists a unique equilibrium capacity and characterize this equilibrium in the following (Liu and van Ryzin 2007):

Proposition 5. *For the region 1 problem, there exists a unique equilibrium capacity which is equal to $\min\{C_E^0, C_s\}$, where C_s is a segmentation threshold capacity* *defined in (15.19), and C_E^0 is called rationing equilibrium capacity determined by*

$$C_E^0 = \frac{N}{\bar{U}}\left(\bar{U} - v_E^0 + (v_E^0 - p_2)\left(\frac{v_E^0 - p_1}{v_E^0 - p_2}\right)^\gamma\right). \tag{15.24}$$

In (15.24), v_E^0 is the solution to

$$\left(\frac{v - p_1}{v - p_2}\right)^\gamma\left(1 + \frac{\gamma(p_1 - p_2)}{v - p_1}\right) - \frac{(p_2 - \alpha)(\frac{1}{\delta} - 1) + \theta(p_1 - \alpha)}{(p_2 - \alpha)(\frac{1}{\delta} - 1 + \theta)} = 0. \tag{15.25}$$

In (Liu and van Ryzin 2007), we further show that the rationing equilibrium C_E^0 decreases in the firm's discount factor δ and the learning speed of customers θ; and the per-stage profit at C_E^0, $\Pi(C_E^0, C_E^0)$, increases in δ and θ. These results are quite intuitive. The larger the firm's discount factor, the more important are future profits. Hence, the long-run benefit of stocking less and inducing more early purchases at higher prices dominates the short-term benefit of stocking more to satisfy the current demand. We therefore expect a lower rationing equilibrium as the firm's discount factor increases. Such a lower rationing capacity induces more customers to buy early at full price and thus improves the long-run profit per stage. Similarly, as customers adapt expectations to the firm's capacity more quickly, it becomes less costly to change customers' expectations. That is, to persuade customers to believe there will not be enough inventory left at low price, the firm can change their beliefs by stocking less in a shorter period of time. Again, the long-run benefit of introducing more customers to buy early at full price exceeds the short-run benefit of stocking more to earn higher revenue for current. Therefore, when customers update capacity expectations faster, the optimal threshold value becomes smaller (i.e., more customers buy early at full price), which corresponds to smaller rationing capacity and higher earning in each stage.

15.3.2.2 Monotone Convergence of Optimal State Paths

We now attempt to "paste" the results for each region problem and derive the equilibrium outcome for the original problem. The key reason that we are able to "paste" results of the subproblems is the monotonicity of optimal state paths for the original problem (Liu and van Ryzin 2007):

Proposition 6. *For the problem (15.20), there exists an optimal monotone state path, namely, given any initial state $\hat{C}_1$, there exists an optimal state path, denoted $\{\hat{C}_t\}_{t \geq 1}$, such that either $\hat{C}_1 \geq \cdots \geq \hat{C}_t \geq \cdots$ or $\hat{C}_1 \leq \cdots \leq \hat{C}_t \leq \cdots$.*

Because the optimal states evolve monotonically, the problem will remain in one region forever once it reaches that region. The equilibrium results for each region-specific problem can then carry over to the original problem. The following proposition shows that the equilibrium of the original problem must be the one solved for either the region 1 or the region 2 problem. This result is summarized in the following proposition (Liu and van Ryzin 2007):

Proposition 7. *For the problem (15.20), given any state $\hat{C}_1 \in [\underline{C}, \bar{C}]$, there exists a monotone optimal state path $\{\hat{C}_t\}_{t \geq 1}$ which converges to either a rationing equilibrium capacity C_E^0 or a low-price-only equilibrium capacity $\bar{C}$.*

This proposition shows that repeated interactions between the firm and its customers lead to an equilibrium, which is either a rationing equilibrium given by C_E^0 or a low-price-only equilibrium without rationing: $\bar{C}$. This result implies the optimal decisions do not oscillate among high- and low-capacity choices. In other words, the firm does not profit from manipulating customers' expectations by alternating between providing high and low availability during markdown periods. This contrasts with the results of Ovchinnikov and Milner (2005), who find that, under their model of rationing and learning, when customers learn by a "smoothing" process (as in our case), it is optimal for the firm to follow a "bang – bang" type policy, in which it alternates between offering high and low availability. Similarly, Gallego et al. (2008) numerically study the dynamic model of discounting inventory when customers learn availability through past experiences. Their examples suggest the firm use a high – low sales limit in alternate periods when customers update their belief quickly; otherwise, the sales limit tend to converge to a constant value. Why does the capacity policy not converge in Ovchinnikov and Milner's model but converge in our model? Mathematically, the difference appears due to the convexity/concavity of the value functions; if the value function is convex (as, for example, in the model of Ovchinnikov and Milner 2005), then it pays to oscillate between high and low availability since the average payoff from being in two extreme states dominates the payoff from being at the average of the two states. When the value function is concave (as in our case in the region where customers segment), the payoff from oscillating between states cannot dominate the payoff from staying in one state. Yet how the particular model primitives in each case induce this convex versus concave payoff is difficult to determine; this is a subject warranting further investigation.

15.3.2.3 Initial Expectations and Equilibrium Outcomes

Both C_E^0 (rationing) and $\bar{C}$ (no rationing) can be equilibria for the adaptive learning model (15.20). Under what conditions does there exist a unique equilibrium? One can show that if a low-price-only equilibrium is more profitable than a rationing equilibrium in the long run, the low-price-only solution becomes the unique equilibrium. However, if rationing is more profitable in the long run, both equilibria can be reached, depending on customers' initial expectations. In fact, there exists a critical value of initial customer expectation. If customers' initial expectations are larger than that value, the long-run equilibrium involves no rationing or segmentation at all. Only if customers' initial expectations are smaller than the critical value does the firm benefit from rationing and the market converges to the rationing equilibrium. This result is established below (Liu and van Ryzin 2007):

Proposition 8. *There exists a critical value of initial customer expectation, denoted $\hat{C}_c$, such that it is optimal to converge to $\bar{C}$ for all $\hat{C} \geq \hat{C}_c$; and it is optimal to converge to C_E^0 for any $\hat{C} < \hat{C}_c$.*

This result suggests one explanation for why retail firms may follow policies of providing high availability that are not necessarily the most profitable in the long run. If customers expect high availability based on a long history of always finding products available during markdown periods and update their beliefs slowly, it can be quite costly to change their expectations to reach a new equilibrium in which they anticipate shortages during markdown periods. Stated in practical terms, changing strategies might require limiting availability for a sequence of seasons during which customers still refuse to buy at full price because they expect products to be available at markdown. It could take several years of experience to convince customers that the firm's availability policy has really changed, and the profit losses incurred during this learning process might simply be too severe to justify the change in strategy. In this way retailers can be saddled by the expectations they have created historically.

We also find numerically that this critical value increases in customers' learning speed, the firm's discount factor, and the degree of risk aversion of customers.

15.4 Relation to Rational Expectation Equilibrium

We now relate the equilibrium outcome under the adaptive learning model to the optimal capacity decision in the rational expectation case studied in Section 15.2. First, note that the following three properties can be easily checked (Liu and van Ryzin 2007):

(1) The rationing equilibrium under adaptive learning, C_E^0, converges to the rationing outcome under rational expectation, C^0, as the discount factor δ approaches 1.

(2) For the adaptive learning model (15.20), if the profit per stage at a rationing equilibrium, denoted $\Pi(C_E^0, C_E^0)$, is less than that at a low-price-only equilibrium, equal to $(p_L - \alpha)\bar{C}$, then the equilibrium is uniquely attained at $\bar{C}$.

(3) For the adaptive learning model (15.20), if the per-stage profit at a rationing equilibrium C_E^0 is strictly larger than that at a low-price-only equilibrium $\bar{C}$, namely, $\Pi(C_E^0, C_E^0) > (p_2 - \alpha)\bar{C}$, then as δ approaches 1, C_E^0 becomes the optimal long-run outcome regardless of customer expectation.

Recall in Section 15.2, we have shown that when customers can perfectly anticipate availability, the optimal stocking quantity is C^0 if $\Pi(C^0, C^0) > (p_2 - \alpha)\bar{C}$; otherwise, the firm stocks $\bar{C}$ without introducing segmentation. We then have the following (Liu and van Ryzin 2007):

Proposition 9. *As the discount factor $\delta \to 1$, the equilibrium capacity under adaptive learning converges to the equilibrium capacity when customers have perfectly rational expectation.*

This result implies that assuming customers have rational expectation is valid even though customers learn adaptively provided the discount factor is close to 1. Our numerical studies (Liu and van Ryzin 2007) show that rational expectation model is a good approximation for an adaptive learning model as long as the discount factor is high enough.

15.5 Conclusions

Our work shows that rationing can be a profitable strategy to influence the strategic behavior of customers. It also provides a behavioral explanation for stocking and inventory service level decisions that are normally explained in terms of holding and lost-sales cost trade-offs.

When customers have fully rational expectations about availability, the trade-off is between the benefits of inducing customers to purchase early at high prices and the cost of lost sales due to rationing. We find whether rationing is profitable or not depends on several market factors. In general, a large high-value customer segment, high levels of risk aversion, and large differences in price over time all tend to favor rationing as an optimal strategy. And when the firm has the ability to choose prices optimally, rationing is always a profitable strategy. This implies with the ability to fine tune price schedules, rationing enables the firm to price discriminate and always emerges as an optimal selling strategy. Our oligopoly analysis shows that competition makes it more difficult to support segmentation using rationing and thus rationing is more likely to be used in cases where a firm has some reasonable degree of market power.

When customers are not able to perfectly anticipate availability, we find that rationing can be sustained as an equilibrium only if changing customer expectations is not very costly. When customers adjust their expectations slowly, future profits are deeply discounted, or customers are not very risk averse, the firm could end up serving the entire market at the discount price, even though rationing is more profitable in the long run. This shows how firms can be indeed saddled with an unprofitable strategy due to their past history. However, when future profits are not discounted, the equilibrium produced by assuming customers adaptively learn is the same as the equilibrium when customers have rational expectations.

There are several directions for potential further research. For example, in our rationing model, we analyze the firm's capacity decision assuming deterministic aggregate market demand. When aggregate demand is uncertain, the firm needs to also consider the trade-off between overage and shortage costs when it makes stocking decision. It would be interesting to see how aggregate demand uncertainty affects the rationing decision. Also, our learning model assumes that all the customers have the same estimate about the firm's strategy. What happens when each customer has his/her own estimate based on their own shopping experiences and hence there are heterogeneous expectations about the firm's capacity decision? Lastly, in the learning model, understanding what fundamental factors in customer behavior and the firm's economics lead to convergence to a single price versus a oscillating high – low availability strategy warrants further investigation.

References

Byers RE, Huff DJ (2005) No soup for you!: Intentionally unsatisfied demand and future production. MSOM 2005 Conference

Ferdows K, Lewis MA, Machuca JAD (2005) Zara's secret for fast fashion. http://hbswk.hbs.edu/tools. February 21

Gallego G, Phillips R, Sahin O (2008) Strategic management of distressed inventory. Production and Operations Management 17:402–415

Greenleaf EA (1995) The impact of reference price effects on the profitability of price promotions. Marketing Science 14:82–104

Liu Q, van Ryzin G (2007) Strategic capacity rationing when customers learn. Graduate School of Business, Columbia University. Working paper

Liu Q, van Ryzin G (2008) Strategic capacity rationing to induce early purchases. Management Science 54:1115–1131

Ovchinnikov A, Milner JM (2005) Strategic response to wait-or-buy: Revenue management through last minute deals in the presence of customer learning. Joseph L. Rotman School of Management, University of Toronto. Working paper

Part V
Pricing Strategies for Managing Rational/Strategic Consumer Behavior

Chapter 16
Shaping Consumer Demand Through the Use of Contingent Pricing

Eyal Biyalogorsky

Abstract In this chapter I assert that revenue management techniques like contingent pricing are not merely an optimal response by firms to exogenous conditions of uncertain demand that is spread over time but that sometimes one of the aims of those techniques is to shape consumer demand in such a way as to create the conditions necessary for successful employment of intertemporal price discrimination. In this view, the interaction between a firm's policies and the strategic response of consumers to those policies leads to consumer arrival processes that are the basis of many revenue management techniques. I consider a model with strategic consumers who can decide when to show up in the market and reveal demand. Using the example of contingent pricing, I investigate how consumers' awareness of the use of contingent pricing affects their decisions regarding when to show up in the market and how, in turn, consumers' responses should affect the firm's use of contingent pricing. I identify the conditions under which it is optimal for the firm to use contingent pricing to induce consumers to arrive at different times in the market. Implications for the design and use of contingent pricing and for public policy are explored.

16.1 Introduction

Revenue management methods have been developed to help a firm improve profits when selling a fixed number of units in a market in which consumer demand is spread over a period of time (i.e., not all consumers appear in the market at the same time). The firm is assumed to face some exogenously given, uncertain demand-generating process. A typical example is air travel, for which the typical (simplifying) assumption is that low-fare leisure travelers tend to appear early in the selling period and high-paying business travelers tend to appear late in the selling period (Wollmer 1992). Revenue management is concerned with deriving how the firm can

Eyal Biyalogorsky
University of California, Davis and IDC, Herzlia, Israel
e-mail: ebialogorsky@idc.ac.il

S. Netessine, C.S. Tang (eds.), *Consumer-Driven Demand and Operations Management Models*, International Series in Operations Research & Management Science 131, DOI 10.1007/978-0-387-98026-3_16, © Springer Science+Business Media, LLC 2009

use capacity allocation, dynamic pricing, and intertemporal price discrimination in the face of this demand-generating process to improve the firm's profits.

The assumption that demand is exogenous is, of course, a simplification and researchers have long recognized that consumers are likely to change or adapt their behavior as a result of revenue management efforts by firms. Researchers have long been concerned with practices of diversion and buy-up when customers are buying lower-fare tickets instead of higher-fare ones and vice versa in response to the availability of open-fare classes determined by the revenue management system (Brumelle et al. 1990, Pfeifer 1989). More recently, there has been much interest in the effects of strategic delay by consumers. Su (2007) considered the case in which some consumers may be patient: if prices at the time they show up in the market are too high, they may be willing to wait until prices drop before making a purchase. He shows that the optimal time path for price depends on whether the high-willingness-to-pay or low-willingness-to-pay customers are more patient. Aviv and Pazgal (2007) assumed that the price path exhibits discounting at some point in time and investigated how strategic delay by consumers should affect the way the seller sets his discount. Koenigsberg et al. (2008) allowed low-willingness-to-pay consumers to strategically delay their purchases and wait for last-minute deals. They showed that EasyJet's "commitment" to increasing prices over time can be an optimal reaction to such behavior and explored when last-minute sales should still be offered. Strategic consumers are likely to learn or anticipate that sellers will offer last-minute deals. Elmaghraby et al. (2009) show that if the amount of bargain hunting consumers is not too high the seller may be better off if consumers were allowed to make an advance reservation to purchase the product if it is still available at the time of the last-minute sale. The volume you are holding in your hand is evidence of the continuing interest in the effects of strategic consumer behavior on revenue management systems.

This chapter extends and complements the work on strategic consumer behavior and revenue management systems by looking at a setting in which consumers can decide when to show up in the market during the selling period,[1] whereas consumers in the previously mentioned papers could delay only the purchase, not decide when to show up. Assuming that consumers can decide when to show up without any restrictions makes the consumer arrival process endogenous and enables exploration of when and how revenue management can be used by firms to shape that process. The underlying motivation is the realization that arrival processes observed in actual situations do not result simply from exogenous factors but also can reflect long-term changes in behavior in response to implementation of various policies by the firm. This raises the possibility that some revenue management techniques are used not only in response to existing patterns of behavior but may represent an attempt to create or influence strategic consumers.

Consider the pattern in which early consumers in a market typically have a low willingness-to-pay and later consumers a high willingness-to-pay, a pattern that is

---

[1] I use the term "show up" to indicate that consumers are not active in the market all the time and choose when to become active. One can compare this to price skimming models in which consumers are active in the market all the time.

typical for air travel. This pattern is usually thought to result from leisure travelers' tendency to plan their trips well in advance while business travelers often need to change their plans on short notice. However, there is some anecdotal evidence that during the recession of the early 1990s the wide availability of "standby" bookings led many leisure passengers to delay purchase until the last moment and even show up at the airport without a reservation. This suggests that the common pattern of arrival may be only partially exogenous and may also depend on airline pricing. In addition, from a consumer behavior perspective, humans' well-known tendency to procrastinate and delay decisions until the last moment (Ariely and Wertenbroch 2002, Anderson 2003) suggests that leisure travelers would naturally wait unless there is a compelling reason to do otherwise. The nonrefundable nature of lower-price early bookings would exacerbate the tendency to procrastinate by creating financial risk if travel plans change. This is not meant to suggest that exogenous factors are not sometimes at work in the arrival pattern we observe in the airline industry, but the pricing patterns the airlines use appear to be a necessary condition for maintaining that pattern. In other words, it is possible that the revenue management systems the airlines use may have, over time, led to consumers adopting the behavior we see today.

This raises the question of whether revenue management can be used profitably to induce certain arrival patterns by consumers and what the implications of doing so are. In this work I take a stab at answering these questions by looking at one specific method—contingent pricing (see Biyalogorsky and Gerstner (2004))—and considering whether, in the face of strategic behavior by consumers, it can be profitable for sellers to use such a price mechanism to induce the low–high arrival pattern typical in the airline industry.

16.2 Contingent Pricing

Contingent pricing mechanisms are arrangements in which a seller agrees to sell a product to a buyer at a somewhat lower price while keeping an option to cancel the sale and instead sell the product to another buyer (Biyalogorsky and Gerstner 2004). Examples of such arrangements include the use of some cancellation clauses in house sales, airlines deliberately overselling a plane's capacity (Biyalogorsky et al. 1999), and underwriting of standby equity rights offerings (Bohern et al. 1997). Contingent pricing can help a seller mitigate price risks such as losing the opportunity to sell at a low price while waiting in vain for a high-willingness-to-pay consumer to show up or committing to sell to a low-willingness-to-pay buyer and losing potential sales to high-willingness-to-pay buyers. Biyalogorsky and Gerstner (2004) showed that contingent pricing can reduce such risks and increase the seller's expected profit, consumer surplus, and economic efficiency. The applicability and usefulness of such arrangements have been greatly extended in follow-up work on callable products (Gallego et al. 2008) and probabilistic selling (Fay and Xie 2008).

The idea behind contingent pricing is to find ways to avoid potentially inefficient use of available capacity. Because demand is spread over time and the seller is uncertain how many consumers will show up, *ex ante* pricing and allocation decisions are inefficient. Contingent pricing allows the seller, at a certain cost, to make decisions that are efficient *ex post*. In the original model by Biyalogorsky and Gerstner (2004), the seller knows the willingness-to-pay of each consumer because the arrival pattern is known and exogenous. However, since the seller is uncertain about whether the high-willingness-to-pay consumer will show up, his optimal decisions may be inefficient *ex post* and contingent pricing provides a solution to this problem.

If consumers are strategic, however, the arrival pattern is no longer exogenous and depends on the seller's price path. As a result, the seller faces the additional problem of identifying which consumers have a high willingness-to-pay and which consumers have a low willingness-to-pay (in addition to the price risks the seller faces in the original model). In the next section I present a model of contingent pricing with strategic consumers to explore how their strategic behavior affects the use of contingent pricing and when it is optimal for a seller to use contingent pricing, not just to avoid inefficient use of capacity but also to induce an arrival pattern that reveals consumers' willingness-to-pay.

16.3 Contingent Pricing with Strategic Consumers

In this section I describe a model of the use of contingent pricing with consumers who behave strategically.

A seller has one unit of a product for sale. As is common in the revenue management literature, there is a selling period of some length of time. Consumers can appear in the market at any point during this period and contract with the seller to purchase the unit. At the end of the period, the unit is delivered to the buyer who arranged to purchase it. The unit has no residual value (zero salvage value).

The major departure of this model from traditional revenue management models is that consumers who are active in the market are strategic and decide when to appear during the selling period. Further, I assume that consumers show up only once and disappear from the market and do not return if they do not contract to purchase the unit. This last assumption keeps in the model the risk of losing customers if the seller does not lock them up once they show up. Implicitly, it assumes that there is competition or other substitutes available to consumers in the market.[2]

Accordingly, the sequence of moves in the game has the seller announcing the price path over the selling period. Based on that, consumers decide when to show up and contract with the seller to purchase the unit. At the end of the period, the unit is delivered to the buyer who purchased it.

---

[2] One can also introduce a cost of showing up into the model. To keep things simple, however, I assume that buyers can show up only once, which, in effect, means that the cost of showing up a second time is infinite.

These assumptions on the strategic behavior of consumers in the market differ from traditional revenue management models, which usually assume that the pattern of consumers showing up in the market is exogenous. Even recent models that allowed for strategic behavior usually assumed that the appearance of a consumer in the market is exogenous and that the consumer can only decide whether to purchase immediately or to wait for a better price later (Koenigsberg et al. 2008, Su 2007). The setup here also differs from models of price skimming (Besanko and Whinston 1990, Jerath et al. 2007). In those models, strategic consumers are constantly active in the market so the seller does not face the risk that consumers who show up and are not served will leave the market.

There are two potential customers in the market: A high-valuation customer (v_h) and a low-valuation customer (v_l). The probability of each type of customer being active in the market is given by q_h and q_l, respectively. The customers' valuations and probabilities of being active in the market are common knowledge. However, the seller cannot identify which customer is which and does not observe the number of consumers active in the market. Both the seller and the consumers are risk-neutral.

In this chapter I explore whether, under this set of conditions, consumers' responses to a contingent pricing mechanism can lead them naturally to choose different times during the selling period to appear and whether it therefore benefits the seller to implement such contingent pricing arrangements.

Since there are only two consumers in the market, the contingent pricing arrangement need only have two price points. The specific arrangement I consider has the seller setting a price of p_l in the first part of the selling period and a higher price, p_h, in the second part of the selling period. In addition, the seller reserves the right to cancel the sale at any point prior to the end of the selling period. Thus, the seller can agree to sell the unit at a price of p_l and then later cancel the initial sale if a high-valuation customer appears and sell the unit at the higher price of p_h. A buyer who agrees to purchase the unit for a price of p_l is not guaranteed to receive it. I assume that compensation, h, is needed to convince a buyer to participate in a contingent contract in which receiving the unit is not guaranteed.[3] The compensation provided to the buyer is discounting of the price to p_l. Thus, the price pattern considered has the characteristics of a "deep discount" contingent pricing arrangement (see Biyalogorsky and Gerstner (2004)) with an increasing price path over time. The reason I concentrate on this particular price pattern is that it provides the stiffest test to the use of contingent pricing in the face of strategic consumers. Other possible price patterns make the seller's problem in using contingent pricing easier. For example, a "consolation reward" contingent arrangement, which is similar to the way airlines deal with overbooking, leads to less severe incentive constraint compared to the deep discount case[4]; a decreasing price path

---

[3] Biyalogorsky and Gerstner (2004) showed how the required compensation can be derived from the buyer's utility function.

[4] Biyalogorsky and Gerstner (2004) showed that with risk-neutral, nonstrategic behavior the deep discount and consolation reward arrangements are equivalent, but that equivalence does not hold in the case of strategic consumers.

over time avoids some of the commitment problems engendered by an increasing path.[5]

What the seller wants to achieve with this contingent pricing arrangement is for the low-valuation customer to appear early and the high-valuation customer to appear late, thus providing the seller with, in essence, two selling opportunities and protecting the seller from the risk of losing customers who are active in the market.

The optimal early price, p_l, must be appealing to the low-valuation customer under the contingent pricing arrangement. It is optimal, therefore, for the seller to set $p_l = v_l - h$ (proof of this and all other derivations can be found in the appendix).

If the high-valuation consumer is active in the market and decides to show up early to take advantage of the early low price, the probability that he will be able to purchase the unit is $1 - \frac{1}{2}q_l$ (assuming that, when the low-valuation consumer shows up, whoever shows up first gets the unit). Therefore, the expected surplus of the high-valuation consumer from showing up early is

$$Exp.\ Surplus_{\text{from coming early, high-valuation}} = (v_h - v_l + h)\left(1 - \tfrac{1}{2}q_l\right). \tag{16.1}$$

The expected surplus from showing up late is

$$Exp.\ Surplus_{\text{from coming late, high-valuation}} = v_h - p_h. \tag{16.2}$$

With the optimal price, p_h, chosen by the seller, the high-valuation consumer will be indifferent about showing up early or late. Therefore, the optimal contingent prices are

$$\begin{aligned} p_h &= (v_l - h)\left(1 - \tfrac{1}{2}q_l\right) + \tfrac{1}{2}q_l v_h, \\ p_l &= v_l - h. \end{aligned} \tag{16.3}$$

Given the optimal prices in (16.3), the expected surplus of the low-valuation consumer from showing up early is

$$Exp.\ Surplus_{\text{from coming early, low-valuation}} = h. \tag{16.4}$$

The optimal surplus from showing up late (note that p_h can potentially be lower than v_l and again assuming that if both the high-valuation and the low-valuation consumers show up late each have the same chance of getting the unit) is

$$\begin{aligned} Exp.\ Surplus_{\text{from coming late, low-valuation}} &= (v_l - p_h)\left(1 - \tfrac{1}{2}q_h\right) \\ &= \left[h\left(1 - \tfrac{1}{2}q_l\right) - \tfrac{1}{2}q_l(v_h - v_l)\right]\left[1 - \tfrac{1}{2}q_h\right]. \end{aligned} \tag{16.5}$$

For the low-valuation consumer who chooses to show up early, the surplus from appearing early has to be at least as great as that for showing up late. This leads to the following condition for the contingent pricing arrangement to induce consumers to show up at different times:

$$v_h - v_l > h\frac{q_h - q_l}{q_l}. \tag{16.6}$$

---

[5] Details of the solutions for alternative contingent pricing cases are available from the author.

Result 1. *Contingent pricing arrangements can induce low-valuation consumers to show up early and high-valuation consumers to show up late in the selling period even when consumers make decisions strategically.*

Result 1 shows that a contingent pricing arrangement can indeed lead to the low-to-high arrival pattern among consumers that was the basis for the original model of Biyalogorsky and Gerstner (2004). Specifically, this chapter shows that a deep-discount contingent pricing arrangement with prices as in (16.3) will cause the low-valuation consumer to show up early and the high-valuation consumer to show up late in the selling period if condition (16.6) holds. Contingent pricing will lead to the low–high arrival pattern if the difference in valuations between the consumers is sufficiently large and the compensation required by low-valuation consumers to agree to the contingent pricing arrangement is small enough. The threshold level of the difference in valuation that starts leading to separation in consumer arrival increases the higher the probability of the high-valuation consumer being active in the market and decreases the higher the probability of the low-valuation consumer being active in the market.

The seller's expected profit under the contingent pricing arrangement is

$$\Pi_{contingent} = (v_l - h)q_l(1 - q_h) + q_h p_h. \qquad (16.7)$$

Under fixed pricing (no contingent pricing), the seller's expected profit is[6]

$$\Pi_{fixed} = \begin{cases} q_h v_h & \text{if } v_h > v_l(1 + q_l(1 - q_h)/q_h) \\ (q_h + q_l - q_h q_l)v_l & \text{if } v_h < v_l(1 + q_l(1 - q_h)/q_h). \end{cases} \qquad (16.8)$$

Comparing the expected profits, the conditions under which the seller will implement a contingent pricing arrangement are

$$\text{i. } v_h < v_l(1 + q_l(1 - q_h)/q_h),$$
$$\text{ii. } v_h - v_l > 2h\frac{q_h + q_l - (3/2)q_h q_l}{q_h q_l}. \qquad (16.9)$$

Result 2. *Contingent pricing arrangements are more profitable than fixed pricing for the seller if condition 16.9 holds.*

Result 2 shows that it can be profitable for a seller to implement a contingent pricing arrangement (specifically, a deep discount arrangement) and induce strategic consumers to show up at different times during the selling season. This shows that it can be profitable for a seller to use contingent pricing arrangements even if all consumers in the market are completely strategic in their behavior.[7] Second, this

---

[6] Without contingent pricing, the seller does not know whether a customer who shows up has a high or low valuation apart from the base rate of the probability of each being active in the market. The seller's optimal strategy is to set the price at either v_l or v_h.

[7] Note that the model precludes some sort of strategic behavior such as collusion. This is not a problem in the airline industry but can be more problematic in other industries.

points to the possibility that firms' pricing arrangements are a factor that, over time, affected consumer behavior and actually created the familiar demand patterns we see in various industries. Thus, the airlines' use of contingent pricing and other revenue management techniques may have led to the low-valuation travelers who reserve flights well ahead of time and higher-valuation consumers who wait (or at least do not make reservations well in advance).

For contingent pricing to be profitable for the seller, the difference in valuations between the high- and low-valuation consumers must be large enough (16.9, part ii) to justify the cost of implementing the contingent arrangement (lower prices for low-valuation consumers). At the same time, the difference in valuations cannot be so high that the seller finds it optimal to ignore low-valuation consumers and restrict sales to high-valuation consumers (16.9, part i). If we compare the conditions in 16.9 to the conditions affecting a seller making optimal fixed-pricing decisions (16.8), we find that

Result 3. *It is optimal for the seller to implement contingent pricing only if the seller's optimal fixed-pricing approach is to set a low price that appeals to both high-valuation and low-valuation consumers.*

Result 3 shows how strategic behavior by consumers limits the value of contingent pricing, both in terms of the range of conditions under which it is optimal for the seller to use contingent pricing and in terms of the overall societal benefits from using it. The range over which it is optimal for the seller to use contingent pricing with strategic consumers is smaller than the range if consumers are not strategic. In particular, if consumers are not strategic in their behavior, contingent pricing can be optimal even when the best fixed-pricing approach is to set the price high enough to appeal only to the high-valuation consumer (Biyalogorsky and Gerstner 2004). When the best fixed-pricing approach is to serve only high-valuation consumers, there is a risk of not selling the available unit at all, a clear waste of resources and an inefficient outcome. As Biyalogorsky and Gerstner (2004) pointed out, one of the important effects of contingent pricing is that it avoids this potential waste, leading to increases in both profits and consumer surplus. Strategic behavior by consumers, however, leads sellers to limit the use of contingent pricing in a way that negates much of its potential positive effect.

16.3.1 Contingent Pricing as a Truth-Revealing Mechanism

There are two basic issues that a seller tries to address with contingent pricing. First, the seller is uncertain about the number of active consumers in the market. Second, consumers' valuations are private information that is not observable by the seller. Thus, the seller does not know if a consumer who shows up has a high or low valuation for the unit. By inducing consumers to separate their appearances in the market based on their valuations of the unit, contingent pricing allows the seller to ascertain what each consumer's valuation is and price accordingly.

The field of mechanism design is concerned with understanding how one can design mechanisms that induce others to reveal private information (Laffont 1989). In the setting considered in this work, contingent pricing provides one such mechanism whereby buyers reveal their valuations through choice of arrival time. One way to assess contingent pricing is to consider how effective it is as a truth-revealing mechanism. Assuming that the revelation principle holds in our setting,[8] (16.10) gives the best feasible pricing structure that is consistent with consumers truthfully revealing their valuations.

$$\begin{cases} v_l & \text{if a buyer identifies as a low-valuation buyer,} \\ v_l + \frac{1}{2}(v_h - v_l)q_l & \text{if a buyer identifies as a high-valuation buyer.} \end{cases} \tag{16.10}$$

Equation 16.10 thus gives the "best" pricing mechanism that can still lead to consumers revealing their valuations and therefore provides an upper-bound benchmark for the potential profits that the seller can achieve. Comparing (16.10) to the contingent pricing mechanism (16.3), we see that

Result 4. *As h goes to zero, contingent pricing converges to the "best" feasible truth-revealing mechanism.*

Per result 4, as long as the compensation (or cost), h, that is required to convince the low-valuation consumer to agree to a contingent pricing arrangement is relatively small, the contingent pricing arrangement basically implements the best possible truth-revealing mechanism and no alternative mechanism that the seller can implement will do better.[9]

The preceding discussion suggests that in many cases contingent pricing could be a viable approach for a seller to implement a truth-revealing mechanism. I will go one step further and claim that it is not easy to come up with other practical approaches that implement the truth-revealing pricing of (16.10). The basic issue with trying to implement the pricing structure of (16.10) is that in order for that pricing structure to induce truth telling by buyers they have to reveal their valuations simultaneously. However, the primary problem facing the seller is that buyers can appear at any time during the selling period. Once the buyers do not reveal their valuation simultaneously, the pricing structure of (16.10) no longer induces truth telling. Consider a high-valuation consumer who decides to lie and pretend to be a low-valuation consumer. If the real low-valuation consumer already appeared in

---

[8] The central result of mechanism design theory is that one can restrict attention to mechanisms under which all players with private information simultaneously and truthfully reveal that information. The conditions under which this holds are specified by the revelation principle. Developing the conditions under which the revelation principle holds in this setting is beyond the scope of this work, though I later discuss issues associated with implementing truth-revealing mechanisms other than contingent pricing.

[9] While we do not know enough to determine what compensation consumers will require to agree to a contingent pricing arrangement, it appears that in many cases the compensation is small relative to the potential benefits to the seller. For example, airline travelers who voluntarily agree to be bumped from a flight usually do so in return for in-kind rewards such as a lower price on a future flight. The real cost of such in-kind rewards for the airlines is much smaller than the stated value.

the market and the seller did not sell the unit to that first low-valuation customer, the seller can do no better than to sell the unit to the second consumer (despite the low price of v_l) because there are no other potential consumers in the market. On the other hand, if the low-valuation consumer has not shown up yet, there is no point in waiting to see if another consumer is active in the market—because if the high-valuation consumer pretends to be a low-valuation consumer, the best the seller can achieve, again, is v_l. Therefore, in order to induce truth telling, the seller must get both buyers to appear at the same time. The most common method to achieve this is to use an auction. Typical auction structures, however, only achieve second best, which in this case, again, is a price of v_l. To implement the price structure of (16.10) through an auction, one would have to use a special form in which bid steps correspond to the price in (16.10). This, for obvious reasons, is probably impossible in practice.

The point of this discussion is not to prove definitively that there is no other mechanism that implements (16.10) but to demonstrate that it is not easy to do so. Therefore, if contingent pricing achieves results that approach those possible using (16.10), it seems reasonable that sellers will use contingent pricing to induce separation and order in the arrival of consumers so they can ascertain the consumers' valuations.

16.4 Conclusion

This chapter shows that when consumers are completely strategic in their decisions regarding when to show up during a selling period the use of a contingent pricing arrangement can cause consumers to arrive in a desired order—specifically, low-valuation consumers first, followed by consumers with a high willingness-to-pay. It also demonstrates that inducing such an ordered arrival pattern can be profitable for the seller and that the profit from a contingent price arrangement can approximate the potential profit from the "best" possible truth-revealing mechanism if the consumer compensation required for implementing contingent pricing is small.

These results demonstrate that sellers can use contingent pricing to influence customer arrival patterns in profitable ways. They point to the intriguing possibility that some of the arrival patterns we actually observe were created over the long term by firms using such revenue management approaches. While this chapter only looked at contingent pricing, it is quite possible that other revenue management techniques can have similar effects. Cho et al. (2009) consider a seller that implements a dynamic pricing approach based on the remaining inventory and time till the end of the selling season. They show that the seller benefits if some consumers are patient and once in the market strategically wait in anticipation of lower prices.

One issue with the optimal contingent arrangement derived is that it requires commitment from the seller to a certain price path over time. Without that commitment, the seller has an incentive to deviate and change p_h (16.3) to v_h. While this is formally true in the static one-shot model presented, I do not consider this a major issue. In real-life situations, contingent pricing is used through repeated interactions with consumers, making deviation unprofitable for the seller. In addition, extending the model to capture other common factors may alleviate the commitment problem. For example, the possibility of having last-minute sales (as in Koenigsberg et al. (2008)) will prevent the seller from raising p_h. Airlines usually set prices in advance and only adjust capacity allocations during the selling period, which in effect creates a commitment device in this particular case.

A more fundamental issue is that consumers have to believe or know that the prices in (16.3) will be in effect. If consumers do not believe that that is the case, they will not respond to the prices in the desired way and will not arrive at the anticipated time. In other words, it is crucial that consumers learn what the price path will be. The implication is that a seller who wants strategic consumers to arrive at a particular time must be consistent and transparent in terms of pricing arrangements. This suggests that making it hard for consumers to learn about prices over time, as many airlines appear to do by creating obstacles and obfuscating the pricing structure, may be counterproductive in the long run because it may lead to an unraveling of the arrival patterns on which many of these pricing mechanisms rely.

Appendix

Proof of $p_l = v_l - h$

First note that the price p_l cannot be higher than $v_l - h$ because of the participation constraint of the low-valuation consumer. Now, consider a feasible contingent pricing arrangement with prices $\hat{p}_l$ and $\hat{p}_h$ such that $\hat{p}_l < v_l$ and $\hat{p}_h < v_h$. Increasing both prices $\hat{p}_l$ and $\hat{p}_h$ by ε does not change the relevant incentive constraints while still satisfying the participation constraints, therefore leading to the same behavior but with higher prices. Therefore, it is optimal to increase the price until the participation constraint is binding at $v_l - h$.

Derivation of Fixed-Pricing Profits

Under a fixed-price policy, the seller keeps the same price throughout the selling period. If the seller sets the price at v_h, he will sell the unit if a high-valuation customer shows up. The expected profit in this case is $q_h v_h$. If the seller sets the price at v_l, he will sell the unit if any customer shows up. The expected profit in this case is $(q_h + q_l - q_h q_l)v_l$. The seller will set the price at v_h if the expected profit from doing this is higher or if $v_h > v_l(1 + q_l(1 - q_h)/q_h)$.

Derivation of (16.10)

The seller announces that the price will be v_l if a buyer identifies as a low-valuation consumer, and p_{hr} if a buyer identifies as a high-valuation consumer, and, in case of a tie, will use a coin toss to determine which buyer gets the unit.

If $p_{hr} > v_l$, the low-valuation consumer will truthfully identify as having a low valuation. The expected surplus of the high-valuation consumer from truthfully identifying is $v_h - p_{hr}$ while the expected surplus from identifying as a low-valuation consumer is $(v_h - v_l)(1 - q_l/2)$. Thus, if $p_{hr} \leq v_l + \frac{1}{2}(v_h - v_l)q_l$, the high-valuation consumer will truthfully identify himself.

References

Anderson CJ (2003) The psychology of doing nothing: Forms of decision avoidance result from reason and emotion. Psychological Bulletin 129:139–167

Ariely D, Wertenbroch K (2002) Procrastination, deadlines, and performance: Self-control by precommitment. Psychological Science 13(3):219–224

Aviv Y, Pazgal A (2007) Optimal pricing of seasonal products in the presence of forward-looking consumers. Manufacturing & Service Operations Management

Besanko D, Whinston WL (1990) Optimal price skimming by a monopolist facing rational consumers. Management Science 36(5):555–567

Biyalogorsky E, Gerstner E (2004) Contingent pricing to reduce price risks. Marketing Science 23(1):146–155

Biyalogorsky E, Carmon Z, Fruchter G, Gerstner E (1999) Overselling with opportunistic cancellations. Marketing Science 18(4):605–610

Bohern Ø, Eckbo BE, Michalsen D (1997) Why underwrite rights offerings? Some new evidence. Journal of Financial Economics 43:223–261

Brumelle SL, McGill JI, Oum TH, Sawaki K, Tretheway MW (1990) Allocation of airline seats between stochastically dependent demands. Transportation Science 24:183–192

Cho M, Fan M, Zhou Y-P (2009) Strategic consumer response to dynamic pricing of perishable products. Consumer-driven demand and operations management models. Eds. Serguei Netessine and Christopher Tang, Springer. 435–457.

Elmaghraby W, Lippman S, Tang CS, Yin R (2009) Will More Purchasing Options Benefit Customers? Production and Operations Management. Forthcoming

Fay S, Xie J (2008) Probabilistic goods: An innovative way of selling products and services. Marketing Science. 27(4):674–690.

Gallego G, Kou SG, Phillips R (2008) Revenue management of callable products. Management Science 54(3):530–564

Koenigsberg O, Muller E, Vilcassim NJ (2008) easyJet pricing strategy: Should low-fare airlines offer last minute deals? Quantitative Marketing & Economics 6(3):279-297

Jerath K, Netessine S, Veeraraghavan SK (2007) Revenue management with strategic customers: Last-minute selling and opaque selling. Working paper, University of Pennsylvania, Wharton

Laffont JJ (1989) The Economics of Uncertainty and Information. Cambridge: MIT Press

Pfeifer PE (1989) The airline discount fare allocation problem. Decision Sciences 20:149–157

Su X (2007) Inter-temporal pricing with strategic customer behavior. Management Science 53(5):726–741

Wollmer RD (1992) An airline seat management model for a single leg route when lower fare classes book first. Operations Research 40(1):26–37

Chapter 17
Strategic Consumer Response to Dynamic Pricing of Perishable Products

Minho Cho, Ming Fan, and Yong-Pin Zhou

Abstract Dynamic pricing is a standard practice that sellers use for revenue management. With the vast availability of pricing and inventory data on the Internet, it is possible for consumers to become aware of the pricing strategies used by sellers and to develop strategic responses. In this chapter, we study the strategic response of consumers to dynamic prices for perishable products. As price fluctuates with the changes in time and inventory, a strategic consumer may choose to postpone a purchase in anticipation of lower prices in the future. We analyze a threshold purchasing policy for the strategic consumer, and conduct numerical studies to study its impact on both the strategic consumer's benefits and the seller's revenue. We find that in most cases the policy can benefit both the strategic consumer and the seller. In practice, the seller could encourage consumer waiting by adopting a target price purchasing system.

17.1 Introduction

Pricing has been an age-old management issue, especially for perishable products facing uncertain demand. Under the common fixed-price scheme, if the price is set

Minho Cho
Department of Information Systems and Operations Management, Michael G. Foster School of Business, University of Washington, Seattle, WA 98195-3200, USA,
e-mail: mc9@u.washington.edu

Ming Fan
Department of Information Systems and Operations Management, Michael G. Foster School of Business, University of Washington, Seattle, WA 98195-3200, USA,
e-mail: mfan@u.washington.edu

Yong-Pin Zhou
Department of Information Systems and Operations Management, Michael G. Foster School of Business, University of Washington, Seattle, WA 98195-3200, USA,
e-mail: yongpin@u.washington.edu

S. Netessine, C.S. Tang (eds.), *Consumer-Driven Demand and Operations Management Models*, International Series in Operations Research & Management Science 131, DOI 10.1007/978-0-387-98026-3_17, © Springer Science+Business Media, LLC 2009

too low, potential revenue will be lost; but if the price is set too high, demand will be low and perishable products may be wasted when they expire. Revenue management (a.k.a yield management) has become an increasingly popular management tool in selling perishable products. It is widely used not only in the hospitality industry (e.g., airlines, hotels, and cruise lines), but also in many other industries where products or capacity are perishable (e.g., golf course reservation, natural gas pipeline reservation, concert and ball game ticket sales, and fashion products). A detailed review on the subject was provided by McGill and van Ryzin (1999). Essentially, revenue management is a method that aims to sell the right inventory unit to the right consumer, at the right time, and for the right price (Kimes 1989). This is mainly achieved through dynamic pricing and inventory allocation. More recently, sellers begin to take advantage of the Internet to sell perishable products online (Choi and Kimes 2002, Liddle 2003). To many sellers, the Internet offers a new opportunity to implement revenue management techniques such as dynamic pricing because price changes are easy, inexpensive, and potentially more effective.

Most of the research on revenue management focuses on developing optimal pricing and inventory allocation policies (e.g., Littlewood 1972, Belobaba 1989, Gallego and van Ryzin 1994, Zhao and Zheng 2000). These models generally assume that consumers are not forward-looking and will purchase the products when the prices are below their reservation values. In contrast, this chapter examines how, by looking forward, consumers can strategically respond to the seller's dynamic prices over time. The growing use of the Internet provides an opportunity for consumers to gather information on sellers' pricing policies and respond strategically. The primary online shopping tools that consumers use today are shopbots that do price comparisons (Montgomery et al. 2004). Traditional shopbots compare prices spatially by checking the prices at various Websites at roughly the same time. They do not anticipate possible future price changes. More recently, researchers have shown interests in developing tools that can also compare prices temporally. One example is the "Hamlet" program[1] that studies past trends in the variation of airline fares and establishes the patterns, which can then be used to decide whether the consumer should make a purchase immediately or wait for possible future price reductions (Etzioni et al. 2003). Many critics doubt the effectiveness and the accuracy of Hamlet's prediction, however, because the underlying factors that determine the prices are not clearly understood (Knapp 2003).

In this research, we examine the behavior of strategic consumers who responds to dynamic prices by timing the purchase. The tradeoff is clear: since the price of a perishable product changes continuously over time, there is a chance to get the same product at a lower price by waiting. On the other hand, there is a chance that the product, which is available and affordable now, may be sold out or become more expensive later if the strategic consumer waits. We develop a threshold purchasing policy that balances this tradeoff and examine its impact on both the consumer and the seller. Focusing on the main factors that influence price, our analytical approach gives simple and effective solutions, and allows us to derive insights. Using

---

[1] This led to the establishment of the website http://farecast.com.

simulation we also find that the strategic consumer delay could benefit both the consumer and the seller. This conclusion is closely related to the reservation option used by the seller in Elmaghraby et al. (2009) which shows the seller can benefit from allowing a strategic customer who delays his/her purchase to reserve the item (the consumer must purchase the item if its prices drops to a lower, previously agreed-upon sales price).

It should be noted that in most existing models, while consumer purchasing patterns can be strategic, their arrivals patterns are usually assumed exogenous. In Biyalorgorsky (2009), the author presents a model in which the customer can decide strategically to show up or not, depending on the offering price. It is shown that the seller can use contingent pricing to influence consumers to show up at the desired time and improve his/her own profit.

The rest of the chapter is organized as follows. In the next section, we provide a brief review of the related literature. In Section 17.3, we derive a threshold policy that helps a single strategic consumer to decide when to purchase. In Section 17.4, we use simulations to evaluate its benefit to both the strategic consumer and the seller. In Section 17.5, we examine extensions to our base model. We make concluding remarks in Section 17.6.

17.2 Literature Review

There is an extensive body of literature on revenue management, mostly in the context of airline ticket sales. For a comprehensive review, see Talluri and van Ryzin (2004). Two different approaches complement each other. The first assumes that consumers can be categorized into different classes (e.g. leisure and business travelers) and focuses the analysis on the allocation of capacity among these classes. Based on the demand forecast for each consumer class, a "booking limit" of perishable products (e.g. airplane tickets) is computed for each consumer type. These thresholds can vary over time as demand unfolds (Littlewood 1972, Brumelle and McGill 1993, Robinson 1995). Literature on capacity allocation usually assumes a monopoly market structure with the exception that Netessine and Shumsky (2005) analyze seat allocation under both horizontal and vertical competitions using a game theoretical model. The second approach in revenue management focuses more on the dynamic pricing aspect of revenue management. Gallego and van Ryzin (1994) analyze the dynamic pricing policy for one type of product and homogeneous consumers. The consumers arrive randomly and their valuations for the product are also random. Important monotonicity properties are derived for the seller's optimal pricing policy. Zhao and Zheng (2000) extend this model to include non-homogeneous demand. Consumers are time sensitive so their reservation price distribution may change over time. None of these models consider consumers' reaction to the seller's pricing strategy, however. In their review of dynamic pricing models, Bitran and Caldentey (2003) point out "incorporating rationality on the behavior of consumers" as an interesting field of research.

Rather than assuming consumers are price takers, some marketing researchers have studied rational shopper behavior in the face of random price variations. In Ho, Tang, and Bell's rational shopper model (1998), the seller chooses one of a finite set of pricing scenarios and rational shoppers react by purchasing more when the price is low and purchasing less when the price is high. They find, among other things, that when price variability is high, the rational shoppers shop more frequently and buy fewer units every time. The type of product under consideration is the daily consumer product, which needs to be purchased and consumed repeatedly and continually over time. Consequently the main trade-off for a rational shopper is between the purchase costs and the inventory holding costs. This differs from the one-time purchase of perishable products, which is the focus of this chapter. Moreover, the price variation in Ho et al. (1998) is random, while the price variation in our chapter follows certain optimally determined curves that are given in the revenue management literature.

Besanko and Winston (1990) study a game between a monopolist, who sets prices for a new product over time, and strategic consumers, who decide whether to purchase now for the sure utility or postpone the purchase so as to maximize the future expected utility. In the equilibrium, the monopolist systematically reduces price over time. Elmaghraby et al. (2008) also study a game where the seller changes price over time and the buyers submit the desired quantities at any given price. Liu and van Ryzin (2005) study a similar problem in a discrete time-period setting, and allow consumers to be risk averse. All three papers are based on the assumption that all consumers are present at the beginning of the game, which results in certain monotonicity properties. In our chapter, consumers arrive randomly over time. Therefore, the optimal price trajectory depends on the realization of the consumer arrival process, and it may experience gradual decrease over time and sudden increase right after a purchase is made.

Aviv and Pazgal (2008) also study the strategic consumer reaction to price variations, and allow consumers to arrive over time. When forward-looking consumers have information about future price discounts, they may decide to postpone their purchases to a later time when discounts are offered. In their model, there are only a pre-fixed number of price changes, and the price-setting seller announces the prices and the price change times ahead of time. While this may represent a retail-type environment, it does not apply to the situations where the seller continuously changes its price in response to the realization of stochastic demands. In addition, in Aviv and Pazgal (2008), the consumers' valuations are homogeneous and decrease over time according to a deterministic function known to the seller. Thus, a consumer who arrives at a certain time will have a deterministic valuation for the product. In contrast, our model assumes heterogeneous consumer valuations and random consumer arrivals. Consequently, the prices consumers face are also stochastic.

Anderson and Wilson (2003) study consumer reactions to the dynamic allocation of airline seats to various fare classes. When all the low-price fares are closed, consumers may decide to wait before purchasing a ticket in the hope that a low-price fare class will reopen. The paper does not model consumer behavior explicitly, however.

The model in our chapter is most closely related to the dynamic pricing model in Gallego and van Ryzin (1994). Gallego and van Ryzin (1994) assume that all consumers are price-takers: those who can afford the price purchase right away and those who cannot, leave. In our model, strategic consumers are patient and would not purchase until the desired time or price of the product is reached. We are interested in the effect of such a strategy on the consumers' utility and the seller's total revenue.

17.3 Strategic Consumer Behavior

17.3.1 Dynamic Pricing Model

We assume that the seller's pricing strategy follows that in Gallego and van Ryzin (1994), which we call the GVR model. Therefore, we begin with a brief review of the GVR model. There is a fixed number, n, of one type of perishable product to be sold during a finite time horizon, T. The product is perishable so all units left at the end of the sales period are worth nothing.[2] Let k denote the number of products left, $0 \le k \le n$, and t the time units left in the sale horizon, $0 \le t \le T$. As is the convention, t gets smaller as time goes by. Therefore, the state of the system can be described by the vector (k,t).

Consumer purchases follow a price-sensitive Poisson process. That is, if price is p, then the instantaneous Poisson arrival rate is $\lambda(p)$, where $\lambda(p)$ is decreasing in p and $\lim_{p\to\infty} \lambda(p) = 0$. There is another way to interpret this consumer arrival process: Let the arrival of all potential consumers follow a Poisson process with a constant rate $\lambda(0)$. Moreover, let each consumer's valuation of the product, v, has the cumulative probability distribution (CDF) $F(p) = 1 - \lambda(p)/\lambda(0)$. Thus, when the price is p, an arriving consumer can afford the product with the probability of $1 - F(p)$. Consequently, the price-sensitive purchase arrival process is Poisson with the instantaneous rate $\lambda(0)[1 - F(p)] = \lambda(p)$. In this chapter, the second interpretation will be used.

In any state (k,t), the seller chooses the best price p – or equivalently $\lambda(p)$ – to maximize its total expected revenue $J(k,t)$. No inventory holding cost is considered for the seller, which is standard in the one-period problem setting. Gallego and van Ryzin (1994) show that $J(k,t)$ is determined by the following equation, with boundary conditions $J(n,0) = 0$ and $J(0,t) = 0$:

$$\frac{\partial J(k,t)}{\partial t} = \sup_{\lambda} [\lambda p(\lambda) - \lambda (J(k,t) - J(k-1,t))], \quad \forall n \ge 1, \forall t > 0,$$

where $p(\lambda)$ is the inverse function of $\lambda(p)$.

The seller's dynamic pricing strategy thus depends on the state status (k,t) and can be summarized in a pricing function $p(k,t)$. Clearly, it is reasonable to expect

---

[2] It will be straightforward to include an end-of-horizon salvage value for each unsold unit.

the price to be higher when fewer units are left or when more time is left. Thus, $p(k,t)$ is decreasing in k but increasing in t. Those properties are proved in Gallego and van Ryzin (1994).

In the GVR model, all consumers are price takers, which we call regular consumers. In this chapter, we assume there are two types of consumers: regular consumers (RC) and strategic consumers (SC). To begin with, in this section and next we will assume that there is only one SC in the system and analyze his/her behavior. In Section 17.5, we study the extension of having multiple SCs in the system.

We assume that the SC, with the help of software agents, is able to collect information about the seller's pricing policy $p(k,t)$ and the demand arrival function $\lambda(p)$, and use them to optimize the timing of her purchase.

The SC exhibits two major differences in her behavior from that of a RC. First, when a RC cannot afford the item, she simply leaves. In contrast, an SC chooses to wait so that, if the price drops later, she may afford it. Second, when a RC can afford the item at the current price, she purchases right away. In contrast, an SC may decide to postpone the purchase so that she may purchase the product at a lower price later.

17.3.2 Threshold Purchasing Policy

When the SC arrives to find the system in state (k,t), the decision for her is whether to purchase at the current price $p(k,t)$ or to wait. If she decides to wait, then what is the desired time or price level to make the purchase? We study the following two policies:

Threshold time policy (TTP). *With k products available, purchase if and only if there are t_k time units or less left in the sales time horizon, i.e., purchase if and only if $t \leq t_k$.*

Threshold price policy (TPP). *With k products available, purchase if and only if the price is below a certain threshold price level p_k.*

Since the SC knows that the seller changes price dynamically, waiting a little bit to purchase may result in a lower price. How long she waits will have to depend on both the number of units left, k, and the time left, t. This results in the TTP. From another perspective, the SC waits till a target price is reached, which is the TPP. Below, we show that the two policies are equivalent. All of the proofs in this chapter are shown in Appendix.

Proposition 1. *The threshold price policy (TPP) is equivalent to the threshold time policy (TTP).*

Because the TTP and the TPP are equivalent, in this chapter we will use them interchangeably.

If the SC arrives with little time but many products left (i.e., small t and big k), the price may already be lower than her target price p_k so the SC will purchase right away. In other situations, the SC may wait. Clearly, during the wait, it is possible that another consumer may arrive and make a purchase. In this case, k becomes $k-1$, and the SC will continue to follow the above policies and wait for t_{k-1} (or p_{k-1}).

Now we study how the SC determines the thresholds. Let her have a valuation of v for the product. The objective for her is to maximize her utility, which is defined to be the difference between v and the price paid for the product. Clearly, the SC will only purchase the product if the price is no more than v (i.e., no negative utility). If the SC ends up unable to purchase the product because the price is higher than v, we say that the consumer receives a utility of 0.

At any time, if the price is below the SC's valuation, she has two options: purchase now and get the sure utility or wait till later to either get the product at a lower price or see the price jump due to other consumers' purchases. The SC must carefully balance the consequences of the two options. We let the threshold t_k be the point at which the SC is indifferent between purchasing now and waiting a little longer. Due to bounded rationality, it is reasonable to assume that the strategic consumer only considers these two options. A more rigorous approach would also consider the option of waiting to purchase at a more distant future time. In this case, although we believe the following Proposition still holds, we can only prove it for some special cases. Even when one considers (17.1) to be a heuristic, our simulations in Section 17.4 show it is very effective.

Proposition 2. *Let t_k be the solution to*

$$\min\{p(k-1,t),v\} = p(k,t) + \frac{\partial p(k,t)/\partial t}{\lambda\left(p(k,t)\right)}. \tag{17.1}$$

If $t_k \geq t$, the strategic consumer will purchase right away; and if $t_k < t$, the strategic consumer will wait and the target purchase time is t_k.

17.3.3 Exponential Valuation of the Consumers

Equation (17.1) can be used to derive the thresholds for any given price strategy $p(k,t)$. To evaluate its efficiency, we will apply it to the case in which v follows an exponential distribution. This is the same distribution used in Kincaid and Darling (1963) and Gallego and van Ryzin (1994).

Let the arrival of potential consumers follow a Poisson process with a constant rate of a. Each consumers' valuation of the product, v, follows an exponential distribution with a rate of α. Consequently, when the price is $p(k,t)$, the probability that an arriving consumer has a valuation v higher than $p(k,t)$ is $e^{-\alpha p(k,t)}$. Hence, the price-sensitive Poisson arrival rate is $\lambda\left(p(k,t)\right) = ae^{-\alpha p(k,t)}$. For simplicity of notation, α is set to one.

Under these assumptions, Gallego and van Ryzin (1994) show that the optimal pricing policy for the seller satisfies:

$$p(k,t) = J(k,t) - J(k-1,t) + 1 \tag{17.2}$$

where $J(k,t)$ is the maximum revenue function for the seller and it satisfies

$$\frac{\partial J(k,t)}{\partial t} = \lambda(k,t) \tag{17.3}$$

and

$$J(k,t) = \log\left[\sum_{i=0}^{k}\left(\frac{at}{e}\right)^i \frac{1}{i!}\right]. \tag{17.4}$$

In what follows, we will further characterize these functions and derive properties that will simplify the analysis of (17.1). To streamline the exposition, we will use $\lambda(k,t)$ instead of $\lambda(p(k,t))$, and define

$$g(k,t) = p(k,t) + \frac{\partial p(k,t)/\partial t}{\lambda(k,t)}.$$

We obtain the following results:

Lemma 1. $p(k,t) + \dfrac{\partial p(k,t)/\partial t}{\lambda(k,t)}$ *increases in t.*

Lemma 2. $p(k-1,t) > p(k,t) + \dfrac{\partial p(k,t)/\partial t}{\lambda(k,t)}.$

Based on Lemmas 1 and 2, we can find the optimal purchasing thresholds.

Proposition 3. *(i) The t_ks for the TTP are solutions to* $v = p(k,t) + \dfrac{\partial p(k,t)/\partial t}{\lambda(k,t)}.$
(ii) A unique finite solution, t_k, exists for every k if and only if $v \geq 1$.

Proposition 3 reduces the computational effort for the time thresholds and facilitates further theoretical analysis. It also has a simple interpretation: When the SC decides not to purchase right now, two things are possible: the price may go up if another consumer arrives and the effect of this is $\lambda(k,t)[p(k-1,t) - p(k,t)]$; or if there is no other arrivals then the price will gradually go down over time and the effect of this is $\partial p(k,t)/\partial t$. Lemma 2 shows that the first, price-jump effect always exceeds the second, time effect. This, together with (17.1), results in Proposition 3.

Therefore, if v is very high, the SC will always purchase immediately. However, the existence of a finite v limits the first effect and makes the waiting option more attractive. One can also easily deduce that the lower the v, the more restrictions it puts on the price-jump effect, and the consumer is more willing to wait. The properties of the TTP are formally stated in Proposition 4.

Proposition 4. *The solution of the TTP has the following properties:*
(i) The t_ks are increasing in v.
(ii) The t_ks are decreasing in a.

Intuitively speaking, when v is small, the utility for the SC is small if she purchases the product right away; so the SC has little to lose if she waits and other RCs make purchases (and the price goes above v), but she has the potential to gain much if the price keeps dropping. On the other hand, the SC with a higher v will have a higher loss if the price jumps if she waits; but her gain from waiting for a lower price remains the same as that with a lower v. As a result, the SC with a higher v will purchase earlier. Numerically, this holds true especially for $k = 1$. For $k > 1$, the t_ks are quite insensitive to v.

Proposition 4 also states that the bigger the arrival rate a, the smaller the t_k. This means that if the product is "hot," then the consumer will want to wait longer. This seems counterintuitive at first, but it makes sense after a careful examination. When the demand rate is high, the seller also knows it. As a result, for the same k and t, the price will be higher for a higher a. Therefore the utility to gain for a consumer with a fixed v is lower. The SC's risk of losing this current utility by waiting is smaller now (since a is larger). So the consumer is willing to wait longer.

When the SC follows the TTP, she needs to estimate the following three parameters to determine her time thresholds:

- t, the time left
- k, the number of products left
- a, the arrival rate

In general, while t is usually easy to estimate, k may not be. If it is a physical item on display in retail stores, the consumers can check the level of inventory. On the other hand, if the product is not a physical item (e.g., air ticket), it may be difficult to obtain the seller's inventory information. However, sellers are increasingly volunteering such inventory information on their website and making it easier for consumers to find.[3] Hence, here we assume consumers can obtain the inventory level information. In Section 17.5, we relax this assumption and examine a policy that does not rely on the sellers' inventory information.

For the arrival rate a, we prove in the following Proposition that when a consumer follows the TPP, there is no need to estimate that parameter at all:

Proposition 5. *The solution to the TPP, p_k, is independent of a.*

From the proof we see that the p_ks are independent of a and the t_ks depend on a only through the product at_k. This makes sense because what is important for the SC, for a fixed inventory level k, is not the arrival *rate* of other consumers, but rather the expected *number* of other consumers who will arrive later. This is the product of the arrival rate and how much time is left, at.

That the threshold prices can be determined with only k and t makes the TPP a lot easier to use. Also, it is worth noting that the use of the TPP is quite similar to that of the limit order in stock trading: a consumer arrives to find the current prevailing market price and decides to transact later when a threshold price is reached. We will have more discussion on this later.

---

[3] For example, AA.com, expedia.com, and Travelocity.com all show how many seats/tickets are still left to potential buyers (sometimes on the first screen after a search). Moreover, on websites such as www.expertflyer.com consumers can get an inside peek into the airline's inventory.

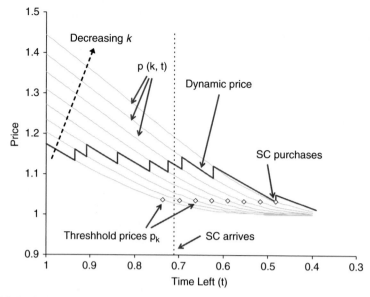

Fig. 17.1 Strategic consumer purchasing policy ($a = 70, n = 25, v = 1.05$).

The example in Figure 17.1 illustrates how the threshold policy works for the SC. Numerical results show that the threshold policy uses a different threshold time (t_k) for each inventory level (k). As shown in Figure 17.1, the threshold time decreases in k (this decrease is also observed in all the numerical tests we carried out for the simulations in the next section), which suggests that when inventory is higher, the SC should wait shorter. The reason is that, when inventory is high, the seller's price will be low, which means the SC does not need to wait long for the price to drop below the threshold level.

17.4 Simulation Results

17.4.1 Benefits to the Strategic Consumer

We conduct simulation studies to examine the benefit of using the TPP to the strategic consumer. The main purpose is to investigate the magnitude of the SC's benefit when different sets of parameters are considered. For every sample path of all consumer arrivals, we run two simulations simultaneously. In Simulation 1, we randomly pick a consumer to be the SC. This SC will follow the TPP. Simulation 2 is identical to Simulation 1 except that we replace the SC with a RC. If her valuation is less than the current price, the RC in Simulation 2 will leave the market while the corresponding SC in Simulation 1 will wait. If her valuation is higher than or equal to the current price, the RC in Simulation 2 will purchase the item right away, while the SC in Simulation 1 may still wait.

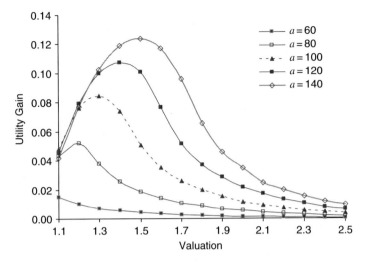

Fig. 17.2 Average utility gain for SC.

We compute two measures of the benefit to the SC. The first is the difference in utility gain between the SC in Simulation 1 and her corresponding RC in Simulation 2. The second is the difference in the probability of obtaining the product between the two consumers. We report the results in Figures 17.2 and 17.3, respectively.

It is worth noting that the price formula in (17.2) yields a minimum price of 1. Therefore, any consumer with valuation of less than 1 will never be able to afford the product. In the simulation tests, we allow the consumer valuations to follow the exponential distribution, but will present only results on the consumers with valuations more than 1.

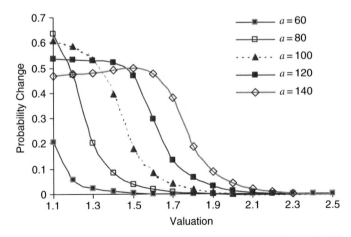

Fig. 17.3 Percentage point increase in the probability of obtaining the product for SC.

As shown in Figure 17.2, the SC consistently outperforms the corresponding RC. The highest performance difference occurs when the SC's valuation of the product is intermediate. Our explanation is that when the valuation is low, the maximum utility that can be obtained by the SC is limited; hence is the difference of utility between the two types of consumers. When the SC's valuation is high, her target prices will also be high. Oftentimes she will purchase the product immediately upon arrival. Thus, the SC does not gain much utility than the corresponding RC. It is also interesting to note that the utility gain increases with the arrival rate. With a higher arrival rate, the average product price will also be higher. The SC's benefit of using the TPP is higher under those situations.

For the SC with a high valuation of the product, she will not improve her chance of getting the product over the corresponding RC by waiting, because both are likely to afford the product. Therefore, it is expected that the improvement in the probability of getting the product mostly occurs when valuations are low. This is confirmed by Figure 17.3.

Figures 17.2 and 17.3 suggest that by following the TPP, the SC may benefit because (1) she may improve her chance of getting the product if she could not afford it upon arrival or (2) she may get a lower price later. The question is which effect is more dominant. To answer this, we perform more detailed analysis. We categorize all the simulation outcomes into two cases. In Case 1, the SC cannot afford the product upon arrival (i.e., $v < p$). In Case 2, the SC can afford the product upon arrival (i.e., $v \geq p$). The corresponding RC, who has the same valuation as the SC, will get a utility of 0 in Case 1. Thus, the SC will always be better off in Case 1. In Case 2, there are three scenarios. First, the SC buys the product immediately. In this scenario, there is no difference on the benefit. Second, the SC manages to purchase the product later. We believe that on an average she will be able to purchase at a lower price and, thus, is better off by waiting. Third, the SC waits but does not get the product. Because the corresponding RC purchases the product, the SC is worse off in this scenario.

The simulation results show that the expected utility gain of SC is positive in both Cases 1 and 2, suggesting that on an average the SC is always better off. Furthermore, we find that the expected gain predominantly comes from Case 1 when the valuation is low and the arrival rate is high. For example, about 99% of the benefit comes from Case 1 when $v = 1.1$ and $a = 140$, while only 12% of the benefit comes from Case 1 when $v = 2.5$ and $a = 60$. When the valuation is low and the arrival rate is high, the price is less affordable, and the TPP allows the SC to have the chance to purchase the product at a price lower than his valuation. When the price is more affordable due to either a lower arrival rate or a higher consumer valuation, a higher percentage of the expected gain comes from Case 2. Table 17.1 provides a summary.

17.4.2 Impact on the Seller

Since the use of the threshold purchase policy benefits the strategic consumer, one may expect that the seller will be worse-off if it continues to use the original dynamic pricing policy. Revenue could decline because strategic consumers will delay

Table 17.1 Sources of expected benefits.

	Scenarios	Change of benefits for SC (%)		
		Average	Max	Min
Case 1 ($v < p$)	Wait and get	64.5	99.4	11.9
			($v = 1.1, a = 140$)	($v = 2.5, a = 60$)
	Wait and not get	0	0	0
Case 2 ($v \geq p$)	Buy immediately	0	0	0
	Wait and get	54.6	236.1	0.6
			($v = 2.5, a = 60$)	($v = 1.1, a = 120$)
	Wait and not get	-19.1	0	-148.0
			($v = 1.1, a = 140$)	($v = 2.5, a = 60$)

their purchases and pay lower prices. On the contrary, we find the sellers by and large do better with a strategic consumer.

Figure 17.4 clearly shows that the impact on seller revenue is non-negative across all consumer valuations. With an SC delaying her purchase, there are two likely effects on seller revenue. First, the SC may purchase at a lower price or not purchase at all if the price increases beyond her valuation. This impact on seller revenue is negative. Second, when the SC could not afford the item upon arrival, her waiting essentially keeps the demand, which would have otherwise been lost, in reserve. Consequently, the seller can both maintain a higher price and reduce the number of unsold items later on. This impact on seller revenue is positive. Our results suggest that the positive effect dominates the negative effect. We also see in Figure 17.5 that the pattern of the increase in sales (number of tickets sold) is consistent with revenue increase, suggesting that sales increase is likely the major cause of revenue increase.

Note in Figure 17.4 that the positive impact is most significant when consumer valuation is low. Because consumer valuations are exponentially distributed, which favors low valuations, the seller's overall revenue increase should be significant. To see that, we conduct further simulations by following a random SC, whose valuation follows the exponential distribution. We find both the average seller

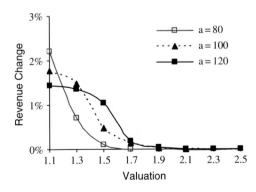

Fig. 17.4 Percentage of revenue change.

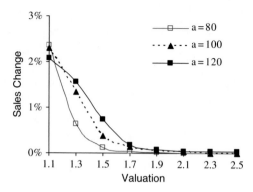

Fig. 17.5 Percentage of sales change.

revenue improvement and average sales improvement increase in the arrival rate (Figure 17.6). Figures 17.2 and 17.6 together suggest that when the product is "hot" (higher demand relative to supply), the use of the TPP results in higher benefits for both the SC and the seller. To explain this, we note first that when the arrival rate is high, the price is also high. Individual consumers are more likely to be priced out of the market when they arrive. This may even happen to high-valuation consumers at the beginning of the sales horizon. With the SC waiting, when price drops below the SC's threshold price, the SC will purchase. Thus, the SC provides a valuable demand cushion for the seller, especially when the arrival rate is high.

Moreover, using standard deviation or CV to measure price volatility in the original GVR model, we find that price volatility increases in the consumer arrival rate (Figure 17.7). Intuitively, with a higher arrival rate, the seller will price products higher. However, if expected demand does not materialize, the seller has to reduce the price more sharply. Therefore, the higher arrival rate leads to higher pricevolatility.

It seems that the increase in both the SC's utility and the seller's revenue can be explained by the increase in price volatility when the arrival rate is high. This is consistent with the results in financial literature on the limit order trading discussed earlier. In general, when the market is more volatile, individual market participants can benefit by being patient and waiting to a threshold price. Essentially, it is a

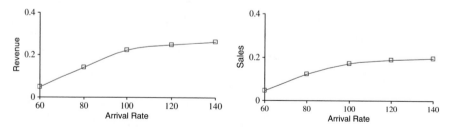

Fig. 17.6 Average revenue and sales increase by arrival rate.

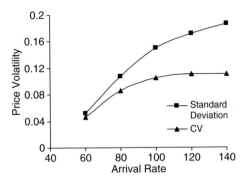

Fig. 17.7 Price volatility and arrival rate ($n = 25$).

form of transferring demand over time. When demand is stochastic, this practice will help improve the overall market performance as well. In financial market, limit orders narrow the bid–ask spread (Chung et al. 1999) and reduce transaction costs. In the market of perishable products studied in our research, the use of the TPP reduces wasteful inventory and increases seller revenue.

17.5 Extensions

17.5.1 Multiple SCs and a Simplified Threshold Price Policy

Realizing that the strategic consumer's waiting could increase sellers' revenue, sellers may develop a system to encourage consumer waiting. An interesting analogy, as mentioned earlier, is that allowing limited orders in financial markets helps to improve the overall market performance (Chung et al. 1999). There are many options to encourage consumers to stay around rather than leave instantly when prices are too high. We consider a simple system that allows consumers to indicate an intention of future purchase. For example, the seller can ask the consumer to create a "wish list" of the product and the target price, as well as the e-mail address where the consumer can be informed when the price is reached.[4]

In this section, we numerically investigate the impact of such a system on the seller's revenue. In Section 17.4, we already studied the impact of a single SC on the seller's revenue; but a target purchase system will be open to all the consumers and there likely will be more than one SC. In our simulations, we let each consumer choose to use such a system with a certain probability and systematically vary this probability. (We will continue to call these consumers SC.) Prior studies have reported that, even after many years in existence, online searching activities are still

---

[4] While this practice is quite common for online retailers such as Amazon.com, it is rare in the airline industry. Recently, however, Travelocity.com introduced a "FareWatcher" feature that allows users to be notified when the ticket price of a particular flight reaches a certain level or drops by a certain amount.

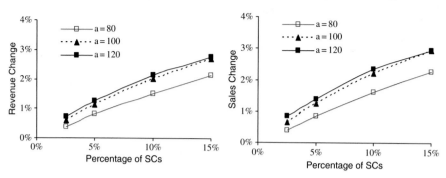

Fig. 17.8 Revenue and sales increase under a single target price. Impatience ratio $= 10\%$.

limited (Johnson et al. 2004, Montgomery et al. 2004). Therefore, we expect the use of such a target purchase system to be limited as well. Consequently, we vary the proportion of SCs from 2.5 to 15%.

For simplicity, the seller allows a consumer to leave only one target price.[5] Therefore, the SCs need to determine an inventory-independent target price. We simplify the TPP heuristic to achieve this: When an SC arrives, she first estimates the average inventory the seller will carry from this time forward, and then use this average inventory and the TPP to calculate her single target price.

Figure 17.8 shows how the proportion of SC impacts the firm revenue and sales. It is clear that more SCs help the seller to increase their revenue more, as they provide a larger demand cushion for the seller so that the price does not drop too low. This also explains the result that the seller will be able to sell more products when the SC proportion increases.

It is an interesting research topic to examine how the seller should react when the portion of SCs is more significant, but we do not pursue this further since it is beyond the scope of this chapter. Interested readers are referred to Su (2007).

17.5.2 Constraints on Strategic Consumer Waiting

Our model so far has assumed an infinitely patient SC who does not incur cost while waiting for the target time/price. In this section, we examine two approaches that incorporate constraints on SC waiting. First, we include waiting cost for the SC. Second, we consider impatient SCs.

In the first approach, we extend the base model by including a linear waiting cost. That is, for every unit of time the SC waits, she incurs a cost of c, which can be a function of the SC's valuation v. For example, if the SC is waiting for an air

---

[5] It is unlikely that the firm will allow the consumers to leave target prices based on the inventory level. Theoretically, the consumer can periodically check the inventory level and modify her target price accordingly. This calls for such a substantial amount of work on the consumer's part that they will not use it frequently in practice. Therefore, to simplify the analysis, we focus on the case where the consumers leave one price and do not change it as time and inventory levels change.

ticket, then while waiting she has to endure and manage the uncertainty imposed on her other activities during the trip (booking hotel, rental car, tour, etc.). It turns out that it is fairly straightforward to extend the base model to include c. The following Proposition parallels Proposition 3.

Proposition 6. *The $t_k s$ for the TTP are solutions to* $v = p(k,t) + \dfrac{\partial p(k,t)/\partial t}{\lambda(k,t)} - c.$

It is interesting to note that, in terms of choosing target times, the inclusion of c effectively makes an SC with valuation v act like an SC with valuation $v + c$ in the base model. Using Proposition 4, we observe that the higher the waiting cost, the bigger the $t_k s$, and the shorter the SC's waiting time. Although intuitive, Proposition 6 provides a way to quantify the effect of c.

Another way to incorporate the constraint on consumer waiting is to explicitly model those consumers who wait but then leave the system before making a purchase; i.e., some SCs are impatient. The difference between this approach and the waiting cost approach is akin to that between abandonment and waiting cost in the queueing literature. We believe that abandonment is a more realistic and robust way to model consumer waiting because the cost of waiting could be difficult to quantify. Therefore, we focus on this approach in subsequent simulation studies.

In the simulations we allow a certain portion of SCs to be impatient. We call this portion the impatience ratio. Those impatient SCs are randomly selected, and each has her own time-to-abandonment which is uniformly distributed between their arrival time and the end of the sales horizon. In addition to consumer impatience level, the impatience ratio can also reflect the level of competition (e.g., how many airlines fly between the city pair on that date) and the level of consumer loyalty (e.g., whether the consumer belongs to a loyalty program). In our simulations we vary the impatience ratio from 0 to 15%.

Figure 17.9 displays the impact of impatience ratio on seller revenue and sales. We set the proportion of SCs of all consumers to 10% and let all the SCs follow a single target price heuristic—the simplified TPP. Not surprisingly, as impatience ratio increases, both revenue and sales increase decrease, but they remain positive.

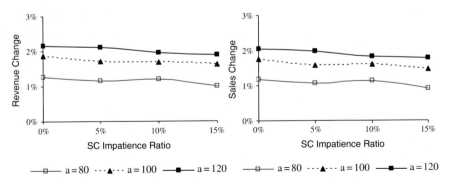

Fig. 17.9 Percentage of impatient SCs and the changes of revenue and sales.

Figures 17.9, together with Figure 17.8, also reveal that the revenue increase with SCs is higher with a higher customer arrival rate. This again suggests that sellers with more price volatility should benefit more by providing a target purchase option to their customers.

17.6 Conclusions and Future Research

In this research, we study the strategic response of customers to dynamic prices of revenue management. The strategic customers wait to purchase at specific target prices (TPP) or target times (TTP) that depend on the customer's valuation of the product and the current inventory level. We conduct simulations to study the performance of TTP/TPP. We show that customers benefit by following these policies. In particular we find that when customer valuation is low or the arrival rate is high, most of the utility gains come from the improved probability of getting the product by waiting (hence, the utility improves to non-zero from zero). When the valuation is high, then most of the benefits come from the lower price strategic customers can expect by waiting. Overall, the benefit is the greatest for low-valuation customers (low v) and hot products (high a).

We show that the firm also benefits from having SCs who follow the TTP/TPP. This result first seems to be counterintuitive until one realizes that this is not a zero-sum game. The firm may benefit because, while RCs will leave the market if they cannot afford the product upon arrival (especially early in the sales period when the product price is usually higher), SCs are kept in the waiting pool. This waiting of SCs provides a cushion to price volatility and prevents the price from falling too low. It also serves as an additional demand that helps to reduce wasted inventory at the end. This benefit is somewhat similar to the benefits of limit orders in stock trading which provide liquidity to the market (Chung et al. 1999, Foucault 1999).

When high-valuation SCs wait and get a lower price, this will negatively affect the firm's revenue. But our results show that, in general, the potential revenue loss from the delay of purchase is limited. High-valuation consumers, as it turns out, have higher target prices, and are very likely to purchase immediately upon arrival. Keeping low-valuation consumers in the waiting pool helps to reduce wasted inventory and prevent firms from deep price discounts toward the end. This could be especially beneficial to industries with a fixed cost for the products, e.g., airline tickets and hotel rooms, where the revenue loss of each wasted inventory is large.

This discovery of benefits to the firm is important as it encourages companies to develop systems that can allow consumers to place a "limit order" for the products or services. Actual implementation can be flexible. Consumers can choose to be notified of price changes through e-mails. A promising direction for future research is to model the impact of such practices on firm's revenue analytically and quantify the trade-offs between the higher sales and the lower prices paid by some consumers.

Appendix

Proof of Proposition 1

Because the pricing curves $p(k,t)$ are strictly increasing in t for the fixed k, it is easy to show that there exists a one-to-one relationship between t_k and $p_k = p(k,t_k)$ such that $t > t_k \Leftrightarrow p > p_k$ and $t < t_k \Leftrightarrow p < p_k$. Thus, there is a one-to-one correspondence between the TPP and the TTP.

Proof of Proposition 2

Suppose that the SC arrives in the state (k,t) and sees the price $p(k,t)$. We denote $q_i(k,t,\Delta t)$ the probability of i consumers arriving during $[t, t - \Delta t]$ who can afford $p(k,t)$. It is easy to see

$$\lim_{\Delta t \to 0} q_0(k,t,\Delta t) = 1, \quad \lim_{\Delta t \to 0} \frac{q_1(k,t,\Delta t)}{\Delta t} = \lambda\left(p(k,t)\right),$$

and

$$\sum_{i \geq 2} q_i(k,t,\Delta t) = o(\Delta t).$$

If the SC purchases the product at t, the realized utility is $v - p(k,t)$. If the SC waits and purchases after Δt, the expected utility is

$$q_1(k,t,\Delta t)\max\{0, v - p(k-1, t - \Delta t)\}$$
$$+ q_0(k,t,\Delta t)[v - p(k, t - \Delta t)] + o(\Delta t). \tag{A.1}$$

At the threshold t_k, the SC is indifferent between purchasing and waiting a little bit. By equating these two utilities and letting Δt go to 0, we obtain

$$\lim_{\Delta t \to 0}\left[\frac{1 - q_1(k,t,\Delta t) - q_0(k,t,\Delta t)}{\Delta t}\right][v - p(k,t)]$$
$$= \lim_{\Delta t \to 0}\left\{\frac{q_1(k,t,\Delta t)}{\Delta t}[p(k,t) - \min\{p(k-1, t - \Delta t), v\}]\right.$$
$$\left. + q_0(k,t,\Delta t)\frac{[p(k,t) - p(k, t - \Delta t)]}{\Delta t} + \frac{o(\Delta t)}{\Delta t}\right\}.$$

This amounts to

$$0 = \lambda\left(p(k,t)\right)[p(k,t) - \min\{p(k-1,t), v\}] + \frac{\partial}{\partial t}p(k,t).$$

Therefore, the time threshold t_k satisfies

$$\min\{p(k-1,t), v\} = p(k,t) + \frac{\partial p(k,t)/\partial t}{\lambda\left(p(k,t)\right)}.$$

Proof of Lemma 1

From (2) and (3),

$$\frac{\partial p(k,t)}{\partial t} = \frac{\partial J(k,t)}{\partial t} - \frac{\partial J(k-1,t)}{\partial t} = \lambda(k,t) - \lambda(k-1,t).$$

We also know that $\lambda(k,t) = ae^{-p(k,t)}$. Therefore, because

$$g(k,t) = p(k,t) + \frac{\partial p(k,t)}{/} \partial t \lambda(k,t),$$

$$g(k,t) = p(k,t) + 1 - \frac{\lambda(k-1,t)}{\lambda(k,t)} = p(k,t) + 1 - e^{-[p(k-1,t)-p(k,t)]}.$$

Therefore,

$$\frac{\partial g(k,t)}{\partial t} = \frac{\partial p(k,t)}{\partial t} + e^{-[p(k-1,t)-p(k,t)]} \left[\frac{\partial p(k-1,t)}{\partial t} - \frac{\partial p(k,t)}{\partial t} \right]$$

$$= \frac{\partial p(k,t)}{\partial t} \left[1 - e^{-[p(k-1,t)-p(k,t)]} \right] + e^{-[p(k-1,t)-p(k,t)]} \frac{\partial p(k-1,t)}{\partial t}.$$

Because $p(k,t)$ is increasing in t and decreasing in k, it follows that $\partial g(k,t)/\partial t \geq 0$.

Proof of Lemma 2

$$\frac{\partial p(k,t)/\partial t}{\lambda(k,t)} = \frac{\lambda(k,t) - \lambda(k-1,t)}{\lambda(k,t)} = \frac{e^{-p(k,t)} - e^{-p(k-1,t)}}{e^{-p(k,t)}}$$

$$= \frac{-e^{-\xi}[p(k,t) - p(k-1,t)]}{e^{-p(k,t)}} = \frac{e^{-\xi}[p(k-1,t) - p(k,t)]}{e^{-p(k,t)}}$$

$$< [p(k-1,t) - p(k,t)], \quad \text{for some } \zeta \in (p(k,t), p(k-1,t)).$$

It is clear then

$$p(k-1,t) > p(k,t) + \frac{\partial p(k,t)/\partial t}{\lambda(k,t)}.$$

Proof of Proposition 3

Lemmas 1 and 2 imply that the LHS and the RHS of (17.1) look like the graph displayed in Figure 17.10.

(i) From Figure 17.10, it is clear that, because $p(k-1, t)$ is always greater than the RHS, t_k is the intersection of v and the RHS. In effect, (17.1) can be simplified to

$$v = p(k,t) + \frac{\partial p(k,t)/\partial t}{\lambda(p(k,t))}. \tag{A.2}$$

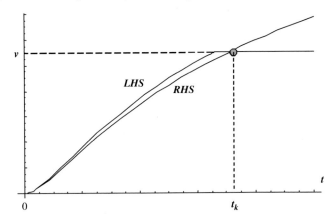

Fig. 17.10 Solution to the threshold policy.

(ii) Next, we prove that the two curves will intersect if and only if $v \geq 1$. Since the RHS is increasing in t, its minimum is achieved at $t = 0$, which is 1. So clearly v needs to be at least one. On the other hand, when t goes to 0, the RHS goes to 1; and when t goes to ∞, the value goes to ∞. Because the RHS is continuous, we conclude that for any $v \geq 1$, there exists a t_k such that the equality holds. The uniqueness follows easily from the monotonicity of the RHS (Lemma 1).

Proof of Proposition 4

Property (i) follows immediately from Figure 17.10. For Property (ii), we note that

$$\frac{\partial g(k,t)}{\partial a} = \frac{\partial p(k,t)}{\partial a} + e^{-[p(k-1,t)-p(k,t)]}\left[\frac{\partial p(k-1,t)}{\partial a} - \frac{\partial p(k,t)}{\partial a}\right]$$
$$= \frac{\partial p(k,t)}{\partial a}\left[1 - e^{-[p(k-1,t)-p(k,t)]}\right] + e^{-[p(k-1,t)-p(k,t)]}\frac{\partial p(k-1,t)}{\partial a}.$$

Because $p(k,t)$ is increasing in a, it follows that $g(k,t)$ is also increasing in a. Clearly from Figure 17.10, as the RHS increases and v stays the same, the intersection point, t_k, decreases.

Proof of Proposition 5

First of all, note the following:

$$p_k = p(k,t_k) = v - \frac{\partial p(k,t_k)/\partial t}{\lambda(k,t_k)} = v - \frac{\lambda(k,t_k) - \lambda(k-1,t_k)}{\lambda(k,t_k)}$$
$$= v - 1 + \frac{\lambda(k-1,t_k)}{\lambda(k,t_k)} = v - 1 + e^{-[p(k-1,t_k)-p(k,t_k)]}. \tag{A.3}$$

Because $J(k,t) = \log\left[\sum_{i=0}^{k}((at/e)^i/i!)\right]$ and $p(k,t) = J(k,t) - J(k-1,t) + 1$, both $J(k,t)$ and $p(k,t)$ depend on a only through the product at. So if we let $x = at$ then both $J(k,t)$ and $p(k,t)$ become functions of only x (i.e., they are free of a). Therefore, we can simply solve (A.2) to obtain $x_k = at_k$ and plug them into (A.3) to compute p_k. The p_ks thus computed are all free of a.

Proof of Proposition 6

This proof is very similar to that of Proposition 2. If the SC purchases the product at t, the realized utility is $v - p(k,t)$. If the SC waits and purchases after Δt, the expected utility is

$$q_1(k,t,\Delta t)\max\{0, v - p(k-1, t - \Delta t)\}$$
$$+ q_0(k,t,\Delta t)[v - p(k, t - \Delta t)] - c\Delta t + o(\Delta t). \qquad (A.4)$$

At the threshold t_k, the SC is indifferent between purchasing and waiting a little bit. By equating these two utilities and letting Δt go to 0, we obtain

$$\lim_{\Delta t \to 0}\left[\frac{1 - q_1(k,t,\Delta t) - q_0(k,t,\Delta t)}{\Delta t}\right][v - p(k,t)]$$
$$= \lim_{\Delta t \to 0}\left\{\frac{q_1(k,t,\Delta t)}{\Delta t}[p(k,t) - \min\{p(k-1, t - \Delta t), v\}]\right.$$
$$\left. + q_0(k,t,\Delta t)\frac{[p(k,t) - p(k, t - \Delta t)]}{\Delta t} - c + \frac{o(\Delta t)}{\Delta t}\right\}.$$

This amounts to

$$0 = \lambda(p(k,t))[p(k,t) - \min\{p(k-1,t), v\}] + \frac{\partial}{\partial t}p(k,t) - c.$$

Therefore, the time threshold t_k satisfies

$$\min\{p(k-1,t), v\} = p(k,t) + \frac{\partial p(k,t)/\partial t}{\lambda(p(k,t))} - c. \qquad (A.5)$$

If $t_k \geq t$, the strategic consumer will purchase right away; and if $t_k < t$, the strategic consumer will wait and the target purchase time is t_k. Also, similar to Lemmas 1 and 2 (the proofs are hence omitted), we can show that

1. $p(k,t) + \dfrac{\partial p(k,t)/\partial t}{\lambda(k,t)} - c$ is increasing in t, and

2. $p(k-1,t) > p(k,t) + \dfrac{\partial p(k,t)/\partial t}{\lambda(k,t)} - c.$

The second result above allows us to simplify (A.3) to

$$v = p(k,t) + \frac{\partial p(k,t)/\partial t}{\lambda(k,t)} - c,$$

which completes the proof. We note, from Figure 17.10, that a positive c will increase the target time $t_k s$, which means the SC is willing to wait less when there is a cost. While this is intuitive, Propositions 3 and 6 show a way to quantify the difference.

References

Anderson CK, Wilson JG (2003) Wait or buy? The strategic consumer: Pricing and profit implications. Journal of the Operational Research Society 54(2):299–306

Aviv Y, Pazgal A (2008) Optimal pricing of seasonal products in the presence of forward-looking consumers. Manufacturing & Service Operations Management 10(3):339– 359

Belobaba P (1989) Application of a probabilistic decision model to airline seat inventory control. Operations Research 37:183–197

Besanko D, Winston W (1990) Optimal price skimming by a monopolist facing rational consumers. Management Science 36(5):555–567

Bitran G, Caldentey R (2003) An overview of pricing models for revenue management. Manufacturing & Service Operations Management 5(2):203–229

Biyalorgorsky E (2009) Shaping consumer demand through the use of contingent pricing, in Operations Management Models with Consumer-Driven Demand, ed. Serguei Netessine and Christopher S. Tang, Springer

Brumelle SL, McGill JI (1993) Airline seat allocation with multiple nested classes. Operations Research 41:127–137

Choi S, Kimes SE (2002) Electronic distribution channel's effect on hotel revenue management. Cornell Hotel and Restaurant Administration Quarterly 43(2):23–31

Chung K, Van Ness B, Van Ness R (1999) Limit orders and the bid-ask spread. Journal of Financial Economics 53:255–287

Elmaghraby W, Gulcu A, Keskinocak P (2008) Designing the optimal preannounced markdowns in the presence of rational consumers with multi-unit demands. Manufacturing & Service Operations Managements 10(3):126–148

Elmaghraby W, Lippman S, Tang CS, Yin R (2009) Will more purchasing options benefit customers? Production and Operations Management. Forthcoming

Etzioni O, Knoblock C, Tuchinda R, Yates A (2003) To buy or not to buy: Mining airfare data to minimize ticket purchase price. SIGKDD'03, August 24–27, Washington, DC, USA

Foucault T (1999) Order flow composition and trading costs in a dynamic limit order market. Journal of Financial Markets 2:99–134

Gallego G, van Ryzin G (1994) Optimal dynamic pricing of inventories with stochastic demand over finite horizon. Management Science 40:999–1020

Ho T, Tang CS, Bell DR (1998) Rational shopping behavior and the option value of variable pricing. Management Science 44:145–160

Johnson E, Moe W, Fader P, Bellman S, Lohse G (2004) On the depth and dynamics of online search behavior. Management Science 50(2):299–308

Kimes SE (1989) Yield management: a tool for capacity-constrained service firm. Journal of Operations Management 8:348–363

Kincaid WM, Darling DA (1963) An inventory pricing problem. Journal of Mathematical Analysis and Applications 7 (2):183–208

Knapp L April 9, (2003) Algorithms key to cheap air fare. Wired News

Liddle A (2003) Using web for discounting clicks with digital diners. Nation's Restaurant News 37(20):172

Littlewood K (1972) Forecasting and control of passengers. 12th AGIFORS Symposium Proceedings. Nathanya, Israel 95–128

Liu Q, van Ryzin G (2005) Strategic capacity rationing to induce early purchases. Manufacturing & Service Operations Management 8(1):110–115

McGill J, van Ryzin G (1999) Revenue management: Research overview and prospects. Transportation Science 33:233–256

Montgomery A, Hosanagar K, Krishnan R, Clay K (2004) Designing a better shopbot. Management Science 50(2):189–206

Netessine S, Shumsky RA (2005) Revenue management games: Horizontal and vertical competition. Management Science 51(5):813–831

Robinson LW (1995) Optimal and approximate control policies for airline booking with sequential nonmonotonic fare classes. Operations Research 43:252–263

Su X (2007) Inter-temporal pricing with strategic customer behavior. Management Science 53(5):726–741

Talluri K, van Ryzin G (2004) The theory and practice of revenue management. Kluwer Academic Publishers, Dodrecht

Zhao W, Zheng Y (2000) Optimal dynamic pricing for perishable assets with nonhomogeneous demand. Management Science 46:375–388

Chapter 18
Strategic Behavior in Supply Chains: Information Acquisition

Karan Girotra and Wenjie Tang

Abstract Reducing the financial impact of supply–demand mismatches is a central objective of supply chain management. Modern supply chains have multiple independent self-interested actors each with different information about the demand uncertainties facing the supply chain. Strategic behavior by these self-interested actors often enhances the supply–demand mismatches in the supply chain. In this chapter, we present the case of a fashion products supply chain with multiple strategic actors each of which has different information. Traditional contracting strategies in this supply chain lead to excessive supply–demand mismatches. We then propose an alternate contracting strategy. Specifically, we propose that the supply chain starts offering "Advanced Purchase Discounts" in addition to the traditional wholesale price based contracts. We demonstrate that strategic responses to these contracts by agents in the supply chain lead to *better information sharing, superior risk bearing, reduced supply–demand mismatches* and can lead to Pareto-improving outcomes for all actors in the supply chain. In contrast with conventional wisdom that strategic behavior in the supply chain leads to poorer supply chain performance, our results illustrate that appropriately designed supply chain practices can actually exploit the strategic behavior of actors to improve supply chain performance. We conclude by illustrating the application of the proposed contracts to our motivating example of the fashion products supply chain.

Karan Girotra
Technology & Operations Management, INSEAD, Fontainebleau, 77300, France,
e-mail: karan.girotra@insead.edu

Wenjie Tang
Technology & Operations Management, INSEAD, Fontainebleau, 77300, France,
e-mail: wenjie.tang@insead.edu

S. Netessine, C.S. Tang (eds.), *Consumer-Driven Demand and Operations Management Models*, International Series in Operations Research & Management Science 131, DOI 10.1007/978-0-387-98026-3_18, © Springer Science+Business Media, LLC 2009

18.1 Introduction

Supply chains are made up of multiple strategic actors – manufacturers, wholesalers, retailers, and most importantly customers. Prevalent macroeconomic trends favoring skill and geographical specialization are making it increasingly common that each of these tiers is owned and operated by different agents. Each of these strategic agents acts independently with its best information to maximize its benefits. As a consequence, such supply chains are often plagued by financial losses due to supply–demand mismatches. Often, different tiers in the supply chain produce, buy or stock too much and are stuck with excess inventory. In other situations, firms produce or stock too little and are consequently unable to meet demand from their customers, thus losing potential profits. Minimizing the financial impact of these supply–demand mismatches is a central objective of supply chain management. In this chapter, we present the case of a fashion products supply chain, that is struggling with extensive losses due to such supply–demand mismatches. We then present a strategy that exploits the strategic behavior of individual actors in the supply chain to mitigate these supply–demand mismatches.

One of the primary reasons for supply–demand mismatch is imprecise demand information – If all agents knew exactly how much demand would be, they would all produce or stock exactly as much as demand and there would be no leftover inventory or unmet customer demand. While each tier of the supply chain individually suffers from the consequences of imprecise demand information, a supply chain with independent strategic actors also suffers from the additional consequences arising out of the lack of information sharing between different tiers of a supply chain. In many instances, the tiers of a supply chain closest to the customer may have the best demand information, but they do not have the incentives to share information with other agents in the supply chain. In other instances, the supply chain tier with the best information may not have the decision rights. Further, at times different tiers may each have some private information and consolidating that information may lead to superior decision making than utilizing the information independently.

We propose a strategy to ameliorate the losses due to lack of information sharing by designing contracts that exploit the strategic behavior of independent actors in the supply chain. Our strategy involves offering "Advance Purchase Discounts" (APDs). Under such a scheme an upstream tier offers downstream tiers the opportunity to place orders well in advance of demand. Acting in its own best interest, the downstream tier uses the best information available to it when making these early orders. From observing these orders, the upstream tier can infer the information available to the downstream tier and can make its decisions on the basis of the demand information inferred and its own private information. The strategic behavior of agents in this setup leads to improved information sharing and consequently, higher profits for the supply chain. Further, these profits can be redistributed to make each agent in the supply chain better off. Finally, such an arrangement also leads to improved sharing of risks in the supply chain; agents that have private information also bear some risks.

The rest of this chapter is organized as follows. In Section 18.2, we present the case of a fashion products manufacturer that motivates this study. In Section 18.3, we survey the relevant literature. In Section 18.4, we provide results from our analysis of a setup where there are multiple independent retailers each selling different products. In Section 18.6, we present the results from applying our model to the fashion products manufacturer described in Section 18.2. We conclude in Section 18.7.[1]

18.2 Motivating Example: Costume Gallery

Costume Gallery is a New Jersey-based manufacturer of dance costumes. In the US market, it is among the top 3 manufacturers of dance costumes. Annual sales in 2005 amounted to about US $30 million. Costume Gallery has been family run since its inception in 1957. The third generation of the family took over in 1997 and has been instrumental in bringing scientific management principles to the enterprise.

Costume Gallery was founded on the premise of excellent customer service. The strategic focus for Costume Gallery has always been on fully satisfying its customers at all costs. This strategic focus translates into a very large assortment of dance costumes available for purchase. At any time, as many as 500 different styles are available for purchase. Further, Costume Gallery meets all costumer demand. If any style is not available in stock, Costume Gallery often produces the style on-order for its customers.

Costume Gallery's supply chain is illustrated in Figure 18.1.

Costume gallery sells most of its merchandise through dance schools. Typically, the end consumer is a student enrolled in dance classes at dance schools. The instructor at a dance school plans a dance production and then decides on the appropriate dance costume. The recommended dance costume is then ordered by the school/instructor from Costume Gallery. Typically, the price of an average costume to students is about $40. The dance instructors/schools typically have a 10% margin on the merchandise. The dance schools do not hold any inventory or bear any of the supply chain risks. All inventory costs and risks are traditionally borne by Costume Gallery. Costume gallery can produce the dance costumes in a couple of different ways. Either the dance costumes can be produced in house or can be sourced overseas. Costumes produced in house cost about US $15 and can be produced with a lead time of 1–2 days. Even very small lots can be produced at Costume Gallery. Alternately, costumes can be sourced from Asia. Typically fashion products can be

[1] The authors would like to thank Ellen and Rick Ferreira from Costume Gallery for numerous useful discussions. Comments from Serguei Netessine, Marcelo Olivares, Yu-Sheng Zheng, Krishnan S. Anand, Karl T. Ulrich, Christian Terwiesch, Terry Taylor, Senthil Veeraraghavan, Xuanming Su, and Nils Rudi have all helped in improving this chapter.

Data presented in this chapter are indicative of the situation at Costume Gallery, a fashion product retailer; but has been completely disguised for business confidentiality reasons. Further, the opinions in this document are not endorsed by or, are an endorsement of Costume Gallery or its business practices.

Fig. 18.1 The dance costume business.

sourced at 30–40% of the in-house production cost however; the production and shipping lead time is as long as 2–3 months. Since there is a substantial cost saving in sourcing from Asia, Costume Gallery would prefer to source as much of its production from Asia as it can.

The dance costume business is highly seasonal with 90% of the annual demand occurring in the second half of April, coinciding with the end of school-year dance performances. The timeline of the dance costume business is illustrated in Figure 18.2.

To meet demand, Costume Gallery typically starts designing costumes in July of the previous year. These costumes are profiled in a catalog that is sent out to dance schools in early August. An illustration of the catalog is shown in Figure 18.3.

Dance schools finalize their enrollment in November and have a good idea of the theme behind the dance performance in December. At this point dance schools have a fair idea of demand for different dance costumes, since they know the size of their classes and the theme of the dance. However, there is still some residual uncertainty due to changing sizes of students in classes and additions or dropouts from classes. Given this residual uncertainty, schools behave *strategically* and do not place any demand orders with Costume Gallery.

To meet April demand, Costume Gallery must place its overseas orders by the month of January (given the 2–3-month lead time). Typically, these orders must be placed before the Chinese New Year holiday that occurs in late January or early

Jun	Jul	Aug	Nov	Dec	Jan	Feb	Mar	April
Costumes Designed	Catalogue Designed & Produced	Students enroll in classes	Dance Theme Finalized	Overseas orders must be placed	Dance Schools Place orders / Chinese New Year Holiday	In-House Production	Deliveries, Dance Performances

DANCE SCHOOLS HAVE DEMAND RELEVANT INFORMATION, BUT ARE NOT SURE

ORDERS PLACED W/O INFORMATION

Fig. 18.2 Timeline of the dance costume business.

Fig. 18.3 The costume gallery catalog.

February. These orders are placed on the basis of the best information that Costume Gallery has about the top selling styles. While dance schools have a far better idea of the demand, they do not have any incentives to place any orders early in the season and bear the risk due to their residual uncertainty in demand. Thus, Costume Gallery's overseas orders are placed without utilizing the demand relevant information available to dance schools. From January to April, Costume Gallery gets more and more accurate demand information and utilizes its in-house production and local contractors to meet demand over and above the quantities sourced from Asia.

In any given year, Costume Gallery is unable to sell as much as 35% of its stocked inventory and often has to produce as much as 20% of its sales at the last minute using the more expensive in-house production resources.

In recent years, Costume Gallery offered a novel discount scheme – orders committed to and paid in full by January 15, received a 15% discount. This "Advance Purchase Discount Scheme" provided dance schools with an incentive to place orders on the basis of their early demand information. While this meant that dance schools had to bear some risk and could potentially have unsold inventory, the discount could significantly increase the margins for the dance schools. Costume Gallery loses some revenues by offering the discount; however, the early demand orders provide valuable information which can be used by it to source more efficiently from the cheapest suppliers. In particular, this information drastically reduced the amount of merchandise that was left unsold by Costume Gallery and also reduced the expensive in-house production utilized by Costume Gallery. Further, by getting dance schools to commit to orders, some of the risk of supply–demand mismatches is transferred to the dance schools.

The two-tier production costs, seasonality in demand, and information asymmetry characterizing Costume Gallery's business are characteristics of the supply chains of many manufactured goods. Advance purchase discounts of the kind offered by Costume Gallery can significantly help such businesses improve their profits. In the subsequent sections, we will develop an economic model that demonstrates the benefits of offering APDs and highlights the drivers of the benefits. We will then employ our developed model to a representative subset of products from the Costume Gallery catalog. In the analysis that follows, we will model Costume Gallery as the wholesaler and various dance schools as retailers.

18.3 Literature Review

There are multiple streams of existing literature that are relevant to this study. Fisher and collaborators (Fisher and Raman (1996), Fisher et al. (1994, 2001), Hammond (1990)) in their celebrated work on skiwear manufacturing at Sport Obermeyer examine a setting where the firm has two production opportunities. The firm uses information from customers that order early to optimize the orders in the second production opportunity. Fisher and Raman (1996) characterize the benefits of such multiple production opportunities. Fisher et al. (2001) provide a heuristic for computing the optimal orders at the first and second ordering opportunity. In all of the above-mentioned papers, while early demand information is utilized by the manufacturer, there are no mechanisms for proactively obtaining this demand information as in the setup we analyze in this chapter. In particular, no advance purchase discount scheme is offered.

Tang et al. (2004) provide the motivating example of Moon-cake sellers. They model a setup where advance booking discounts are offered directly to customers. Customers can order well in advance of demand and deliveries, and obtain a discount; or customers can order closer to demand and pay full price. The customers fully know their demand and respond to the discount as a function of their time sensitivity. McCardle et al. (2004) extend this analysis to a competitive setting with retail competition. Dana (1998) also considers Advance Purchase Discounts offered directly to customers. Again, the customers are aware of their demand and the advanced purchase discount scheme serves as a price discrimination mechanism to separate between heterogeneous customers. Finally, Gundepudi et al. (2001) examine the case of selling *information* goods directly to customers. In contrast with above detailed body of work, in the setup proposed in this chapter, the discount is offered to a *retailer who in turn sells to customers*. The retailer *does not* fully know her demand. Further, in our case, she decides to hold inventory and ends up sharing supply–demand mismatch risks due to these discounts. The models presented in this chapter can be viewed as a multitier extension of the models presented in Tang et al. (2004).

Cachon (2004), like our setup, considers a setting where Advance Purchase Discounts are offered by an upstream supply chain agent (wholesalers) to a downstream agent (retailers). The allocation of inventory risk is the central focus of this paper. However, both retailers and wholesalers have the same information in this setup. In contrast to this, we assume that retailers by virtue of their being closer to customers have some private information. Thus, in our chapter Advance Purchase Discounts serve an additional purpose – they influence the transmission of information and the allocation of inventory risks in the supply chain. Not surprisingly, as a consequence of this information asymmetry the economics of offering these discounts are modified in our setup.

Li and Zhang (2008) analyze the transmission and sharing of information in a supply chain. They impose exogenous informational conditions, such as agreements on confidentiality or information sharing. They then examine and compare the performance of supply chains under the different informational conditions. In contrast with this work, our research endogenizes the informational conditions, or in other words, strategic agents in our models decide whether to share information or not. We examine specific incentive mechanisms such as Advance Purchase Discounts, which influence these choices.

18.4 Independent Retailers and Products

We consider a setup where one wholesaler can sell products through multiple retailers. We assume that each retailer sells the product in an independent market. Further, we assume that each product is sold by only one retailer. Under these assumptions, each retailer is effectively independent of the other retailers, and the economics of the relationship between each retailer and the wholesaler can be examined individually.

18.4.1 Model Setup

Consider the supply chain illustrated in Figure 18.4.

Customer demand is given as $\tilde{D}$, and is assumed to be distributed normally with mean μ and variance $\sigma^2 = 1/S$. The parameter, S, can be interpreted as the precision

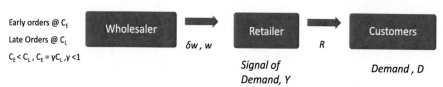

Fig. 18.4 The independent retailer model.

or the quality of the demand estimate available. The retailer sells this product at price R. The retailer can purchase the product from the wholesaler at the full wholesale price w. Alternately, the retailer can participate in the advanced purchase discount scheme. Under the advanced purchase discount scheme, orders placed and paid for in full by a particular cut off date, can be bought at a discounted wholesale price, δw. The wholesaler has two potential production sources: the wholesaler can source the product from a local production facility or he can source the product from an overseas supplier. Sourcing from the overseas suppliers involves longer lead times and thus, overseas orders must be placed well in advance of deliveries. The local production, on the other hand, has shorter lead times and orders for local production are placed much closer to the required delivery date. The in-house production costs are denoted by C_L. The overseas production costs are γC_L, where $\gamma < 1$. We assume that $\gamma < \delta$, or in other words, the difference between local and overseas sourcing costs is larger than the discount offered under the advanced purchase discount scheme. Fashion garments, which are the primary application of this model tend to be highly labor intensive and for such products, the difference between local and overseas sourcing costs is very high. For the organization described in Section 18.2, the costs for overseas production are typically around 80% lower than local production costs ($\gamma = 0.2$). On the other hand, retailers are typically offered around 15% discount on orders that are committed early ($\delta = 0.85$).

The timeline of actions is illustrated in Figure 18.5.

First, the retailer receives a demand signal Y. Next, the wholesaler announces the terms of the advance purchase discount scheme, and the wholesale prices, δw and w. The retailer then decides if she would participate in the discount scheme or not. If the retailer decides to participate in the scheme, she incurs a participation cost, K,[2] and she orders a quantity $Q_E > 0$ at a price δw, otherwise $Q_E = 0$. The wholesaler observes these orders and places an order P_E at a price γC_L. Then, demand D is

| Retailer Receives Demand Signal, Y | Wholesaler offers price w, δw (APD) | Retailer orders Q_E @ δw, Wholesaler procures P_E @ γC_L | Demand D is realized | Retailer orders Q_L @ w, Wholesaler orders P_L @ C_L | Sales/Deliveries @ R |

Fig. 18.5 Timeline of actions.

---

[2] This captures the administrative burden of participating in the advance purchase discount scheme: collecting early demand information, blocking capital, and placing orders.

realized. Based on observation of demand, the retailer orders Q_L at a price w. The wholesaler then orders a quantity P_L at a price C_L. Finally, the wholesaler delivers the products to the retailer and the retailer in turn, delivers them to the customers. In our model, the wholesaler proposes the discount parameter δ, as a take-it-or-leave-it offer that the retailer can only accept or reject. This allows the wholesaler to choose whatever value of δ that works best for him as long as it ensures that the retailer will participate in the scheme. The retailer decides to participate in the scheme as long as her gains from participating in the scheme are more than the profits if she stays out.

As mentioned before, demand is distributed normally with mean μ and variance $1/S$. The signal of demand, $\tilde{Y}$, conditional on demand taking a value D, is also distributed normally with a conditional mean D, and variance $1/T$. Applying Bayes theorem, we obtain the distribution of demand conditional on observation of the signal Y, which is also normal, with the following mean, $\mu_{D|Y}$, and variance, $\sigma_{D|Y}^2$.

$$\tilde{D}|Y \sim N\left(\frac{S\mu + YT}{S+T}, \frac{1}{S+T}\right) \tag{18.1}$$

where Y is the observed value of the signal. Note that the posterior distribution has lower variance or is more precise than the prior distribution. This is a consequence of incorporating the information contained in the demand signal.

Next, we examine the retailer and wholesaler's profits under two conditions: (1) when Advance Purchase Discounts are either not offered or the retailer decides not to participate in them and (2) when Advance Purchase Discounts are offered and the retailer participates in them.

18.4.2 Case 1: No Advance Purchase Discounts

We first consider the setup where no Advance Purchase Discounts are offered, or $\delta = 1$.

Retailer's choices: The retailer faces demand $\tilde{D}$ and obtains the signal of demand Y before the demand is realized. Since there are no Advance Purchase Discounts, the retailer has no incentive to place any early orders, $Q_E = 0$. The late orders Q_L are made after demand is observed, and are thus equal to demand D. It follows that the retailer's expected profit is

$$E\left[\Pi_R^{NOAPD}\right] = (R - w)\mu \tag{18.2}$$

Wholesaler's choices: The wholesaler has two decision variables, P_E, the quantity procured from overseas suppliers, and P_L, the quantity produced in-house. The decision P_L is made after observation of demand, whereas P_E is made before observation of demand. The wholesaler faces demand, $\tilde{D}$, that is passed on by the retailer. The wholesaler's choice of P_E is like a traditional newsvendor choice.

Demand is distributed normally with mean μ and variance $1/S$. We denote $\Phi(\cdot)$ and $\phi(\cdot)$ as the cumulative distribution function (CDF) and probability distribution function (PDF), respectively, of the standard normal distribution. If the wholesaler orders too many units of the good from the overseas supplier, he suffers an overage cost that is equivalent to the price of the good, γC_L. If the retailer orders too few units of the product, he has to produce the excess demand using the in-house production and this entails an additional cost of $C_L - \gamma C_L$. The optimal choice of P_E and P_L is thus given as

$$P_E = \mu + \frac{1}{\sqrt{S}} z_\gamma, \quad \text{where} \quad z_\gamma = \Phi^{-1}(1-\gamma)$$
$$P_L = (D - P_E)^+$$

Consequently the profits earned by the wholesaler are given as

$$E\left[\Pi_W^{NOAPD}\right] = \mu w - \gamma C_L \mu - \frac{1}{\sqrt{S}} C_L \phi_\gamma \tag{18.3}$$

where ϕ_γ is the PDF of the standard normal distribution function computed at $\Phi^{-1}(1-\gamma)$.

18.4.3 Case 2: Advance Purchase Discounts are Offered

Now, consider the case where the wholesaler offers a scheme where early orders, Q_E, can be bought at a price δw. Orders placed late, Q_L, can be bought at a price w.

Retailer's Choices: In such a setup, the retailer faces demand $\tilde{D}$, and can choose Q_E and Q_L. Q_L is chosen after observation of demand, whereas Q_E is chosen after observation of the signal but before demand. Theorem 1 provides the optimal retailer choices and her maximized profits.

Lemma 1. *1. The retailer's optimal choices are given as*

$$Q_E = \mu_{D|Y} + \sigma_{D|Y} z_\delta$$
$$Q_L = (D - Q_E)^+$$
$$E[Q_L] = \sigma_{D|Y} L(z_\delta)$$

where $L(\cdot)$ is the unit normal loss function and $z_\delta = \Phi^{-1}(1-\delta)$.
2. The retailer's optimal expected profit is

$$E\left[\Pi_R^{APD}\right] = (R - \delta w)\mu - w\sigma_{D|Y}\phi_\delta, \tag{18.4}$$

where ϕ_δ is the PDF of standard normal distribution function computed at $\Phi^{-1}(1-\delta)$.

Proof. The retailer chooses Q_E to maximize

$$E_Y \left\{ E_{D|Y} \left[RD - \delta w Q_E - w (D - Q_E)^+ \right] \right\}$$
$$= (R - \delta w) \mu - E_Y \left\{ E_{D|Y} \left[(w - \delta w)(D - Q_E)^+ + \delta w (Q_E - D)^+ \right] \right\}$$

which has a standard newsvendor solution with demand normally distributed, mean $\mu_{D|Y}$, and variance $\sigma_{D|Y}^2$. When demand is realized, retailer makes late order $Q_L = (D - Q_E)^+$. The result is as follows.

Theorem 1. *If the retailer participates in the advance purchase discount scheme, the retailer's signal, Y, can be inferred by the wholesaler.*

Proof. Observe that all quantities in Q_E are known besides Y. Y can thus be inferred from observation of Q_E.

Wholesaler's Choices: As a consequence of Theorem 1, the wholesaler infers all the information that is available to the retailer. Further, his demand can never be lower than Q_E, the order quantity already committed for purchase by the retailer. Thus, the demand facing the wholesaler is given as $\max \left(\tilde{D}|Y, Q_E \right)$. The choices available to the wholesaler are the overseas production quantity, which can now be made with the inferred knowledge from the demand signal, but still before observing actual demand. After demand is observed, the wholesaler may utilize in-house production, if there is more demand than the production available at hand. The wholesaler's optimal choices are given in Lemma 2.

Lemma 2. *1. The wholesaler's optimal choices are given as*

$$P_E = \mu_{D|Y} + \sigma_{D|Y} z_\gamma$$
$$P_L = (\max (D, Q_E) - P_E)^+$$

2. The wholesaler's expected profit under optimal order quantity is

$$E \left[\Pi_W^{APD} \right] = (\delta w - \gamma C_L) \mu - C_L \sigma_{D|Y} \phi_\gamma + w \sigma_{D|Y} \phi_\delta, \qquad (18.5)$$

Proof. The wholesaler faces a demand of $\max \left(\tilde{D}|Y, Q_E \right)$. She chooses $P_E \geq Q_E$ to maximize

$$E_Y \left\{ E_{\tilde{D}|Y} \left[\delta w Q_E + (\tilde{D} - Q_E)^+ w - \gamma C_L P_E - C_L \left(\max (\tilde{D}, Q_E) - P_E \right)^+ \right] \right\}$$
$$= E_Y \left\{ E_{\tilde{D}|Y} \left[\gamma C_L \tilde{D} + \delta w Q_E + (\tilde{D} - Q_E)^+ w \right] \right\}$$
$$\quad - E_Y \left\{ E_{\tilde{D}|Y} \left[(C_L - \gamma C_L)(\tilde{D} - P_E)^+ + \gamma C_L (P_E - \tilde{D})^+ \right] \right\},$$

which is a standard newsvendor problem with demand normally distributed, mean $\mu_{D|Y}$, and variance $\sigma_{D|Y}^2$. The result then follows from our earlier assumption that $\gamma < \delta$.

Taking the retailer's optimal order quantity into account, the wholesaler chooses a δ to maximize his expected profit while ensuring that the retailer participates in the discount scheme. The following theorem presents the equilibrium discount parameter:

Theorem 2. *If Advance Purchase Discounts are offered by the wholesaler and are used by the retailer,*

1. *the expected profit of wholesaler is monotonically increasing in discount parameter δ;*
2. *the wholesaler's equilibrium choice of δ, δ^* is*

$$\delta^* = \left\{ \delta \,\middle|\, w(1-\delta)\mu - w\sigma_{D|Y}\phi_\delta = K, \quad 0 < \delta < 1 \right\}$$

Proof. Rewrite the first-order condition for the retailer's optimal order quantity as $\Phi(z) = 1 - \delta$, where $z = (Q_E - \mu_{D|Y})/\sigma_{D|Y}$, then (18.4) becomes

$$R\mu - w\mu\left(1 - \Phi(z)\right) - w\sigma_{D|Y}\phi(z) = (R-w)\mu + w\mu\Phi(z)\left(1 - \frac{\sigma_{D|Y}\phi(z)}{\mu\Phi(z)}\right).$$

Since the inverse hazard rate $\phi(z)/\Phi(z)$ is decreasing for normal distribution, the expression is increasing in z which is decreasing in δ as long as $1 - \sigma_{D|Y} \cdot \phi(z)/(\mu\Phi(z))$ is positive, which is true if $Q_E > 0$. Applying the same logic to the wholesaler's profits, we can show that the wholesaler's expected profit is increasing in δ. Thus, in equilibrium, wholesaler sets δ^* as provided earlier.

The above results provide the profits for the retailer and the wholesaler, under Advance Purchase Discounts and when Advance Purchase Discounts are not offered. In the next section, we examine the implications of employing advanced purchase discounts in the supply chain. We will examine risk sharing in the supply chain and the benefits of participating in the proposed scheme for both the retailer and the wholesaler.

18.5 Advance Purchase Discounts: Risk Sharing and Supply Chain Performance

The first metric that we examine is mismatch cost, which includes the losses from leftover inventory and the opportunity cost of lost sales. Mismatch costs are directly related to the risk arising out of demand uncertainty. Consequently, a comparative examination of the mismatch costs that each tier of supply chain incurs, helps us understand how Advance Purchase Discounts influence risk sharing in the supply chain.

Theorem 3. *If Advance Purchase Discounts are offered and the retailer participates in them,*

1. *The mismatch costs for the supply chain are shared between the retailer and the wholesaler. They are given as*

$$MC_S = C_L \sigma_{D|Y} \phi_\gamma$$
$$MC_R = w \sigma_{D|Y} \phi_\delta$$
$$MC_W = C_L \sigma_{D|Y} \phi_\gamma - w \sigma_{D|Y} \phi_\delta$$

where the subscripts S, R, and W refer to the supply chain, retailer, and wholesaler, respectively.
2. *Both the total supply chain mismatch cost and the retailer's mismatch costs are decreasing in the retailer's information precision, T.*
3. *For given parameters γ and δ, the wholesaler's share of mismatch cost is constant.*

Proof. Rewrite retailer, wholesaler, and supply chain's objective function and apply optimal order quantity. Note that $\sigma_{D|Y}$ is decreasing in T. The results are as follows.

Theorem 3 shows that with increasing quality of the retailer's information, T, the supply chain has lower mismatch costs; however, the retailer bears less and less of this mismatch cost. As a result, with better information from the retailer, the wholesaler benefits from diminishing total mismatch costs in the supply chain, but transfers a smaller fraction of these mismatch costs or risks to the retailer. As a proportion, the share of the mismatch costs borne by the retailer and wholesaler remains the same.

Next, we compare the profits of the supply chain, the retailer, and the wholesaler in a setup where Advance Purchase Discounts are offered, with a setup where no Advance Purchase Discounts are offered. This helps us understand the incentives for the retailer to participate in the advance purchase discount scheme and for the wholesaler to offer the scheme. We denote the difference between the profits under APDs and without APDs as the "benefit" from participating in Advance Purchase Discounts.

Theorem 4. *The benefits from participating in advanced purchase discounts in a supply chain are given as:*

$$B_W = \left(\sigma - \sigma_{D|Y}\right) C_L \phi_\gamma - w(1-\delta)\mu + w \sigma_{D|Y} \phi_\delta$$
$$B_R = w(1-\delta)\mu - w \sigma_{D|Y} \phi_\delta - K$$
$$B_S = \left(\sigma - \sigma_{D|Y}\right) C_L \phi_\gamma$$

where the subscripts W, R, and S denote the wholesaler, retailer, and the supply chain.

The benefits, as written above, have an interesting interpretation. For the wholesaler, the first term denotes the benefit from making his ordering decisions under better information. This benefit depends on (a) the difference between the standard deviation of the prior of the demand distribution and the standard deviation of the posterior of the demand distribution, or the *quality of the signal*; and (b) the costs savings from early sourcing or the *degree of informational advantage* that the early information can provide. The second term captures the loss due to the discount and is a direct function of the market size and the amount of the discount offered. Finally, the third term captures the benefits from transferring the risks to the retailer. As discussed above, this depends on the discount offered and the quality of retailer's signal. For the same quality of the retailer's information, if a higher discount is offered, more risk (mismatch cost) can be transferred to the retailer.

For the retailer, her benefits have three terms: (a) the advantages of sourcing at the lower price, (b) the losses from bearing some of the mismatch costs, and (c) the administrative costs of placing early orders. Finally, as for the supply chain, it is always better off due to better sharing and utilization of information, the benefit being a function of the quality of the information and the financial advantage from early sourcing.

These two results bring some clarity into the mechanisms by which Advance Purchase Discounts operate. A critical decision for the supply chain is the quantity to be sourced from the long lead-time supplier. Advance purchase discounts lead to the sharing of the retailer's private information with the wholesaler and he can consequently make this decision with all the information available in the supply chain. However, to obtain this information he has to pay a price to the retailer in form of the discount. The retailer while availing the benefits from the discount, must also pay a price, by bearing some of the supply–demand mismatch risk. Put simply, the benefits of APDs *arise out incentive compatible strategic behavior* by different tiers of the supply chain which leads to *sharing of information*, which leads to making critical *supply chain decisions under superior information*.

18.6 Application at Costume Gallery

In this section, we illustrate the gains from deploying an advance purchase discount scheme. Further, we try to build an understanding of the on how characteristics of different products and retailers influence these benefits. Understanding the drivers of these benefits can provide guidance on a strategy for implementation of these policies. We present our results for a wide representative range of products, and retailers that Costume Gallery deals with.[3] In the following examples, unless stated otherwise, we set $\mu = 50000$, $R = 50$, $w = 35$, $C_L = 30$ and $\delta = 0.85$, $T = 0.001$, $S = 10^{-9}$, $K = 0$, and $\gamma = 0.5$.

Different products in the Costume Gallery catalog have intrinsically different demand characteristics. In addition to obvious difference in demand characteristics

---

[3] The numbers used in this section are representative of the setup at Costume Gallery, but for business confidentiality reasons, they have been disguised. The disguising of these numbers does not drive or influence any of the arguments made in this section.

(a) Predictable Demand:
Style "Feminine"

(b) Unpredictable Demand:
Style "Low Red Moon"

Fig. 18.6 Costume styles with different uncertainty in demand.

due to price, demand characteristics may also be different depending on the use of the product. The following illustration demonstrates this.

Consider products in a similar price range. Some of these products are "basics" used in a wide variety of dance performances such as a black shirt, a pair of black pants, and tutus. On the other hand, certain products are used only in very specific costume ensembles. These products are expected to have high sales if fashion trends support the particular style or costume, but may have very low sales otherwise. Not surprisingly, one can use the sales data from previous years, and reasonable expectations of demand growth to predict the sales of basics. On the other hand, there are limited forecasting models that can predict the trends for the latter category of products. As an example consider the two costumes illustrated in Figure 18.6. The first costume in Figure 18.6a is a timeless ballet costume used in dance performances. On the other hand, the costume in Figure 18.6b is based on a specific fashion trend and concept. Consequently, one would expect that the quality of prior demand estimates, S, is higher for the first costume than that for the second costume. More importantly, it is useful to understand how these differences in demand characteristics influence the benefits from offering Advance Purchase Discounts. Table 18.1 illustrates this for a representative sample of costumes, along with the estimated uncertainty in prior demand estimates.

Offering advanced purchase discounts on costumes with low quality of prior demand estimates leads to the highest performance gains for the wholesaler. On the

Table 18.1 Percentage gains in profits: Quality of demand estimates.

Product name	Quality, $S\left(10^{-8}\right)$	Wholesaler (%)	Retailer (%)	Supply chain (%)
Low Red Moon	0.05	58.70	34.97	44.05
Rich Girl	0.10	18.66	34.97	27.58
Beloved	0.15	6.73	34.97	21.43
Feminine	0.20	0.69	34.97	18.03
Euro tutu	0.25	−3.05	34.97	15.82
Black shirt and pants	0.30	−5.64	34.97	14.25

other hand, basic costumes for which accurate estimates are already available do not benefit much by additional information, and the losses due to the discount outweigh these benefits.

Costumes sold by Costume Gallery vary greatly in the manufacturing processes employed. Certain product types such as basic shirts and pants, can be cut and to an extent can even be stitched by machines. On the other hand, costumes with sequin, rhinestone, foil, fringe, feather, etc. cannot be manufactured by automated processes and must be worked on by skilled labor. Consequently, the labor content of the former category of costumes is low and the labor content of the latter category is high. Further, since the main advantage of sourcing from overseas suppliers tends to be driven by different labor costs, the benefit of overseas sourcing is higher for costumes that have higher labor content or γ *is lower*. As an example, consider the two costumes shown in Figure 18.7.

(a) Low labor costs:
    style "Play it Again"

(b) High labor costs:
    style "All Eyes on Me"

Fig. 18.7 Costume styles with different labor costs.

Table 18.2 Percentage gains in profits: Labor content.

Product name	γ	Wholesaler (%)	Retailer (%)	Supply Chain (%)
All Eyes on Me	0.1	−41.07	34.97	16.92
Nouveau Riche	0.2	1.11	34.97	25.66
I am an Illusion	0.3	18.20	34.97	29.43
Dancing Queen	0.4	21.51	34.97	29.69
Hit It	0.5	18.66	34.97	27.58
Lady	0.6	13.28	34.97	23.88
In the Money	0.7	6.94	34.97	19.16
Play it Again	0.8	0.27	34.97	13.72
Black shirts and pants	0.9	−6.69	34.97	7.62

The first costume (Figure 18.7a) has a low labor content, whereas the second costume (Figure 18.7b) is highly labor intensive. To examine the economics of Advance Purchase Discounts for costumes that differ in the above-described respect, we compute the profit gains from deploying Advance Purchase Discounts for a representative sample of costumes with different labor content (Table 18.2).

For costumes that have very low labor content, the benefits of early sourcing are small, γ is high, consequently the acquisition of information does not have significant value and the costs of offering the discount outweigh the benefits of superior information. Further, it is interesting to note that when the same percentage advanced purchase discount is offered on costumes with the same sales price but very different labor content, the wholesaler could be worse off for costumes where the benefits of overseas sourcing are the largest. Essentially, for these costumes, the costs of ordering too much are not significant for the wholesaler and therefore the benefits from obtaining early information are outweighed by the relatively large discount given (since the discount is offered as a constant percentage of a constant high sales price).

Costume Gallery partners with a wide variety of dance schools. These dance schools vary greatly in their structure. Some dance schools have been in operation for a longer period of time, have more experienced teachers, start classes earlier, etc. Such schools are better at predicting students' demand for a certain costume and thus have more precise demand information or signals. On the other hand, some dance schools employ more liberal cancellation policies for students' enrollment, have not been in operation for long, and have relatively under-developed information processing systems. Their information tends to be less precise. In Table 18.3, we illustrate the economics of offering Advance Purchase Discounts to schools which differ on the dimension discussed earlier. Again, we use a representative sample of partners from Costume Gallery to demonstrate our results.[4]

While the dance schools discussed in Table 18.3 vary greatly in the quality of information, the profit gains are not significantly different.

The results described above provide guidance for maximizing the benefits from implementation of Advance Purchase Discounts for a portfolio of products and

---

[4] Names of Dance Schools are disguised.

Table 18.3 Percentage gains in profits: Different retailer characteristics.

Dance school	$T\left(10^{-4}\right)$	Wholesaler (%)	Retailer (%)	Supply chain (%)
A	0.5	18.59	34.85	27.48
B	1.0	18.62	34.89	27.52
C	1.5	18.63	34.91	27.53
D	2.0	18.63	34.92	27.54
E	2.5	18.64	34.93	27.55
F	3.0	18.64	34.94	27.55

retailers. Wholesalers can increase their profits by more selective and targeted offering of Advance Purchase Discounts. If Advance Purchase Discounts were to be offered selectively, perhaps the most gains can be realized from focusing on a subsample of products. More specifically, products with poor quality of prior demand estimates and intermediate labor content benefit the most from an offer of Advance Purchase Discounts.

18.7 Conclusions and Future Work

In this study, we analyzed the economics of offering Advance Purchase Discounts in a supply chain. We found that there exist schemes under which all agents in the supply chain are better off. We then analyzed the economics of offering Advance Purchase Discounts and provided suggestions for efficient implementation of Advance Purchase Discounts. These results focus on the analysis of a firm offering products to independent retailers. While demand for single products demonstrates substantial uncertainty often the demand for products offered in an assortment is even more uncertain. This is especially true in catalogs of fashion products. This setup is not captured in the models presented above and is an interesting avenue for future work.

Optimally utilizing the information obtained from early orders also remains an interesting question. While inferring the signal from the newsvendor model and the above modeled Bayesian update scheme provides guidance, it assumes prior knowledge of the properties of the information structure such as information precision. A scheme for empirically estimating both the parameters of the information structure and then utilizing the signal to obtain forecasts of future sales is an interesting extension.

References

Cachon GP (2004) The allocation of inventory risk in a supply chain: Push, pull, and advance-purchase discount contracts. Management Science 50(2):222–238

Dana Jr JD (1998) Advance-purchase discounts and price discrimination in competitive markets. Journal of Political Economy 106(2):395–422

Fisher M, Rajaram K, Raman A (2001) Optimizing inventory replenishment of retail fashion products. Manufacturing & Service Operations Management 3(3):230

Fisher M, Raman A (1996) Reducing the cost of demand uncertainty through accurate response to early sales. Operations Research 44(1):87–99

Fisher ML, Hammond JH, Obermeyer WR, Raman A (1994) Making supply meet demand in an uncertain world. Harvard Business Review 72:83

Gundepudi P, Rudi N, Seidmann A (2001) Forward vs. spot buying of information goods on Web: Analyzing the consumer decision process. Journal of Management Information Systems 18(2):107–131

Hammond JH (1990) Quick response in the apparel industry. Harvard Business School Note 690-038

Li L, Zhang H (2008) Confidentiality and information sharing in supply chain coordination. Management Science 54(8):1467–1481

McCardle K, Rajaram K, Tang CS (2004) Advance booking discount programs under retail competition. Management Science 50(5):701

Tang CS, Rajaram K, Alptekinoglu A, Ou J (2004) The benefits of advance booking discount programs: Model and analysis. Management Science 50(4):465

Index

Early Titles in the
INTERNATIONAL SERIES IN
OPERATIONS RESEARCH & MANAGEMENT SCIENCE
Frederick S. Hillier, Series Editor, *Stanford University*

Early Titles in the
INTERNATIONAL SERIES IN
OPERATIONS RESEARCH & MANAGEMENT SCIENCE
(Continued)